This modern text is designed to prepare you for your future professional career. While theories, ideas, techniques, and data are dynamic, the information contained in this volume will provide you a quick and useful reference as well as a guide for future learning for many years to come. Your familiarity with the contents of this book will make it an important volume in your professional library.

EX LIBRIS

BUSINESS POLICY:

Administrative, Strategic, and Constituency Issues

BUSINESS POLICY:

Administrative, Strategic, and Constituency Issues

Second Edition

Curtis E. Tate, Jr.
The University of Georgia

Marilyn L. Taylor
The University of Kansas

Frank S. Hoy
The University of Georgia

BUSINESS PUBLICATIONS, INC.
Plano, Texas 75075

© BUSINESS PUBLICATIONS, INC., 1983 and 1987

Acquisitions Editor: John R. Weimeister
Developmental Editor: Rhonda K. Harris
Project Editor: Jane Lightell
Production Manager: Bette Ittersagen
Compositor: Bi-Comp, Inc.
Typeface: 10/12 Caledonia
Printer: Arcata Graphics/Halliday

ISBN 0-256-06215-3

Library of Congress Catalog Card No. 87–73027

Printed in the United States of America

1 2 3 4 5 6 7 8 9 0 H 5 4 3 2 1 0 9 8

Preface

The study of *business policy* and *strategic management* can be a challenging experience. Using cases in this study provides opportunities for integration of materials learned in previous courses, for learning and practicing analytical skills, and for an exposure to a wide variety of business activities. This course may be a first and, often, only opportunity for formal training in business policy and strategic management. The concepts are intriguing and the field's rapid development exciting.

This course is a "capstone"; that is, it ties together the various areas in the business curriculum. The text (Chapters 1–6) is organized to give the reader the necessary skills and information to approach analysis of the cases effectively. The first five chapters provide a conceptual foundation for the cases that follow. Chapter 6 deals with case analysis and discussion techniques, providing guidance for case preparation, class participation, and case report writing.

The introductory chapters (1–6) should be read before attempting analysis of any of the cases. As the various cases are analyzed, the material from the chapters relevant to the case may be reviewed.

We have revised the text chapters considerably from the first edition. The changes partially reflect suggestions from faculty and students who have used the book, but are mostly a response to the evolving field of strategic management. Among the topics that we thought needed additional attention are mission statements and goal setting, strategy implementation, and the impact of constituents on strategic management. Readers of the first edition will find minor modifications in the "Case Analysis and Presentation" chapter (Chapter 5 in the first edition, Chapter 6 in this edition).

In this revised edition, approximately 85 percent of the case material is new. This new material was collected in a different manner. Persons recognized for their skills in quality case research and case writing were invited to prepare an exclusive case for inclusion in this book. The authors made a special effort to include cases not found in other policy and strategic management texts.

The organizational structure of the case material has been reformulated. Early in the collection of the case materials, the authors became aware that the cases would fit into topical modules. Thus, the cases were assembled into 12 such modules.

The case organizational structure topics used in the first edition have been restructured into a grid pattern. The grid is used to introduce the case section.

You will find that the cases contain a diversity of managerial information accompanied by supporting data.

ACKNOWLEDGMENTS

Completion of this book has been accomplished with the support and assistance of many people. The association of the coauthors in this endeavor has been a meaningful experience for each of us. We are grateful for the contributions by many of our academic mentors, as well as the many practitioners who have added to our base of knowledge.

We are grateful to those who performed the case research and prepared the case material with an accompanying teaching note. Surely, we would be remiss if we failed to acknowledge the many contributions of the North American Case Research Association, the Midwest Case Writer's Association, and the Eastern Case Association, and their memberships. We appreciate Robbie Boggs's cover design and useful comments from Oakland University.

A number of persons provided secretarial assistance in the development of the manuscript. They are: Billie Najour, Sharon Cheeley, Karen Turner, and Melanie Blakeman. Editorial assistance was provided by: John Lough, Marie Rock, and Elena Whitehead. Development of graphic material was done by Lynn Manzione.

We are grateful for the support we received from our spouses: Mary Jim Tate, Bob Taylor, and Patricia Hoy.

Curtis E. Tate, Jr.
Marilyn L. Taylor
Francis S. Hoy

Contents

CASE CONTRIBUTORS

Robert Anderson
Jaynelle Ashley
McRae Banks
Thomas Bashuray
Kenneth Beck
Joyce Beggs
William Boulton
Larry Boyd
Betsy Boze
Ken Boze
Robert E. Callahan
Robert P. Crowner
Emit Deal
Robert R. Dince
Jack Ferner
June Freund
James Graham
Otha Gray
Walter Greene
James Harbin
Harry Kuniansky
Donald Kuratko
Don Law
Clint Le Noir, Jr.
Nanette Levinson
Michael Lubatkin

Harry McAlum
M. Blaine McCormick III
Robert McGlashan
Thomas McKinnon
William Naumes
Eugene Nini
Lee Owens
Judith Pierce
John E. Pierey
William Rice
Marie Rock
Eleanor Schwartz
Donald Scotton
John Seeger
Timothy Singleton
Lynette Solomon
Robert H. Solomon
Edward Stead
Jean Carver Stead
Patricia Stephens
Curtis E. Tate, Jr.
Marilyn Taylor
George Thompson
Thomas Urban
James Verbrugge
Charles W. White

Introduction

What is business policy and why should you take a course in this subject before you receive a degree in business administration? The policy course lifts you from the operational applications you have studied in prior classes and places you in the role of the general manager. In doing so, this course asks more of you than to memorize and give feedback. You are required to project yourself into a situation that some real manager at some real time faced when decisions had to be made and organizational resources had to be committed. This is a course, then, that asks you to think. It demands that you make decisions and develop strategic plans under conditions of uncertainty, with few parameters and no absolutes. Many students find this course frustrating, yet it is one of the most powerful tools we have for teaching you the reality of organizational management.

At most institutions, the business policy course serves three purposes. First, it is the *capstone* of the curriculum in business administration. By that we mean that it places the final touch on your education. Without the course in policy, your preparation for a managerial career will not be complete. Second, the policy class enables you at last to *integrate* all the functional material to which you were exposed in previous courses. Experience has shown that students often absorb knowledge in courses in marketing, economics, finance, and so on as though the pieces of information were independent from one another. In the policy course, you will be asked to draw from these disciplines and apply what you learned from a variety of sources to a single case.

Finally, the policy course offers you the opportunity to learn *substantive* material. Ideas and concepts are presented that you did not learn in earlier courses. These include such subjects as the role of the general manager, methods of decision making at top levels of organizations, mechanisms for formulating strategic plans, and others.

THE BUSINESS POLICY COURSE

Business policy, as a course and as a field of study, has passed through an evolutionary process since the American Assembly of Collegiate Schools of Business[1] cast it into a significant and permanent role in school of business curriculum. The business policy course was originally conceived as an integrative course for the undergraduate business major. Since that time, business policy has developed as a separate discipline within the broader field of business administration. The extent of emphasis varies from school to school. Some schools have only one course, while others have several such as strategic planning, environmental analysis, and industry analysis for strategic planning. The business policy course has maintained a prominent role in the curriculum.

Policy as an Integrative Course

At the graduate and undergraduate levels, the course is integrative and intended to broaden the students' horizons. At the undergraduate level, policy is generally scheduled during the last quarter or semester. The rationale for this position in the curriculum is that the course's purpose is to provide a series of integrative experiences. The integrative experiences often consist of cases each of which involve several functional areas or disciplines. Such cases may require taking on the role of the chief executive officer or another general manager position. In some institutions there is a heavy reliance on simulations or computerized games. In other institutions there is greater reliance on conceptual material.

Business policy is equally important in the graduate business program. The differentiating factor is that the graduate courses tend to use more sophisticated tools for case analysis, and the cases tend to involve issues of greater complexity.

---

[1] The American Assembly of Collegiate Schools of Businesses (AACSB) is the national accrediting agency for schools of business. AACSB reviews curriculums, facilities, and faculty of accredited schools on a regular basis and on request by schools that desire accreditation. In addition, AACSB, from time to time, revises curricular requirements after extensive study by task force committees. In 1959, the Ford Foundation funded a study that indicated that curriculums in schools of business resulted in students understanding content from the various disciplines (accounting, finance, marketing, etc.) only in isolation. This study gave impetus to the requirement that schools of business initiate an integrating course.

Purposes of This Course

One purpose of this business policy course is to provide practice in decision making.[2] The course prepares the user to be a facilitator of decision making and to seek simplification, conservation of time, and greater consistency in the decision-making process. This text provides opportunities to (*a*) make and evaluate decisions within the existing strategic framework and (*b*) evaluate and modify the strategic framework itself.

Throughout this text, the concept is stressed that in policy formulation and implementation, consideration must be given to all pertinent functional areas. For example, what effect will the decision under consideration have on the firm's financial status, marketing activities, personnel operations, accounting, engineering department, risk management, manufacturing operation (production), corporate planning (economics), and procurement section?

In this course, you will also be exposed to content areas specific to the field of business policy or strategic management. You will learn about mission statements, organizational goal setting, techniques of strategy formulation and implementation, and the influences of organizational constituents on the entire process.

This text is not designed to prepare you to step immediately into a strategic management position in a major corporation. Few students will be faced with such an opportunity on completion of this course. To qualify for general management responsibilities, you can anticipate the need to acquire significant and meaningful experience as well as additional education. One quarter or semester of business policy is not adequate to provide you all the knowledge and experience required to manage large complex organizations. You will gain in this course, however, a better understanding of the demands on the general manager. You will learn how all members of an organization affect and are in turn affected by corporate policies and strategies, thus enabling you to make a greater contribution to your organization in whatever initial assignment you accept.

PREPARATION FOR THE POLICY COURSE

In considering the cases in this text, your concern is how you as a senior executive would best approach the issues. For example, not only must you give consideration to the formulation of policy and strategy (the focus of Chapters 2 and 3), but also to implementation (the focus of Chapter 4). It is critical to anticipate the reception any

---

[2] *Business policy* is used here to refer to the course that has various titles, including "Problems of General Management," "Administrative Policy," and "Strategic Management."

EXHIBIT 1   Information Checklist

Accounting	_____	Budgets	_____
Economics	_____	a. Operating	_____
Engineering	_____	b. Cash flow	_____
Environment	_____	c. Capital	_____
Ecology	_____	Management	_____
Finance	_____	Marketing	_____
Government regulation	_____	Production	_____
Information system	_____	Personnel	_____
Risk management and insurance	_____	Organization	_____

individual executive decision may receive. If a decision is rejected by the affected personnel, it is not likely to be implemented.

The most important prerequisite for business policy is to have completed the core curriculum in business administration. It is difficult for you to integrate knowledge that you have not acquired. Generally, students are most likely to be prepared to take the policy class during the final semester or quarter before graduation.

Additionally, many students suffer from what may be called a societal information deficit. In the classroom, students often demonstrate a lack of awareness of their surroundings, of history, of current events, and so on. To successfully complete business policy, you must have the information at your command that will enable you to respond intelligently to assignments. When the course concludes, you should be able to interpret the economic environment in which you must function.

Policy and Information

As you begin to analyze the cases, you will define the information you will need to facilitate the decision process. The checklist in Exhibit 1 suggests some categories of information that may be needed. Refer to the checklist and review those areas in which you may need some conceptual reinforcement. Some useful references are found at the end of this Introduction.

You have observed by now how the departments within a school of business parallel functional departments in corporations. Business policy, by its very nature, affects all of the functional areas, either individually or collectively. In the formulation of business policy, it is important for the policymaker to be sensitive to the relationship between a particular policy's implementation and the functional areas of the firm.

DEFINITIONS

In this section, we differentiate between the terms *policy* and *strategy* as they will be used in this text.

There are numerous definitions of the term *business policy*.[3] For this book, an appropriate definition for policy is a guide to action in areas of repetitive activity. Unless an event or activity occurs with significant frequency, there is no justification for the establishment of a policy. Policy is for people; policies are directed toward people and their actions. Because of the actions people take, policies may involve money, things, or people. Policies may be established for a variety of purposes. One firm may have a policy of selling for cash. Another may encourage credit sales. One firm may hire students directly out of college and use extensive resources training the recruits. Another firm may prefer to hire only people with several years of experience.

In addition, policies may be either limited or global in effect. In this text, we differentiate between the limited and the more global by referring to the first as policies and the last as strategy. Strategy involves the long-term objectives of the firm and the means or set of functional policies by which it intends to get there. More succinctly,

> Strategy is most usefully thought of as its [a firm's] key operating policies in each functional area of the business and how it seeks to interrelate the functions. This strategy may be implicit or explicit—one always exists in one form or another.[4]

Strategic management involves continuous appraisal of the firm's environment and modification of the firm's objectives and policies to take advantage of opportunities in that environment. In the words of two other theorists, strategy is "the basic characteristics of the match an organization achieves with its environments"[5] and strategic management is the "process of continuously adapting to changes in the firm's environment."[6]

The following quote captures the differentiation between policy and strategy:

> It seems wise here to emphasize the distinction between the formulation of policies and procedures and their implementation. The formulation of policies and procedures can be defined as either strategic or tactical. Strategic decisions are concerned with the long-term health of the

---

[3] Milton Leontiades, "The Confusing Words of Business Policy," *Academy of Management Review* 7, no. 1 (1982), p. 45.

[4] Michael Porter, *Competitive Strategy* (New York: The Free Press, 1980), p. 63.

[5] C. W. Hofer and D. E. Schendel, *Strategy Formulation: Analytical Concepts* (New York: West Publishing, 1978), p. 4.

[6] D. E. Schendel and C. W. Hofer, *Strategic Management: A New View of Business Policy and Planning* (Boston: Little, Brown, 1979).

enterprise. Tactical decisions deal more with the day-to-day activities necessary for efficient and smooth operations. But decisions, either tactical or strategic, usually require implementation by an allocation or reallocation of resources—funds, equipment, or personnel.[7]

The tactical decisions referred to are what we call policies. We use *strategy* to refer to the global orientation of the firm. Thus, the term *business strategy* is global while *business policy* is more constrained.

OVERVIEW OF THE BOOK

You will discover that in this text the term *strategy* occurs more frequently than *policy*. We find that by the time students are ready for the capstone course, they have been well grounded in policymaking, or tactical decisions, in the functional disciplines. In Chapter 1, we examine in greater depth the concepts that are reencompassed by the strategic management process. You will see that this process occurs at four levels in complex organizations: enterprise, corporate, business unit, and operational (or functional). Most of your attention in prior courses has been directed toward operational or functional levels of analysis. You have learned about policies and tactical decisions in accounting, finance, marketing, and so on.

We have already emphasized the importance of these functional areas, and you can expect to apply what you learned to the cases you will analyze for this course. The primary level of analysis for this text is the *strategic business unit* (SBU), focusing on its relationship with its environment. We explain in Chapter 1 that your perspective in most cases will be that of the *general manager,* that is, the chief executive responsible for policy development and strategic management of an organization or a major, relatively autonomous unit within a larger organization. You will be learning about strategies that enable SBUs to cope within competitive industries.

This text does not exclude public-sector organizations. Chapter 1 explains how business policy and strategic management apply in the public sector. You have undoubtedly noticed that public-sector organizations, such as colleges and universities, struggle in environments that may be every bit as competitive as those of private enterprise.

Chapter 2 is devoted to mission statements and goal setting. Strategies represent courses of action, implying some desired outcomes toward which resources are being mobilized. Policies cover routine activities and must be written within a framework that determines

---

[7] Alfred D. Chandler, *Strategy and Structure* (Cambridge, Mass.: MIT Press, 1962), p. 11.

what is routine for the organization. Missions and goals are prerequisites for strategic management. Chapter 2 addresses the role of dominant coalitions consisting of those who band together to exert power and influence in defining the mission and goals of organizations.

The formulation of strategy is the subject of Chapter 3. We look in some depth at strategic planning and how it differs from short-term managerial planning. Various generic strategic alternatives available to general managers are introduced.

Plans are not complete if they are not successfully implemented. Chapter 4 explains how to manage the organizational changes that are inherent in the implementation of strategies and policies. We also address fitting the structure of the organization to the proposed strategy, and vice versa. Measuring the effectiveness of strategies and controlling for the achievement of goals are also discussed in Chapter 4.

Next, in Chapter 5, you will study the vital role of constituents in the survival and success of an organization. Many organizations measure their effectiveness by their ability to satisfy constituents such as owners, employees, creditors, suppliers, customers, and government. Constituents not only influence strategy formulation and implementation, but also are themselves the targets of strategies and tactics developed by the general manager.

Chapter 6 focuses on the process of analyzing cases and your role as a member of case discussion classes. As you read through the chapters and work on the cases, you will find there is not a one-on-one relationship between the chapters and the case sections. The learning experience will be enhanced by reading entirely through the chapters and then returning to review one or more sections that are appropriate to the case at hand.

The cases that follow Chapter 6 are organized with several interests in mind. First, while we expect you to draw on the text material in your case analyses, we did not match cases to chapters. Strategic management is complex, and that complexity is reflected in each case. You will find that the policy and strategy concepts emphasized will vary from case to case, but virtually every case can be examined using material from more than one chapter. We have attempted to arrange the cases from the relatively simply to the relatively complex. Effecting this arrangement has been our attempt to group the cases in meaningful ways. For example, some cases are organized by industry, such as banking or airlines. Alternatively, we have grouped other cases by issue, such as international business or legal problems. If your instructor chooses to cover all cases in a section, you will be able to examine an industry or issue in great scope and depth from a strategic management perspective.

We again remind you that this text does not propose to cover all aspects of strategic management, nor does it expose you to all contingencies faced by senior managers. It is designed to explain the most critical elements of the strategic management process and to place students into roles in which typical general managers have had to deal with uncertain situations and reach decisions with significant consequences for their organizations.

1

Policy and Strategy: The Management of Organizations

An executive's effectiveness is dependent on his or her ability to deal simultaneously with many elements of the firm's environment. Many of these critical elements exist within the firm. However, decisions, whether of a policy or strategic nature, are not made in a vacuum. As the American economy has matured, external environmental factors have assumed greater influence in organizational decisions. The importance of external environmental factors will become evident in this chapter. In addition, and perhaps even more important, is the matching of internal with external elements. The firm that has achieved a fit with its environment is far more likely to be successful.[1]

ROLE OF THE GENERAL MANAGER

We use the term *general manager* when we refer to the chief executive responsible for policy development and strategic management of an organization or a major, relatively autonomous unit within a larger

---

[1] A person responsible for policy and strategy information and administration must be able to manage the multiple elements of the firm's environment simultaneously. You might compare the situation with that of a pedestrian trying to cross the Los Angeles freeway—a lot of elements must be considered simultaneously—the kinds of vehicles, the density of the traffic, the speed of the traffic (all external elements) and the agility of the pedestrian (a critical internal element). Just as the pedestrian's survival is dependent on his ability to negotiate the complexity of the traffic, so an administrator's effectiveness is dependent on his ability to maneuver the firm through the "traffic."

EXHIBIT 1–1 Management

Management is:
1. doing through others
2. decision making
3. resource allocation

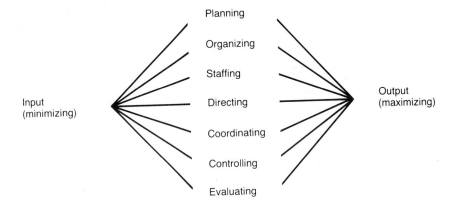

organization. The study of business policy, therefore, requires an understanding of the role of the general manager. First and foremost, policy administrators *are* managers. An overview of the managerial process is shown in Exhibit 1–1. You will note in the upper *left-hand corner* of Exhibit 1–1 that there are three items used to define management. The items in the middle of the exhibit are the management functional areas.

One of the key factors of being a manager is your ability to get things done through others. This is true whether we are entrepreneurs or professional managers. In the role of a professional manager, we hold ourselves out as persons with the skills to get things done through others. If we fail to prevail on others to do our bidding, then we have failed as managers. Key elements that contribute to effective managerial performance are personal security and personal self-confidence, that is, you believe that within yourself you have the ability to manage the activities of others; and you have the skills to delegate activities to others to perform.

A basic tenet of *decision making* is that factual information be viewed objectively. We are aware that decision making does not always occur in this manner. We observe that there are occasions when personal bias intrudes into the decision process. In order to counter the personal bias effect we need to develop an analytical framework for use in achieving an objective decisive conclusion. Yet, the subjectivity of decision making, especially at top levels of organizations, must never be ignored. Ultimately, decisions are implemented by people. What analysis shows us to be the "best" decision is not always the one that will be carried out most successfully.

The field of economics teaches us that managers must allocate scarce resources among alternative ends of consumption. Often the most critical policy decisions involve determining the mix of resource allocation. Resource allocation requires both efficiency and effectiveness. Efficiency can be defined as "doing things right" and frequently reaps the greatest rewards in the short run by achieving the greatest output on minimum inputs. Effectiveness, alternatively, is "doing the right thing," and leads to long-run success. Efficiency and effectiveness are not always compatible and strain resource allocation decisions.

The functional areas of management listed in Exhibit 1–1 are the basic means by which managers perform their responsibilities.

Planning

In dealing with this subject in a classroom, frequently an analogy of a flight plan is used. The proficient airplane pilot always prepares for a flight by making a flight plan. This includes distance, weather information, navigation instrument checkpoints, and so on. It is equally important for the general manager to formulate a plan of action. Only by planning can the criteria for the formulation and implementation of policies be met.

Organization

The formalized organizational structure is an essential ingredient in the functioning of the managerial process. The formal structure defines roles, relationships, responsibility and authority, and channels of communication.

You may view the formalized structure as the *conduit* through which flows the fluid of policy. It is the structure that facilitates the effectiveness of any organizational policy.

Staffing

In giving consideration to staffing, you should avoid confusing the *staffing* function with the *staff* function. In the last sense we think of the staff function as a service element of the organization, whereas we think of *staffing* as personnel procurement and assignment in an organization.

Directing

The *directing function* concerns itself with direction of personnel toward the achievement of their assigned roles. In fulfillment of these roles, affected personnel are expected to comply with the appropriate policy.

Coordinating

In an academic environment, we tend to discuss the managerial functional areas independently. However, in the "real world," we should recognize that functional activity tends to occur simultaneously and in some related manner. Because of these relationships it is desirable to coordinate the functional activities and the affected policies.

Controlling

Again, we will use the parallel analogy of the airplane pilot. If the pilot and aircraft are to arrive at a predetermined destination, the aircraft control system must function effectively. The same is true for an organization. There exists a need for a system of controls for personnel, operations, and financial activities. This is essential if preconceived objectives are to be achieved.

Evaluating

In the control systems, various elements of information are generated. As managers, if we are to function effectively, it is essential that we process and evaluate these various elements of information. Based on the conclusive results of the evaluation process, we should recognize what action is needed. It is essential that we formulate policy performance criteria so that we may make an appropriate managerial response.

CONTEXT OF POLICY

The general manager formulates and implements policy in a broad context with management at its core. This places demands on the general manager beyond those of others in supervisory positions.

Scope of Impact

Policymaking is organizationwide in scope. You must assess the consequences of your policy decisions beyond their direct and obvious impact. There *will* be a ripple effect. Policy decisions influence the future direction of the organization and will be long lasting in their effects.

Functional Requirements

Students are frequently taught the various business courses in a compartmental manner, applying only to the individual discipline/functional area.

You must, however, consider the influence of policy decisions on the organization's financial status, marketing activities, personnel operations, accounting, engineering department, risk management, manufacturing operation (production), corporate planning (economics), and procurement section. The functional knowledge required is portrayed in Exhibit 1–2. Note the centrality of management in this exhibit. Exhibit 1–3 offers a checklist that you may use to assess your own functional expertise at this stage. To analyze cases for this course, you will draw on the various types of information included on this list.

Technical Requirements

Management is often taught as if it were universal. Learn a set of skills, and you can transfer them with ease from organization to organization. There are classic examples where this has been the case. George Romney was successful first as chief executive officer of American Motors, then as governor of Michigan; Admiral Bobby Inman is achieving success in the private sector after having been an effective administrator in the Central Intelligence Agency. The failures are far more numerous, though. Successful policymakers are steeped in an understanding of the technical aspects of the products and services their organizations offer. Executives who manage their companies as though they were making investment portfolio decisions seldom formulate policies that achieve long-term success given the resources that make up those companies.

Industry Requirements

Closely associated with technical expertise is the knowledge of the industry in which the firm must compete. Each industry has its own history and characteristics that impinge on the policies of firms within that industry. Policies must be formulated within the context of the industry environment if they are to accomplish their predefined objectives.

EXHIBIT 1-2

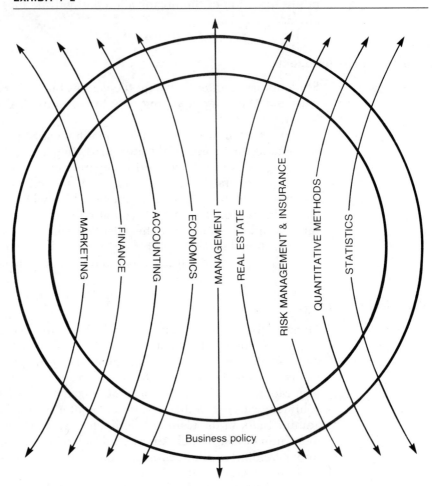

Business policy

External Environments

In addition to the industry, there are numerous other environmental constraints on policy formulation and implementation. The general manager must scan and assess the legal, cultural, economic, technological, and other environments that influence the organization's capacity for survival. The manager devises strategies by which the organization relates to its environment.

Do Not Use

~~MILITARY DERIVATION AND ANALOGY~~

Much of what we have learned and apply in business policy has been derived from military organization and practice. Countless genera-

EXHIBIT 1–3   Classified Information Checklist

Accounting	_____	Budgets	_____
Economics	_____	a. Operating	_____
Engineering	_____	b. Cash Flow	_____
Environment	_____	c. Capital	_____
Ecology	_____	Management	_____
Financial	_____	Marketing	_____
Government regulation	_____	Production	_____
Information systems	_____	Personnel	_____
Risk Management and insurance	_____	Organization	_____

tions of military commanders have been called upon to set organizationwide objectives, drawing on functional and technical knowledge and experience while making decisions and implementing strategies in hostile environments.

Just as generals establish the overall objectives of war, companies too establish their overall objectives. The Pentagon (or its equivalent in another country) may set out to acquire additional territory, reestablish an old boundary line, or defend existing territory against enemy forces. A company may set out to acquire additional market share, recapture previously held market share, or defend existing market share against the renewed aggressiveness of competitors. Business goals of efficiency and profitability also find comparabilities in military objectives of efficient and effective deployment of resources.

What are the resources or weapons that will be used to attain those objectives and how will they be deployed? In other words, how is the firm (or military power) going to get where it aims to go? Economics categorizes basic business resources as land, labor, and capital. Refined and expanded, the list of company resources, or "weapons," includes:

1. Marketing: products, distribution channels, pricing, and advertising.
2. Production: manufacturing, raw material procurement, and distribution capabilities.
3. Finance: debt and equity resources.
4. People: executives, salespeople, factory workers, engineers, accountants, clerks, and secretaries.

Analogies with military resources are readily apparent:

1. Marketing:
   a. Distribution: deployment capabilities.
   b. Promotion and advertising: generation of social and political support.

2. Hardware (production): airplanes and missiles.
3. Financial resources: the ability to persuade the legislature to tax or borrow.
4. People: army, navy, and air force personnel.

Admittedly, the analogy breaks down. Deployment in the military usually refers to ability to get personnel (e.g., troops) and hardware (e.g., tanks and jeeps) in the appropriate locations at the right time. Distribution in business terms has a more limited meaning and usually refers to having goods on the shelves when and where the customer wants them.

Most students may be familiar with the nursery rhyme

> For want of a nail the shoe was lost.
> For want of the shoe the horse was lost.
> For want of the horse the leader was lost.
> For want of the leader the battle was lost.
> And all for the want of a nail!

Among the stories of a modern corporation losing the battle on the basis of distribution, perhaps none is more to the point than Polaroid's war with Kodak for the instant camera market. The two companies pitted the low-priced Polaroid One Step camera and the Kodak Handle camera against each other in the marketplace. The customers seized the opportunity. Kodak, however, won this particular battle, partially because of more effective deployment. Kodak's Handle was on the shelf when the customer, lured by a Polaroid at $40, found the One Step out of stock. Polaroid's planning system had failed to predict the high level of demand and the company was unable to produce in sufficient quantities to meet the demand.

An example of a corporation winning the battle of sales and profits based on distribution may be found in a *Forbes* article relating to Wal-Mart stores.[2]

> "With the plans in place today," says analyst Bernard Sosnick, "Wal-Mart will generate $33 billion in sales by the end of 1990."
>
> How? A key element is his warehouses. Wal-Mart's "saturation policy" calls for clustering scores of stores throughout a 200-square-mile area around the distribution points. Deliveries of goods can be made every day. Wal-Mart stores get 77 percent of their merchandise from the company's warehouses; other chains' stores are forced to get much more of their goods from higher-priced middlemen. Keeping its stores close to each other and the distribution centers also helps Wal-Mart keep advertising costs to 0.6 percent of sales, compared with 2 percent to 3 percent for other discount chains.
>
> Late in 1985 Walton approved three distribution centers, each larger than several football fields. But that was only the beginning. Wal-Mart is

---

[2] Howard Rudnitsky, "Play it again, Sam," *Forbes*, August 10, 1987, p. 48.

now building two more distribution centers, including a mammoth 1.5 million-square-foot center in South Carolina, with a third planned for 1988. Each center is capable of servicing between 150 and 200 stores in the 23 southern and southwestern states Wal-Mart now serves. All told, Walton plans to double distribution space, to around 10 million square feet, within 30 months, at an estimated cost of more than $200 million.

Walton equips his distribution centers and his stores with the latest in optical scanning devices and automated materials handling equipment. A new satellite communications network connects most stores with his nine distribution centers.

At Wal-Mart, squeezing costs is a near religion. The efforts show. Wal-Mart's distribution costs, at 3 percent of sales, come to about half of most chains' cost. That's a substantial saving when you are dealing with 24 percent gross margins. Retailing analysts point out that other discounters like Woolco, TG&Y, and Kuhn's Big-K failed in recent years because they were unable to remain cost-competitive.

This military example raises another issue for you to keep in mind as you read this text. Although we have titled the book *Business Policy*, you will find that the concepts and analytical techniques you learn in this course are every bit as appropriate for public-sector organizations as for private firms. For that reason, we prefer the term *organization* to *firm* or *corporation* and have included several cases on not-for-profit, or more appropriately, tax-exempt organizations.

POLICY AND STRATEGY DEFINED

We have now complicated the study of business policy by introducing the concepts of public-sector policy and military strategy. Some authors use the terms *policy* and *strategy* interchangeably, or neglect to differentiate them. We attach distinct definitions to each, which we believe will clarify the subject you are studying and enhance your ability to analyze cases.

Policy is a guide to action in areas of repetitive activity. Unless an event or activity occurs with significant frequency there is no justification for the establishment of a policy. A trite but simple and meaningful statement is: policy is for people. Policy is directed toward people and their actions. Because of the action people take, however, policy may involve money, things, or people.

Alternatively, *strategy* refers to the long-term objectives of an organization and the means by which the organization interacts with its environment in its efforts to attain those objectives.

The primary focus of policy is internal—the rules, procedures, and guidelines that enable an organization to function. Strategic management is an externally focused activity. Information about the external environment is constantly collected and processed for the organization to behave in appropriate reactive and proactive modes.

LEVELS OF ANALYSIS

Policy formulation and strategic management occur at different levels within organizations. This is an important fact to recognize because, as we shall see in subsequent chapters, relevance of information and choices of alternatives will vary by the level of analysis at which the key decision maker is functioning. We identify four levels of policy: enterprise, corporate, business unit, and operational.

Enterprise strategy is the most encompassing. At this level, executives ask why are we in business? And what function does our organization serve in society? Enterprise level strategies are devised to enable an organization to cope with volatile environments over long periods of time. They are concerned with meeting the responsibilities the organization has to its numerous stakeholders.

Since the mid-1960s, American business has become more concentrated. The period of the late 1960s and early 1970s, as mentioned earlier, is often referred to as a period of conglomerate fever. Numerous companies reveling in extended periods of successful growth were flush with cash or intoxicated with their high price-earnings ratios.[3] Many of these companies, assuming their managerial staff was invincible, purchased unrelated companies. Some of these companies have remained successful growth companies. Raytheon, for example, began its diversification in the 1960s with a base of electronic products manufactured for government contracts. Today, Raytheon still manufactures a wide range of sophisticated technological products, including missiles for government contracts. However, Amana (kitchen appliances), D. C. Heath (book publisher), and Beech Aircraft (general aviation aircraft) are among Raytheon subsidiaries. Textron is a conglomerate whose subsidiaries include Bell Helicopters, Speidel watchbands, and Correc-to-Type! ITT is another successful conglomerate.

Corporate level strategy for businesses such as the examples above involves asking the question what business are we in, which implies the follow-up question, should we be in this business? Managers at the corporate level of analysis make portfolio decisions: whether to purchase Company A, whether to divest Company B.

In multibusiness or diversified companies strategic planning is carried out at the business unit and corporate levels. The determination of basic objectives and the establishment of tactical and policy decisions by which these objectives will be met is often delegated to the division or business unit. Approval of the business unit's strategic

---

[3] A high price-earnings ratio allows a company to issue stock to purchase another company with a lower price-earnings ratio without unduly diluting ownership control or earnings per share.

plans is made at the corporate level. Approval at the corporate level is usually accompanied by decisions regarding financial allocation.

When a company produces one product or a set of products so closely related they belong in the same industry, we can talk about strategic planning at the business unit or strategic business unit (SBU) level. At the business unit level, strategic planning focuses on orienting the firm to take advantage of external environmental opportunities efficiently and effectively. Concern is focused on establishing (or modifying) the product, R&D, production, finance, marketing, personnel, and accounting policies in such a way that each is consistent with the others and the company's overall objectives are likely to be met. Basic questions include: Are we producing appropriate products or providing appropriate services? What pricing and promotion are appropriate? Should we make or buy? How should this effort be financed (e.g., reduce expenditures on other products, reduce dividends, sell off some marketable securities, ask for better terms from suppliers until the product generates the expected inflow, seek intermediate term financing or new equity)? Are the current sales force and distribution channels appropriate?

Operational policies address issues facing functional or product divisions within SBUs. For example, one firm that made the "Chevrolet/Pontiac" of the industry was offered the opportunity to purchase the "Oldsmobile/Cadillac" product line. The company opted for the opportunity since it allowed them to serve their current clientele even better with appreciable modifications in the existing plant and with little retraining of the same sales force. Moreover, the company knew that no other firm in the industry would be able to match the breadth of their augmented product line and that they themselves would require years to develop a comparable set of products.

Strategic product planning also occurs when a company is deciding what new products to introduce in future years. Specialty producers, for example, spend considerable time analyzing the competition's product lineup and expected additions so that they can determine where the niches are for new product designs. For example, many companies make belt buckles; however, one small company designs specialty belt buckles with corporate logos for companies.

American Motors Corporation as the "giant killer" for years has tried to find those narrower and narrower market segments for which they might introduce new automobiles. They were successful with the Gremlin but the Pacer was another story. Hesston, a specialty producer of agricultural implements, has marketed numerous innovations—usually for small market segments. Once Hesston introduces a product, the company hopes the new addition will not be so successful that it attracts the attention of the long-line producers such as John Deere!

This is the level at which efficiency issues often predominate. The general manager is frequently concerned with how to achieve maximum sales from given inputs in advertising and promotion or increased production with minimum waste.

While all four levels of policy analysis will be given attention in both text and cases, the emphasis we have chosen is on the business unit level. By the time most college graduates participate in enterprise and corporate level decisions, they will have had the opportunity to extend their educations well beyond a single course in business policy. For operational level analysis, you will draw from material you learned in various discipline-specific courses, such as marketing, production/operations, finance, real estate, and others. Assessing and formulating policies for SBUs is the capstone activity of your business degree. At this level, you integrate knowledge previously learned and develop your conceptual and analytical skills by evaluating the decisions and behaviors of general managers in single-industry environments.

STRATEGIC PROCESS

The following four chapters introduce you to the strategic management process. Exhibit 1–4 displays a model of this process. Although the process is, as the model shows, circular, it may be useful to consider goal setting as the starting point. The organizational mission establishes the context for goals, which may be revised based on changes in the environment or assessments or current strategy.

Strategy formulation is a planning process that selects from among viable options and results in policies and procedures. The implementation of these policies must consider the structure of the organization. The general manager evaluates the strategy and makes modifications as necessary. All aspects of the process are subject to influence by the various constituents, internal and external, who have a stake in the organization or its products and services.

SUMMARY

In this chapter, we have described the role of the general manager in formulating policy and implementing strategies in organizations. The centrality of management to business policy has been established. Policy and strategy have been differentiated based on their respective internal and external orientations. We have introduced you to four levels of policy and explained that our attention will be directed in greater part to the business unit level. Finally, we have given you a brief overview of the strategic management process. This allows us to turn now to setting goals and objectives for organizations.

EXHIBIT 1–4   Strategic Management Program

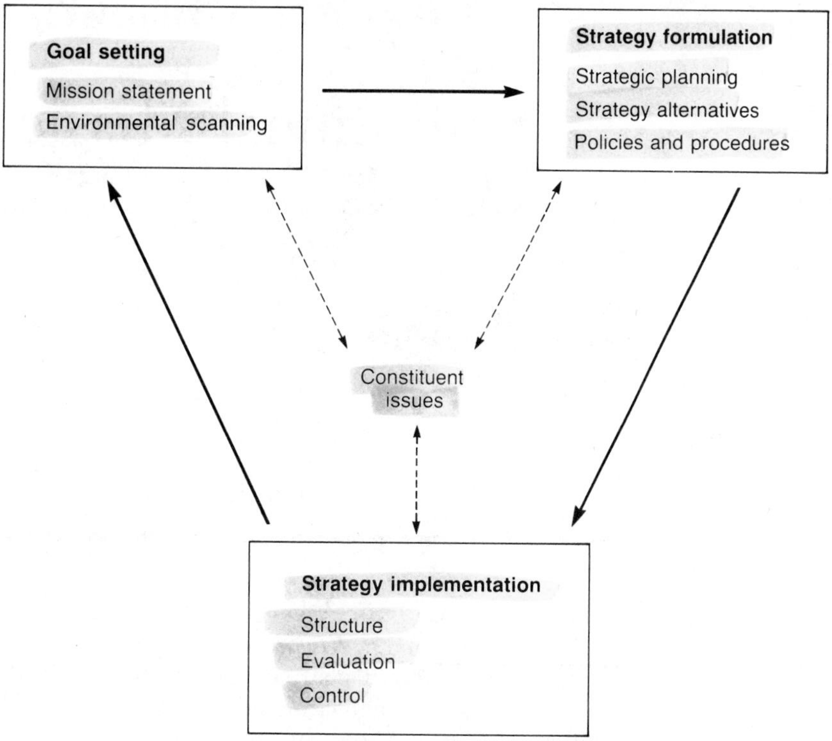

Goal setting

Mission statement
Environmental scanning

Strategy formulation

Strategic planning
Strategy alternatives
Policies and procedures

Constituent
issues

Strategy implementation

Structure

Evaluation

Control

2

Organizational Missions and Goals

In Chapter 1 we defined the role of the general manager and the terms *policy* and *strategy*. We presented you with a three-stage strategic process sequence of goal setting, strategy formulation, and strategy implementation, each affected by organizational constituents. It is critical to hold in mind that strategic management and policy formulation and implementation occur with the context of an organization.

In this chapter, you will learn about missions, goals, and objectives. From a policy perspective, you develop mission statements, set goals, and target objectives to mobilize organizational resources to fulfill your mission and achieve your goals. Thus, we begin with the concept of the organization.

ORGANIZATION

An organization is the joining together of a group of people for a common purpose and for the achievement of common objectives. Organizations have three characteristics.

1. They are goal directed, that is, they behave as though their activities are directed toward some common purpose.
2. They are activity systems, that is, they possess technologies or techniques for manufacturing goods or performing services.

3. They maintain boundaries although those <u>boundaries may be more or less clear to an observer</u>.[1]

The boundaries of some organizations are quite clearly defined. In other instances, organizational boundaries are difficult to ascertain. Many volunteer organizations, for example, find it difficult to determine who is a member and who is not. One of the authors of this text, for example, is still a "member" of a church not attended for the last 20 years! This example is also included as a reminder that organizations, as we use the term, refer to public and tax-exempt entities as well as private companies.

MISSION

Important portion of Company or organization.

need etters in memo

Mission states what the objective is of the organization.

examples

The notion of a common purpose leads us to mission statements of organizations. <u>Put simply, a mission statement defines the ultimate purpose of an organization.</u> It describes <u>why the organization exists</u> and <u>its long-term function</u> within <u>its environment</u>. More narrowly, a mission is the mechanism for achieving objectives. It is the framework against which you can test whether a goal or objective is within the scope of the organization and whether proposed strategies for achieving goals fit the purpose of the organization.

The mission statement of an organization currently directed by one of the authors reads as follows:

> The Small Business Development Center program is a management and technical assistance program designed to improve the economic climate of the United States through strengthening the contribution of small business to the economic system. It is a cooperative venture by local, state, and federal governments; universities and colleges; and the private sector.
>
> The purpose of the SBDC in Georgia is to serve small business owners, managers, and prospective owners through a statewide network. This University System-affiliated organization provides counseling and continuing education services, which are made available through regional and district centers. Additionally, specialized divisions of the SBDC place particular emphasis on minority enterprise, international trade, business and economic studies, student education, and information dissemination.

The mission of the Small Business Development Center is:

1. To assist existing small businesses to function more efficiently and effectively.
2. To aid the establishment of new businesses.

---

[1] Howard E. Aldrich, *Organizations and Environment* (Englewood Cliffs, N.J.: Prentice-Hall, 1979), pp. 4–5.

STRENGTHS
WEAKNESSES
Opportunities
Threats

3. To encourage participation in the business system by disadvantaged groups, such as minorities, females, and veterans.
4. To increase market opportunities for Georgia-based business by increasing involvement in international trade.
5. To provide students with the opportunity to learn about and participate in small business.
6. To provide information that will improve the start-up and operation of small business to communities, state and local organizations, trade associations, and other interested parties.
7. To serve as an advocate of the small business community.

As you can see, this statement explains what the organization is, why it exists, and lists mechanisms by which its purposes are achieved.

In your studies you may find some corporations whose mission statements are identical with their strategies and others that have been drafted more for public relations than for actual guidance. In the first instance, the mission loses its timelessness, its value in articulating long-term purposes. In the second, managers must perform their duties without the parameters of a legitimate statement of their ultimate goals. Statements should be written to aid the general manager in establishing priorities, assessing trade-offs, and evaluating the demands of constituents.

STRATEGIC THINKING

A mission statement forces you to think strategically, first in writing the statement itself, then in formulating and evaluating policies and strategies. There are three characteristics of strategic thinking: (1) a long-term orientation, (2) a broad scope of organizational activities, and (3) a focus on the fit of the organization to its external environment.

The ability to think strategically does not evolve naturally among managers. In fact, the daily experiences you acquire in organizations may train you against developing this skill. For example, rewards in the form of recognition, raises, and advancement often are based on short-term accomplishments rather than your long-term plans. Additionally, the more expertise you gain in your work, the more specialized you may become, rather than obtaining a broad-based view of your firm. Finally, your daily activities are most likely spent within the boundaries of your company, sometimes leading you to be negligent in scanning the changes occurring in your environment.

To think strategically, you must consciously work to develop your perceptual and intellectual skills. An important step is to recognize that all organizations possess both internal and external environments, inextricably linked to the mission of the enterprise.

INTERNAL AND EXTERNAL ENVIRONMENTS

Talks about SWOT — Hard to Define.

As a person responsible for policy formulation and administration you might compare your situation with a pedestrian trying to cross the Los Angeles freeway—a lot of things are coming at you. Just as the pedestrian's survival is dependent on the ability to handle the traffic, so is the policy administrator's survival dependent on the ability to deal with the many elements of the administrative environment.

How do you distinguish the boundaries between a firm's internal and external environments? One author suggests that finding the boundaries of an organization is somewhat like determining the boundaries of a cloud.[2] Measuring a cloud involves measuring moisture density or particles, but measuring an organization is more difficult. What kinds of "particles" does one measure—employees, stockholders, customers? And what interactions should be considered?

Consider a firm's external environment. The external environment of a firm is comprised of other organizations or clusters of individuals whose common interests lead them to act like quasi organizations. Determining where one organization stops and another begins is difficult. Moreover, the boundaries of an organization are fluid and depend on the perspective of the investigator and the issues involved in the investigation.

Another way of looking at this issue is through the use of the constituency concept. The constituency concept suggests that a firm must be responsive to the needs and demands of those who have a vested interest in the company. Stockholders constitute a legitimate constituency for any publicly or privately held company. But employees, creditors, and suppliers also have stakes in the outcomes of a company.[3] The issues become fuzzier and consequently more hotly debated when those with less directly affected interests are considered. Many organizations, particularly in the public sector, measure their success by their ability to satisfy this multitude of constituents.

How responsive, for example, should a mining company be to the townspeople where one of its operations are located? Milton Friedman in a classic article[4] argued that the responsibility of a company is to make a profit. Under this guideline, the company should close down a marginal plant if the decision makers can demonstrate that the company as a whole would be more profitable without the plant. Un-

---

[2] William H. Starbuck, "Organizations and Their Environments," in *Handbook of Industrial and Organizational Psychology*, ed. Marvin D. Dunnette (Chicago: Rand McNally, 1975).

[3] The constituency concept is also referred to as the stakeholder concept. See, for example, Eric Rhenman, *Industrial Democracy and Industrial Management* (London: Tavistock. 1968), pp. 24–26, 110–12.

[4] Milton Friedman, "The Social Responsibility of Business Is to Increase Its Profits," *New York Times Magazine*, September 13, 1970, pp. 33, 122–26.

EXHIBIT 2–1 Organizational Environments

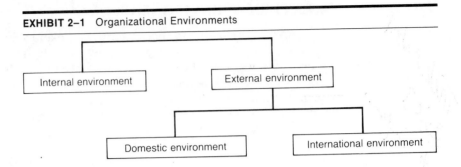

der these circumstances, what was the responsibility of the Anaconda Copper Company to the people of Anaconda and Great Falls, Montana, when it closed smelting and refining operations in the two towns? In Anaconda about 82 percent of the city's primary and secondary employment depended on the company's smeltering activities. In addition to a severance package for all employees, the company set up a $5 million fund to pay for the community's adjustment to the closing.[5]

Environmental issues relevant to a firm are broader than constituency or stakeholder theory, however. There are several ways of categorizing the environmental elements organizational decision makers must consider. One way of conceptualizing these various environments is given in Exhibit 2–1. Some elements, the firm's raison d'être, its objectives, its orientation and culture, are clearly internal elements. Others such as the economic cycle, industry structure and culture, the broader social milieu, the religious, political, and cultural, ethnic, and regulatory environments are more clearly external elements. Others, such as the financial and technical elements, are both external and internal.

INTERNAL ELEMENTS

The Firm's Raison d'Être

As a practicing executive, have you identified your firm's "reason for being"? Many executives plod their merry way without ever stopping to question, "What is this company's reason for being (raison d'être)? If they do ask the question, can they correctly answer it? The answer

Why is the Company here?

---

[5] "Anaconda to Close Two Montana Units over Pollution Rules," *The Wall Street Journal*, September 30, 1980, p. 10. "Anaconda Shuts Refinery Here," *Great Falls Tribune*, 1980. "Anaconda Co. Aid May be $1.5 Million," *Great Falls Tribune*, December 4, 1980. Last two articles courtesy of Great Falls Area Chamber of Commerce.

is not always the obvious; sometimes it appears more implied. If you are to direct the firm's activities toward its appropriate objectives, then you must understand the reason for its existence and move toward fulfilling these objectives. ✗✗

The Firm's Objectives

To function effectively as an executive you must define objectives. Otherwise, you might be as a log adrift in the current of the Mississippi River whose direction is dependent on the buffeting wind and current of the river. You might have some general idea of your potential destination but, knocked about by a complex set of environmental forces, you have no idea where you might get stuck! You want to adjust to these environmental forces, but at the same time direct and control the firm toward its predetermined objectives, whether those objectives are profit, profitability, growth, acquisition, or diversification. Whatever the objectives, you will want to stay in control.

Orientation of the Firm

Observation of a variety of firms suggests that, in some instances, the firm's objectives and its actions are in alignment. In other instances, we find that the firm may be giving lip service to a list of objectives, while in practice it is pursuing something entirely different. The executive's responsibility is to determine the realities of the situation, making these distinctions within the firm's operating environment, if control and direction are to be maintained.

Specific elements of a firm's orientation may be found among the items that follow. What is the firm's _profit posture_ and what efforts are being made in this direction? Is there evidence of efforts being made by the firm to achieve an _image of prestige and status?_ Are there indications of obvious efforts being made by the firm toward making a _social contribution to society?_ In some instances the firm's management appears strongly directed toward _personal satisfaction._ Some firms appear oriented toward maintaining a posture of status quo, that is, do not touch a thing, leave it be, let it run like it is running. Other firms appear to have a strong orientation toward entrepreneurship and growth (this growth may be reflected by increased profits, sales, market share, product line, physical facilities, stockholder equity, price of company stock, etc.). The greatest concern of some firms appears product related. In such instances, we would consider the firm to have a _product orientation._ In recent times, we have found a number of firms with an _acquisition_ or _merger_ orientation. In addition, there are the firms who seem to have a strong _R&D (research and development)_ orientation (a great deal of America's future is dependent on the quality of its firms' R&D effort, as well as the quantity of new or improved technology the effort produces). It appears that some firms perceive their niche to be accommodated by an orientation toward *diversification*, while other firms appear to have a *profit* orientation. The questions here are: are they thinking of *profit* in the *short run* or *long run*, and is *profit keeping up with or surpassing inflation?*

A firm's orientation is also revealed by the competencies it has developed. Some firms are skilled at advertising. Some have excellent research and development programs. Others have highly developed distribution channels. Still others operate efficient manufacturing facilities. Orientations, revealed by the development of distinctive competencies, have come about because of previous commitments by the firm of resources in a particular direction. Often a firm is forced to reevaluate its situation because its distinctive competence or orientation is no longer appropriate in the environment in which it currently competes.

The Financial Environment

The executive must also consider the financial circumstances of the firm. A number of relevant issues are summarized in Exhibit 2–2. With knowledge of the financial environment shown in Exhibit 2–2, the executive should be able to determine what the firm can do and thereby formulate policy more successfully.

EXTERNAL ELEMENTS

How important are external environmental forces to an organization? One theorist put it this way:

> A particular technology is effective only insofar as it is appropriate to the environment an organization faces. . . . No matter how internally efficient the tech-activity system, the loss of external relevance dooms an organization to inferior status unless it has other sources of power over its environment. . . . Most organizations have only a limited degree of freedom from environmental forces.[6]

Another writer distinguished between

center firms: those with the power to shape their environments
and
periphery firms: those only able to respond to rather than influence their environments.[7]

Large organizations are less likely to fail and have the power to influence their environments whereas smaller organizations (of which there are a far greater number) have a significantly higher probability

(handwritten margin note: Question to ask or answer for term paper. ✱ R.O.I.)

EXHIBIT 2–2 Financial Considerations for the Firm

Sales
1. What are the annual sales of the company?
2. What are the annual sales for the industry?
3. What are the sales trends for the company?
4. What are the sales trends for the industry?

Growth
1. Is the company's net worth growing?
2. Is the company's stockholder equity growing?
3. What is happening with the company's asset value?
4. What are the trends in these areas for the last 10 years?

Profit
1. What is happening to company profits?
2. Are profits keeping ahead of inflation?
3. What are the profit trends for the last 10 years?

Receivables
1. Is the volume of accounts receivable stable or is it changing?
2. Is there a correlation between the volume of accounts receivable and sales volume?
3. What are the trends in the volume of accounts receivable?

Payables
What are the trends in accounts payable?

Inventory
1. What is the status of the volume of inventory?
2. What is the rate of inventory turnover?
3. What is the trend in inventory investment?

Cash
1. What is the cash position?
2. What is the pattern of cash flow?
3. What are the trends in cash flow?
4. Does the company's cash position make it a potential candidate for acquisition take-over?

Retained Earnings
1. What is the company's retained earnings position?
2. What is the trend in retained earnings?

---

of failure and a higher turnover rate. However, larger firms are not immune to failure. The Penn Central collapse, the difficulties faced by Boeing several years ago, and the current uncertainty about the future of Texaco and Bank of America underscore that bigness alone does not ensure survival.

External environmental analysis has become increasingly important in recent years because of the increasing rate of environmental change often coupled with uncertainty about the directions of change in the future. Adherence to a consistent strategy often is difficult, if not

---

[6] Howard E. Aldrich, *Organizations and Environments* (Englewood Cliffs, N.J.: Prentice-Hall, 1979), p. 18.

[7] Robert Averitt, *The Dual Economy* (New York: W. W. Norton, 1968).

impossible, for a firm under such conditions. Organizations, especially larger ones, constantly monitor various elements of their environment. The elements most carefully monitored by a firm are the ones having the greatest impact on outcomes for the firm.[8]

Environmental forecasting has been implemented by several firms. Included are forecasts about societal demands and technological changes. Firms that are adaptive under conditions of uncertainty and rapid change can take advantage of the elements of their environments. We now turn to a discussion of these various external elements.

Economic Environment

In looking at the economic environment, there are many facets with which an executive must be concerned. Always in the forefront is the nature of the market. What is the level and rate of growth of demand? Does the firm dominate its market or markets or is its share of the market on the low side? Is the industry embryonic, youthful, adolescent, mature, or declining? Is there an adequate supply of labor available? Is the available labor unionized or nonunionized? What is the status of the wage rates? What are the implications of the shift in the United States from a manufacturing to a service economy? Today, the general manager must be concerned with international competitiveness, the level of productivity, and the closely related state of technology, inflation, interest rates, and availability of capital.

Industry Structure and Company Position

Two other business environmental concerns are the structure of the industry and the position of the company in that industry. Does the firm have many competitors, few, or none? If there are competitors, is the firm one of the more prominent companies? Does it fall in the medium-sized range of the industry? Or is it one of the less important companies in the industry? Understanding the industry is important as a basis for planning the company's future policy and strategy.

The Social Environment

The concern with the social environment has to do with people, their interrelationships, and the impact these factors have on the company's operation. Since policy is a people matter, a decision mechanism, the *policymaker* should be concerned with the *ramifications* imposed by

---

[8] Liam Fahey and William R. King, "Environmental Scanning for Corporate Planning," *Business Horizons*, August 1977, pp. 61–71.

the *social environment*. In viewing the sensitivity of people and their responsiveness to the social environment, it seems necessary for the policymaker to be aware of the social environment's influence on the subordinate's behavior.

Religious Environment

It has been observed that in some circumstances, the religious environment seems to have little if any impact on the behavior of the subordinate. There are, however, circumstances, given the tenets some religions impose on their parishioners, where it will be observed that the employee may respond positively or negatively to a policy, based on the tenets his or her religion imposes. In such situations, it becomes important for the executive to be cognizant of the potential influence the religious environment may have on managerial results.

Political Environment

In contemporary times, and possibly throughout history, business has been affected by the political environment. In some instances, executives may be able to mold the political environment to favor their objectives and their special needs. In other circumstances, the executive cannot (or will not, as through bribes) affect political outcomes and consequently must then find ways of conforming to the *political* circumstance. The executive should always be sensitive to the political environment to be able to interpret the significant meanings and to take appropriate action.

Two examples follow that show two different approaches that were used relating to a national political circumstance.

Two senators, belonging to the president's party, went to an opposing senator's home state on a quiet speaking tour. During the tour they raised $400,000 to be used two years hence to support a candidate from their party to oppose the incumbent. When the senator arrived home to start his speaking tour or "constituent pulse taking," he discovered to his chagrin what had happened. The opposing party senators informed him that unless he supported the president's legislative program they would fund the opponent's political campaign in the next election. This intimidation coerced the senator to yield to the opposition.

Chief executive officers from a number of major companies were invited to Washington. The purpose of their visit was to call on those congressmen representing districts where each company had plants located. Surely the congressmen would not want it said that plant closing was the result of lack of cooperativeness. The consequence of these visits was the gaining of additional support for the president's program.

Cultural Environment

One of the lessons learned in recent times is the importance of the *cultural environment* on *managerial action*. It is essential, therefore, for the executive to be sensitive to the cultural environment and to be able to interpret its meaning. There are many examples of American business firms having moved abroad while lacking an understanding of their new cultural environment. The consequence, unfortunately, has been failure. Similar examples may be found in the United States where firms have opened new plants in new sections of the country, locations with pronounced cultural differences.

Ethnic Environment

In America, through the years, various ethnic groups have presented executives with a series of interesting challenges. More recently, it appears that there has been a greater melding of ethnic groups into the traditional American population. It is not uncommon to find first-generation Vietnamese, Chinese, East Indians, Hispanics, and other ethnic groups in areas that formerly were inhabited by those Americans whose heritage in America covered a number of generations. It should be understood that these various ethnic groups bring with their immigration a different culture and lifestyle. It is not uncommon to find conflicts between the natives and the new Americans. Witness the conflict that occurred between the native Texas shrimpers and the Vietnamese shrimpers. The executives finding themselves enmeshed in this type of environment must find the means to effectively deal with these people and their behavior.

The "Now Group" in the Environment

This is a group that may not be easily identified since the group's composition and reason for being tends to shift from time to time. As an executive, if you are to deal effectively with such groups, you must recognize *what* it is that a particular group has on its *now agenda*. In this recognition, it seems necessary to be able to *evaluate* and *determine* the *significance* of the now group's objective and define its importance to your mission.

An example of a now group is the dissident student groups found on college and university campuses during the 1960s. At one point, their want-it-now objective was to immediately have campus residence halls officially open to coeducational living. Surely in today's world you can identify other examples of now groups with different "now objectives."

After having used these series of questions, the financial status of the company should be evident. With this knowledge of the financial environment, the policy executive should be better able to formulate policy successfully.

Technology

The technologies with which a firm is concerned include product and process technologies. Product technology is concerned with how products are designed; process technology is concerned with how products are manufactured and delivered to the consumer. Technologies can change rapidly or slowly. Firms can strive to be in the forefront of technology, thereby increasing their risk and potential return. Or firms can deliberately choose to follow the leader, thereby dampening the risks associated with technological innovation and probably potential profitability and margins as well. A danger facing many firms today is technological obsolescence. The orientation and values of key executives can lead to critical decisions with negative future outcomes. For example, Romney, head of American Motors Corporation, preferred to avoid debt. When AMC enjoyed a period of considerable success, Romney chose to retire debt rather than to reinvest in research and development—a decision that later cost the company heavily in the marketplace.

Demographics

Population characteristics and movements are part of the external environment. You must be sensitive to changes and trends if your firm is to survive. Migrations from the Snow Belt to the Sun Belt have brought failure to some companies and prosperity to others. Recent projections suggest a slowing and possible reversal of this trend. Gerber adjusted to the aging of the baby boomers and the arrival of the baby bust years by initiating insurance sales to offset the flattening and prospective decline of its baby food line.

Domestic Setting

Finally, we must note two special subsets of the external environment: domestic and international. You will find that different techniques may be required in scanning these two environments and that your organization may need to respond differentially to the stimuli of these environments.

In the domestic setting, the executive administrator is concerned with local as well as regional and national factors. The set of factors in the domestic setting is similar to the set in the international arena, though the information relating to each is different. In viewing the domestic setting, executives need to understand the relationships of the following to their organizational responsibilities: the cultural environment, the firm's relationship with various levels of government, and the political environment. The effectiveness of the executive is dependent on his or her ability to cope with these environmental aspects.

International Setting

In recent times, it has been necessary for many firms to expand their business activities beyond the national boundaries to achieve desired growth. At the same time, American firms have been confronted with competition from foreign firms in domestic markets as well as in international markets. Competition between firms in highly industrialized nations is very visible. Most Americans are acutely aware of the impact on the American automobile industry of competition from Japanese, German, and Swedish automobile manufacturers. Just as critical is the impact on the United States steel, watch, shoe, and textile industries.

The situation becomes increasingly complex as executives creatively consider the worldwide implications of their actions over a longer period of time. The world is not just composed of industrialized and nonindustrialized countries or of haves and have nots. Instead, it may be useful to distinguish among (a) OPEC countries, which are still underdeveloped but in some ways quite wealthy; (b) underdeveloped and poor countries sometimes referred to as the Third World; and (c) the Fourth World, made up of those 15 countries so desperately poor that their populations are literally starving to death (per capita annual income of less than $100). We can also talk of NICs (newly industrializing countries), which are suddenly competitive on world markets in certain sectors and which have grown rapidly. Another recent designation is nopecs, referring to those less developed countries that, having no oil, are in serious financial problems. We talk of North-South relations, meaning the capitalist and very rich countries versus the less developed countries. We can also refer to the MSAs (most seriously affected) in referring to the group of underdeveloped countries particularly hard hit by the raising of oil prices. None of these terms refers to quite the same set of countries, but they all have their special advantages—depending on the particular topic under discussion.

What nations can provide to world markets is dependent on a variety of factors. There are resource-rich poor countries (the OPEC bloc is the best example), and labor-rich, rapidly developing countries (Hong Kong, Singapore, Korea, Mexico, Brazil, Taiwan) that have done quite well in world trade. Other poor or developing countries may have as much labor, but no growth is occurring. There are market-rich developing countries, such as Brazil, Mexico, Philippines, and Argentina, with sufficient purchasing power to attract light industry, and other countries such as China, with the world's largest population, an unattractive market because the people have no purchasing power.[9]

DOMINANT COALITIONS

Who determines the mission of the organization? Who defines the relevant environmental components toward which organizational resources will be directed? Who sets the goals that organizational members will strive to achieve? In most organizations of any size, the answer to those questions will be more than one person.

Choices are made within organizations by those in power. The individuals involved in influencing these choices are often referred to as the dominant coalition. The involvement of the dominant coalition is critical to acceptance and implementation of major policy and strategic choices. Indeed, as suggested earlier, implementation is not a clear-cut phase but rather begins from the moment the idea or proposal surfaces. As suggested by the discussion of the informal organization, those who are in power, the dominant coalition, may be difficult to identify. As one writer put it,

> The dominant coalition may be the owners or founders of an organization, but it may also be any other group in an organization that has achieved power through control over critical contingencies or essential resources.[10]

SHARED VALUES

Cornerstone of Well managed Comp.

You become part of a coalition because you share values with other members of the organization. Dominant coalitions attempt to extend their values organizationwide. These extended values establish the *culture* of the organization, which then either facilitates or impedes the achievement of stated goals.

Peters and Waterman have shown us that *excellent* companies are characterized by a few shared values, which are both understood and believed in by company employees.[11] The shared values of the excellent companies provide a framework within which managers can exer-

---

[9] We are indebted to John Garland, Assistant Professor of International Business at the University of Kansas, for these insights.

[10] Aldrich, *Organizations and Environment*, p. 138.

[11] Thomas J. Peters and Robert H. Waterman, Jr., *In Search of Excellence: Lessons from America's Best-Run Companies* (New York: Harper & Row, 1982).

cise practical autonomy. These values form a culture with an external focus from which employees desire to provide the best in quality, service, and innovative problem solving in support of their customers.

If a mission statement represents the true long-term purpose of an organization, it will reflect the shared values of organizational members, particularly as articulated by the dominant coalition. The coalition will set goals for the organization which, in turn, reflect the intent of the mission statement.

GOALS AND OBJECTIVES

goals flow from the mission

We have defined policy as a guide to action in areas of repetitive activity and strategy as the means by which an organization interacts with its environment to attain long-term goals. Both policy and strategy demand the existence of goals. Goals answer the why of organizational activity—Why must we adhere to Policy A? Why must I allocate my resources to Strategy B?—because the policies and strategies have been designed as mechanisms to accomplish goals.

In this text, we have used two labels, goals and objectives, which may appear interchangeable. Many authors consider them synonymous. In practice you will find that executives use them to describe the same result, or perhaps use one label as broader and more encompassing than the other. For the purposes of this book, we define goals as being more global than objectives. Generally, the term *goal* is associated with strategy and is the *purpose* toward which an endeavor is directed, giving a basic sense of direction for an organization's activities. An objective is more specific and associated with policy. An *objective* is the *desired outcome* of a business plan, an *identifiable end* that also serves as a *tool for measuring performance.*

The general manager has the responsibility for establishing organizational goals. As we have previously explained, however, the general manager does not function in isolation and may be one among several in a dominant coalition. Further, in setting goals, you must be sensitive to a variety of other influences on your decision. Exhibit 2–3 shows some of the factors affecting goal setting in organizations.

You must weigh the resources and competencies your organization possesses before you establish a goal. If you do not currently have the competencies on staff, do you have adequate resources to obtain them? We have examined the effects of shared values on the firm. Does your goal reflect these values? Will accomplishment of the goal satisfy or infringe on the obligations of your company to its constituents? This will be discussed more fully in Chapter 5. Are you addressing realistic threats and opportunities in your environment in the goals you establish? Finally, test the goal against your mission state-

EXHIBIT 2–3 Influences on Goal Setting

```
┌──────────────┐  ┌──────────────┐  ┌──────────────┐  ┌──────────────┐
│ Competencies │  │ Values and   │  │ Obligations  │  │ Opportunities│
│ and          │  │ aspirations  │  │ to           │  │ and          │
│ resources    │  │ of           │  │ constituents │  │ threats      │
│              │  │ management   │  │              │  │              │
└──────────────┘  └──────────────┘  └──────────────┘  └──────────────┘

                        ┌──────────────┐
                        │  Strategic   │
                        │    goals     │
                        └──────────────┘

                        ┌──────────────┐
                        │   Mission    │
                        │  statement   │
                        └──────────────┘
```

ment. Is it a fit or is it in contradiction? Do changing events require a
modification in either or both?

Questions to ask regarding objectives that you are setting include:

- Is the objective compatible with organizational policies?
- Is it understandable by those charged with the responsibility of
  achieving it?
- Is it measurable?
- Is its accomplishment cost effective?

KEY RESULTS AREAS

A final note on goal setting is that you should address your efforts
toward what we call _key results areas._ Organizational goals must not
be trivial. You should not waste your time developing vague, ill-de-
fined goals (e.g., to provide a quality product) that are written more for
morale than for mobilizing resources. Alternatively, do not, at the
policy level, select goals only because they are concrete and measurable (e.g., reduce copy machine expenses by one half percent per
month for the next six months).

Key results areas represent the goals from which an organization
can expect the greatest payoffs. They are critical to the survival,

growth, and success of the organization. The focus of key results areas is *results*, not activities. Categories of key results areas include customer satisfaction, productivity, innovation, resources, human resource development, public responsibility, organizational image, and others. Identifying key results areas is part of your responsibility to prioritize. This will be dealt with in greater detail in Chapter 3.

SUMMARY

Goal setting can be viewed as the first step in the strategic management process. The goals you establish are an extension of the mission of your organization. Comprehension and fulfillment of the mission requires knowledge of the elements of both the internal and external environments of your organization. In this chapter, we have defined goals and objectives. We have also explained how they are influenced by resources, values, obligations, and opportunities. In Chapter 3, we turn to the formulation of strategies for attaining your goals.

3

Formulating Strategies

Continuing need for environmental scanning

By formulating we mean creating or developing the strategies an enterprise will apply in relating to its external environment and the policies it will establish to guide internal functioning. Strategies are formulated to carry out the mission of the organization and achieve its goals. Strategies must be subordinated to missions and goals. You may discover your goals are impossible to attain or your mission has become obsolete. If so, redefine your mission statement and draft new goals. Do not formulate a strategy without a clear sense of purpose for your firm.

Know →

In this chapter, we examine the strategic planning process that will result in a course of action for the organization. We shall discuss various strategic options available to the general manager and consider selected factors that influence strategy formulation.

PLANNING

Most executives do plan; that is, they establish an outline for future action. During this century, companies, especially the larger firms, have become increasingly committed to formal planning activities. There are, however, various kinds of planning activities carried out in firms, including strategic, operational, and budgetary planning.

Strategic planning activities are longer term in nature, involve top-level executives, and are more global in their effect on the firm. Operational planning and establishing major policies are also plan-

EXHIBIT 3–1   Relationships of Major Planning Activities

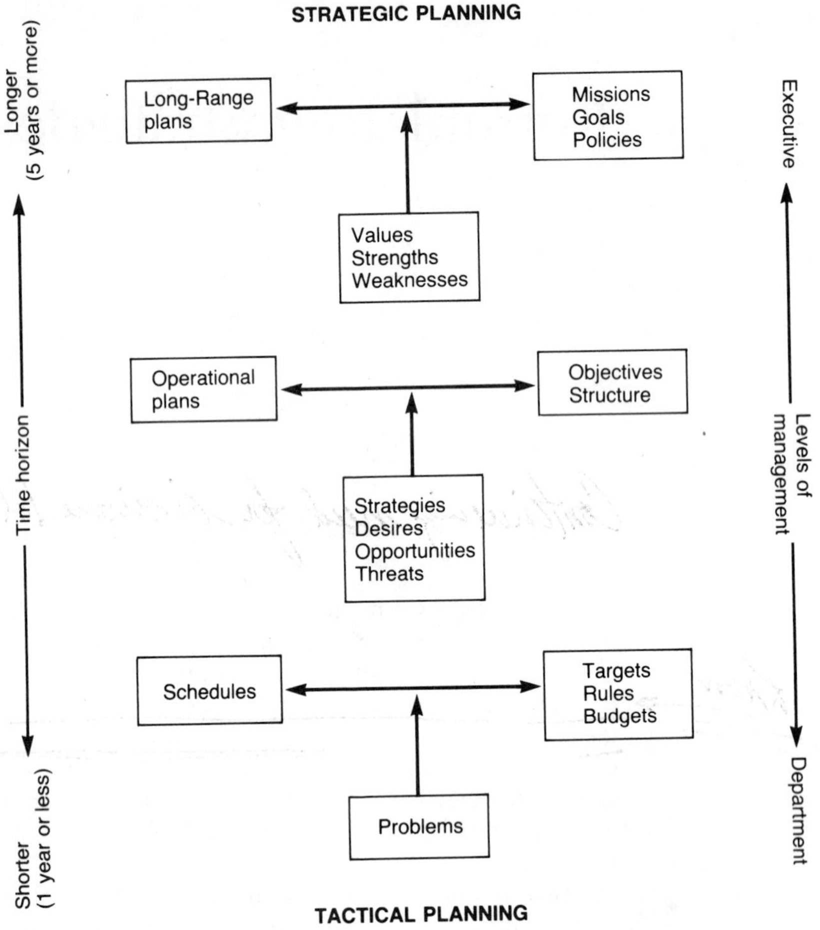

STRATEGIC PLANNING

TACTICAL PLANNING

ning activities that are longer term and broader in effect. However, operational planning (e.g., planning for major facility additions) and policy formulation (e.g., establishing whether the firm will continue to market through manufacturing representatives or initiate its own sales force) are usually carried out within a broader strategic framework.

Planning activities also include establishing budgets, schedules, and departmental policies. These activities involve a shorter term focus and lower level managers. Planning, therefore, involves all levels of an organization's management. The relationships among these various planning activities is given in Exhibit 3–1. As indicated, planning activities can be initiated from the top—top-down planning—or from the bottom—bottom-up planning. Exhibit 3–1 also shows that each planning level is affected by subjective influences. It would be misleading to suggest that missions, objectives, targets, and even budgets are objectively determined, although they may appear to be when read by one who did not participate in the planning process. We mentioned earlier the effects of the values of the dominant coalition on an organization. These values, along with top management's perception of organizational strengths and weaknesses, lead to strategy formulation. Those strategies, the desires of relevant managers, and assessments of opportunities and threats affect medium-range objectives and the structure designed to implement strategies. In the short range, the daily choices by managers of problems and priorities to address affect targets, rules, and budgets.

By now you should readily conclude that strategic planning is not a one-year budget. Even so, the one-year budget should reflect the strategic plan. Nor is the strategic plan that marvelous five-year forecast. Again, however, the five-year forecast (of sales, profits, production capacity, budgets, sales force, or what have you) should reflect the strategic plan. These forecasts and long-range budgets are operational plans. In other words, operational plans, especially long-range plans, emanate from the overall strategic plan.

Difficulties with Planning

A number of difficulties occur with planning. Three of the most common are (*a*) failure to take significant factors into account, (*b*) implicit planning, and (*c*) exclusive focus on the short run.

Ignoring Significant Factors

Many firms are guilty at some point of ignoring significant factors. Significant factors can be internal and external. Edwin Land of Polaroid provides a vivid example. Shortly after World War II, Edwin Land, founder, director of research and development, president, and chairman of the board of Polaroid, became convinced that people would want instant photography. For the most part, Land's "visions," which emanated from his R&D lab, found a ready market among the American people—at least until Polaroid introduced an instant development movie system that the company called Polavision. Had Polavision preceded video, it might have enjoyed extensive if short-lived demand. However, lack of demand, mainly attributable to video's competitive prices, combined with inappropriate channel of distribution (Polavision did not sell well in drugstores!), led to Polaroid's biggest failure.

Implicit Planning

However, Edwin Land did not make the classic entrepreneurial planning error. Unlike the executive in the next example, Land's company carried out explicit planning. Many entrepreneurs, however, only plan implicitly. The courses of action to unfold their visions remain where the visions originated—in the entrepreneur's head! Plans can and should provide direction and cohesion for the firm. To do so, they need to be explicit.

For example, the president of a medium-sized manufacturing company was, most agree, a man of brilliance. Unfortunately for his firm and those associated with it, his flashes of brilliance occurred in his moments of solitude—usually when others were sleeping. The president would appear in the morning and snap out orders. However, the course of action he intended to follow was never clear to those whose coordinated activities were necessary. This man planned, but the planning process could not provide direction and cohesion for his firm.

At this juncture, however, we should point out that we are not advocating inflexibility in the planning process. It has been observed that managers often do carry their best strategies around in their heads.

> For example, having presided over the development of a process that produced extremely fine metal fibers, one manager was assigned the task of establishing a business unit that was to supply manufacturers of filtration equipment. Some time later, noting that demand was considerably short of what the corporation had come to expect, he changed his plan in a sudden but timely way. He radically restructured the nature of his business unit to include the control of fluid control as well as the manufacturing of fluids, all of which was done to complement the production of the filter fibers. This led to the acquisition of several filter and valve manufacturers, and provided the necessary growth for his company. His plan was not as tightly thought out or voluminously detailed as those that commonly appear in planning documents. It couldn't be; rigidity of that kind would not have helped him adapt to changing circumstances.[1]

Short-Term Focus

The third critical error made in the planning process is exclusive (or concerted) focus on short-term planning. This criticism is frequently leveled at American business as a whole today. Judging executive performance on the basis of quarterly reports, earnings per share, and Wall Street reports on the price-earnings ratio contribute to the

---

[1] John M. Strengrevics, "Corporate Planning Needn't Be an Executive Straitjacket," *The Wall Street Journal*, September 26, 1983, p. 28.

myopic focus. There is often a significant time lapse before policies can be formulated and implemented. There is additional time before the full effects of major policy change can be observed. One rule of thumb for CEOs is that three years may elapse before the effects of major policy and strategic changes are experienced. Many executives are in or looking for new positions before the full effects of their programs have an impact on company performance!

One of the senior financial managers of Hallmark, Inc. (the card company) recently extolled his company's long-range viewpoint. Hallmark is one of the largest privately held companies in the United States. Its growth rate over more than the last decade is estimated at greater than 15 percent per year. All of the company's growth has been supported by internally generated funds—a remarkable record indeed! Said the financial executive: "We can take a long-range viewpoint since we do not have to respond to Wall Street fluctuations and stockholders demanding quarterly results." Some critics of the American system predict that the country is undercutting its future as a world economic power because of its myopic short-term viewpoint.

WHAT IS STRATEGIC PLANNING?

excellent definition

Strategic planning is a decision-making process that leads to the selection of a course of action by which an organization will fulfill its mission and strive toward its goals within its environment. Objectives and action plans should be established only after careful assessment and prediction of the future states of relevant environmental factors. For example, ABC Company decided to develop a new technology and planned to achieve dominance in this new area by using the distribution channels and sales forces of several established companies. The company also decided to rely on outside suppliers for most component parts and on another manufacturer for final assembly. If demand developed as the company anticipated, consideration would be given to developing the company's own assembly plant, although most components would continue to be purchased during the foreseeable future. Funds were to come from three sources: (*a*) initial limited financing from the owner-founder, (*b*) subsequent inflow of debt and equity by the company undertaking the final assembly, and (*c*) subsequent offerings of equity to the public.

The preceding statement delineates the basic strategic plan for ABC Company. The plan was a high-risk one since the company knew that other larger companies were developing competing technologies. It was, therefore, a race to see who made it to the market first!

DEF Company is a contrasting example. DEF Company committed itself to maintaining a long-established tradition of unexcelled quality. Its basic strategic plan can be described as follows: The company produces a limited number of products of unexcelled quality. Production is carried out by finely trained craftsmen. Some limited automation is introduced each year but only after extensive testing to assure maintenance of superb quality. The company makes most of the component parts in its own factory and tests each product for a significant period of time after completion. All rejected pieces are disassembled; no second-quality units are sold. The company's small sales force services a set of limited and carefully selected distribution outlets, most of which have long-established names of their own. Only one or two outlets are added each year, and these only when another outlet has ceased operation. The company carries out limited advertising in magazines normally read only by the upper level socioeconomic classes. Ownership is held by the fifth generation of the family. Recently, a portion of ownership was given to the first nonfamily member who assumed the post of managing director.

The two strategic descriptions reflect very different companies indeed! The two illustrations show that strategic planning involves establishing the overall identity of the company, deciding on the strategic alternatives the company will follow, and choosing the tactics or weapons that the company will emphasize.

STRATEGIC PLANNING SEQUENCE

Although we are about to list a series of steps for you, it is rare for managers to be as sequential and discrete in planning as this process implies. Some firms formalize strategic planning, employing professional staffs or scheduling executive retreats. Nevertheless, even in these instances, there is negotiation and compromise among participants. There is disorder and there are tangential diversions during the discussions. There is subsequent input from others who become significant in implementing strategies. And there is reactive as well as proactive decision making toward events that affect the company.

Despite these complications, analytical evaluation of the planning process can help you ensure that critical steps will not be omitted. Further, for years, researchers have found that companies that engage in formal planning outperform those that do not.[2]

Strategic planning includes the following activities:

1. Ensure a *strategic fit*.
    a. Is your mission statement current and accurate?
    b. Have you reached agreement on critical, long-term goals?

---

[2] See, for example, Stanley S. Thune and Robert J. House, "Where Long-Range Planning Pays Off," *Business Horizons*, August 1970, pp. 81–87; and Patrick H. Irwin, "Romulus and Remus: Two Studies in Corporate Planning," *Management Review*, October 1976, pp. 24–26.

2. Conduct a *forecast*.
   a. What is the current status of the organization?
   b. Have you scanned the environment to anticipate probable changes?
   c. What will happen if you make no changes in present strategy and activities?
3. Perform a *strategic analysis*.
   a. Internal: What resources does the organization have available?
   b. External: What are the states of your relevant environments?
4. Generate options.
   a. Should you *specialize?*
   b. Should you *diversify?*
   c. Should you *divest?*
5. Evaluate options.
   a. Does the option fit strategically with your mission, goals, and other strategies?
   b. What are the costs and benefits of the option?
   c. How will your competition react?
   d. Can you measure progress toward your goals?
   e. Will organization members be committed?
6. Select the strategy.

The questions you ask and the factors you consider in proceeding through these planning steps vary depending on the stage of life cycle of your organization and its major products or services.

ORGANIZATIONAL STAGES

In firms or divisions operating with a fairly focused product line or within a particular industry, various functions tend to predominate at various stages in the product (or industry) life cycle. The stages and typical functional dominance are depicted in Exhibit 3–2. In the introduction phase, particularly for highly technical products, R&D may be the dominant function. Later, in the growth phase, as demand materializes and accelerates, production may become paramount. In the mature phase, market segmentation may take place, and marketing may be cast into a paramount role. When demand for the product wanes and the firm begins to withdraw resources from the activities devoted to that product or service, finance may play a dominant role. This discussion is somewhat simplistic since firms choose different strategies in various phases of the product life cycle. Depending on the strategy followed by the firm, however, various functional areas dominate.

EXHIBIT 3–2 Typical Functional Dominance at Various Product Life Cycle Stages

Product life cycle stage

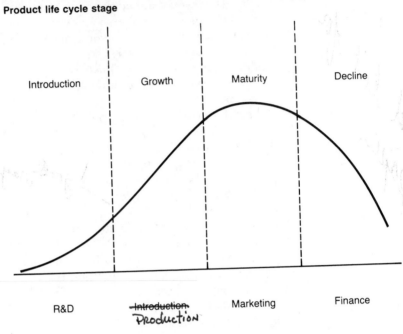

Typical functional dominance

Do not be fooled by the lines between the stages into thinking that there are quick discrete steps. In fact, the transition periods may be longer than the stages themselves. The transitions are often arduous and fraught with peril. During periods of transition, conflicts between old dominant groups and new dominant groups are common. It is also important to recognize that strategies developed by a general manager may be influenced by his or her own life cycle or by the stage of his or her immediate family's development.

SWOT ANALYSIS

A procedure used by strategic planners in assessing the relevance of life cycles to strategic options as well as the influences of other factors is referred to as SWOT analysis. SWOT is an acronym for strengths, weaknesses, opportunities, and threats. As you can see in Exhibit 3–3, a SWOT analysis demands that you focus on both the internal and external environments of the firm to determine your capability of adopting a given strategy.

EXHIBIT 3–3 Evaluating a Firm's Strategic Capability

**EVALUATION OF THE FIRM'S
INTERNAL ENVIRONMENT**

**EVALUATION OF THE FIRM'S
EXTERNAL ENVIRONMENT**

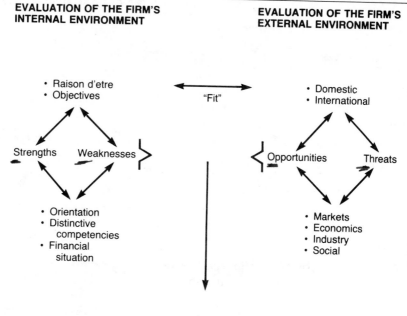

Strategic Capability

The analysis is both quantitative and qualitative. The internal analysis examines existing resources to ascertain if proposed strategies can be implemented. Strengths and weaknesses of all appropriate resources, human, capital, and material, are considered. The external analysis addresses opportunities and threats posed by relevant environments (e.g., technological, legal, economic) and constituents (e.g., customers, suppliers, community). Analysis and evaluation of the internal elements of a firm's environment must consider the firm's strengths and weaknesses relative to (*a*) what the firm wants to be or do and (*b*) the threats and opportunities in the firm's external environment. Ultimately, of course, the results the firm will achieve will be determined by the fit between the elements of its internal environment and the elements of its external environment. It is this fit as depicted in Exhibit 3–3 that determines a firm's strategic capability.[3]

---

[3] This term is used by R. T. Lenz in "Strategic Capability: A Concept and Framework for Analysis," *Academy of Management Review* 5, no. 2 (1980), pp. 225–34 as "the capability of an enterprise to successfully undertake action that is intended to affect its long-term growth and development," (p. 226).

BASIC STRATEGIC ALTERNATIVES

A firm may pursue one of three basic strategies:

1. Specialize
2. Diversify
    a. Related
        (1) Horizontal
        (2) Vertical
    b. Unrelated
    c. Geographical
        (1) Regional
        (2) National
        (3) International
3. Divest

Each of these is discussed in the following sections.

Specialization

Specialization usually refers to a focused product line. In fact, the history of most firms begins with one or two products or services. Ford began with the basic black Model-T. Culpepper Tackle has chosen to concentrate on fishing gear. Marion Laboratories, Inc. began with Oscal. A firm that markets a related set of services or products is usually referred to as having a single business focus.

In addition to *product specialization*, however, firms can also decide to engage in *market specialization* by channel of distribution ("We use only manufacturers' representatives"), geographical area, ("We distribute only in the Northeast"), market segment ("Our eating establishment attracts middle-class families"), choice of media ("We advertise strictly through local newspapers") and so on. Baskin-Robbins, for example, specializes in ice cream sold through brand name stores that are primarily franchised units. Still other companies choose to use only manufacturers' representatives or only their own internal salespeople. One casualty insurance company for many years used independent insurance agents to sell its insurance and service established clients. In the last several years, the company decided to replace the independents with company agencies. This change created considerable dismay among the independents—many of whom had a long-standing relationship with the company and a firmly established clientele.

Companies may specialize by geographical area. A number of family owned beer companies held major market shares for many years in localized areas or within narrowly defined regions. Still other companies may specialize in their production capabilities. Many companies choose to be assemblers rather than manufacturers. Others choose to specialize in location. Coors, the beer company, for many years continued to enlarge its plant outside of Denver until it had the largest beer manufacturing facility in the world. The company's advertising, "Brewed with Pure Rocky Mountain Water," emphasized the unique quality of the water. Only in recent years did the company consider building another facility. Still other companies have firmly established financial policies to use only equity in their long-term capital base (e.g., Hallmark).

Specialized companies, even with coherent strategies, can discover themselves in trouble if their products or technologies become obsolete or if competitors gain a comparative advantage. Companies that concentrated on mechanical typewriters (e.g., Underwood) or calculators (e.g., Burroughs) were outdistanced by competitors who brought in the electronic age. Now typewriters and IBM are almost synonymous, and today's major competitors did not even make typewriters 15 years ago!

Diversification

The larger firms in the United States today have typically diversified away from a single business focus. The following discussion is focused primarily on diversification of product lines but refers, broadly, to all the major activities of the business.

Firms may diversify into related product lines. The new product lines may or may not be related. Gerber, for example, diversified from a focus on baby food to other products appropriate for infants and Gerber's channel of distribution. The Gerber expansion is referred to as horizontal diversification. For example, sports equipment manufacturers and retail dealers have added fashion sportswear. Where slack production capacity existed, companies have added products that could be made with existing equipment. For example, one small metal fabricator operated most of its machinery at about 60 percent of its one-shift capacity. By adding people, scheduling carefully, and aiming at products using the equipment with the greater slack, the entrepreneur was able to improve sales, margin, and personnel use. In undertaking the diversification of Holbrook Tire Service into Charlestown Accessories and Equipment, the president, Neil Bergh, aimed to serve a customer base to whom he sold tires, namely, trucking companies.

In other instances, companies add channels of distribution. For example, products that were sold only through department stores are now found in supermarkets. Other companies add channels of distribution to reach additional customer segments.

Vertical integration. Companies that pursue vertical integration typically move forward to secure more control of their channels of distribution (forward integration) or backward to secure supplies of raw materials (backward integration). A manufacturer who purchases or establishes a chain of retail outlets is an example of forward vertical integration. A local dairy, for example, has a chain of combination convenience store-ice cream specialty shops.

A manufacturer who purchases a raw materials supplier is an example of backward vertical integration. Most of the major oil companies are "wholly integrated"; that is, their range of activities encompasses exploration, wellhead production, transportation, refining, and marketing. In fact, most of the independents, that is, those companies that are not wholly integrated, have either purchased or been purchased by firms whose activities brought the combined activities closer to total integration.

Generally, in undertaking related diversification, companies seek synergism. Synergism refers to the phenomenon of the whole being greater than the sum of its parts. In vertical integration, for example, firms usually hope to attain greater control and eliminate some marketing or procurement costs. Greater revenues and profits should result from a lowered asset base. As with a good marriage, firms undertaking related diversification expect that the new combination of activities will yield more to the whole than either activity by itself. In other words, the company hopes two plus one will equal four or, at least, three and a half!

Unrelated diversification. Other firms have diversified into unrelated activities. Unrelated or conglomerate diversification has been rampant in the United States at least since the latter part of the 1960s. Marion Laboratories, like many firms in the late 1960s and 1970s, undertook diversification only moderately related to the firm's initial focus. Marion Laboratories was not the only company—either cash rich or enjoying a high price-earnings ratio[4]—that caught "conglomerate fever" at the time!

Unrelated diversification has come under attack for two reasons. In the first place, there is concern about the concentration of power in the hands of a few. The power to shift financial resources has the potential to affect significantly the future of a nation or nations. In the second place, unrelated diversification has tended to be less profitable in the long run than related diversification.[5] Critics suggest that unre-

---

[4] A high price-earnings ratio allows a company to issue stock to purchase another company with a lower price-earnings ratio without unduly diluting ownership control or earnings per share.

[5] See, for example, Richard Rumelt, *Strategy, Structure and Economic Performance* (Harvard Business School, Harvard University, 1974).

lated diversification is motivated by top management's desire to enhance its power base. Managers who enthusiastically engage in unrelated diversification too frequently get themselves into businesses about which they know little or nothing. Thus, they cannot make adequate judgments about financial allocations (investment), let alone strategic and policy decisions.

In the face of these two well-founded criticisms of conglomerates, several observations can be made. While conglomerates have indeed great potential power, they also offer the potential for more efficient allocation of resources. Similarly, facilities and, to some extent, labor redeployment can also be more efficient. One of the reasons Beech Aircraft Corporation was interested in merging with Raytheon in 1978 was that Raytheon had excess capacity in some areas while Beech was bumping up against the limits of capital facilities and labor supply in several locations. The problems of labor redeployment are more difficult in technologically sophisticated industries. Retraining takes time, and highly skilled employees may prefer to change location rather than to start at the bottom of the ladder in another skill.

The other criticism of unrelated diversification, that it is less profitable than related diversification, is debatable. Advocates suggest that a potential strength is to even out the cyclical fluctuations inherent in many industries. The success of several highly visible firms, including Raytheon, ITT, and Textron, support this contention.

Conglomerate diversification does not usually provide synergism in the same sense related diversification does. However, it does provide opportunity for more efficient reallocation of resources, especially financial resources. In addition, unrelated diversification can increase the resilience of the firm by decreasing its vulnerability to economic fluctuations.

Geographical diversification. Opening a new plant or a new retail outlet, marketing existing products in another region, or establishing an export department are all examples of geographical diversification. Geographical diversification can include expansion into another region, across the country, or into international markets.

Coors (the beer company) was once a regional brewer, distributing only in Colorado. From a centralized plant the company moved into states adjacent to Colorado. In military analogy they continued to capture contiguous territories. Today, Coors is a nationally known brand name. H & R Block, the income tax preparation firm, started in Kansas City and today has offices throughout the United States and Canada. With the deregulation of banking, more and more banks are establishing branches offering essentially the same services in a different area. Other banks are considering horizontal combinations or mergers to combine financial resources and spread the cost of specialized services over an increased customer base. Wal-Mart, one of the fastest growing retail chains, has concentrated its efforts for a number of years in small growth towns. Until recently, this retail firm did not move beyond a 450-mile radius from corporate headquarters and the company's distribution centers in Arkansas. Finally, in 1980 the firm added a second distribution center in Texas.

International diversification. Of all the geographical diversification alternatives, expanding internationally is probably the most complex. The markets for many goods or services are saturated in the United States. As the rate of growth of demand for these goods or services diminished in the United States, companies often looked abroad for new markets. United Telecommunications, the third largest U.S. telephone company, looks to international markets for the growth. United Supply, their subsidiary, purchases telephone and communications equipment from many sources and supplies a wide range of equipment to telephone companies throughout the world.

One small company, Tec Tank, Inc., made bolted steel storage tanks for petroleum, agricultural, and chemical companies. The number of competing firms in the United States was small. Most, however, were considerably larger than Tec Tank. As Tec Tank grew, it began to confront its competition more intensively. The firm began marketing efforts in South America to continue its phenomenal growth record and maintain margins.

Manufacturing firms typically follow a four-stage sequence as they enter international markets. First, the firm exports goods requested by customers abroad. Second, the firm initiates marketing activities abroad. Third, the firm establishes other functional activities, such as manufacturing, in host countries. A firm that has extensive operations abroad is referred to as a multinational organization or MNO. Some firms have moved to a fourth stage internationally. These firms, referred to as transnationals, have become so widespread in their operations and use people from so many of the countries in which they operate that they can no longer be identified with a particular country. Many companies have been impressed by the influence of these transnational companies on the world scene since they are not controlled by any particular government. Indeed, their revenues exceed the GNP of many of the countries within which they operate! To people of the United States, IBM is perhaps the best known of these transnational companies. Among others, the automobile industry, which is undergoing consolidation, will ultimately be composed of several transnational companies.

Divestment

How does a company get rid of a portion of its activities? One way, of course, is to liquidate. *Liquidation* occurs when the company shuts down operations and sells off the assets. A firm might also sell off the unit as an ongoing enterprise. Another form of divestment is a *spin-off*. A *spin-off* occurs when the parent company separates from a unit so that each become free-standing companies. Individuals who held stock in the original consolidated company then hold stock in two companies. Another form of divestment occurs when a firm plans to decrease activities over an extended period of time. Usually, the firm withdraws its investment from those activities (inventory, accounts receivable, plant, and equipment) and invests the freed up resources and the profits from that business or division into other units. This process is often referred to as *harvesting*. Another method gaining popularity is the *leveraged buyout*. This involves the purchase of a subsidiary from a parent company, often by the managers of the subsidiary, using the assets of the unit to finance the purchase.

Which Alternative?

Which alternative should a firm choose? The alternative chosen is influenced by the firm's past history, the values of the top executives, as well as an analysis of its internal and external environments. We shall now consider several factors that impact on your choice of a strategy.

FACTORS AFFECTING STRATEGY OPTIONS

There are various forces at work that propel organizations toward or away from their goals. Exhibit 3–4 represents some of these forces, categorizing them as impetus factors, which press for action, and enabling factors, which facilitate or constrain actions.

Enabling factors such as government, coalitions, and competitors play on the strategic decision of whether to seek *growth* or *stability*. Growth is most often sought through a diversification strategy. Some of the strategic options available using this strategy include:

1. *Acquisition,* or purchase of an existing business.
2. *Corporate venturing,* or *intrapreneurship*, involving the initiation of a new enterprise by a parent corporation.
3. *Merger,* the absorption of one company by another.

Of course, these options could be chosen by a firm following a specialization strategy as well. Companies that specialize generally *concentrate* their product/market efforts, generate their expansions in the introduction and growth stages internally, and seek stability, or change to a diversification strategy.

Specializing companies sometimes select *retrenchment* (i.e., implementing efficiency measures and eliminating waste) options. More

EXHIBIT 3–4 Factors Affecting an Organization's Strategic Alternatives

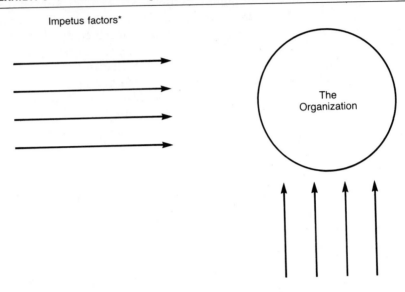

Impetus factors*

The Organization

Enabling factors*

Impetus factors: Factors that broadly impel the organization to act and give direction
to the action.
  Social milieu: The setting in which the organization finds itself including its multiple constituents.
  Government action: Expected or current government laws, regulation of "jawbon-
  ing."
  Identity of the organization: The firm's orientation, mission, or identity and its fit
  with the strategic alternative.
  Coalitions within the organization: Lower level groups can coalesce to gain power
  and influence over alternatives or smaller groups of more powerful individuals may
  coalesce to support or resist an alternative.
  Competitor's action: To preempt a competitor's anticipated actions, a firm may
  initiate a particular alternative.
  Attitude and behavior of organizational leader: Because of experience or deep-
  seated values, an organization's top leadership may support or resist an alternative.

Enabling factors:
  Financial resources: Without financial resources, a firm cannot pursue other than
  strictly survival activities.
  Available personnel: Unless the organization has in-house skills or can attract
  needed expertise, it may be unable to pursue a given strategy.
  Stability within the organization: If the organization's resources—financial manpower and emotional—are diverted to dealing with intra- or extraorganizational
  turmoil, the organization cannot readily pursue other issues.

  * These factors may be positive or negative in effect.
  SOURCE: Derived from Marilyn L. Taylor, "Implementing Affirmative Action: Impetus and Ena-
bling Factors in Five Organizations," *Research Issues in Social Responsibility* (Greenwich, Conn.:
JAI Press, 1981).

often, there are strategies adopted by diversifying companies that find themselves overextended. These options are, in reality, variations of divestment strategies. *Bankruptcy* is normally considered, like liquidation, an ultimate form of divestment strategy. Many firms are now using bankruptcy as a survival strategy rather than a form of exit. Manville Corporation sought protection under Chapter 11 of the Bankruptcy Code as a result of the huge volume of asbestos related suits filed against it. Continental Airlines purportedly filed for bankruptcy to terminate union contracts. More recently, Texaco took the bankruptcy option to avoid being forced to pay a multibillion dollar court settlement to Pennzoil.

Other questions that must be resolved in the formulation of a strategy under any of the three major strategy alternatives include:

- Should we emphasize price or quality?
- Should we seek to *differentiate* and expand our products and services, or *integrate* to achieve synergy?
- Shall we be a follower or leader in technology in our industry?
- What level of risk are our owners and managers prepared to accept?

A number of models have been developed to aid in the strategy formulation process. Your instructor may wish to introduce you to some, such as the General Electric Nine-Cell Planning Grid or McKinsey & Company's 7-S Framework. We shall briefly explain one widely used model as an example.

BCG MODEL

The BCG model was initially developed by Bruce Henderson, president of the Boston Consulting Group. BCG specializes in strategic planning. Underlying the BCG model are two basic concepts: product (or industry) life cycles and experience curves. The product life cycle (PLC) concept is used to provide guidelines for marketing strategy. PLC assumes that over time a product goes through four phases: introduction, growth, maturity, and decline (see Exhibit 3–2). Sales or market growth depends heavily on the PLC stage.

In the early stages of the product life cycle there is often heavy emphasis on R&D and education of the consumer. In a later stage the emphasis may shift to production as the company attempts to meet the demand it has created or to become more efficient than competitors. In a still later stage the emphasis may shift to marketing as there is often brand proliferation and finer market segmentation. In the final stages of the product life cycle, the emphasis may switch to financial aspects as the company withdraws its resources from a product in a declining market.

EXHIBIT 3–5 BCG Model

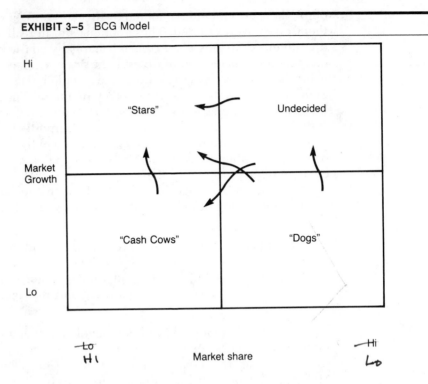

The experience curve concept, in its simplest form, suggests that, as production doubles, costs decline by a relatively constant proportion. The concept can be extended to other functions such as advertising, sales, and distribution. The dominant companies then are those that, having achieved the highest market share, have the widest margins. Such firms can, therefore, afford to stay in an industry/product line for the longest period of time.

The BCG model essentially divides the businesses managed by the company into strategic business units (SBUs) that fall into one of four categories indicated in Exhibit 3–5. The specific category depends on the growth of the market and the company's market share. Exhibit 3–5 displays the basic concept. The four quadrants in this exhibit are discussed in turn.

Stars

Business units with dominant positions in attractive (growth) markets are referred to as *stars*. Most of these subsidiary companies are growing as fast or faster than their markets and have either leading market shares or are among the leading companies. In some instances, these companies generate sufficient capital resources to support their own growth.[6] In other instances, the subsidiary company will need infusions of new capital. The decisions made by top officers in diversified companies are those of capital resource allocation among the subsidiaries. The arrows in Exhibit 3–5 indicate capital flows.

Cash Cows

Companies that are earning good margins but whose growth rates are slow enough that they produce more than sufficient cash flow (net income plus noncash expenses) are referred to as *cash cows*. These businesses are usually in mature industries. The freed financial resources can be used in subsidiaries where infusions are needed. The flow of these funds is indicated in Exhibit 3–5 by the curved arrows.

Dogs

The term *dogs* refers to subsidiaries where the company has a poor market position in a no-growth or declining market. The product(s) or industry is very late in the life cycle. The company wants out. The strategy referred to as *harvesting* is used to shrink assets and gradually phase out the business, liquidate, or sell. The financial resources can then be deployed in other operations.

Undecided

Undecideds are those subsidiaries about which the company has to make a critical decision: Should they get in—or out? The company may bump up against established competitors. To win away market share the company may have to accept a lower margin because it will need to employ strategic or tactical "weapons" more intensively. The company will have to use more advertising, greater intensity of sales effort, better after-sale service, attractive price offers to end users and/ or intermediaries, distribution on demand, attractive product features or other effort that, especially in the short run, can be expected to shave margins.

The BCG Model and Strategic Planning

The BCG model has been most extensively used by diversified companies. However, the model is also applicable to firms with a focused set of products. In addition, the model is also used when examining individual product lines, even those that are closely related. Procter &

---

[6] Students will recognize from constructing pro formas that there is, over the longer term, a more or less constant ratio between assets and sales.

Gamble, for example, recently has made decisions to put resources into some of its product lines, allow some to die a slow "natural" death, and withdraw more quickly from others.[7]

A Word about Managing Cows and Dogs!

A recent criticism leveled at business policy courses is the heavy emphasis on growth goals. Growth, according to some, became the panacea for all ills, the end for all means. The BCG model clearly illustrates that growth is not and indeed should not be the goal for all business entities. However, managers who are programmed for growth often have a difficult readjustment to make if the subsidiary or business needs to be pruned or managed at a different rate or activity than originally planned. Imagine the shock of a manager hired to head a subsidiary slated for growth, who discovers, two weeks after moving his family from one coast to the other, that the parent company has reversed its decision about this subsidiary. The subsidiary was to be trimmed (assets shrunk) in preparation for sale. A similar example occurred when RCA closed its computer operation. In the process of writing off $700 million, RCA terminated employees, some of whom had given up jobs with competitors and had arrived as recently as the day before the announced closure. Significant redirections of companies' strategic plans can raise critical ethical and moral issues!

Sophisticated companies recognize that managing dogs and cows is different from managing stars. Accordingly, these companies fit the person to the job carefully. They select the manager, not just based on managerial ability or industry knowledge, but also based on the individual's emotional response to the task. Managing a dog is not unlike tending a terminally ill patient. The task requires a person who can understand and respond to the needs of such a "patient." In addition, companies modify their control and reward systems. Instead of being measured heavily on profitability, dog managers may be measured and rewarded heavily on the basis of "free cash flow"; that is, the level of resources returned for use to the parent company. In addition, the parent company should provide a sympathetic and knowledgeable managerial and staff superstructure.

Application to the Cases

The BCG model will be applicable to a number of the cases in this text. Depending in which quadrant the company categorizes its divisions or business units, the firm may choose among the basic strategic

---

[7] Carol J. Loomis, "P & G Up Against Its Wall," *Fortune*, February 23, 1981, pp. 49–54.

alternatives—specialization, diversification, or divestment. Some cases will require you to evaluate the current strategy and consider other strategic alternatives. Still others will require you to make policy decisions within the current strategy. Modifying policy requires considering whether policy changes may ultimately lead to strategic changes. Strategic change, on the other hand, requires consideration of the policy changes that will need to be made.

HIDDEN FACETS OF FORMULATION

Earlier, we discussed organizational values, dominant coalitions, and the subjectivity of planning. Strategy formulation is a process of human endeavor, with all the attendant strengths and flaws. Strategies that managers formulate may be implemented as written; they may not be taken seriously by their drafters who, if the truth were known, do not believe in plans; or they may be intended for public consumption while actual plans are carefully disguised.

George Steiner observed that mission statements are written for the public, often as public relations statements.[8] Business plans, however, are proprietary and confidential. Thus, can we invariably assume that a published mission statement actually represents the long-run commitment of the company? Archie Carroll has argued that it should. If the positive results that successful companies have achieved from planning are to be obtained by your organization, your strategy formulation process must have integrity.[9] This means that the plan must be free from defect, error, or fallacy, requiring therefore that it be an outgrowth of an honest mission statement and realistic goals. This can only occur if top management is committed to the process. Managers may operate from a *secret agenda* in formulating strategy, while presenting a *public agenda* to competitors and other relevant outside parties. If the secret agenda moves too far from the organization's defined mission, however, the integrity of the planning process will be lost.

SUMMARY

This chapter has described the process of strategy formulation. You have learned that planning is a critical activity in establishing a firm's strategy. There are, however, many forms of planning. Short-term plans including budgets, schedules, and operational plans must be in harmony with strategic plans. Although strategic planning is fre-

---

[8] George A. Steiner, *Top Management Planning* (New York: Macmillan, 1969).

[9] Archie B. Carroll, "Put Integrity into Your Planning Process," *Planning Review*, July 1984, p. 4.

quently a messy confused process, we can break it down into a logical sequence of steps. There are a number of alternatives firms may choose in achieving their objectives. Basic among these are specialization, diversification, and divestment. The BCG model is an example of one tool a firm can use to decide which of the basic alternatives it may want to pursue.

Finally, many aspects of strategy formulation are hidden from public view, for both good and bad reasons. Make integrity integral to your planning process if you expect meaningful results.

4

Implementing Strategies

largely related to people

implement in stages — set specific goal — do environmental scanning to determine needed changes.

Do not be misled by our separate chapters on goals, formulation, and implementation into thinking that the strategic management process is a series of discrete steps. In fact, these activities, if successful, are inextricably intertwined. An effective general manager anticipates problems in the implementation phase from the very beginning of formulating a new strategy. As one set of authors put it, "Commitment to a strategic decision begins to evolve during the early phases of the decision (rather than after the decision is made)."[1]

In this chapter, we give special attention to the aspects of strategy implementation and to the factors you must consider to ensure that your policies and strategies will be carried out so that goals and objectives are achieved. One factor is the ability of personnel to adjust to the changes that inevitably accompany a new strategy. We shall examine the human resource aspects and techniques for gaining cooperation. This chapter also covers the issue of matching organizational structure to strategy decisions.

STRATEGY AND CHANGE

You have learned that strategies are designed to enable corporations to compete in changing environments. The implementation of a strat-

---

[1] V. K. Narayanan and Liam Fahey, "The Micro-Politics of Strategy Formulation," *Academy of Management Review* 7, no. 1 (January 1982), p. 32.

egy also requires change within the organization. The ability and willingness of relevant personnel to accept and adapt to changes can determine whether the new strategy will succeed or fail.

"If it ain't broke, don't fix it" is a popular cliché used to support the status quo. It is important for you to remember that resistance to change can be a valuable behavior in your organization. Why are people resisting your proposal for a strategic change? Maybe your decision won't work! Resistance forces you to reexamine your premises and reassess probable outcomes. Strategic management concerns itself with major resource allocations across a broad scope of the organization. Decisions must be carefully evaluated before being implemented, time permitting.

It is well also to remember that in our complex world, there is no such thing as a true status quo. Conditions, events, people, and so on will change. Rest assured that the only results of unmanaged change are disorder and chaos. Thus, while you may not seek "change for the sake of change," you would be similarly foolish to attempt to prevent change in your firm.

How can you gain acceptance to a change in strategy? Recall that successful implementation begins in goal setting and strategy formulation. We have all heard and read about consensus decision making in Japanese corporations. Studies of American firms have shown that superior performance can be achieved when key parties arrive at a consensus on both goals and the means for attaining them.[2] Failure to agree on strategies, even though goals are mutually accepted, is associated with poor performance.

You can debate whether change can best be effected by global revolutionary strategy implementation or by a slower incremental process. Some researchers argue that the slower process fails to result in significant changes in behavior.[3] Others have found, however, that strategic changes that superficially appear to represent quantum leaps, on examination, can be broken down to a series of steps. James Brian Quinn has made a persuasive case for gaining consensus on strategy implementation by logical incrementalism:[4]

1. Develop informal networks to sense the need for change.
2. Seek wider organizational support by building awareness, concern, and interest before initiating action.

---

[2] L. J. Bourgeois, "Performance and Consensus," *Strategic Management Journal* 1 (1980), pp. 227–48.

[3] D. Miller and P. H. Friesen, "Momentum and Revolution in Organizational Adaptation," *Academy of Management Journal* 23 (1980), pp. 591–614.

[4] J. B. Quinn, "Managing Strategic Change," *Sloan Management Review* 21 (1980), pp. 3–18.

3. Build credibility by making symbolic moves that show top management's commitment.
4. Legitimize new perceived risky options by encouraging their open discussion.
5. Experiment with partial changes that may appear to be tactical adjustments to existing strategies.
6. Obtain political support through committees, task forces, and retreats.
7. Involve key personnel in "no lose" situations in which they implement partial nonthreatening strategies.
8. Design flexibility into the implementation process since you cannot anticipate all events involved in the change.
9. Prepare to react to external events that may precipitate strategy implementation, such as new technology or legislative changes.
10. Solidify progress toward implementation through exploratory projects, focusing on critical points, and managing coalitions.
11. Formalize commitment by placing power in the hands of those who will champion the new strategy.

An understanding of power and conflict is essential to the successful implementation of a strategic change.

Power

The internal politics of the organization are multifaceted. The groupings and subgroups have numerous purposes, some complementary, others negative and contradictory. It should be understood that a general manager does not arrive at his or her position lacking political skills. In fact, attainment of political skill is one of the requisites for moving up through the organization. Only in rare instances is a chief executive officer (CEO) removed by an opposing faction. The effects of these political battles often have disruptive side effects for the organization. To be successful in the organizational environment requires an understanding of how to build coalitions. In organizational settings, coalitions are the mechanisms through which organizational political objectives are achieved.

We have previously described the notion of dominant coalitions and their roles in establishing the values and climates in their organizations. Coalitions can accrue their power in a variety of ways. Often, power is legitimate, inherent in the position an individual holds, derived from the resources that he or she controls. Power can also come from organization around special interests of the coalition. An individual can obtain power because of his or her particular expertise or competence, or due to occupying a pivotal role, frequently a communication link, in the system. Strategy implementation can be a nonrational process. You need to be prepared for the effects of powerful coalitions on implementation. General managers become skilled in the art of negotiation in the political environment internal to the organization. Inherent in the negotiation process is the possibility of conflicts.

Conflict

While organizations are the conduit for formulating and implementing strategy and policies, the existence of the conduit does not mean it will always function effectively. In fact, various organizational groupings may react to a specific policy or strategic redirection in a negative and antagonistic manner while others may be totally supportive.

Moreover, there are situations in which basic conflicts exist among various organizational groupings. Conflicts occur when a policy or strategy facilitates the purpose or objective of one organizational grouping but conflicts with the purpose or objective of another. In addition, conflicts may emanate from contradictions in the objectives of various groups. On occasion, organizational conflicts result in charges of prima donnas—the building of empires or other forms of defensive/aggressive activities that prove disruptive to the formal organization.

Managers at the same organizational level may find themselves in conflict because tasks and responsibilities overlap. The overlap may occur by deliberate design or because of the managers' perceptions of their spans of control. Personnel given overlapping task assignments will find themselves in conflict with each other. The conflict is likely to involve the organizational layers above and below the level at which the overlap actually occurs. It is important to be able to identify and diagnose these kinds of situations. If policy and strategy are to function effectively, hierarchical conflicts must be minimized.

Often there are gaps in the assignment of tasks within organizations. Such organizations are susceptible to the aggressiveness of an ambitious personality. The gaps make it easy for the ambitious empire builder to operate without restraint. Some CEOs think of this environment as ideal, that is, they see it as a situation encouraging competitive aggressiveness and expansiveness. They perceive this environment as conducive to growth, increased production, increased sales, and ultimately increased profits. Overlooked is that this free-ranging ambitious personality irritates those with whom he or she comes into contact. This type of manager creates conflict, resulting in dampened effort instead of positive performance. These results may be felt throughout the organization.

For example, one owner-founder of a smaller company had two sons. One of these he appointed as vice president–operations and the other as executive vice president. The responsibilities of the two positions were never clearly drawn, and the situation was described by one observer as "analogous to putting two two years olds in a small room with a limited set of toys." The elder brother eventually left the company when his alcoholism prevented him from functioning effectively. The younger brother became president after the father died.

The negative outcomes from various forms of organizational conflicts include disruption of forward momentum toward the attainment of objectives. In these circumstances, personnel begin to take issues personally. Often, the objectives and purposes of the organization are cast aside and replaced by personal objectives. Such conflicts tend to destroy the effectiveness of the organization.

On the other hand, conflicts can have positive benefits for the organization if they raise for explicit reexamination issues critical for a healthy organization and if organizational members are willing to confront these issues creatively. One set of researchers, for example, described three modes of dealing with intraorganizational conflict.

1. Confronting: Active and open exploration of conflicts and various alternative resolutions.
2. Smoothing: Use of various tactics to reduce the anger without dealing with the basic sources of the conflict.
3. Forcing: Use of power to resolve the situation to one's advantage.[5]

In this study, the firms that predominantly used confrontation to resolve internal conflicts tended to have better financial results. In summary, conflicts are inherent in various organizational situations. They cannot always be resolved and, more frequently, must be actively managed.

REACTION TO POLICY CHANGES

In policy formulation, you should remember that policy is for people. If those to whom policy applies reject the policy, the policy will not be implemented. In the formulation and implementation of policy, it is important to keep the human dimension in perspective.

It is difficult to overemphasize the human element in describing strategy implementation. We have introduced you to nonrationality in strategic decision making and have stressed the need for commitment. Top managers may mislead themselves by assuming that they have articulated a clear strategy that others in the organization understand

---

[5] Paul R. Lawrence and Jay W. Lorsch, *Organization and Environment: Managing Differentiation and Integration* (Homewood, Ill.: Richard D. Irwin, 1969).

and use. This can occur only with effective internal communication, and with reward systems that reinforce the implementation of strategy. Unit missions and job responsibilities should be linked to strategy.[6] Linkages can be established through action plans, which list the activities necessary to achieve specific objectives, the resources required to carry out and perform the activities, the person responsible for each objective, starting and ending dates, and results.

Feedback to organizational members regarding compliance with strategies should be built into reward systems. It is not the purpose of this section to go into any depth about various compensation and motivation schemes. There is, however, one overriding principle: The data gathered must be used to justify the rewards allocated, and the rewards must be designed to fit behavior consistent with organizational goals, strategies, and policies. Nowhere has this fit been so severely tried as in executive compensation systems. Among other factors, the changing tax laws and IRS regulations have wreaked havoc with companies' ability to design coherent systems oriented toward longer term performance. The major difficulties with most systems is that they have been put together incrementally over many years and are short term in focus.[7]

One warning: Monitor the rewards system to verify that results are being achieved, not mere commitment to strategy. Some organizations have made the mistake of reinforcing, and thus escalating, commitment to a losing course of action.[8]

The reward system is one subsystem among many that makes up the structure through which an organization implements its strategy.

STRATEGY AND STRUCTURE

The relationship between strategy and structure is controversial. Some executives and scholars argue that in the strategy formulation process you determine the appropriate structure for implementing the strategy, then design the organization appropriately. Others contend that it is naive to attempt to implement a new strategy via a theoretically single best organization structure. The organization exists and functions because of the people who work in it. Strategic thinking will be framed by the structure and will be more effective if implemented in existing structural dimensions.

The point is that strategy and structure impact on one another and

---

[6] A. Brache, "Strategy and the Middle Manager," *Training* (April 1986), pp. 30–34.

[7] David J. McLaughlin, "Reinforcing Corporate Strategy through Executive Compensation," *Management Review*, October 1981, pp. 8–15.

[8] G. Whyte, "Escalating Commitment to a Course of Action: A Reinterpretation," *Academy of Management Review* 11 (1986), pp. 311–21.

EXHIBIT 4–1 Centralized Organization (Layered Triangle)

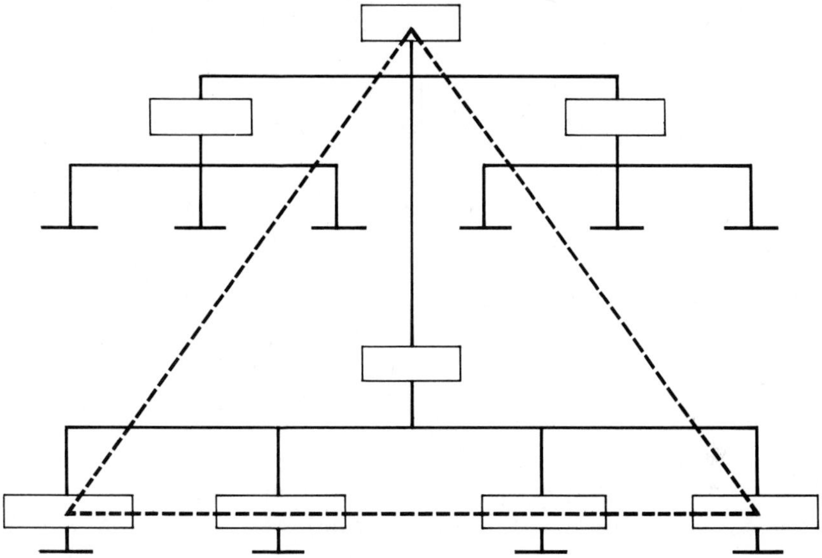

cannot be considered in isolation. Organizations can be structured in a multitude of ways. Structure is influenced by an organization's size, strategy, tradition, and values of the dominant coalition. Major strategic elements of structure include *centralization, formalization,* and *complexity.*

Centralization

In strongly centralized organizations, decision and actions are controlled from the top. Information flows upward to the appropriate place in the upper echelon of the organization. Sometimes this configuration may be referred to as the layered-triangular type of organization depicted in Exhibit 4–1. Note the layers and the dotted line triangle. The span of control tends to be narrow. Decisions are made and disseminated downward for implementation.

One of the major difficulties in this type of organization is that it usually has many layers. The distance between operating levels and responsible top management is often great. This distance contributes to frequent breakdowns in the flow of information from top to bottom or from bottom to top. Another difficulty is the integrity of the information; if information is distorted, the quality of top-level decision making naturally suffers.

In a decentralized organization, each subentity is self-contained. Typically, key decisions are made at the unit level. For example, a

EXHIBIT 4–2 Decentralized Organization

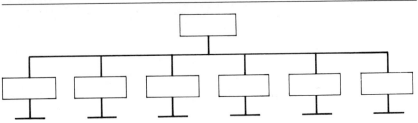

retail firm with geographically dispersed stores operating in relatively heterogeneous markets may give a great deal of latitude to the store manager in choosing the product lines to be offered in that unit.

Exhibit 4–2 depicts a decentralized organization. The decentralized organization tends to have fewer staff positions at the corporate level. Rather, a decentralized unit may have its own staff units performing staff functions that are appropriate for that division. In such instances, the subunit may be designated as a profit center responsible for its own budget and profits accompanied by appropriate accountability.

In a decentralized organization, the upper echelon staff tend to function more in a consultive manner and less in a line-staff role. The span of control is broad. An executive can manage many profit centers if they are operating as autonomous systems but only a few managers in a more centralized organization where more guidance is needed to coordinate the efforts of lower level units.

Formalization

An organization is formalized to the extent that it uses rules and procedures to prescribe behavior. Thus the more explicit and the more enforced company policies are, the more formalized that organization's structure becomes.

The formal organization defines the expected or required relationships between various organizational tasks and positions. It defines lines of authority and sets of responsibilities.

The organizational chart is the most usual method of depicting the relationships within an organization. It is a skeletal picture of these relationships. It defines the responsibilities, roles, channels of communications, and other internal organizational relationships. Not all companies, however, have organizational charts. Many businesses, especially smaller ones, perform quite effectively without an organizational chart. In these instances, face-to-face communication enables members of an organization to form a fairly clear picture of the organization within which they work and to negotiate the relationships needed to perform the required tasks.

Informal organization refers to organizational relationships resulting from personal relationships among people. Generally, there exists a common denominator that brings individuals into an informal grouping. On occasion the common denominator may be a feeling of being threatened by the formal organization; the informal group provides its members with a sense of security. In other instances, the informal organization evolves to meet the needs of its members for affiliation or esteem.

The informal organization is sometimes referred to as a *clique;* the word has negative implications. Whether the perception is negative or positive is in part determined by the actions and attitude of the formal group toward the informal organization. Properly approached, the informal organization may be an effective mechanism for communication of policy and strategy information. The informal organization may also encourage the acceptance of the formal policies and strategies by its membership.

Some companies have formalized the informal. For example, under the self-managed groups concept, work teams are sometimes allowed to choose their own coordinator or supervisor. Such groups often choose the informal leader to fill this position. The evaluation of the informal organization must, therefore, be based on its effect on the organization both in implementation as well as formulation of policies and strategy.

You may expect that the more formalized an organization is, the more its strategies will be implemented incrementally, to merge with existing rules and procedures. There is a danger that the rules can themselves become objectives and cause resources to be misallocated. Existing policies can also set parameters on the interaction of the organization with its environment.

Complexity

Complexity is closely related to size and refers to the number of components of an organization and to the interrelatedness of those components. An organization can be complex in its number of management levels, its number of divisions, and its number of geographic locations. The more complex an organization is, the more difficult it is to achieve consensus and to communicate the content and purposes of a strategy. In complex organizations, negotiation skills are critical in obtaining commitment to strategies among various coalitions.[9]

---

[9] Expected relationships among structural variables and strategy are discussed more fully by J. W. Fredrickson, "The Strategic Decision Process and Organizational Structure," *Academy of Management Review* 11 (1986), pp. 280–97.

Computer Technology

The traditional relationships of centralization, formalization, and complexity with strategy are undergoing change with advanced developments in computer technology. Increases in capability, flexibility, and data access combined with reduced cost and innovative software have resulted in the viability of computer applications to virtually all organizations. Significant implications for structure include the following:

1. Increased ability to centralize due to the availability of detailed and timely information to top management *versus* increased ability to decentralize due to extended access of information and knowledge of other organizational components by unit managers.

2. Pressure toward formalization as top management uses computers to issue policies and directives *versus* pressure from formalization as unit managers can provide central offices with on-line information of their activities and initiate actions more quickly in response to local conditions.

3. Greater complexity permitted by compiling information about corporate activities across organizational levels, boundaries, and geography *versus* reducing complexity by integrating activities through greater knowledge and awareness by unit managers of one another's responsibilities.

Life Cycle

In Chapter 3, we addressed organizational and product life cycles as they affected strategy formulation. Similarly, the successful implementation of a strategy is dependent on the stage of development of a firm, which may be reflected in its structure.

Stages and Structures

Organizations change as they grow, mature, or redefine their mission. Some of the largest organizations in the United States have followed predictable patterns in changing their formal organization. Four common structural arrangements appear to accompany the growth and maturity of organizations.[10] These are the "hub of the wheel," functional specialization, divisionalization, and matrix arrangements.

In the earliest structural form, the CEO is often the hub of the wheel (Exhibit 4–3). In a hub of the wheel, all information flows to the CEO, and most decisions are made by the CEO. The firm is highly

---

[10] See Alfred D. Chandler, *Strategy and Structure* (Cambridge, Mass.: MIT Press, 1962); and Bruce R. Scott, *Stages of Corporate Development* (Cambridge, Mass.: Harvard University Press, 1971).

EXHIBIT 4–3 Hub of the Wheel

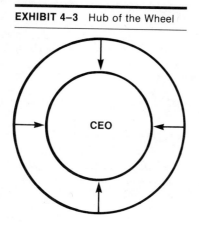

centralized. A firm is composed of three levels of decision makers—strategic, managerial, and operational (or programmatic). In the smallest of firms, the CEO is all of these! Several of the cases in this text illustrate companies in which the owner manages the company in this structural arrangement.

As firms grow, however, there usually is specialization by functional area and delegation of responsibility as suggested in Exhibit 4–4. The CEO's task becomes more strategic. The primary tasks of the CEO are establishing overall direction and coordinating among functions. The managerial and operational levels are differentiated from top-management tasks.

If the firm continues to grow and diversify, the formal organization may require restructuring. The third form depends on the strategy followed by the firm in its growth. Geographical diversification, for example, is likely to require restructuring into geographical divisions (Exhibit 4–5). Exhibit 4–5 is not unlike the model followed by Sears and other national retailers as they spread throughout the United

EXHIBIT 4–4 Functional Specialization

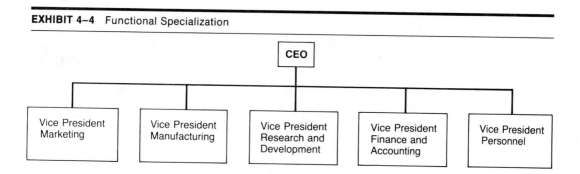

EXHIBIT 4–5 Geographical Divisionalization

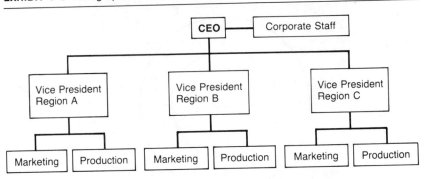

States. The geographical divisionalization shown in Exhibit 4–5 is accompanied by functional specialization at the next level.

On the other hand, firms may grow by adding additional product lines, resulting in product divisionalization (Exhibit 4–6). Still another divisional variation is process divisionalization as depicted in Exhibit 4–7. Process divisionalization is the basis on which many integrated oil companies have established their formal organization.

These three stages—hub of the wheel, functional, divisional—require different modes of managing. There are difficulties in transcending stages.[11] One of the most frequent criticisms of a CEO in a firm moving from the first stage (hub of the wheel) to the second (functional), for example, is inability to delegate. The CEO wants to be involved in everything! Moving from the functionally oriented

EXHIBIT 4–6 Divisionalization by Product

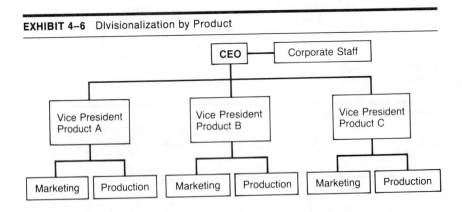

EXHIBIT 4–7 Divisionalization by Process

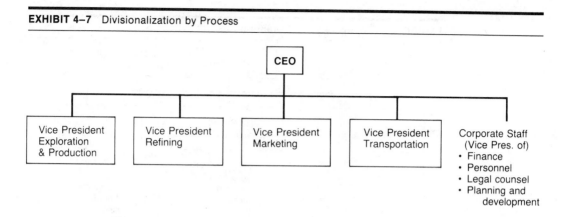

stage (which varies in centralization) to divisionalization (which is decentralized) often requires that even more autonomy be vested in the divisions. In some conglomerates, for example, strategic directions and policies are established at the divisional level whereas the corporate level is concerned primarily with allocating the firm's financial resources.

A fourth organizational form, the matrix, is found with many multinational corporations and large public-sector bureaucracies. This form overlays one structure on another. In Exhibit 4–8, the typical form of a major land-grant university is diagrammed. There are three strategic divisions in this example: teaching (academic affairs), research, and public service. The ideas of the various functional specialties report primarily to the vice president for academic affairs, but have obligations and reporting relationships to the other vice presidents as well. The matrix structure must be managed with care as conflict is unavoidable. It is designed to ensure that multiple organizational missions are carried out by personnel with appropriate expertise.

ACTION PLANS

To implement strategy successfully, the general manager must develop an organizational structure and climate that match the proposed strategy. With reference to the general strategy, medium- and short-range tactics are then devised and employed. These represent the action plans described earlier in this chapter. Action plans define duties, responsibilities, deadlines, performance measures, and results to be achieved, generally within an operational or functional unit. Action plans must be consistent with internal policies and external strategy.

EXHIBIT 4–8 Matrix of a Land-Grant University

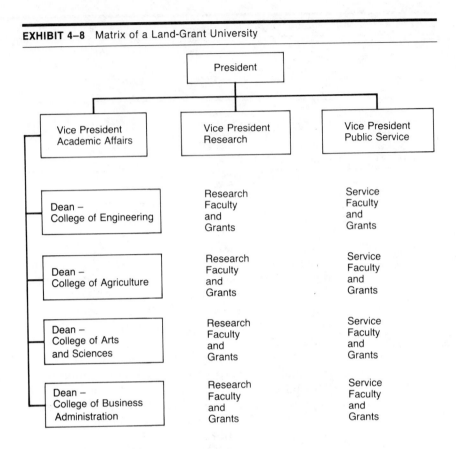

Resource Allocation

It is the responsibility of the management person to determine the mix of resource allocation. You should understand that both policy and strategy, each in its own way, influence the organization's resource allocation. The effectiveness of any organization is, to a great extent, determined by the proportionate manner in which its resources are allocated.

Resource allocation involves the assignment of human, financial, and physical (equipment, facilities, etc.) resources to tasks and courses of action as appropriate to the strategy. You can see why it is so important to reference these plans to the larger strategy to verify the most efficient and effective allocation of resources at the disposal of management.

Tactical Focus

Managers who implement strategies through action plans are almost certain to focus predominantly on the internal organizational environment. Your daily activities are usually inside your company, and it becomes your point of reference. Resources to be allocated may, especially in the short run, be exclusively internal to the organization. The long-range strategy, however, may require that your tactics include boundary-spanning activities, that is, those activities that cause you or members of your staff to cross organizational lines and deal with legislators, competitors, customers, and others external to the firm.

Functional Activities

Finally, action plans may serve as mechanisms to facilitate cooperation with other functional divisions of your organization. One of the most difficult problems associated with implementation is coordination among units within organizations. You may, for example, need to develop tactics for transferring innovations in your research and development department into commercial applications via production and marketing.

STRATEGIC CONTROL

No strategy will work in practice precisely as it has been designed on paper. A strategy must permit corrective action for goals to be achieved. Control mechanisms are, therefore, integral components of a fully developed strategy. This means that you integrate control systems into the strategy formulation process.

A complete system of strategic controls enables you to:

1. Periodically reevaluate the mission of your organization in relation to changing environments.
2. Systematically evaluate your success in achieving organizational goals.
3. Modify objectives in accordance with changing conditions.
4. Examine policies to ensure their consistency with objectives.
5. Examine resource mix to consider possible reallocations.

An effective strategy builds in control standards against which subsequent performance may be measured.

ORGANIZATIONAL PERFORMANCE

How do you know if your organization is performing effectively? Is effectiveness measured by sales? by profits? by return on investment? by market share? by employee satisfaction? or by some other criterion? Measures of effectiveness are elusive and are best made organization specific. For a small business, success may mean survival. For a multinational corporation, it may mean market penetration in targeted countries. Effectiveness for one hospital may be measured by quality of patient care, while for another it may be the level of physician satisfaction.

At the corporate strategy level, financial indicators are the most frequent measures of performance. General managers use "portfolio" analysis tools, such as the Boston Consulting Group's matrix described in Chapter 3, to make resource allocation decisions among subsidiaries. Decisions to purchase or sell units may turn on comparison of rates of return on investment or market share trends.

Strategic business units, alternatively, often measure their effectiveness by their ability to satisfy or maintain adequate relationships with their major stakeholders or constituents. These include owners, employees, customers, suppliers, government, creditors, and many others. The significance of constituents to strategy formulation and implementation is discussed in greater detail in Chapter 5.

Performance measures at the operational level should be functions of SBU or corporate strategy. Standards of performance are most likely to be internal efficiency measures: reduction of waste and damage, reduced lead time, increased productivity per employee, reduced inventory costs. A reminder: These standards are not objectives, merely tools to assess whether efforts are on track to accomplish objectives. Operational measures of performance should help determine whether strategies are being properly implemented and if they are successful.

Effectiveness is, by its nature, a subjective phenomenon. We attempt to make it objective by applying dollar signs to various outcomes. The values imposed by dominant coalitions are more indicative of the success of any given organization. If those values stray too far from broad societal norms, however, action may be taken to overturn the dominant coalition and redirect strategies. Such actions may be represented by union strikes, hostile takeovers, government lawsuits, consumer boycotts, and many other examples.

COMPETITOR REACTION

You have not completely implemented your strategic change if you have not assessed and prepared for competitor reactions. You share your external environment with your competitors. Your strategy alters their environment. They will not observe your actions idly if they anticipate those actions will impact negatively on theirs.

Questions you should be able to answer about your competitors include:

- Who are your major competitors?
- What is their market share?
- What are their strengths and weaknesses?

- What are the trends in your competitive environment?
- What are your plans to offset probable competitive threats?

Competitor reactions to your strategies can take many forms. Competitors can counter your action with changes in price, promotion, number, and quality of products and services, channels of distribution, and many other elements. Your responsibility is to be prepared for these reactions by (1) anticipating them in formulating your strategy, and (2) implementing a strategy that is flexible enough to adjust to unforeseen and harmful reactions.

SUMMARY

In this chapter we have examined the factors that influence the implementation of a strategy. Implementation is not an addendum to the strategic management process, but an integral component that must be considered when setting goals and formulating strategies.

Implementation demands change in an organization. Change can be traumatic and should be addressed strategically. A new strategy may lead to structural changes. Care should be taken to match the strategy and structure of an organization.

Strategy implementation can never ignore the human dimension. Reactions of organizational members, constituents, and competitors all influence the success or failure of a strategy. The human element is also evident in control systems. You establish control procedures to determine if organizational performance is effective, yet the notion of effectiveness is subjective and may be defined in many different ways by the firm's stakeholders. Ultimately, you have implemented strategies successfully if your organization adapts to the demands and changes of its environment.

5

Organizational Constituents

The strategic management process is described in Chapters 2, 3, and 4. This process is *not* totally logical and objective. The general managers cannot free themselves from their own values and subjective perceptions. Neither can they avoid pressures and constraints imposed by influential individuals and groups who profess an interest in the actions and outcomes of the organization.

These individuals and groups, which we label *constituents* or *stakeholders*, are the subject of Chapter 5. We shall examine who the constituents are, their effects on goals and strategies, and approaches to addressing their needs and demands. The issues of corporate social responsibility and management succession are also addressed based on constituencies.

CONSTITUENTS AND STAKEHOLDERS

Formulation, implementation, and outcomes of policies and strategies are influenced by parties who have a "stake" or vital interest in the organization. Stakeholders are generally assumed to derive benefits from the success of the firm, although different parties define success in different ways. Shareholders, for example, benefit from positive returns on investment, whereas success to a cognizant government agency may be measured by jobs created. Stakeholder analysis is usually directed at policies and the internal environment of the firm.

We prefer to use the term *constituents* to imply a broader definition of those affected and affecting organizational activities and results. Constituents, therefore, include not only investors, employees, customers, suppliers, and so on, but also consumer groups, environmentalists, organized labor, takeover specialists, even on occasion, competitors.

CONCERN WITH CONSTITUENTS

You have learned about your role, as general manager, in setting goals and formulating strategy. We have introduced you to dominant coalitions as sources and mediators of power in organizations. And you have read about the need to consider the members of the organization who will participate in the implementation of a strategy. Why do we now ask you to concern yourself with a multitude of constituents?

There are many reasons for concern. They vary from organization to organization and constituent to constituent. Stockholders ultimately determine the fate of general managers in corporations, but are irrelevant to administrators in a municipal government. Your concerns for your employees relate to morale, cost, and retention, while for the community you strive to be perceived as a good corporate citizen.

Constituents impact on the organization and its strategies in a variety of ways. Most obvious is *survival*. Failure to satisfy customers or to repay creditors can lead to bankruptcy. Some organizations address constituents in their mission statements. Management may stipulate a goal of maximizing the return to shareholders. Thus, those constituents represent the very *purpose* of the organization. As we mentioned in Chapter 4, the satisfaction of constituents is one means of measuring the *effectiveness* of an organization. As you shall soon see, strategies to satisfy constituents can conflict with one another.

Finally, you may be concerned with constituents to the extent that you perceive an *obligation* to act responsibly toward the constituent. An organization has four levels of responsibility toward its constituents: economic, legal, ethical, and discretionary.[1] An enterprise must fulfill its economic obligations to its investors, creditors, employees, suppliers, and so on to survive. It must carry out its mission legally or be subject to fines, closures, or other actions. There are several theories supporting the need to behave as an ethical corporate citizen for the long-range benefit of the organization, its customers, and the community it serves. There remain discretionary areas in which management may choose to take on additional obligations, such as affirmative action or support for the arts.

---

[1] A. B. Carroll and F. Hoy, "Integrating Corporate Social Policy into Strategic Management," *Journal of Business Strategy*, Winter 1984, pp. 48–57.

It must be noted that the demands of these diverse constituencies can place constraints on the firm. In particular, they can inhibit your ability to induce change through a new strategy. We examined the effects of employees and competitors on implementing strategy in the last chapter. Lawsuits filed by government agencies and environmentalists, for example, to delay the construction of nuclear power plants are other indications of how constituents can constrain management. Contracts with labor unions may be written to limit change in internal personnel policies. We live in a complex society in which no general manager may totally disregard the influence of constituents on his or her actions.

WHO ARE YOUR CONSTITUENTS?

To oversimplify, you can divide your constituents into two groups: those whose primary interest is in your organization's basic economic function and those whose interest is not primarily in your economic operations. We have already identified several parties in each category and given examples of their influence on the strategic management process.

Constituents with an economic interest in the firm include the owners (stockholders, inventors), employees, suppliers, creditors, customers, unions, competitors, and families of the owners and employees. As you can see, not all constituents have goals that consistently or invariably converge with positive financial returns. You will also find that the impact of family members is seldom explicitly addressed in strategy formulation and implementation. Yet family influences can be among the most powerful in our lives.

Other constituents unquestionably have interests in the economic functioning of the firm, but that interest may not be perceived by the constituent or may be perceived as secondary in importance. Constituents such as government agencies and community members may have an interest in the economic contribution made by a corporation, but not necessarily in the specific operations of the firm. Trade associations and various special-interest groups fall into this category. Let us digress a moment to a few constituents that may be hostile toward corporate strategies.

External Antagonistic Organizations

Critics of democracy accuse it of being a system resulting in tyranny of the majority. They complain that minority rights are ignored or trampled by a homogeneous and monolithic majority of the population. Recent history indicates that just the opposite occurs in a large complex society such as ours. Citizens are concerned with multiple and diverse issues. They are constantly forming, disbanding, and reforming into special-interest groups. Special-interest groups appear to carry the image of being totally self-serving and working against the common good. In fact, it is through special-interest groups, often several working together to achieve a goal, that minority rights are protected. They mobilize action and public opinion where otherwise nothing may have occurred. Their effect has both positive and negative implications for general managers.

Business organizations have special-interest groups of their own. The Corporate Roundtable, the U.S. Chamber of Commerce, the American Petroleum Institute, and the National Federation of Independent Business, for example, each attempts to influence events on behalf of its members. Individual companies sometimes organize political action committees to support candidates that they expect will be sympathetic to the companies' positions when in office.

Similarly, people band together outside business organizations to achieve other purposes. They join the National Association of the Advancement of Colored People to foster social and economic progress for ethnic minorities. They join the Sierra Club to protect the natural environment. They join Greenpeace to protest the construction of nuclear power facilities.

These special-interest groups may interfere with your ability to implement strategy, which could be harmful not only to your company, but to the general population as well. For example, it has been shown that changes in the natural environment are not all negative. Removal of timber often creates a better habitat for wildlife. In the natural wild area, the animal population is much lower than in the areas where timber has been selectively harvested.

The fish population has been found larger in embankments/streams where power plant hot water has been discharged. An area in western Tennessee where the river channels have not been kept open, that is, an area free of drifts and beaver dams, has resulted in the loss of live timber. This economic loss to individual landowners has amounted to thousands of dollars.

Alternatively, special-interest groups can serve as a checks and balances system on corporate management. Antinuclear groups, as an example, may have value as society's watchdogs to ensure against careless and indifferent operations of plants. In one well-known case, the primary and backup control systems for the power plant were placed in the same environment. An unfortunate incident resulted in both systems being destroyed. A major catastrophe was narrowly averted; at the time the plant was brought back under control, meltdown was but a few short hours away. No one can support the argument that top management may be allowed to formulate and implement strategy without restraints.

Internal Antagonistic Organizations

Hostile constituents are not always outside the organization. Occasionally you will find that members of your organization actively work at cross purposes to what you consider the organization's mission. Earlier we examined the effects of the dominant coalition and the informal organization on strategy. Now we introduce the *secret organization* and the *hidden organization*.

The Secret Organization

At first glance, one might assume that the secret organization belongs in the category of the informal organization. However, where it exists, it generally functions within the confines of the formal organization but should not be assumed to be congruent with the formal organizational structure. While its members are part of the formal organizational structure, in the secret organization they may be found to bypass or short-circuit the formal structure, and may in a sense, sabotage the direction and efforts of the formal organization. An example follows.

> Some years ago it was purported that one of the military service schools contained a secret organization whose members continued to participate after they graduated from the academy. According to this report, it was indicated that the members of this secret organization were most highly favored throughout their careers in the formal military organization, with favored promotions and assignments. In addition, there were other special favors accorded the members of this secret organization. The investigators concluded in this instance that the secret organization may not have been in the *general interest* of *this arm* of the *military service* and the *nation's defense*.

Each secret organization needs to be evaluated on its own merits. However, it may be concluded that given the nature and purpose of secret organizations, they tend to perform an abortive role in relationship to the formal organization.

The Hidden Organization

The hidden organization is not to be confused with the secret organization. There are similarities with the informal organization but noticeable differences. Typically, the hidden organization exists within the hierarchical framework of the formal organizational structure. It is not unusual for the hidden organization to have a disruptive influence on the effectiveness of the formal organization operation. An example found in one of the air force's AMA's:

> A manager at level 1 (for our purposes here, we will use number designations to indicate level relationships) was a good fishing buddy of the manager at level 4. The managers at levels 2 and 3 did not communi-

cate their wishes upward to the manager at level 1; instead they communicated downward to level 4, who in turn communicated upward to level 1. After typing a case written by a fifth party concerning this circumstance, an enterprising secretary mailed a copy to the base commander.

The base commander became distressed to learn that his formal organization was being bypassed, called in the four offenders, each of whom feigned surprise and innocence when approached by the base commander.

Another example is found at the same installation.

It was apparent to many civilians, as well as military personnel, that four "longtime" civilian staff employees had formed an alliance of significant power and influence. Many of these personnel had learned from unpleasant personal experiences that one did not challenge the turf of these four without paying the unpleasant consequences.

Public versus Private Organizations

We have already explained that different organizations must address constituents in different ways. These differences are particularly significant when comparing private-sector to public-sector organizations. With rare exceptions, private companies must answer to two primary constituents: owners and customers. The latter are the focus of the strategy and are unlikely to participate actively in its development. Most businesses in the United States are small, organized as proprietorships, partnerships, or closely held corporations. Thus, the owners may not even be concerned with boards of directors or shareholders.

General managers of public-sector organizations, however, face a far broader array of significant constituents. Public-sector, or tax-exempt, organizations frequently obtain operating revenues from several sources: taxes, foundation grants, corporate donations, user fees, fund-raising events, and many others. Each source may expect a voice in the strategy or even operations of the organization. Additionally, because of their public accountability, these organizations may invest a sizable portion of their resources complying with notorious red-tape requirements: adhering to strict rules of operations and documentation of expenditures (i.e., paper trails). We have addressed nonrationality in the strategic decision process, but this is compounded in the public sector by the multitude of constituents. Negotiation and compromise are essential in satisfying political and emotional demands placed by constituents on top management.

BALANCING CONSTITUENTS

While you may assess your effectiveness based on constituent satisfaction, it is impossible to maximize the satisfaction of all parties who have a stake in your organization. Some constituents are clearly more influential to your survival and success than others; therefore, their goals must be weighted more heavily. Concern for the well-being of the owners almost invariably supersedes concern over satisfying your suppliers, although you will usually find actions to satisfy both are harmonious.

Unfortunately, goals of your constituents can also be in conflict with one another. This can be true even with a single constituent. Owners may desire profit and growth. In the short run, it is probably impossible to maximize both. Add another constituent, and you add complexity to the situation. Can you function as a good corporate citizen in your community—participating in United Way campaigns, sponsoring public education programs, contributing to downtown renovation projects—and still increase the return on investment to your stockholders? The successful manager accurately weighs the relative value of diverse constituents' goals by their relevance to the organization's mission, assesses the true needs of the various constituent groups, and negotiates compromise. This may be achieved through coalition building.

Coalitions

The dominant coalition is not the only coalition of which you should be aware. Borrowing a leaf from the political scientists' book, if we are to be successful in the organizational environment, we need to understand the finesse of building coalitions. In an organizational setting, a coalition is the mechanism through which we achieve organizational political objectives. This is not to say that through coalitions we achieve those objectives to the fullest; of necessity, the art of compromise becomes a key element of the political interplay that molds the coalition into its best acceptable form.

It should be understood that the very nature of a coalition casts it into a role of conflict with other coalitions. You should keep in mind that through negotiation you wish to gain the most advantage and give up as little of the desirable as possible. Therefore, the art of negotiation becomes another key ingredient in the organizational political environment.

At this point, it should be recognized that in this negotiation process there exists an inherent possibility of conflict. It is hoped that in this process the least damage to the organization will occur.

Conflict Disruptions

The unfortunate result of the various organizational conflicts is the disruptive intrusion it creates. This result affects the achievement of specific organizational purposes.

One observes that in circumstances of this type, ultimately constituents begin to take issues personally. Consequently, the objectives and purposes of the organization are cast aside to be replaced by the selfish personal objectives of the various involved individuals. In such situations, these conflicts tend to destroy the effectiveness of the organization.

You may call on organizational members to subordinate their interests to the long-run needs of the enterprise, but you cannot exercise comparable control over external constituents. Thus your strategies must be sensitive to the impact of the organization on those constituents and must anticipate their perceptions of your actions. Thus, again, constituents either actively participate in strategy formulation and implementation, or passively influence it as you fine-tune your strategy as you prepare for its effects.

ETHICS AND RESPONSIBILITIES TO CONSTITUENTS

It is not enough to give mere consideration to constituent reactions to policies and strategies. Policies and strategies must be designed ethically and with integrity. How many chief executives are going to publish a mission statement that describes unethical behavior? As we explained in Chapter 2, mission statements are often written for public relations purposes. Yet if they have no integrity in charting the direction of the company, it is impossible to derive valid policies and strategies.

The cover of the May 25, 1987, issue of *Time* magazine asks the question, "What Ever Happened to Ethics?" Stories in the magazine address corruption in government, religious institutions, and corporations.

> Not since the reckless 1920s and desperate 1930s have the financial columns carried such unrelenting tales of vivid scandals, rascally characters, and creative new means for dirty dealing (insider trading, money laundering, greenmailing). Consider these episodes, all hard to believe, all matters of record:
> A widely admired investment banker with a yearly income said to exceed $1 million sneaks into Wall Street alleys to sell insider tips, for which he later collects a briefcase stuffed with $700,000.
> Savings and loan officers in Texas, all with six-figure salaries and bonuses, loot their institution to buy Rolls-Royces and trips to Paris.
> A defense contractor with $11 billion in annual sales charges the government $1,118.26 for the plastic cap on a stool leg.[2]

Firms with vocal constituencies often have epithets such as "unfair," "unethical," or "immoral" hurled at their management. How-

---

[2] S. Koepp, "Having It All, Then Throwing It All Away," *Time*, May 25, 1987, p. 22.

ever, even where the social responsibility of a firm is confined to its legal obligations, there are circumstances in which managers respond illegally or in a socially irresponsible manner. Why do companies—and their executives—succumb to the temptation of illegal or immoral acts? Many individuals respond, "It depends on the innate honesty of the people in charge," or "It depends on the top executive's ethical sense." Certainly organizational leaders are responsible for defining objectives, purpose, mission, strategies and policies—all of the issues with which this text is concerned—but other factors are also at work. One is the effect of information inductance. Another is the hostility of the environment within which the organization competes and still another is the anonymity of the large, administrated, systems-rich firm.

Information Inductance

Information inductance is the process by which the providers of information are influenced by requests for information.[3] The simple act of requesting certain data suggests that behavior associated with the information is important. Financial rewards, status rewards, commendations or other forms of feedback may be associated with specified or relative levels of performance. If so, the importance of meeting those specified or implied standards can become important. To meet the standards individuals may choose a variety of actions. They can modify the data, perhaps by recategorizing the information or forging data, or they can, if possible, modify the behavior described by the data. These aspects of the information inductance process are important to those who design control and reward systems—whether financial and quantitative or qualitative systems.

Hostile Environments

If the current performance is not up to par, organizational members, units, or the organization as a whole may modify their behavior—if possible. However, there is evidence to indicate that where environmental opportunities are the leanest, organizations and their participants are likely to make questionable ethical choices. Staw and Szwajkowski (1975) studied 105 companies involved in possible antitrust and FTCA violations from 1968 to 1972. These researchers compared the environmental capacity of the industries of these firms with all other Fortune 500 companies. "The crucial comparison between cited

---

[3] M. S. Barr, *Some Impacts of a Management Information System on Subunit Behavior: A Contingency Approach* (Unpublished doctoral dissertation, University of Kansas, 1982).

industries and all firms in the Fortune 500 list showed that return on equity and sales were significantly lower for the cited industries."[4]

Anonymity—Its Effect on Morality

Generally, the larger the firm, the more difficult the task of pinpointing responsibility. The situation is exacerbated by the complex decision-making systems in place in many of today's larger companies. Alfred Sloan was the genius behind GM's innovative organizational systems design.[5] GM's systems of managing as originally designed by Sloan were the cornerstone on which the company survived the depression and subsequently built its multinational empire. Yet this same system gave rise to such fiascoes as the Vega decision and the difficulties experienced with the Corvair.[6]

Social Responsiveness

Historically the demands on business organizations have broadened, but the arguments still rage about how socially responsive they should be. The arguments form a wide continuum. On one hand are those who argue that the social responsibility of business is to be concerned about business profits and shareholder wealth.[7] Others argue that business must respond to the legal obligations placed on it. (See Exhibit 5–1.) Going beyond these minimum obligations dilutes business' purpose as an economic institution, is simply too costly for business alone, is beyond the skills of business, places firms at a competitive disadvantage, and results in poor social control since the means of making business economically accountable are available whereas the means of accounting for social responsibility are not. Those who argue for a broader definition of the social responsibilities of business suggest that:

1. Social expenditures today result in greater profits for the company in the long run.
2. Stockholders have interests other than direct profit maximization.
3. Society created business as one of its institutions; therefore, its demands are legitimate.

---

[4] Barry Staw and E. Szwajkowski, "The Scarcity-Munifence Component of Organizational Environments and the Commission of Illegal Acts," *Administrative Science Quarterly* 20 (September 1975), pp. 345–54.

[5] Alfred P. Sloan, *My Years with General Motors* (New York: Doubleday Publishing, 1963).

[6] Patrick Wright (with deLorean), *On a Clear Day You Can See GM* (Grosse Pointe, Mich.: Wright Enterprises, 1979).

[7] See Milton Friedman's classic article, "The Social Responsibility of Business Is to Make a Profit," *New York Times Magazine*, September 13, 1970, pp. 33, 122–26.

EXHIBIT 5–1 Corporate Social Responsibility: A Step-by-Step Course of Action

Step	Step Classification

1. An enumeration of community problems—as perceived by the community.	A company sponsored undertaking aimed at:
	a. Identifying and defining the "community."
	b. Identifying community information sources to be surveyed, along with determining survey methods to be used.
	c. Formulating the specific instruments through which community sources are able:
	  (1) to list social problem areas.
	  (2) to identify by rank order the intensity of the respective problem areas.
	d. Conducting the community survey.

2. A corporate study of community opinion.	By the corporation a. The consolidation and publication—for internal review—of information obtained through the community survey. b. A critical appraisal of the survey findings.
3. A reformulation and an updating of corporate social responsibilities.	Statements by the company setting forth: a. Social responsibility areas in which the firm will commit itself. b. The rank order or priority it will place on the respective responsibility areas.
4. The establishment of corporation goals in each program area of responsibility.	In each priority area, the corporation will state a specific goal or goals—in quantitative terms where possible.
5. A determination of corporate resources to be committed in attempting to achieve social goals.	An explanatory report identifying by problem area and activity the specific human, financial, and material resources to be utilized by the corporation. *Note:* Where possible, quantitative data should be supplied that list resource costs, direct and indirect, assumed by the corporation.
6. The corporation's implementation of commitments.	Corporate action aimed at concrete goal accomplishments: The application of resources in the direction of attaining specific goals.

7. The corporation's monitoring and control of social performance.	The corporation should aim to accomplish the following:
	a. Measure the company's performance in social responsibility programs.
	b. Compare performance to goal standards (the standards formulated in Step 4), and ascertain the difference, if any.
	c. Take remedial action where unfavorable deviations from goal standards exist and
	  (1) change certain specific target goals (frequently, in a downward direction).
	  (2) initiate appropriate action to raise performance where previously determined target goals are judged valid and attainable.

8. Statements by the corporation revealing accomplishments and/or progress toward the achievement of social goals.	The writing of a summary document describing in quantitative measures and narrative statements the extent of corporate involvement in social problem areas, and the accomplishments and/or progress attained.

SOURCE: J. Carroll Swart, "Corporate Social Responsibility: An Action Model," *Academy of Management Proceedings*, 1981, pp. 114–19.

4. All institutions in the social system are interdependent; if business is not socially responsive, there are two long-run outcomes: (*a*) the negative impacts will ultimately directly or indirectly affect the firm's own performance; and (*b*) other organizations will require the firm to shoulder its "fair share."
5. If business does not balance its power with responsibility, other groups will step in to assume the power and the responsibility.
6. Some other institutions have tried and failed; business ought to have the opportunity to try.
7. Business has the resources and talents to solve many social ills.
8. Socially responsible behavior enhances the public image of business.
9. If business does not act in a socially responsible manner, government regulation will ultimately force response.[8]

Exhibit 5–1 suggests the steps an organization might follow in establishing its responsiveness to its community. Organizations, of course, have to determine whether their posture will be to drag their feet, be reactive, or be proactive with regard to various issues.

How Organizations Respond

Organizations respond to social responsibility issues in at last three steps.

1. Initiation: The stage in which the need for change is recognized and initial proposals are made with regard to accomplishing the change.
2. Adoption: The stage in which a course of action is selected and resources are committed.
3. Implementation: The stage in which procedures are introduced and changes are made in the organization.[9]

A similar way of categorizing an organization's response process is:

1. CEO involvement: The CEO must become aware of and publicly committed to the issue.
2. Appointment of a staff specialist: The CEO must appoint a staff executive to coordinate the corporation's activities in the area: The specialist becomes, in essence, an extension of the president's earlier interest, although the new appointee may

---

[8] Franklin Strier, "The Business Manager's Dilemma—II. Arguments Pro and Con Social Responsibility," *Journal of Enterprise Management* 2 (1979), pp. 11–23.

[9] Kenneth E. Marion, "Organizational Structure and Environmental Adaptation: A Case of Regulatory Compliance," *Academy of Management Proceedings*, 1979.

not directly report to the CEO and may be drawn from internal or external applicants.

3. Institutionalization of the issue: Ultimately the issue must become part of the processes through which resources are allocated and careers decided.[10]

The dilemma in the second stage is whether to hire someone from outside the organization who knows the issue or to use an employee who knows the organization but may not be familiar with the issue. The third stage is concerned with working the issue into the warp and woof of the organization. This third stage will consist of:

> An information system [that] must be devised [to] track the performance of the relevant operating units. Staff specialists may be assigned to the operating units. Committees may be formed to afford representation and expertise. Operating procedures [hiring practices, controls on polluting machinery, improving the quality of the product, increasing plant safety, and so on] are reviewed and changed if necessary. Finally, performance on the relevant dimensions of the new policy is made subject to executive evaluation.[11]

Moving from the second to the third stage is problematic. Raymond Bauer, an observer of social responsibility processes in organizations, notes:

> We have not found any divisionalized firm that has successfully institutionalized a major social policy in less than five or six years. Eight to ten years is more usual. . . . Our judgment is that in divisionalized firms the response process cannot be considered complete until it has moved through the first two stages and landed solidly in stage three.[12]

Of course, socially responsive action may be confined to actions at the corporate level. But, to confine such acts to the top assures that the organization will not respond consistently over the longer term. Ultimately the managerial system must be responsible and responsive. As one executive put it: "Our middle managers are critical to the implementation of the program, but it's in the foxholes of the supervisory level that a program is made or broken."

SUCCESSION

Another issue that both affects and is affected by constituents is the problem of succession to general management positions. It has been

---

[10] Robert W. Ackerman, "How Companies Respond to Social Demands," *Harvard Business Review*, July–August 1973, pp. 92–94.

[11] Raymond A. Bauer, L. Terry Cauthorn, and Ranne P. Warner, "Auditing the Management Process for Social Performance," *Business and Society Review*, Fall 1975, pp. 43–44.

[12] Ibid., p. 44.

observed that organizational succession problems may, in fact, have little or no relationship to age. Surely, there are situations where age is a factor, that is, a circumstance where the degeneration of attitudes, of health, and mental abilities interfere with the functioning of the individual. Even so, it is not always easy to prevail on this individual to "move out" so that a more vigorous person may move into the position.

The greater or more difficult problem appears to take one of two forms: the competition for position between two or more personalities, or the manager who feels threatened by the ability of an underling.

An example of the last situation was the dialogue overheard between an ad hoc committee of a board of directors of a well-known multinational corporation's subsidiary. In discussing the subsidiary's future, their obvious concern was the future quality of leadership. In the past, the subsidiary had filled its organizational pipeline with outstandingly qualified personnel. However, of more recent date, it had been observed that this pattern had changed. An expressed concern was the exit of the subsidiary's CEO's understudy—an obviously desirable personality for the CEO's slot but this fact became a liability, a threat to the CEO. The committee's concern was not for the immediate but more for the long-run implications of this situation and how it might best be resolved.

Succession decisions are often a function of the coalition-building process described earlier that involves persistent negotiation and compromise. Coalitions may include external constituents, such as bankers or venture capitalists who have vested interests in the decisions made by top management.

TAKEOVERS

If management fails to satisfy key constituents, internal succession decisions may become academic as external constituents effect changes at the top.

The corporate financial environment of the post–World War II era has witnessed an ever-increasing incidence of corporate mergers and acquisitions. This has frequently been facilitated by the individual corporate managements adopting a corporate strategy of portfolio management. These actions may be divided into two groups: the friendly takeover and the unfriendly takeover.

The Friendly Takeover

In the friendly takeover, frequently the circumstance is one of mutual benefit. The benefits take a variety of forms: an increased market capability; access to needed new technology; increased research and development capability; increased production capability; access to needed material resources; acquisition of needed management personnel (Kennecott and Carborandum); and access to needed financial resources.

Even in the friendly takeover, seldom is there a situation in which some conflict does not arise. Management philosophies, style, objectives, and actions tend to be different. This in itself is a basis for conflict. As the new entity, growing out of the merger/acquisition, takes shape, the opportunity and need for personnel changes/reduction comes into focus. This occurs in spite of the fact that at the time the merger/acquisition process was occurring, there were vocal statements being publicized that "no management or personnel changes were anticipated on completion of the merger/acquisition."

Adversary Takeovers

In the adversary takeover from the outset, the present board of directors and management oppose any encroachment by outside interests seeking control of the firm by way of merger/acquisition. Examples of this in recent times are Texas International's move to acquire Continental Airlines, or more recently, the Mobil effort to acquire Marathon Oil. In some instances, there exists some doubt relating to the conduct of some management personalities in a merger or acquisition circumstance. While it is often difficult to prove/substantiate, it is thought there are cases where the present management "caves in for a price" to the incoming corporation. In so doing, questions of ethics, integrity, and conflicts of interest arise.

Historic fact raises some interesting questions relating to the benefits of mergers/acquisitions. Seldom are there the kind of benefits purported to result in premerger/preacquisition. There are also the questions related to the book value of the acquired firm. Just what is the true dollar value of the firm allocated on a per-share basis? These are facts that are difficult to derive. Be that as it may, this does not remove the responsibility from existing corporate management to come up with these facts if economic justice is to be served.

Finally, the monetary costs associated with an adversary merger/acquisition should be considered. Frequently, the legal and investment banker fees on both sides run into the millions of dollars.

STRATEGIC MANAGEMENT OF CONSTITUENTS

What must you know about your constituents to be an effective manager of corporate strategy? What information will enable you to satisfy constituent needs and demands when appropriate, or anticipate and preempt constituent actions when necessary? The management of constituents is comparable to other strategy processes discussed in this text. You are expected to develop policies for handling routine relationships with constituents and devise strategies that will lead to survival and success in environments in which multiple and contradictory constituencies provide both stimuli and impetus to your actions.

Questions to be answered in dealing with constituents include:

1. Who are the constituents of this organization?
   a. Who benefits from its success?
   b. Who benefits from its failure?
   c. Who is impacted by the results we achieve?
   d. Who is questioning your actions?
   e. Are there latent or emerging groups that may become constituents if you change strategies?
2. What do these constituents want from this organization?
   a. Do they expect economic gain from your normal operations?
   b. Do they expect gains from your profitability?
   c. Do they expect social or other noneconomic benefits?
   d. Are there specific identifiable outcomes desired by a particular constituent?
   e. Are you evaluating their wants from their stated positions or behaviors that you can observe?
3. How do you prioritize your need and ability to satisfy constituents?
   a. How vital is this constituent to the survival and success of your firm?
   b. How vital is the issue of interest to this constituent to the survival and success of your firm?
   c. What are the costs of satisfying a constituent?
   d. What benefits can be expected from satisfying the constituent?
   e. What are the anticipated penalties if the constituent is not satisfied?
4. What actions are required for an effective constituency strategy?
   a. How large is the area of overlap of positive benefits to be derived by your constituents from your success?
   b. How large is the zone of indifference, that is, that area in which you may take action without dissatisfying your constituents?
   c. What is encompassed by the territory that remains, that is, areas of potential negative impact?

      d. How vital to you are those constituents that are likely to be negatively affected by your strategy?

      e. Are there coalitions that you can build to strengthen your support from your vital constituents?

      f. What can you compromise to build those coalitions?

  5. What strategies will enable you to provide the greatest benefit to the largest number of key constituents in such a way as to merge them into a coalition that will assist you in achieving organizational goals?

SUMMARY

Managers can be compared to politicians. Both must decide what constitutes their relevant set of constituencies. With limited resources, both must decide which of the constituents will receive attention. To be effective, today's managers must be aware of various kinds of typical extraorganizational objectives and a general course of action. Finally, managers must be aware of situations that engender socially irresponsible or unethical behavior on the part of the firm's managers. Equipped with this basic knowledge and skills the manager can guide his or her firm to an effective role in today's—and tomorrow's—social milieu.

6

Case Analysis and Presentation

The professor turned to a student seated on the far right. "Well, Jill, what should Mr. Cobb recommend to Dixie's loan committee?!" Jill was in a quandary. Indeed her quandary was that experienced by Mr. Cobb. What *should* she recommend?

The student in a case classroom—unlike one attending a lecture—is usually an active participant in the learning process. As in a problem-solving class in statistics where the instructor says, "Jill, put problem number 15 on the board," Jill is on the spot! Unlike the situation in the long-past "stat" course, however, Jill has at least three answers she can choose. Whether Jill's choice is "right" depends on her analysis and how she organizes the data from the case in support of her answer.

What is a case? How does one analyze a case? What does it take to be a good class participant? How does one write a strong case analysis paper? This chapter is intended to give you some general guidelines for these issues. In the conclusion of the chapter, we try to answer the question, "What does one learn from studying an unending succession of business situations, each one unique in many respects?"

DEFINITION OF A CASE

A case is a capsule of events that occurred at some point in time. In this text a case is a description of a business situation as viewed through the eyes of the case writer. As such, the case is biased by the perceptions of the writer and by any limitations placed by the company. A case usually has one or more issues or problems requiring decisions and actions on the part of the chief executive officer or some other executive. The job of the case reader is that of an outside consultant or decision maker whose job is to analyze carefully the total situation and make recommendations based on that analysis.

This discussion refers to cases in this book and in many other texts used in "capstone" courses. However, cases differ in complexity and purpose. In some classes, "cases" are more like the problems found at the conclusion of the chapters in a college algebra book. They are short and succinct, and give an opportunity to practice formulas and techniques. On the other hand, some cases are more complex and sometimes less organized in presentation of data. In some instances, the case may have a right answer, and the reader is expected to practice the process of getting there. In some instances, the reader is expected to evaluate a solution or recommendation made by others. In others, like those in this text, the reader is confronted with a sometimes bewildering array of data and is expected to identify the problems and issues to be addressed. The reader is then expected to design solutions that are tailored to the situation.

Cases and Cadavers

A business student working on a case in a capstone course is like a medical school student in anatomy—working with a case is like working with a cadaver. The decision has been made, and the fate of the patient is determined.[1] But the case worker is asked to treat the patient as though it is still living, use the symptoms to diagnose the diseases, and recommend treatment. In cutting up the cadaver and performing the lab work (e.g., financial ratios), what the worker sees is not always entirely correct. For example, the bottom line of the income statement may indicate a net margin of 5 percent—a reasonable figure at first glance. A little digging, however, may indicate certain company operations are in the red, and the company has kept in the black by renting out unutilized warehouse space or receiving healthy dividends from securities. A number of years ago an established woolen mill was sold to a new set of principals. All previous financial data indicated it was a profitable operation. Some months later the profitability had not proven out. Further investigation indicated that the previous profitability was attributable to the original owner's success in commodity trading.

---

[1] Occasionally professors get the opportunity to present cases about unresolved situations. However, companies are often, understandably so, concerned about the proprietary nature of the data or the sensitivity of people inside (and outside) the firm about unresolved issues.

Symptoms and diseases.   The case analyst rarely has all the information he wants. A cadaver does not talk. The medical student cannot know whether a lightly coated set of lungs exists because the patient was a light smoker or worked in a household or office of heavy smokers though the recommendation will be affected by which. In a similar vein, a slowdown in inventory turnover is easily identified, but the causes may not be. In other instances, future actions or outcomes of circumstances beyond the company's control will affect the longer-term viability of the decision made today. For example, a company owns AM/FM radio and VHF television stations in several cities, and the FCC proposed a rule requiring divestment in situations where companies own radio and TV in the same market. Recently, the FCC relaxed the rule somewhat so that a company can own AM/FM combinations and UHF stations in the same market. Another hearing is in the offing, but it is unclear whether the rule will be relaxed further. The company has a buyer for one of its TV stations. Should it sell?

Use of assumptions.   Analyzing cases under certain conditions requires judicious use of assumptions. Where information is *unclear* (what did the company's salesman mean when he said, "We attack the easy marks?"), or *missing* (who owns this company? where are the financial statements?) or based on projections (will government regulations change? will demand develop for a product like this?), it is necessary to make assumptions. However frustrating this may be in working on a case, it is no more so than what the executive experiences everyday.

One renowned teacher of business policy regularly points out to his students that the difference between business leaders who make outstanding contributions and those who never rise above the crowd is "vision." He means that executives utilize their assumptions, especially about the future, to determine the directions their company takes. In this respect, a case approaches reality; it requires making a decision under conditions of uncertainty.

Additional information.   In some instances, your instructor may encourage you to seek additional information about the environment or about the particular company *up to the time of the case.* There is temptation to go beyond and find out "what the company really did"! The danger is that the outcome is not always the "right answer."[2] The real challenge of the case is utilizing the information—partial and fragmentary though it may be—to come to the best possible decision for action.

---

[2] Professors will sometimes give the class an update. Indeed students often clamor "What happened?" Many of us lack tolerance for ambiguity. We prefer situations with precise and complete information which can be resolved or brought to closure in fairly short periods of time. We demand the closure and are often quick to accept actions that result in "successful" outcomes as the "right" choices.

EXHIBIT 6–1 Outline for Studying Cases

Step 1 First Reading	Step 2 Second Reading/ Beginning Analysis	Step 3 Thorough Analysis	Step 4 Recommendations
Skim or read lightly to learn basic facts and the layout of the case. That is, *where* facts are. Identify the major issues.	Read carefully. Examine exhibits to understand importance. Conduct financial analysis. Be creative in analyzing other quantitative information.	Identify exhaustive list of issues. Prioritize (most important, less important, etc.) and indicate amount of control company may have over situation. List the relevant facts and factors. Compare quantitative and qualitative data. Indicate which data are most critical for firm.	Develop a list of alternatives. Indicate the arguments for and against each option. Make commitment to preferred action.

Cases and Skill Building

Working on a case, therefore, is an experience closely akin to learning by doing. The skill of a top-notch surgeon is acquired only by diligent practice. So, too, the skill of a top-notch administrator is acquired only by doing. Cases have limitations for learning by doing. One cannot be sure until after the "operation" what will be the actual effect on the patient. However, even when a "living, breathing" patient expires (or recovers), it often is difficult to separate the effects of the physician's treatment from the actual cause of death (or recovery). The best one can do is examine the evidence carefully and make a judgment. Cases provide opportunity for exercising that kind of judgment as well as improving other skills.

Dr. Wescoe, chairman of Sterling Drug Company and formerly dean of the University of Kansas School of Medicine, recently reviewed a list of skills he felt medical school training fostered. Dr. Wescoe gave six major aims of a medical school curriculum: (1) to listen; (2) to observe; (3) to analyze facts; (4) to ascertain when one or more consultants may be needed; (5) to take full responsibility for the decision, action, and outcomes; and (6) to take action when needed even if all information is not available. The list is almost identical with the list of skills that the current course is designed to enhance.

CASE ANALYSIS

Okay, now you have your cadaver. What now? (See Exhibit 6–1.) The assignments may be general such as, "What are the issues and problems in this situation and what would you do about them?" Or more focused as, "XYZ company has to decide whether to enlarge and modernize their plant facilities. Make recommendations."[3]

Whether the assignment is structured or somewhat ambiguous, there are some general guidelines that are helpful. Each case will require that you:

1. Study: Know case facts thoroughly.
2. Analyze: Break down, synthesize, evaluate, and prioritize the data.
3. Decide: Make a commitment.

Study Your Case

First reading. A general or cursory examination of the case the evening before class is not sufficient. Enhancement of learning and exciting class dynamics depends on *everyone's* thoroughly understanding the case—instructor and students alike.[4] Thorough understanding takes at least two readings. The first reading should give a general view of the case, a "feel" for the basic issue, and a road map of the various pieces of information. For the analysis, you will need to be aware of the critical data which are available.

Second reading. The second reading should occur the following day, or at least several hours later. As you go through the case this second time, move much more slowly. You will already be into the analysis phase. Since you "know" the basic facts from your first reading, you need to dig into the case. For example, work with the numbers. There are rarely magic formulas, so use your common sense and be creative. In some instances as you push your pencil (and your calculator), you will find yourself in blind alleys. In other instances, you will feel the joy of that "aha" feeling! For example, graphing quantitative data (e.g., company revenues or market demand) will allow you to see what a percentage analysis would tell you, but perhaps not so forcefully.

Preliminary analysis. Go over each exhibit. Write the main points in the margin in qualitative terms. Writing your analysis down helps to clarify your logic and to commit you to a position. Spend time running important ratios in the financial statements (see Exhibit 6–2). Collect essential points about the emerging (or assigned) major issues in your notes or in the margins of the case. For example, if the president of the company is optimistic about a new product line, but elsewhere in the case an industry expert sounds a note of caution about

---

[3] In some instances the decision will be described and you may be asked to evaluate it.

[4] One of the biggest thrills professors who use cases can have is an (albeit occasional) class that "teaches itself"; that is, with little or no orchestration by the instructor the class identifies the major issues, lays out the options, and evaluates the various courses of action.

EXHIBIT 6–2 Financial Analysis—Selected Issues*

---

1. Profitability:
   a. gross and net margins; expenses as percent of sales
   b. profit after tax as percent of assets and owner's equity (ROA and ROI)
2. Liquidity:
   a. current ratio
   b. quick ratio
   c. days of cash
3. Turnover (as measures of efficiency of asset use):
   a. accounts receivable
   b. inventory
   c. current liabilities
4. Other:
   a. Earnings per Share (EPS)
   b. Price to Earnings (P/E)
   c. Debt to Equity (D/E)
   d. Cash flow
   e. Funds flow (especially *major* sources and uses)
5. Evaluate 1–4 by:
   a. looking at the company's historical trends
   b. using industry data
   c. using other companies as a benchmark
   d. using rules of thumb (if all else fails), e.g., a C.R. < 1; a D/E ratio over 1 is probably okay if revenues and profits are unstable; the D/E ratio might be over 2 if they are stable; use the current savings account interest as a guide to evaluating ROA and as an absolute floor for ROI; use the current return on high yield bonds to evaluate ROI.

---

* See Appendix to this chapter for formulas. The following are references for further review: Maurice Joy, *Introduction to Financial Management*, rev. ed. Homewood, Ill.: Richard D. Irwin, 1980; John A. Tracy, *How to Read a Financial Report*. New York: John Wiley & Sons, 1980; and James C. Van Horne, *Financial Management and Policy*, 5th ed., Englewood Cliffs, N.J.: Prentice-Hall, 1980.

---

the long-term potential for this kind of product, take note! The case is the data bank of information. Make sure you have collected the relevant facts and organized them to make as convincing an argument as possible.

Examine statements by individuals in the case. The president of the company says it would take sales of $700,000 to break even in a new plant. Your projections indicate the company can probably reach $600,000 three years from now. Decision? Do not build the plant. But wait, reexamine that break even with your own numbers. In other words, where the information is critical to the decision, *do not* accept statements as facts if they can be refuted by evidence from other parts of the case.

Analysis

There are no hard and fast rules for good analysis, but a few simple (sometimes time-consuming) techniques are useful. To some extent,

EXHIBIT 6–3   List of Problems or Issues

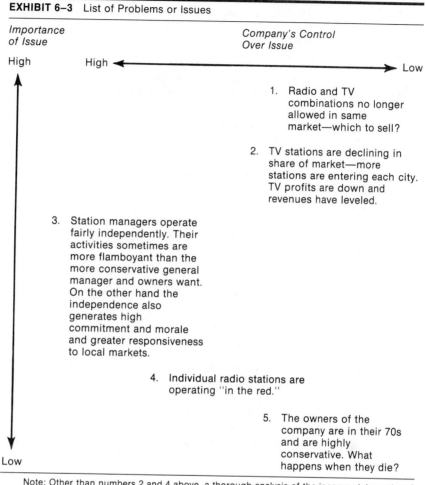

*Importance
of Issue*

High

*Company's Control
Over Issue*

High ←————————————————————→ Low

1. Radio and TV combinations no longer allowed in same market—which to sell?

2. TV stations are declining in share of market—more stations are entering each city. TV profits are down and revenues have leveled.

3. Station managers operate fairly independently. Their activities sometimes are more flamboyant than the more conservative general manager and owners want. On the other hand the independence also generates high commitment and morale and greater responsiveness to local markets.

4. Individual radio stations are operating "in the red."

5. The owners of the company are in their 70s and are highly conservative. What happens when they die?

Low

Note: Other than numbers 2 and 4 above, a thorough analysis of the income statement and balance sheet reveals no difficulties. Overall profitability, liquidity and use of assets appear in good shape and the company may have considerable debt leverage if the conservative owners are not opposed to increasing the financial risks.

what you do will depend on the assignment the instructor gives you. First, develop an exhaustive list of the problems or issues that this company or executive must handle. Some of these may "pop out" easily (e.g., the "hero" tells you his number one concern is . . . *and* the other information given in the case supports his contention). Put these issues/problems in a priority list *and* indicate how much control the company has over each. For example, your list from the broadcasting company might look like Exhibit 6–3.

For each issue you have identified, make a list of important factors to consider. Let's reexamine the radio-TV company. If you've assumed

EXHIBIT 6-4 Evaluation of Alternatives

Priority Number I—Problem:

  Alternative A:
    1. Advantages (or supporting data)
    2. Disadvantages (or data that argues against)
  Alternative B:
    1. Advantages
    2. Disadvantages

Decision:

that the FCC ruling will require divestment of either radio or TV where the company owns both in the same market, your notes might look like the following:

  Facts/Factors:
    1. Radio sales and profitability are increasing steadily.
    2. TV sales growth continues at a decreasing rate while profits are declining.
    3. TV contributes the lion's share of the company's revenues and profits.
    4. TV stations are losing market share; this appears to be because the competition is increasing in each of its markets. The radio stations are increasing their market share or holding their own.
  Note: It took a little time to compute the numbers that demonstrated points 1–4 convincingly.
    5. The company has demonstrated its ability to buy rundown (low-market share) stations and rebuild them (demonstrated in the numbers *and* in a case statement).
    6. The president of the company has led the company in a six-year period of building from a beginning base of one TV station and one radio station to the ownership of two TV stations and six radio stations. (The current FCC allows ownership of a maximum of seven each.)
    7. The owners of the company are elderly and conservative. They are somewhat more concerned with influencing public views than with the level of profitability as long as the latter is positive.
    8. The owners are financially conservative and have limited access to internally generated funds.

Items 1–8 above are a much abbreviated summary of the facts and factors you might make in your notes. Once the summary is complete, go on to the next phase and develop two or more options for action for each issue. Outline the data that are supportive and nonsupportive for each option (Exhibit 6–4).

Recommendation

Designing a solution to your case consists of committing yourself to the alternative about which you feel most comfortable (or least uncomfortable) defending. After completing the broadcasting company case, you could make one of several recommendations using the arguments suggested below.

1. Sell the TV stations: using points 2 and 4 above as primary support. Look for a replacement radio station and a replacement TV station. The company's revenues would be much smaller than before. In addition, the owners might not "buy" this recommendation since their influence would be significantly lessened (one of the TV stations is in their hometown and radio appeals to segmented audiences).

2. Sell the radio stations: using points 1, 3, and 7 as primary arguments. The company could then buy three potential stations from the funds generated from these good stations (a good student would demonstrate higher than average sale price, e.g., if usual sale price was 10 times profit before tax then these should bring 12 to 15 times profit before tax. Buying several run-down stations at less than 10 times profit before tax should not be too difficult).

3. Do not do anything—lobby the FCC. This would be a high-risk strategy. The owners risk the possibility of an FCC required "fire sale" of two stations (or, at best, a trade with someone). However, the case indicated several individuals associated with the company had strong contacts in the industry, in Washington, and in the state.

Now that you have read and analyzed the case thoroughly and committed yourself to one or more recommendations, you are ready for the next step—either participating in the class discussion and/or writing up your case analysis.

PARTICIPATING IN CLASS

The Classroom Process

Just as there are no firm rules concerning case analysis, there are no firm rules concerning participation in class. One general rule is *Be Prepared!* A second suggestion is always to bring a set of written notes and a well marked-up case to class. With these in hand, you are likely to have more confidence in your ability to participate constructively in the class process.

The roles taken in case classes varies considerably. Exhibit 6–5 suggests some of these varieties in style and the roles possible for

EXHIBIT 6–5 Varieties of Professor and Student Classroom Roles

Direction of discussion	Certain			Less certain
Ambiguity for student	Low			High
Amount of "air time" taken by professor	High			Low
Amount of "air time" allocated to students	Low			High
Professor's role	Typically lecture format.	Shorter lectures. May ask questions of students.	Lectures may be confined to points of elaboration or summarization. Keep students to relevant topics.	May initiate class with a broad general question and summarize at end of class.
Student's role	Ask good questions for elaboration or clarification. Professor may be open to illustrating applications.	Students demonstrate their application of techniques to assigned problems.	Lots of questions. Students' responses and debate are utilized to demonstrate the application of techniques and concepts.	Similar to leaderless group dynamics. Students must initiate topics, keep discussion on track and probe each other's assumptions.
Quality of learning for student	Depends on professor.			Depends heavily on students.

student and instructor. The following comments assume that the class is discussion oriented and summarizes the various ways of participating observed among students.

Student's Role

Students in a case discussion class can be classified by (a) their amount of preparation, (b) the amount of "air time" they take, and (c) the degree of initiative they undertake. These three factors are related. That is, people who are thoroughly prepared will tend to take more air time and are more likely to initiate discussion. However, many quiet people *are* well prepared and will take air time—if called on. And some who are not very well prepared at all may initiate freely and speak at length or in spurts. Hence Exhibit 6–6 seems applicable.

Remember that you are not alone in feeling strange about the dynamics of case discussion. If you are in a school where most of the

EXHIBIT 6–6 Interaction of Student Preparation, Initiation, and "Air Time"

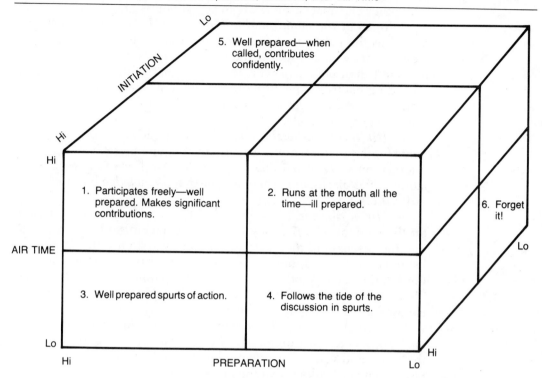

professors use a lecture format to deliver the content of the course, a case discussion class may feel very strange—at least for a while. You may find too that while you were considered "quite a talker—even took the professor on once" in a small or moderate size class, you now feel tongue-tied in a larger class. In addition, you may have spent hours working on the case, only to have the first three participants contribute points you did not even think about! Relax. Most professors will admit they did not think of all the points raised in the first 15 minutes by a well-prepared class.

The following discussion suggests the benefits and risks or disadvantages for each type of participation depicted in Exhibit 6–6. While not exhaustive, these descriptions will give you some idea of the tactics or strategies you can use in class.

1. *Participates freely:* This tactic runs the risk of both impressing and alienating students and professors alike. The professor may have a need (for personal or pedagogical reasons) to orient the class. Suggestion: If you are usually well prepared, like to talk before a group, and have no difficulty initiating, then participate! Be careful not to dominate two classes in a row. By all means check with the

professor to see if the role you are playing is dysfunctional. Check too with other classmates. Be ready to adjust your style.

2. *Runs at the mouth and not always well prepared:* This student runs the risk of alienating fellow students and professor. There are students who can follow the logic of a class discussion for some time and then chime in with comments that synthesize or contrast preceding contributions. Woe to the student, however, whose comment is based on assumptions counter to the case data or is a repeat of some other's comments.

3. *Hit 'n run but well prepared:* A significant proportion of students (unfortunately) are constantly adding one more fact or piece of information without helping very much to add warp or woof to the fabric of the discussion. They demonstrate *knowledge* but not necessarily *thinking.*

4. *Hit 'n run and ill prepared:* This is probably the best tactic for the student who read the first three paragraphs of the case—get into the discussion; then get out. Another way to use this tactic is to listen very hard and then compare or contrast two or more contributions to the class. Another mode is to stop action with an unsolicited, "I do not understand," when someone is obtuse. Be prepared to be exposed as ill prepared, however.

5. *Well prepared but contributes confidently only when called on:* So, you are just quiet. The world (alias the discussion class) is the loser, and you can conduct a lengthy debate at home before the mirror. The difficulty is that the professor never sees the performance, and you leave yourself wide open to be called upon at the professor's option. If this is you, do listen to the flow of discussion, and do conduct those postmortem bathroom mirror debates, *but* go two steps further: (1) ask another member of the class to discuss the case with you *before* class to increase your confidence, and (2) volunteer information in class discussion as appropriate.

6. *Rarely participates and ill prepared:* This student's chief contribution is adding warmth in the classroom in the late fall or early winter before the central heat is turned on!

If participation is at your initiative, you stand a higher chance of making a significant contribution regardless of whether you have prepared thoroughly or not. If you are reticent about initiating your participation in class, the best defense is definitely good preparation. The well prepared are generally a delight, regardless of whether they initiate their part in the discussion or have to be called on.

WRITING UP THE CASE ANALYSIS

In most case classes, you will be asked for one or more written case analysis. Some instructors may ask only for an analysis; others may define the problem(s) and then ask for analysis and recommendations; still others may ask you for a definition of the problem(s) and analysis and recommendations. Whatever the assignment, the following comments are relevant.

First of all, good spelling, sentence structure, and paragraph structure are necessities for good papers. The writer must give attention to transitions between paragraphs and between major themes and issues in the paper. Furthermore, the logic of the entire paper must form an identifiable whole; what you write must "hang together."[5]

Good papers are *concise,* even if no maximum page length is specified. To be concise, *avoid repeating the case.* Some students use a page or more to describe (not analyze) the history or product lines of the company. It is far better to demonstrate analytic understanding by pointing out the boundaries within which your report is constrained because of historical conditions. If, for example, the company has been wholly owned by five generations of a family with absolutely no intent of selling any of that ownership, there are constraints thereby imposed on future action (e.g., "the family's desire to retain control limits expansion or replacement of capital equipment to $1 million per year of internally generated funds and, currently, $10 million of debt capacity"). It is wasteful to start with a long family history.

Make your reader aware to whom you are writing the report. If, for example, you are writing to a nonfamily member of the firm, the essence of the report may be the same as if you were writing to a family member. However, the influence that the individual has to decide on an issue may be markedly different. Understanding of and empathy with the individual you are advising should be clearly demonstrated, although usually implicitly.

Headings and Exhibits

The longer the paper, the more need there is for headings. Use them for each major section of your paper. In addition, exhibits may be useful in presenting supporting material, although exhibits should not simply be copied from the case. The best exhibit is a very simple one helping the writer to support a point. If sales are declining at an increasing rate, a graph may depict the current situation and demonstrate pictorially several possible future growth patterns. Net income might be charted on the same or an accompanying graph to demonstrate the relationship between the two. An exhibit can also be used to summarize data scattered throughout the case or to compare or contrast data in a manner not previously presented.

---

[5] Kate L. Turabian, *A Manual for Writers* (Chicago: University of Chicago Press, 1967) and Arno Knapper and R. Bruce McAffee, *A Style Manual for Written Communication,* 2d ed. (Columbus, Ohio: Grid Publishing Co., 1982).

Exhibits *must be integrally related* to the case. Whatever their message they must clarify, support, or illustrate the analysis and recommendations. The exhibits must also be referred to explicitly. For example, students sometimes refer vaguely to the "solid financial health of the company as depicted by several ratios. . . ." The professor discovers, *after* reading the student's analysis, that the last page is an exhibit containing the financial analysis for the company complete with carefully documented and graphed trends, contrasted with industry averages and color coded to demonstrate strengths, weaknesses, and potential difficulties! Be creative with exhibits, *but* make sure they are *linked* with *your analysis explicitly.*

SUMMARY—LEARNING WITH CASES

Cases are exciting; each is a new and different situation. There is greater variety in the cases you are studying this term than most class participants will encounter in a whole career! On the other hand, cases are frustrating. Each case is, to a great extent, unique. What, therefore, can you carry away to your own career/situation that is useful?

In the first place, you practice the skills of identifying problems, carrying out analyses, and making decisions. Second, a number of generalizable concepts may be drawn by cross comparisons of several cases. The discussion in class can be much enriched if you are able to say, "That is similar (or completely opposite) to the case we studied earlier."

In some instances your cases will require you to formulate a strategy for the company as a whole or for a product line. In these instances, you will be concerned about marketing strategy including product positioning, pricing, promotion, and distribution channels. In addition, you will probably be concerned about margins or contributions; the amount of total financing or, at least, working capital needed; manufacturing the product (make or buy decisions, for example) or deliver the service; and the kinds of people, reward, and information systems needed to implement these new strategic directions. These questions cannot be answered unless you know something about the environment. Exhibit 6–7 summarizes several important environmental dimensions, their potential effects, and some possible applications. It should be evident from even a cursory reading of the exhibit that the environmental dimensions may be highly interrelated. Demand, for example, may be related to any or all of the other categories.

In other instances, the issues of the case may center around a specific administrative decision within the framework of an existing

EXHIBIT 6–7 Environmental Dimensions, Potential Affects, and Generalizeable Examples of Applications

Environmental Dimension	Potential Affect	Example
1. Outlook for demand	Affects financing needs, expected margins, choice of channels, etc.	Slow growth may mean slimmer margins but less need for investment in company.
2. Changes in societal structure or expectations	May affect demand or government regulations.	The "graying of America" phenomenon will mean a long-term shift in purchase allocations by individuals.

3. State of technology
  a. product
  b. process
	Will directly affect decisions about how to produce.	If product becomes rapidly obsolete or out of fashion we may not want expensive automated equipment.

4. Economic cycles	Affects demand.	The larger ticket items tend to be more highly affected by downturns and to move sharply up in good times.
	Affects bond rates, equity prices, and willingness of suppliers to extend trade credit.	May be difficult to expand during economic downturn even if long-term demand looks good.
5. Competition	Affects product positioning, pricing, promotion.	If we are the "little guy" among giants, our best gambit is probably to specialize in a narrow market segment and pray the market doesn't develop enough to attract the "big guys."

strategy. Dixie National Bank, for example, is a city bank attempting to maintain its ties with the rural and agricultural economic interests through its correspondent banks. The current decision by itself would not alter the bank's identity. However, it does run the risk of endangering relationships with one of the correspondent banks (and thus others?) and with a large depositor (and thus others?). The decision to make the loan may not hinge on the bank's current strategy or the creditworthiness of the loan applicant, but rather Dixie's willingness to risk alienation of a large customer (Hooker) and an industry colleague (Winton). Weighing these risks requires judgment.

Similarly, political considerations do not easily fall into the categories shown in Exhibit 6–7 but rather depend on the situation. Your list of political considerations and how you rank them is unlikely to be just like your neighbors'.

Case learning is, therefore, both unique and judiciously generalizable. Thorough preparation, active class preparation, and careful attention to written assignments can reap significant dividends—now and in your future career years!

APPENDIX Financial Ratios

Ratio	Formula
1. Net profit to net worth	Net profit before taxes/Net worth
2. Net profit to net sales	Net profit before taxes/Net sales
3. Net sales to fixed assets	Net sales/Fixed assets
4. Net sales to net worth	Net sales/Owner's equity
5. Current ratio	Current assets/Current liabilities
6. Acid test	(Current assets—inventory)/Current liabilities
7. Receivables to working capital	Accounts receivable/Working capital
8. Inventory to working capital	Inventory/Working capital
9. Collection period	Accounts receivable/Average daily credit sales
10. Net sales to inventory	Net sales/Inventory
11. Net sales to working capital	Net sales/Working capital
12. Long-term liabilities to working capital	Long-term liabilities/Working capital
13. Debt to net worth	Total liabilities/Net worth
14. Current liabilities to net worth	Current liabilities/Owner's equity
15. Fixed assets to net worth	Fixed assets/Owner's equity

REFERENCES

Edge, Alfred G. and Denis R. Coleman. *The Guide to Case Analysis and Reporting.* Honolulu: System Logistics, Inc., 1978.

Handspicker, M. B. "How to Study a Case." Harvard Business School, Boston, Mass.: Intercollegiate Case Clearing House Number 9–376–661.

Neely, A. "Cases: What They Are and How to Study Them." Harvard Business School, Boston, Mass.: Intercollegiate Case Clearing House Number 9–479–668.

Ronstadt, Robert. *The Art of Case Analysis.* Dover, Mass.: Lord Publishing, 1978.

Shapiro, B. P. "Introduction to the Case Method." Harvard Business School, Boston, Mass.: Intercollegiate Case Clearing House Number 9–576–031.

```
                        ┌─────────────────────┐
                        │   Case Analysis     │
                        │      Issue          │
                        │  Considerations     │
                        └─────────────────────┘
```

Internal and External Environmental Analysis	Strategic Alternatives and Strategic Planning	The Formulation and Implementation of Strategy and Policies
Social Responsiveness— A Knotty Problem	Case Analysis and Presentation	Strategic Decision Making at the Programmatic Level
Enterprise Evaluation— Stage I Firms	The Smaller Firm in Transition	Global Enterprise Evaluation
Evaluating the Firm and Its External Environment	Organizational Issues	Constituency Issues in Strategic Decision Making

In performing the case analysis of the cases that follow, you may find it appropriate to give consideration to the issues stated in the grid above. These items are considered to be pertinent to your course's content. If so, then it is essential for you to relate these issues to your analysis.

Business and the Free Enterprise System

1. Metal Specialties

Metal Specialties, Inc., manufactured a series of proprietary metal fabrication items as well as a line of competitive products. For several years annual sales volume had been approximately $1 million per year. The company was closely held by the Jason brothers, John and Bill. During 1977, the company decided to construct a fabricating plant adjacent to their existing plant and operate it as a new activity, to be designated as Fabricators, Inc. It was thought that existing management personnel could be spread over both operations thereby reducing overhead and increasing profits. The building plan called for the use of existing personnel in the planning and construction process. In exchange for this effort the personnel would receive shares of stock in the new operation. Each person saw an opportunity for a special reward for his contribution.

Unfortunately, the new plant was not ready for production until almost the middle of 1978. The equipment for the new plant had been designed by personnel of the parent company and it had been fabricated by the shop people. From the outset, production was impaired by the crudeness and ineffectiveness of the equipment. This hampered production and required modification of the production equipment. During this period waste and labor costs were excessive.

About the time the new plant was conceived, George Kelly, an "Ivy-leaguer," had been brought in as director of corporate development. John Jason, corporate president, had felt that if the company were to overcome growth and profit problems such a person must be brought in from the outside to breathe new life into the company.

For a number of years Tim Smith had been sales manager for the company. Smith was a good salesman and was very conversant with the industry; there was some question, however, as to whether he had the managerial ability to direct a sales force. He was always optimistic in developing the annual sales forecast. In fact, his figures usually ran about twice the sales achieved. In late summer 1978 Smith was relieved of the sales management responsibility and assigned the task of managing the new fabricating plant activity, including production and sales. It had become apparent that the split responsibility of other personnel was interfering with the production and efficiency of both

---

This case was prepared by Curtis E. Tate, University of Georgia.

operations. Also, the fabricating plant was in serious difficulty. It continued to be plagued with production problems, excessive waste, and an inability to meet delivery schedules. The impact was a sharp reduction of morale in both organizations.

When Smith became general manager of Fabricators, Kelly was given a special assignment to take over as sales manager for Specialties. He was given specific instructions to develop a sales force, including a new person to fill the sales manager's slot. Kelly started with one salesman in addition to himself.

TERMINATION OF THE NEW OPERATION

The failures at Fabricators had imposed such a drain on Specialties' resources that in early 1980 a composition of creditors took place. The terms of this arrangement called for equal monthly payments on the outstanding indebtedness for 24 months. If at any time the company were to lose money for three consecutive months the creditors would take over the operation of Specialties. In addition, the arrangement required the termination of Fabricators and its subsequent liquidation.

An outside group had been appointed as directors to complement the inside group in early 1978. They had foreseen the demise of Fabricators as early as September. They had suggested the activities of Fabricators be terminated, but their entreaties had fallen upon deaf ears.

The termination of Fabricators placed Smith in the role of liquidator. However, upon completion of this activity he was left on the payroll of Specialties as manager of special projects. In effect, this left him with little but frustration. John Jason felt a special affinity for Smith because of his long years of loyalty and was reluctant to terminate his services.

During the last half of 1978, Kelly and his one salesman plodded the territory and brought in sufficient orders to keep the company in the black. However, as time passed he became more unhappy with his personal situation. On more than one occasion, Kelly visited with the outside board members and voiced his displeasure. During this period the board of directors was not meeting. The target date for having a sales organization established passed. Kelly still had his one salesman and he was becoming more vocal concerning his unhappiness.

In early December 1980, the board of directors met for the first time in a year. One of the actions at this meeting was to appoint an ad hoc committee to formulate a remuneration plan for Kelly. Professor Joe Sexton of State University was appointed chairman of the committee. Kelly had earlier presented his demands to John Jason. He requested that he be given 51 percent of company stock and that his salary be increased from its current annual rate of $30,000. Kelly's rationale for these demands was that he had made a significant contribution to salvaging the company.

It was decided that the three-member committee—Joe Sexton, Ed Snow, and Jack Phillips—would meet weekly until a plan had been formulated for remunerating Kelly. Due to miscommunication, Phillips was not present at the first meeting. After some discussion between Sexton and Snow, it soon became apparent that the committee's assignment had more ramifications than Kelly's problems. The whole company's future was at stake as was the welfare of both John and Bill Jason. It seemed that Kelly was completely ignoring the efforts and contributions that John Jason had made to the company. To submit to Kelly's demands would certainly be inequitable to John. In addition, Kelly lacked a track record.

The ad hoc committee continued its weekly meetings exploring an ever-widening series of issues. In early January, Snow related an incident to Sexton concerning a meeting between John Jason, George Kelly, Tim Smith, and Roy Page, the technical director. The subject of the meeting was a bid Kelly had made for a large order. Kelly had bid 50 cents per pound when he knew the competition was bidding 48 cents. The material cost to Specialties was 38 cents a pound plus 3 cents for container and 8 cents for transportation; direct labor costs were negligible, and less than the latter two cost items. This action of Kelly's distressed the other executives. December sales had been low and the company had suffered a substantial loss.

At the next meeting, the committee agreed upon remuneration for Kelly. His salary would be $30,000 per year for the first $100,000 profit. For the next $100,000 profit, he would receive another $10,000; and for the next $100,000 profit, he would receive an additional $10,000. He would be given an option to purchase stock from John and Bill Jason. The initial payments for this stock would be used to retire personal notes held by the company against John and Bill.

FURTHER INVESTIGATION AND VIEWPOINTS

A formal report was submitted to John Jason including this and other recommendations of the committee. Later Sexton received a call from Kelly requesting a luncheon appointment. As they sat down to lunch, Kelly began to push Sexton for information concerning the committee's recommendations. Sexton replied that the committee had finished its report, and it was the responsibility of John Jason to communicate it to him. This left Kelly in not too happy a state, but Sexton tried to convince Kelly that it was John's responsibility to make the interpretation. Sexton indicated that he thought the committee had come up with an equitable solution to Kelly's dilemma.

Later Sexton received a call from Kelly indicating a conversation with John. The proposal John had tendered in no way was in accord with the committee's report. Sexton called John to discuss the discrepancy with him. During the conversation, John proposed that Sexton meet on the next Saturday individually with Smith, Page, and Kelly to determine what each thought his potential was in the company and the contributions that he could make. John also reported that sales and profits during the first two weeks of January were off more than in December. Following this conversation, Sexton did some informal questioning and was told by a reliable source that Smith was an excellent salesman. The source believed that the company was hurting itself by not utilizing his service in a sales capacity.

The Saturday meeting began with an interview with Smith. He was very vocal in expressing his frustration because of the lack of a definitive assignment. At the same time, he expressed his loyalty to the company and his strong belief that he could make a contribution to rebuilding the company. When asked if he would like to return to the road as a salesman, his face broke into a joyous grin with an affirmative answer. Next in order came Page. He initially discussed the opportunity for savings through changed purchasing procedures. He was very vocal in expressing his confidence in Smith's loyalty and capability. Page appeared to lack confidence, however, concerning Kelly and spoke in reserved terms. The matter of the high bid was discussed freely and Page felt that such actions would destroy the company.

When Kelly came in after lunch, he had a chip on his shoulder. He opened, "Why in the hell should we go over this again? We've already been over it." Sexton said, "OK, but there is one thing I want to know. Why did you bid 50 cents on the XCO order?" Kelly snapped, "I wanted to put the competition on notice that we are not in the price-cutting business." Sexton, after further conversation, thanked Kelly for his time and told him that was all for now. Kelly again expressed interest in the terms of the committee proposal but Sexton told him again that information would have to come from John.

Sexton—mentally reviewing his discussions with Smith, Page, and Kelly—went into John Jason's office to seek his views. He told John that six more weeks of losses and the creditors "will take over and put the company up for sale." Sexton, after briefing John on the three discussions, inquired especially about the role that John had planned for Kelly at the time he had brought Kelly into the company. John reiterated his belief that Kelly had the background that could have helped breathe new life into the company. He mentioned also the value of Kelly's contacts and the influence that Kelly's father had as a member of one of the major investment banking houses. Admittedly disappointed in Kelly's failure to develop the sales force, John did express the view that Kelly's sales had helped keep the company in the black for several months and that Kelly had given him some good ideas. "In fact," said John—pointing to a list of "managerial do's" given to him earlier by Kelly—"I think I'd better start using some more of them right away." The first item on the list was that a manager should delegate; the second item was that a manager should pull back his delegation in a time of crisis.

"This sounds like the second item applies," Jason stated. "Anything else you learned that I'd better keep in mind as I start changing things?"

Sexton mentioned again his thoughts about Smith's assignment, the need for getting everyone on the road who could sell and Smith's feelings about being a salesman. He also pointed out that Kelly seemed to believe that "the company will have plenty of orders in April and May." "But," Sexton noted, "it will be too late by then. And if he handles any more bids like he did that XCO order, he won't get the orders even then." Concluding his remarks, Sexton told John, "I agree you'd better start changing things—and I think a key decision you must make is what role, if any, you let Kelly play!"

2. Funware, Inc.

Michael Brouthers, the 23-year-old founder of Funware, Inc., a firm that manufactured computer game programs, faced an important decision. Two investors had offered to buy his company, which had not yet reached the break-even point.

Should Funware be sold? It was an agonizing decision! Selling the fledgling company would enable Brouthers to pay his creditors and would ensure a high return to stockholders. He had been guaranteed a long-term contract as president of the company at a substantial salary, and further high financial rewards for himself and the other stockholders were a distinct possibility. Yet, he believed the company he founded had great potential, and he hesitated to lose his own independence as a small businessman.

What should he do?

BACKGROUND

By the time he was a junior at Southern Methodist University, Michael knew that he preferred to lead rather than to be led. The quickest way to do this was to go into business for himself. He had observed the freedom of his father, who was an independent businessman. Additionally, he had become actively involved in extracurricular activities and found that he enjoyed the challenge of decision making and leadership. As he commented to a friend, "It is not the need for power but the enjoyment of making decisions and making things happen that excites me."

While still a student, Michael started thinking about the possibility of starting a business. After he graduated in 1980 with a degree in management systems engineering, he accepted employment with the research division of Texas Instruments with the thought that at the earliest possible opportunity he would resign and go into business for himself.

Two ideas—one for a computer store and one for a hand-held computer game center—were developed into business plans and then rejected on the advice of his wife. Then, during the Christmas season

---

This case was prepared by James E. Piercy of John Carroll University as a basis for class discussion. It was accepted by the refereed Midwest Case Writers Association Workshop in 1986. All rights are reserved.

of 1981, he noted the sale of home computers and visualized the home computer replacing the video game machine. The situation, he realized, provided a ready market for home computer game cartridges. Thus, Brouthers conceived the idea of starting a company to produce and market game cartridges for the Texas Instruments 99/4A home computer.

THE PRODUCT

Most home computer games can be grouped into distinct categories, such as maze games, chase games, adventure games, speed games, "shoot-'em-ups," and "point of view" games. The number of variations of these categories is limited only by the creativity of the designer.

Once a game concept is selected, the program storyboard is designed. The storyboard includes a description of the game play, the peculiarities of the game, and drawings of the game boards. Together, these tell the programmer what the screen should look like and how the game should play. The programmer uses the appropriate assembly language to turn the program ideas into an action game. Next, the completed program is put on printed circuits.

The assembled game modules consist of a hard plastic case, the printed circuit board, and the circuits needed to run the software. An instructions manual or leaflet is included in the protective box for each module.

THE MARKET

Prominent manufacturers of home computers included Commodore, Apple, Texas Instruments, and Warner Communications (Atari). Estimates placed the sale of home computers at 2.25 million units, valued at $1 billion, in 1982. Sales were expected to increase to 5 million units, valued at $2.1 billion in 1983, and possibly to reach 8 million units in 1984.[1] Surveys revealed that approximately 50 percent of all home computer time is used in playing games and that purchasers of home computers would buy 5 to 10 games during their first six months of ownership.[2]

In 1979, the Texas Instruments 99/4 home computer sold for well over $1,000 and was not widely accepted. However, changes in hardware design and appearance and pricing for the mass market led to a surge in sales. Estimates indicated that by the end of 1982, about 250,000 new TI 99/4A home computers would be sold and another

---

[1] *Cleveland Plain Dealer,* November 25, 1983, p. 24–C.
[2] *St. Petersburg Times,* July 17, 1983, p. 19H.

quarter of a million would be sold during 1983. Game modules retailed for about $35. Thus, if each new TI 99/4A owner purchased six games, the potential market for game software would exceed $100 million.

Texas Instruments had written and produced its own game software. However, less than a dozen games were available, and they were considered to be of inferior quality. As sales of the 99/4A increased, the need for additional game software became evident, and the hardware was modified to enable outside firms to produce game modules which used standard hardware and a well-known programming language.

TIMING

In early 1982, Brouthers started examining the market more carefully. During his evenings and spare time he investigated production costs and put together a reasonable estimate for developing and manufacturing the cartridges. The potential was there, but when would the market take off? He concluded that if he were going to get into the business he should have games in the marketplace for the 1982 holiday season. This meant that he needed to move quickly to have the company in full operation by September 1, 1982.

KEY PERSONNEL SUPPORT

While Brouthers was familiar with the development of computer games, he needed technical expertise in order to produce high-quality games. He discussed his idea with Ted Carter, a 21-year-old electrical engineer. As a teenager, Ted had become interested in electronics and had formed his own company to produce electronic components. While continuing to operate his company, he had graduated from the University of Texas with a degree in electrical engineering. Carter had extensive experience in both computer hardware and software, including the assembly language used in the TI 99/4A. He shared Brouthers' enthusiasm and agreed to join him in a part-time capacity if a company were formed. He also contacted two expert programmers who had a keen interest in computer games and they indicated a willingness to join the venture.

THE BUSINESS PLAN

With key personnel support assured, Brouthers proceeded to develop a business plan. A skeleton plan was developed concurrent with continuing market analysis and investigation of various production and marketing costs. The plan was completed by mid-June 1982, leaving about 10 weeks to raise capital, form and locate the company, and start production. The September start-up date was significant, since Brouthers felt the timing would allow him to have games on the market for the holiday season and would provide an advantage of 6 to 12 months over other companies entering the TI 99/4A market.

His market strategy was to produce high-quality games and distribute them nationally through major retailers, such as K mart, Target, and Best. He also wanted to establish a national system of local distributors. Additionally, he would provide programming and production support on a contractual basis to other home computer game firms.

Advertising and promotion were to play major roles in the marketing effort with about 20 percent of sales allocated for this purpose. Initial advertising was to be in trade publications and specialty magazines in order to create an awareness of Funware by 99/4A distributors. Eventually, the firm would advertise directly to the consumer through consumer magazines, radio, and television.

Initial staffing for Funware would consist of Brouthers, Carter, two programmers, and one part-time employee to handle graphics and sound. As sales developed, additional personnel would be added. Production of the modules after completion of programming would be contracted out. Brouthers had developed an estimate of $10 per module for production.

The business plan contained a pro forma cash flow analysis based on both a pessimistic and an optimistic sales forecast for a two-year period. The first year analysis, based on the pessimistic sales forecast, is shown in Exhibit 1. By the end of the second year, gross profits approaching $200,000 were anticipated. The optimistic forecast projected reaching the break-even point at the end of nine months and realizing gross profits of about $1 million at the end of the second year. An estimated $300,000 in capital would be required to put the plan into action.

PUTTING THE PLAN INTO ACTION

With $300,000 required for start-up and operating capital, financing was a crucial issue. To raise the capital, Brouthers turned to friends and relatives who could help him to develop a list of wealthy individuals who would be willing to take risk with the possibility of a high payoff. He located one individual who agreed to put up one half of the required capital. The investor then convinced two others to put up the remaining 50 percent of the equity.

Since the total capital would not be needed immediately upon start-up, Funware was capitalized with $180,000. The remaining capital was available for loan on an "as-needed" basis.

EXHIBIT 1 Pro Forma Cash Flow Based on Pessimistic Sales Forecasts (000s)

Month	September 1, 1982											
	1	2	3	4	5	6	7	8	9	10	11	12
Unit sales					3.0	3.6	4.3	5.2	6.2	7.5	9.0	10.7
Sales dollars[a]					57.0	68.4	81.7	98.8	117.8	142.5	171.0	203.3
Cash in[b]	120.0					45.6	66.1	79.0	95.4	114.0	137.6	165.3
Accounts receivable[c]					57.0	79.8	95.4	115.1	137.6	166.1	199.5	237.5
Cost of goods sold[d]					12.0	32.4	38.8	46.6	56.0	67.2	81.0	95.6
Start-up and tooling	10.0	10.0	5.0	6.0				8.0				
Salaries[e]	5.8	5.8	8.1	8.1	8.1	11.0	11.0	11.0	11.0	14.0	14.0	14.0
Benefits[e]	1.1	1.1	1.5	1.5	1.5	2.1	2.1	2.1	2.1	2.7	2.7	2.7
Programmer royalties[f]					15.0	2.8	6.6	8.7	25.4	12.6	15.1	18.1
Rent			1.0	1.0	1.0	1.0	1.2	1.2	1.2	1.2	1.6	1.6
Miscellaneous operating expenses			1.0	1.2	1.2	1.2	1.4	1.4	1.4	1.5	1.7	1.8
Interest expense[g]						0.5	0.8	0.9	1.1	1.5	1.7	1.8
Marketing expenses[h]	2.0	2.0		15.0	25.0	10.0	10.0	15.0	20.0	25.0	25.0	30.0
Cash out[i]	18.9	18.9	16.6	32.8	63.8	61.0	71.9	94.9	118.2	125.6	142.3	165.0
Cash flow[j]	101.1	(18.9)	(16.6)	(32.8)	(63.8)	(15.4)	(5.8)	(15.9)	(22.8)	(11.6)	(4.7)	0.3
Cumulative cash flow[k]	101.1	82.2	65.6	32.8	(31.0)	(46.4)	(52.2)	(68.1)	(90.9)	(102.5)	(107.2)	(106.9)
Loan amount					31.0	15.4	5.8	15.9	22.8	11.6	4.7	
Cumulative loan amount					31.0	46.4	52.2	68.1	90.9	102.5	107.2	107.2

[a] Unit sales times average unit sale price of $19.
[b] Based on estimate of 80 percent within 30 days; 100 percent within 60 days.
[c] Projected as 100 percent of present month's sales and 20 percent of previous month's sales.
[d] Projected as $10 per unit with 40 percent due currently and remaining 60 percent due in 30 days.
[e] Calculated as 19 percent of salaries for first year; 20 percent after first year.
[f] Calculated as 5 percent of sales due 30 days after sales.
[g] Based on 20 percent annual rate on borrowed funds.
[h] Includes advertising, promotion, and travel and based on 20 percent of sales.
[i] Total of cost of goods sold, general and interest expense, and marketing expense.
[j] Calculated by subtracting Cash out from Cash in.
[k] Current running total of company's cash. When cumulative cash flow is negative, funds are required in the form of a loan.

START-UP

A royalty agreement was signed with Texas Instruments to manufacture and market games for the TI 99/4A home computer, and Funware was started on September 1, 1982. The corporate form of organization was chosen with Brouthers, as president, owning 51 percent of the stock. Carter, as vice president, was given a small minority interest, and the three investors received the remaining shares based on the proportion of capital each had invested or pledged. Brouthers handled all marketing and production activities, while Carter supervised the programming and technical aspects of game development. The group planned to make three games available for the holiday season with about a dozen to follow in 1983.

The most pressing problem was lining up distributors. This lengthy and time-consuming process occupied most of Brouthers' time during the early months of operation. While the three games were completed and ready for distribution by early December, the lack of a distribution network resulted in only a trickle of sales.

Brouthers attended the winter electronics show in early January, completed arrangements for distributors, and sales began to increase. By March, sales had reached 2,000 modules and for the succeeding months, they approached the projected level. However, a second problem—cash flow—emerged.

CASH-FLOW PROBLEM

Brouthers' business plan had been based on an assumption that 80 percent of accounts receivable would be paid within 30 days and the remaining 20 percent would be paid within 60 days. In actuality, only about 20 percent was paid within 30 days, and many accounts exceeded the 60-day period. On the other hand, the various contractors that produced the cartridges, as well as the advertising agencies, had to be paid immediately. Moreover, payroll and other operating expenses had to be paid. And Brouthers, insisting on high-quality advertising (see Exhibit 2), had underestimated the cost of preparing copy.

The $120,000 available for loan was quickly dissipated. Brouthers turned to banks for capital, but was refused because of the outstanding loans already incurred by Funware. After several weeks of uncertainty, he was able to resolve the problem by pledging his home as collateral to a local bank.

THE FUTURE BRIGHTENS

Although the first few months of 1983 had been trying ones for Brouthers, he was optimistic about the future. By June the cash-flow

EXHIBIT 2

problem had been eased, although accounts receivable continued to be much larger than anticipated. Sales continued to meet expectations, new games were introduced, and the picture brightened. Brouthers' projection that home computer games would replace the standard video games proved to be accurate. Soon, by mid-1983, the home game consoles were being outclassed by home computers and home computer games. Independent game manufacturers began to shift their emphasis away from conventional systems and toward home computers.[3]

Brouthers, asked what he would do differently if he started over, replied, "I would be very conservative in my cash-flow analysis and then double the amount of projected capital needs."

---

[3] *The Wall Street Journal*, September 21, 1983, p. 31.

TI's CHANGE IN STRATEGY

Program cartridges for the 99/4A contain an electronic circuit known as graphic read only memory (GROM). Using a counting technique, GROMs move electronic images from the program cartridge to an extra memory within the computer, enabling the computer to draw far more pictures on the video screen and to run more complex programs than would otherwise be possible.

In March 1983, Texas Instruments announced a change in strategy for TI 99/4A software. TI would alter the computer so that cartridges without GROMs would not work, and the company would no longer license their GROM technology. Instead, those who wished to publish cartridge programs for the 99/4A would give TI the rights to make and sell the cartridges and TI would pay the program authors a royalty. As part of this new strategy, the computer price was lowered to $149 after a $100 rebate in the hope that sales would be sharply increased and the many new owners would purchase attachments and programs. The strategy would give TI a major advantage over other home computer companies, such as Atari, Commodore, Tandy, and Timex.

The president of TI's consumer group, William J. Turner, explained TI's strategy by saying, "We understand how to take software to the market. We intend to earn our money from the authors, not just take it away from them."[4]

Some software manufacturers, such as Creative Software, CBS Software, Spinnaker Software, and Imagic, objected to the change and questioned TI's strategy. Others, notably Milton Bradley, Scott, Foresman, and Walt Disney Productions, agreed to develop 99/4A cartridge programs for TI to make and market.

Prior to the change in strategy, Funware had signed an agreement with Texas Instruments to produce and market cartridge programs for the 99/4A. Thus, the firm would be in an enviable position if the change led to sharply increased sales of the 99/4A.

TO SELL OR NOT TO SELL

In May 1983 a major independent software company approached Brouthers with an offer to purchase Funware. In June a second suitor appeared. Brouthers carefully weighed the two offers. The more attractive one involved a seven-figure purchase price to be paid in four equal annual payments. Brouthers would be given a four-year contract as president of Funware with a six-figure annual salary. Other

---

[4] *The Wall Street Journal*, March 4, 1983, p. 19.

Funware personnel would be retained under existing terms of employment. Funware would develop the game programs while the manufacturing, marketing, and distribution functions would be carried out by the parent firm.

The pros and cons of selling were discussed with Carter and the other stockholders, but the final decision rested with Brouthers and time was running out.

3. Central Carpets

HISTORY

In the summer of 1984 the two Jones brothers, David and Lewis, decided to form a partnership and open a retail outlet for the purpose of selling and installing floor covering. Lewis had been in the floor covering installation business for almost 30 years. David had a long history of experience in sales management. The two decided their experience and knowledge would easily combine, and Central Carpets was initiated.

The city in which Central Carpets is located is the county seat of an average size mid-Texas county. The town has a population of 3,500. There is one metropolitan center located at a 25-mile distance with a population of 35,000. Within a 50-mile radius there is an estimated total population of 60,000. The economy of the area centers primarily on farming and ranching with some related industries. Most of the clientele of Central Carpets are either farmers, ranchers, or agriculturally oriented. The economy fluctuates with the agricultural cycle and climate. The cycle seems to be on average five years. One year extremely good, one bad, and three average.

The company began modestly with only $15,000 in capital, each partner contributing $7,500. A building was rented in a small Texas town, which was the home of both brothers. The building was converted into a showroom, warehouse, and sales office with less than 1,200 total square feet. The company started with a few hundred samples of carpet and linoleum. If a customer decided to buy from the selection of samples offered, an order for the merchandise selected would be placed with one of several major distributors located in a large city 150 miles away. When the merchandise arrived, it was then installed in the customer's home.

The business soon outgrew the building in which the Jones's originally started. In the fall of 1985 a new building with 3,400 square feet of warehouse and 1,600 square feet of showroom was leased and the company moved to its new location. The company is prospering

This case was prepared by William L. Boyd and Charles W. White of Hardin-Simmons University as a basis for class discussion rather than to illustrate either effective or ineffective handling of an administrative situation.

well and in 1986 had a net income of $44,526.15 on sales of $276,522.60.

OPERATING CHARACTERISTICS

Personal

David and Lewis are both in their 50s. Neither finished high school and neither has any formal education on the college level. Their knowledge and abilities come from years of experience in business and floor covering for other business concerns. Both men are bright and energetic. Both are married with stable families and grown children. Both were born and raised in the central Texas town where Central Carpets was started. The families are well known and well respected in the area.

Marketing

"When we began," states David Jones, "we had very limited capital and knew we could not survive any type of price war with our competitors. Thus from the outset we decided our policy would be to emphasize service and quality." The company has pursued this objective by stressing 30 years of experience and emphasizing quality whenever possible. David further states, "The best advertising we have is by word of mouth. If your customer is satisfied, he will tell another and word gets around pretty quickly. I question the advisability of spending much money for commercial advertising."

Lewis Jones commented, "Our showroom is the best within a 100-mile radius. We have a lot of room for display and expansion. We are getting a lot more walk-in traffic since we moved. These people have not decided on their product or even if they should buy new floor covering at all. They are just walking in and looking around. We have to do the selling once they come in."

"Another approach we use in selling our products," comments David, "is giving a rebate to building contractors. If they are building a new home or remodeling an old one, they advise their customers to come see us for selection of their floor covering. If the individual does purchase the floor covering from us, we give the contractor a 10 percent rebate on all material cost. This, of course, cuts into our profit margin but we have had quite a few sales from this approach."

With the move to a new building the company has expanded its inventory and product line. They now have over $20,000 in carpet and linoleum inventory on display for immediate selection and installation. With the additional room, they have also added some complementary products. The company purchased a binding machine which is used to bind the edges of remnants left from carpet installations. These are then sold as small area rugs. The company has also started selling name-brand vacuum sweepers. Other incidental items now being sold are floor care products, and door or porch mats. David Jones states, "Some people have suggested we move into custom-made drapes. Several seem to think they go hand in hand with selling new carpet. But I'm not an interior decorator and I don't think people out here would use the service even if we offered it."

Management

"I run the office, order merchandise, measure jobs, and do a great deal of the selling," comments David Jones. "My brother Lewis takes care of all installation work. He works two men besides himself. The company considers all installation work to be contract labor. We pay Lewis $3.10 per yard of material laid. From this $3.10 he pays his crew and supports himself. The company also pays Lewis $375 per month truck expense for the use of his vehicle." David further states, "The company pays me $275 per week and also buys gas and oil for my vehicle. We have a lady who works in the afternoon Monday through Saturday. She takes care of the showroom and sells merchandise when I'm not in. We pay her $4.15 per hour. We've taken very little else out of the company. Most all the other profits have been reinvested in inventory and equipment."

David Jones supplements his income through providing a janitorial service for the local telephone company. He and his wife spend about eight hours per week cleaning offices and various small telephone equipment buildings scattered throughout the county. He receives $600 per month for this service. David comments, "I could do a lot more if I only had the time. I've turned down several other requests for my cleaning service." David further supplements his income with a carpet-cleaning service. "I don't use the steam cleaning equipment. All I have is one of the old type rug shampooers. But I still have more business than I can handle. I've considered buying a new cleaner but they cost a lot of money and I just don't have the time to pursue the cleaning end of it like I should."

Neither David nor Lewis have had formal training in management and do not understand many of the basic concepts of management and small business. As with many small businesses, the owners can be classified as doers and not managers in the textbook sense.

Financing and the Future

"We started with very little," comments Lewis Jones, "but in 18 months we've done very well. We've worked hard, taken little out of the company, and built up our inventories and cash balances. But David and I are both getting on up in years and are going to have to start slowing down. What we would like to do is start planning for our retirement. My son Billy is already working in our installation crew and David's son Ray has talked about coming back and working for us when he is discharged from the navy. Both David and I would like to gradually work them into the company. But when you think about living on just your social security check you decide that retirement is still a long way off."

Since Central Carpet Company and its owners are searching for ways to raise revenue and increase profits, the owners feel they should explore the marketing of indirectly related products if the situation warrants. Many areas could, of course, be examined that would be indirectly connected to floor covering, but the present partners wish to limit any considerations to products and/or services that would require little or no technical training.

FEASIBILITY OF OFFERING WINDOW COVERINGS

One product that fits the above criteria is draperies. At first contact with this proposal it was assumed that skill in interior decorating would be needed, but pursuit of the matter has shown that this is not true. According to Mr. Patrick V. Myers, sales manager of Interior Fabric Company, the sales of floor covering and the sales of draperies go "hand-in-hand." When the housewife is deciding on her new carpets, quite often she is in the act of redecorating part of her home. She did not consult an interior decorator to choose her carpets; chances are she will not consult one to choose her draperies either. If the carpets and draperies are available at the same location, each draws customers from and for the other. As the business presently exists the addition of a line of draperies would surely create some "automatic" sales as well as enhancing the present sales.

According to Mr. Myers, a wholesaler for custom-made draperies, virtually no investment or prior knowledge is required to successfully offer his line of draperies. As time passes and sales are made, some expertise would naturally be acquired, but no schooling is needed to get started. Interior Fabric Company offers a package display at a cost of $200 to the retailer. In this package is a mobile display rack exhibiting 15–20 miniature drapery combinations complete with various types of rods for hanging the drapes. The exhibit is quite attractive and sells itself. Also included in the package are several sample books of the various types and colors of fabrics available from Interior Fabrics. The package offers explicit instruction to the retailer for measuring and pricing the sale. This $200 investment is virtually the entire cost of entering the business. Some money could be spent on hand

EXHIBIT 1 Carpet-Cleaning Machine Cost Data

Cost $3,600

Estimated life   5 years   no salvage value

Assumptions:
  Variable costs
   Direct labor
    $12 per machine hour (6 cents per square foot of carpet cleaned)
   Overhead
    Advertising $60 per month
    Maintenance   60 per month
    Materials   40 per month (compute at 5 cents per sq. ft. of carpet
                       cleaned)
  Fixed costs
   Depreciation $60 per month

tools for installation purposes, but most businesses already have hammer, screwdrivers, and small drills on hand.

In the literature to the retailer, Interior Fabrics requests a 2–3 week turnaround time from receipt of order to shipment. In practice delivery takes only 2–3 days. An order received on Monday or Tuesday is usually shipped no later than Thursday. In short, service is fast and reliable.

Profits on this venture are the most attractive part. A retail price of $100 costs the retailer only $50 from Interior Fabrics. In other words any suggested retail price in the price catalog is 50 percent profit or 100 percent markup on cost. From this, of course, would have to be deducted vehicle allowance and installation costs, but these would be small in relation to the markup. The venture appears to be highly lucrative and the costs to enter quite low.

FEASIBILITY OF NEW CARPET-CLEANING MACHINE

The partners have discussed buying a new carpet-cleaning machine for the business. This would require David to give up his sideline business now being operated. The carpet-cleaning function does seem to mesh very well into their current product line and both partners seem willing to consider its feasibility. The following data was compiled for analysis by the partners (see Exhibit 1).

Assumptions

Revenue of 20 cents to 30 cents per square foot cleaned is based on past experience with a rug shampooer which is presently used by David Jones. He estimates that a 600-square-foot job of carpet cleaning can be completed by two men working three hours or a total of six

EXHIBIT 2

**Income Statement
Jones Janitorial Service***

Sales		$5,640.00
Expenses		
Auto†	$1,480.00	
Labor‡	239.00	1,730.00
Net income before taxes		$3,710.00

* This statement is derived from Mr. Jones's current janitorial service and shows the net income derived from the already existing service.

† 7,400 miles at 20 cents per mile.

‡ Mr. Jones performs most of his own labor.

man hours. The $6-per-hour wage figure is quite liberal considering the employment market in the county. This total cost of $36 in labor has been reduced to 6 cents per square foot of carpet cleaned.

Advertising costs in the area are quite inexpensive. A small but effective advertisement in area newspapers costs about $10 per month per newspaper. The only radio station in the county charges $3 per spot. Initial advertising costs could exceed the $60 per month allowance but should level out to a maximum of $60 once the carpet-cleaning service availability has become known to the public.

Maintenance and materials are a raw estimate based on prior experience in this area. It has been set up on a per foot basis so that it is variable with the amount of work done. Vehicle expenses have been purposely omitted in this analysis.

FEASIBILITY OF JANITORIAL SERVICE

Assumptions

1. Return of $14.10 per hour of cleaning based on sample of four prospective clients and what they are currently paying for cleaning service and the amount of time per month it takes two men to service these clients.
2. An hourly wage expense of $4.50 per worker.
3. With a concentrated effort the service could capture 25 percent of the market the first year and 50 percent of the market the second year.
4. An estimated 15,000 miles per year on a vehicle costing 20 cents per mile in operating cost.

Based on the above assumptions, compiled by the partners, and Exhibit 2, the data suggest that a janitorial service, vigorously pursued, is not only feasible but also a potentially profitable endeavor.

EXHIBIT 3

**Income Statement of
CENTRAL CARPETS
For Period Ending
December 31, 1985***

Gross sales	$79,834.63	
Sales returns and allowances	56.60	
Net sales		$79,778.03
Merchandise inventory:		
Purchases	52,875.90	
Less ending inventory	10,647.50	
Cost of merchandise sold		42,228.40
Gross margin		37,549.63
Expenses:		
Freight	2,317.93	
Office supplies	193.70	
Advertising	1,290.25	
Contract labor	16,251.88	
Samples	1,071.63	
Taxes	2,296.00	
Bookkeeper	112.50	
Depreciation expense	39.70	
Rent	1,900.00	
Labor	1,887.15	
Insurance	352.50	
Miscellaneous	1,429.48	
Utilities	$ 989.60	
Total expenses		30,132.30
Net income		$ 7,417.33

* It should be noted that Central Carpets was in operation only six months in 1985.

David Jones is currently operating a janitorial service as a supplement to his income (see Exhibits 3, 4, 5, and 6). He has been asked to do several other buildings in the area, but for reasons of lack of time he has either turned the offers down or referred the prospective clients to other people who might do the work.

Currently there is no service of this type in the county. Based on this fact, plus the requests Mr. Jones has received to expand his service, it would seem to be a reasonable assumption that there would be a high demand for a janitorial service in the area. If a vigorous campaign to sell the service was initiated, it is felt that 25 percent of the potential market could be captured the first year and 50 percent or more of the market captured in the second year.

The final discussion with David and Lewis Jones ended with the comment, "It's difficult to know what to do. If we only had proper financial and managerial advice. We are reluctant to do anything for fear of doing the wrong thing." See Exhibit 7.

EXHIBIT 4

**Balance Sheet
CENTRAL CARPETS
December 31, 1985***

Current assets

Cash	$ 7,088.03	
Inventory	10,647.50	
Deposits	150.00	
Total current assets		$17,885.53
Plant assets		
Store equipment	410.63	
Less accumulated depreciation . .	39.70	
Total plant assets		370.93
Total assets		18,256.46
Liabilities		
Sales tax payable		1,678.66
Capital		
D. T. Jones	8,288.90	
L. W. Jones	$ 8,288.90	
Total		16,577.80
Total liabilities and capital		$18,256.46

* It should be noted that Central Carpets was in operation only six months in 1985.

EXHIBIT 5

Income Statement of
CENTRAL CARPETS
For Period Ending
December 31, 1986

Gross sales.	$276,522.60	
Sales returns and allowances	1,979.23	
Net sales.		$274,543.38
Merchandise inventory		
Beginning inventory	10,650.00	
Purchases	153,799.40	
Merchandise available for sale.	164,449.40	
Less ending inventory.	20,375.00	
Cost of merchandise sold		144,074.40
Gross margin.		130,468.98
Expenses		
Freight.	4,727.78	
Office supplies	403.10	
Rent.	4,287.50	
Labor	6,716.33	
Samples	632.95	
Advertising.	1,565.25	
Miscellaneous expense	4,004.50	
Insurance	435.00	
Utilities.	2,642.75	
Taxes	8,728.35	
Bookkeeping.	562.50	
Depreciation expense.	129.25	
Contract labor	$ 51,107.58	
Total expense		85,942.83
Net income.		$ 44,526.15

EXHIBIT 6

Balance Sheet
CENTRAL CARPETS
December 31, 1986

Current assets		
Cash	$21,026.43	
Inventory	21,445.88	
Deposits	150.00	
Total current assets		$42,622.31
Plant assets		
Store equipment	1,477.88	
Less accumulated depreciation	168.95	
Total plant assets		1,308.93
Total assets		43,931.23
Liabilities		
Taxes payable		3,187.70
Services payable		112.50
Total liabilities		3,300.20
Capital		
D. T. Jones	20,315.50	
L. W. Jones	$20,315.53	
Total capital		40,631.03
Total liabilities and capital		$43,931.23

EXHIBIT 7 Central Carpet's Store Layout

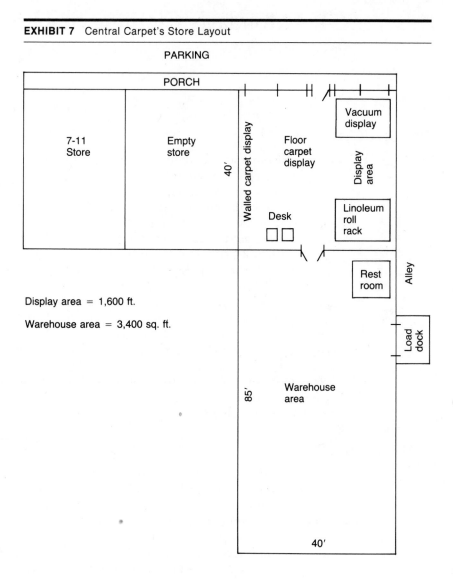

Display area = 1,600 ft.

Warehouse area = 3,400 sq. ft.

4. Monday's Clothing Store

INTRODUCTION

Edith Fitzsimmons and Jo Ann Woodward are equal partners in a small clothing store called Monday's in Granton, West Virginia. Monday's carries a wide variety of styles for both men and women. The women's clothing are both dressy and casual with sizes ranging from half sizes, misses, juniors, to petites. In addition, complementing accessories are sold. The men's line includes suits and leisure apparel, along with belts, ties, socks, and swimwear. In general, the clothes are stylish, well made, moderately priced, and popular branded.

In mid-1985, Edith and Jo Ann were faced with some serious problems. Allowing credit approved customers to open interest free credit lines without scheduled payments led to a high accounts receivable balance (see Exhibit 1). As a result, the store had difficulty paying wholesalers for merchandise purchased for the current season. Although all payments were made, Monday's was unable to take advantage of an 8 percent discount offered by wholesalers for prompt payment. Moreover, complications resulted from the lack of formal guidelines for advertising.

COMPANY HISTORY

In 1885, the Monday family rented one of their downtown buildings to the proprietors of Archdeaton's, a retailer of fine men's clothes. In 1973, Archdeaton's added a fine line of women's clothes. In August 1983, the current owners of Archdeaton's moved and closed their successful business of almost 100 years. Two of Archdeaton's employees formed a partnership and reopened the clothing store in November 1983. Jo Ann had worked for Archdeaton's for 10 years, and Edith had worked there 2 years.

A financing arrangement was made for a $60,000 loan with a local bank at 13.5 percent interest rate. The Monday family, owners of the Archdeaton's store building, generously loaned an additional $30,000 to be paid quarterly at 10 percent interest rate. Consequently, the store was named Monday's to show their gratitude. However, the

---

This case was prepared by Joyce M. Beggs of West Virginia University with the help of Rhonda Nancarrow and Beth Dugan as a basis for class discussion. The case is not designed to present either correct or incorrect handling of administrative problems.

EXHIBIT 1 Monday's Balance Sheet

	10/31/84	10/31/83
Assets:		
Cash	$ 7,360	$60,000
Accounts receivable	13,943	
Inventory	58,911	
Current assets	80,214	60,000
Fixed assets		
Furniture and fixtures	7,500	7,500
Depreciation	−600	
Total assets	87,114	67,500
Liabilities:		
Accounts payable	21,659	
Notes payable (over 1 year)	25,951	25,000
Total liabilities:	47,610	25,000
Net worth	39,504	42,500
Total liabilities and net worth	$87,114	67,500

financial agreement was not the only reason for the name choice. The Monday family was very well known and respected in the Granton area where they have large land holdings. Naming the store Monday's not only honored the family but also established the image of quality.

Background of Granton

Located in Tanlor County, Monday's is on the main street in the shopping district of Granton. Along this street are a number of run-down buildings and 10 stores which are operating. These stores include a five-and-dime store, a drugstore, a jewelry store, a florist, a few diners, and a clothing store.

This downtown area is also plagued with very limited parking. In addition, the local police department follows a strict procedure of giving parking tickets when metered time expires. Consequently, this has resulted in a large number of parking tickets being issued to downtown shoppers. Thus, a combination of limited parking spaces and generous ticketing practices has inhibited customers from shopping downtown.

Monday's is open Monday through Thursday from 9:30 A.M. to 5:00 P.M. and to 8:00 P.M. on Friday and Saturday. Major competitors include a dress shop named the Benerly Shop, a brand-name factory outlet in the suburbs, and the clothing stores in neighboring malls. The Benerly Shop essentially caters to the same customer group as Monday's. However, the merchandise may be more conservative and geared to an older age group. Moreover, the Benerly Shop is smaller and does not sell men's clothing but does offer interest-free charge accounts. The local factory outlet specializes in branded men's, women's, and junior clothing, along with shoes and accessories at discounted prices.

Approximately 22 miles from Granton are two malls which draw many Tanlor County residents. Both malls house a variety of specialty stores that cater to all age groups. A popular trend seems to be shopping in neighboring malls rather than shopping in downtown areas. The residents of Granton may be influenced by the ease of parking and the variety of merchandise offered at the malls.

The apparel industry is characterized by rapidly changing buyer needs and tastes that result in high levels of obsolete merchandise. There has been an expansion of discount chains, self-service discount departments, and off-price divisions. Off-price chains are also expanding and should account for 25 percent of the apparel market by 1990. Their pricing policy is to cut 20 to 70 percent off the prices of brand name items due to low operating costs.

The main employer of Tanlor County is the Baltimore and Ohio

EXHIBIT 2 Monday's Income Statement for 12 Months Ending 10/31/84

Income	
Cash and charge sales	$131,609
Returned sales	5,721
Net sales	125,888
Cost of goods sold	67,326
Gross margin	58,562
Expenses	
Wages	17,635
Utilities	3,294
Telephone	1,079
Vehicle-gas, repair	576
Buying trips	932
Office supplies	896
Supplies	4,096
Alterations	1,663
Advertising	2,885
Taxes	2,098
Interest	6,396
Insurance	1,234
Laundry, cleaning	308
Freight, express	1,009
Accounting, legal	1,087
Employee benefits	112
Maintenance, repair	461
Depreciation	600
Total expenses	46,361
Net Profit	$ 12,201

EXHIBIT 3 Monday's Income Statement from Origin to Present

	5/85	4/85	3/85	2/85	1/85	12/84	11/84	10/84	9/84	8/84	7/84	6/84	5/84	4/84	3/84	2/84	1/84	12/83	11/83
Income																			
Cash	$7,004	$6,909	$4,881	$4,464	$3,759	$17,211	$7,514	$4,677	$6,422	$7,363	$6,593	$5,966	$4,891	$6,844	$4,516	$3,562	$5,240	$14,334	$7,290
Charge	3,045	6,947	4,432	3,953	2,332	8,706	6,123	5,494	5,106	5,409	3,415	5,043	7,225	6,476	3,442	2,169	1,107	5,110	3,913
Returned sales	−755	−730	−649	−300	−848	−1,931	−357	−627	−290	−439	−431	−423	−771	−297	−220	−726	−552	−945	
Net sales	9,294	13,126	8,664	8,117	5,243	23,986	13,280	9,544	11,238	12,333	9,577	10,586	11,345	13,023	7,738	5,005	5,795	18,499	11,203
Costs of goods sold	5,112	7,219	4,765	4,464	2,888	13,193	7,107	5,594	6,340	6,783	5,267	5,822	6,240	7,163	4,376	2,753	3,187	10,695	6,161
Gross margin	4,182	5,907	3,899	3,653	2,355	10,793	6,173	3,950	4,898	5,550	4,310	4,764	5,105	5,860	3,362	2,252	2,608	7,804	5,042
Expenses																			
Wages	1,442	924	1,772	1,180	1,207	1,450	1,347	1,207	1,315	1,977	1,120	1,135	1,135	1,773	1,147	1,120	1,165	1,895	2,756
Utilities	627	631	462	400	505	271	20	180	171		383	224	258	605	463	337		613	60
Telephone	106	74	66	62	70	67	91	82	56	63	84	82	133		65	51	85	78	301
Travel, auto	27	139	26	200	194	62	238	93	10			225		174	75	20	195	71	444
Freight	255		166	46	359	160	22	116	237		39	74	86		349	55			53
Advertising	87		119	18	223	295		219	103	455	167	82	181	66	53	480	125	444	
Rent	235	235	235	235	240	230	230	230	230	230	230	230	230	230	230	230	230	230	230
Supplies			33	59	552	60	103	177		68	43	16	121	169	62	62		793	382
Cleaning, laundry	9	26	50		15	3	15	17				23	20		6	6		14	
Alterations	173	203	166	72	211	166	17	223	222	135	104	154	121	28	75	75			
Legal, accounting	60	60	60	60	60	150	116	60	60	60	60	60	60	217	60	60	100	159	106
Interest	340	339	374	340	341		60	400	400	346	1,886	355	346	120	47	1,098		145	401
Insurance	202	233	202	202	502	202	341	438			184	64	187	693	363	363	698		349
Office supplies	22	20	70	2	20	31	202	226	20		23	22	24		46	30			285
Maintenance		30	30	5	26		9			91	28			24	116	2		404	315
Taxes		513			510	515		515			1,243		723	132		30	440	69	26
Total expenses	3,585	3,427	3,831	2,881	5,035	3,147	3,379	4,183	2,824	3,425	5,594	2,746	3,625	4,231	2,594	4,019	3,038	4,915	5,708
Net profit	$ 597	$ 2,480	$ 68	$ 772	$(2,680)	$ 7,646	$ 3,379	$ (233)	$ 2,074	$ 2,125	$(1,284)	$ 2,018	$ 1,480	$ 1,629	$ 768	$(1,767)	$ (430)	$ 2,889	$ (666)

Railroad. Recently, the railroad has drastically reduced the number of people it employs. The breakdown of Tanlor County's major sources of income are transportation (26.8 percent), government (25.6 percent), manufacturing (15.5 percent), retail trade (10.1 percent), services (7.3 percent), and other (14.7 percent).

In fact, the economy of the state of West Virginia could be described as "treading water" according to the chamber of commerce. As compiled by the Bureau of Labor Statistics, the unemployment rate for January 1985 was 15.9 percent of the total labor force. This compares to an unemployment rate of 8 percent for the United States. Some feel that the West Virginia rate is actually higher since many have ceased actively looking for work. The coal industry has been stagnant and is suffering from the decreased price of oil. As a result of downturns in the coal industry, the railroad business is adversely affected. In addition, foreign oil activity has unfavorably impacted the oil and natural gas extraction business in West Virginia. This downward business trend is reflected in no building permits being issued for Granton in 1984 or 1985.

In 1984, the population of Tanlor County was 17,756 and was expected to grow at a decreasing rate to reach 20,853 by 1995. There are 6,512 housing units in the county which has increased 26 percent since the early 1970s. Tanlor County has five major age segments that Monday's services. These include the 15–24 age group at 16 percent of the population, the 25–34 age group at 15 percent, the 35–44 age group at 11 percent, the 45–54 age group at 10 percent and the over 55 age group at 24 percent (see Exhibit 4).

There are 7,909 passenger cars which has increased 7 percent since 1979. Therefore, there are 1.2 cars per household. This appears to indicate that a number of wives or husbands stay home during the day, giving the spouse the car for work.

Forty-one percent of Tanlor County reside in urban areas while 59 percent live in rural areas. There is a relatively even split between genders with 49 percent male and 51 percent female (see Exhibit 5).

Granton has one newspaper (*The Mountain News*), whereas there are five other newspapers located within delivery distance. In addition, Granton has two radio stations. However, there are eight other radio stations and two television stations within the Granton broadcasting range.

The average income earned by households in Tanlor County is $16,179. Approximately 39 percent of Tanlor County households make under $10,000 per year, whereas 19 percent earn $10,000–$15,000 per year. The remaining households earn as follows: $15,000–$20,000 as 15 percent, $20,000–$30,000 as 18 percent, $30,000–$40,000 as 6 percent, $40,000–$50,000 as 2 percent, and over $50,000 as 1 percent (see Exhibit 5).

EXHIBIT 4

Total Population of Tanlor County and Surrounding Counties by Age Group

County	Total Population	Age Groups (percentage)												Median Age
		0–4	5–9	10–14	15–19	20–24	25–34	35–44	45–54	55–59	60–64	65–74	75 and Over	
Barter	16,639	7	8	8	10	9	15	10	9	5	5	8	6	30.1
Hanten	77,710	7	8	8	9	8	15	10	10	6	5	9	5	32.8
Martin	65,789	7	7	8	9	9	15	10	10	6	5	9	5	32.4
Monga	75,024	6	6	6	11	18	18	9	8	4	4	5	5	26.0
Prenton	30,460	8	8	9	9	8	15	11	10	5	4	8	5	29.8
Tanlor	17,756	7	8	9	9	7	15	11	10	6	4	8	6	31.4

Female Population of Tanlor County and Surrounding Counties by Age Groups

County	Total Population	Age Groups (percentage)												Median Age
		0–4	5–9	10–14	15–19	20–24	25–34	35–44	45–54	55–59	60–64	65–74	75 and Over	
Barter	8,652	7	8	8	10	9	14	10	9	5	5	9	6	31.0
Hanten	41,186	6	7	7	8	8	14	10	11	6	6	10	7	34.6
Martin	34,868	6	7	7	8	8	14	10	11	6	6	10	7	34.4
Monga	37,512	6	6	6	11	17	17	9	8	5	4	6	5	27.1
Prenton	15,230	8	8	9	8	8	15	10	10	5	5	8	6	30.8
Tanlor	9,055	7	7	8	8	7	15	10	10	6	5	9	8	33.5

EXHIBIT 5

General Population Characteristics of Tanlor County and Surrounding Counties by Residence, Sex, and Race

County	Total Population	Residence		Sex		Race		
		Urban Percent	Rural Percent	Male Percent	Female Percent	White	Black Percent	Other
Barter	16,639	19	81	48	52	99	1	
Hanten	77,710	45	55	47	53	98	1	1
Martin	65,789	41	59	47	53	96	3	1
Monga	75,024	43	57	50	50	96	2	2
Prenton	30,460	9	91	50	50	99	1	
Tanlor	17,756	41	59	49	51	98	1	1

Distribution of Households of Tanlor County and Surrounding Counties by Income in 1979

Income (percentage)

County	Under $10,000	$10,000–$15,000	$15,000–$20,000	$20,000–$25,000	$25,000–$30,000	$30,000–$40,000	$40,000–$50,000	Over $50,000	Median Income
Barter	42	19	15	10	7	5	1	1	$11,996
Hanten	37	17	15	12	7	7	2	3	13,794
Martin	35	17	15	12	8	8	3	2	14,418
Monga	39	16	12	11	7	8	4	3	13,371
Prenton	40	17	16	11	7	6	2	1	12,979
Tanlor	39	19	15	11	7	6	2	1	12,678

Background on Monday's

Edith and Jo Ann pride themselves on Monday's quality image and the personal service offered to their customers. Consistent with this image are Monday's display windows which are very attractive. Equally inviting is the store entrance and the abundant floor space which is uncluttered and used to accent the store's elegance. Customers, many of whom were loyal to Archdeaton's, are loyal and shop on a frequent basis.

Edith has lived in Granton for 20 years, and Jo Ann is a lifetime resident. The two other employees are the daughter of one partner and a part-time sales clerk. Therefore, they know most of the customers by name, which enhances Monday's friendly atmosphere.

Monday's has an attractive leasing arrangement, as they pay only $235 a month for a site with excess capacity that allows for future expansion. In fact, the store has ample space (5,300 square feet), which makes a spacious layout plan and extensive use of displays possible. Their rent expense is 2.2 percent of net sales, which is less than the apparel industry average of 7.2 percent. The location of the store, on the most highly traveled street, must be considered as an advantage. However, the downtown area is deteriorating as shoppers tend to prefer malls.

The owners' originally attended buying shows in Atlanta, New York, Dallas, and Pittsburgh. Due to the high costs of these trips, buying trips are now limited to 10 trips to Pittsburgh with occasional trips to Atlanta. The owners appear to be quite in tune with current trends in fashion and customer needs.

Since staggered display showings are used, Monday's constantly has new stylish clothes to offer its customers. In the past, the store tried unsuccessfully to sell a cheaper line of clothing. However, it appeared that the community had a preference for the higher quality of clothing even if it meant higher prices. A keystone pricing policy is followed that involves a 100 percent markup over costs. However, this does vary to allow prices to be lower than competitor stores at the malls.

The products are divided into five separate departments. Department 1 consists of men's clothing which includes suits, sports jackets, shirts, slacks, ties, socks, and belts. Indeed, many of the suits are made and labeled especially for Monday's. Prices range from $2 for socks to $200 for suits. The sales of Department 1 contribute 21 percent to total sales. Monday's is the only store that sells men's clothing in downtown Granton. Department 2 is comprised of women's straight sizes and includes jeans, suits, evening wear, and other casual wear. This department contributes over 38 percent to sales. In Department 3, there are junior sizes and newly introduced half sizes. Department 4 caters to a more specific group of women—the petites—since the clothing is made for smaller women. Prices in these three departments range from $20 for jeans to $150 for evening wear. In addition, Department 3 contributes 21 percent to total sales, whereas Department 4 contributes 14 percent. Department 5 houses women's accessories that include belts, purses, jewelry, and a perfume made especially for the store. Prices range from $4 to $26, and the contribution to sales of Department 5 is 5.5 percent.

Simple alterations such as hemming are offered free of charge. However, more complex alterations are offered at a minimum charge. The seamstress is paid on a piece-rate basis.

Sales are made on a cash basis or on a credit basis of two types. First, major credit cards are accepted; and second, customers are offered an interest-free line of credit. To obtain a line of credit, customers complete an application form that is verified through a credit agency. An unwritten policy is that credit customers should pay 10 percent of their balance each month. However, this policy is not strictly enforced. In addition, credit customers are allowed to take merchandise home on a three-day approval. Moreover, a very lenient return and refund policy is practiced.

Like most stores, Monday's participates in holiday and end of the season sales. Promotions for these sales is done mainly through the Granton paper, *The Mountain News*. The newspaper's circulation is limited to Tanlor County, and 52 percent of those households receive the publication. Generally, advertising lower prices on quality merchandise is avoided in order to maintain their image.

No formal advertising budget has been established, and expenditures vary from month to month. However, 10 percent discount coupons are offered regularly in the Thursday and Friday editions of *The Mountain News* but are rarely redeemed. Some advertising is done on the two Granton radio stations with the greatest response being from the country station.

There are a number of community organizations in Granton. Edith and Jo Ann have held fashion shows for some of the associations using organization members as models. However, the Downtown Merchants Association is the only association to which Edith and Jo Ann are members. The association attempts to lure customers to downtown by offering merchandise as a prize for visiting stores and by entering contests with no purchase required. These promotional practices do not seem to attract the middle income market to which Monday's caters. The association appears to be somewhat disorganized and lack creativity, but little has been done to remedy its problems or those of the depressed downtown areas.

5. The Athletic Club

The 11 general partners of the Athletic Club, a health and recreation facility based in Fairbanks, Alaska, met recently to consider restructuring their business. Several partners suggested incorporating the business, and one member said that it seemed to be the right time to make a change.

"We are in our seventh year of operation," he said, "and we are in an ideal position to incorporate our business. Cash flow is positive, although we are still in a tax loss position because of depreciation and amortization expenses.

"If our income continues to rise, each one of us will have a personal tax liability rather than a tax write-off. If we incur a tax liability, no cash will be available from the club to meet it, nor would we want it to be available. Frankly, I do not like the loan guarantee liability each one of us faces as a partner!

"Now is the time to sell stock outside the partnership and use the proceeds to pay off our long-term debt. We are currently paying more than $11,000 per month in principal and interest. Also, the club has grown sharply over the last three years and should be perceived by the public as an attractive investment possibility."

A CASE STUDY

Is incorporation the logical solution to the club's situation? An analysis of the details of this case study may suggest the answer.

THE FAIRBANKS COMMUNITY

Fairbanks, with a metropolitan population of 75,000, is located in the geographic center of Alaska, about 150 miles south of the Arctic Circle. Temperatures range from 50 degrees below zero in the winter to 90 degrees above zero in June. The community, founded in the gold rush days of the early 1900s, has retained its frontier flavor. Oil discov-

Copyright © 1986 by Marvin J. Andresen and Ken M. Boze. Andresen, associate professor of business administration (and a partner in The Athletic Club) and Boze, assistant professor of accounting, are both of the School of Management, University of Alaska, Fairbanks. This case study was prepared as a basis for class discussion, rather than as an illustration of either effective or ineffective management.

eries on the north slope and the construction of the Trans-Alaska pipeline stimulated population growth in the late 1970s and early 1980s, but little growth has occurred in 1985.

Several diverse factors affect the Fairbanks community. Government spending comprises approximately 50 percent of the Fairbanks economy. The University of Alaska and two large military bases located near Fairbanks provide a relatively stable payroll and a rapid turnover of population—the average length of residence is three years. Recently, declining oil royalty and severance tax revenues for the state have reduced the payroll and spending of the university. However, in 1987 and 1988 the army will move 2,000 soldiers and their families into the area as part of a rapid-deployment force, and an economic revival is expected. Tourism is another major source of income; the community welcomes approximately 250,000 visitors each year.

BACKGROUND OF THE COMPANY

In January 1978, Marvin Andresen was visiting Hawaii and met Don Moody, a friend who had taught at the University of Alaska from 1962 to 1964. The men discussed possibilities for a joint business venture and decided to build modular free-standing, single-unit racquetball courts that could be combined in many different arrangements for customers. Over the following six weeks, Moody's construction company designed and erected a prototype court.

At Andresen's suggestion, a racquetball friend from Fairbanks visited Moody and played on the prototype court; he was very impressed. Andresen, the friend, and others from Fairbanks decided to form a group to build an eight-court racquetball facility. Time was of the essence and many decisions were made very rapidly. The partnership was formed in June, and an architect and a site were selected in July. Moody's company was authorized to build eight modular courts, targeted for delivery in Fairbanks by September 1, 1978.

Demographic studies indicated that four times the industry's recommended number of people aged 18 to 28 lived within a 10-minute drive of the site selected for the club. Area financial conditions seemed favorable: the state collected considerable revenues from oil royalties and severance taxes as the pipeline began to move oil from the north slope to Valdez. Based upon the prospect of obtaining a good racquetball facility and a projection of cash flows provided by a local accountant (see Exhibit 1), a partnership of 12 members was formed in the summer of 1978 to build the club for an estimated $820,000. The partners planned to provide $120,000 in cash and to borrow another $700,000 from a local bank.

Three voting groups emerged within the partnership: the businessmen (43 percent ownership), the physicians (24 percent owner-

EXHIBIT 1 Athletic Club Cash Flow Projection, 1980–1984

	1980	1981	1982	1983	1984
Cash receipts	$325,280	$441,725	$548,100	$612,550	$650,355
Cost of sales	33,000	46,000	52,000	56,000	60,250
Gross profit	292,280	395,725	496,100	556,550	590,105
Operating expenditures	210,690	227,610	246,230	265,750	287,190
Cash from operations	81,590	168,115	249,870	290,800	302,915
Other expenditures:					
Land mortgage	25,960	25,960	25,960	25,960	25,960
Interim mortgage interest	78,700	–0–	–0–	–0–	–0–
Equipment contracts	420	390	–0–	–0–	–0–
City assessments	270	270	270	270	270
Payments on proposed					
refinancing loan	50,000	144,000	144,000	144,000	144,000
Total other expenditures	155,350	170,620	170,230	170,230	170,230
Excess (or deficit) cash flow	$ (73,760)	$ (2,505)	$ 79,640	$120,570	$132,685

SOURCE: Accountant's projections.

ship), and the dentists (33 percent ownership). The last two groups frequently voted together as one bloc. All partners were in high-income tax brackets and could profit from a tax shelter, but did not expect to invest large sums of money in the club. One of the original 12 partners was bought out by the remaining 11 after the first year.

A banker who was also a racquetball player guided the group through the financing of the preconstruction and construction phases, arranging long-term financing with his bank. Although he did not believe the venture would be highly profitable, he felt the club would be a good addition to the community. Construction progressed rapidly in order to enclose the building by the middle of October. However, several unforeseen design changes and other problems significantly increased costs above the original estimates. Soon the partnership had invested $325,000 for 56,000 square feet of land, $1,050,000 for the 16,500 square-foot building, and $270,000 for eight prefabricated courts. By the club's opening in February 1979, the partners had contributed more than $600,000 and were each having cash calls of $1,000 to $5,000 per month, for total costs of $1.7 to $1.8 million.

Managerial dilemmas plagued the partnership from the beginning. The first club manager, hired on a trial basis, was supposed to arrive in January to market club memberships. (Prime racquetball season is September through April.) By early February, however, the manager had not started a serious marketing effort. He was dismissed on April 1, and Andresen directed the club on a temporary basis until a permanent manager could be found. Partner morale was very low.

An executive committee of four partners was formed, consisting of three dentists and one businessman. Although they met periodically to direct the business, they knew little about club business and considered their other jobs and activities more important. Their philosophy was to cut costs, which was partially accomplished by reducing the hours the club was open.

The club endured several local interim managers until a professional was hired through a trade journal advertisement in the spring of 1980. During the next two years he carried out the executive committee's policy of reducing spending. Staff and membership attitudes at the club were not warm or friendly, and cash losses of $10,000 per month occurred with continued cash calls to the partners. Membership was never more than 200. One partner wryly observed that he "belonged to a very expensive, very exclusive club."

By spring 1982 the dentists, exhausted by their committee experience, were replaced by two businessmen and one physician. Fortunately, the dentists had contacted a group led by a CPA that had successfully managed a similar club in Anchorage. After several months of negotiations, the Anchorage people agreed to lease the Fairbanks club for one year with an option to purchase it for $1.5 million.

The Anchorage people immediately made two managerial changes. They changed the club from a single-purpose, racquet facility to a broad-spectrum athletic and health club. Top-line Nautilus equipment was purchased, and a sun-tanning bed was added. Also, monthly dues, rather than court fees, became the major source of revenues.

Under the enlightened leadership of the Anchorage group, membership rapidly increased to about 450 members and financial conditions vastly improved. The Anchorage group, which had some internal problems, did not exercise their option to purchase the club in July 1983. However, they had thoroughly trained a manager with their policies and methods; he remained when the Fairbanks people regained control. There were no calls for cash after January 1984.

CLUB OBJECTIVES

The partnership has two primary objectives. First, it seeks to maintain a high quality racquetball/health club in Fairbanks for the fun and fitness of the members. Second, it wants to avoid cash losses and provide tax shelters for the partners.

FINANCING AND OPERATIONS

The Athletic Club was originally financed by partner contributions, two notes carried by sellers of land to the partnership, and a bank loan for the building and facilities. Each individual partner fully guaran-

EXHIBIT 2 The Athletic Club, 1981–85: Net Cash Flow and Net Taxable Income

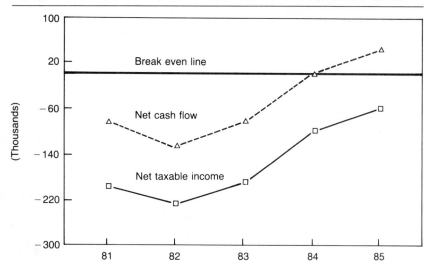

tees the total bank loan. Operating losses through 1983 required cash contributions from the partners of $1,000 to $10,000 per month. In 1986 the firm's equity became positive because cash contributions from the partners, previously classified as loans, were reclassified as capital.

Appendixes A and B provide data from IRS Form 1065, U.S. Partnership Return of Income. Athletic club industry data are set forth in Appendixes C and D, and E.

Three exhibits focusing upon various aspects of cash flow are included. Exhibit 2 is a graph showing recent taxable income and cash flow. Notice how cash flow is positive in 1985 while income is still negative and the trend is up. Exhibit 3, a bar chart, identifies the three major sources of revenues: monthly dues, membership fees, and court fees for members and guests. The major source of income has shifted from member court fees to dues, a more stable source of revenue. Exhibit 4, a graph showing monthly gross revenues from 1981 to 1985, is divided into three periods: the time of manager K, the period the club was managed by the CPA from Anchorage, and the time manager D was in charge. The yearly cyclical nature of the club is similar to that shown by most athletic clubs; during the summer months, few people wish to spend time indoors, and revenues and the number of memberships decrease.

By the end of 1985 the partners were tired of their partnership. They had not liked the continual cash calls, the problems, and the liability risk they faced for member injury or employee negligence. Now, with business improving, the partners faced another challenge:

EXHIBIT 3 The Athletic Club, 1981–85: Changes in Major Sources of Revenue: Initiation Fees, Court Fees, and Dues

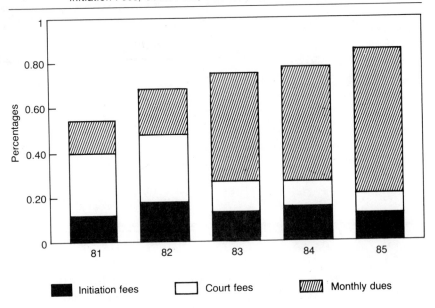

EXHIBIT 4 The Athletic Club, 1981–85: Monthly Gross Revenues

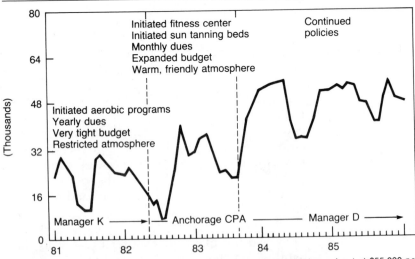

Note: (1) Seasonal nature of income. (2) Revenues seem to have topped out at $55,000 per month. (3) Difference between summer low and winter high has decreased.

the potential of income tax liability from future profits and the likelihood of no cash distributions from the partnership. The introduction of new equity financing, they felt, would reduce the large debt and protect the interests of the partners. Incorporation of the business appeared to be the only alternative.

CONCLUSIONS OF THE 1986 MEETING

The partners' meeting early in 1986 considered the possibility of incorporation. What were its benefits?

1. In the present partnership organization, each partner faces a high risk in personal injury liability. Each partner is jointly and severally liable for any and all actions by employees and other partners. Personal injury liability insurance costs are very high.

2. As a corporation, the club would be easier to sell; the terms of a sale and a selling price could be more readily determined and implemented. At present, the 11 partners are often out of town and they frequently disagree on business decisions.

3. The club would be more efficiently managed. A fully empowered board of directors could make decisions and binding agreements more quickly. In addition, outside talent could be brought in to serve on the board. This option is not possible with the executive committee.

4. On a limited basis, stock could be sold to others without registration of the securities. The funds would be used to reduce the fixed debt. With the debt reduced or paid in full, each partner would be free of the contingent liabilities of the personally guaranteed debt. One plan would be to register the securities and sell about 40 percent to 45 percent ownership in the club for about $950,000 and retire the existing debt. As stockholders, individuals could not be assessed for operating shortfalls. Then, with no interest and/or principal payments, the club could operate profitably on considerably less cash flow per month.

5. Personal tax liability will soon be a factor in the depreciation/amortization situation. Each partner faces a personal tax liability from the operation, and there will probably be no cash distribution from the club to the partners to pay the tax. In other words, the tax shelter aspect is gone.

6. The partners could sell more of their own shares in the corporation to new members. The partners could recover some of their cash investment, and the club would gradually be transformed into a member-owned/operated organization.

The partners adjourned their meeting with no clear decision, except to seek additional information before taking any action.

APPENDIX A Tax Basis Income Statements for the Athletic Club—1978 to 1985

	1978	1979	1980	1981	1982	1983	1984	1985
Gross receipts	$ 200	$225,881	$273,883	$271,755	$123,698	$169,030	$553,694	$585,104
Cost of sales	–0–	30,736	24,996	18,125	12,604	11,674	36,945	29,595
Gross profit	200	195,145	248,887	253,630	111,094	157,356	516,749	555,509
Interest income	–0–	156	27	–0–	–0–	–0–	2,212	1,001
Total income	200	195,301	248,914	253,630	111,094	157,356	518,961	556,510
Salaries and wages	–0–	77,639	94,095	87,518	48,021	62,187	162,510	139,479
Rent	528	956	84	–0–	–0–	–0–	–0–	–0–
Interest	5,113	101,829	135,420	110,438	99,601	100,378	99,836	94,720
Taxes	25	13,387	21,637	16,289	15,741	17,893	29,640	24,806
Repair and maintenance	–0–	–0–	21,613	8,900	5,793	11,963	30,305	22,475
Depreciation	133	103,921	119,011	105,144	94,615	95,495	94,849	94,710
Amortization	1,820	7,281	7,698	7,698	7,698	7,698	6,150	6,150
Other deductions	14,680	109,765	123,225	112,399	67,634	51,309	196,632	372,730
Total deductions	22,299	414,787	522,783	448,386	339,103	346,923	619,922	615,591
Ordinary income/loss	($22,099)	($219,486)	($273,869)	($194,756)	($228,009)	($189,567)	($100,961)	($59,081)

source: IRS Form 1065, U.S. Partnership Return of Income.

APPENDIX B Tax Basis Balance Sheets for the Athletic Club, 1978 to 1985

	1978	1979	1980	1981	1982	1983	1984	1985
Assets:								
Current assets								
Cash	$ 11,026	$ 11,192	$ 3,725	$ 9,265	$ 119	$ 25,526	$ 11,572	$ 17,857
Receivables	–0–	–0–	–0–	–0–	3,058	–0–	–0–	–0–
Inventories	–0–	–0–	–0–	–0–	–0–	4,559	4,523	4,068
Other current assets	3,075	6,990	9,687	9,227	1,882	1,621	4,809	3,023
Buildings and depreciable assets	32,000	1,596,164	1,616,730	1,616,730	1,616,730	1,665,229	1,680,910	1,705,238
Less: Accumulated depreciation	(2,133)	(108,054)	(227,004)	(332,148)	(426,763)	(522,258)	(617,107)	(705,816)
Land	278,247	281,458	281,458	281,458	281,458	281,458	281,458	281,458
Intangible assets	11,629	52,178	52,178	52,178	52,178	52,178	52,178	52,178
Less: Accumulated amortization	(1,820)	(9,101)	(16,799)	(24,496)	(32,194)	(39,876)	(46,026)	(52,176)
Other assets	712,161	–0–	–0–	–0–	–0–	–0–	–0–	–0–
Total assets	$1,044,185	$1,830,827	$1,719,975	$1,612,214	$1,496,468	$1,468,437	$1,372,317	$1,305,830
Liabilities and capital:								
Accounts payable	$ –0–	$ –0–	$ –0–	$ –0–	$ –0–	$ –0–	$ –0–	$ –0–
Mortgages— due in one year	656,335	6,933	315	–0–	–0–	–0–	–0–	–0–
Other current liabilities	–0–	7,704	1,208	1,578	683	3,691	3,500	1,358
Mortgages— due after one year	207,500	1,063,236	1,082,846	1,054,774	1,035,360	1,005,904	975,375	970,111
Other liabilities*	–0–	774,200	865,721	980,733	1,113,305	1,301,289	1,336,851	–0–
Total liabilities	863,835	1,852,073	1,950,090	2,037,085	2,149,348	2,310,884	2,315,726	971,469
Partner's capital	180,350	(21,246)	(230,115)	(424,871)	(652,880)	(842,447)	(943,408)	334,361
Total liabilities and capital	$1,044,185	$1,830,827	$1,719,975	$1,612,214	$1,496,468	$1,468,437	$1,372,318	$1,305,830
Reconciliation of capital:								
Beginning balance	$ –0–	$180,350	($21,246)	($230,115)	($424,871)	($652,880)	($842,447)	($943,408)
Add: Contributions	202,449	17,890	65,000	–0–	–0–	–0–	–0–	1,336,850
Income (loss)	(22,099)	(219,486)	(273,869)	(194,756)	(228,009)	(189,567)	(100,961)	(59,081)
	180,350	(21,246)	(230,115)	(424,871)	(652,880)	(842,447)	(943,408)	334,361
Less: Withdrawals	–0–	–0–	–0–	–0–	–0–	–0–	–0–	–0–
Ending capital	$180,350	($21,246)	($230,115)	($424,871)	($652,880)	($842,447)	($943,408)	$334,361

* Note: Loans from partners.
SOURCE: IRS Form 1065, U.S. Partnership Return of Income.

APPENDIX C 1985 Membership Profile of the Club Industry

	Tennis Facilities	Racquetball Facilities with Staffed Fitness Centers	Multirecreation	
			with Indoor Pool	Other
Number of respondents	39	31	67	54
Average club memberships				
beginning of fiscal year	736	1,542	1,156	1,779
Average memberships added during year	211	903	572	804
	947	2,445	1,728	2,583
Average memberships dropped during year	150	509	366	591
Average memberships end of fiscal year	797	1,936	1,362	1,992
Percentage of increase in membership				
During past fiscal year	8.3%	25.6%	17.8%	12.0%
Estimated for next fiscal year	14.4	21.6	19.7	11.7

SOURCE: International Racket Sports Association 1985 Industry Data Survey.

APPENDIX D Industry Balance Sheets and Key Ratios, 1985

	Tennis Facilities	Racquetball Facilities with Staffed Fitness Centers	Multirecreation	
			with Indoor Pool	Other
Balance sheets (averages):				
Current assets:	$157,895	$ 79,000	$ 262,146	$ 114,000
Property, plant, and equipment	974,248	1,204,688	2,203,115	1,590,000
Accumulated depreciation	(367,495)	(298,424)	(639,752)	(471,000)
Property, plant, and equipment, net	606,753	906,264	1,563,363	1,118,000
Other assets	48,798	54,465	98,587	17,000
Total assets	$813,446	$1,039,729	$1,924,096	$1,250,000
Current liabilities	72,149	373,229	298,234	147,000
Deferred revenues	40,381	5,608	116,348	46,000
Long-term debt	481,988	712,315	1,447,162	803,000
Total liabilities	594,518	1,091,152	1,861,744	997,000
Net worth (equity)	218,928	(51,423)	62,352	253,000
Total liabilities and net worth	$813,446	$1,039,729	$1,924,096	$1,250,000
Key ratios (industry averages):				
Current ratio	2.19%	0.21%	0.88%	
Long-term debt to equity	2.22	—	23.21	
Net PPE to equity	2.77	—	25.07	
Net PPE to long-term debt	1.26	1.27	1.08	
Net income to total revenues	8.6	4.7	7.7	
Payroll, payroll taxes, and benefits to total				
revenues	28.8	29.1	29.8	
Management fees to total revenues	7.2	4.0	3.9	
Rent to total revenues	10.5	21.3	8.7	
Interest expense to revenues	11.4	8.6	11.4	
Depreciation and amortization to revenues	8.3	9.1	9.6	

SOURCE: International Racket Sports Association 1985 Industry Data Survey.

APPENDIX E Underwriters' and Investment Advisors' Advice on Initial Public Offerings

Several key areas deserve consideration in an investor's decision to acquire newly issued stock. Advice from noted securities underwriters and investment advisors was excerpted from "Stock Market Pros Offer Some Tips On Judging Initial Public Offerings," *The Wall Street Journal,* February 21, 1986, p. 25. These are identified below with brief comments:

Market Conditions
The first red flag is a booming market since many new issues are snatched up at inflated prices.

Offering Price
Established companies go public for $10 per share or more. Prices of less than one dollar carry "an extraordinary amount of risk." Stocks with prices from one to five dollars are "very speculative."

Rules of Thumb:
1. Price-earnings ratio < 1/2 growth rate income.
2. Offering price/sales < 2.7.

Industry Group
Two common sense rules:
1. Is this a market that makes sense?
2. Is what the company offering in any way unique?

Track Record
Avoid start-up companies and those in development stages due to lack of history.

Use of Proceeds
Use should be for company expansion, not to repay debt or to invest in securities.

Management
Ideally, current managers should be responsible for company's success. Experience is important; you don't want a young inexperienced MBA running the company. Look at the reputation of outside directors to see if the firm can attract competent, honest people.

Underwriters
Look at how the underwriter's recent issues traded.

Other Considerations
"Take a list of IPOs (initial public offerings), put it on the wall, throw 20 darts at it, and put $5,000 in each stock. You're in just as good shape as anything else."

6.   Midcity Pawn Shop

Midcity Pawn Shop, a family business for three generations, has been in operation for more than 50 years. Located in Shreveport, Louisiana, which has a trade area population of 500,000, Midcity is a leader among the dozen or more pawn shops in the city.

LOCAL ECONOMY

The divestiture of AT&T nationwide has directly influenced Shreveport's economy. AT&T Consumer Products Division, one of the city's largest employers, has fired more than 6,000 people in six months and moved many business operations overseas.

The price of oil dropped from $26 a barrel in July 1985 to less than $10 a barrel in July 1986—a crippling situation for an economy dependent upon oil and gas drilling.

Unemployment in the area is currently 13 percent. Although a high rate of unemployment is bad for the local economy, it is good for business at Midcity Pawn Shop.

HISTORY

Midcity Pawn Shop, started by an immigrant family in the 1930s, was located in the downtown business district at the intersection of three busy streets. After the discovery of oil and gas in the area, the town grew. The business, which was well located, also prospered. Also in the neighborhood were a large church with a congregation of more than 5,000 and several successful businesses, including a hotel, a home decorating center, and a record store. When the street traffic became too busy for on-street parking, a parking lot was added behind the pawn shop.

The business has been passed down through the sons in the family. Members of the family, who do not want to attract too much attention to a service some associate with loan sharking, keep a low profile in the community. Midcity is now managed by Tony, a personable

---

This case was prepared by Betsy V. Boze, assistant professor of business, Centenary College of Louisiana, and Ken M. Boze, assistant professor of accounting, University of Alaska, Fairbanks. It was designed as a basis for class discussion, rather than as an illustration of either effective or ineffective management.

man in his mid-30s, who makes the customers feel comfortable and secure in dealing with him. He is successful: He drives a new Volvo and sends his children to the best private schools. Tony keeps his two lives—one as a pawnbroker and the other as a socialite—as separate as possible.

HOW THE BUSINESS WORKS

Midcity is a typical pawn shop. People bring in merchandise and leave it as collateral on loans. When they do not pay the loans, the collateral becomes inventory the pawnbroker can sell. Inventory items include cameras, watches, jewelry, firearms, musical instruments, stereo components, televisions, and even lawnmowers, bicycles, and heavy equipment. Interest rates are high and very little of the merchandise is ever redeemed by the owners.

Merchandise is held for 60 days before it is available for sale; typically it is held longer. Jewelry is usually held for one year, although it is seldom claimed. Tony cooperates with local law enforcement officials and does not believe that his merchandise is stolen. Most merchandise, he claims, is brought in by people who need money quickly or are leaving the area. Loan value on the items is low (10 to 15 percent of the original retail value), but the merchandise is not new and cannot be sold as new.

THE CURRENT SITUATION

Although Midcity is successful as a loan service, Tony is concerned about his retail sales. The downtown business district has moved two miles to the other end of town, and the neighborhood has deteriorated. Many boarded-up vacant buildings surround the shop. The alley behind the store is a dangerous-looking area; even walking from the parking lot to the shop is a frightening experience for customers who do not frequent that part of town.

Tony has recently added a free-standing branch location in a fast-growing industrial/residential district on the outskirts of town. The suburban store does a fair amount of business, but is not as prosperous as the downtown store.

THE MARKETING MIX

Tony is not academically trained in retailing or marketing, but he has grown up in the shop and knows his trade. He believes the principles of marketing apply to the retail end of the business. He does not know the four Ps of marketing by name, but does know the information they cover: product, price, place, and promotion. He also knows his customers, who are primarily the poor people who live near the old downtown area, middle-class customers who do not want anyone to know they visit pawn shops, and a few nonprofit groups.

PRODUCT

The merchandise that is brought to him is usually personal, high-priced consumer goods. Although he sells used merchandise, Tony offers a 60-day store warranty to his customers. Any item that does not function satisfactorily can be exchanged or returned for a full refund.

PRICE

Tony compares prices at traditional retail stores and sells his merchandise at about one third its retail value. He matches the prices of other pawn shops in the area and lets his customers negotiate their purchases. Sample prices include brand name (Cannon, Nikon, etc.) 35-millimeter SLR cameras with lenses for $100 to $150, color televisions for $50 and up, and lawnmowers for $35 and up. Discounts are offered to churches and nonprofit organizations.

PLACE

The location is still easily accessible and highly visible; in fact, Midcity's name recognition exceeds that of all the retailers in the area with the exception of the major department stores. The suburban store, while newer, cleaner, and in a more desirable neighborhood, is virtually unknown.

PROMOTION

Tony markets the business by the methods his family has used for 50 years. He hangs a large sign in front of the downtown store, uses window displays, and buys a half-page advertisement in the Yellow Pages. But Tony is not satisfied. Although his loan business is thriving, retail sales are slow. The people who come into his store are selling, not buying. People with cash (his target market) do not come to his store. He has advertised in one of the two daily newspapers and offered discount coupons, without much response.

TONY'S DILEMMA

Tony's inventory is overflowing his store and the warehouse is bulging. He wants to make selling pawned items his business, rather than the loan business, Midcity's main source of revenue. In other words, Tony needs to stimulate retail sales.

7. Buckhorn Welding Supply Company

The position Bob Ridgeway found himself in was certainly not unique. His firm, Buckhorn Welding Supply Company, was once a prosperous family business. But sharp competition and the indifferent management style of his uncles, Ben and Jake Smith, had taken their toll. The business declined, and the uncles sold out to their nephew.

BACKGROUND

After the war, Ben and Jake worked for a wholesale grocery company while their father managed the family firm. They learned the practical aspects of the grocery trade, not the details of running a small business. As Jake explained the situation:

> When Ben and I came home from the war, we went to work for a big grocery wholesaler. We unloaded boxcars, stacked merchandise, loaded trucks. We drove forklift trucks. We moved pallets around. We counted inventory. We reclaimed returned goods. We learned truck loading and dispatching. We learned a lot about grocery distribution while our dad ran the welding supply company. One day our daddy died.

In 1960, Ben and Jake inherited Buckhorn Welding Supply Company. At first, the merchandising challenge of their central Texas store interested the two brothers. Eventually, however, they grew tired of opening each day for business. Their sales declined when competitors joined big regional chains. They could not collect from many contractors who went bankrupt. They no longer made punctual customer deliveries to distant job sites. As a result, the once prosperous business slowly became less profitable.

After 20 years of frustration, both brothers were ready to sell.

"Another year like the last one and I'll be fit for the trash pile," Jake said one day. "I just don't know how the little guy can compete with the big chains."

This case was prepared by Dr. George Thompson, Trinity University.

His brother agreed.

"I'd say sell this business if we could find a buyer," Ben replied. "It's good to be your own boss, but the ups and downs drive you nuts. You wonder if you're ever really in control. The family has owned this business for a very long time and we really ought to keep it in the family. Still. . . ."

The idea of keeping the business in the family appealed to their sister (and Bob's mother) Sarah.

"I'm proud to see my brothers run the family business," Sarah said. "I just wish that their children or my son Bob would take an active part working in it. Once it supported us quite well, and I'm sure it could do better again. If Bob took over, I'd finance him for awhile."

Bob had a degree in mechanical engineering from State University and had gained valuable experience in planning and control in the face of scarce resources in the Korean War. He mustered out as a captain and immediately was hired as a production engineer by a Fortune 500 company. Bob, who had both technical and managerial skills, rose quickly through middle management ranks.

Although he had a promising future with the industrial giant, Bob was excited about the possibilities of running the family business. He felt certain that he could make the firm prosperous again. After all, his uncles had never really understood the technical details of the business—and the business showed it.

Ben admitted as much.

"We really didn't understand the business," Ben said. "It's one thing to know how to run people, to count stock, to borrow money. It's something entirely different to talk to customers about product complaints, to figure trade-in values on used welding equipment, and to guess when the latest technology will make some of your stock obsolete."

When his uncles asked him to head the business, Bob left his job with the Fortune 500 company. He bought the incorporated firm from the family estate for $200,000, payable out of company income at $23,000 a year for five years, then at $17,000 a year until the debt was cleared.

The company continued to lose money for the first three years under Bob's management. It broke even the fourth year, and net income has risen each year since (see Appendix A).

FIVE MAIN PROBLEMS AND SOLUTIONS

From his association over the years with other business owners, Ridgeway learned that they all faced many of the same problems. He worked diligently to find the reasons for his firm's decline. In his analytical way he identified five problems that plagued Buckhorn and other small businesses as well. He listed these problems and offered possible solutions for each problem.

1. *Too little working capital.* The gap between paying bills and receiving payment from customers is widened by customers who take the full period for payment or extend it even further.

Solution: Increase customer cash discounts to induce earlier payment. Penalize late payments and print a warning on all invoices. Time the paying of accounts payable to take full advantage of supplier terms (i.e., do not pay early). Screen new customers carefully in order to identify those who will pay late. Contractors, for example, have to wait until all phases of a building contract are completed before they collect their money and pay their bills. Accordingly, limit the number and size of credit sales to contractors.

2. *Thin profit margin.* Costs rise steadily but customer resistance keeps prices from going up.

Solution: Contain costs wherever possible. Convince employees that they should waste nothing, especially their time.

3. *Competitors reduce prices.* Prices fall so low that no one can make a profit. Competitors go out of business, or use backlog capital from retained earnings, or gain working capital from the volume of business that the price reduction generates.

Solution: Study the market constantly and price at market. Create an atmosphere in which everyone's ideas are received with respect and attention. Do not reward occasional suggestions, but insist that the survival of the firm depends upon profit-making suggestions from everyone all the time.

4. *No customer loyalty.* The firm finds it very hard to build up or to keep loyal patrons. People are very price conscious these days and shop around for the cheapest price.

Solution: Combine a high level of customer service with prompt deliveries and swift equipment maintenance in the field. Listen to customers' complaints and resolve them quickly.

5. *Lack of control.* Ridgeway lacks external control over finances. Although he constructed the working paper (Appendix A), he does not know how to convert it into action. He lacks customer related control over stocking and demand forecasting. He lacks internal control over the day-by-day activities of the firm because of poor bookkeeping services and sparse information flow. The outside CPAs he has hired are remote, incomprehensible, and standoffish and offer no strengthening of control. Bob retains hands-on authority, as Exhibit 1 suggests, but still has difficulty monitoring all activities.

Solution: Appoint a deputy and delegate these fiscal responsibilities to him. Ask the CPAs to interpret the figures each month. Ask a banker for assistance in financial interpretation and planning. Make

EXHIBIT 1 Buckhorn Welding Supply Company: Function Chart

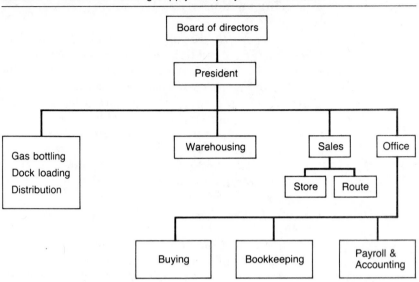

an ABC analysis on product lines. For A items, track actual demand against forecasts. Place a microcomputer in the loading dock area and network it to the deputy's office for online updating of receiving and shipping schedules by products, vendors, and customers. Track daily performance against promised schedules.

FACTORY SUPPLIES

Ridgeway's trucks make two-day hauls from factories and plants within a radius of 200 miles. The factories supply directly or through distributors, as indicated by Exhibit 2. Buckhorn buys a variety of items (listed in Appendix B) to operate its extensive truck fleet and its busy salesroom, office, and warehouse.

LIMITING CAPACITIES

Ridgeway realizes that profitability and growth depend upon his making effective use of the company's resources despite several limiting capacities. He wants to attract loyal customers, but feels restrained by certain limitations. He feels frustrated at his inability to maintain a high level of customer service.

The welding supply company president has identified seven areas of limitation.

EXHIBIT 2 Factory Supply Lines

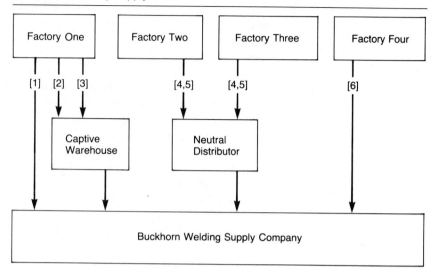

[1] Gases
[2] Welding machines
[3] Wire
[4] Equipment
[5] Expendable supplies
[6] Fiber metal

1. Distribution capacity. Gas cylinders weigh 155 lbs. full and 135 to 140 lbs. empty. The cylinders weigh 87 percent of the hauled out load; the gas weighs 20 lbs. (13 percent of the load).

2. Direction. How many customers does Buckhorn serve in one direction; how many in another? Do trucks backhaul empty too often?

3. Premise storage capacity. Three trucks are at the dock. The dock holds 500 oxygen cylinders and 1,500 other cylinders, which are nine inches in diameter, of various heights, for acetylene, nitrogen, argon, chlorine, ammonia, and mixed gases. Helium cylinders, which are of small diameter, take up little room. Bulk oxygen presents no storage or loading problems.

4. Dock-loading capacity. The dock services three or four vehicles at a time in a turnaround time of five minutes. Monday is the firm's busiest day, followed by Wednesday, Thursday, Tuesday, and Friday. Customers may return cylinders only on Thursday; the firm knows when the customer intends to return empty cylinders.

On a typical day between 8 A.M. and 9 A.M., the dock is clogged with impatient customers. Throughout the rest of the day, customers arrive at different times, and the dock is not crowded. Buckhorn's own trucks have radio contact and stay away if customers clog the yard.

5. Loading rate. The janitor loads 50 cylinders per hour. A full manpower load is 100 cylinders per hour.

6. Demand. The purchase price that the vendor charges for one million cubic feet of gas per month affects demand. "Priority lists," consisting of store counter demand lists and telephone order lists, drive the daily operation. The demand for either is not high enough to develop a constant rate of service. Counter service is interrupted by incoming telephone calls from customers placing orders and requesting technical information or chatting with friends on duty at the counter.

7. Cylinder fleet (9,000 in all). Full cylinders are kept on hand; empty cylinders, amounting to 35 percent of the total, are maintained in-house in order to support a certain number in the field.

RIDGEWAY'S PHILOSOPHY

Commonsense directives characterize Ridgeway's managerial philosophy. Short-run profits are plowed back into the company. And, as the company's manager and owner, he tries to "hire good people, train them right, and then leave them alone." His rationale is to "hold out for long-run growth, meet all commitments promptly, and plan for the years ahead." The long view, Ridgeway firmly believes, is more profitable in the end.

"Training personnel in vendor schools," he says, "reduces short-term profit, but builds up employee morale and makes more money in the long run. Sales are expanded when salesmen are hired at some expense, well trained, assigned a definite territory, and given time.

"Managers," he adds, "must qualify their objectives. Are they people oriented or profit oriented? Long-range or short-range?"

PLANNING HORIZONS AND CYCLES

Ridgeway believes very strongly in planning. He has established a series of horizons and cycles in which he identifies times for purchasing, packaging, mixing, testing, certifying and/or distributing his company's various products. These divisions are as follows:

One-week plans: Chlorine for water purifying for swimming pool companies. Blood gases, special mixes for analyzers, "zero" gases (referee gases for use as standards), and mixed gases. Five-day lead time.

Two-week plans: Research institute gases (expensive).

Three-month plans: Basic supplies, such as welding helmets, goggles, and face shields. These supplies remain constant in different seasons and take up much space.

Six-month plans: Electrodes in 20,000 lb., 40,000 lb. (boxcar) lots.

One-year plans: Welding wire. Four or five base variables, but factories manufacture only one type (like low carbon wire or nickel-alloy wire) at a time. Vendors allocate to customers.

Ridgeway believes this type of planning, although helpful, is incomplete. He seeks, in addition, a business plan that would serve two functions. First, it would identify internal operations cycles, such as total inventory timing and product lines timing. Second, it would define external cycles, such as marketing and distribution. More complete business planning, he believes, would allow him to schedule better and would help him to save money.

APPENDIX A   Buckhorn Welding Supply Company: Working Paper

	1981	1982	1983	1984	1985	1986
Net sales	1,018	939	1,011	1,138	1,068	1,367
Gross margin (%)	37.3	34.3	29	31.6	36.6	37.4
Gross profit	383	322	293	361	391	511
Cylinder income	(50)	(3)	(5)	6	29	63
Operating expense	305	294	323	328	357	470
Other expense	20	20	14	17	18	34
Operating income	8	5	(47)	23	45	70
Payments, estate	23	23	23	23	23	17
Net Income	(15)	(18)	(70)	0	22	53
Extraordinary expense				9	6	
Extraordinary credit				29	11	
Net after extraordinary items	(15)	(18)	(70)	20	27	53
Accounts receivable	129	153	195	189	172	170
Accounts payable	104	110	217	153	114	173
Inventory, start	133	175	153	176	178	185
Inventory, end	175	153	176	177	185	228
Cash on hand	44	25	27	2	14	40
Balance bank loan	80	70	60	40	20	0

(Numbers to the nearest $1,000)

APPENDIX B   Buckhorn's Purchased Items

Trucks and cars
Truck two-way radios, salesmen's beepers
Fuel for trucks and cars
Tires
Maintenance of truck and cars
Truck rental with operator—professional leasing
Utilities
Advertising
Uniform service
Office supplies
Purchased computer, paper, and software
Computer rental
Air conditioning, heating and plumbing service
Maintenance supplies and service
Commercial refuse disposal service

Farmer's Group

8. Taylor Farm Equipment Manufacturing Company

BACKGROUND

Lloyd Taylor, age 67, could be considered a true entrepreneur. His closely held business, Taylor Farm Equipment Company, had grown over the past eight years from producing farm implements in the back of his retail farm equipment store into a $5 million per year manufacturing company.

Mr. Taylor purchased half interest in a Brisco farm equipment retail store in 1955 and in 1962 acquired sole interest after his partner died. Having a flair for inventing things, Mr. Taylor, in the summer of 1968, developed a simple reliable method for planting agricultural seeds. He incorporated this technique into a planter and shortly thereafter obtained a patent. In 1969, production of Taylor's planters began in the service area of his retail store. The planters were built utilizing the spare time of his service store employees.

The Taylor planter proved to be successful and sales grew from $85,000 in 1971–72 to approximately $5,175,000 in 1976–77. The retail store was sold in 1972 to devote full time to planter manufacturing. At this time, the name of the company was changed to the Taylor Farm Equipment Manufacturing Company. The future indeed appeared bright for the man who had grown from a middle income background into a respected and moderately successful independent businessman.

Taylor Farm Equipment Manufacturing Company was located in Exter, Arkansas, a town of approximately 25,000 people. It was the largest city in an 80-mile radius. Exter, until 1970, had been a predominantly agricultural community with cotton, soybeans, rice, and corn being the principle crops. Over the past eight years, several major industrial companies had located in Exter with others seriously considering such a move. A plentiful work force, lower wage expectations, local tax incentives, a university, a clean city with a low crime rate, and a good family environment were Exter's drawing points. Arkansas's being a right-to-work state also added to Exter's attraction as an industrial location.

This case was prepared by James Harbin and June Freund of Missouri Southern State College.

EXHIBIT 1 Taylor Farm
Equipment Company
Sales (1971–1977)

Year	Sales
1971–72	$ 85,000
1972–73	107,000
1973–74	425,000
1974–75	1,110,000
1975–76	2,748,000
1976–77	5,175,000

PRODUCT

Planters were Taylor's major product, and the planter industry was under intense pressure to keep up with recent and potential future innovations. The 1970s brought enormous advances in planter design. Recent engineering revolutions in seed metering and depth control had opened the door for extremely versatile planters capable of providing accurate seed placement even under adverse field and management conditions. It was expected that planters in the future: (1) would be built for versatility; (2) would be built increasingly for no-till planting (particularly due to increased fuel costs); (3) would have sharpened depth control (one major farm implement producer had recently made the first major breakthrough in this concept); (4) would be wider in terms of rows; (5) would be able to plant faster and longer; and (6) would utilize more automatic monitors and controls.

Most planters had the same basic design. They were built for 2, 4, 6, 8, 10, and even 12 rows of planting. With only minor parts substitution, such as switching seed plates at the bottom of the planter hopper, a farmer could change from planting corn to cotton, cotton to soybeans, etc.

Taylor expanded production into other farm-related products as manufacturing sales increased (see Exhibit 1). This broader line of products resulted first from the similarity and ease of shifting production between planters and other farm related items, and second to provide a greater depth to the Taylor product line. These other products consisted of such items as discs, harrows, plows, and cultivators. The majority of Taylor's products were rather simple to build and to assemble.

Steel, castings, plastic, and fiberglass were the main components of Taylor's products. Quality control was the responsibility of the respective supervisors. Inspections were handled in an unsophisticated "eyeball" manner. If it looked good and fit into the other parts, it passed inspection. However, on the whole the company had few customer complaints, and those received were expeditiously and courteously handled.

The nature of the product and sales made the work at Taylor highly seasonal. Attempts to even out this seasonality were made, but the cost of carrying inventories, little storage space, and volatility of orders limited the success of such attempts. Preliminary sales orders (usually about 20 percent of the annual year's volume) could be expected starting in October–November. Customers were encouraged to order early, but there was little incentive to do so. The majority of the year's orders (approximately 50 percent) were received in January–February with the remainder tapering off from April to July. The bulk of planter shipments were made during March–April.

Work slowed to a snail's pace during the summer months of June through August, and only a skeleton crew of hourly employees were retained. Design changes, clean-up maintenance work, and minimum production took place during these slow months. During this period, all supervisors could take several weeks off (without pay) for vacations and were encouraged to do so. With a few exceptions for extremely valued employees, only those hourly workers whose skills and talents deemed them to be indispensable to year-round operations were retained during these months.

SALES

Planters represented approximately 80 percent of Taylor's yearly sales over the past six years. It was Mr. Taylor's "opinion" that nonplanter sales, however, provided the company with a slightly higher profit margin.

Sales in the early years of Taylor's existence were generated by Lloyd Taylor and Harry Johnson. Harry was the sales and service manager for the retail business. By loading up the store truck with planters and selling to increasingly larger areas, Lloyd and Harry were gradually able to expand sales utilizing the contacts they had made in the retail store.

In 1972, the Brisco Tractor Company learned of the Taylor planter through their local sales representative. At this time, Brisco had 6 percent of the tractor market and ranked seventh in the farm equipment business. Prior to 1972, Brisco had not offered a full array of farm implements to complement their tractors. Shortly thereafter, Taylor entered into an informal agreement to supply Brisco with planters for their retail outlets. Most of the other major tractor manufacturers produced their own planters and farm implements. These planters were to be marketed under the Brisco label. The only basic difference between a Taylor planter and a Brisco planter was the color and brand labels. Orders for Taylor's products were placed by Brisco's home office, who in turn passed them on to Taylor. Payment for shipments were made by the Brisco Tractor Company. This association with a major manufacturer and retailer provided Taylor with the volume, outlets, and stability deemed necessary for the growth of the company.

Brisco sales averaged roughly 70 to 80 percent of Taylor's total sales. Sales expanded so rapidly that Taylor was unable to supply all of Brisco's orders in 1975–76. Brisco then turned to Seon Company to supply those orders that Taylor could not. Seon was a multifaceted company with about $30 million a year in sales. It was believed, however, that Brisco preferred Taylor to Seon because of lower prices and a better bargaining position.

The farming implement industry is highly competitive with the top seven companies dominating the market. The planting industry consisted of 50 to 70 producers with about 25 of them specializing in a particular product. Customers attributed their purchases of farm products to brand loyalty (his father had always bought brand X), compatability of equipment to brand of tractor (although all the implements were basically interchangeable), price, and loyalty to dealership. Many customers preferred the major brands because of warranties, parts, and service. The importance of these attributes, however, tended to be a highly personal matter.

Retail prices of planters tended to fluctuate widely. Depending upon the versatility and sophistication of the planter, prices in 1976 could range from $400 to $1,000/foot. Bargaining with the retail dealers on price was a tradition much like that in the automobile business.

PERSONNEL

Harry Johnson, 64, was Lloyd's right-hand man and a personal friend. He had been with Lloyd since the start of the retail business and was regarded as a knowledgeable and loyal employee whom everyone naturally liked. Anyone wanting to know Mr. Taylor's thinking or having new ideas or suggestions would usually speak with Harry first. Harry would either give his opinion concerning how Lloyd would react, or, if one were lucky, he would introduce the idea to Lloyd, thereby increasing the chance for its acceptance.

Harry thought very highly of Lloyd as a boss first and a friend second. He knew just how far Lloyd could be pushed or persuaded, when to suggest or to back off, and was usually an insider to privileged information or thoughts. Lloyd trusted Harry and valued him as an employee. Lloyd had the final say-so and Harry accepted that, yet Harry was not a typical yes-man.

The marketing efforts of the company centered around Harry. It was still common for Harry to load up the company truck and promote their products during the off-season. Harry would promote only the Taylor label. Promotion of the Brisco planter was handled through Brisco's sales representatives. Since the Brisco arrangement, Harry's marketing efforts were curtailed to a few times a year. An elderly manufacturing representative for the Brisco Tractor Company provided the Taylor Company with the only other internal marketing efforts. Taylor sales generated by this representative to date were only a minor amount of Taylor's total sales. His primary responsibility was to Brisco Tractor Company, but because of his long association with Lloyd, he promoted Taylor's products as a favor and as a second source of income.

Harry's daily activities presently centered around accepting, logging, and coordinating orders with the production schedule. He insured the shipment of orders at the proper times. In addition, Harry handled all service related questions or problems. Travel was sometimes necessary to handle problems experienced. Lloyd would often ask Harry to handle miscellaneous tasks as well.

In 1974, Lloyd's son-in-law, Leroy Howard, was encouraged to enter the business as the general plant manager. Leroy had a mechanical engineering degree with six years experience in an unrelated type of business. However, Leroy had no managerial experience. Leroy possessed an energetic personality with a direct manner. He seemed to enjoy the position of plant manager. Yet, in some cases, there appeared an uncertainty on his part concerning the extent of his authority and responsibility. Lloyd, on his many frequent trips through the plant, would often change an operation or production schedule without notifying Leroy or his subordinates.

Leroy's activities involved overseeing the day-to-day operations of the plant, a task Lloyd did not particularly enjoy. Lloyd retained authority for the financial function of the business. Approximately 30 to 40 percent of Leroy's time was spent handling personnel matters. This was particularly true during the company's peak work season. Interviewing seemed to be a necessary but never-ending task due to the large amount of employee turnover. Leroy seemed to enjoy this role in particular and interviewed almost anyone who walked in off the street. If there was an opening, the applicants applying that day would invariably get the job. In fact, on several occasions a prospective employee would walk in for a job application and go to work the next day, often without any real concept of the type of work they were expected to perform.

Jay Mueher joined the Taylor Company in the summer of 1975. His initial duties were truck driver and general errand man. Jay, 24, was not a typical hourly employee and quickly moved into the front office. He gradually assumed the production and inventory control duties of the business. Later, Jay also started placing some of the material orders under the close supervision of Leroy. Jay's personality was unpretentious, but he had an innate ability for grasping figures and planning.

Sally Kreps had been with the Taylor Company for the last six years. Her responsibilities included all the in-house bookkeeping. Decisions of any scope were referred to Lloyd. The payroll cards and verification of hours worked were Sally's responsibility. The actual computation and issuance of checks was performed through the services of a local computer company on a time-sharing basis. Sally was a rather likable, introverted, conscientious person. In 1976, Sally enrolled in a night principles of accounting class at the local university and was experiencing some difficulties comprehending the mechanics of the course. However, this did represent her first attempt at college classes.

The receptionist, June Simmon, handled the telephone switchboard and performed the necessary typing. Lloyd, Harry, Leroy, Jay, Sally, and June comprised the Taylor team until the fall of 1976. At this time, it was the consensus decision of Lloyd, Harry, and Leroy that there was a need to expand the management staff so as to relieve their increasing workload demands.

Tim Berry, 30, was employed in the fall of 1976 to help provide expertise in the materials planning and scheduling functions of the business. Tim had five years experience in the production and planning departments of two manufacturing companies and was completing his MBA degree at night. Initially, Tim and Jay worked together to formally organize the production control function. Gradually Tim took over and expanded the purchasing function leaving Jay with the production and control function. Tim had worked closely with the purchasing departments in his two previous positions.

Richard Youst, 35, was employed as a part-time person to assist in the accounting function. He possessed 14 years experience in the military as helicopter pilot and was presently in the process of earning his MBA degree. Richard had developed an interest in accounting in his previous job. The primary responsibilities of Richard, as a part-time employee, were to work with Sally in trying to improve the organization's bookkeeping function. Richard also subbed in a variety of other tasks, one of which was as a time-study man. Recognizing that standards were essential to costing, pricing, and planning decisions, Richard convinced Lloyd and Leroy of the standards necessity. A large percentage of Richard's time was devoted to performing time studies. In the spring of 1977 and coinciding with his graduation, Richard was offered and accepted a full-time position with Taylor as controller. At that time, he was promised that he would have the authority in his new position to carry out necessary reforms in the accounting department.

A plant superintendent was also sought in the spring of 1977. Bill Adams, an engineer with eight years of varied experience, was employed by Taylor for this position. Bill, 39, and recently divorced, was an individualist, easy to relate to, and a husky sort of person. He proved to be very popular with the majority of the plant supervisors who reported to him. Several enjoyed off-duty activities with Bill. He impressed one on the surface, at least, as capable of performing the tasks assigned to him.

A search for a personnel manager took place in the summer of 1977. Ron Temple, 38, possessing four years experience in personnel, was chosen. Prior to his leaving his present job, Ron was injured in a car accident that prevented his starting to work with Taylor for the next nine months.

In the spring of 1977, Dave Bartlett, 33, a talented mechanical engineer, was added to the Taylor team. Dave had previously been employed by MCC, a major producer of a variety of agricultural and military products, which was also located in Exter. The justification for hiring Dave was Lloyd's inability to perfect a new method for planting. Lloyd had devoted much of his time in the past 14 months to this project. Lloyd felt this new concept in planting could have a revolutionary effect in the industry.

Many of Dave's activities centered around the development of this new planter. Several other projects cut into his time, such as the construction of a new conveyor for the painting of Taylor's parts. This system (which was built in-house) was completed during 1977 and much of its success was attributed to Dave. The new system replaced a very inefficient one.

The hourly work force consisted of predominately young first-time workers, unskilled workers, and temporarily unemployed workers. Because of the harsh working conditions, few women tended to stay with the company. During the busy season of 1977, the number of employees reached 210, an all-time high for the Taylor Company. Turnover ran at approximately 175 percent for 1977, which was slightly higher than in previous years.

While there was no organization chart per se in the company, Exhibit 2 represents a fairly accurate picture of the management team as of 1977.

COMPENSATION AND BENEFITS

Pay and benefits at the Taylor Company were established at below average scale for the local geographical area. This was also true for the recently hired new manager. The only exception to this policy was Dave, the new engineer. Dave's salary was slightly above the going salary in the area. Lloyd felt this to be justified because of the need to develop the new planter. The possibility of getting in on the ground floor of a fast-growing industrial concern appeared to be a prime at-

EXHIBIT 2

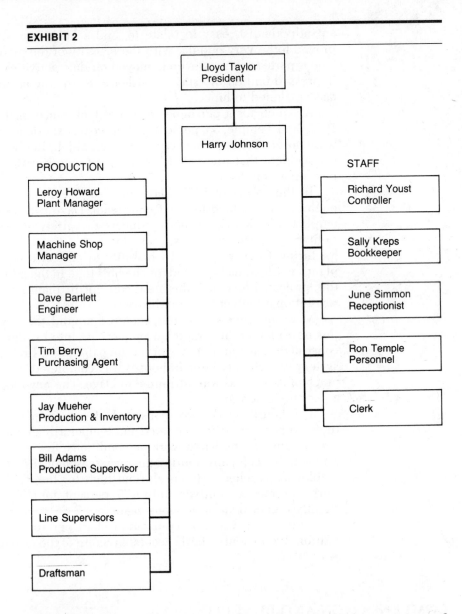

traction for the new managers and seemed to balance the inequities of lower salaries.

Compensation for the hourly ranks was established slightly above minimum wage. Certain key positions paid more, such as welders, skilled machinists, etc.; but again these were still below average scale for the area. This was partly attributed to Lloyd's cost-conscious philosophy and partly to an assumed conclusion that there was no need to pay more. The logic for this assumed conclusion was: (1) the simplicity of the operations; (2) an adequate labor supply; (3) a short training time for new employees; and (4) little loss of productivity due to labor turnover.

Injuries were a common occurrence within the plant, ranging from minor cuts to lost fingers. Medical insurance was provided; however, workers were not fully compensated for lost work time. There was a rather unhumorous remark once made that, "we should start an injury-of-the-week club."

STANDARDS

Standards for production did not exist until the fall of 1976. Pricing of the products was accomplished through the "gut" feelings of Lloyd, Leroy, and Harry. It was Lloyd's philosophy that pricing be comparable to other producers, and he usually attempted to price below the major producers. There was room for price flexibility depending on the need for sales and the bargaining position of his customers.

The lack of a basis for realistic pricing procedures was brought to the surface largely through the efforts of Richard while he was still a part-time employee. With his clipboard and stopwatch, Richard developed a record of "averages" for time spent in production for as many parts as time permitted. Production time of less expensive parts was estimated until Richard could observe them. The standards and efficiency hours generated by Richard resulted in some pricing revisions of Taylor products. Several products in the Taylor line were either overpriced or underpriced.

FINANCES

The financial condition of Taylor Farm Equipment Manufacturing Company was considered to be a private matter. A local CPA firm generated the income statements, balance sheets, capital statements, and tax returns. A line of credit assumed to be sufficient was established with a local bank and had not been increased in the last two years. On several occasions, when financial statements were requested by potential suppliers, Taylor refused to supply such information and insisted that his line of credit with the local bank should provide sufficient information.

Checks for payments to suppliers required Taylor's signature. His philosophy on accounts payable was unusual to say the least. Payments were delayed as long as possible. Notices of payments past due were ignored, and calls from credit managers were diverted by Sally if possible. Payments occurred only when final credit threats were made. Taylor viewed this delaying tactic as a form of leverage.

In the past eight months, several of Taylor's suppliers would ship only on a COD basis. Among those demanding a COD policy were all existing steel suppliers. (Steel was the primary raw material cost of Taylor's products.)

In November of 1976, Leroy called a meeting with Jay, Tim, and Harry to discuss purchases and production schedules. At this meeting, Leroy stated that while there was no danger of inability to meet payroll expenses, other expenses should be kept to a minimum for the next three months. This meant that all possible purchases and receipts of goods should be postponed. Production should center around only those items necessary for immediate shipment or absolutely necessary to generate work for existing personnel. Leroy attributed the money crunch to an excessive amount of in-house inventory.

SAN SALVADOR

In the spring of 1977, Lloyd and Leroy flew to San Salvador to participate in an international showing and demonstration of agricultural products. An assortment of the Taylor line was displayed at this exhibit. International marketing agents and sales representatives, as well as agricultural officials from over 40 countries, were present to inspect and purchase farming implements.

At this showing, an informal agreement was established between the Sanger Marketing Corporation and Taylor Farm Equipment Manufacturing Company. The Sanger company was to market the Taylor line of products in foreign countries. This company was acknowledged as a leader in international marketing circles.

As a result of this showing and association with Sanger, orders were being received from overseas countries as indicated by $35,000 from Jordan, $47,000 from Israel, and $52,000 from Spain. Sanger further informed Mr. Taylor that several other foreign officials were impressed with the planter, and that overseas sales could quite shortly accelerate.

PLANS FOR THE FUTURE

In early summer of 1977, Leroy rented a motel conference room for what was to be the company's first formal planning session. Harry, Jay, Tim, Dave, and Leroy spent a day mapping out future needs and projections. Anticipated sales and production projections were discussed at length. It was the consensus of those attending that sales could be expected to increase considerably in the future, although perhaps not at the rate they had in the past four years.

Some of the more important recommendations were:

1. An additional (50 percent more) production space to include warehouse capacity should be rented within the next six months;

2. An additional (50 percent minimum) increase in hourly workers would be necessary by next year.
3. A greater emphasis should be placed on cost efficiency.

THE BLOW

In late summer of 1977, Lloyd and Leroy made their annual trip to
Brisco's headquarters to meet with the marketing department to get an
estimate of projected sales to Brisco's retailers for the next year. Lloyd
and Leroy returned to Exter a very surprised and disappointed pair.
Brisco had decided to drop Taylor Farm Equipment Company in the
coming year as its prime supplier of planters in favor of Seon Company. The reasons given for discontinuing the Taylor-Brisco arrangement were rather nebulous, although pricing was mentioned by the
Brisco executives. As an act of conciliation, Brisco did say that Taylor
could expect to receive orders for discs, plows, harrows, etc., and even
a few planters. Brisco implied that the arrangement with Seon might
not be a permanent one and that things could change in the future.

APPENDIX A   Selected Farm Machines and Equipment Shipments: 1960 to 1976 (in millions of dollars; excludes tractors and irrigation systems.)

Product	1960	1965	1970	1972	1974	1975	1976
Total	$1,001	$1,432	$1,553	$1,981	$3,637	$4,179	$4,481
Farm machines and equipment (complete units)	798	1,169	1,271	1,616	3,042	3,485	3,726
Attachments and parts	203	263	282	365	595	693	755
Complete units, attachments, and parts:							
Plows	61	96	76	99	182	250	267
Harrows, rollers, pulverizers, stalk cutters	86	133	153	189	395	476	478
Planting, seeding, and fertilizing equipment	98	140	161	197	354	480	517
Cultivators, weeders, sprayers, dusters	96	122	115	138	302	383	383
Harvesting and haying machinery	464	651	631	834	1,501	1,735	1,944
Machinery for preparing crops for market	38	59	85	111	255	262	234
Farm poultry equipment	29	45	73	63	76	70	100
Farm dairy machines and equipment	20	31	42	61	80	68	77
Hog and other barn equipment	44	67	114	135	213	175	220
Farm elevators and blowers	28	37	35	52	92	100	88
Farm wagons and other transportation equipment	37	51	69	104	186	179	173

SOURCE: U.S. Bureau of the Census, Current Industrial Reports, Series MA–35A.

General Farm Machinery and Equipment Statistics by Employment Size: 1972

	Establishments	Capital Expenditures (millions)	End of Year Inventories (millions)
Total establishments	1,547	$115.6	$640.0
Establishments with an average of:			
1 to 4 employees	551	1.1	.6
5 to 9 employees	216	1.4	.9
10 to 19 employees	217	7.1	.9
20 to 49 employees	266	6.1	4.1
50 to 99 employees	141	7.5	13.0
100 to 249 employees	101	11.7	31.9
250 to 499 employees	21	5.4	38.6
500 to 999 employees	12	13.1	116.1
1,000 to 2,499 employees	15	10.7	207.3
2,500 employees or more	7	51.5	226.6

SOURCE: Census of Manufacturing, 1972.

General Statistics of Planting, Seeding, and Fertilizing Machinery: 1972

	Establishments (number)	Value Added by Manufacturer (millions)	Cost of Materials (millions)	Value of Shipments (millions)	Capital Expenditures (millions)
Planting, seeding, and fertilizing machinery establishments	50	$149.7	$107.0	$209.9	$3.3
Establishments with 75% or more specialization	28	20.1	22.8	42.4	.8

SOURCE: Census of Manufacturing, 1972.

9. Holland Farm Products

John Holland's thoughts had been miles away from the golf course all day and his score showed it. Holland, president of Holland Farm Products, Inc. (HFP), was not accustomed to losing so badly to his regular partners. The lack of concentration was not surprising. On Holland's mind was the deal with Colliers which could virtually turn his business around.

HFP had experienced excellent profits and growth in the late 1960s and early 1970s. But in 1976, sales volume dropped off dramatically and the company incurred large losses. In fact, the report Holland's financial vice president had given him early that morning for the current six months just ended showed more red ink. Granted the six-month period was the slack time in a very seasonal business, but the losses were larger than he had anticipated and were putting a real strain on working capital. Holland was beginning to feel desperate to get back to the days when the company was profitable and in a stronger financial position.

As he prepared to hit his approach to the 18th green, Holland decided to stop by the office on the way home from the club. He wanted to spend a little more time analyzing the proposed agreements with Colliers.

HISTORY

In 1935, Oliver Holland, John's father, founded Holland Farm Products in Augusta, Georgia. In 1979, company headquarters were still located in Augusta. The elder Holland began in business by supplying tobacco farmers in Georgia and South Carolina with tobacco curing equipment. His father before him had been a tobacco farmer, and it was Oliver Holland's knowledge of the tobacco industry that enabled him to understand the needs of the grower.

The tobacco season begins in February when farmers plant seeds in their greenhouses. During March and April the fledgling tobacco plants are moved outside to the fields. There they are allowed to grow until time for harvest, generally between late June and September.

This case was prepared by Jack D. Ferner with the assistance of Frank L. Horne, Jr., and Lenoir C. Kessler, Jr., all of Wake Forest University.

During the harvest season, the tobacco leaves are pulled from the plants and put in barns, where they are dried by means of tobacco curers. Once cured, the tobacco is taken to market, graded, and sold.

Tobacco curing in the past has been done by burning a wood fire in a barn where the leaves hung on poles. The process was slow and the fire hazard was ever present. Oliver Holland, who had sold propane and butane bottles gas, began the design of an improved tobacco curer which burned propane gas. The curer stood on the floor of the tobacco barn and radiated heat which could be adjusted by thermostat. The heater was innovative in that it not only reduced the curing time but also decreased the fire hazard.

The elder Holland formed a business in 1935 to market his tobacco curer. He traveled throughout Georgia and South Carolina to tell farmers about its advantages. The business grew and prospered over the years until, in 1965, HFP was the largest supplier of this type equipment.

In 1960, John Holland joined his father at HFP. The two men had an understanding that in time, Oliver Holland would turn over management of the concern to his son.

In the late 1960s, the technology of tobacco curing changed. A new method of curing tobacco—bulk curing—was introduced. Bulk curing involved a self-contained structure which could hold as much as 5,000 pounds of tobacco. The structures, called "barns," closely resembled mobile homes in both appearance and specifications. These buildings were 18 feet by 48 feet with a large gas or oil furnace attached to the back. These new barns were designed to be movable and airtight. The latter feature enabled them to better maintain constant temperature.

HFP was late in reacting to this new direction in the industry. In 1972, the company introduced its first bulk curing device. At the outset, an old converted warehouse in Aiken, South Carolina, was leased to build these barns. As sales for the new structures grew, HFP built a permanent manufacturing plant in Florence, South Carolina. These bulk barns accounted for 80 percent of the company's tobacco equipment sales in the mid-1970s. The remaining 20 percent came from sale of the more conventional curing equipment—floor heaters.

EXPANSION

In 1969, when Oliver Holland became ill and was forced to retire to Florida, John Holland took over the family business. More ambitious than his father, John Holland decided it was time to expand geographically into the rich tobacco belts in North Carolina and Virginia. There were only two bona fide competitors in these areas and Holland believed the market opportunities were considerable. Up until that time, over 95 percent of the company's sales had come from Georgia and South Carolina.

Due to the seasonality of the tobacco curing equipment industry (mainly spring and summer), Holland sought a countercyclical product utilizing similar technology. He developed a line of gas-fired, infrared space heaters for both home and industrial use. Although the original cost of the equipment was higher than competitive heating systems, fuel costs were low and the demand came mainly in fall and winter. In 1967, Holland formed a Canadian subsidiary to manufacture and market this type heating equipment with a specialized application in raising chickens.

This expansion into North Carolina and Virginia and the addition of the new heater line took HFP from $209,000 in sales in 1960 to peak sales of almost $12 million in 1975. (See Exhibits 1 and 2 for the most recent financial statements of the company.)

MARKETING

The marketing function at HFP consisted primarily of supporting the company's distributors who in turn sold the products to the farmers. These distributors were mostly gas and fuel oil dealers who carried not only HFP's line of products but also those of competitors. To provide incentives for sales, HFP set up a cooperative advertising campaign, and sponsored holidays for the distributors to resort areas such as Myrtle Beach, South Carolina.

The sales force supporting the distributors reached a peak of eight in 1975, but was cut to four when sales and profits declined. Salespersons traveled to small towns in tobacco-growing regions and made calls on gas and fuel oil dealers. The company had its own in-house advertising department. The principal media were trade journals, radio, billboards, and television in the prime market areas.

MANUFACTURING

The company operated two plants in the United States in addition to the one in Canada. The company built a 50,000 square foot facility in Florence, South Carolina, in 1974 to supply the then large demand. This plant came on stream in 1975 and initially operated on a year-round basis, making and shipping the structure to house the tobacco.

EXHIBIT 1   Holland Farm Products, Inc.   Consolidated Balance Sheets, September 30, 1973–1978

	1978	1977	1976	1975	1974	1973
Assets						
Cash	$ 164,586	$ 17,711	$ 395,127	$ 75,557	$ 171,739	$ 50,623
Accounts receivable	646,488	911,845	872,923	1,404,630	1,011,610	1,035,587
Inventories.	1,344,646	1,531,687	1,477,347	2,009,030	1,537,887	1,210,916
Prepaid expenses	56,947	66,996	38,085	25,902	15,335	11,119
Refundable income taxes. . . .		111,343	20,605	3,400		
Total current assets	2,212,667	2,639,582	2,804,087	3,515,119	2,739,971	2,308,245
Plant and equipment (net) . . .	571,263	666,418	$ 739,131	805,998	370,072	315,318
Other	94,504	74,331	53,289	72,123	297,015	63,275
Total assets	$2,878,434	$3,380,331	$3,596,507	$4,393,240	$3,407,058	$2,686,838
Liabilities and owner's equity						
Bank overdraft.		45,787		41,251	47,203	105,145
Notes payable-secured	993,595	1,253,958	1,027,751	1,474,502	950,000	384,947
Accounts payable	276,858	216,868	219,485	487,959	346,552	332,705
Current portion long-term debt	8,771	7,940	7,187	63,944	58,692	58,664
Other current liabilities	86,629	169,621	192,139	477,262	216,853	195,931
Total current liabilities	1,365,852	1,694,174	1,446,526	2,544,918	1,619,300	1,077,392
Long-term debt	772,751	776,513	775,633	457,499	531,463	508,225
Deferred income taxes payable	81,473	48,645	40,991	14,246		
Total liabilities	2,220,076	2,519,332	$2,263,186	3,016,663	2,150,763	1,585,617
Common stock.	257,076	257,076	257,076	257,076	257,076	257,076
Retained earnings	401,282	603,923	1,076,245	1,119,501	999,219	844,145
Total owner's equity	658,358	860,999	$1,333,321	1,376,577	$1,256,295	1,101,221
Total liabilities and OE	$2,878,434	$3,380,331	$3,596,507	$4,393,240	$3,407,058	$2,686,838
Net sales	$5,606,559	$5,371,246	$7,885,673	11,968,657	$7,109,861	$4,945,581
Cost of sales.	4,711,940	4,753,329	6,440,583	9,719,039	5,406,018	3,443,202
	$ 894,619	$ 617,917	$1,444,820	$2,249,618	$1,703,843	$1,502,379
Operating expenses:						
Selling expense	$ 142,606	$ 90,569	$ 353,800	$ 759,873	$ 651,002	$ 610,584
G & A expense.	649,260	755,104	780,836	909,281	594,756	448,117
Interest expense	137,461	167,949	190,408	146,208	144,476	78,983
Engineering expense.	130,858	157,150	174,234	155,275	138,119	145,742
	$1,060,185	$1,170,772	$1,499,278	$1,970,637	$1,528,353	$1,283,426
Operating profit	(165,566)	(552,855)	(54,458)	278,981	175,490	218,953
Other-foreign exchange	(4,247)	(21,378)	17,341	(12,974)	(5,244)	–0–
Profit before tax	(169,813)	(574,233)	(37,117)	266,007	170,246	218,953
Income taxes	32,828	(101,911)	6,139	145,725	85,772	108,929
Net income (loss)	(202,641)	(472,322)	(43,256)	120,282	84,474	110,024
Retained earnings B.O.Y.. . . .	603,923	1,076,245	1,119,501			
Retained earnings E.O.Y.. . . .	401,282	603,923	1,076,245			
Earnings per share.	$ (0.81)	$ (1.89)	$ (0.17)	$ 0.48	$ 0.34	$ 0.44

EXHIBIT 1 (concluded)   Selected Notes to Financial Statements

Note a.   Inventories:
Inventories at September 30, 1978 and 1977, consisted of the following:

	1978	1977
Parent company:		
Finished goods	$ 175,281	$ 175,635
Work in process	61,701	40,815
Raw materials	805,016	1,032,318
	1,041,998	1,248,768
Subsidiaries	302,648	282,919
	$1,344,646	$1,531,687

Note b.   Manufacturing/office facilities

	Augusta	Florence	Canada
Production and storage (sq. ft.)	37,700	43,419	9,600
Office space (sq. ft.)	6,764	1,662	1,000
Total number employees	40	35	15

Note c.   Pledged assets:
Substantially all accounts receivable, inventories, and fixed assets of the parent company and of its Canadian subsidiary are pledged as collateral for bank loans and mortgages.

Note d.   Long-term debt:
At September 30, 1978 and 1977, the company's noncurrent debt consisted of the following:

	1978	1977
15 year mortgage on land and building in Florence, S.C., at 10 percent interest rate	$ 191,163	$ 199,933
Note payable, due in 1986, to the Holland Company (an affiliate), unsecured	273,000	240,000
Note payable, due in 1981, to the Holland Company (an affiliate), unsecured	266,307	294,490
Deferred noninterest-bearing account payable to the Holland Company (an affiliate) with no stated due date	42,281	42,090
	$ 772,751	$ 776,513

Note e.   Subsequent to this statement the company has entered into an accounts receivable financing agreement with Multi-National Corporation. The agreement has an upper limit of $200,000.

During 1978, the Florence facility operated at less than 50 percent capacity. The Augusta plant built the furnaces and steel baling devices and shipped them to the Florence plant for installation.

A third plant had been leased in Aiken, South Carolina, in 1972. However, the drop-off in sales which started in 1976 forced HFP to let the lease expire and close the facility down.

The plants were assembly operations. Parts were bought from regular suppliers. Certain items for the heaters had long lead times (up to a year) while components for the barns could be obtained in a month or so. The finished products were assembled and delivered to the distributors, who in turn sold to the farmer.

EXHIBIT 2 Holland Farm Products, Inc.

Monthly Income Statements: Actual October 1978–March 1979 and Estimated April–September 1979
(internal—unaudited—Canadian subsidiary not included) ($000)

| | Actual | | | | | | Estimated | | | | | | 1978/1979 |
	Oct.	Nov.	Dec.	Jan.	Feb.	March	Apr.	May	June	July	Aug.	Sept.	Total
Net sales:													
Infrared space heaters	211.1	296.6	265.7	302.0	197.9	56.5	41.5	7.7	15.3	144.4	174.2	174.2	1,887.1
Tobacco curing	82.7	.5	55.9	4.9	86.7	405.0	343.5	355.4	634.7	653.8	390.4	9.4	3,022.9
Prefab buildings	42.1	12.2	26.1	10.6	2.4	6.5	19.6	17.5	17.5	17.5	17.5	17.5	206.0
Other sales	10.0	10.4	21.3	23.3	14.6	12.6	2.4	1.2	5.3	.7	2.0	1.0	104.8
Total	345.9	319.7	369.0	340.8	301.6	480.6	406.0	381.8	672.8	816.4	584.1	202.1	5,220.8
Cost of goods sold													
Direct material	226.6	213.3	231.9	213.6	195.1	317.1	270.2	236.6	413.9	489.8	350.6	121.9	3,280.6
Direct material—													
Augusta	15.8	20.9	18.9	17.3	12.8	14.1	13.1	13.0	13.0	13.5	14.0	14.0	180.4
Direct labor—Florence	7.9	10.0	8.3	10.4	11.2	11.7	16.0	16.5	16.0	16.0	15.0	6.0	144.9
Factory overhead—													
Augusta	24.5	24.8	25.5	29.7	26.4	27.6	22.6	27.3	27.5	27.5	27.0	16.0	306.4
Factory overhead—													
Florence	18.9	19.7	17.7	24.9	21.7	22.1	19.5	20.0	22.0	21.0	21.0	9.0	237.5
Purchasing	2.5	3.0	3.6	3.0	3.0	3.2	3.0	3.3	3.1	3.2	3.0	2.5	36.4
Total	296.2	291.7	305.9	298.9	270.1	395.8	344.4	316.7	495.5	571.0	430.6	169.4	4,186.2
Gross profit	49.7	28.0	63.1	41.9	31.5	84.8	61.6	65.1	177.3	245.4	153.5	32.7	1,034.6
Operating expense													
Engineering	10.7	9.5	10.1	12.6	12.5	11.5	12.1	11.6	11.8	11.4	12.0	11.6	137.4
Selling	21.8	33.1	27.7	35.9	26.2	27.4	25.0	24.0	26.0	24.5	25.0	20.0	316.6
Delivery	(1.5)	7.3	3.4	6.7	.9	(.9)	6.3	1.0	.5	1.5	2.0	2.1	29.3
Administrative	35.0	48.1	41.7	61.5	45.8	49.1	46.3	47.5	46.0	45.0	47.8	25.0	538.8
Operating profit (loss)	(16.3)	(70.0)	(19.8)	(74.8)	(53.9)	(2.3)	(28.1)	(19.0)	93.0	163.0	00.7	(26.0)	12.5
Other income (expense)	(10.6)	(11.5)	(11.3)	(12.2)	(12.7)	(11.6)	(12.7)	(10.4)	(10.1)	(9.8)	(9.8)	(10.0)	(132.7)
Net profit	(26.9)	(81.5)	(31.1)	(87.0)	(66.6)	(13.9)	(40.8)	(29.4)	82.9	153.2	56.9	(36.0)	(120.2)

FINANCIAL

The last few years had not been good ones for tobacco farmers. Cancer scares, antismoking campaigns, recessions, inflation, and decreases in price supports had made the already conservative farmer more conservative.

The decline in the tobacco industry had disastrous effects on HFP's financial position (see Exhibits 1, 2, and 3 for financial data). The resulting pressures on working capital caused Holland to borrow heavily, and the company had become highly leveraged. In 1979, HFP had almost $1 million in short-term secured notes outstanding. In the past, the company simply rolled this debt over each year. In addition, there was over three-quarters of a million dollars in long-term debt on the balance sheet.

The bank was uneasy about the situation, and anxious for HFP to retire some of its debt. Aside from the bank, much of the borrowing

EXHIBIT 3   Holland Farm Products, Inc.

	1978 HFP	73–78 HFP avg.	1978 Beatty	Ind. Htr. ind. avg.	Fab. Steel ind. avg.
Balance Sheet Ratio Comparisons					
Current ratio	1.62	1.57	2.33	2.10	1.60
Quick ratio	.64	.69	1.35	1.00	.85
Debt/assets	.77	.68	.46	.51	.56
Inventory turn	4.2x	4.6x	14.5x	5.9x	7.2x
Average collection period	41.5 days	52.0 days	28.6 days	53.0 days	32.0 days
Fixed asset turn	9.8x	13.0x	13.4x	10.8x	10.5x
Total asset turn	1.9x	2.0x	3.8x	1.9x	2.3x
Return on sales	(3.6%)	(0.9%)	3.9%	3.4%	1.7%
Return on assets	(7.0%)	(1.1%)	14.7%	6.5%	3.8%
Return on equity	(30.8%)	(8.0%)	27.0%	11.9%	10.0%
Net working capital/sales	.15	.15	.09	.17	.11
Net income/net working capital	(.24)	(.06)	.41	.20	.10
Current debt/assets	.35	.32	.05	.12	.12
Income Statement Ratio Comparisons					
Net sales	100.0%	100.0%	100.0%	100.0%	100.0%
Cost of sales	84.0	79.4	70.8	74.5	77.7
Gross margin	16.0	19.6	29.2	25.5	22.3
Selling expenses	2.5	6.1			
			21.9		
G & A expenses	11.6	9.6			
Engineering expenses	2.3	2.1		19.4	20.1
Interest expense	2.5	2.0	0.7		
Other expense	0.1	0.1	0.3		
Profit before tax	(3.0)	(0.3)	6.9	6.1	2.2
Income taxes	0.6	0.6	3.2		
Net income	(3.6)%	(0.9)%	3.7%		
Earnings per share	$(0.81)	$(0.27)	$1.00		

had come from the Hollands themselves through an affiliated investment company called Holland Company.

Holland was not convinced that his company's unsatisfactory financial condition was solely the result of the recent poor years for tobacco farmers. Specifically, he suspected that internal operating inefficiencies could be at least part of the overall problem. Exhibit 3 presents a comparison of HFP financial ratios with those of similar—though not identical—industries.

MANAGEMENT AND OWNERSHIP

HFP was a family business both in terms of historical development and current management. John Holland and his younger brother, Otis, held equal ownership of the company's privately held stock, but not equal responsibilities. Otis Holland directed engineering and new product experimentation. John was responsible for managing the entire company. John also maintained close contact with the company's distributors.

In addition to the Hollands, a general manager and a vice president for finance completed the top management team. John Holland was considering changes in the organization.

> As you can see from our organizational structure [see Exhibit 4], we are not really divided along traditional lines. The general manager Otis and I work in tandem handling all of the day-to-day operating problems. I think we are a good team, but I know we could use some help in some areas. My problem is that until business improves, my hands are tied as far as hiring any new people.
>
> I can envision three functional areas of finance, sales, and production. The general manager and I concentrate on sales and day-to-day operations of the business, while Otis spends most of his time with the engineers—developing new products and improving old ones. The four sales people report directly to the general manager or myself, depending on who is in the office that day. The vice president of finance coordinates all purchasing, bookkeeping, and accounting functions. The plant managers run their respective operations as they see fit. They receive orders from the general manager. The advertising manager runs the actual printing and media buying for the company. The people in the advertising department report to the general manager and myself, while the engineers are Otis's domain. I'm not really sure that this is the best organization we can come up with, but I do know that we cannot afford to hire any new people.

JOHN HOLLAND

John Holland was a well-respected member of the Augusta community—as a person and as a businessman. He was active in the city's Little League baseball program and had chaired Augusta's United

EXHIBIT 4 Holland Farm Products Organizational Structure

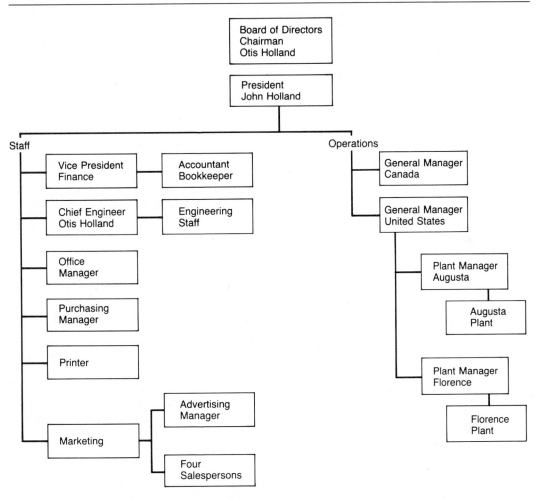

Way campaign in the late 1960s. His involvement with community affairs had dropped off as the company's problems developed.

Customers of HFP were strong supporters of Holland. One long-time distributor for the company had this to say about him:

> John Holland is a fine man, a fair man. And he is a great salesman. He knows my problems and what I need. His products have always been well made and reliable. And he's got the kind of integrity I wish everybody had. When I'm short of money because the farmers are slow in paying, he always is understanding. He says I can pay my bill late, and lots of times that saves me. Lots of other businessmen wouldn't let me do that. I enjoy doing business with him.

A banker friend offered this comment:

> The Holland family and HFP had been customers of ours for many years. Until the last few years, John has had a carte blanche agreement with us—what he feels he needs, he gets. But the company has become too highly leveraged to continue that policy, so we have to be more formalized now in our dealings. In my opinion, he needs to do a couple of things. First, he should restructure his debt. The long-term debt on his balance is actually money loaned by Holland Company, a corporation put together for tax purposes to act as an investment organization for the two Holland brothers. When times started getting bad, the Hollands found it necessary to plow back all of this company's assets into HFP. Since the long-term debt is really owed the two Holland brothers, for all intents and purposes all of HFP's debt is short term. Secondly, John is sacrificing working capital due to sloppy receivables collection. I also suspect that he is holding more inventory than necessary. If he could get these two items in line, then he could afford to pay down his debt to us.

CURRENT SALES OUTLOOK

John Holland had always taken a heavy part in the selling effort and the decline in sales had been a shock. He knew the future of HFP would depend on current market factors and short-term sales prospects. Below is his summary of the situation:

1. Tobacco curing equipment. Historically the major product line. Sales off sharply from a high of approximately $10 million annually to $2 million to $2.2 million. Expected to stabilize at about this volume. Low growth potential but profitable if able to hold these sales without financial drain of the underutilized Florence plant.

2. Infrared space heaters. Sells through manufacturers' agents throughout the United States. Largest backlog of preseason orders. Peak shipping time August–January. U.S. energy situation favors use of this type of heating for large industrial and commercial buildings. Previously higher cost of equipment versus low cost of fuel made growth slow. Now high cost of fuel and conservation makes infrared heating much more competitive and attractive for both the new and replacement market. Our product enjoys a strong industry position in this field. Excellent growth potential with little or no requirement for additional capital expenditure to accommodate accelerated demand. Sales approximately $2 million in this fiscal year (October 1978–September 1979). A growth situation with possibilities of a 20 to 30 percent annual rate.

3. Wholly owned Canadian subsidiary. In strong growth and profit pattern. Sales in fiscal 1978–1979 over $1 million. Out-

look strong. Supplies chicken-rearing market with breeding equipment for Canadian market and export. Has developed excellent system that can be introduced into U.S. market. Also sells industrial and commercial heating market in Canada.

NEW PRODUCT OPPORTUNITY

Uncertain about prospects for the tobacco industry and realizing the risk of being dependent on only a couple of products, Holland had been on the search for additions to the company's product line. In late 1977, he came up with an idea that was adaptable to HFP's manufacturing capabilities. Since the curing barns were essentially prefabricated in the plants, Holland felt the same concept could be applied to outdoor utility/storage rooms. The components—doors, walls, and roof—could be manufactured in the plant, and then shipped to the distributor. When a sale had been made to a user, the structure could be assembled on a concrete pad at the site.

Holland knew the Beatty Company had been successful with a similar product in another part of the country. He was able to get information about that firm, its products, and its manufacturing process from trade journals like *Automated Housing*. Holland saw no reason why the same product concept would not be accepted in the Georgia-Carolinas-Virginia region.

After investigating the manufacturing aspects of the new product, Holland turned his attention to the question of marketing and distribution. Initially, he approached the same fuel oil and gas dealers who were already distributing tobacco-curing equipment. He was able to convince three of these to sell the new product. However, because the utility/storage buildings did not constitute their main line of business, the distributors were unable to give the buildings proper attention.

Next he approached people in real estate/construction. During a space of six months, he reached agreement with 15 parties who said they would push the product. Out of the original group, only 5 remained at the time that talks with Colliers began.

During the winter of 1978, Holland contacted Colliers, a large well-known hardware and building supplies retailer in the South. Holland knew that Colliers had sold a similar product in the past, and felt that HFP's concept was superior in quality and value. He also knew that Colliers had the network of stores necessary to provide distribution and the available resources to promote the buildings.

Colliers evaluated the product concept and concluded that it was viable and that HFP could provide the quality of workmanship that was associated with their other product lines. In order to assess the market size, Colliers requested 18 of its store managers in the South Carolina region for an estimate of the number of buildings they felt

EXHIBIT 5 Holland Farm Products, Inc.—Colliers' Store Managers' Estimates Prefabricated Utility Building

Location	Maximum per Month	Minimum per Month
Aiken	3 or 4	1
Columbia #1	4	1
Columbia #2	2	1
Orangeburg	3	1
Sumter	4	1
Manning	2	1
Florence	1	1
Conway	4	1
Myrtle Beach	4 to 6	1
Charleston	3	1
Hartsville	1	1
Dillon	4	1
Marion	4	1
Camden	3	1
Rock Hill	3	1
Lancaster	3	1
Bennettsville	3	1
Chester	3	1
Total	54–57	18

could be sold through their store per month. Each store manager submitted a minimum and maximum estimate. These projections are found in Exhibit 5. Colliers' management felt that by the sixth month of the program, total unit sales for the 18-store region would amount to 34 per month.

Sufficiently encouraged by its findings, Colliers then drafted a proposal agreement. They would begin marketing the product in the 18-store South Carolina region. If the product line was successful after a six-month trial, the program would be expanded to their other stores.

The utility/storage buildings would be available in five sizes. Holland knew that certain models would be more popular than others and estimated the average selling price (HFP to Colliers) at $3,400. He estimated the margin (selling price minus all direct costs) in this type business would run 20–22 percent.

IMPLICATIONS FOR HFP

Holland felt that with luck this new project could increase the company's annual sales by almost 50 percent and perhaps bail them out of their present problems. On the other hand, Holland was concerned about the following:

1. With liquidity presently strained, would HFP be able to meet the additional working capital requirements necessary for the project?

2. Was there sufficient manufacturing capacity at the Florence plant to handle the sales orders from Colliers?
3. How would this new product line fit into the present organizational structure? Would it be necessary to appoint a coordinator to oversee the entire project?
4. If Colliers wanted exclusive distribution rights, what would be done with the five remaining distributors?
5. If the program began to go well for both parties, what could HFP do if Colliers later threatened to squeeze the company's margins?

Holland wondered also whether the utility buildings fit into the company's strategy. In view of the uncertainty surrounding the future of the tobacco industry, he questioned whether he was just fighting fires with this new product.

THE CANADIAN DISINVESTMENT

Although the Canadian subsidiary began operations in 1972, its first profitable year was 1977. The profit in 1978 was $75,000. Holland attributed the early losses to management problems associated with his being so far away.

For a year and a half, Holland had considered selling the concern and using the proceeds from the sale to retire part of HFP's outstanding debt. He felt he could net $400,000–$450,000 if the company were sold. After having almost made the decision to accept one offer, the possibility of financial relief from the Colliers deal convinced him to reconsider. The offers were not all that attractive, and he firmly believed the company would grow in profitability.

STRATEGIC DECISIONS

Holland knew that internal controls had suffered badly during the last few years when he had been on the road so much. He was distressed with the losses and heavy reliance on borrowed funds for working capital. He knew he had some important decisions to make—soon. John Holland had these thoughts:

> The Colliers thing is a tremendous opportunity for us—if we can handle it. And whether or not we can handle it depends a lot on finding a solution to our financial problems. If the bank won't lend us any more money, then we'll have to find the working capital internally. I would like very much to find the necessary funds internally, so we can avoid taking on more debt or selling the Canadian subsidiary.

Business and the Law

10. The Technical Trap

INTRODUCTION

The phone rang in Dr. Zoro's office on Tuesday, April 23, 1983. His wife Mary was on the other end of the phone line. She was very upset. "Autumn Lee's Health Spa is being sued," she said. "Being sued? By whom? Why? Who would sue us?" responded Dr. Zoro. Mary, still very upset, said, "We are being sued for false advertising and for charging interest when we say we do not charge interest." Dr. Zoro said, "That is absurd! We do not charge interest or any finance charges, so how can we falsely advertise about it?" Mary responded, "That is what I say. It is ridiculous. We have never charged interest or a finance charge." Dr. Zoro said, "Well, calm down, don't get all worked up. Bring the complaint home. I will read it. I am sure there must be some mistake."

HISTORICAL SETTING

Autumn Lee's Health Spa was organized in Bolivar, Tennessee, in 1971, under the name of Fourth Street Health Spa. Ten years later, in 1981, the spa moved from Fourth Street, a low-traffic density street, into a new building on Adams Street, a heavy traffic main thoroughfare. In the same year, the name of the spa was changed from Fourth Street Health Spa to Autumn Lee's Health Spa.

Autumn Lee's Health Spa is a mom and pop business—owned by Mary and Bill Zoro. Autumn Lee's is for females only and is managed by Mary. Bill is a state employee. His main contribution to Autumn Lee's is in keeping the books, establishing policy, developing strategy, and doing much of the repair work on the club equipment and building.

Autumn Lee's sells four major types of memberships. These are: (1) a six-month membership for $43 per month, (2) a one-year membership for $36 per month, (3) a two-year membership for $31 per month, and (4) a three-year charter membership for $39 per month. The three-year charter membership may be renewed each year after

This case was prepared by S. Lee Owens of Tennessee Technological University, Allan Reddy of Valdosta State College, and Michael L. Menefee of Tennessee Technological University.

the first three years for $120 per year. From time to time, one or more of each of these memberships is placed on sale. When this happens, prices are usually reduced 20–25 percent. From 1971 to the time of this court case there had always been a one-time $10 bookkeeping fee. The bookkeeping fee was not charged if the member elected to pay in advance for the membership. Other than these there were no other charges.

Most health spas receive payment for memberships up front—all at once. The way this works is that most health spas run their membership paper through a bank or some other lending institution. This means the health spa receives 100 percent of their money up front. It also means the new member has borrowed, through the health spa, from a lending institution the money to pay in advance the cost of his/her membership.

Autumn Lee's does not work this way. Autumn Lee's does not run membership paper through the bank. Thus, the member does not borrow the funds to pay in advance for her membership. However, she may if she likes, pay in advance for her membership. Less than 1 percent of Autumn Lee's members pay their membership in advance. Thus, 99 percent or more of Autumn Lee's members pay monthly, not the lending institution, but directly to Autumn Lee's. Except for late payments, members pay in the month they use the services of Autumn Lee's.

THE PROBLEM

Dr. Zoro read the complaint. He discovered Autumn Lee's was being sued in the United States District Court for the Middle District of Tennessee Southeastern Division by a member, Miss Doris Balo. Miss Balo had purchased a membership on April 10, 1983, from Autumn Lee's. She had gotten behind on her monthly payments and her overdue amount had been turned over to a collection agency. In purchasing this membership, she claimed she had entered into a consumer credit transaction with the defendant in which she had been extended consumer credit. Also, she claimed Autumn Lee's knowingly violated and continues to violate the disclosure requirement of the Truth in Lending Act and Regulation Z. Autumn Lee's is doing this by failing to disclose the terms *finance charge* and *annual percentage rate* (together with corresponding amounts of percentage rate), as required to be disclosed by the act, in violation of Regulation Z. [1]

The plaintiff was requesting the following relief:

1. Award plaintiff actual damages.
2. Award the plaintiff twice the finance charge in connection

with this transaction, as provided under Section 130(a) of the Truth in Lending Act. [2]

3. Award the plaintiff costs and a reasonable attorney's fee as provided under Section 130(a) of the Truth in Lending Act. [3]
4. Award the plaintiff one thousand eight hundred dollars ($1,800) persuant to ACA 47-18-109 of Tennessee Consumer Protection Act of 1977. [4]
5. Award such other and further relief as the court deems just and proper.

AUTUMN LEE'S EARLY RESPONSE

Mary and Bill, after getting over the original shock, delivered the document to their lawyer Jonathan Morgan, who read the document and asked a series of questions. Jonathan said, "I think this is absurd. I think they have a very weak case, but let me file a document denying all charges, and then I will get back in touch with you."

THE PLAINTIFF'S CASE

Doris Balo, the plaintiff, was still angry over her account being turned over to a collection agency, and she was worried. She was sitting in the attorney's office talking to her attorney, Ben Winum. Doris said, "Are you sure that the $10 bookkeeping fee charged by Autumn Lee's is a finance charge or interest charge? The $10 fee is so small, will the judge think it is foolish? Also, please outline again for me the major arguments you plan to present to the court."

Ben responded, "Let me respond to your questions one at a time. First, I believe the $10 bookkeeping fee is a finance charge, and I will tell you why in a moment. Second, the judge may think the $10 fee is small; however, the Truth in Lending Act, as detailed by Regulation Z, exempts a fee of $7.50 or less, so he will be forced to admit this case. The major arguments I plan to present to the court are as follows:

1. Miss Doris Balo purchased from Autumn Lee's a two-year membership on credit for $624 to be paid for by the month. Miss Balo was charged a $10 bookkeeping fee.
2. Autumn Lee's advertised in the newspaper and on a large exterior sign that they charged no finance or interest charges. Autumn Lee's does not deny this.
3. Miss Balo was told when she signed the membership form that there were no interest or finance charges. Autumn Lee's admits this.
4. We argue that the $10 bookkeeping fee was a hidden finance charge because:

     a. It is charged only to those who pay by the month;

     b. It is not charged to those who pay in advance; and

     c. This, by definition, forces it to be a finance charge and not a bookkeeping fee.

5. The Truth in Lending Act clearly requires that certain fees, such as insurance fees and others, be included in computing interest and finance charges.

6. In selling to Miss Balo a two-year membership to be paid for by the month, Autumn Lee's has in fact extended to Miss Balo credit—in fact, she owed $624 minus $26, or $598. These payments were to be paid for monthly at the rate of $26 per month.

7. Congress clearly intended, in the Truth in Lending Act, that Miss Balo be able to compare credit charges. [5] Miss Balo was told that there were no finance or interest charges. Therefore, she could not compare interest charges.

8. In the same law, Congress clearly stated that a part of the purpose of the law was to protect consumers from 'uninformed use of credit.' Miss Balo was told that she was not being charged a finance charge or interest. Therefore, she was uninformed and paying a finance charge."

AUTUMN LEE'S CASE

Some 10 weeks later, Mary Zoro said to Bill, "It seems to me, according to the way he talks, that our attorney may not be putting enough research into our case. You have brought up more points than I have heard him mention. Do you agree?" "Well, I don't know," said Bill. Mary said, "You have a Ph.D., you know how to do research. Why don't you go to the library and see if you can find some pointers that may help us win this case?" Bill said, "That's a good suggestion; I think I will do just that. If I do, do you think it will offend Jonathan?" Mary responded, "No, I don't think it will offend Jonathan; he doesn't get offended easily." Bill went to the law library to see what he could find.

After having done his research at the library, Bill made an appointment with Jonathan. At the appointment Bill said, "Jonathan, I hope what I am about to say will not offend you. I have gone to the law library and have tried to find some references which I hope may be of some value in our case. I have come up with several. You probably have thought of most or even all of them, but if I may, let me present them to you. If you can use one or more of them, fine; if not, fine." Jonathan said, "It will not offend me; I need all the help I can get."

Bill said, "Jonathan, here are some 10 points I hope you will, if you think they will help, present to the judge in our case."

1. If the court rules our $10 bookkeeping fee is a finance charge, could the plaintiff have found a lower finance charge? A part of the purpose in the Truth in Lending Act is "so that the consumer will be able to compare more readily the various credit terms available to him [5]. Plaintiff purchased a two-year membership on April 10, 1983. The membership was on sale; it cost $624 plus $10 bookkeeping fee. She paid one payment of $26 plus the bookkeeping fee of $10; the unpaid balance was $598. Using the below listed formula where i = the annual interest cost, m = the number of payments in one year, D = the actual interest or finance charge in dollars, n = the total number of payments, and P = the actual amount of the principal borrowed, we find i = 1.7 percent per year.

$$i = \frac{2mD}{P(n-1)}$$

In 1983 the best possible loan from a bank or lending institution would have been at an annual interest cost of 16–26 percent. Sixteen percent is 9.41 times higher than 1.7 percent. Thus, $10 × 9.41 = $91.10. We think if she had borrowed the $598 from a bank or other lending institution, she would have had to pay a minimum of $94.10 for this unsecured loan. Therefore, even if she had compared our $10 bookkeeping fee with other loan rates she could not have found a better deal. Incidentally, in 1983 the federal government was paying 9–13 percent annual interest.

2. Has Autumn Lee's engaged in unscrupulous and predatory credit practices? Several court cases point out that the major purpose of the Truth in Lending Act is to "prevent unscrupulous and predatory creditor practices." [6, 7, 8] Since Autumn Lee's was opened in 1971, we have charged a $10 bookkeeping fee; it had not been changed until May 1983. There were no other charges except the monthly membership fee. The consumer price index increased about 130 percent during this period, yet Autumn Lee's did not increase their bookkeeping fee.

3. Is a bookkeeping fee always a finance charge? We have always thought a bookkeeping fee was a bookkeeping fee and not a finance charge. There is a precedent for charging fees for services. Banks often charge a fee for stop payment on a check, for overdraft, for returned checks, a fee if an account falls below a given level, say, $500. The federal government and most state governments charge a fee for copies of some documents and for other services. At least one court ruled that some fees "may be excluded from it, provided they are properly itemized and disclosed to the customer." [9] The Truth in Lending Act says one "may permit the use of terminology different from that employed in this subchapter if it conveys substantially the same meaning." [10]

4. Did Autumn Lee's lend funds to Doris Balo? Did a bank or other lending institution lend funds to Miss Balo for her to use to pay in advance for her membership? The answer is no. At Autumn Lee's, with one exception, all payments are paid to Autumn Lee's in advance of the service being rendered. This exception is late payments. If all payments are paid in advance can there be: an extension of a loan, interest cost, finance charges? We believe not.

5. Has a dichotomy been created by the federal government? On one hand, in Autumn Lee's case, if the court decides the $10 book-keeping fee is a finance or interest cost, the federal government is saying that our memberships sold are loans to the member to pay off her membership. Another branch of the federal government seems to be saying that when not paid for up front, membership sales are not loans to the member. This branch is the Internal Revenue Service.

A loan extended by a lender is always an asset to the lender. Autumn Lee's is on the cash accounting basis. This means among other things that the Internal Revenue Service will not permit us to list accounts receivable of memberships sold as assets, or to write off uncollected accounts as bad debts. Thus, the federal government seems to be saying on the one hand that our noncash sales are credit (loan) sales, and, on the other hand, they seem to be saying that they are not. Is it fair for the federal government to have it both ways?

6. Is the federal government treating mom and pop-type merchants as second class citizens? The Truth in Lending Act is administratively enforced by several different federal agencies. The major two of these are the board of directors of the Federal Reserve System and the Federal Trade Commission. [11] The act clearly states "in cases where an annual percentage rate or finance charge was inaccurately disclosed, the enforcing agency shall notify the creditor of such disclosure error and is authorized in accordance with the provisions of this subsection to require the creditor to make an adjustment to the account of the person to whom credit was extended." This seems to suggest that banks and larger lending institutions are often given a chance to correct any deficiencies before they are taken to court. In Autumn Lee's case, no second chance was given. Instead, bang! Off you go to court. Therefore, we feel the federal government is treating mom and pop merchants as second-class citizens.

7. The court system seems to be using two different sets of standards, one for robbers, murderers, rapists, and a second for businesses like mom and pop merchants. Normally, the former are considered innocent until proven guilty. For the latter, the reverse seems to be the case. According to most weekly reports in newspapers and magazines, courts often seem to lean over backward in trying to find a technicality that lets criminals go free. When one reads court decisions in the Truth in Lending Act, one rapidly detects what seems to

be a very strong bias against the lender. The predominance of court decisions makes statements similar to the following: "This subchapter is a remedial statute and should be construed liberally in favor of the consumer" [12] or "This subchapter should be strictly enforced by the courts." [13] Indeed the courts seem to search for technicalities to find the lender guilty. This is the very reverse of what the courts often do in the case of criminals. We strongly believe mom and pop merchants should not be treated more harshly than criminals.

8. Was this case brought to obtain an unjust gain? The management of Autumn Lee's believes this case was brought not to force Autumn Lee's to disclose something they would be very happy to disclose or to gain lower finance and interest cost for the public or because Autumn Lee's has been unscrupulous or predatory, but to obtain an unjust gain. How could an alleged interest rate or finance charge of 1.7 percent offend anyone? And if Congress was trying to get a better deal for consumers, how could they get a better deal than 1.7 percent? As a comparison the rate the owners pay J. C. Penney's is a 21 percent annual interest rate. Would a court decision for the plaintiff result in a lower rate for the consumer? Autumn Lee's feels the plaintiff was not misled, but that she wanted to obtain an unjust gain. Some court decisions have warned against this. "The district court will construct provisions of this subchapter against borrowers who were not misled, but merely seeking a windfall for finding a technical defect in the disclosure form which could not conceivably have influenced his choice of credit." [14] Also "Debtor should not win recovery of finance charges and attorney's fees under this section unless there is some relationship between alleged violation of this subchapter and congressional purposes of meaningful disclosure and fully informed debtors." [15]

9. Autumn Lee's did not intend to violate, if indeed we did violate, the Truth in Lending Act. We disclosed all we knew to disclose. We thought and still think we did not lend funds to the plaintiff to pay off her membership and, therefore, did not charge any finance or interest charges. Why would anyone be ashamed of a 1.7 percent finance charge when the market rate is 16–26 percent? Some court decisions have given weight to unintentional violations. For example, the term *intentional*, as used in subsec. (c) of this section, removes liability for creditor whose violation was not intentional, and limits to voluntary and deliberate acts and omissions. [16] Also, the "intent of Congress" is "to set standards to achieve meaningful truth in lending and not to deviously set traps by which windfalls can be reaped." [17] Thus, Autumn Lee's requested the court to give weight to the fact that Autumn Lee's did not intend to violate the Truth in Lending Act.

10. Autumn Lee's believes Congress did not intend that a federal court case be made over a $10 bookkeeping fee. Surely, the court's

time could be used to greater advantage. Think of the time, energy, and resources required over $10.

Jonathan listened as Bill listed each of these suggested points. After the last point was listed, Jonathan said, "I agree with the logic of many of these points, and I will consider them. However, I think the case is going to hinge on the time sequence relationship. By the time sequence relationship, I mean that only those that were paying by the month paid the $10 bookkeeping fee. However, first I want to see if the plaintiff is willing to settle out of court."

REFERENCES

1. U.S. Regulation Z, Section 226.17(a) [12C.F.R. 226.17(a)].
2. U.S. Truth in Lending Act, Section 130(a) [15 U.S.C. Section 1640(a)], 1968.
3. U.S. Truth in Lending Act, Section 130(a) [15 U.S.C. Section (a)], 1968.
4. Tennessee Consumer Protection Act, A.C.A. 47-18-109, 1977.
5. U.S. Code Annotated [15 A 1601(a)], 1968.
6. *Little Field* v. *Walt Flanagan and Co.*, C. A. Colo., 1974 F. 2d., 1133.
7. *Public Loan Co., Inc.* v. *Hyde*, 1979, 390 N.E. 2d., 1162, 47 N.Y. 3d., 41 N.Y.S. 2d., 238.
8. *Lincoln First Bank of Rochester* v. *Rupert*, 1977, 400 N.Y.S. 2d., 618, 60 A.D. 2d., 193.
9. *Souife* v. *First National Bank of Commerce*, New Orleans, La., D.C. La., 1978, 452 F. Supp. 818.
10. U.S. Code Annotated (15-1632a), 1968.
11. U.S. Code Annotated [15-1607(a)(c)], 1968.
12. *Dorsey* v. *Beads M.D.* 1980, 416 A 2d., 739.
13. *Shields* v. *Valley National Bank of Arizona*, D.C. Ariz., 1971, 56 F.D.R. 448.
14. *Dixie* v. *Idaho First National Bank*, D.C. Idaho, 1981, 505 F. Supp. 846.
15. *Dzadovsky* v. *Lyons Ford Sales, Inc.*, D.C. Pa., 1978, 452 F. Supp. 606, Affirmed 593 F. 2d., 538.
16. *Haynes* v. *Logan Furniture Mart, Inc.*, C.A. Ill., 1974, 503 F. 2d., 1161.
17. *Andrucci* v. *Gimbel Bros., Inc.*, D.C. Pa., 1973, 365 F. Supp. 1240, Affirmed 505 F. 2d., 729.

11. The Playboy Emblem: A Case of Trademark Infringement

THE LETTER

On August 26, 1982, a disturbing and almost unbelievable letter arrived certified mail (return receipt requested) at Bunny's Tavern, Brookfield, Illinois. The letter to tavern owner John P. Browne stated:

> Re: RABBIT HEAD Design Trademark Infringement
> Bunny's Tavern, Brookfield, Illinois

> Gentlemen:

> It has been brought to our attention that Bunny's Tavern has painted on the outside wall of its establishment a rabbit head design virtually identical to our company's RABBIT HEAD design trademark. The RABBIT HEAD design is a trademark owned by Playboy Enterprises, Inc., and Bunny's unauthorized use of our mark constitutes trademark infringement and unfair competition. Bunny's continued use of our mark is likely to cause confusion to the general public in that the public could consider Bunny's Tavern as being in some way sponsored by or otherwise associated with our company.

> Unless Bunny's Tavern immediately and permanently ceases and desists its unauthorized use of our company's RABBIT HEAD design trademark or any other mark or design similar thereto owned by or associated with our company within 10 days of the date of this letter, we will recommend to management that legal action be taken against it to protect our company's rights.

> Should Bunny's Tavern wish to avoid the possibility of future unpleasantness and the needless expense of litigation, please have an authorized representative sign, date, and return the enclosed copy of this letter. Such signature will evidence Bunny's agreement to settle this matter according to the terms of this letter.

This case and the accompanying teaching note are intended to be used as a basis for class discussion. They were copyrighted by Donald F. Kuratko (1986) and accepted by the refereed Midwest Case Writers Association Workshop (1986). All rights are reserved.

Should Bunny's Tavern continue its unauthorized use of our company's mark, it does so at its own risk.

Very truly yours,

PLAYBOY ENTERPRISES, INC.

Harriet E. Earle
Trademarks Coordinator

BACKGROUND: JOHN P. BROWNE AND HIS TAVERN

In November 1948, John P. Browne opened a small neighborhood tavern on 47th Street in Brookfield, Illinois (a western suburb of Chicago). His facilities included a room with 16 barstools (no tables) and a few arcade games (bowling and pinball) for the entertainment of his clientele.

For more than 34 years the tavern operated successfully. The customers were neighborhood friends and workers from the Electromotive and Material Service factories, which were located nearby. The clientele was loyal, and a strong rapport was established through the years between Browne and his customers. Browne handled most of the bartending duties himself, aided in later years by his father Patrick J. Browne. The tavern, a place for drinking and relaxing in a neighborhood atmosphere was appreciated by the Brookfield population of 21,000. And its owner became a well-liked and respected businessman in the local community.

John P. Browne has been known all his life as "Bunny Browne." The name was coined 63 years ago by a nurse in a Chicago hospital who thought he was as "cute as a bunny." The nickname stuck through his early years, and when he became a lightweight boxer in the Chicago area Golden Gloves, it characterized his bouncing style. Later, when John opened his establishment in 1948, he adopted the popular name for his tavern, calling it officially Bunny Browne's Tap.

THE RABBIT HEAD EMBLEM

The idea of painting an emblem on the side of the tavern was conceived five years after the tavern opened. In 1954, one of the tavern's patrons, Joe Karasek, painted the emblem as an expression of friendship and gratitude to his friend Bunny Browne. Karasek and Browne discussed many possibilities and agreed to use a simple rabbit's head to advertise the tavern. Such an emblem, they felt, would be easy to distinguish at a distance and would clearly represent Browne's nickname Bunny.

Thus, Karasek, in the summer of 1954, began his decorating task. He painted the east side of the tavern black and then superimposed a white rabbit head on the black background.

It may be noted here that Playboy Enterprises developed its rabbit head design in 1953. Arthur Paul designed the emblem, and Playboy had it registered as a trademark that same year—1953. It became a protected property item for Playboy, and served for more than 30 years as the Playboy symbol.

BUNNY'S RESPONSE

Browne was astounded that Playboy had perceived his emblem as a threat to its powerful sexual domain. Surely his tavern could not be construed as a copy, a replica, or even a poor imitation of the Playboy clubs. At 63, Bunny was often the youngest person in the bar; thus, his customers had little in common with the Playboy clientele. How could he, the sole proprietor of a small local tavern in existence before Playboy started its empire in 1953, be guilty of unfair competition through trademark infringement? At first, he did not take the letter seriously.

"I thought it was a joke," he said. "After all, it has been up there for nearly 30 years, and I am unaware of anyone ever having confused my establishment for the Playboy Club." He added, "Basically, I feel I'm absolutely no threat to their organization. They are simply nitpicking."

Believing that a simple letter of clarification would resolve the situation, Browne wrote to Playboy's chief executive officer on September 3, 1978. He hoped to clear up the misunderstanding and remove the threat of legal action. The letter, to Christine Hefner, read:

Dear Ms. Hefner,

Enclosed is a copy of a letter I received by certified mail from the office of your general counsel. As you see, it is addressed to Bunny's Tavern and says that my modest tavern, place of business, is guilty of unfair competition, and the use of a rather tired looking emblem I have on the side wall could confuse the public, and cause the public to believe that my little tavern is associated with Playboy Enterprises, Inc.

In a way it is flattering to be considered a competitor of a giant enterprise, but it is disturbing to read the reference to expensive litigation and unpleasantness.

When you read what is involved (and I hope you will be given this letter) you, too, may feel that your lawyer's letter does not express your feeling and does not reflect favorably on Playboy Enterprises.

I was first called Bunny by a nurse in the hospital where I was born over 63 years ago. I have been known as Bunny all of my life. I have lived my life in Brookfield (pop. 21,000) and very few of the people in the village know me as John. I began my business as Bunny's in November 1948 and have operated it continuously since that time. My tavern is not large (16 stools and no tables). My trade is from Brookfield and the surrounding neighborhood. The emblem of Bunny has been on the wall since the 1950s. It is inconceivable that anyone would confuse my emblem and tavern with the Playboy Club. My patrons and the people of Brookfield would, I know, be astonished to learn of Playboy's fears and I am sure would be upset to learn that I have fears of future unpleasantness and expensive litigation.

Ms. Hefner, I hope you will inform me that you consider the action of your lawyers to be unnecessary and in this case not in the best interest of Playboy.

Sincerely,

John P. Browne
Bunny's Tavern
9536 W. 47th Street
Brookfield, Illinois 60513

THE MEDIA REACTION

The controversy of the look-alike rabbit heads spread throughout the community of Brookfield, the surrounding suburbs, and finally into Chicago. The newspapers perceived the disagreement as an attack by big business on "the little guy." Articles quickly appeared in local newspapers and were followed by editorials by noted columnists Art Petacque and Hugh Hough of the *Chicago Sun Times* and Mike Royko of the *Chicago Tribune*.

SPLITTING HARES: Bunny's Tavern, a neighborhood bar in west suburban Brookfield, has never been mistaken for a Playboy Club by its beer-quaffing customers. But that didn't stop Playboy Enterprises from threatening legal action against the bar's owner, John P. "Bunny" Browne . . .   (Petacque & Hough—*Chicago Sun Times*)

There was a duel between Playboy Enterprises and a neighborhood tavern in Brookfield called Bunny's.

For three decades, the Bunny's tavern had a big painting of a rabbit head on the side of its building.

Then Playboy decided that the tavern's rabbit looked too much like Playboy's rabbit symbol and threatened to sue.

It seemed unfair, because the tavern sells booze, not Hefner's kinky fantasies.
(Royko—*Chicago Tribune*)

The news traveled as far as Natchez, Mississippi, by October 1982, where Browne's friends included Ben Chase Callun and Tony Byrne, the mayor of Natchez. Bunny, after years of visits, had been fondly dubbed an "honorary citizen" of Natchez. Thus, the Natchez paper carried an article concerning Playboy's squabble over Bunny's emblem.

Soon the local television stations sent crews to film the tavern and interview Bunny over the Playboy incident. While the television interviews were brief spots on the evening news, the interest in this little tavern in Brookfield, Illinois, was astounding. Visitors came from all over the city and suburbs to see the tavern and its famous rabbit head. Having a beer at Bunny's became a popular diversion—at least for a brief period of interest and curiosity.

BUNNY'S DILEMMA

The fanfare subsided in a few weeks and Bunny Browne's Tap returned to its normal routine and loyal clientele. The customers, proud of their tavern meetingplace, urged Bunny to take a stand against Playboy. "Let's fight 'em all the way, Bunny!" they shouted. Retorted Bunny, "Maybe I'll have to get in the ring and box with Playboy's best—like the old Golden Gloves days!" The bar cheered and toasted Bunny.

But the reality he faced was a different dilemma from his fighting days—and Bunny knew it. As he closed up the tavern on a late November evening, he reflected on the rabbit head painting that had been his "friend" for 30 years and now seemed to be the center of so much controversy. His emblem, unretouched in 30 years, was peeling badly and gradually fading away. Yet it had aroused the ire of the powerful Playboy empire. As he turned off the tavern lights, Bunny knew he must make a decision.

12. Mid-State Enterprises

Mid-State Enterprises
Post Office Box 9000
Colby, Oklahoma 72426
June 15, 1985

Ms. Susan Smith
Account Officer
FDIC
P. O. Box 2000
Colby, Oklahoma 72426

Dear Ms. Smith:

Please consider the attached proposal to settle the following:
I. Debt which was contracted with First National Bank of Colby and later remitted to the FDIC after the failure of said bank. Total principle debt $797,000.
II. Bank loan reference numbers:
   1. 264-310-18
   2. 265-310-34
   3. 265-310-42
   4. 265-505-18
   5. 265-505-26
   6. 267-895-18
   7. 108-840-18
   8. 821-060-18 Paid in Full February 25, 1985.

Sincerely,

Andrew Crockett
Owner

AC:kp

This case has been disguised. It was prepared by Eugene Nini of the University of Texas, Permian Basin, Texas.

PROPOSAL—MID-STATE ENTERPRISES

I. RECAPITULATION
II. FINANCIAL POSITION
    1. Historical
    2. Present
    3. Loss of Income
III. WORKOUT PROPOSAL

RECAPITULATION

The following is a chronological recapitulation of the events immediately preceding the demise of the First National Bank of Colby and the events which transpired after its failure up to the present time.

However, before I recapitulate I would like to make a brief statement concerning my relations with said bank prior to its failure.

I began banking with First National in 1969. From that time through May 1983, I borrowed and paid back in a timely fashion hundreds of thousands of dollars. To the best of my knowledge I was considered a valued customer of the bank.

My banking philosophy had always been to work with the loan officer to structure my banking needs *before* I ever consummated a business transaction. During the first quarter of 1983 I was following the procedure stated above with the loan officer, Mr. John Atwood. I was told to proceed with normal business activity while we worked out a loan consolidation plan (including working capital) which was to allow a minimum of five years to amortize the planned financial restructuring. Since my loan request was within the credit-granting limits of my loan officer I knew, as had been the procedure in the past, that my loan had been approved and the only thing remaining for the bank to do was complete the administrative details. In fact, my loan documentation was being processed at Mid-State Abstract when the following "nightmare" began. (The following events were taken from logs I personally prepared at the time the events were transpiring.)

April 25, 1983. Rumors were running rampant about the financial condition of FNB. I began to notice that FNB personnel were acting in a manner inconsistent with the past. As a prudent businessman, I felt that I should seek alternative financing. This act was traumatic because I had never done business financing with any other bank. In fact, I was a stockholder in FNB.

May 12, 1983. I went to Clementon to meet with the National Bank of Clementon to seek alternative financing. Since two banks had already failed in the area and the energy recession was already underway, I felt it was prudent business judgment to make our financial request outside the area. Since my financial "track record" was excellent and my businesses were still financially sound, I did not think I would find any difficulty.

May 26, 1983. FNB held its annual stockholders meeting which was one month late. Rumors were still "running wild," and the National Bank of Clementon had a reasonable time to respond. Again I thought it prudent to seek alternative financing. Since I am a working person and not a financial wizard I did not know where else to seek help but locally. As a result, I met with Mr. James Bryant, vice president, Benson National Bank. The meeting with Mr. Bryant took place on June 2, 1983.

June 3, 1983. During this period of time I tried to conduct my ongoing business in a normal fashion. I knew (even though the general public did not) that there were two distinct facets to the oil business—drilling and production. The energy recession devastated the drilling business but did not have nearly the same effect on the production side of the business. Since my primary thrust in the energy business relates to oil production I would have been able to function profitably during this time period if FNB had fulfilled their financial commitment to me. Since they did not meet their commitment I was forced to struggle financially. The financial obligations I had entered into were in full agreement with the FNB loan officer and in conformity with the financial commitment he had made to me as an agent of FNB.

October 6, 1983. There was a financial "run" on FNB.

October 12, 1983. The National Bank of Clementon, Clementon, Oklahoma, turned down my request for a loan. During the four months from our initial request and their denial of my loan request there had been many telephone calls, requests for information, and they even conducted a reservoir study. The bank's attitude went from very positive to very negative. Their denial of credit was apparently predicated on the fact that FNB was failing and the National Bank of Clementon was nervous about any loans presently housed in a failing bank. I think it is again important to point out that I would not have committed to the business ventures I was pursuing if it had not been for the financial commitment given me by FNB in the first quarter of 1983.

October 13, 1983. During the previous six months I continued to try to resolve the problem with my loan request at FNB. I was informed that since the "rules" had changed I met this day with Mr. John Atwood, my loan officer of long-standing, to attempt again to structure a financial plan plan to be presented to FNB's new president Mr. Rogers. It seems incomprehensible now, after the fact, that this meeting took place.

October 14, 1983. FNB was declared insolvent by the FDIC.

October 17, 1983. Liberty Bank—FNB opened this day. At this point Liberty Bank began to analyze the FNB loan portfolio to determine which loans they were going to buy. Also on this date I had a buyer for one of my companies (Mid-State Petroleum Services). I called Liberty Bank and they were not releasing any titles on anything regardless of the circumstances, thus negating the sale.

January 17, 1984. Liberty Bank, after being granted an extension of time by the FDIC, made its decision concerning which FNB loans it would purchase.

January 30, 1984. After two and one-half additional months of being in limbo (which now made a total of nine and one-half months) concerning my bank loan position I was notified that the FDIC was now the owner of the loans I had contracted with FNB. It seems little wonder that Liberty Bank did not purchase the loans of Mid-State Enterprises. To them, I am sure all they saw was nonperformance for nine months. However, during the same time period all I saw was indecision, broken commitments, rules changing, confusion, and no direction concerning who and when to pay. I am aware that it was a difficult time for FNB, but it was a set of circumstances I did not create. However, their difficulties created a set of circumstances which prevented me from maintaining and adding to my asset wealth, which could have caused Liberty Bank to purchase our FNB loans.

February 2, 1984. I went to the FDIC office on the 19th floor of the FNB building. I was given financial statement forms and told the first order of business was to prepare said forms. I began working on said forms today.

February 8, 1984. Completed financial statement forms today.

February 9, 1984. Called Ms. Helen Jackson with FDIC Install-ment Loan Department. I confirmed the status of these installment loans and have continued to make timely payments on this debt. These loans are not a part of the commercial loans.

February 23, 1984. I had my first meeting with FDIC account officer Mr. Jerry Street. My hope and desire was to establish a loan consolidation and amortization plan similar to the one promised by FNB so that I could proceed with my normal and previously success-ful business activity. I discovered again that the "rules" had changed and that I was starting over again as if I were a "brand-new" client. Mr. Street followed up my meeting with a letter dated March 2, 1984. In his letter Mr. Street made the following three stipulations:

1. Current financial statements, both personal and on each busi-ness entity.
2. A written proposal outlining what you are willing to do in order to satisfy and/or work out your debt situation.
3. At least three "turndown" letters evidencing your attempts to move your debt to other financial institutions.

I had no problem with requirement number one. In requirement number two he said "satisfy and/or work out." Since I informed him I was not liquid enough nor could I get liquid enough to immediately satisfy my debt, a "workout" is our only alternative. As a matter of record a workout is what I have been striving for for the previous nine and one-half months. Requirement number three appears to be a "catch 22" situation. It is easy to get three turndown letters because it has been made clear to me from other financial institutions that they ordinarily will not seriously consider FDIC clients unless the FDIC has already approved a workout plan. Their thinking appears to be that since Liberty Bank did not purchase the loan then they are by edict bad loans. In addition, Mr. Street asked us for additional collateral. I indicated to him that I did not feel this was a legitimate request since the original collateral was sufficient to get the original commitment from FNB. The fact that FNB failed to honor their commitment, through no fault of ours, should not change the agreement. One further point: Mr. Street's letter stated that my per diem interest was approximately $279. I took exception to that stipulation at the time and still feel that interest on a loan I was prevented from servicing is not legitimate. At that meeting and until very recently I was laboring under the assumption that our account officer or at least the Colby office of the FDIC could make a decision concerning our loan workout proposal. Now I understand that all loan workouts in excess of $250,000 must be submitted and approved by the Dallas and Washington office of the FDIC.

March 6, 1984. Called Mr. Jerry Street and discovered that he had been transferred. I would be assigned a new account officer.

March 15, 1984. I talked to our new account officer by phone—Ms. Susan Smith.

Ms. Smith indicated I needed to make a written proposal outlining our ideas for a workout. This made the second person to tell me I needed to submit a written proposal; however, neither party would suggest any guidelines I might follow. (I found out in March 1985 that it is apparently against FDIC rules for account officers to suggest possible solutions.) Ms. Smith told me I must also submit tax returns for 1981, 1982, and 1983. This presented a problem for me since my CPA, Mr. Wayne Jones, had not completed our 1983 tax return. As a matter of record, Mr. Jones did not complete our 1983 return until August 1984. Even though I continued to work with Ms. Smith I had no way of forcing Mr. Jones to accelerate his work on our 1983 tax return.

March 16, 1984. In accordance with Mr. Street's letter of March 2, 1984, we secured two bank turndowns on requests to move our debt from FDIC. I was turned down by Union Bank and Liberty Bank, both of Colby, Oklahoma.

March 27, 1984. Obtained the third bank turndown as requested by the FDIC. Commerce Union Bank said no today. (It seems ironic that we are seeking bank rejections for a loan FNB had previously committed to and at the same time I am struggling for financial stability at a time when I could be making significant financial progress.)

April 10, 1984.   Ms. Smith called today in reference to her letter of March 26, 1984. She reiterated that the FDIC wanted current appraisals, at my expense, of the property they hold as collateral. The request for appraisals is the second new item added to the items requested originally by Mr. Street. It still seems to me that all of the guidelines for a written workout proposal should have been given to me at the outset. Each new request causes a delay over which I have no control. I also responded with a letter on this date.

April 16, 1984.   Called Ms. Smith to inform her that I will submit my written proposal to her on approximately April 20, 1984. Ms. Smith said she will call me back to confirm a date for submission.

April 19, 1984.   FDIC had appraisers from Fred Singleton begin appraising our property.

April 20, 1984.   Ms. Smith called and suggested I submit my written proposal to her on April 23 or 24, 1984.

April 24, 1984.   Submitted my written workout proposal to Ms. Smith on this day. Since I have never submitted a workout proposal and since I was given no guidelines for such document I did the best I knew how in all good faith. Without being given any idea whatsoever (other than immediate full cash payment) concerning what would satisfy the FDIC, my proposal was predicated on what I thought was fair taking into consideration what FNB's failure did to my ability to maintain normal business activity. Even though I was advised to the contrary, I submitted additional collateral.

April 27, 1984.   Ms. Smith called requesting information on installment notes.

May 10, 1984.   Received letter from Ms. Smith dated May 2, 1984. Again she is asking for additional information. I truly wish the FDIC would allow its account officers to tell their clients precisely what is required a priori. In paragraph two Ms. Smith asked again about encumbering our oil properties. I had previously stated many times that I will not encumber my oil properties which are in partnership. I am finding it more and more difficult to keep from going bankrupt because I have no borrowing power and I am spending so much time educating the FDIC about me and my business activity. I spent 12 years establishing a rapport with FNB and the FDIC does not seem to care who I am. (What happened to the banker's adage that character was the primary consideration in making a loan?) In paragraph three Ms. Smith says "are you able to cover the cost we are incurring on these certificates and appraisals?" It seems she is implying that if I cannot "cover the costs" the FDIC will. I have, however, been forced to pay all expenses caused by the FDIC. (Again it seems so unjustified to undergo the expense and expenditures of time [which is so costly to a small operation like mine] to rejustify a loan request which was previously approved by FNB.)

May 14, 1984. Received letter from Ms. Smith dated May 9, 1984. Another request—another unavoidable delay.

June 4, 1984. Received another letter from Ms. Smith dated May 31, 1984. (In retrospect this letter proved to be the most critical piece of correspondence I received from the FDIC.) In paragraph two Ms. Smith said "If the information requested is not received by June 15, I will have to take action necessary to protect our interest." Please allow me to put forth the following facts:

1. Ms. Smith's letter was dated May 2, 1984. Ms. Smith's letter was postmarked May 8, 1984. Ms. Smith's letter was received May 10, 1984.
2. I began May 10, 1984, gathering the information she requested. (Apparently I should have called to notify her that I had received her letter and that I was gathering information.)
3. When I waited three and one-half months (October 14, 1983 to January 30, 1984) to hear from someone telling me the status of and who owned my bank debt, I did not deem it necessary or appropriate to threaten legal action. Throughout this whole process I have been victimized by circumstances I did not foster or create yet I have never deemed it necessary to imply and/or threaten legal action. The FDIC insured a bank in Colby, Oklahoma, which is its primary business activity as stipulated by law in 1933. The insured bank failed. To the best of my knowledge I did not cause the energy economy to destruct or said bank to fail.
4. From this point forward the whole atmosphere changed. The rumors which were repeated so often on "the street" took on new significance to me. Maybe the "government" in the form of the FDIC was going to "get me" as nearly everyone in Colby was saying.
5. I had, prior to receiving Ms. Smith's letter dated May 31, 1984, responded to her requests in our letter dated June 4, 1984. However, I had also called Ms. Smith on May 18, 1984, June 1, 1984, and June 4, 1984.

June 5, 1984. At my request I had a meeting at the FDIC with Ms. Smith and her section chief, Mr. Sam Watson. Since Mr. Watson was new to my case I spent at least one hour rehashing the details of the case. Ms. Smith followed up this meeting with a letter dated June 8, 1984. In the last paragraph of her letter she stated that the ". . . FDIC is willing to work with you; however, your full cooperation is essential." To the best of my knowledge I have not withheld one degree of my cooperation. I have, however, been denied the ability to function in a normal business fashion as a result of circumstances I did not create. For example, as I told Ms. Smith and Mr. Watson (as noted in Ms. Smith's June 8, 1984, letter) the Rich land was to be sold in a trustee's sale that day at the county courthouse because I was not making timely payments. If I would have lost that land it would have been as a direct result of the broken commitment of First National Bank of Colby.

June 8, 1984. Ms. Smith called asking us to prove we had paid the taxes on the Raleigh farm.

June 11, 1984. Typed new financial statements on me personally and Mid-State Petroleum Services as requested in June 8, 1984, letter from Ms. Smith.

June 12, 1984. Delivered financial statements and property descriptions to Ms. Smith as she requested in her June 8, 1984, letter.

June 14, 1984. Mid-State Petroleum Services received a letter from Ms. Katie Hatley of the FDIC stating that they had no record of insurance on two trucks and trailers. Again I was threatened with legal action if I did not respond in 10 days. I immediately called our insurance agent Bob Morris to provide the necessary proof of coverage so that I would not be sued by the FDIC for something I did not know they did not possess.

June 15, 1984. Mailed letter, dated June 14, 1984, to Ms. Smith and also called her. In my letter I have tried again to explain my situation and to get some clearly delineated rules and/or boundaries of what is expected of me. It seems to me that nearly every game that is played has specific guidelines which clearly define the rules to the players. Since I am not now, nor have I ever been, a professional workout proposal writer I am forced to constantly ask for direction.

June 19, 1984. Received letter from Mr. Sam Watson dated June 16, 1984. The letter was nice but still quite vague as to specific requirements concerning the workout proposal. My thoughts at this time are: I appreciate his defense of my criticisms of Ms. Smith but my criticisms of her are only a normal human reaction of her unjustified criticisms of me.

July 16, 1984. Equipment appraisers came by office. Took photographs.

July 19, 1984. Met today with Commerce State Bank in an attempt to move FDIC debt.

July 24, 1984. Called Ms. Smith today. She indicated she had not heard anything on our workout proposal. This is confusing to me because I am in the process of preparing a proposal right now.

July 27, 1984. Hand delivered to Ms. Smith my written workout proposal dated July 26, 1984.

July 30, 1984. Called Ms. Smith at 3:22 P.M. and she set our meeting for July 31, 1984, at 10 A.M.

July 31, 1984. Met at FDIC with Ms. Smith and Mr. Sam Watson. We went over my proposal and answered a few questions. They said they would present my proposal to Dallas but it might take a month to get an answer.

August 20, 1984. Mr. Wayne Jones, CPA, finally completed our 1983 tax return. We had tried every imaginable way to hurry Mr. Jones but to no avail.

October 8, 1984. Called Ms. Smith today but FDIC had a holiday.

October 9, 1984. Ms. Smith called today at 1:40 P.M. She informed me that my workout proposal had been declined. (My thoughts: Mr. Sam Watson was certainly correct in paragraph three of his letter dated June 26, 1984. He said "We agree with you that it appears to be a lot of paperwork; unfortunately that is one of the handicaps that we are forced to operate under. It was much easier for the bank to 'cut a deal' than for the FDIC.") This time it took the FDIC two and one-half months to say no. I was informed in our July 31, 1984, meeting that it might take a month to get an answer. I am curious to know if the FDIC would pay rent (vis-à-vis interest) on a building they were planning to lease while the landlord took two and one-half months to make up his mind.

October 10, 1984. Called Ms. Smith. She was not in.

October 12, 1984. Received letter from Ms. Smith dated October 10, 1984. She indicated our proposal had been turned down and suggested additional information I need to prepare. However, there was no indication whatsoever as to what they might accept. There was no counterproposal of any kind. They seem to be inviting me into a Chapter 11. Also, got together information for Mr. Henry Scott, CPA, so that he could prepare information requested in Ms. Smith's letter.

October 17, 1984. Met with Henry Scott regarding preparation of information requested by FDIC.

October 26, 1984. Scheduled meeting with Ms. Smith and Mr. Watson for October 31, 1984, at 3:30 P.M.

October 31, 1984. Mr. Scott, my CPA, called this morning and said there is no need to prepare separate financial statements since our income tax returns clearly state our financial position. We, along with Mr. Scott, met with Ms. Smith and Mr. Watson at 3:30 P.M. at the FDIC. A possibility of a $700,000 cash settlement was mentioned by Mr. Sam Watson. We submitted my last written proposal dated October 31, 1984.

November 2, 1984. Called Ms. Smith and gave her property descriptions on commercial property on Cherry Lane and 205 Rome Street property.

November 15, 1984.   Called Ms. Smith.

November 17, 1984.   Received letter from Ms. Smith dated November 15, 1984.

November 26, 1984.   Called Ms. Smith to inform her that I am still trying to find a bank to move FDIC debt. I am still getting the same vibes from bankers. They will not be interested until the FDIC has approved a workout plan. CATCH 22 AGAIN!

November 29, 1984.   I met with Mr. James Bryant of Benson Bank in another attempt to satisfy the FDIC loans.

December 3, 1984.   Sent letter to Ms. Smith informing her of our meetings with Mr. James Bryant of Benson Bank.

December 10, 1984.   Ray Johnson, Bill Johnson, and I met with Jim Bryant of Benson Bank regarding the Johnsons' purchase of Mid-State Petroleum Services and the satisfaction of our FDIC debt.

December 11, 1984.   Delivered appraisals to Mr. Bryant of Benson Bank. I am afraid to get my hopes up but he is talking very, very positively.

December 14, 1984.   Received letter from Ms. Smith dated December 12, 1984.

December 17, 1984.   Mr. Bryant of Benson Bank informed me that they have approved a loan to the Johnsons to buy Mid-State Petroleum Services. (Maybe things are finally beginning to break my way!)

December 28, 1984.   Called Ms. Smith to inform her that Henry Scott's office will be closed until after January 1, 1985. She insisted that I spend the money for a CPA-prepared financial statement even though Mr. Scott informed her and Mr. Watson in our meeting of October 31, 1984, that to prepare one would be a redundancy.

January 14, 1985.   Jim Bryant of Benson turned down my loan request. He indicated that his bank does not want to work with the FDIC because it is too time consuming. My thoughts: Benson was so positive and then turned negative so quickly I suspect that I am not being told the real reason Benson turned me down. We have heard rumors of an unfriendly meeting between Jim Bryant and Susan Smith.

January 15, 1984.   Called Ms. Smith to inform her of my turndown by Benson Bank.

January 18, 1984.   I met at the FDIC with Ms. Smith and her new section chief, Mr. Charles Switzer. I agreed to submit a new proposal on January 23, 1985. Mr. Switzer emphatically stated that he had the authority to settle my account and that he would do so very quickly "one way or another."

January 22, 1985.   Ms. Smith called to postpone our January 23, 1985, meeting.

January 24, 1985.   Met with Ms. Smith and Mr. Switzer and submitted our written proposal.

January 29, 1985. Ms. Smith called to inform me that the FDIC needs new appraisals. More expense for which I do not feel responsible.

February 5, 1985. Called Charles Switzer three times today without success.

February 6, 1985. Called Charles Switzer to inform him that if FDIC did not speed up its processing of Mid-State Petroleum Services sale the Johnsons were going to back out of deal. Mr. Switzer also said he and Ms. Smith were meeting on our proposal that day and they would be in touch.

February 8, 1985. Ms. Smith called and requested a meeting on February 11, 1985, at 9 A.M.

February 11, 1985. Ms. Smith and Mr. Switzer informed us that our January 25, 1985, proposal had been turned down. They said I needed to make "good faith" payments; however, every attempt I had made in the past to make good faith payments was summarily rejected.

February 13, 1985. Ms. Smith called concerning Johnson sale.

February 14, 1985. Received letter from Ms. Smith dated February 12, 1985. Called Ms. Smith today. Her line was busy and receptionist said she would call back.

February 16, 1985. Received letter from Ms. Smith dated February 14, 1985, concerning Johnson sale.

February 18, 1985. Fred Singleton did another appraisal on 2007 Wood.

February 19, 1985. Sent letter to Ms. Smith on Johnson sale. Also on this date I took a statement to the FDIC office stating that Benson National Bank would furnish the funding for the sale of Mid-State Petroleum Services and I would give the FDIC a certified check for $26,940.08.

February 21, 1985. Talked to Ms. Smith today. She said that if I did not pay for the $200 appraisal on Mid-State Petroleum Services for the FDIC that they could not approve the sale to the Johnsons. I agreed to pay said appraisal.

February 25, 1985. Ms. Smith called and said she could meet with me to consummate the sale of Mid-State Petroleum Services. I met and consummated said transaction. (From that date the Johnsons agreed to buy and secured financing it took the FDIC 71 days to consummate the sale. During that period I almost lost the sale twice.)

February 28, 1985. Met with Dr. John Lyle, professor of business, Middle Oklahoma State University, to see if he could help us write our next proposal. Since I cannot seem to satisfy the FDIC I am looking for help.

March 1, 1985. The appraisers came today for yet another appraisal of the 150 acres of farmland.

March 19, 1985. The appraisers came today for yet another appraisal of the Mimosa Street property. Ms. Smith called today.

March 20, 1985. Engaged Dr. Lyle to help us.

March 21, 1985. Dr. Lyle had meeting with Ms. Smith. (Dr. Lyle had a meeting with Mr. Roy Yates and Mr. George Walker of the FDIC so he asked Mr. Walker to introduce him to Ms. Smith.) He informed her he was not acting as an attorney and was not there in an adversarial role. He stated he was there just to let her know he was going to help me write my next proposal.

March 23, 1985. Met with Dr. Lyle to discuss his meeting with Ms. Smith on March 21, 1985.

March 25, 1985. Called Ms. Smith. She said I must give her a power-of-attorney before she would release any information to Dr. Lyle. I tried to explain (probably unsuccessfully) that Dr. Lyle would not be asking them directly for anything and that he was not their enemy—he is just going to help me write a proposal.

April 25, 1985. Ms. Smith called Clayton office. I have leased that office.

April 30, 1985. I called Ms. Smith. Ms. Smith again derisively questioned the fact that I had engaged Dr. Lyle.

May 1, 1985. Mr. Charles Switzer called Clayton office at 10 A.M. I called Mr. Switzer this evening after he got in from the field. Mr. Switzer was quite upset that I had called in "outside people." I explained that in my business all professional people were outside people because my staff did not include lawyers, accountants, consultants, engineers, etc. Mr. Switzer responded by saying (I interpreted his comment to be a threat) that if I were going to call in "outsiders or heavy artillery" that maybe he should turn our case over to the legal department. I assured him I was working as rapidly as I could and that if he felt he should "call in" their lawyers then he should run his business as he sees fit to do so. He also informed me that I must call Ms. Smith. (From March 21 to today has to be the most bizarre period I have ever experienced. I have been turned down, belittled for my inability to understand what they want, criticized for submitting inadequate proposals [but remember Ms. Smith has said repeatedly that she is not allowed to help us structure a proposal], and now they are acting churlishly when I ask someone to help me. I am at a complete loss as to what to do. If I continue to use Dr. Lyle then I feel they may turn me over to their legal department—whatever that means.)

May 2, 1985. Called Ms. Smith as required by Mr. Switzer. Ms. Smith was still upset over our use of Dr. Lyle and insisted that we have a meeting. I informed her that Dr. Lyle was working as diligently and as rapidly as possible on my proposal. However, if she insisted I would have a meeting to go over historical information. Ms. Smith agreed that would be nonproductive but said that Washington was putting the heat on Dallas, and Dallas was putting the heat on Colby and thus on the legal staff (we assumed this was another threat). We set a meeting for May 10, 1985.

May 8, 1985.   I called Ms. Smith to tell her that Dr. Lyle could not meet on May 10, 1985. Together I set an alternate date on May 21, 1985.

May 13, 1985.   I called Ms. Smith and they set the time for the May 21 meeting at 9 A.M.

May 20, 1985.   Ms. Smith called and said she could not meet with us on May 21 and the meeting was rescheduled for May 22.

May 22, 1985.   Meeting at FDIC at 9 A.M. attended by me, Dr. John Lyle, Ms. Susan Smith, and Mr. Bill Burke. Dr. Lyle explained the approach he was taking in the preparation of our workout proposal and indicated he would try to be finished by June 5, 1985. Mr. Burke did two things of significance: (1) he lectured us on what the FDIC is and how it operates, and (2) he told Dr. Lyle to include in the proposal a cash settlement option.

FINANCIAL POSITION

Historical

MID-STATE ENTERPRISES
EQUIPMENT, PIPE & SUPPLY
Income Statement
For the Period Ending December 31, 1980

Sales		$277,122.03
Less: Cost of goods sold		201,273.06
Gross profit		$ 75,848.97
Operating Expenses:		
Advertising	$ 904.27	
Car and truck expenses	7,072.68	
Commissions paid	7,882.55	
Depreciation	27,750.00	
Insurance	10,526.56	
Interest	12,615.27	
Laundry	326.38	
Legal	764.82	
Office supplies	734.41	
Postage	90.00	
Repairs	5,135.19	
Taxes	1,834.54	
Telephone	3,462.67	
Travel and entertainment	1,180.00	
Utilities	1,509.03	
Wages	18,238.22	
Equipment lease	7,343.86	
Janitorial service	270.00	
Total expenses		107,640.45
Net operating loss		($ 31,791.48)
Other income		5,400.00
Net loss		($ 26,391.48)

MID-STATE ENTERPRISES
EQUIPMENT, PIPE & SUPPLY
Income Statement
For the Period Ending December 31, 1981

Sales		$2,079,724.93
Less: Cost of goods sold		1,659,694.91
Gross profit		$ 420,030.02
Operating expenses:		
Advertising	$ 1,527.80	
Car and truck expenses	48,846.62	
Commissions paid.	21,704.22	
Depletion	29,220.07	
Depreciation	62,807.50	
Freight	13,417.91	
Insurance.	16,442.03	
Interest on business indebtedness . . .	29,366.80	
Laundry and cleaning	409.22	
Legal and professional services	10,752.62	
Office supplies and postage	2,041.71	
Taxes.	59,328.75	
Travel and entertainment	6,225.86	
Utilities	8,754.91	
Wages	34,562.69	
Windfall profit tax withheld in 1981. . .	17,109.02	
Equipment leasing	8,749.44	
Janitorial service	1,196.17	
Maintenance	24,993.10	
Disposal fees	5,705.20	
Well workover.	5,481.61	
Pipe testing.	12,672.08	
Total expenses		421,315.33
Net operating loss.	($	1,285.31)
Other income		7,250.00
Net profit or (loss).	$	5,964.69

MID-STATE ENTERPRISES
EQUIPMENT, PIPE & SUPPLY
Income Statement
For the Period Ending December 31, 1982

Sales		$979,699.00
Less: Cost of goods sold		643,373.00
Gross profit		$336,326.00
Operating expenses:		
Advertising	$ 1,027.00	
Car and truck expenses	27,584.00	
Commissions paid	13,413.00	
Depreciation	57,641.00	
Freight	2,034.00	
Insurance	22,924.00	
Interest on business indebtedness	41,155.00	
Legal and professional services	826.00	
Office supplies and postage	1,802.00	
Rent on business property	1,010.00	
Taxes	55,835.00	
Travel and entertainment	5,103.00	
Utilities and telephone	8,445.00	
Wages	47,271.00	
Equipment leasing	1,684.00	
Janitorial service	464.00	
Maintenance	19,929.00	
Disposal fees	1,809.00	
Total expenses		309,956.00
Net operating profit or (loss)		$ 26,370.00
Other income		–0–
Net profit or (loss)		$ 26,370.00

MID-STATE ENTERPRISES
ANDREW CROCKETT COMPANY
Income Statement
For the Period Ending December 31, 1982

Sales		$146,829.00
Less: Cost of goods sold		135,749.00
Gross profit		$ 11,080.00
Operating expenses:		
Car and truck expenses	$ 7,714.00	
Depreciation	42,985.00	
Interest on business indebtedness	34,190.00	
Legal and professional services	1,524.00	
Office supplies and postage	319.00	
Supplies	3,101.00	
Taxes	8,023.00	
Travel and entertainment	3,301.00	
Windfall profit tax withheld in 1982	1,820.00	
Contract labor	6,438.00	
Materials and supplies	21,803.00	
Less amount allocated to overhead	−50,149.00	
Total expenses		81,069.00
Net operating loss		($ 69,989.00)
Other income		–0–
Net profit or (loss)		($ 69,989.00)

MID-STATE ENTERPRISES
CROCKETT PIPE & EQUIPMENT SALES
Income Statement
For the Period Ending December 31, 1983

Sales		$327,046.00
Less: Cost of goods sold		205,284.00
Gross profit.		$121,762.00
Operating expenses:		
Advertising	$ 2,349.00	
Car and truck expenses	71,168.00	
Commissions paid.	7,537.00	
Depreciation	69,937.00	
Freight	75.00	
Insurance.	29,409.00	
Interest on business indebtedness . . .	20,871.00	
Legal and professional services	10,475.00	
Office expense	2,844.00	
Taxes.	4,893.00	
Travel and entertainment	13,718.00	
Utilities and telephone.	10,148.00	
Wages	70,663.00	
Equipment leasing	4,144.00	
Consulting fees	26,107.00	
Janitorial service	239.00	
Disposal fees	28,093.00	
Total expenses		370,670.00
Net operating loss.		($248,908.00)
Other income		–0–
Net profit or (loss).		($248,908.00)

MID-STATE ENTERPRISES
CROCKETT COMPANY
Income Statement
For the Period Ending December 31, 1983

Gross receipts.		$605,553.00
Operating expenses:		
Depletion	$ 1,160.00	
Depreciation	88,458.00	
Supplies	18,804.00	
Taxes.	23,752.00	
Utilities	1,667.00	
Windfall profit tax withheld in 1983 . . .	8,012.00	
Contract labor.	18,818.00	
Lease use—gas	20.00	
Propane	2,263.00	
Operating expenses	134,515.00	
Dry hole cost	109,010.00	
Other depletion expenses	2,268.00	
Total expenses		408,747.00
Net operating profit or (loss)		$ 96,806.00
Other income		–0–
Net profit or (loss)		$196,806.00

MID-STATE ENTERPRISES
CROCKETT PIPE & EQUIPMENT SALES
Income Statement
For the Period Ending December 31, 1984

Sales.		$13,488.81
Less: Cost of goods sold		4,000.00
Gross profit		$ 9,488.81
Operating expenses:		
Advertising	$ 204.87	
Bank service charges	66.51	
Car and truck expenses	631.89	
Depreciation	12,050.00	
Insurance	1,284.60	
Interest on business indebtedness	5,511.61	
Legal and professional services	221.50	
Office expense	467.51	
Rent on business property	412.04	
Taxes	2,529.95	
Travel and entertainment	150.00	
Utilities and telephone	1,528.36	
Wages	5,000.00	
Labor	988.89	
Materials	1,336.91	
Freight	86.20	
Janitor	417.90	
Gas and oil	1,772.45	
Postage	40.00	
Licenses, tags	3,053.66	
Total expenses		37,754.85
Net operating loss		($28,266.04)
Other income		−0−
Net profit or (loss)		($28,266.04)

MID-STATE ENTERPRISES
ANDREW CROCKETT COMPANY
Income Statement
For the Period Ending December 31, 1984

Gross receipts		$233,848.32
Operating expenses:		
Advertising	$ 87.40	
Bank service charges.	76.00	
Car and truck expenses	4,976.60	
Depletion (gross × 15% + 13,487.00 carryover) . . .	48,574.25	
Depreciation.	72,494.00	
Insurance	17,525.81	
Legal and professional services.	13,915.81	
Office expense.	128.59	
Rent on business property	1,011.75	
Taxes	11,021.53	
Travel and entertainment	2,880.35	
Utilities and telephone	4,169.87	
Wages.	50.44	
Gas reimbursement	1,297.38	
Labor	9,471.91	
Materials and supplies	6,420.89	
Tags and taxes.	1,279.33	
Commissions	712.61	
Fuel.	32.42	
Janitor	35.00	
Gas and oil	2,892.43	
65% limitation depletion	(48,574.25)	
Total expenses.		150,480.12
Net operating profit or (loss)		$ 83,368.20
Other income		12,328.51
Net profit or (loss)		$ 95,696.71

MID-STATE ENTERPRISES
Statement of Cash Receipts and Disbursements
(Consolidated)
Five Months Ended May 31, 1985

January 1–May 31
1985

Cash receipts

Oil and gas production	$ 88,892.24
Pipe and equipment sales	35,225.00
Rent income—houses	1,200.00
Rent income—commercial properties	9,050.00
Farm income	5,532.31
	$139,899.55

Cash disbursements

Materials and supplies	5,127.49
Farm expenses	30,499.10
Lease use tax	2,747.29
Freight	—
Commissions and finder's fees	1,600.00
Truck and vehicle expenses	4,497.39
Insurance	4,562.38
Telephone	—
Janitorial service	—
Legal and professional fees	4,130.00
Utilities	440.92
Advertising	—
Office supplies	—
Gasoline, oil	2,644.56
Equipment leases	358.91
Office rent	—
Disposal fees	11,356.28
License tags and taxes—trucks	907.30
Postage	97.35
Bank fees	67.00
Travel	600.00
Wages	744.75
Contract labor	13,453.00
Note payments	13,984.31
Internal Revenue Service and payroll	3,656.65
Materials and supplies—oil wells	—
PPS debt retirement	7,574.62
Jones suit settlement	2,000.00
Property taxes	1,611.30
Rental—insurance	—
Rental—advertising	123.64
Rental—materials	1,423.14
Rental—utilities	309.62
Rental—taxes	1,235.96
Rental—repairs	3,489.45
Rental—cleaning	40.00
Rental—trash	—
Rental—office supplies	—
	$119,282.41
Excess of cash receipts over disbursements	$ 20,617.14

MID-STATE ENTERPRISES
Statement of Cash Receipts and Disbursements
(Consolidated)
Twelve Months Ended December 31, 1984

	Year to Date
Cash receipts	
Oil and gas production	$226,481.27
Pipe and equipment sales	85,105.97
Other oil and gas income	12,328.51
Rent income—houses	3,980.00
Rent income—commercial properties	15,300.00
Farm income	2,392.41
	$345,588.16
Cash disbursements	
Materials and supplies	$ 15,460.99
Farm expenses	35,329.54
Lease use tax	32.42
Freight	86.20
Commissions and finder's fees	1,071.71
Truck and vehicle expenses	11,453.20
Insurance	23,704.84
Telephone	3,955.23
Janitorial service	501.40
Legal and professional fees	14,161.92
Utilities	1,743.00
Advertising	381.59
Office supplies	840.00
Gasoline, oil	8,722.65
Equipment leases	972.59
Office rent	600.00
Disposal fees	15,090.96
License tags and taxes—trucks	4,822.18
Postage	188.24
Bank fees	152.51
Travel	3,280.35
Wages	20,355.50
Contract labor	18,992.65
Note payments	76,078.81
Internal Revenue Service and payroll	10,173.63
Materials and supplies—Oil wells Clayton operating .	16,839.75
PPS debt retirement	18,138.56
Haywood suit settlement	—
Property taxes	—
Rental—insurance	657.66
Rental—advertising	438.02
Rental—materials	3,348.27
Rental—utilities	815.48
Rental—taxes	2,922.03
Rental—repairs	3,205.22
Rental—cleaning	1,470.00
Rental—trash	—
Rental—office supplies	194.69
	$316,181.79
Excess of cash receipts over disbursements	$ 29,406.37

Loss of Income

In this section I feel compelled to indicate to the FDIC the burden that befell me when the FDIC was forced to take on my loans from First National Bank of Colby, Oklahoma.

Contrary to many (possibly most) of the loans not purchased by Liberty Bank from the insolvent First National, my loans were not in default. In fact, I do not at the present time consider my loans in default. I had a legitimate, legal, verbal contract with First National Bank of Colby on a consolidated loan which I was prevented from receiving (thus, making timely payments on) by the demise of the bank. I feel extremely confident that I would have paid the approximately $10,000 per month for the previous 25 months on the consolidated loan committed to me by First National Bank of Colby, Oklahoma.

As the FDIC is well aware, there are two distinct facets to the energy industry. One is drilling and the other is production. The drilling facet was devastated by the energy downturn but the production facet was not.

My business endeavors were concentrated in the production area of the energy industry as follows:

1. Buy and sell all types of equipment and pipe which was used to *maintain existing* oil producing wells and facilities.
2. Buy, sell and/or maintain oil producing properties.

Since I operated a small family-intensive operation I could operate much more efficiently than a large business. This approach, in conjunction with legitimate income tax provision, allowed me to build my business and operate quite profitably.

From my federal income tax return I submit the following information:

Year		Net Profit/Loss
1980	Pipe and equipment business	($26,391)
1981	Pipe and equipment business	$ 5,964
1982	Pipe and equipment business	$26,370
1982	Oil and gas production	($69,989)

The table above shows that my pipe and equipment business got better in 1981 and made a profit in 1982. The consolidated loan committed to me by the First National Bank of Colby in the first quarter of 1983 was to provide working capital for the pipe and equipment business and to complete the following projects approved by the bank:

1. Subdivide and sell Rich property.
2. Construction and sale of homes in Raleigh Country Club.

3. Working capital financing for the pipe and equipment business.

When First National broke its commitment to me I was left without a bank and the needed funding which would have enabled me to carry out my normal business operations. Without the promised working capital funds and the funds promised to complete bank approved projects, I was forced to use all available resources to maintain a status quo on partially funded projects and to pay normal business creditors in our pipe and equipment business. The effects of the preceding were disastrous as shown from the following:

Year		Net Profit/Loss
1983	Pipe and equipment business	($248,908)
1983	Oil and gas production	$196,806
1984	Pipe and equipment business	($ 28,266)
1984	Oil and gas production	$ 95,697

It appears to me that I have been damaged at least $1,500,000 as a result of the broken loan commitment by First National Bank of Colby and the fact that the federal government allowed Liberty Bank to refuse to purchase our loans. Through no fault of my own making, I was left without the means to maintain what I had worked so hard to accomplish.

WORKOUT PROPOSAL

A. Proposal Number One—Because I feel I have been financially damaged and because I feel I was prevented (through no fault of our own) from maintaining the value of my assets I will settle our alleged entire debt with the FDIC for a sum of $419,989. We have a bank committed to loan us the required $419,989.

B. Proposal Number Two—In this proposal I will arrive at a loan balance which I will be willing to amortize.
    1. I do not dispute the principal balance of my loans from First National Bank of Colby which totals $797,000.00.
    2. I do contest the amount of interest I allegedly owe. During the periods I stood ready and willing to perform on the consolidated loan committed to me by the First National Bank of Colby but I was prevented from doing so through no fault of my own. Therefore, I contend that I do not owe interest for the following periods:
        4-25-83 thru 10-14-83: During this period I was told I had a loan consolidation. I performed all the necessarily pru-

dent actions required of a bank borrower. In my opinion I had an executory contract with First National Bank of Colby and consummated said contract by executing what was expected of me. (173 days.)

10-15-83 thru 1-30-84: During this period of time the only information I could get concerning my debt position with the bank was what I read in the papers and "street" rumors. From information I could gather it was stated that Liberty Bank had 30 days to analyze the FNB loan portfolio to determine which loans they would purchase from the FDIC. As I understand it Liberty Bank asked for and was granted two extensions of that time period and decided on approximately January 17, 1984. On January 30, 1984, I was informed that Liberty Bank had not purchased my loans. (108 days.)

3-6-84 thru 3-15-84: On March 6, 1984, I was told my first account officer was transferred and I was not notified who my new account officer was until March 15, 1984. (10 days.)

4-20-84 thru 4-24-84: I was prepared to submit my first written proposal but my account officer would not meet with me until April 24, 1984. (5 days.)

5-10-84 thru 7-27-84: I spent this entire period trying to satisfy the FDIC's request for additional information concerning my workout proposal. If I had been given clear and complete instructions prior to April 24, 1984, I would have submitted the necessary information negating the delay of this period. (79 days.)

8-27-84 thru 10-9-84: When I submitted my written proposal on July 27, 1984, I was told that I could expect an answer in one month. This time period represents the excess time period over and above one month before I received an answer. (44 days.)

11-19-84 thru 1-18-85: I spent this time period trying to move our FDIC debt to Benson National Bank. I feel the time was wasted for two reasons: (1) Trying to move FDIC debt without a workout plan accepted by the FDIC is a catch 22 situation; and (2) Part of the reason for my turndown resulted from a rumored unfriendly meeting between our FDIC account officer and the Benson Bank officer I was negotiating with. (61 days.)

1-24-85 thru 2-11-85: Spent this time waiting to be turned down again. Again I was given little indication of what to include in my proposal. (19 days.)

2-12-85 thru 3-20-85: During this period of time I had no idea what to do next. On March 20, 1985, I engaged Dr.

SCHEDULE 1 Mid-State Enterprises

Obligor	Principal	Note Date	Accrued Interest as of 5-31-85	Reciprocal Factor to Represent the 536 Days Interest Is not Owed	Interest Owed
Andrew Crockett					
264–310					
18	$ 85,000	2-23-83	$ 27,948	.35	$ 9,781
34	110,000	11-18-82	33,669	.42	14,141
42	57,000	12-21-82	24,744	.35	8,660
Clayton Building					
265–505–					
18	$175,000	2-10-82	$ 50,546	.56	$ 28,306
26	61,000	11-01-82	16,549	.43	7,116
Andrew Crockett					
267–895–	209,000				
18	$209,000	11-30-82	$ 67,074	.41	$ 27,500
Clayton Energy					
108–840–					
18	$ 70,000	8-17-82	$ 30,315	.47	$ 14,248
	$767,000		$250,845	Total interest owed	$109,752
			Grand total $1,127,537		

Lyle and we have been working diligently to prepare a workout proposal. (37 days.)

C. Recapitulation—In accordance with the preceding I feel I do not owe interest for 536 days from the period April 25, 1983, through March 20, 1985. Therefore, if you do not accept our cash settlement offer we propose the following workout proposal:

1. Principal amount due: $797,000
2. Interest due: $109,752 (see Schedule 1).
3. Total amount due $906,725

I propose to pay the $906,725 by paying $7,556 per month for 10 years. My cash flow (see pages 232 and 233 of section II) before normal living expenses is approximately $4,123 per month. Even though the $4,123 is not sufficient to cover the proposed $7,556 I would be willing to sell off assets to maintain my proposed payment schedule.

I suggest the FDIC accept either proposal number one or proposal number two for the following reasons:

1. My cash settlement offer was arrived at in the following manner. I took the present value of $906,725 for 10 years at an average treasury bill rate of 8%:
   a. Present value: $419,989
2. If the FDIC takes my $419,989 cash settlement and invests in U.S. Treasury bonds at 11 percent interest, it will yield

$1,192,525 in interest earnings over 10 years. This is total, not interest.

3. If the FDIC does not accept one of my two proposals then I will be left with no other recourse but to seek redress in the courts.

   a. From what the legal community tells me it will take at least two years to reach an accord in the courts and would cost the FDIC at least $100,000 in legal fees.

   b. The collateral presently held by the FDIC consists of the following:

Collateral	Present Value
2006 Wood	$200,000
Green Addition, Lot 90	35,000
Rich Farm—Lacy Survey (152 acres)	152,000
4500 Erath Highway	125,000
1800 Erath Highway—office building	150,000
Mimosa Street—homestead	95,000
Total	$757,000

Since the Mimosa Street property is my homestead and 1800 Erath Highway is my business homestead, both must be released as collateral. The removal of these two pieces of property reduces the FDIC's collateral value to $512,000 to cover the FDIC's alleged debt of approximately $1 million. If we go to court the FDIC collateral will probably deteriorate for two reasons: (1) as a result of the declining nature of the Oklahoma economy, and (2) the physical deterioration of the property from lack of upkeep.

   c. The oil and gas production revenues we are relying upon to service our proposal number two possesses a normally declining nature.

   d. If I am forced to seek redress in the courts I am told by our legal counsel that I should request damages for loss of income as stipulated on page 235 in Section II of this proposal.

Nonprofit

13. "That's Not What I Thought": American Association of University Women—Staff Reorganization

The American Association of University Women is the largest and oldest national organization devoted to concerns for women. The organization began in January 1882 in Boston. At that time, women were excluded from the mainstream of contemporary life, and academic pursuits were dominated by men. A leading physician of the time declared that "education for women impaired their physical health."[1] In 1885, this infant organization supported the first research study on health of women college graduates which disproved popular opinion that higher education adversely affected women's health.

The present AAUW headquarters—The Educational Center— was built in 1958 without ever carrying a mortgage. It was financed solely by funds raised and contributed by members. The center is in Washington, D.C., conveniently located a short walk from the Kennedy Center, the Watergate complex, and the Lincoln Memorial. A professional staff of 80 persons work in this center to provide services to members and to assist in the implementation of policy and program.

UNIQUE PROBLEM

AAUW, like all volunteer organizations, has a board of directors composed of unpaid members. The staff is a group of paid professionals. The special relationship of a professional staff and a volunteer corps of association officers is the focus of this case. In 1979, the board of

The research and written case information were presented at a Case Research Symposium and were evaluated by the Case Research Association's editorial board. This case was prepared by Lynnette K. Solomon and Robert H. Solomon of Stephen F. Austin State University as a basis for class discussion.

Distributed by the Case Research Association. All rights reserved to the authors and the Case Research Association. Permission to use the case should be obtained from the Case Research Association.

[1] American Association of University Women, "The AAUW Story," Washington, D.C., 1979. Appreciation is expressed to Mary A. Grefe, president, and to Quincalee Brown, executive director of AAUW for permission to use materials and resources generated by the staff of AAUW.

directors of AAUW realized that the character of its membership was changing and undertook a reorganization of the staff designed to more efficiently accomplish association goals.

The case centers around the difficulties of developing and implementing a restructuring of the program staff. To understand the problems involved, it is first necessary to look at the purpose of volunteer organizations in general and the structure of AAUW specifically.

BACKGROUND OF PROBLEM

Associations exist for a number of reasons. The trade or professional associations have long histories of accomplishments for members through collective action. Many associations were formed to serve government relations purposes. Some provide marketing services while others serve professional needs, such as education and training or professional recognition.

The purpose of an association is reflected in its program. Some come into being and exist for a single task, and involvement in that task becomes its exclusive activity. Usually, however, an association is organized to support and facilitate a group or profession with whatever activities seem appropriate. This latter reason fits the purpose for the existence of AAUW.[2]

The necessity of responding to member needs in a dynamic society had generated an evolution in the structure of AAUW. The leaders of the organization were aware of the changing composition of membership and the changing views of members. For example, just after World War II, the typical AAUW member was an urban housewife. In 1980, over one half of the membership was employed outside the home.

In recent years, all not-for-profit organizations have come under some scrutiny. The public, whether member or taxpayer, was demanding a higher level of accountability of all nonprofit organizations whether it be association, trade union, government organization, educational institutions, etc.

The not-for-profit sector has responded to criticisms by becoming more "management conscious." In all nonprofit organizations, concepts and tools of business management have become more and more popular. These are wide in range and include management training and development, systems analysis, planning, management by objectives, project management, and participatory management techniques.

---

[2] American Society of Association Executives, *Principles of Association Management*, 1977.

The management of a not-for-profit organization may think that "not-for-profits are different and cannot be managed like a business." Although there are significant differences between profit-making and nonprofit-making businesses, management techniques and styles in both have common elements. There is uniqueness in the not-for-profit sector; however, the important thing is to recognize that the uniqueness is not a single unit standing alone but is part of a large process. Not all business management techniques will work in the nonprofit sector, but it is important to recognize that some business management techniques are, in fact, working very well in a variety of organizations within the not-for-profit sector.[3]

UNIQUE RELATIONSHIPS FOR A NOT-FOR-PROFIT ORGANIZATION

Power in AAUW lies for the most part in the hands of its board of directors which is the decision-making body. While it is the function of the professional staff to carry out these decisions, and the formal working rules generally substantiate the "implementation" role of the staff, some problems began to arise because it was not exactly clear where the decision-making power lay. As with many nonprofit associations, there is a crucial relationship between the volunteer members, the board of directors, and the employed staff. These relationships generate the difficulty encountered in implementing change when the management is a group of volunteer members.

Members of the AAUW board of directors serve for two-year terms. In some bienniums, members of the board might have little experience or skill in the tools of management. Those members on the board who did have some management skills recognized, in 1979, that the organization needed to develop some viable ways of looking at itself, educating itself about management tools, and developing appropriate applications for the organization.

In a profit oriented organization, management personnel as well as management style can be expected to remain somewhat stable over time. However, with a volunteer organization, there can be a radical change in management philosophy every two years. This possibility can generate a great deal of anxiety and uncertainty among the professional members of the paid staff.

In 1979, the AAUW board of directors (volunteers) and the program staff (salaried professionals) became increasingly concerned with whether or not the current organization, especially the program department, was efficiently and effectively responding to the needs of

---

[3] Diane Borst and Patrick Montana, eds., *Managing Nonprofit Organizations*, American Management Association, 1977.

the members. The structure of the organization in 1979 is described in Exhibit 1.

ORGANIZATION OF THE ASSOCIATION

The basic unit of the association is the local branch. Branches range in size from 15 to 1,200 members with each branch having its own distinctive characteristics and personality. The second level of organization for the association is the state division. As the number of members and branches grew, the division came to play an increasingly important role. State divisions are grouped in 10 geographical regions. In 1979, each region was represented on the association board of directors by a vice president from that region.

At the highest level is the association with the Board of Directors composed of both elected and appointed officers. The elected officers, who were the Executive Committee, included the president, 3 vice presidents, recording secretary, treasurer, and 10 vice presidents from the regions. In addition to the elected officers, there were 11 appointed members of the board. An organization chart for the association board is shown in Exhibit 1.

ORGANIZATION OF PROFESSIONAL STAFF

The association staff is housed in the eight-story education center in Washington, D.C. The staff is organized into nine units.

The executive director. Chief administrative officer of the staff which serves the board of directors and the educational center. She may make recommendations to the association board relating to the program, policies, and activities of the association and is responsible for the execution of plans and policies officially adopted by the association or the board and for coordinating the various interests of the association.

Office of controller and membership services. Responsible for accounting, purchasing, and investments; receiving dues payments, supervising AAUW sales office, handling membership records and mailing lists; responding to questions regarding group insurance programs; arranging AAUW tours; and handling inquiries about financial matters.

Office of the board of directors. Responsible for all board related communications; arranging board meetings, conventions, and conferences; and administering the AAUW travel program. All association board, staff, and committee members serve as travel consultants in response to requests by division and/or regions.

Office of development. Fund-raising activities, administration of special gifts and bequests, and fund-raising workshops are in the pur-

EXHIBIT 1 American Association of University Women Board of Directors

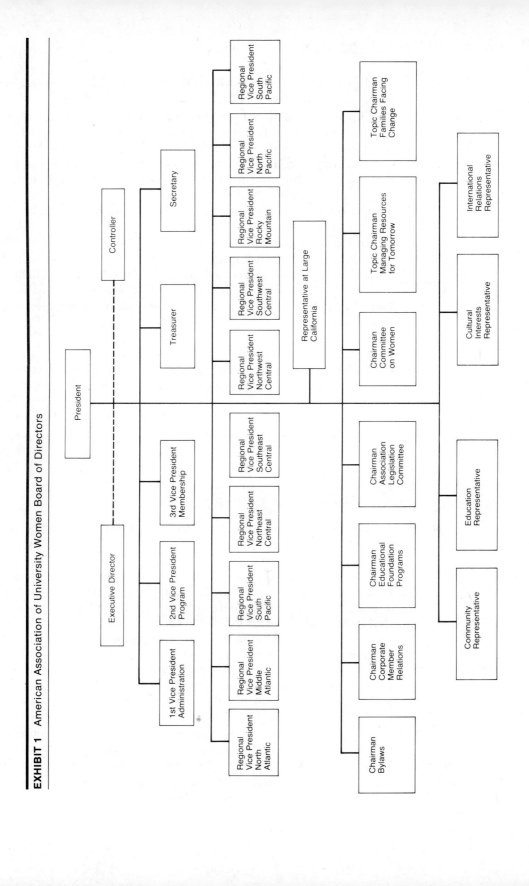

view of this department. All funds generated by the development office go to the educational foundation program.

Office of educational foundation programs. Administrant of fellowships program; research and projects grants; African educators program; and recognition awards. The AAUW educational foundation was incorporated in 1958 to promote the association's activities through fellowships and other educational awards, demonstration projects, public service activities, and research. In 1980, this endowment fund stood at $20 million, and in that year, over $1 million in awards and grants were made.

Office of program. Responsible for all aspects of the AAUW program; legislation, study topics, areas of interest, and higher education.

Office of publications and public information. Publishes the AAUW *Graduate Woman* magazine and all other publications, contacts the media, issues press releases, arranges press conferences, and sends out vitae for association personnel.

Library. Houses the books and reference materials of the association; maintains the archives.

Office of employee relations and administrative services. Has the responsibility for coordinating personnel matters; operating the educational center building and facilities such as food services and parking; coordinating all functions held at the educational center.

An organization chart for the professional staff is found in Exhibit 2.

ORGANIZATION OF PROGRAM DEPARTMENT

As seen from the organization chart, the largest staff was that of the program department. This sector covers a very significant segment of total AAUW activities. The relationship with the program staff and components of the program development committee which is composed of volunteer members is shown in Exhibit 3. This program development area was where the major 1979–80 reorganization of staff occurred.

Volunteer positions in program development. The program development committee (volunteers) was responsible for coordinating and assessing all program activities of the organization and participating in long-range planning for future program directions. The committee was involved in planning programs for all national-level conventions, conferences, and workshops. The second vice president was the committee chairman and thus provided leadership in identifying issues and developing study-action topics to be adopted each biennium. The program development committee was the planning unit for all program activities. In the organization chart above, the volunteer ele-

EXHIBIT 2 Professional Staff Organizational Chart

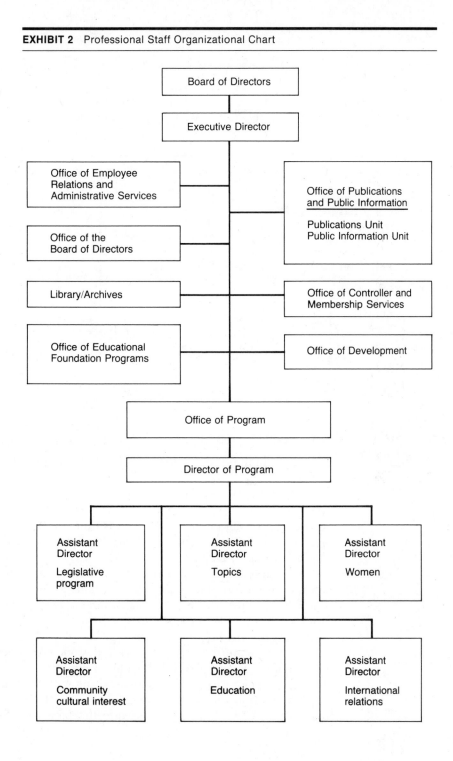

EXHIBIT 3 Organizational Structure of Program Department/Program Development Committee

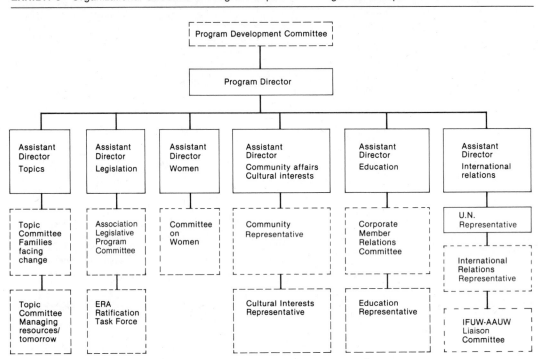

ments are in the dashed boxes while professional staff positions are in solid lines.

Job descriptions of program staff. The function of the program department was to provide staff support for the board of directors and all association committees. Part of this function involved representing AAUW at the many forums, seminars, conferences, etc. which occur in the Washington, D.C., area.

Although all local branches of the association had a great deal of latitude in formulating their own programs, some structure did exist. Each biennium, the association program development committee, from a survey of members, developed action/study topics to direct emphasis toward broad national issues.

Topic committees were appointed from volunteer ranks to develop materials and methods for implementation of these topics. The staff had a major responsibility in assisting with the development and implementation of these ideas. Also, it was the staff responsibility to get the materials printed and into the hands of the local branch members.

The program staff served as an "anchor" in that they were in a permanent location at the educational center, and they were permanently employed while the board was elected for two-year terms. Volunteers served on all association committees with the volunteer positions paralleling somewhat that of the professional program development staff.

REORGANIZATION PROCESS

The difficulty in developing and installing a new staff structure began in 1979 when the board of directors conducted an assessment of the relationship between the volunteers and the program staff. One problem seemed to be the narrow focus of the staff in specified issue areas. A perception began to develop that perhaps the staff should be organized around "functions" rather than issues. The staff had a very narrow view of what constituted their area and in some cases were reluctant to "cross over" into another issue. Also, one problem seemed to be that each volunteer chairman or representative became personally and firmly attached to one staff person and lost the benefit of using expertise from all six of the staff persons. This "attachment" frequently led to conflicts both between and among volunteers and staff.

One of the most difficult problems in a not-for-profit organization is maintaining the delicate balance of responsibility for the volunteer board members and the professional staff. The board members are usually active task oriented persons who sometimes find it difficult to maintain the appropriate posture with the professional staff.

The program staff began the laborious job of identifying their tasks. From this self-analysis, they concentrated on four "functional" areas which to them seemed to be logical.

A great deal of time and effort went into the development of this reorganization plan. The staff members exchanged ideas, disagreed, argued, evaluated, reevaluated, and at last finalized their plan. The staff felt that the plan was a strong one and would allow them to carry out effectively the functions of the program development department. Exhibit 4 below was their final product as presented to the board of directors.

The staff visualized the department being organized into a management team with the director and four assistant directors. The four assistants would provide suggestions, ideas, and recommendations for planning, goal setting, policies, and procedures. Although final decisions would be with the director, the staff felt that coordination, effort, and flexibility would allow effective accomplishment of the necessary tasks.

Five interlocking functions were identified to be shared by the assistant directors.

EXHIBIT 4 Proposed Design for AAUW Program Department[4]

The program department staff, after determining its mission and goals, makes the following recommendations for the design of the Program Department. These recommendations emerged from the functions that the program department staff expects and anticipates will need to be performed. The design accommodates both a clear division of labor and integration and coordination when the task(s) require it. [The graphic illustration is found on page 252.] An explanation of the functions of each of the parts of the design appears below.

Program Outreach. The purposes of this function are to provide direct contact with the members to promote their intellectual growth by setting priorities, evaluating sources and methods of presentation, and bringing materials together in a meaningful presentation on all aspects of AAUW's program, especially the topics, AAUW's areas of interest, and the committee on women. Specific activities of this function include written publications for the membership; personal contact in workshops, conferences, conventions; response to member requests; assistance in mobilizing member action; serving special constituencies such as corporate members and IFUW, as well as other groups to be defined.

Public Policy. The purposes of this function are to prepare and deliver expert testimony on the Hill; manage the lobbying function; create comment on federal regulations (agencies); create and have input into federal agencies and international organizations; monitor and track legislation which reflects the priorities of AAUW; secure federal-level appointments for AAUW members; develop political alliances and create an effective and responsive network of AAUW members to support all the above activities.

Training and Development. The purpose of this function is to provide an ongoing plan for organizational self-renewal. Commitment to individual and organizational renewal suggests that plans will be translated into action and the organization will be flexible enough to change plans when better ones are found, so that the plans are fit to people, not vice versa. A program of training and development might include preservice training, start-up support, maintenance-of-effort training, periodic review and feedback, and transition training. The function would identify and administer then, the training and development activities of the association. These activities would include, but not be limited to, the following skills development for AAUW members; political action, group leadership, interpersonal, self-development, program development, knowledge acquisition, networking, group process, problem solving and organizational effectiveness.

Research and Evaluation. The purpose of this function is to provide both short-term and in-depth policy research capabilities for the program department. This function will provide expertise on issues which we have positions on (and forward them to the public policy unit for strategic use in carrying out their responsibilities on the Hill and to the membership); provide technical skills to do research including statistical, library, field and survey; develop, conduct, and disseminate research; provide program evaluation data collection processes and prepare in-depth analyses for future planning.

Office of the Director of Program. The purpose of this function, the director of program, is to provide leadership based upon strong management and intellectual skills. The director of program needs to be skilled in the following areas; team leader and staff advocate, committee liaison (representative to the board through the executive director for the staff and coordinator with the second vice president for program of the work of the program committees of the association); departmental personnel relations, human resources management, staffing and training, development and supervision; organizational development, office management; resource allocation and management; conflict management (intrastaff and interstaff and volunteer leadership); planning (long and short term) and budgeting; interdepartmental communications; arbitration; monitoring and feedback; source of information and accountability (with adequate authority as well as responsibility) for the functioning of the department; and liaison with outside organizations (manages the liaison function, delegating appropriate liaison activity to other program staff professionals).

---

[4] Permission for use granted by president of AAUW.

1. Information gathering in the Washington, D.C., community, promoting association purposes at conferences, meetings, and governmental briefings, and impacting on legislation.
2. Serving as a liaison to AAUW members and outside organizations and promoting AAUW visibility through speeches, panel presentations, etc.
3. Making contact with governmental and nongovernmental organizations for the purpose of identifying potential funding sources and establishing AAUW credibility as a grant recipient.
4. Analyzing and evaluating developments in the field to shape policy and strategies for new program direction.
5. Supervising staff and interns and distributing assignments appropriately.

IMPLEMENTATION OF REORGANIZATION PLAN

In November 1979, the AAUW board of directors voted to implement the suggested reorganization plan and proceeded to develop job descriptions and qualification requirements for the newly designed positions. However, the perceptions of the plan by the board and staff were not the same. For example, in the process of implementation by AAUW administrators, a decision was made to develop the "legislative" or "public policy" segment of the program into a separate department. This decision was discussed at length with the program staff and the rationale for the change covered in meetings with individual members and with the total program staff. As the discussion developed, a frequently heard comment was "That's not what I thought" from both board and staff members.

Despite communication efforts, the staff felt that their own plan was based on a team concept and that now one of the team members suddenly had been elevated to a new higher status above the others. The staff members could not see how the public policy department could function without involvement of the program staff. They felt strongly that public policy was a part of program. In the past, the legislative function had been on the same level with the other program segments. This change in the organization plan seemed to undermine staff support of its own plan. As shown in Exhibit 5 the program staff had seen the four assistant directors of program working as a team and now that there would be a director of public policy on the same level with the director of program, that team concept was destroyed.

Because of the perception that the old staff would be reshuffled into the new positions, there was no doubt concern over who of the

EXHIBIT 5   Proposed Design for Program Department Structure

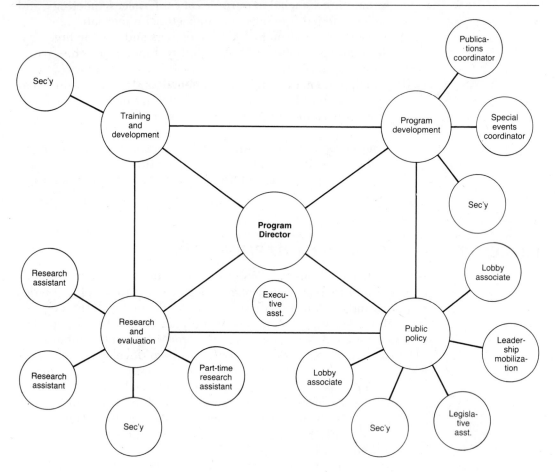

existing six assistant directors would now be at the higher level. However, the Executive Committee of AAUW made the decision to open
all the new positions to outside applications. Again, the executives
were faced with a response of "That's not how we understood things
were to be done." The executive committee had realized that the
skills and talents for the new positions were not the same as for the old
alignment and were concerned with obtaining the best possible
talent.

Only two of the six assistant directors of program shown in Exhibit
3 became a part of the reorganization. The former assistant director for
women was appointed to assistant director for program development
and the former assistant for cultural interest and community was ap-

pointed to assistant director for training and development. Three of the former assistant directors left the association staff and one was given a new assignment.

The administration of AAUW is now interested in reviewing events and assessing what, if anything, might have been done to avoid the difficulties encountered in the transition.

14. North Urban Private Industry Council (NUPIC) (A)

Sarah Washington recognized her own mixed emotions as she thumbed through the 25-page report which had just arrived from the Planning Department. This was a draft of her organization's new two-year plan, and her first reaction was a feeling of pride in the progress it reflected. Mingled with pride, however, was apprehension. It was January of 1987, and times were hard. Of the 15 organizations like hers in the Commonwealth of Massachusetts in 1986, only 10 would survive the new fiscal year. Sarah Washington, manager of service delivery for the North Urban Private Industry Council, wanted NUPIC to survive.

NUPIC, formerly the North Urban Manpower Administration, served one of 15 "service delivery areas" in Massachusetts. Its mission, under the federal Job Training Partnership Act (JTPA) was to recruit unemployed and underemployed people, train them in skills needed in their local economies, and place them in unsubsidized jobs in the private sector of the economy. In its mission, NUPIC was similar to its predecessor organization, the North Urban Manpower Administration. In its implementation and its content, however, there were substantial differences. Sarah Washington commented:

> The mission in manpower development programs has always been the same, even back in the Office of Economic Opportunity days. The money was granted to change the poverty cycle—to get people out of the cycle. I have actually seen that work, although the percentages were not what the government wanted. It was popular to say the OEO program didn't work, but the successful parts of it were carried over into CETA, just as the things that were good in CETA were carried over into JTPA.
>
> JTPA is different from CETA. Our clients aren't *paid* to be trained; in CETA they were. Now training and development are required by law to be funded through private industry councils. Those represent private industry, so we're dealing with a business philosophy. The key is *private*. That's where the jobs are. Businesses aren't human services agencies, and that's our point of view too.

This case was prepared by John A. Seeger, associate professor of management at Bentley College and Marie Rock, MBA, to serve as a basis for class discussion. Permission to republish should be obtained from the Case Research Association and from the authors. Copyright © 1987 by John A. Seeger.

For the first year and a half, it was very difficult to get that concept over to the public. It was just as difficult for those of us who worked in CETA to adjust to a business philosophy; we were used to the government point of view.

Federal guidelines originated in the Department of Labor and imposed performance measures which were monitored by the states. Funds came to the states as block grants, administered through executive offices chosen by the governors. In Massachusetts, the executive office of economic affairs channeled the funds to the service delivery area organizations such as NUPIC. The office of training and employment policy collected and reviewed performance measures from all the SDAs. Exhibit 1 reproduces one such report, showing statewide statistics. Exhibit 2 shows costs per trainee actually placed for the 15 SDAs. Washington spoke of the measurements:

> What we're doing, of course, is trying to keep our figures high—have to be out there recruiting and keeping our promises—placing our people in unsubsidized jobs. The entered employment rate has to be high and our cost per placement has to be low. We have to place people at the highest wage rate and, as we understand it for the new year, retention will also be important. We need to place people at a higher wage than they could earn before. The state sets the goals, and then we have to set our own goals in our two-year plan. In some programs it's very hard to measure achievement. In the summer youth program, for example, we're just beginning to measure changes in competence. Up to now, it's been whether they got a job. Now we're starting to administer before-and-after competency tests.

Although quantitative measures of program results were available, they did not capture the staff's perceptions of qualitative changes. Washington said:

> You get a sense of personal accomplishment, seeing people come through and changing their life cycle . . . going on through high school, through college. And some who've gone to prison, of course. I've had the whole gamut.
>
> Many clients took advantage of the system in CETA. Now that system is changed: There is more control over students and there is much less use of the grievance process. Standards are set at the beginning of each program. Clients now know what is expected of them, and what they can expect from their teachers. We try to reach some form of agreement with every client. It doesn't have to be rigid, but there has to be some kind of contract.

NUPIC's programs all documented their rules and procedures for attendance and student behavior. Exhibit 3 shows excerpts from the six-page *Student Handbook* used in the clerical skills training program. In addition to rules on punching the time clock, absences, and tardiness, NUPIC was explicit in standards of dress, use of profanity,

EXHIBIT 1 JTPA Quarterly Report on Participant Characteristics

Title: II-A   Period Covered: 10/1/83 to 6/30/84   Service Delivery Area: All Massachusetts

Line No.		Characteristics	Participants	Terminations	Entered Employment	Employment Enhancement	Average Placement Wage	Line No.
1	Total		11,441	7,690	5,465	242	$4.81	1
2	Sex	Male	5,297	4,285	3,144	122	$4.97	2
3		Female	5,514	3,405	2,321	120	$4.60	3
4	Age	14–15	81	59	5	53	$3.53	4
5		16–19	2,992	1,817	1,238	158	$4.04	5
6		20–21	1,320	925	671	31	$4.63	6
7		22–39	5,760	4,008	2,943		$5.07	7
8		40–44	539	364	256		$5.36	8
9		45–54	484	329	221		$5.29	9
10		55 & over	265	188	131		$5.50	10
11	Race/Ethnic Group	White (non-Hispanic)	6,915	4,651	3,447		$4.88	11
12		Black (non-Hispanic)	2,529	1,750	1,186		$4.75	12
13		Hispanic	1,467	949	597		$4.44	13
14		American Indian or Alaskan native	42	27	16		$5.30	14
15		Asian or Pacific Islander	488	313	219		$5.08	15
16	Education Status	School Dropout	3,738	2,619	1,673	138	$4.52	16
17		Student (high school or less)	1,205	539	361	88	$3.75	17
18		H.S. graduate or equivalent	4,706	3,315	2,488	15	$4.92	18
19		Post high school attendee	1,792	1,217	943	1	$5.52	19
20	Labor Force Status	Unemployed	9,164	6,275	4,467	132		20
21		Employed	1,065	659	513	23		21
22	Public Assistance Status	Adult cash public assistance	2,653	1,723	1,097		$4.82	22
23		a. AFDC	1,992	1,225	777		$4.78	23
24		1. WIN	849	515	328		$4.83	24
25		b. General assistance	583	438	283			25
26		c. Refugee assistance	80	60	37			26
27		Youth welfare recipient	1,301	750	454	86	$4.12	27
28	Other	U.I. Claimant	933	626	507			28
29		Limited English speaking	983	621	419		$4.68	29
30		Handicapped	1,084	747	525		$4.66	30
31		Offender	1,878	1,534	1,107		$4.64	31
32		Economically disadvantaged	11,066	7,431	5,241		$4.80	32
33		Single head of household with dependent children under 18	2,570	1,553	988			33
34		Other:						34
35		Other:						35

SOURCE: Commonwealth of Massachusetts, Executive Office of Economic Affairs.

EXHIBIT 2 Title IIA Performance Standard Comparison—Adult Cost per Entered Employment

Service Delivery Area	PY'84 Actual Performance	PY'84 Model Standard	No Governor's Factor	PY'85 Model Standard	Governor's Factor (X1.08)	PY'86 Model Standard
Area I	2,549	3,456		4,864	5,253	4,622
Area II	5,981	4,040		4,089	4,416	4,220
Area III	3,835	4,459		4,431	4,786	4,754
Area IV	5,536	3,274		5,375	5,805	4,735
Area V	4,841	3,990		4,052	4,376	4,257
Area VI	1,824	4,729		4,379	4,729	4,310
Area VII	3,363	4,837		4,877	5,267	5,619
Area VIII	5,626	4,375		4,264	4,605	4,858
Area IX	2,565	2,639		3,215	3,472	3,871
Area X	5,448	4,907		4,832	5,219	4,947
Area XI	3,026	3,777		3,279	3,541	3,674
Area XII	3,080	3,172		3,814	4,119	3,785
Area XIII	4,543	4,136		5,288	5,711	5,504
Area XIV	4,604	3,726		4,478	4,836	4,147
Area XV	5,691	2,354		4,450	4,806	4,154
Massachusetts state average	3,629	4,088		4,336	4,682	4,506
DOL national standard		5,704			5,704	4,374

PY'84 actual data used for all models. CY'83 area wage used. CY'84 wage in PY'85 model would raise average by $110. CY'85 wage in PY'86 model would raise average by $275.

EXHIBIT 3 Excerpts from *Student Handbook*

General Guidelines
1. Students are docked for tardiness.
2. Once students punch in, they are expected to go to their work stations and begin work.
3. Students are responsible for the amount of time spent in class; therefore, each student is responsible for his or her own time card.
4. Based on a six-hour training day, there are two breaks, each of *fifteen* minutes duration.
5. The lunch period is from 12–12:30 P.M. Failure to return promptly at 12:30 constitutes tardiness, and students will be docked accordingly.
6. The training day ends at 3:20 P.M.

Specific Guidelines
1. If a student is going to be absent or tardy, for any reason whatsoever, he or she *must* call in to notify the instructors *before* 9 A.M.
2. Whenever a student is tardy or absent, his or her absenteeism percentage will be affected and the following corrective measures will be taken:

Ten percent	Verbal warning issued
Fifteen percent	Written warning issued
Twenty percent	Subject to termination

3. If a student is absent from class for three or more consecutive days, a doctor's note is required to allow the student to return to class.
4. Students will receive attendance credit for holidays *only* if present in class the last day prior to the holiday and the first class day after the holiday.

eating and drinking in classrooms, gum chewing, smoking, personal use of telephones, and loud talking.

> It can be done. You have to have the mentality to understand that people *are* motivated and can be motivated to do it for themselves. To see there is some sunshine—something up there for them. That's why I think and I know it can be done if we give people an opportunity to do it. You'll still have those people who aren't going to make it. You'll always have some of those. But it's a smaller group.

In 1986, Massachusetts boasted one of the lowest unemployment rates in the country (just over 3 percent). Manpower agencies had a smaller pool of applicants. At the time when high placement rates were most difficult to achieve, manpower agencies were under pressure from Gramm-Rudman budget cuts at the federal level and from administrative cuts at the state level. Within the next few months, Massachusetts' 15 service delivery areas would be consolidated into 10. Comparative measures were public information, so NUPIC staff knew they stood above average now. But performance in the next quarter would be crucial to the survival decisions at the state level. Washington commented:

> Gramm-Rudman is devastating. In the first cutback we lost seven people. Still the same work has to be done. The remaining staff is shuffled around and has to take on the burden. And more cutbacks may still be coming.
>
> The heat is on all the agencies. Business is slow for us and probably slow for the others. We all need clients coming in the door. We're all in competition. We have to be more aggressive than they are. We're out hunting for grants from a variety of sources, to hold the staff together—to keep the people operating.
>
> Our two-year plan concerns JTPA funding. Grants are outside of that. That's where we can be aggressive. We already have grants from the Department of Education and the Department of Public Welfare. We're proposing to run training programs for local business groups, and for trade associations. In order to do this our staff has to be flexible, to keep up with changing times.
>
> There is a real change going on in our economy, in terms of service jobs. We're trying to train for the jobs that will be available. In the future, the clients may have no choice. There's going to be competition, even for the service jobs.

NUPIC also faced competition from other local institutions. The public school system, under pressure from state government to reduce the number of dropouts, had recently incorporated special programs to serve young people. Community colleges in the area offered training programs in clerical skills, drafting, adult basic education and high school equivalency education. Sarah Washington offered her opinion:

The public school program is very good, but the clients have to be very motivated for that. We do the best job for our clients. The others are good, but we do the best.

Just as economic times were changing, so were parts of the social environment. Washington went on:

With the economy as good as it is, we're dealing with people at lower levels of formal education, and it's very very difficult. We're going to have to adjust our curricula—slow them down and do more individualized training.

We now get people who really have problems and need to be worked with before they can make it on their own. There are reasons for their problems—family history, lack of examples in their own families. They haven't any idea what it's like to work because they've never worked. We need to give preemployment services. Train them that they have to get up every morning at the same time—that it's important to call into work—that they have to do what's expected of them—that no one is going to do it for them—to leave the barrage of excuses at home—you have to be *reliable*. And this *can* be taught. But it takes time. We help but they have to do things too. It's a contract. They have to prepare themselves. You have to stop pampering them.

But why not give them the help? It's so much better than giving them furniture to sit down on at home and be comfortable.

15. North Urban Manpower Administration (B)

Carol Wong sipped her tea and reflected upon her long association with federally sponsored manpower training programs. After working over 10 years in such programs, with 7 of them in management positions, she was considering moving to private industry. A friend who worked in a Fortune 500 company had told her of an opening for a training manager and Wong had concluded, as did many of her government colleagues, that if she could work for agencies governed by the Comprehensive Employment and Training Act (CETA), then she could work anywhere. She wondered, though, if she could make the adjustment from working with essentially underprivileged individuals to working with people who by comparison were worlds apart.

It was January 1983, and NUMA staff had just learned of the impending replacement of CETA by the new Job Training Partnership Act. It was clear that over the next year most programs would change dramatically; some might even be dissolved. It appeared probable that some manpower administrative centers would be consolidated. Carol Wong and many of her colleagues, recognizing that their jobs were in jeopardy anyway, were considering changing vocations. She reflected upon the purpose of manpower programs and the difficulties with their implementation.

> CETA has been regarded by many legislators as being a cure-all to the nation's unemployment problem, but it was really only a stopgap measure. If you were to look at the old federal regulations, you might see the characteristically verbose explanations of the program's purpose, like: "To recruit, hire, and train all persons meeting such-and-such eligibility requirements as specified under Title II of the Comprehensive Employment and Training Act and to actively promote and expand entry of such persons into all job classifications regardless of race, color, religion, sex, age," and so on. The program really seemed to be a wonderful idea. It actively took into account the Civil Rights Act of 1964, equal employment opportunity laws and the concept of affirmative action. It gave many people a chance to attain a higher level of education, such as a high

This case was prepared by Marie Rock, MEA, and John A. Seeger, associate professor of management at Bentley College, to serve as a basis for class discussion. Permission to republish should be obtained from the Case Research Association and from the authors. Copyright © 1986 by John A. Seeger.

school diploma or a training certificate, and it particularly helped female heads of household—those who had been left by their husbands—to gain some confidence and skills, provided that they completed their work or training program.

NORTH URBAN MANPOWER ADMINISTRATION

North Urban Manpower Administration (NUMA) was formed from a unification of several government-sponsored social and employment programs within the city. Funding for NUMA, as for hundreds of similar agencies throughout the United States, came directly to its city from the Department of Labor under the Comprehensive Employment and Training Act of 1973.

Housed in a low-rent, two-story brick building, a former office supplies warehouse, NUMA served the residents of an old textile manufacturing city and 10 neighboring towns in northern Massachusetts. By the time of its inception many of the old industries, which had attracted thousands of immigrants, had gradually died out. Although there were still some clothing manufacturers in the area, much of the industry had been damaged through the introduction of low-cost imports into the American marketplace. Within NUMA's territory, thousands of stitchers, cutters, sewing machine mechanics, and other blue-collar workers were permanently laid off. According to Nick Giovanis, an employment counselor who had worked at NUMA for several years:

> Whenever a major layoff happened, it effectively split up a lot of families. More women who had never worked in their lives became the heads of their households. And those who *did* have work experience, such as stitching, were not in demand. Many men found that they couldn't get a job because they didn't have the requisite technical skills. These people represented two of our recruited target groups: the technologically displaced and female heads of households. There were others such as Vietnam-era veterans, handicapped persons, minorities, people who had been seasonally laid off, and so on. It was our job to see that these people received some kind of marketable training; or if they hadn't worked before or had poor work histories for a variety of reasons, then we tried to provide them with short-term work experience so that they could develop the skills and self-assurance to find and hold onto a job.

In 1978, NUMA received the highest level of funding it was ever to obtain: approximately $3 million in federal funds. Most of the money went to clients who were paid a weekly stipend to attend one of five specific programs. NUMA's service area included a population in excess of 250,000. The city alone was home to more than 100,000 people and the director of NUMA was appointed by its mayor, as provided for within the CETA federal regulations. NUMA served approximately 2,000 adult applicants and 1,200 youth applicants in 1978, most of whom became participants once they were deemed eligible for a training or employment program.

Fluctuating funding levels of CETA affected the organization's structure, its staffing, and its service levels dramatically from one quarter to the next. The program itself was continually threatened with congressional refusal to continue its operation in the next fiscal period. NUMA often lacked funds for basics such as pens and paper; employees provided their own.

INTAKE AND ASSESSMENT

Under CETA rules, each NUMA applicant was required to complete a 19-page form, documenting proof of residency, underemployment or unemployment status, handicap status if applicable, and so on. The most controversial requirement was proof of annual income. Applicants were required to provide enough information for an intake clerk to determine if they met the guidelines for being economically disadvantaged, that is, at either the poverty level or at certain percentages of the lower living standard index (LLSI). An applicant who was able to prove handicap status was automatically deemed eligible. Each intake clerk at NUMA kept at least one 80-page copy of the CETA regulations in his or her desk in order to answer eligibility questions. Many applicants exceeded the income guidelines and were turned away while others were extremely "system-wise" and were able to work their way through loopholes in the eligibility requirements. Many applicants considered themselves "entitled" to whatever NUMA could offer, and were prepared to file formal complaints if services were denied.

Petra Diomedes, intake and assessment manager, recounted her experience with one of NUMA's more challenging applicants:

> I remember one instance in which a businessman who had had a successful partnership wanted to get five of his seven kids into the summer youth employment program. He drove up in his Mercedes station wagon and herded the kids into the intake office. He gave us this song and dance about how his partner had taken off with the revenues from the business after changing the locks. The businessman claimed that he hadn't had any income for the past seven months and that his children were therefore qualified for the program.
>
> But, the burden of proof is always on the applicant. When questioned, this businessman eventually admitted that there was actually some sort of court injunction prohibiting him from entering his former business office and that, in fact, his father had loaned him several thousand dollars on which to live and support his family. I required that he produce a notarized copy of the loan agreement, the court injunction order, and all bank

statements and passbooks, along with a copy of the previous year's income tax statements. It turned out that the businessman *was* eligible and that his teenagers were employed for that summer in the youth program. The representative from the Department of Labor who monitored the program was very satisfied with the documentation. After all, we *did* prevent even the appearance of fraud by the client.

After being determined eligible, an applicant became a "participant" and advanced to the assessment phase, to be interviewed by a screening counselor who recorded work history and stated abilities and interests. The screening counselor might refer the client to another agency, to CETA work programs and services, or onto the assessment counselor for further evaluation services, especially if the client expressed an interest in a training program.

ADULT WORK EXPERIENCE (AWE) PROGRAM

At NUMA, adult work experience was a six-month public employment program geared specifically toward participants who had never been employed or who had been out of the work force for more than one or two years and needed to reestablish basic work habits. Usually clients assigned to this program needed the most supportive services available under CETA, such as additional counseling, adult basic education, child-care services, and a very supportive public agency which had been selected as a work site. The typical client might be someone who had been referred by the state welfare department, area correctional institution, or mental health facility. Nick Giovanis described his experiences as a counselor for the program.

We would place inexperienced people in low-level jobs in a public agency such as a police department or public housing agency. Usually they would do things like basic typing or yard care. Sometimes they were able to take on a lot of responsibility and work themselves into a long-term public job, but rarely did this sufficiently prepare them for a job in private industry.

They were supervised by people from the public agencies and their time was routinely tracked, but these supervisors had no incentive to really monitor a client's hours and work activities. After all, the AWE client was being paid with federal tax dollars and not that worksite's municipal monies. So if a client wanted to stay home with her sick children, the supervisor usually looked the other way. I saw this often enough whenever I visited certain worksites. We tried to impress our clients with the fact that this was *not* acceptable behavior in the real world. But what incentive did they have? Welfare represents security and a definite way of life. It was just expecting too much of us and of them to try to break the dependency. We had no authority to discipline people as an employer would in private industry; clients could file a grievance at the drop of a hat if they felt pressured by their counselor.

PUBLIC SERVICE EMPLOYMENT (PSE) PROGRAM

This program was designed to provide employment to people who already had job skills but who were laid off during economic recessions. In most cases they were rehired by their former employer nine months to a year later. In many ways, PSE was very similar to AWE in that the client was placed at a similar, if not the same, worksite as the AWE clients. More often than not, a person applying for a PSE position at a particular municipal worksite might have a relative or friend working there. Federal regulations prohibiting nepotism attempted to guard against the appearance of favoritism of any kind.

In general, the maximum length of time a client could spend in PSE was 18 months; this was reduced to 1 year in early 1980. The typical PSE client was assumed by worksite supervisors to be a step up in skill level and maturity from AWE clients. For many counselors, however, the difference was negligible. Counselor Pat Murphy recounted this experience.

> One of my clients worked at a local elderly services agency as a file clerk. One day she came to my office—I had already been called by her supervisor who had reported her absence. Anyway, she was disoriented and had a bloody gash on her left cheek. She told me that her ex-boyfriend had broken down the door to her apartment—he had actually removed the hinges—and then he had slashed her with a disposable razor and pushed her into the bathtub where she had really knocked her head. He had threatened to come back and kill her if she didn't agree to live with him. I took her to the hospital and stayed with her for about four hours until one of her brothers finally came to pick her up. She had refused to file charges against her boyfriend and I never saw her again. She left town. This sort of crisis was common and expected in AWE, but not in PSE.

Alleged abuses in the public service employment program drew widespread media attention in the late 1970s, and mounting political pressure resulted in cancellation of the program in the closing months of the Carter administration in 1980. Current PSE client employees were terminated then and offered job development services; NUMA staff members were reorganized in a general reduction in force.

CLASSROOM TRAINING PROGRAM

Under certain funding titles of CETA, NUMA was able to provide promising clients with a variety of programs and services. Services included tutoring, academic and career counseling. Classroom programs ranged from English as a second language instruction to technical training, such as computer technician, operator, or programmer training. As with other programs, each client was allotted a training stipend based on the amount of hours spent in training per week. These stipends amounted to approximately $85 per week, depending upon attendance.

Although classroom training was typically no more than 30 hours per week, participants were not allowed to supplement their subsidized training income with a non-CETA-funded job because this would mean that they had attained employment in the private sector, requiring their termination under CETA rules.

Sometimes a client was permitted to enroll in more than one training program. This would be especially applicable to a client who lacked academic skills to advance through a technical or skilled training program. For example, a client who lacked basic education, that is, less than the eighth grade, would be enrolled in an adult basic education program. Upon completion of ABE, which might take from three to nine months, the client might advance to a general equivalency diploma program for an additional three to six months. The GED is a state-certified diploma and is the equivalent of a high school diploma. After attaining this diploma, the client's classroom training counselor could recommend the client for technical or skilled training, which might be for anything from air conditioning mechanic to computer programmer.

Clients who were able to successfully complete a technical training program that required above average verbal, quantitative, and analytical skills were often able to enter positions in private industry that offered substantial starting salaries.

Technical training programs were the most sought after programs at NUMA and therefore their selection criteria were the most stringent, requiring that the classroom training counselor and the assessment counselor meet in a closed conference, after the client was interviewed and tested, to discuss the likelihood that he or she would successfully complete the program. After this conference, the client met with both counselors together, to review test results and the counselors' recommendations, which might or might not include a referral to the desired program. In the event that the client was dissatisfied with the recommendations, then he or she could appeal to the training manager, and/or file a grievance.

ON-THE-JOB TRAINING (O-J-T) PROGRAM

On-the-job training was considered to be the most successful of all the training programs funded through CETA with respect to placing clients permanently in private industry. O-J-T counselors contacted area employers to negotiate a contract in which a client would learn a skilled trade on the job over a nine-month period. During that time, half of the client's wages would be paid for by the private employer, the other half by NUMA with CETA funds. The wages were set by the employers in accordance with their regular wage guidelines, not those of the federal government. Some clients were able to earn over $10 an hour in O-J-T. On the other hand, employers had the authority to hire, discipline, and terminate clients according to their own procedures as long as the equal employment opportunity law was not transgressed. If, at the end of the contracted training period, the private employer was satisfied with the performance of the client, then he or she was hired permanently by the employer. Clients who went this route for training were usually not seen again by NUMA counselors for additional programs. Sometimes, though, the bureaucracy at NUMA thwarted the ambitions of both the clients and the counselors. Beth Hansen was an O-J-T counselor for three years at NUMA before achieving a management position. She described a "typical" encounter with bureaucracy that bore some tragic results.

We had set up an O-J-T for a client who had a record for burglary. George had a very engaging personality and he was well liked by NUMA counselors due to his sincerity and because he was putting in a lot of effort to become employed. He was hired for the O-J-T but because of a delay in the paperwork in another department, his starting date was put off. He asked me and another counselor if we could do something to speed up the processing because he was getting desperate for money and he was fearful that he would have to resort to illegal activities.

You have to understand that he hadn't eaten in two days and was living out of an abandoned car. That was his address: abandoned Chevy on such and such street. You had to see this young man. Whenever he had an appointment he was punctual and pleasant, and he always wore the same clothes when he came to NUMA but they were always clean. He managed to keep himself and his clothes clean by using the public lavatories, and a nurse at City Hospital gave him haircuts. We referred him to the Salvation Army for food and shelter, but he had had some personal conflicts there with other clients so he didn't go, and he couldn't collect welfare because he didn't have an official address. "Abandoned Chevy" just didn't qualify.

Anyway, we put pressure on people in the delaying department by going over their heads to their manager and we were not liked for doing this, but as far as we were concerned, the stakes were high. Well, two days later we heard on the local radio station that George had broken into a furniture store and had been caught. A clerk in the department that held us up said that at least now George would be getting his food and shelter. To top that off, three months later we read in the newspaper that George had been killed in a drug deal that turned sour while he was an inmate in a notoriously overcrowded correctional institution. It's things like this, clients who were crushed by the system, directly or indirectly, that make the job seem futile at times.

Although the O-J-T program was purported to have a high place-ment retention rate, it didn't receive as much CETA funding as most of the other programs and services.

JOB DEVELOPMENT SERVICES

Job development services were provided to all eligible CETA clients who were "participants," whether or not they entered and completed a program. If a client dropped out of a work or a training program, then job development was immediately initiated by his or her program counselor in collaboration with a job development counselor. Like-wise, if during the assessment phase it was determined by either the screening or assessment counselor that the participant already pos-sessed marketable job skills, then he or she would be routed directly to job development services. Only in exceptional cases, as when a client produced medical certification of a new disability, were the job development services waived. Otherwise, each client was expected to participate actively in these services, the last phase of programs and services funded through CETA and administered by NUMA.

At NUMA, job development was stressed as the final instrument which could catapult a client into a job. All counselors were required to work with the job placement specialists in developing job leads for their clients. As a part of job development, program counselors deter-mined if their clients needed supplemental services such as job-seek-ing skills (JSS) or job retention skills (JRS) seminars, which were originally conducted by local consulting firms. By 1981, these semi-nars were phased out in favor of individual counseling by NUMA staff.

In general, job development consisted of allowing each client a limited use of telephones to set up job interviews with potential em-ployers; use of the "job market" bulletin board on which were posted selected ads cut from the "help wanted" sections of area newspapers; and the client's follow-up of job leads provided by NUMA's place-ment specialists. These specialists worked with as many as 60 to 100 clients, attempting to place them during the 90 days following com-pletion of a final program or service. After that time period, federal regulations required that the client be terminated completely from the CETA program and services.

Clients received no stipends during the job development phase, but frequently put little effort into their own searches. They com-monly expected NUMA to provide private-sector or municipal jobs as a matter of entitlement. In an effort to place responsibility for finding work squarely on the client's shoulders, NUMA developed an "assis-tance agreement" to be signed by all clients (this form is reproduced

---

EXHIBIT 1 Job Development and Placement Assistance Agreement

I understand that the intended result of my CETA participation is to change my current status as a temporary and subsidized CETA participant to that of a permanent and unsubsidized employee.

To this end, I agree to work with my developer and placement specialist to secure unsubsidized employment. This cooperation on my part will consist of actual participation in all job placement and job development services provided for me. It is further understood that I will not refuse any suitable job interview or job offer provided it meets the criteria established by the subgrantee. The criteria is defined as:

1. Suitable occupations consistent with client's skill level, training, and prior experience in accordance with the demands of the labor market.
2. The minimum wage upon placement will be $3.50 per hour, except for the following:
   a. A placement wage of less than $3.50 will be acceptable if the placement is within an occupation that has a prevailing occupational wage of less than $3.50 per hour.
   b. A job with a wage of less than $3.50 per hour must include such fringe benefits, employer retention wage, union benefits, or other factors that would enhance the quality of the job.

I further understand that failure to abide by this agreement on my part will result in termination from the CETA program and may result in disqualification for unemployment insurance benefits. I further understand that my CETA participation is not to be considered guaranteed employment and that the efforts of the subgrantee are directed toward placing me in unsubsidized employment at the earliest possible opportunity. I understand and accept the conditions of this agreement

_____   _____
Participant Signature   Date

_____   _____
Placement Specialist   Date

SOURCE: North American Manpower Administration.

---

as Exhibit 1). After about two years' use, the form was dropped because of its legal implications.

Placement manager Sarah Washington commented on the frustrations induced when clients circumvented the system.

> We had one man who was known to be a highly skilled small-appliance repairman. Well, he signed this assistance agreement and went on interviews to all the employers we had contacted. The trouble is that during every interview he just sat like a lump and showed no interest at all in the job, and an employer won't hire someone like that. So he was never hired. He just stayed on welfare and worked under the table. After all, he had 10 kids and a wife to take care of. He would sit here and explain to me that the job couldn't possibly support 12 people, but that taking it would mean losing welfare support. He would do everything the signed agreement demanded: He'd go on every interview we arranged—but he wouldn't answer the employers' questions with anything more than a mumble.

PLACEMENT RATES

As with other CETA-funded agencies in the United States, NUMA's financial survival depended upon its placement rate, which represented the number of positive terminations of clients. According to the federal regulations, client terminations were categorized within three general headings: positive terminations, such as "secured permanent employment" or "entered the armed forces"; neutral terminations such as "moved from the area"; and negative terminations such as "refused to continue."

There were several CETA-funded agencies in Massachusetts, each covering a particular geographic section of the state and each in competition with others regarding the placement rate. If an agency's placement rate was low relative to a neighboring agency, then that agency would probably acquire the territory of the low performer, which would then be closed. Job developer Jake Smith commented on the drive for a high placement rate at NUMA.

> We took some placements which in my mind are ethically questionable. I remember my boss telling me to take a positive termination on a client who had only worked at one place for an hour and then quit. I thought the boss was joking. After all, there was still enough time for us to work with the client on getting some viable employment leads. But, no, the placement rate had to be raised, so I was directed to give him positive termination status. That's the way it was to maintain our administrative centers. You have to realize that if our territory was ever taken over by another agency, then the possibility of being transferred was slim. Every agency suffered from the budget cuts and a threat of a takeover meant that our jobs were at stake.
>
> Sometimes trying to place our clients was a continuous exercise in futility. We devised a method of counteracting the futility when we finally realized a different way to increase our placement rate and to help people at the same time. Instead of increasing our positive placements, we began to reduce our negative results by excluding the clients least likely to succeed. It's called "creaming." That is, we referred the really hard-to-place people to other agencies like Massachusetts Rehabilitation Commission. Those who were marginal risks were sometimes referred to the Mass Division of Employment Security. We concentrated on helping those people who already had the motivation and skills to get a job on their own. A lot of times we knew we were training people who could get a job *without* the training. It's too bad that we had to take this attitude, but with budget cuts always hanging over our heads, we creamed. We never had problems placing a laid-off teacher or a computer programmer.

While creaming was accepted unofficially as the preferred method of ensuring placements at NUMA, there were other ways such as official loopholes in the regulations. One of the youth work experience (YWE) counselors described a well-used loophole.

We had a sparse YWE program except in the summer, when we were deluged with kids. The rest of the year we got part- and full-time employment for about 80 school dropouts. And if an older teenager completed one of the youth programs and then decided to return to school, that person would be counted as a positive termination. This was a particular boon when close to 1,500 teenagers completed the summer youth employment program and returned to school each fall. If the teenager was 18 or 19, then he or she could be counted as an adult placement. And that's what happened: Adult job development services robbed the youth program of its placements.

RETENTION RATES

Retention records were not required by the federal regulations. Informal tracking of clients by program managers and counselors happened on an infrequent and unsustained basis. Placement manager Sarah Washington noted that many NUMA staff members never saw the results of their training and counseling efforts.

I'm a career person in manpower, and I've *seen* it work. But it takes years and years. I know a *doctor* who started out in the old Office of Economic Opportunity program as a trainee. A couple of lawyers . . . many college graduates. I've seen these programs change people's lives.

Most of our staff, though, only work here three or four years. That's not long enough to see what happens. It's too bad. Staff people tend to burn out. They get a double whammy, from the clients on one side and the administration on the other.

DISCIPLINARY AND GRIEVANCE PROCEDURES

Adverse Action Procedures

The nature of NUMA's participants made it likely that corrective measures or disciplinary actions would be necessary during the program. Extensive documentation was essential to justify any adverse action dealing with attitude problems, lack of training, interpersonal difficulties, or patterns of unexcused absences. Warnings or disciplinary actions were required under CETA rules to be recorded in triplicate, including details on the infraction and corrective measures taken and proposed. Either the form of this record or its content might be subject to grievance.

In general, before being placed on probation, suspension, or termination, a client received a written warning from the employer or training agent. This warning outlined the steps to which the client, the employer/training agent, and a NUMA representative complied prior to the implementation of any adverse action. A classroom-training counselor voiced his opinion of the procedure's effectiveness.

You would think that the disciplinary procedure would be straightforward and that some immediate action could be taken. But that's not how it really is. It is a convoluted system that does nothing to resolve the situation. The client always comes up with some sob story for not being able to attend the informal conference. Everyone has to juggle their schedules and sometimes the issue is dropped altogether.

Grievance Procedures

The grievance procedure at NUMA was also designed in accordance with federal regulations. Each applicant at NUMA was given a copy of *How to File a Grievance,* along with the 19-page CETA application. Documentation that the applicant had received the written grievance procedures was recorded by the intake clerk on a form which was then signed by the applicant. Although counselors and other staff members tried to resolve issues and conflicts at the lowest level possible, the client was never overtly dissuaded from filing a grievance by a NUMA staff member; to do so could instigate a civil lawsuit. NUMA insured any staff member who had regular contact with the public for $100,000 liability.

Once a client initiated the grievance procedure by filing a grievance with NUMA's affirmative action officer, and notice was filed with the appropriate parties, a formal hearing took place at the local level. This hearing was tape recorded and all parties could be represented by counsel and supported by witnesses if they chose to do so. After the hearing, the director of NUMA and counsel made a determination, including any corrective action to be taken by NUMA and employers/ training agents such as the reinstatement of the client into a program, payment of back wages, damages, etc. All affected parties were then notified of the determination. If the client still felt aggrieved after this, he or she could escalate the grievance to the federal level.

Carol Wong, training manager, shared her impressions of the procedure.

It's like living in a glass house. We are really reluctant to put any pressure on trouble-making clients to conform to the rules. Ironically, the clients who need some disciplinary action are the ones we're afraid to discipline because of the grievance procedure. We had one client who hopped from program to program. Everyone hated to deal with him. In the end, he filed a grievance, just as we expected.

CONCLUSION

Carol Wong, still considering the training manager position in private industry, commented on her career.

You know, this opportunity has really made me sit back and think about where I've been and where I'm going with my career. I never really thought of working here as a career, anyway; I've always thought of it as some sort of mission. It took my friends to make me remember that there was a considerable amount of danger to working with some clients. I've been threatened with physical violence a number of times by people I turned away from training programs. I've had clients who have put their fists through walls, pounded on desks, threatened to bomb the building, followed me out to my car, and so on. Other clients have deteriorated into psychotic states, complete with a variety of hallucinations. But most are striving to rise up from the state of depression that people fall into when they have been unemployed for months or years.

If you asked me if I like it, I would have to say no to the bureaucracy and yes to the people. I love finding out about people. I have conducted over 3,000 interviews and I have met people from all over the world—Southeast Asians, Middle Easterners, Europeans, South Americans, just a great variety of interesting people.

And I have met and hopefully helped people who have been at the door of hell, like the 33-year-old toothless bag lady who washed her hair in the toilet of the ladies' room, or the man who was looking for his first job after spending 20 years in prison.

All in all, I have to say that my colleagues and I are regularly faced with some dilemmas that are atypical, not your everyday fare. Your own standards, your values, everything that you have selectively assimilated from your parents, teachers, and significant others comes into play. And if your standards are in deep conflict with the system, well, then you decide whether to stay or to leave.

Higher Education

16.　Cleveland State University

Cleveland State University is an urban institution, and the only state university in the Cleveland metropolitan area.

Created by the Ohio General Assembly in 1964 to provide Clevelanders with a quality education at a reasonable cost, the University is 1 of 10 institutions of higher education in Cuyahoga County, Ohio's most populous area. Tuition is about one third that of the area's private institutions and more than twice that of the community colleges. The university offers undergraduate and graduate programs through its College of Arts and Sciences, Business Administration, Education, Engineering, Law, and Urban Affairs. Much of its faculty research, public service activities, and instructional programs relate to its urban environment. The College of Urban Affairs directly addresses urban concerns in the Cleveland community.

Almost all of the university's 17,500 students commuted in 1977; less than 2 percent lived on campus. About 87 percent of its students were from Cuyahoga County; about 10 percent from nearby Medina, Summit, Portage, Geauga, and Ashtabula counties.

THE PROBLEM

In the mid-1970s, demographic studies showed that the number of traditional college-age youths was declining at a greater rate in Northeast Ohio than in the state or nation. Projections indicated a 50 percent decline in the number of high school graduates by 1995 in Cuyahoga and contiguous counties, and a 15.7 percent overall population drop in Cuyahoga County by 1990. Only the 30–34 age group was expected to grow.

More than 90 percent of the university's students fell into the 15–24 age group. This group was expected to begin declining significantly by 1985. This decline would have a twofold impact on the funding of Cleveland State University: a decrease in fees received from students, and an even greater decrease in subsidy received from the state of Ohio. Moreover, competition for students among Ohio

This case was prepared by Eleanor Schwartz, Vice Chancellor for Academic Affairs, the University of Missouri, Kansas City, and Don Scotton, Cleveland State University.

colleges and universities was intensifying with increased advertising and other recruiting techniques.

A second dimension of the problem derived from the newness of Cleveland State University. The youngest of all the institutions of higher education in the Cleveland metropolitan area, it has a lesser identity than the other institutions.

INTERIM ACTION

The university president assembled a task force to evaluate the situation. Upon recommendation of the task force's study, he appointed a university recruitment committee of faculty and administrators to assess and improve ongoing student recruitment efforts and to develop new strategies. The committee also was to enlist faculty and administrative recruitment support and to encourage faculty awareness of the importance of program responsiveness and adaptation to the community needs.

COMMITTEE CONCLUSIONS

The Committee, with a recruitment strategy focus, immediately began a situation analysis to determine ongoing recruitment efforts, student and other perceptions toward the university, and significant factors in students' choices of colleges/universities. Recruitment and retention experiences were assessed to identify areas for improvement of current efforts and for direction in the development of other approaches. Student categories analyzed included (1) admitted applicants who enrolled/did not enroll, (2) transfers, (3) freshmen who continued into their sophomore year, (4) withdrawals, and (5) underrepresented target groups (e.g., minorities and adults).

To facilitate faculty support and to encourage awareness of program responsiveness and adaptation needed to attract and retain students, the committee formally established a faculty liaison in each college. The faculty liaison in each college evaluated efforts that related to the university admissions office; reviewed college attrition rates; and pinpointed areas for improvement and/or new approaches. Faculty liaisons were expected to accomplish several other goals; for example, faculty involvement in and awareness of the need for recruitment and retention efforts; better interpersonal communication (academic advising, career counseling) between faculty and students; and information exchange among academic and nonacademic units.

As a result of a situational analysis,[1] the committee changed its focus from a recruitment to marketing approach. To maintain a strong enrollment position as a young university which needed to build a

---

[1] See Appendixes A–H for graphic depiction of areas the committee analyzed.

definitive quality image, the committee identified five fundamental factors the university must address.

1. Overall coordinated integration of the university unit's communications efforts.
2. Ongoing systematic information upon which policy, program, and recruitment decisions are based.
3. An established university position for long-run direction and image building.
4. Focused communication strategies that appeal to target markets.
5. Satisfaction of people's educational needs and concerns through program content, delivery modes, and student services.

A marketing approach was deemed crucial as a framework for integrated actions that achieved long-run cumulative results (e.g., image and reputation; student attraction, enrollment, satisfaction, and retention; and therefore the greatest return for dollars spent).

The committee recommended to the president that the marketing function be incorporated formally into the university's organizational operation. To implement this, the committee further recommended the appointment of a marketing director. A knowledgeable, experienced marketer was considered essential for effective ongoing development, coordinated implementation, control, and evaluation of the university's diverse marketing efforts. Specifically it was recommended that the director initiate an information system tailored to specific recruitment/retention information needs; and a position statement from which an image strategy could be developed.

Within overall university objectives, the director should work directly with academic and nonacademic units to tailor plans to target markets. These plans should be based upon internal retention and external market information for strategies to take advantage of new and/or existing market opportunities.

Annual marketing plans should move the university forward each year toward long-range goals. These plans should include a focus communications campaign (that combined mass media, internal, and interpersonal contacts) integrated by an overall theme that increased awareness of the many advantages derived from attending Cleveland State University.

DECISION DILEMMA

The president, contemplating the committee's report and recommendation, had several questions.

Can a marketing approach work in a university setting? The university community traditionally views "recruitment" as the sole responsibility of admissions staff and "marketing" as either advertising, publicity, or public relations—something that only university relations staff do.

Should the university attempt to market itself? Can a university use the same marketing concepts and techniques profit oriented firms use? Does it require appointment of a marketing director?

What decision should I make? What difference will a marketing approach make?

APPENDIX A Phase I: Activities and Recommendations

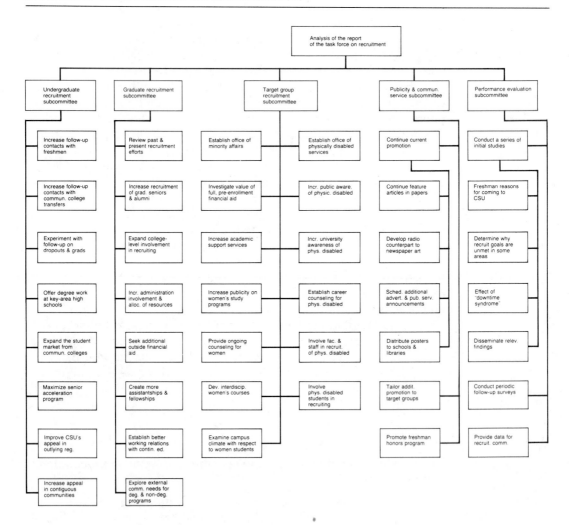

APPENDIX B Phase II: Activities and Recommendations

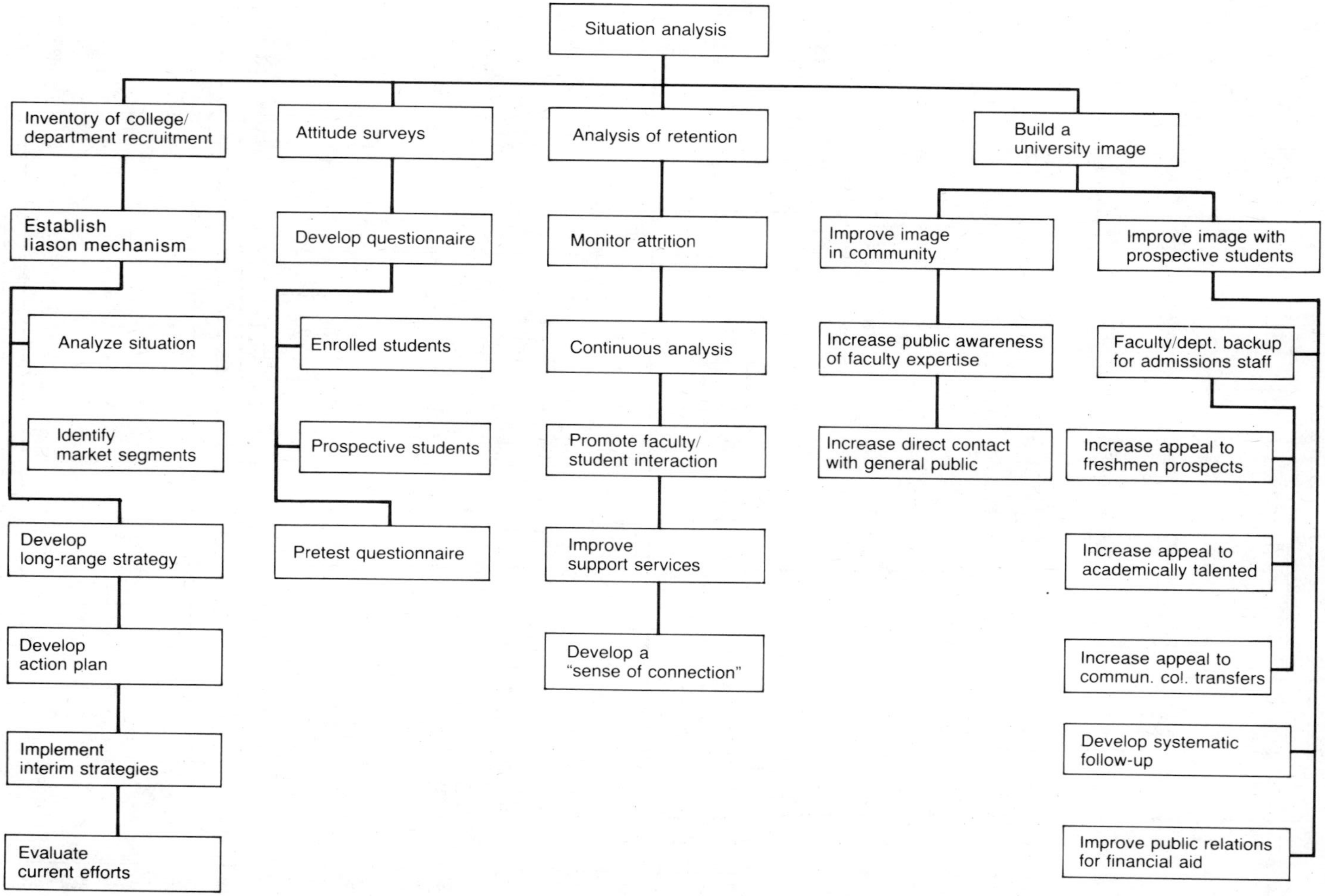

- Implementation of phase I and II recommendations
  - Analysis and long-range
    - Under-represented target groups
      - Adults (particularly women)
      - Analysis of 1977 survey findings
      - Minorities
        - Analysis of minority enrollment
        - Review of minority retention
      - Recommendations for improved support services
      - Recommendations for direct marketing
      - Strategies for targeted marketing
    - Data base
      - Analysis of surveys
      - Admitted but not enrolling prospects
      - CSU freshmen
      - Transfer students
      - Withdrawing students
      - Graduate students
      - Strategy for ongoing data base
  - College liaison and recruitment
    - First college
      - Arts and sciences
      - Recruitment committee
    - Faculty/student recruitment committee
    - Graduate studies
      - Business administration
      - Identification of goals
    - Support for department and college recruitment
    - Law
      - Education
      - Recruitment coordinator
    - Admissions Council
    - Urban affairs
      - Engineering
      - Determination of market segments
    - Communications officer
  - Long-range action plan
    - Coordinated integrated marketing
    - Marketing director
    - Institutional position
    - Focused communication
    - Alternative delivery modes
  - Recruitment of new students
    - Letter campaign half day on campus
    - Increased print medium communication
    - Enhancement and consolidation of CSI image
    - Coordination of publications
    - Increased radio/TV exposure
  - Retention of enrolled students
    - Increased opportunity for interpersonal involvement

APPENDIX D Phase IV Plan

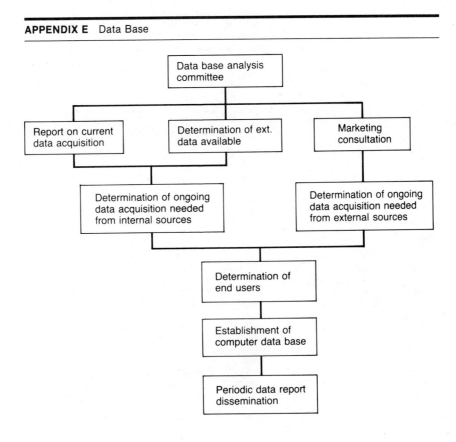

APPENDIX E Data Base

APPENDIX F Position Statement

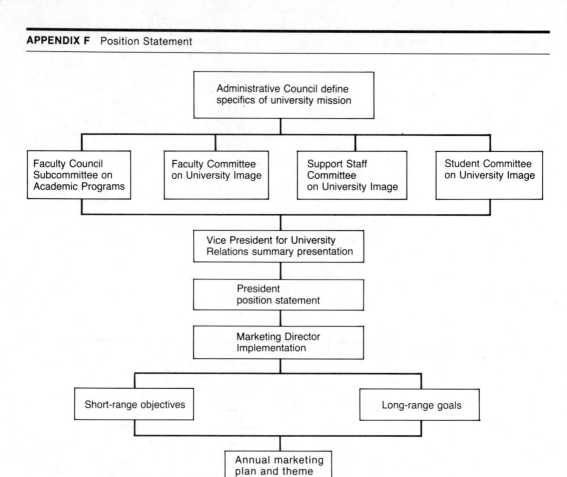

APPENDIX G Focused Communication

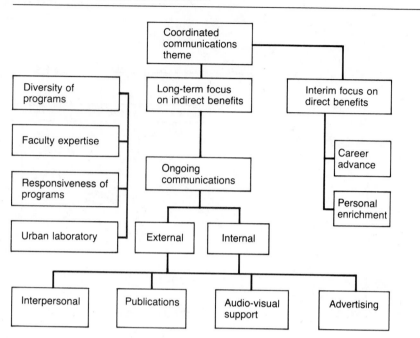

APPENDIX H Communications Strategy, 1980–81

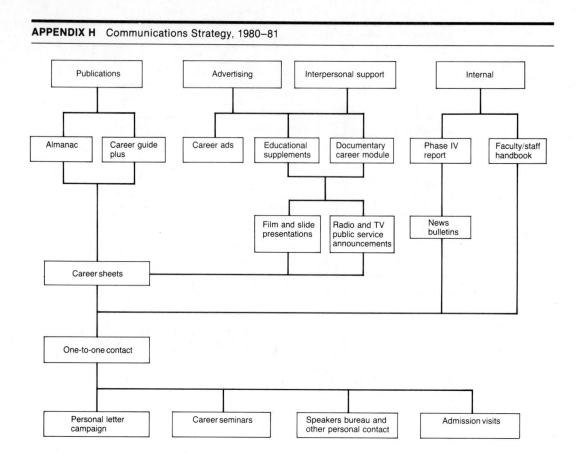

17. Central State University: Resource Reallocation in Times of Uncertainty

After more than 50 years of successful operation Central State University (CSU) faced a bleak picture with the opening of the 1986–87 academic year. The Texas state legislature was convened in special session, with the House and Senate deadlocked on whether to enact massive cuts in state services including higher education; levy new state taxes; approve other forms of revenue enhancement; or combine the measures to cope with a projected $3.5 billion shortfall in state revenue.

Founded as a state teachers' college, Central State gained university status during the decade of the 1960s and enjoyed consistent increases in enrollment due in large part to its reputation for academic excellence, beautiful residential campus, and proximity to major metropolitan areas. University enrollment grew from 2,000 students in 1960 to over 12,000 by mid-decade of the 1980s to make Central State one of the major state universities governed by its own board of regents and outside the University of Texas and Texas A&M systems.

THE STATE BUDGET CRISIS

The Texas legislature budgeted to spend just under $6 billion for higher education in the 1986–87 biennium (beginning September 1, 1985, and ending August 31, 1987), compared to $5.8 billion in 1984–85 and $4.7 billion in 1982–83. The rate of increase dropped from 22.7 percent to 3.2 percent as state revenue growth would no longer permit the same level of enhancement. The share higher education was to receive of the state budget fell also, from 18.8 to 16.3 percent, because of other state spending priorities. Legislators had already raised a number of state fees, including tuition rates at universities and professional schools to balance the state budget. Tuition rates had remained the same for nearly three decades, with the result that Texas taxpayers paid a handsome subsidy for a student's education.

But the budget failed to stay balanced. The collapse of the OPEC price structure—which dropped the spot market selling price of oil from more than $26 per barrel to a low of under $10 per barrel in only a few weeks—precipitated a state budget crisis with the total dollar amount of the deficit described as a "moving target." The target was first pegged in early 1986 at a projected $1.3 billion loss in state tax revenue and subsequently revised upward to a $3.5 billion projected loss to occur during the remaining year of the biennium. The biennial budget suffering erosion was set by the Texas state legislature in its regular session convened in January 1985. It was only shortly after the budget period began in September 1985, therefore, that the forces were set in motion for the OPEC crisis.

The governor called for a voluntary 13 percent spending cut by state agencies in February 1986, when the deficit appeared to be $1.3 billion. In that he also requested no layoffs of personnel or cuts in programs, there was mixed response to the appeal. Faced later with the more dire predictions, however, the Texas legislature was called into special legislative session by the governor in August 1986, to deal with the projected $3.5 billion shortfall for the period ending August 31, 1987. The state comptroller was further predicting a deficit of between $5 to $8 billion when lawmakers were scheduled to return in January 1987, for the regular session which would be charged with approving the budget for the 1988–89 biennium.

With the state treasurer warning that the state would run out of cash within a year unless the legislature raised additional revenue during the special legislative session, the governor—up for reelection in November 1986—was calling for a boost in taxes in conjunction with spending cuts to meet the budget deficit. The treasurer admonished the Senate Finance Committee that "It's time for you to fish or cut bait," and suggested a combination of at least $869 million in new revenues through December 1987, which would translate to an increase to 5 percent in the state general sales tax; budget cuts of at least $1.2 billion; and delays in cash payments to various retirement funds of $744 million.

Though the majority of the Senate members seemed to favor a combination of spending cuts and revenue enhancement, the House stood firm on slicing state spending by over $700 million with no increase in revenue proposed. With the House proposal higher education would suffer to the tune of 13 percent of its appropriation plus a penalty for any part of the 13 percent cut requested by the governor the previous February but not realized.

Amid all this uncertainty and speculation, Central State University was scheduled to open its doors to another predicted record student enrollment. A hiring freeze signed by the governor, however, left doubt as to whether or not unstaffed faculty positions (both full- and part-time) could be filled in addition to those of classified staff (secretaries, etc.), student, and graduate assistants. Beyond opening the doors for the fall semester, administrators pondered the potential impact of the varying levels of projected cuts.

STATE INITIATIVES FOR HIGHER EDUCATION

Like many other states, Texas was "not doing nothing" with respect to the status of higher education in the state. Public interest in higher education actually surged in 1985 following previous efforts to improve the public schools. The increasing revenue gap only exacerbated public and legislative concern. Lawmakers knew that demands on the shrinking funds would be even more difficult to satisfy in light of the lack of options available to the state due to constitutionally dedicated funds, court-ordered programs, and other factors.

In light of all this, the Select Committee on Higher Education was established in 1985 with a charge to make an interim study on the needs of the state college and university system and how to meet them efficiently. The blue-ribbon committee included the governor, lieutenant governor, House speaker, chairmen of the Senate education and House higher education committees, the coordinating board chairman, and 13 members appointed by the top 3 state officials. The governor appointed the coordinating board chairman to head the committee.

Ordered to report its findings to the 70th legislature for possible action in 1987, the committee was responsible for engaging in "serious consideration and long-range planning" in order that higher education would be postured to meet the needs of the growing state population and make "a positive contribution to economic and quality of life in the state." Stipulated for inclusion in the study were "funding; cost-effective alternatives for maintaining the higher education system; curriculum requirements; undergraduate, graduate, and professional education programs; and technology." The committee was further instructed to pay particular attention "to issues of long-term enrollment projections; the distribution, production, and excellence of academic programs; projected appropriations; and the projected needs for higher education programs, research, and facilities of Texas."

Another state initiative for higher education began when voters repealed in 1982 the state ad valorem tax which was used to fund college and university construction projects. The 1983 legislature in turn created a new funding plan, placed it on the November 1984 ballot, and saw the amendment win a majority in every Texas county, resulting in approval by nearly 72 percent of voters overall.

The $100 million annual higher education assistance fund which resulted from the overwhelming approval of the constitutional amendment was to be distributed to universities outside the University of Texas and Texas A&M systems. The amendment provided for all institutions in the UT and Texas A&M systems to participate in the income of the Permanent University Fund (PUF). Before passage of the constitutional amendment, income from the PUF was available only to

The University of Texas at Austin and Texas A&M University. The major intent of the new funding plan was to make campus construction funding more stable and equitable and reduce the need for universities to compete for legislative appropriations.

The framework for distributing the $100 million annual fund called for assigning a specific amount to each of 26 institutions annually for 10 years using an allocation formula based on space deficiency, condition of facilities, and "institutional complexity." The coordinating board was charged with reviewing the formula prior to the 1989 legislative session and recommending any needed adjustments for the five-year period beginning in 1990.

Central State University received its first allocation from the higher education assistance fund (commonly referred to as Proposition II or Prop II funds) in the 1985–86 academic year. As would be expected, demands on the funds far exceeded those available, but the monies provided a welcomed infusion during a very tight budget period. Any pool of money, however, was considered fair game by the legislators as they sifted through their legal alternatives for means by which to solve the state budget crisis. This only added, therefore, to the uncertainty and speculation engendered by the special legislative session as CSU prepared for fall 1986. Could or would Prop II funds be endangered?

ROLE OF COORDINATING BOARD

Created by the Higher Education Coordinating Act of 1965, the coordinating board of Texas was established in an effort to bring order to what was considered at the time to be an inevitable rapid growth of higher education. That rapid growth did in fact occur. In 1965, with a state population of 10.3 million, Texas counted 22 public senior colleges and universities and 32 public junior colleges. By 1985, state population climbed to 16.2 million and supported 37 tax-supported state university campuses and 49 public community college districts with 62 separately identified campuses. During this 20-year period enrollment in the public and private institutions in Texas increased two and a half times—from 292,253 in 1965 to 745,187 in 1985.

The 18-member coordinating board focused the majority of its attention in the early years on increasing the availability of higher education; meeting programmatic and facility needs; and providing a diversity of degree programs. In later years, however, with diverse and accessible programs and a prediction of a downward trend in enrollment through the mid-1990s, the coordinating board concerned itself more with policing new degree programs, campus construction, and the overall quality of higher education. The later board concerns were charted from the beginning, though, as the legislature stated that the purpose of the creation of the coordinating board was:

To establish in the field of public higher education in the state of Texas an agency to provide leadership and coordination for the Texas higher education system, and institutions and governing boards, to the end that the state of Texas may achieve excellence for college education of its youth through the efficient and effective utilization and concentration of all available resources and the elimination of costly duplication in program offerings, faculties, and physical plants.

Some of the more specific statutory responsibilities of the board are to:

Develop and recommend formulas to the governor and Legislative Budget Board for use in determining legislative appropriations and equitable financing of institutions of higher education.

Recommend tuition policies for public institutions of higher education.

Prescribe a uniform system of reporting for institutions of higher education and collect comprehensive data to aid in higher educational decision making.

Conduct studies pertaining to institutional efficiency, administrative costs and assignments, and educational work and standards.

Monitor the Texas Equal Educational Opportunity Plan for Higher Education.

Plan and publish recommendations concerning the public universities, health science centers, community colleges, and technical institutes.

Prescribe changes in the role and scope of public universities and health science centers.

Approve or disapprove requests for new degree and certificate programs and administrative changes.

Review periodically all degree and certificate programs offered by public institutions to assure that they meet present and future state needs.

Order the initiation, consolidation, or elimination of programs as needed to achieve excellence or when judged to be in the best interests of the institutions or general requirements of the state.

Approve or disapprove certification of certain private institutions to offer degrees or courses leading to degrees.

Approve or disapprove off-campus and out-of-district course offerings of public colleges and universities.

Approve or disapprove course offerings in Texas by out-of-state institutions.

Develop transfer curricula to promote free transfer of credits among Texas institutions.

Approve or disapprove property acquisition and major construction and building rehabilitation at public institutions of higher education, except projects specifically approved by the legislature or otherwise exempted.

Recommend policies regarding efficient use of construction funds and orderly development of physical plants and prepare biennial recommendations for the governor and legislature in regard to physical needs at each campus.

EXHIBIT 1 Appropriations by Function and Percent of Total

Function	1981–82	1982–83	1983–84	1984–85	1985–86
General administrative and student services	$ 1,693,371	$ 1,815,255	$ 2,039,679	$ 2,083,159	$ 1,953,626
Percent	6.56	7.88	7.61	7.60	8.63
General institutional expense	384,049	406,768	480,085	492,033	472,916
Percent	1.49	1.77	1.79	1.79	2.09
Staff benefits	585,432	707,112	912,280	1,091,340	1,236,744
Percent	2.27	3.07	3.40	3.98	5.46
Resident instructional expense	14,075,466	15,196,245	17,668,951	18,041,347	17,948,332
Percent	54.49	66.01	65.96	65.81	79.29
Vocational teacher training	20,537	22,324	23,001	23,354	0
Percent	.08	.10	.08	.08	0
Library	1,353,063	1,524,129	1,779,990	1,821,910	1,688,723
Percent	5.24	6.62	6.64	6.64	7.46
Organized research	67,997	67,997	70,431	72,136	67,221
Percent	.26	.30	.26	.26	.29
Physical plant operations	4,270,570	4,734,633	5,330,152	5,684,725	5,706,284
Percent	16.53	20.57	19.78	20.73	25.21
Special items	346,636	371,661	539,202	379,529	340,561
Percent	1.34	1.61	2.01	1.38	1.50
Replacement and rehabilitation	3,031,700	0	0	0	0
Percent	11.74	0	0	0	0
Less: estimated other funds	NA	(1,875,500)	(2,025,900)	(2,275,900)	(6,779,199)
Percent	NA	(8.15)	(7.56)	(8.30)	(29.9)
Plus: adjust pay appropriations	NA	51,892	0	0	0
Percent	NA	.22	0	0	0
Total	$25,828,821	$23,022,516	$26,787,871	$27,413,633	$22,635,208

Administer federal programs relating to facilities construction and equipment grants.

In carrying out many of the above responsibilities, the coordinating board acts in an advisory capacity to both the governor and the legislature, who have final authority on issues such as legislative appropriations, establishment of new public institutions, and discontinuance or combining of public institutions.

STATUS OF CENTRAL STATE UNIVERSITY

For the five-year period between 1981–82 to 1985–86, Central State University recorded state appropriations from a high of $27,413,633 in 1984–85 to a low of $22,635,208 in 1985–86 (see Exhibit 1). The lion's share of the appropriation always goes to "resident instructional ex-

EXHIBIT 2   E&G Summary of Estimated Income and Budget Requirements

	1981–82	1982–83	1983–84	1984–85	1985–86
Unappropriated balance Estimated Balance on 9/1	$ 300,000	$ 380,000	$ 350,000	$ 650,000	$ 435,789
Estimated income					
State appropriation	24,181,321	23,022,516	26,787,871	27,413,633	22,635,208
Federal Revenue Sharing	0	0			
Comptroller Account for					
salary increases	NA	NA	NA	NA	440,707
Local:					
Tuition and Fees	1,411,600	1,441,600	1,629,800	1,638,900	5,418,471
Sales and Service	483,000	522,500	646,100	637,000	1,360,728
Proposition II					
Transfer	NA	NA	NA	NA	845,446
Total funds available	$26,375,921	$25,366,616	$29,413,771	$30,339,533	$31,136,349
Estimated requirements	(26,061,200)	(24,977,530)	(24,977,530)	(29,063,771)	(30,700,560)
Unappropriated balance Estimated Balance on 8/31	$ 314,721	$ 389,086	$ 350,000	$ 455,798	$ 435,789

pense," which includes faculty salaries, departmental operating expenses, instructional administration, and organized activities relating to instruction. When other income items were added to state appropriations, the "educational and general" (E&G) estimated income and corresponding budget requirements showed a less pronounced difference between the 1984–85 and 1985–86 budget years (see Exhibit 2). Increased local income from tuition, fees, sales, and service acted to offset the drastic drop in state appropriations. Budgets by academic schools showed only small variations in percent-to-total figures over the corresponding five-year period (see Exhibit 3).

Degrees awarded by schools presented a slightly different picture, however. As Exhibit 4 shows, only the School of Business recorded a significant increase in the number of degrees awarded between 1980–81 and 1984–85. The increase in the School of Applied Arts and Sciences beginning in 1983–84 was due to the move of the Department of Communication from the School of Fine Arts to the School of Applied Arts and Sciences.

A related phenomenon is evident by looking at Exhibit 5, which shows the School of Business again with the only significant percentage increase at the undergraduate level in majors between 1981 and 1985. The Schools of Liberal Arts and Sciences and Mathematics both showed some increase in percentage of graduate majors.

As would be expected, the increase in the number of majors shown by the School of Business produced the most significant universitywide increase in semester credit hours generated between 1981 and 1985. As shown in Exhibit 6, hours generated by the School

EXHIBIT 3 Budgets by School and Percent of Total

School	1981–82	1982–83	1983–84	1984–85	1985–86
Applied Arts and Sciences					
Amount	$ 389,686	$ 399,112	$ 493,601	$ 910,376	$ 927,949
Percent	3.3	3.2	3.8	6.6	
Business					
Amount	1,705,012	1,895,299	2,140,021	2,279,641	2,363,389
Percent	14.6	15.1	16.4	16.6	17.1
Education					
Amount	2,616,526	2,798,506	2,974,149	3,093,574	3,154,773
Percent	22.5	22.3	22.7	22.5	22.8
Fine Arts					
Amount	1,472,904	1,583,020	1,613,243	1,310,494	1,330,802
Percent	12.6	12.6	12.3	9.5	9.6
Forestry					
Amount	517,330	552,033	601,024	607,011	595,314
Percent	4.4	4.4	4.6	4.4	4.3
Liberal Arts					
Amount	2,665,915	2,861,359	2,807,482	2,895,784	2,889,431
Percent	22.9	22.8	21.4	21.1	20.8
Sciences and Mathematics					
Amount	2,283,645	2,464,735	2,458,594	2,620,636	2,596,236
Percent	19.6	19.6	18.8	19.1	18.7
Total	$11,651,018	$12,554,064	$13,088,114	$13,717,516	$13,857,894

NOTE: Amount includes salaries, teacher salaries, wages, and operation and maintenance. Dean's offices are excluded.

EXHIBIT 4 Degrees Awarded by School and Percent of Total

School	1980–81	1981–82	1982–83	1983–84	1984–85
Applied Arts and Sciences					
Undergraduate	68	54	66	151	171
Masters	0	0	0	8	5
Total	68	54	66	159	176
Percent of total	3.3	2.9	3.1	7.2	7.9
Business					
Undergraduate	467	470	541	560	653
Masters	21	36	26	20	21
Total	488	506	567	580	674
Percent of total	23.4	26.8	27.1	27.5	30.1
Education					
Undergraduate	480	459	433	466	497
Masters	349	293	401	380	343
Total	829	752	834	846	840
Percent of total	39.7	39.8	39.8	40.1	37.5
Fine Arts					
Undergraduate	166	125	143	62	59
Masters	20	20	27	21	21
Total	186	145	170	83	80
Percent of total	8.9	7.7	8.1	4.0	3.6

EXHIBIT 4 *(concluded)*

School	1980–81	1981–82	1982–83	1983–84	1984–85
Forestry					
Undergraduate	92	64	52	45	41
Masters	13/1	12/1	12/2	10/0	9/1
Total	106	77	66	55	51
Percent of total	5.1	4.1	3.1	2.6	2.3
Liberal Arts					
Undergraduate	167	132	158	141	130
Masters	31	29	30	39	30
Total	198	161	188	180	160
Percent of total	9.5	8.5	9.0	8.5	7.2
Sciences and Mathematics					
Undergraduate	183	162	185	186	221
Masters	28	31	20	26	35
Total	211	193	205	212	256
Percent of total	10.1	10.2	9.8	10.1	11.4
All schools					
Undergraduate	1,623	1,466	1,578	1,603	1,772
Masters	461/1	421/1	516/2	504	464/1
Total	2,086	1,888	2,096	2,107	2,237

EXHIBIT 5 Fall Enrollment by School, Number, and Percent

School	1981	1982	1983	1984	1985
Applied Arts and Sciences					
Undergraduate number	212	242	346	911*	1020
Undergraduate percent	2.2	2.3	3.1	8.3	9.5
Graduate number	6	8	2/5	21/10	38
Graduate percent	.5	.5	0	1.8	2.3
Business					
Undergraduate number	3,102	3,560	3,904	3,930	3,888
Undergraduate percent	32.2	34.0	35.5	36.0	36.1
Graduate number	93	115	115	116	136
Graduate percent	7.3	7.6	7.5	6.7	8.2
Education					
Undergraduate number	1,786	1,870	2,000	2,046	1,877
Undergraduate percent	18.5	17.9	18.2	18.7	17.4
Graduate number	650	776	786	865	707
Graduate percent	50.9	51.4	51.2	49.9	42.7
Fine Arts					
Undergraduate number	820	891	897	421*	381
Undergraduate percent	8.5	8.5	8.2	3.8	3.5
Graduate number	61	70	75	113	78
Graduate percent	4.8	4.6	4.9	6.5	4.7
Forestry					
Undergraduate number	412	327	287	255	218
Undergraduate percent	4.3	3.1	2.6	2.3	2.0
Graduate number	73/4	50/4	46/7	50/1	53/2
Graduate percent	6.0	3.6	3.5	2.9	3.3

EXHIBIT 5 *(concluded)*

School	1981	1982	1983	1984	1985
Liberal Arts†					
Undergraduate number	2,051	2,207	2,226	2,142	2,260
Undergraduate percent	21.3	21.0	20.3	19.6	20.9
Graduate number	293	359	354	378	473
Graduate percent	22.9	23.8	23.0	21.8	28.6
Sciences and Math					
Undergraduate number	1,250	1,382	1,326	1,233	1,137
Undergraduate percent	13.0	13.2	12.1	11.3	10.5
Graduate number	99	128	107/39	180	167
Graduate percent	7.7	8.5	9.5	10.4	10.1
Total Schools	10,912	11,989	12,522	12,672	12,435
Undergraduate number	9,633	10,469	10,986	10,938	10,781
Undergraduate percent	88.3	87.4	87.7	86.3	86.7
Graduate number	1,275/4	1,506/4	1,485/51	1,723/11	1,652/2
Graduate percent	11.7	12.6	12.3	13.7	13.3

* Communications moved to Applied Arts and Sciences.
† Includes all undecided students and also those who have not declared a major.

EXHIBIT 6 Semester Hour—Ratio*—Cost Summary by School and University Fall Semester

School	1981	1982	1983	1984	1985
Business					
Hours generated	29,190	31,496	35,008	34,778	36,415
FTE student	1,946	2,100	2,332	2,318	2,428
FTE faculty	70.9	71.2	75.0	82.3	82.0
Student/faculty ratio	27.8	29.5	31.5	28.2	29.6
Teaching salary	$764,634	$820,579	$988,297	$1,074,018	$1,092,143
Average FTE salary	$10,923	$11,525	$13,177	$13,045	$13,319
Faculty cost per hour	$26.20	$26.05	$28.23	$30.88	$29.99
School/university†					
Hourly cost	$.75	$.76	$.73	$.79	$.76
Education					
Hours generated	26,252	29,595	31,222	30,275	28,945
FTE student	1,750	1,973	2,079	2,018	1,930
FTE faculty	96.5	99.8	108.0	105.4	104.8
Student/faculty ratio	18.1	19.8	19.2	19.1	18.4
Teaching salary	$1,138,538	$1,229,508	$1,505,451	$1,405,706	$1,421,521
Average FTE salary	$11,798	$12,320	$13,939	$13,336	$13,568
Faculty cost per hour	$43.37	$41.54	$48.22	$46.43	$49.11
School/university					
Hourly cost	$1.25	$1.22	$1.25	$1.18	$1.24
Fine Arts					
Hours generated	11,180	11,081	13,809	9,140	10,685
FTE student	745	739	919	609	712
FTE faculty	52.5	55.0	60.3	49.3	49.8
Student/faculty ratio	14.2	13.4	15.2	12.3	14.3
Teaching salary	$588,091	$664,069	$768,037	$619,102	$632,784
Average FTE salary	$11,201	$12,074	$12,737	$12,543	$12,704
Faculty cost per hour	$52.60	$59.93	$55.62	$67.73	$59.22
School/university					
Hourly cost	$1.52	$1.76	$1.44	$1.73	$1.50

EXHIBIT 6 *(concluded)*

School	1981	1982	1983	1984	1985
Forestry					
Hours generated	3,030	2,531	2,503	2,255	2,092
FTE student	202	169	166	150	139
FTE faculty	23.3	18.6	19.2	19.9	19.8
Student/faculty ratio	8.7	9.1	8.6	7.5	7.0
Teaching salary	$235,709	$217,828	$314,237	$256,897	$263,687
Average FTE salary	$10,116	$11,711	$16,366	$12,896	$13,344
Faculty cost per hour	$77.79	$86.06	$125.54	$113.92	$126.50
School/university					
Hourly cost	$2.24	$2.52	$3.26	$2.90	$3.20
Liberal Arts					
Hours generated	38,369	43,551	42,781	42,102	40,017
FTE student	2,558	2,903	2,849	2,806	2,668
FTE faculty	108.7	112.3	114.6	113.9	103.5
Student/faculty ratio	23.5	25.8	24.6	24.6	25.8
Teaching salary	$1,225,134	$1,320,223	$1,447,644	$1,456,235	$1,405,021
Average FTE salary	$11,375	$11,756	$12,523	$12,776	$13,570
Faculty cost per hour	$32.14	$30.31	$33.83	$34.59	$35.11
School/university					
Hourly cost	$.93	$.89	$.88	$.88	$.89
Sciences and Math					
Hours generated	32,395	36,942	36,132	34,575	33,013
FTE student	2,160	2,463	2,407	2,305	2,201
FTE faculty	86.5	92.7	99.8	105.4	101.3
Student/faculty ratio	25.0	26.6	24.1	21.8	21.7
Teaching salary	$934,411	$1,039,102	$1,186,331	$1,208,082	$1,221,855
Average FTE salary	$10,802	$11,209	$11,887	$11,464	$12,067
Faculty cost per hour	$28.84	$28.13	$32.83	$34.94	$37.01
School/university					
Hourly cost	$.83	$.83	$.85	$.89	$.94
Applied Arts and Sciences					
Hours generated	2,254	2,328	2,610	8,948	8,974
FTE student	150	155	173	596	598
FTE faculty	6.6	8.1	10.5	65.1	26.0
Student/faculty ratio	14.0	16.2	16.5	9.1	23.0
Teaching salary	$61,938	$78,745	$100,488	$331,813	$292,706
Average FTE salary	$9,384	$9,722	$9,570	$10,292	$11,228
Faculty cost per hour‡	$42.48	$46.10	$38.50	$37.08	$32.62
School/university					
Hourly cost	$1.22	$1.35	$1.00	$.94	$.83
University					
Hours generated	142,670	157,524	164,065	162,013	160,141
FTE student	9,511	10,502	10,925	10,801	10,737
FTE faculty	448.3	459.2	488.4	508.6	487.1
Student/faculty ratio	21.2	22.9	22.4	21.2	21.9
Teaching salary	$4,948,455	$5,370,054	$6,310,485	$6,351,853	$6,329,717
Average FTE salary	$11,039	$11,694	$12,921	$12,488	$12,992
Faculty cost per hour	$34.68	$34.09	$38.46	$39.21	$39.53
School/university					
Hourly cost	$1.00	$1.00	$1.00	$1.00	$1.00

* Ratio and FTE based on funded hours only.
† This figure represents the school cost per hour based on each $1 of university cost per hour.
‡ Distorted because of nonassigned faculty and dean's assignment.
NOTE: Faculty salary represents fall semester only. Cost calculations based on faculty salary.

EXHIBIT 7 Faculty Headcount by Department: Fall Semester Only

Department	1981 Full Time	1981 Part Time	1981 Full Time Equiv-alent	1982 Full Time	1982 Part Time	1982 Full Time Equiv-alent	1983 Full Time	1983 Part Time	1983 Full Time Equiv-alent	1984 Full Time	1984 Part Time	1984 Full Time Equiv-alent	1985 Full Time	1985 Part Time	1985 Full Time Equiv-alent
Business															
Accounting	12	3	13.0	13	2	13.8	14	4	15.8	15	3	16.0	15	2	16.0
Computer Science	8	6	11.0	7	8	11.0	9	7	12.5	10	9	14.5	9	10	14.0
Economic/Finance	13	0	13.0	13	0	13.0	13	0	13.0	14	0	14.0	16	0	16.0
Management/Marketing	14	11	19.1	15	10	19.2	17	6	19.7	18	7	21.3	18	6	20.8
Administrative Services	13	2	14.0	13	2	14.2	13	3	14.0	15	3	16.5	14	3	15.2
Total	60	22	70.1	61	22	71.2	66	20	75.0	72	22	82.3	72	21	82.0
Education															
Agriculture	8	1	8.5	8	1	8.5	8	1	8.5	9	0	9.0	9	1	9.3
Elementary Education	20	1	20.3	19	4	20.5	22	10	25.2	22	6	23.7	18	10	23.2
Secondary Education	13	4	14.9	12	7	15.1	13	5	15.2	12	9	15.7	12	6	14.3
Health and Physical Education	14	23	26.5	14	27	27.8	15	30	30.4	14	29	28.3	15	30	29.7
Home Economics	10	2	11.5	11	1	11.7	11	1	11.7	11	1	11.7	11	2	11.9
Total	78	36	96.5	79	44	99.8	83	52	108.0	82	50	105.4	79	53	104.8
Fine Arts															
Art	14	5	16.1	14	6	16.0	13	9	16.8	13	10	16.6	14	7	16.6
Music	16	10	19.4	18	11	21.9	18	15	24.6	20	12	26.0	19	17	27.3
Communications	16	10	19.4	18	11	21.9	18	15	24.6	*	*	*	*	*	*
Theater	3	3	4.3	3	4	4.7	3	4	5.3	4	6	6.7	4	5	5.8
Total	42	26	52.5	44	31	55.0	43	38	60.3	37	28	49.3	37	29	49.8

Liberal Arts															
English/Philosophy	28	28	43.3	35	21	46.3	33	27	48.0	35	21	46.0	26	25	40.6
History	16	4	17.6	17	4	18.1	17	3	18.1	16	7	19.3	15	6	17.8
Language	9	4	10.0	9	4	10.7	9	5	11.0	9	4	10.7	15	4	11.0
Political Science/Geography	16	1	16.5	15	2	15.7	15	2	16.0	15	2	15.7	15	0	15.0
Psychology	11	4	12.0	11	2	11.5	11	3	12.0	12	3	12.7	10	5	11.3
Sociology	8	2	8.8	9	0	9.0	8	3	9.5	8	3	9.4	7	2	7.9
Bible	0	2	1.0	0	2	1.0	0	2	1.0	0	2	1.0	0	2	1.0
Total	88	45	108.7	96	35	112.3	93	45	114.6	95	42	114.8	82	44	104.6
Forestry															
Total	10	29	23.3	9	23	18.6	12	18	19.2	14	15	19.9	11	19	19.8
Sciences and Mathematics															
Biology	17	18	25.6	17	18	25.6	17	16	24.9	16	18	24.5	15	22	25.3
Chemistry	8	3	9.2	8	3	9.5	9	4	11.0	9	5	11.5	9	5	11.5
Geology	8	10	11.6	8	15	12.9	9	18	16.0	7	19	14.0	6	18	13.1
Mathematics	23	8	26.6	19	15	27.8	23	13	31.8	27	13	35.6	27	11	32.7
Physics	7	6	9.5	7	7	10.6	8	5	10.5	8	9	12.7	8	7	11.7
Nursing	4	0	4.0	7	0	7.0	6	0	6.0	7	0	7.0	7	0	7.0
Total	67	45	86.5	66	56	92.7	71	58	99.8	74	65	105.4	72	63	101.3
Applied Arts and Sciences															
Applied Arts and Sciences	1	1	1.2	1	1	1.2	1	1	1.3	1	1	1.3	1	1	1.3
Communication	*	*	*	*	*	*	*	*	*	12	16	19.2	13	10	17.7
Criminal Justice	3	1	3.3	3	2	3.5	3	1	3.2	3	2	4.0	2	3	3.2
Social Work	2	1	2.1	3	2	3.4	3	0	3.0	4	1	3.5	3	2	3.7
Military Science	2	4	4.1	0	7	1.5	0	0	0	1	4	3.5	0	5	0.8
Total	8	7	10.7	7	12	9.6	7	2	7.5	21	24	32.2	19	21	26.1
University															
Total	353	210	448.3	362	223	459.2	375	231	484.4	395	244	508.6	372	250	487.2

* Communication moved from Fine Arts to Applied Arts and Sciences.

EXHIBIT 8 Percent of FTE Faculty Tenured by Department and School (fall semester)

Department/School	1981	1982	1983	1984	1985
Applied Arts and Sciences	9.3%	20.8%	40.0%	20.0%	20.0%
Applied Arts and Sciences	0	0	0	0	0
Communications				*25.0	26.0
Criminal Justice	30.3	28.6	61.5	20.0	20.0
Military Science	0	0	0	0	0
Social Work	0	29.4	33.3	20.0	20.0
Business	44.9	49.0	51.9	44.6	40.8
Accounting	30.8	29.0	38.1	33.3	35.2
Computer Science	18.2	27.3	32.0	26.3	26.3
Economics/Finance	69.2	76.9	76.9	78.5	62.5
Management/Marketing	39.1	41.0	45.1	36.0	29.1
Administrative Services	64.3	70.4	71.4	61.1	58.8
Education	62.8	57.8	57.5	49.2	47.7
Agriculture	41.2	29.4	64.7	55.5	50.0
Elementary Education	78.8	73.2	59.4	57.1	57.1
Secondary Education	74.8	75.8	78.2	61.9	66.6
Special Education	72.6	72.2	75.3	68.4	66.6
Health and Physical					
Education	50.0	46.8	42.8	30.2	28.8
Home Economics	52.2	42.7	34.0	41.6	38.4
Fine Arts	69.8	63.1	56.2	41.5	42.4
Art	74.5	56.2	56.1	56.1	43.4
Communications	63.0	64.5	58.9	*	*
Music	67.8	64.8	52.4	40.6	36.1
Theater	81.4	74.5	67.1	40.0	44.4
Liberal Arts	75.3	72.5	69.6	59.2	61.9
Bible	0	0	0	0	0
English/Philosophy	56.6	51.1	52.1	42.8	47.0
History	98.4	96.4	92.4	78.2	85.7
Languages	80.0	74.8	72.7	53.8	61.5
Political Science/Geography	97.0	97.1	96.9	94.1	93.3
Psychology	66.7	78.3	66.7	63.6	53.3
Sociology	90.9	80.8	68.7	63.6	66.6
Sciences and Math	63.5	55.8	51.0	38.1	38.5
Biology	60.5	66.3	63.2	45.7	43.2
Chemistry	87.0	63.2	63.6	50.0	50.0
Geology	51.7	46.5	33.8	19.2	20.8
Math/Statistics	68.6	64.7	56.7	42.5	44.7
Physics	64.7	39.6	42.9	35.2	40.0
Nursing	25.0	14.3	16.7	28.5	14.2
University	62.1	60.1	57.5	45.3	45.3

NOTE: Percent calculated by dividing FTE tenured into total FTE figure. Percent tenured is based on teaching appointment only. Faculty members appear in department of their major appointment.

  * Communications added to School of Applied Arts & Sciences.

of Business rose from 29,190 in 1981 to 36,415 in 1985—a 24.7 percent increase. It should be noted that the student/faculty ratio as calculated in Exhibit 6 is not truly representative of what occurs. The ratio is based on a state-required assumption that each faculty member teaches 15 semester credit hours when in fact 12 hours is the standard teaching load. Many faculty teach fewer hours due to graduate teaching, extremely large sections, and other teaching related assignments. The net effect of this, therefore, is to understate the student/faculty ratio.

Changes in faculty headcount by department and school did not necessarily parallel the changes in majors nor semester credit hours produced, as can be seen in Exhibit 7. For example, full-time equivalent (FTE) faculty in the School of Business rose from 70.1 in 1981 to 82.0 in 1985. During the same period, sciences and mathematics faculty rose from 86.5 to 101.3. The mix in part-time (PT) versus full-time (FT) faculty, however, also showed some interesting changes.

An important factor in reviewing any data related to university faculty is tenure status. As Exhibit 8 clearly reflects, there were significant variations in the percent of tenured faculty by school, with the School of Liberal Arts being the most highly tenured, and the youngest and smallest School of Applied Arts and Sciences the least tenured.

A TIME FOR EVALUATION

A crisis in the state budget. Potential for significant changes in the higher education scene based on developing state initiatives. A stable to slightly increasing universitywide enrollment. An internal shift in student demand for degree programs. All these factors combined to raise serious and challenging questions as CSU faced the beginning of the 1986–87 academic year. How would the state legislators resolve the budget crisis? What impact would the resolution have on higher education in general and CSU in particular? What effect might recommendations from the select committee have on the role and scope of CSU? Would student demand for degree programs remain the same or change dramatically? Were answers to any or all of these questions within the purview of CSU administrators? Or were these the questions they should be asking? Where should they go from here?

Health Service Activities

18. Valley Orthopedic Associates

BACKGROUND

Valley Orthopedic Associates, P.C. (VOA), is a medical group practice consisting of five physician partners and one physician employee. The practice began in 1973 when Dr. Omdahl opened a solo practice office with two employees in a general office building in downtown Bismarck, North Dakota. Approximately one year later, in July 1974, Dr. Omdahl moved his office into the newly constructed medical arts building, located conveniently within walking distance of the two Bismarck hospitals. It was at this time Dr. Omdahl incorporated his practice under the name Lloyd G. Omdahl, M.D., P.C.

In July 1977, Dr. Peterson joined Dr. Omdahl's practice (with the understanding that, within one year, he would become a full partner). In July 1978, Dr. Bloomquist joined the clinic and the name of the corporation was officially changed to Valley Orthopedic Associates, P.C. One year later, Dr. Bloomquist became a full and equal partner.

By 1980, the clinic had an annual income of $1.2 million and 12 employees. A plot of land adjacent to the medical arts building was acquired and a new building was constructed to house the practice. At this time, the first professionally trained manager was hired. Exhibit 1 shows the organizational chart as it existed in May 1980.

The clinic continued to prosper. In July 1982, Dr. Steinmetz joined the clinic, followed by Dr. Navarra in July 1983. They became equal partners one year after their joining the practice.

In July 1986, the clinic had grown to employ 23 workers and had an annual income of $2.5 million. At this time the sixth physician, Dr. Johnson, joined the practice with the understanding that he would become a full and equal partner in July 1987. During this period the first manager (administrator) resigned and was replaced shortly thereafter. Exhibit 2 shows the organizational structure as of 1985.

This case was prepared and submitted by M. Tom Basuray, Management Department, Towson State University.

EXHIBIT 1 Organizational Chart, 1980

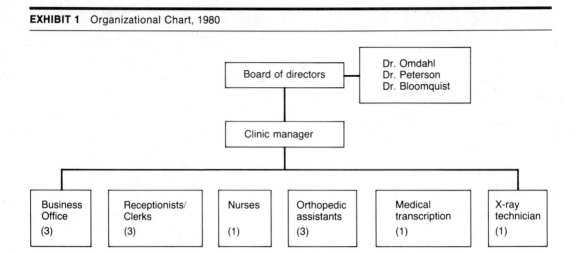

CURRENT STATUS

The clinic currently finds itself with a strong position in the market-place, but at the same time it is concerned with increasing competition and is very aware of the expansion and consolidation trends occurring in both the national and local health care industry.

In the local community of Bismarck-Mandan (approximate population 60,000), there is only one other practicing orthopedic surgeon with whom the clinic maintains a cordial relationship. He is employed by Q&R Clinic, a large multispecialty clinic which has never made a secret of its plans to recruit more orthopedists. The only other competition in the local area is a board-certified hand and plastic surgeon. There are also numerous chiropractors and a podiatrist in the Bismarck area. However, one of the two full-service hospitals in the city is recruiting for two orthopedic surgeons.

In North Dakota, patients often travel a great distance for specialist care, such as orthopedics. For a number of years, orthopedists have been located in the following areas: 6–7 in Grand Forks, 250 miles to the northeast; 8–10 in Fargo, 200 miles to the east; 3–4 in Minot, 110 miles north; and 1 in Jamestown, 100 miles east. In the past two years, two more orthopedists have located in Jamestown, two more in Minot, as well as one in Dickinson, 95 miles west, and one in Williston, 270 miles northwest. While these numbers are not alarming, they do signal a possible trend. As orthopedists become more numerous in both the country as a whole and in North Dakota specifically, they are moving to smaller communities, previously thought to be too small to support a high-earning orthopedist. More significantly, a dent has been put in the referrals from the western part of the state. Previously, the nearest orthopedist to the west was located in Billings, Montana,

EXHIBIT 2   Organizational Chart, 1985

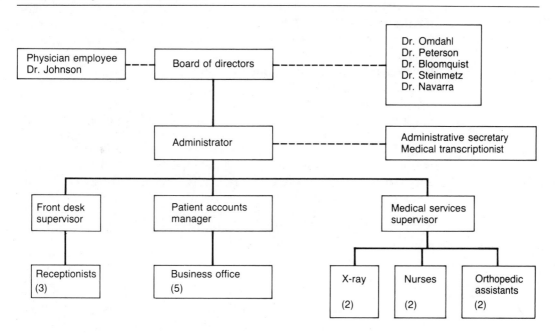

over 600 miles away. VOA is concerned about the out-of-area referrals because only 50 percent of their present patients are from the Bismarck-Mandan area.

The greatest asset of the clinic is the quality and type of physicians who have joined the clinic. The original physician, Dr. Omdahl, is a general orthopedic surgeon with the least amount of specialized skill. His greatest strength may be his desire to establish an orthopedic center in Bismarck and his selection of qualified partners. He was instrumental in establishing a busy solo practice and a good reputation in the community. Dr. Peterson, the second physician, has excellent patient rapport and specializes in treatment of the knee, especially sports related disorders. Dr. Bloomquist also relates very well with patients and specializes in surgery of the hand and upper extremity. Dr. Steinmetz is very high-strung, sometimes moody, and specializes in trauma treatment and care. Dr. Navarra, while also moody, can be very personable. He is highly trained in the latest reconstructive surgery techniques. Dr. Johnson is inexperienced in clinic practice, but plans to specialize in pediatric orthopedics, including foot care and back care.

This has resulted in a very well-rounded specialty clinic, with subspecialists in most orthopedic areas. All orthopedists do spend a good deal of time dealing with general orthopedic care, but they attempt to spend at least 50 percent of their time in their speciality areas. This pattern of subspecialist care has a number of advantages for the clinic. It aids the establishment of a reputation as a quality provider of care. If one physician is unable to provide the proper care, or is unsure of the proper course of treatment, he has other physicians to whom to refer or with whom to consult. This increases the quality of care and lessens the risk of a malpractice occurrence. It also enables the clinic to receive referrals from other orthopedists.

So far, these practice-building techniques and attempts to build the clinic into a major referral center have been very successful. The clinic has never had a problem attracting patients. In fact, the opposite is true. Often, it is several days before a new patient is able to get an appointment. New patients are typically "put off" for three to four weeks or worked in to be seen in a "waiting appointment." This type of patient often waits one to two hours before being seen, disrupting the flow of the regular clinic schedule. This situation has created a reputation that the clinic is inefficient.

INTERNAL OPERATION

The activity within the clinic may be described as anything from "fast-paced" to hectic. The two major elements of the workload are the patient flow and paper flow.

The patient flow consists of the main function of the clinic, namely, having the medical staff examine the patient. On a typical day, two physicians will staff the clinic, seeing 30–40 patients, for a total of 60–80 for the day. Exhibit 3 diagrams the patient flow from the time the patient enters the clinic and checks in with the front desk to the time he or she leaves the office. During this process, the patient will come into contact with 4–6 different members of the clinic staff. At any one time, all 10 exam rooms may be full, 2–4 patients may be checking in or out, and an additional 10–12 patients may be sitting in the waiting room.

The paper flow may be viewed as the method of recording and organizing the patient flow. It is an essential part of the clinic process since no patient can be seen without a medical record present. Also, no revenue will be produced if the charge ticket is not present. Exhibit 4 diagrams the paper flow process from the time the patient schedules the appointment until the patient's medical record is filed. During this process, seven to eight employees handle the medical record and charge ticket. This daily paper flow function does not include the insurance filing and monthly billing statements which are sent out by the business office.

Surgery, which is the most significant factor in terms of revenue production, has little effect on office activity. Surgery is conducted at

EXHIBIT 3   Patient Flow

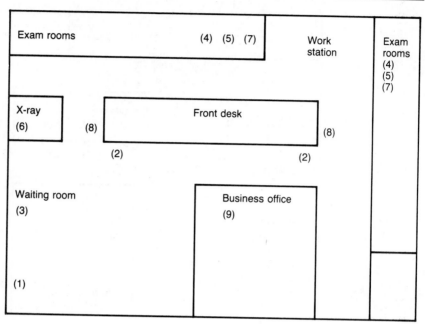

Entrance

(10)

1) Enter clinic
2) Check in at front desk
3) Wait in waiting room
4) Be escorted into exam room
5) Be seen by physician/nurse
6) Have X-ray taken
7) Be seen again by physician
8) Check out at front desk
9) Stop at business office
10) Leave clinic

one of the two local hospitals. Once the office has scheduled the surgery, it has no responsibility or control over it.

As stated earlier, the physicians are the greatest asset of the clinic. In the same manner, the office staff are the most essential part of the clinic operation. As shown previously in Exhibit 2, there are four major areas of office staff: the front desk, the business office, the medical staff, and the small, but important, department of transcription.

The front desk handles the patient check-in and check-out functions, phone answering, appointment and surgery scheduling, and message taking for the physicians. The medical staff handles all support functions for the physicians including taking of X-rays, assisting

EXHIBIT 4 Paper Flow

Exam rooms (4) (5) (7)	Work station (6) (8) (9)	Exam rooms
Work station (6) (8) (9)		
X-ray (7) Front desk (1) (4) (5) (10)		
Waiting room	Business office Files (13) Data input (12) Printer (3) Medical records (2) (14)	Medical trans− cription

1) Patient schedules appointment
2) File clerk pulls medical record of patient
3) File clerk prints charge ticket for patient on computer printer
4) Medical record and charge ticket are taken to front desk
5) Patient checks in
6) Chart (M.R. & C.T.) delivered to work station
7) Chart taken to X-ray with patient
8) Chart returned to work station
9) Physician dictates note on office visit
10) Patient checks out. Chart returned to front desk and copy of charge ticket is given to patient
11) Medical transcriptionist types office note in medical record
12) Patient registration and charge information entered into computer
13) Charge ticket original is filed
14) Medical record is filed

with dressing changes, removing of stitches, applying casts, giving injections, and assisting with surgery. The business office handles all aspects of accounts receivable including charging, insurance filing, billing, and collecting. The medical transcription department documents all office visits as dictated by the physician. Accuracy in this position is vital for both medical and legal reasons.

Human resource maintenance has traditionally been a neglected area of the clinic. Personnel management has been controlled by Dr. Omdahl, who has maintained a veto power on salary increases and who governs employees with the same high standards he sets for himself.

The need to motivate employees has been virtually ignored by management. Dr. Omdahl is an individual who has worked extremely hard to achieve financial and professional success. He feels employees should be sincerely motivated to strive for excellence without rewards offered by management. Items such as good working conditions, good fringe benefits, job security, and friendly work groups are not common elements of the clinic environment. The clinic's physical setting is generally pleasant. The building was constructed in 1980 and has most of the modern amenities. However, the pace of work is fast and hectic. The staff compensation, including salaries and other fringe benefits, are marginal at best. Furthermore, higher order needs, such as esteem and self-actualization, are rarely met at the clinic. The physicians do not show respect for the workers. A well-done job is simply considered to be expected, while mistakes by the staff are chastised. Because of the size of the clinic, promotions are rare and salary increases are typically "across the board" cost of living increases as opposed to merit increases. The job tasks are demanding, mainly because of the work load, but they are also routine, not allowing workers to use their creativity.

Over the past five years at VOA, the work load has steadily increased. This is evidenced by the fact that revenue and patient visits have increased at a faster rate than the number of employees. Since pay increases are based on the cost-of-living index, employees feel they are doing more work for the same pay. Therefore, the employees feel underrewarded. A decrease in the quality and quantity of their work is a logical outcome. The staff turnover rate for VOA for the past three years has been averaging 20 percent.

Despite increased client bookings, the 1986 financial results have been below the partners' expectations. Income statements for 1984 and 1986, as well as the balance sheet as of December 31, 1986, are shown in "Financial Data" at the end of the case. At its annual board meeting held in January 1987, the four partners asked Dr. Omdahl, the chairman and senior partner of the board, to investigate the situation and to prepare a strategic plan for VOA for the next few years. Dr. Omdahl, after consulting with other partners and the clinic administrator, decided to approach the faculty from the College of Business Administration at the University of North Dakota in Grand Forks, North Dakota, for help in evaluating VOA's opportunities and constraints.

Balance Sheet
As of December 31, 1986

Assets			*Liabilities*	
Current assets			Current liabilities	
Cash.	$ 105,000.00		Mortgage payable, current	
Accounts receivable	482,600.00		installments	$ 127,000.00
Prepaid expenses.	9,400.00		Notes payable, current	
Inventory.	87,100.00		installments	86,750.00
Total current assets.	$ 684,100.00		Accounts payable.	143,450.00
			Accruals, local and federal	
Property and equipment			taxes	120,093.00
Land.	$ 200,000.00		Total current liabilities	$ 477,293.00
Building	1,000,000.00			
Less: Depreciation	(67,000.00)		Long-term debt	
Equipment	1,253,086.00		Mortgage payable, deferred	
Less: Depreciation	(125,309.00)		installments	$ 795,000.00
			Notes payable, deferred	
Book value of property and			installments	1,170,491.00
equipment	$2,260,777.00		Total long-term debt	$1,965,491.00
Total assets	$2,944,877.00			
			Capital	
			Capital, Dr. Omdahl.	$ 80,000.00
			Capital, Dr. Peterson	80,000.00
			Capital, Dr. Bloomquist	80,000.00
			Capital, Dr. Navarra.	80,000.00
			Capital, Dr. Steinmetz.	80,000.00
			Total paid-in capital	400,000.00
			Partner's drawing A/C	102,093.00
			Total capital	$ 502,093.00
			Total liabilities	$2,944,877.00

Financial Data
Income Statement

	1986	1985	1984
Income			
Income, professional fees.	$2,164,200.00	$1,898,400.00	$1,680,000.00
Income, ancillary laboratory	181,500.00	173,800.00	168,464.00
Income, ancillary, X-ray.	262,400.00	227,808.00	205,738.00
Gross income	2,608,100.00	2,300,008.00	2,054,202.00
Uncollectible.	168,000.00	113,900.00	109,600.00
Net income	$2,440,100.00	$2,186,108.00	$1,944,602.00
Expenses			
Professional and medical:			
Salaries, doctors.	$ 538,500.00	$ 418,100.00	$ 386,900.00
Taxes and fringe benefits.	188,475.00	146,335.00	135,415.00
Insurance	184,025.00	125,430.00	100,594.00
Travel	26,905.00	23,508.00	22,680.00
Consultants, physicians	64,100.00	53,278.00	50,120.00
Laboratory, outside service.	28,300.00	16,700.00	18,450.00
X-ray, outside service.	37,400.00	22,450.00	21,725.00
Total professional and medical expenses	$1,067,705.00	$ 805,801.00	$ 735,884.00

Financial Data
Income Statement

	1986	1985	1984
Income			
Personnel expenses:			
Salaries, employees	$ 323,000.00	$ 310,500.00	$ 298,900.00
Taxes and fringe benefits.	80,750.00	77,625.00	74,725.00
Insurance	52,500.00	37,260.00	35,868.00
Travel	4,200.00	3,421.00	4,050.00
Contract labor	32,000.00	26,547.00	26,925.000
Total personnel expenses.	$ 492,450.00	$ 455,353.00	$ 440,468.00
Supplies:			
Laboratory supplies	$ 191,376.00	$ 149,726.00	$ 142,329.00
Laundry, cleaning, linen	25,000.00	22,150.00	22,500.00
Maintenance supply	23,500.00	20,800.00	18,665.00
Medicine and drug supplies	60,700.00	50,300.00	51,540.00
Printing and office supplies	24,000.00	21,000.00	20,675.00
Professional supplies.	12,000.00	8,000.00	8,068.00
Total supplies	$ 336,578.00	$ 271,976.00	$ 263,777.00
General and administrative expenses	254,043.00	190,163.00	136,100.00
(includes legal, property taxes, postage, automobile, accounting, data processing, fees and licenses, property insurance, interest, and miscellaneous)			
Total expenses.	2,150,776.00	1,723,293.00	1,576,229.00
Profit before taxes	$ 289,324.00	$ 462,815.00	$ 368,373.00

TECHNICAL NOTE: THE EVOLUTION OF PHYSICIANS' GROUP PRACTICE

In the United States the physician's office plays a vital decision-making role concerning the further utilization of the health care system's various components. This is so because in the United States ambulatory medical care accounts for the majority of provider/patient contacts within the health care delivery system and the physician's office is generally the initial point of contact between the patient and the providers within the health care system.

In response to the growing complexity of the health care delivery system, physicians' group practice as an accessible, continuous, and efficient operational model has grown in the United States in the last three decades. Within the group practice setting, physicians are able to carry on their professional work in contiguous offices with certain shared facilities such as examination and/or consultation rooms, laboratory and radiographic equipment, reception areas, and a business office. A single medical record can be maintained for each center patient and, while each patient may identify primarily with one physician, the physicians as a group can coordinate coverage for professional services, including referral, consultation, and peer review.

In contrast to the group practice trend, at the beginning of the 20th century, the dominant medical mode was solo practice by the physician. The solo practice framework was imported from Europe to the East Coast. In this framework, the patient health care was delivered by the single physician in a particular neighborhood. Such physician was more than likely to be a general practitioner who established a close personal working relationship with his or her clients and developed an attitude for individualized personal health care.

However, even at the turn of the century, the social forces were working toward the establishment of group health care. The westward movement and the subsequent industrialization created a shortage of physicians in remote areas of the country. In the newly developed areas distance and other factors made the framework of solo practice impractical.

Along with industrial revolution, the technology of health care also made quantum leaps. The difficulty of coping with the complexities of modern medical science, as well as the prohibitive capital investment required to provide modern health care, began to loom as significant constraints to solo practice. Also, the time required to complete medical education in the United States and the general shift toward medical specialization and separation of surgical practice from general practice has brought increasing pressures for shift from solo to group practice.

CLASSIFICATION BY FUNCTION

Today, the physicians' group practice may be classified as therapeutic, consultative, diagnostic, or some combination of these, depending upon their primary function. A practice offering general medical services to a continuing patient clientele is considered to be a therapeutic group. Within this classification are the diagnostic and consultative functions usually required in the examination and treatment of patients. Consultation groups are often found within a single specialty practice and function primarily on a referral basis offering the benefits of specialized opinion or treatment for specific and limited health problems. Upon termination of the referred service, the patient resumes general care from the primary physician. The third classification of group by function is diagnostic. These groups limit the scope of their activities to examination and diagnostic services and refer patients to their primary physicians for follow-up management. Specializations such as radiology, pathology, and anesthesiology are usually classified in this category although some of the activities performed by these specialists may also fall in the other two classifications cited above.

TABLE 1 Percentage Breakdown of Total Groups and Full-Time and Part-Time Group Physicians by Type of Service Group

| Type of Group | Groups | Group Physicians | | | |
		Total	Full Time	Part Time	Time Unknown
Total	100.0	100.0	100.0	100.0	100.0
Single specialty	54.2	35.3	39.7	19.4	15.3
General specialty practice	10.7	5.9	6.5	2.6	4.7
Multispecialty	35.1	58.8	53.8	78.0	80.0

SOURCE: American Medical Association survey, 1982.

CLASSIFICATION BY SERVICES RENDERED

Another means of classifying groups is according to type of services rendered. As an outgrowth of specialization, *single-specialty groups* are composed of practitioners representing only one of the variety of medical specialties. Single-specialty groups are usually consultative or diagnostic in nature. Such groups tend to be small (three to five physicians) and are popular practice settings for anesthesiology, orthopedics, pathology, and radiology. On the other hand, *multispecialty group* includes two or more medical specialties. The majority of these groups function as therapeutic groups embracing the concepts of primary care with built-in internal mechanisms for specialty consultation. Multispecialty groups tend to be larger than the single-specialty groups, averaging around 13 physicians per group. Finally, the *general practice* group is composed solely of general medical practitioners and, as such, resembles a single-specialty group. It functions, however, primarily as a therapeutic group and in that way resembles the multispecialty group. Such groups are small in size—three or four physicians. Table 1 shows the percentage breakdown of group physicians by specialty grouping in the United States in 1982.

PHYSICIAN GROUP LEGAL ENTITIES

The organizational forms of physicians' groups generally fall into the categories of sole proprietorship, partnership, corporation, or association. *Sole proprietorship* implies that the legal ownership of the groups rests with one individual. Under this form, the sole proprietor employs additional physicians on a salary basis to assist him or her in the practice. This form of organization is used less frequently than are other forms. A *partnership,* as an organizational form, is the most traditional and currently the second most frequently employed method of organization. Essentially, a partnership is a legal agreement between two or more physicians who are co-owners of a business.

TABLE 2 Percentage Breakdown of Total Groups by Form of
Organization and Type of Service Group

Form of Organization	Total	Type of Group		
		General Practice	Single Specialty	Multispecialty
Total	100.0	100.0	100.0	100.0
Sole proprietorship	1.6	1.6	0.8	2.8
Partnership	27.2	44.0	22.0	29.9
Corporation	61.0	45.1	69.3	53.5
Association	6.4	7.0	5.8	7.1
Other	3.7	2.4	2.1	6.8

Total percentages may not add to 100.0% due to rounding.
SOURCE: American Medical Association survey, 1982.

Partners agree to pool resources and to share, by some predetermined formula, in the profits and losses of that business. All coowners in the partnership usually share unlimited liability and are legally liable for acts committed by any of the partners in the conduct of the partnership's business. The *corporation,* as a form of medical organization, has increased in use among group practices. Economics, the growth of group practice, malpractice litigation, removal of restrictions from state laws of professional incorporation, and taxation have influenced this trend. The corporation is a legal entity unto itself and, as such, is subject to taxation on the income of the practice. Corporation laws generally provide for limited liability of shareholder physicians with respect to the acts of other shareholders, but retain unlimited liability provisions for the shareholder's own acts toward his or her patients. The *association* form of organization includes some of the benefits of the corporation while excluding the unlimited liability feature of the partnership. Table 2 exhibits the percentage breakdown of total groups by form of organization and type of group in 1982.

TYPES OF OPERATIONAL CONTROL

The operations of the physicians' groups are generally managed by a medical director, a partnership, a board of directors, or an executive committee. The governance of a group is closely associated with its organizational form and ownership. With a group practice, the medical director usually serves as chief executive and usually is charged with the responsibility of overall clinic management. Regardless of whether the position is appointed, elected, or assumed, the medical director retains ultimate responsibility for policy development and execution. Governance by a partnership involves the sharing of overall management responsibility between two or more partners in the

TABLE 3 Allied Health Personnel per Physician in Group Practice in 1982

Type of Group	Total	RNs	LPNs and Nursing Aids	Laboratory and X-ray Technicians	Clerical	Other
All groups	2.51	.40	.31	.52	.95	.33
Single specialty	2.26	.31	.15	.60	.92	.28
General practice	2.78	.52	.57	.40	1.07	.22
Multispecialty	2.73	.46	.44	.45	.95	.43

group. Partners may act jointly on policy decisions or may delegate specific areas of responsibility among themselves.

A board of directors may be composed of members of the group, sponsors of the group, or some combination of these. Although the board may appoint a medical director to recommend professional policies and/or may employ an administrator to implement policies and procedures, the board itself retains ultimate responsibility for overall management. Finally, the executive committee, although similar in many respects to a board of directors, does vary, in that management responsibility and accountability are vested in a body elected solely from the owners or partners of the practice. Usually, it is an executive committee that operates through a medical director and/or administrator, as in the case of a board of directors.

Data from the 1980 American Medical Association (AMA) survey indicate an average group size of 7.7 physicians. Multispecialty groups with an average 13.0 physicians tend to be larger than single-specialty groups (5.1 physicians) or general practice groups (4.4 physicians). A review of the 1980 AMA survey data indicates the specialties of internal medicine, general surgery, and obstetrics and gynecology to be the three largest in terms of numbers of specialists in group practice. Also, internal medicine, surgery, and radiology comprise the three specialties having the greatest number of board-certified practitioners in group practice. Table 3 indicates the number of allied health personnel (registered nurses [RNs], licensed practical nurses [LPNs], and nursing aides, laboratory and X-ray technicians, clerical, and other) per physician in group practice in 1982. The majority of allied health personnel employed in group settings in 1982 were categorized as clerical.

GROUP PRACTICE TRENDS

There has been a steady increase in the numbers of practicing physicians' groups in the United States in this century. Precise measurements of this growth are difficult to assemble due to the lack of a common definition of a medical group. In 1975, the AMA published

TABLE 4 Group Practice Growth, 1959–1975

	1959	1956	1969*	1975*
Total number of groups	1,546	4,289	6,162	7,733
Total number of physicians	13,009	28,381	38,834	59,809
Percentage of physicians practicing in groups	8.0	15.6	17.6	18.5

* Data adjusted by the AMA to provide comparable information.

group practice growth data. This is shown in Table 4. The 1969 and 1975 data shown in Table 4 were adjusted by the AMA to assist in drawing comparisons with previous surveys. These adjusted figures demonstrate an average annual increase of 9.5 percent in number of groups between the years 1965 and 1969. This compares to an annual average percentage gain of 18.5 percent in the total number of groups between the years 1959 and 1965. The rate of annual average percentage increase between 1969 and 1975 is 3.9 percent.

Thus average annual percentage increase in physicians' group practice shows increase at a decreasing rate.

Events of the past century have contributed to major changes in the health care system of the United States. The practice of medicine has relied increasingly upon a scientific base, and the sole practitioner has found himself surrounded by a variety of formal and informal associations of interdependent practitioners. Institutions have replaced homes and offices as hubs of medical activity, and improved lines of communication and transportation have rendered these institutions more accessible. The education of health care providers has changed and new types of providers are being relied upon to assist the physicians. Innovative organizational systems have been developed to meet local health needs, and the financing of health care has changed from self-financing to support by third parties such as employers, government, and private insurance companies. Gradually the federal government has become involved in the health affairs of the nation, thus moving from private sponsorship and control toward public regulation.

The consumer of health services today is more aware, more enlightened, and more demanding. The average consumer wants comprehensiveness and continuity in medical care. The multispecialty groups provide the framework in which to respond to these consumer needs. Groups in the future can anticipate greater involvement in community health and can expect consumer input into the planning of services.

As specialization increases and technological sophistication expands, pressures for cost control will increase. Recent escalation of awards in malpractice suits and the ensuing rise in insurance premiums have added to the public's expenses for medical care. The mandate is cost control. Theoretically, the multispecialty group offers the environment within which the mandate may be answered. Modern equipment requires capital investment beyond the resources of most individual physicians. Thus, the pooling and sharing of resources are effective cost-control methods. By delegating appropriate tasks to allied health professionals, physician productivity and professional talent and time may be used more economically. Administrative costs generated by the necessity to comply with new governmental and insurance programs are increasing rapidly. Improved management systems are within the capabilities of the groups and have the potential of reducing administrative costs over the long run.

In the future, those groups that have the ability to provide required services and hence are able to negotiate with major purchasers of medical care will possess an important advantage. Consumers today are seeking ways to budget for health care expenditures. The private health insurance industry, prepayment, and government plans gradually are increasing their coverages to include more comprehensive benefits. Groups can expect that a substantial portion of a patient's medical bill will be covered by insurance programs or prepaid plans. Groups can look for heightened interest in the prepaid mode of group practice stimulated in large part by HMO legislation. Eventual passage of a national health insurance law most certainly will influence future group operations through marked increase in demand for services along with associated administrative burdens. Future health care groups also can expect greater involvement of all third-party payers in the planning, organizing, and controlling of their purchased services.

19. King County Paramedical

In cardiopulmonary crises, medical care must be given within minutes if the patient is to survive, or survive without massive brain damage resulting from lack of oxygen. During the 1960s and 1970s, major cities in some of the world's developed countries established a variety of programs designed to meet the need for prompt care in such crises. All of these programs have as a common denominator the creation of a paramedic service—a system centered on dispatching a team of skilled semiprofessional medical personnel *to* the victim. The establishment of paramedic service in King County began in Seattle in 1969. By the latter part of the 1970s, the western half of the county was served by six paramedic units outside of the Seattle city limits. In 1980 a number of issues faced the county council and county executive especially in the Valley, Highline, and Auburn-Federal Way areas (see maps of King County in Appendix A). This case reconstructs the establishment of the paramedical program in King County and the issues confronting the program as it entered the decade of the 1980s.

ORIGINS

The King County paramedic program had its beginnings in a similar program developed in Seattle, the major city within the county. The Seattle program had its origins in Belfast, Ireland. A leading cardiologist on the staff of a major Seattle hospital had observed the Belfast program during its experimental phase. A feature of the Belfast approach to delivering crisis care was the inclusion of a physician on the team that was dispatched to the patient. The Belfast program was highly successful as judged by the principal criterion of lives saved, but its cost-effectiveness record was poor. The Seattle cardiologist realized that in a city the size of Seattle, the cost-effectiveness picture could be even worse. His objective was to design and implement a program that would be medically effective at a price the city could afford.

The cardiologist was well acquainted with the chief of the city's fire department. The fire department provided general emergency

This case was prepared by Robert E. Callahan of Seattle University and Judith Pierce of King County Emergency Medical Services Division.

services, including first aid, and had a well-developed communications system. The two men concluded that adding a paramedic team to the fire department would be the best way to meet the city's need for cardiopulmonary crisis care. Augmenting the fire department with a paramedic team would minimize costs and reduce the need to educate the public about what agency to call in this type of medical emergency.

The addition of the paramedic program promised to mitigate a crisis which the fire department itself faced. During the 1960s, thanks to effective enforcement of fire-prevention regulation, the city had fewer fires. Consequently, the fire department had fewer opportunities for heroic action. The firefighter was being supplanted by a more stringent building code, and the department's budget, long inviolable, was threatened by city council deliberations. Basing the paramedic program in the fire department would give the department the chance to build up its public image and, at the same time, prevent the continuing erosion of its budget.

In 1969 the city authorized the fire department to begin a pilot program modeled after the one in Belfast. At first physicians were dispatched with the team. However, cost-effectiveness was soon improved by removing physicians from the mobile unit. Instead, in-hospital physicians advised paramedics who were dispatched to patients in a van-type minihospital. The program was officially named Seattle Medic One.

Medic one proved a tremendous success. It served as a model for paramedic programs in other areas, including Los Angeles County. Los Angeles County also attached its paramedic service to its fire department. The LA County paramedic service gained wide fame through the television series "Emergency." (For more on Seattle's medic one, see Appendix B.)

DEVELOPMENT OF THE KING COUNTY PROGRAM

The city of Seattle extends "psychologically" far beyond its official boundaries to include virtually all of King County and the southern part of Snohomish County, which borders King County on the north. The fact that residents throughout this large area think of themselves as living "in Seattle" has long been an asset to cultural and civic organizations based in the city (such as the symphony orchestra and United Way), but it has posed problems for city and county administrators. As soon as the medic one program was underway, people in the entire area demanded its services. It was by no means unusual for a resident in, for example, Edmonds (Snohomish County) to call the telephone operator in an emergency and ask for medic one. If it was difficult for residents of Snohomish County to accept the fact that being a subscriber to a Seattle daily newspaper and holding a season ticket to the opera did not entitle one to service by the city of Seattle fire department, it was virtually impossible for King County residents living closer to the city limits to do so.

Members of the King County Council were soon compelled by public demand for medic one's services to determine how the county could develop and implement a paramedic program. In December 1974, County Executive John Spellman appointed a paramedic program planning task force to prepare a program for recommendation to the county council.

Among the considerations behind the task force's proposed plan was the county government policy of not providing services that local (city) governments could provide. Another was the wide demographic disparity of the county population, ranging from the highest to the lowest socioeconomic levels, and distributed in densities ranging from moderately high to very low. (See Appendix A for maps indicating various services and demographic information.)

Still another important consideration was the fact that the county itself did not have a fire department. The proposed, and eventually implemented, plan utilizing local fire districts compensated for the absence of a countywide fire department while accommodating the public habit of "calling the fire department" in emergencies. Because it would have been highly impracticable (indeed, financially impossible in most cases) for each fire district or department to operate its own paramedic program, the plan called for six "provider groups" or local consortiums. These consortiums consisted of fire districts/departments, incorporated communities, and local hospitals, with each of the six provider groups coordinating and administering a paramedic program in one area of the county. The task force expressed its rationale for the plan in the following way.

> The resources and talents required to make medic one work are now held by a number of different governments; the problem is to create a legal entity that will allow these governments to pool their individual assets and to provide a permanent funding source for medic one services. To such a consortium hospital districts can bring their medical experience, fire agencies their emergency experience and aid car resources, and the county its financial resources and ability to coordinate services.

The county was to provide funding on a per capita basis and each provider group was to be responsible for raising whatever balance was needed to meet the total cost of its program. The county, through its division of emergency medical services, also set minimum standards for medical care and response time. Finally, the county assumed responsibility for ensuring that the communications systems used by the six provider groups would be compatible with the existing fire district dispatch system, while providing a channel exclusively for communication between supervising physicians and paramedics.

The county council authorized funding for the six provider groups as identified by the task force. These six groups operated in the areas shown on Map 4, Appendix A. Two of these—Evergreen and Bellevue—had, in fact, been established in response to local demand before the county became involved, and their service areas and administrative structures were left essentially unaltered by the task force-recommended program. The other group in the northern part of the county, Shoreline, began operations in September 1977, as did two of the south-end groups, Valley and Highline. Auburn-Federal Way did not begin operations until approximately a year and a half later (April 1979).

The long interval between identification of the provider groups and their provision of medic one service resulted from several factors. It was first necessary to develop an administrative structure between local hospitals, fire districts, and incorporated areas. Responsibility had to be fixed for hiring paramedics, supervising program services in the area, setting up a communications system, and handling such administrative matters as employee insurance benefits and liability protection for the provider group. It was also necessary to design a selection process for paramedics, including choosing appropriate tests of mental and physical ability. The selection process itself required some four or five months. After trainees were selected, approximately a year's training ensued before they were ready to work in the field. (A brief description of paramedic training and responsibilities is provided in Appendix C.)

PROBLEMS WITH THE PLAN

In 1980 at the time of this case, the county was faced with the need to make a decision about restructuring the paramedic program. The three northern provider groups—Shoreline, Bellevue, and Evergreen—were operating satisfactorily, providing cardiopulmonary crisis and trauma care and raising adequate funds to provide the services desired by residents. Shoreline, like Bellevue, based its program primarily within a fire district emergency aid service (Fire District 4). The Evergreen program was based in a local hospital.

Problems, however, had developed in the southern areas. None of these groups had been successful in identifying an adequate and stable source of revenue. The cities, fire districts, and hospital districts made no financial contributions to the paramedic programs, and the provider groups relied on county funds and on community donations. The donated funds were small compared with those in the northern areas. As one official put it, "Fund-raising activities such as bake sales are an unstable basis on which to run a critical public safety system."

At the same time, administrative costs were much higher than in the north, and were increasing annually far beyond what could be attributed to inflation. Faced with a 200 percent increase in demands on the county by two of the south-end programs for radio-dispatch fees, and demands for administrative payments nearly three times greater than the total requested by the three groups in the north, the county executive needed to look for alternative approaches to administering paramedic services in the south.

One reason that costs increased was that services that could have been handled by member agencies of the provider groups were being directed to the paramedic program. For example, a fire department aid car could handle a call for emergency aid, but a paramedic team would be dispatched instead and the county billed. Even greater costs were incurred for personnel. The northern groups met much of the need for support personnel by using existing employees and deriving a small portion of their salaries from the paramedic budget (e.g., 10 percent of a secretary's salary might come from the paramedic budget, the other 90 percent from the fire department or hospital). In the south, some full-time positions (including program administrators) were created for the paramedic program, often because none of the local agencies were willing to share their employees with the program. The costs for supplies and equipment were similar.

In essence, the communities and agencies in the south end of the county did not recognize the partnership concept underlying the plan developed by the county administration. Rather, they considered supplying paramedic services to be "the county's job" and did not appear to feel challenged to demonstrate that they could operate a program as successfully as their northern counterparts. In January 1978, the fire chiefs of valley paramedic service area formally recommended that responsibility for the program be transferred to the emergency medical services division of King County, effective April 1, 1978.

The Auburn-Federal Way area did not have a paramedic team in the field until the spring of 1979, but problems at the administrative level were being reported in the press some 18 months earlier. Arguing that the area was too big for a single paramedic unit to cover, the communities of Auburn and Federal Way proposed that the per capita funds designated for the paramedic program be used instead to pay for the current emergency services. The current services were provided by fire department aid cars. The aid cars were manned by emergency medical technicians (EMTs) who received 80 hours of training prior to certification. County council members did not consider this proposal an acceptable alternative.

While the new paramedic team scheduled to begin work in Auburn-Federal Way was completing its training, personnel problems rose in several areas, especially in the south. The complaints attracted the attention of the news media. The new team wanted to know who their employer would be: the provider group or the county. During training, their salaries were paid by the provider group, but the responsibility for negotiating salaries and benefits once the paramedics started work was not fixed. At the same time, Highline, Valley, and Shoreline paramedics were negotiating for increased wages and benefits. They also discovered that there was no clear identification of their employer.

The paramedics appealed to the state public employees relations commission for a ruling on who their employer was. The situation was complicated by the fact that some paramedic units were fire department based while others had civilian affiliation. The affiliation, of course, depended on the configuration of the provider group, based on the fact that some funds were provided by the county and the fact that the county had made stipulations concerning paramedic eligibility for the firefighters' retirement system. PERC ruled that the county was *an* employer. Armed with the ruling, the paramedics threatened to bring suit in order to have the county designated as their coemployer. The county was alarmed at the possible ramifications of such a designation since the county could have legal and administrative responsibility as an employer for any program it provided funds for.

Some of the physicians involved in the program were also interested in the question of who the employer was. Their interest was related to concerns about terminating paramedics thought to be incompetent or insubordinate. Who would do the firing?

For their part, the paramedics were dissatisfied with the attitudes and practices of some physicians and hospitals. Complaints came primarily from the southern provider group areas. Some physicians were not aware of the extensive training the paramedics had completed. As a result there were disputes over autonomy and decision making in the field between the paramedics and physicians. There were also problems with orders to send or not send patients to the trauma unit at Harborview Hospital in Seattle. The paramedics claimed the decisions were made in the immediate interests of the physicians at the local hospitals rather than on the basis of patient need.

The paramedics also wanted better coordination (in some areas there was none) between the program administrator and medical supervisor. Having been trained by the well-administered Seattle Fire Department medic one program, the King County paramedics were highly sensitive to administrative inadequacies in the local provider groups.

Population and Population Density of King County by Paramedic Service Area,
Fire Districts, and Fire Departments

Agency	Number, 1979*	Number, 1980†	Square Miles	Density‡
FD 4	76,100	53,000	13.5	5,637
FD 16	19,800	17,000	9.0	2,200
Total Shoreline Area	95,900	—	22.5	4,262
Bothell	11,300	16,000	20.0	565
Kirkland	46,500	59,000	20.0	2,325
Redmond	26,700	45,000	48.0	556
FD 36	12,300	15,000	30.0	410
Total Evergreen Area	96,800	—	118.0	820
Bellevue	85,600	96,100	30.7	2,788
Mercer Island	20,900	23,000	6.25	3,344
Total Bellevue Area	106,500	—	36.95	2,882
FD 1	2,200	3,420	4.5	488
FD 2	28,300	35,200	8.5	3,329
FD 11	44,600	50,000	11.5	3,877
FD 18	3,900	10,000	2.5	1,560
FD 24	16,300	23,000	10.0	1,630
FD 26	17,000	20,000	5.5	3,090
Total Highline Area	112,300	—	42.5	2,642
Kent	50,000	75,000	53.0	943
Renton	25,700	30,800	15.3	1,680
Tukwila	3,600	3,600	4.3	837
FD 20	12,900	15,000	2.8	4,607
FD 25	21,600	20,000	29.0	745
FD 40	17,300	25,000	12.0	1,442
Total Valley Area	131,100	—	116.0	1,130
Auburn	32,300	30,000	22.0	1,132
Pacific	1,800	2,200	1.0	1,800
FD 39	53,400	65,000	36.0	1,483
Total Auburn-Federal Way Area	87,500	—	59.0	1,483
Enumclaw	9,900	23,000	85.0	116
Issaquah	5,400	5,160	6.0	909
Black Diamond	2,500	5,500	17.0	147
FD 38	3,100	?	17.0	184
FD 10	20,100	25,000	105.0	191
FD 13	8,200	10,000	50.0	164
FD 27	3,000	3,000	34.0	88
FD 35	3,800	4,500	88.0	43
FD 43	14,000	20,000	55.0	25
FD 44	9,400	9,700	25.0	376
FD 45	1,900	3,300	80.0	23
FD 46	2,900	4,500	15.0	193
FD 47	1,000	1,100	26.0	39
FD 49	100	?	6.0	16
FD 50	600	600	120.0	5
Total Rural Area	85,900	—	712.0	117

* Approximate, based on King County Emergency Medical Services Division population figures for Basic Life Support funding, 1979.
† Estimated, based on 1980 Basic Life Support funding applications submitted by agencies.
‡ Per square mile.

Median Income by Fire District and Fire Department

Fire District	Median Income	Fire Department	Median Income
1	11,427	Auburn	11,110
2	13,186	Bellevue	16,996
4*	13,479	Bothell	12,402
10	13,112	Duvall	11,043
11	10,676	Enumclaw	11,093
13	11,367	Issaquah	14,506
16*	13,642	Kent	11,870
17	11,223	Kirkland	12,988
18	11,023	Mercer Island	17,452
20	13,005	North Bend	11,385
24	12,486	Pacific	10,310
25	13,592	Redmond	14,305
26	13,560	Renton	12,492
27	11,537	Snoqualmie	11,385
35	10,620	Tukwila	11,156
36	12,736		
39	12,526		
40	12,423		
43	11,737		
44	11,366		
46	11,407		
47	10,661		
49	12,667		
50	11,750		

* Including Lake Forest Park.
SOURCE: 1970 census.

Median School Years Completed by Fire District and Fire Department

Fire District	School Years	Fire Department	School Years
1	12.3	Auburn	12.1
2	12.6	Bellevue	15.3
4*	12.7	Bothell	12.6
10	12.8	Duvall	12.3
11	12.1	Enumclaw	12.2
13	12.6	Issaquah	12.9
16*	12.9	Kent	12.5
17	12.2	Kirkland	12.8
18	12.3	Mercer Island	15.2
20	12.5	North Bend	12.1
24	12.5	Pacific	11.8
25	12.9	Redmond	13.1
26	12.7	Renton	12.4
27	12.3	Snoqualmie	12.1
35	12.3	Tukwila	12.0
36	12.7		
39	12.6		
40	12.1		
43	12.3		
44	12.4		
46	12.3		
47	12.1		
49	12.4		
50	12.1		

* Including Lake Forest Park.
SOURCE: 1970 census.

1979 Assessed Property Values by Paramedic
Service Area, Fire Districts, and Fire Departments

Agency	Assessed Property Value
Shoreline	
FD 4	$ 635,549,931
FD 16	290,471,535
Total	$ 926,021,466
Evergreen	
Bothell (FD 42)	$ 169,469,284
Kirkland (FD 41)	642,409,273
Redmond (FD 34)	527,233,245
FD 36	209,274,967
Total	$1,548,386,669
Bellevue	
Bellevue FD	$1,747,922,542
Mercer Island FD	448,093,469
Total	$2,196,016,011
Highline	
FD 1	$ 167,355,600
FD 2	439,883,618
FD 11	409,238,699
FD 18	43,366,212
FD 24	219,295,886
FD 26	154,106,259
Total	$1,433,246,274
Valley	
Kent (FD 37)	$1,005,580,705
Renton FD	833,542,660
Tukwila FD	362,641,366
FD 20	116,576,856
FD 25	228,007,994
FD 40	210,536,705
Total	$2,756,886,286
Auburn-Federal Way	
Auburn FD	$ 484,657,824
Pacific FD	12,075,322
FD 39	734,204,177
Total	$1,220,067,323
Rural Areas (EMT Service Only)	
FD 10	$ 294,569,594
FD 13	150,450,200
Black Diamond (FD 17)	32,483,421
Issaquah	90,691,358
FD 27	26,128,963
Enumclaw (FD 28)	142,044,141
FD 35	25,790,796
FD 38	81,170,855
FD 43	170,504,462
FD 44	106,082,058
FD 45	32,242,681
FD 46	34,331,578
FD 47	5,439,016
FD 49	8,972,026
FD 50	11,715,816
Total	$1,222,643,965

MAP 1 Paramedic Areas in King County

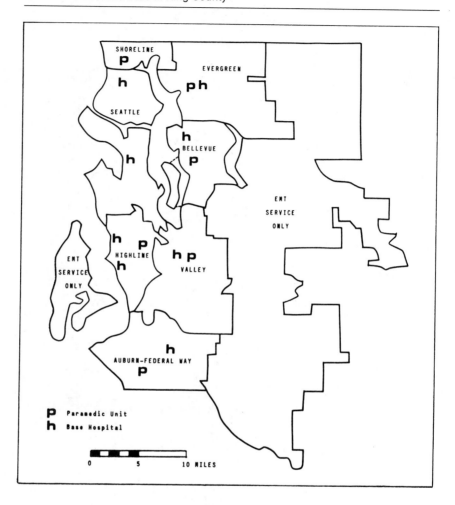

MAP 2   Fire Districts and Fire Departments in King County

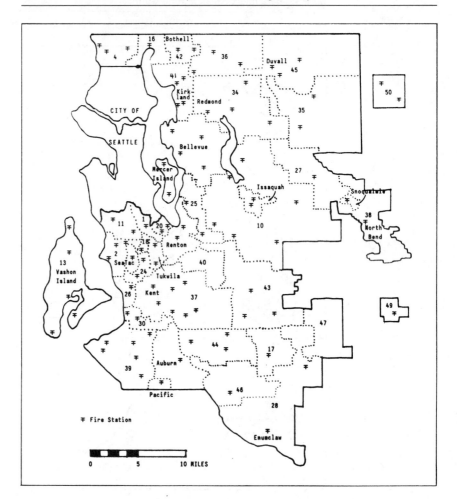

MAP 3 Population Distribution in King County by Fire District and Fire Department

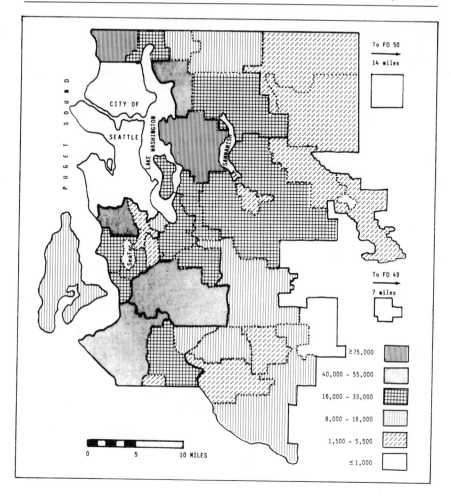

MAP 4 Paid, Mixed, and Volunteer Fire Districts/Departments in King County

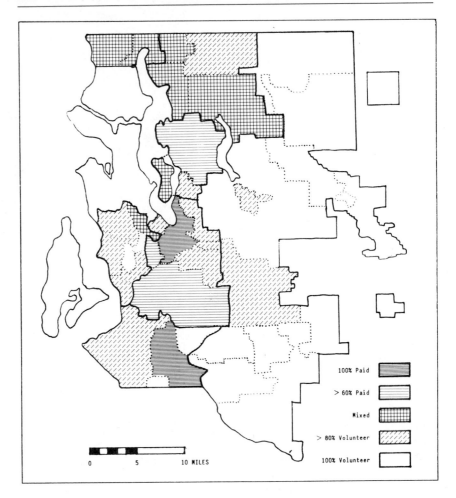

> 100% Paid
>
> \> 60% Paid
>
> Mixed
>
> \> 80% Volunteer
>
> 100% Volunteer

0   5   10 MILES

APPENDIX B "Seattle's Medic One: Paramedic Program Draws Global Acclaim"*

What is it about the medic one system that has made Seattle, as one observer put it, "the best place to have a heart attack"? The answer seems to lie in a number of factors, the overriding one being the manner in which the program is run. Those same people who praise medic one . . . also refer to its organization as "paramilitary" and to its administration as "one of the few dictatorships left in this country."

. . . the benevolent dictators are the program's director, Dr. Leonard Cobb

. . . and [deputy program director and director of paramedic training] Dr. Michael Copass.

. . . neither is paid for his role in the paramedic program, but their authority is absolute.

"Our program is run by two physicians. . . . There isn't a board, there isn't a committee, there's two people, period. They run the program and they make the decisions. I think that's the real key to how it works."

* * * * *

As it stands now, the lines of responsibility are clearly defined. While the city's 49 paramedics and more than 400 EMTs are all firemen, they report directly to Cobb and Copass in all medical matters.

* * * * *

When state law in the mid-1960s permitted . . . training firemen in cardio-pulmonary resuscitation (CPR), Seattle [established] a system of aid cars . . . manned by CPR-trained firefighters. A few years later, Seattle joined Los Angeles, Jacksonville, Florida, and Columbia, Ohio, in pioneering the para-medic concept and the paramedic program was simply grafted onto the existing aid car program.

* * * * *

That residents care about the paramedic program was evidenced early in its history when the federal and city funds supporting the program ran out and the local politicians apparently were willing to let it die. A well-orchestrated public relations campaign . . . generated $225,000 in public donations, most of it in $1 to $10 contributions, Copass said.

"This was enough to keep the program going and also told the city fathers that this was a popular public service which the citizens themselves would not tolerate monkeying around with," Copass said. Today, the program re-mains relatively inexpensive, taking just $1.3 million of the fire department's $26.5 million budget. . . .

* * * * *

According to [Seattle surgeon Dr. Jay] Kranz, the program's success is due not only to close connection between all components of the [emergency med-ical service] system but also to its operational management.

"It's paramilitary, it's very tight, it's very closely supervised; a physician is on top of every move these guys make," he said. "Their reports are reviewed every day and I don't know of another paramedic program in the whole country in which every run is reviewed every day by the medical adviser."

* * * * *

. . . In order to even qualify for paramedic training, a fireman must have three years in the department, must have served at least one year on an aid car, must be a certified EMT, and must have the recommendation of his superiors in the department.

* * * * *

. . . There is disagreement over whether a similarly successful system could be established elsewhere based on the Seattle model. Kranz thinks not.

. . . "There are many local peculiarities that make this particular method and these particular operational techniques appropriate here and they would not be appropriate anyplace else."

---

* *Los Angeles Times*, August 13, 1979, pp. 3; 14–15.

APPENDIX C Training of King County Paramedics

LENGTH OF TRAINING PROGRAM: 11 to 14 months **STIPEND:** $1,000 monthly

CURRICULUM: Lectures, 110 hours; formal lab and tutorials, 87 hours; informal labs, 538 hours.

INTERNSHIP: 12 shifts per student under veteran Seattle Fire Department paramedic supervision. Twelve shifts per student under physician supervision.

TRAINEES WILL RECEIVE INSTRUCTION IN, BUT NOT LIMITED TO, THE FOLLOWING:

Assessing patient's condition and need for treatment by acquiring history and performing physical examination and vital signs in the field.

Instituting treatment of patients according to observations and the Emergency Department physician's interpretation on report via radio contact, including but not limited to:

Perform CPR (cardiopulmonary resuscitation) in the event of cardiac arrest; initiate intravenous fluid therapy according to patient's needs from observations and direction of Emergency Department physician via radio contact; maintain patient's airway and respiratory function; use of portable cardiac monitor to read rhythms that may need emergency treatment; in conjunction, use of a cardiac defibrillator to correct life-threatening arrhythmias; administer certain emergency drugs intracardiac, through the chest wall; deliver newborn infants in the event of emergency childbirth, and proceed with definitive care of mother and child; deal with psychologically or emotionally disturbed individuals in crisis situations; control hemorrhage with dressings and bandages; immobilize fractures and dislocations with splints, backboards, etc.; assist with extrication of individuals who are trapped in automobiles, machinery, etc.; operate and maintain emergency vehicle and all equipment.

DESIRABLE QUALIFICATIONS: Certification as an EMT, or equivalent, such as a college degree in nursing, and two years (24 months) work experience in an emergency medical services area, of which at least one year must include providing emergency medical services "in the field" (outside of hospital setting) as an EMT or equivalent. MUST BE IN EXCELLENT PHYSICAL CONDITION. MUST POSSESS VALID WASHINGTON STATE DRIVER'S LICENSE PRIOR TO TRAINING.

EXAMINATION: The selection process will be competitive, to include an evaluation of the application and self-rating evaluation form. The applicants receiving a passing score on the self-rating evaluation will then be required to pass additional examinations, which may include a written exam, physical performance, and an oral exam. Applicants selected will also be required to pass a medical examination, including X-ray of the lower back, prior to being accepted in the training program.

20. Oklahoma Children's Memorial Hospital

INTRODUCTION

In June 1985, Ms. Cathy Wilson, consultant to the Oklahoma Department of Human Services (DHS), was considering what recommendation to make to Mr. Lloyd Rader, DHS director, concerning the housekeeping department at Oklahoma Children's Memorial Hospital (OCMH). Housekeeping at OCMH was contracted to a professional cleaning service. However, the housekeeping contractor was not providing adequate service, and Ms. Wilson wondered if the housekeeping functions might be administered more effectively if the hospital developed its own department.

The situation was complicated by the controls the state legislature applied to the Department of Human Services, including annual limitations in hiring. Any housekeeping personnel hired by the hospital would be state employees, and as such would enjoy generous benefits. Because of this, DHS could probably subcontract services less expensively. The savings might come at the expense of service, however, and the hospital had recently lost the malpractice protection it had enjoyed by being part of a state agency. Thus, Ms. Wilson's recommendations had to set priorities for the department's functions.

THE HOSPITAL HOUSEKEEPING INDUSTRY

Most home or office environments are considered clean if they are tidy looking and free of dirt. Institutions such as hospitals are primarily concerned with sepsis[1] and therefore have higher standards for cleanliness. Different techniques and supplies are needed for this type of cleaning.

This case was prepared by Patricia Stevens of East Central State College of Oklahoma.

[1] Sepsis is a toxic condition resulting from the spread of bacteria from an infected source.

If in-house services are used, housekeeping departments are usually headed by an executive housekeeper who reports to the hospital administrator. Frequently these housekeepers are certified by the National Executive Housekeeping Association (NEHA), a trade organization which sponsors a 360-hour training program twice a year. Although the NEHA certificate is not officially recognized by the American Hospital Association, it is a well-known qualification, and in many hospitals it is a requirement for the job of executive housekeeper.

Most executive housekeepers have some college training in addition to their NEHA certificate. They usually start in an assistant housekeeper role, receive their certificate, and then move into the position of executive housekeeper. The director of supply for OCMH, Mr. Kelly Roach, who directed the hospital's housekeeping department before OCMH contracted the services, says:

> It's a thankless job. A housekeeper has to maintain high standards of aseptic cleaning while contending with an administration that sees your workers as a bunch of deadbeats and doctors that see your workers as interrupting their job. Those people think they are experts in our field because they clean their own homes. They have no appreciation of the different techniques that are necessary. They constantly question my budget because I am a cost center. Under those conditions, housekeepers are maids, not an important part of the patient care team.

There are several advantages to having in-house services. Keeping control over cleaning services means the hospital administration has better control over the quality of services and greater flexibility in the tasks performed. For example, workers can be assigned to help move patients in case of a disaster.

Another advantage of in-house services is the training of the workers. In-house housekeeping puts the training function in control of the executive housekeeper, who very likely has been trained by the NEHA. In most hospitals, workers are trained in a classroom for several days, then have a week of one-to-one, on-the-job training before taking on a ward individually. The cost of training and service is known to the hospital, thus giving a level of accountability that is unavailable from contract cleaners. This is particularly important since the average worker performs approximately 2,000 tasks a week, doing 15 to 20 base cleaning operations on as many as 200 pieces of equipment.

Because of the unpleasant nature of the tasks they perform, motivation of housekeeping employees is very important. If the hospital administration shows respect for the role of housekeeping, other departments are more likely to support the workers in their tasks. This simple appreciation of the importance of their job makes the house-keepers much easier to motivate. Workers with higher morale are more likely to do quality work.

There are several disadvantages to in-house services. Good executive housekeepers are hard to attract, and command salaries comparable to MBAs. They tend to move from hospital to hospital in order to move up in their profession. Having a boss with no loyalty to the institution can adversely affect the attitudes of the workers. Also, if hospital employees enjoy generous benefits, in-house services can be as much as 20 percent more expensive than contract services.

The cost of contract services can be very competitive, and some hospital administrations prefer not to bother with in-house services. Although the exact number of hospitals that contract housekeeping services varies every year, an informal sample of children's hospitals around the country showed that most prefer in-house services. Results are shown in Exhibit 1.

The contract cleaning end of the business is dominated by two large companies, Servicemaster and American Management Services Company (AMSCO). Both offer two basic kinds of cleaning services. A hospital can contract total responsibility to the company, who then hires supervisors and workers. Or the hospital can contract for only the management of the department, and hire their own workers. The extent of services provided is determined by the individual contract.

Contract services offer several advantages. First, most large contract-cleaning companies have broad experience in the industry. They can accommodate special needs, and have good knowledge of the newest techniques in cleaning. Second, their size allows them to purchase supplies in quantity. This allows hospitals who contract for supplies separately to receive lower prices on those supplies. Hospitals who include supplies in the work contract also receive lower quotes. Lastly, contractors assert more efficient management of their workers. Because they are working for profit, they concentrate on scheduling the worker for maximum productivity. For example, they may schedule part-time help during peak periods. This may result in lower costs for the hospital, and provides lower labor costs for the contractor.

Frequently, contract services are considerably less expensive than the hospital's own employees would be. Contract housekeepers are paid close to minimum wage and receive few if any benefits. Turnover of workers is a problem in the industry and many administrators find it more convenient to let the contractor handle the problems of absenteeism.

Some problems arise with contract cleaners. For example, con-

EXHIBIT 1 Housekeeping at Children's Hospitals, 1979–80: Survey Results

Hospital	Number Beds	Service	Number Cleaning Employees	Shift Coverage	Housekeeping			Ward Construction
					Functions	Organization	Benefits	
St. Louis Children's	182	In-house	37	2 shifts	Integrated positions, job descriptions	Nonunion	Job rotation every year	Most semiprivate, few private
Children's Hospital and Medical Center, Boston, Mass.	335	In-house	125	3 shifts	Same as St. Louis	Nonunion	3 weeks paid vacation, "enlightened bosses"	All semiprivate
Children's Hospital of Michigan, Detroit, Mich.	320	Contract (Servicemaster on a 2-yr. contract)	102	3 shifts	Segmented job, & job descriptions	Union	1 week paid vacation after 1 yr. of work	All semiprivate
Children's Hospital of Pittsburgh	242	Contract (Servicemaster on a 3-yr. contract)	56	3 shifts	Same as Michigan	Nonunion	Same as Michigan	Semiprivate, few 4 and 6-bed wards
Le Bonheur Children's Medical Center, Memphis, Tenn.	225	In-house	55	3 shifts	Same as St. Louis	Nonunion	2 weeks paid vacation every year	All semiprivate
Children's Orthopedic Hospital & Medical Center, Seattle, Wash.	195	In-house	64	2 shifts	Same as St. Louis	Nonunion	2 weeks paid vacation, full insurance package for dependents	80% private, 20% semiprivate
Children's Hospital of Buffalo, Buffalo, N.Y.	246	In-house	75	2 shifts	Same as St. Louis	Union	Not available due to union rules	All semiprivate

SOURCE: Telephone interviews by the casewriter with executive housekeepers at each institution.

tractors save money by providing quartenary[2] cleansers instead of phenolic.[3] Because generic products are often used, it is difficult for the hospital to spot and correct this. Occasionally absenteeism presents a serious problem and the contractor will be shorthanded for a few days. This is disastrous in a septic environment. Training is hard to enforce, especially when the contractor is shorthanded. Also, a contractor's personnel often do not conform to the personnel policies of the hospital.

THE DEPARTMENT OF HUMAN SERVICES

In 1936, amendments to the Oklahoma State Constitution made provisions for the Oklahoma Department of Public Welfare. The department was to be financed by revenue collected from a 1 percent state sales tax. Funds collected from the tax would be deposited with the state treasurer in a fund known as the State Assistance Fund, and were to be used exclusively by the Department of Public Welfare. It soon became apparent that a 1 percent sales tax was insufficient to support the financing of state programs, and the tax was increased to 2 percent. This sales tax was the only source of state funding for aid programs.

The constitutional amendment creating the department stipulated that funds generated from the sales tax had to be disbursed within that fiscal year. The legislation was intended to prevent the Department of Public Welfare from spending the taxpayer's money before it was collected. Because of this provision, all contracts with DHS could be no longer than one year's duration. The amendment also stipulated the state legislature would set, once a year, an allowance for the department's salary and wage expenditures and establish a figure for the allowed number of employees.

The department began operation in 1936, administering state and federal programs such as Old Age Assistance (social security payments) and Aid to Families with Dependent Children. Over the years, many programs were added to the department's jurisdiction.

In 1970, the name was changed to reflect the change in focus from a "pension" and "welfare" agency to an "umbrella" administrative agency. The name became the Department of Human Services (DHS). By 1985 the department's budget exceeded $206 million. At this time DHS administered funds to 13 institutions and several hundred aid programs (see Exhibit 2 for an organizational chart).

---

[2] Quartenary cleansers are ammonia based. They are safe to use against bare skin. They are incomplete disinfectants, not germicides. They do not kill germ spores.

[3] Phenolic cleansers are carbolic-acid based and are powerful antiseptics. They are extremely poisonous and must be handled with rubber gloves. This is the only type of cleaner that will kill many germ spores.

EXHIBIT 2 Oklahoma Department of Human Services: Organizational Chart, 1985

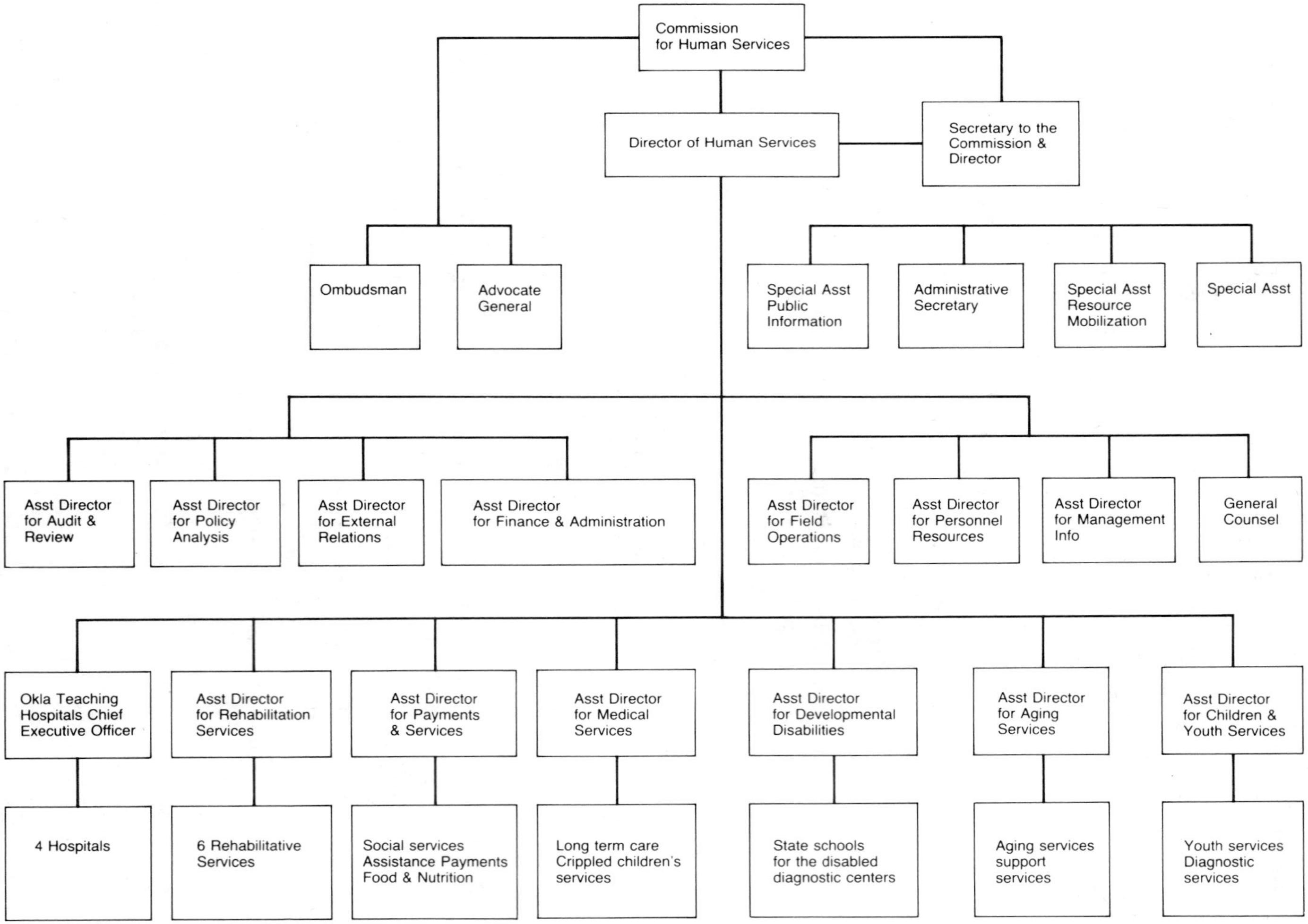

Commission for Human Services

Secretary to the Commission & Director

Director of Human Services

Ombudsman

Advocate General

Special Asst Public Information

Administrative Secretary

Special Asst Resource Mobilization

Special Asst

Asst Director for Field Operations

Asst Director for Personnel Resources

Asst Director for Management Info

General Counsel

Asst Director for Audit & Review

Asst Director for Policy Analysis

Asst Director for External Relations

Asst Director for Finance & Administration

Okla Teaching Hospitals Chief Executive Officer

Asst Director for Rehabilitation Services

Asst Director for Payments & Services

Asst Director for Medical Services

Asst Director for Developmental Disabilities

Asst Director for Aging Services

Asst Director for Children & Youth Services

4 Hospitals

6 Rehabilitative Services

Social services
Assistance Payments
Food & Nutrition

Long term care
Crippled children's services

State schools
for the disabled
diagnostic centers

Aging services
support services

Youth services
Diagnostic services

OKLAHOMA CHILDREN'S MEMORIAL HOSPITAL

The hospital was founded in 1928 as Crippled Children's Hospital for the treatment of tuberculosis and polio. It was part of the University of Oklahoma Health Sciences Center. In the early 1970s the Health Sciences Center encountered financial problems which necessitated the transfer of Crippled Children's Hospital to the Department of Human Services. The transfer was effective July 1, 1973.

At the time of the transfer, the name was changed to Oklahoma Children's Memorial Hospital. One of the first operational changes DHS made was the institution of a 24-hour emergency room to replace the 8 A.M. to 5 P.M. emergency clinic. Under the terms of the transfer, all hospital employees who wished to stay on were integrated into the state merit system, which was the performance measure used to award raises and promotions.

In 1974, DHS allocated $22.6 million to build a seven-story addition and to renovate the existing buildings and equipment. This would bring the hospital to 255 acute-care beds and 108 convalescent beds. In addition, the original building would be restructured to house two floors of clinics. All rooms were to be private or semiprivate, making OCMH one of the largest hospitals in the Midwest.

By the end of 1975, every ward had been remodeled. The hospital had grown to 363 beds and encompassed 700,000 square feet. Medical services delivered had increased outpatient visits by 24 percent and inpatient visits by 10 percent, even though the construction was constant and dust and paint were everywhere. Construction was due to continue through 1980, at which point OCMH would be the largest hospital for children in the world.[4]

In June 1975, the legislature limited the number of employees at OCMH to 1,510. This created a squeeze for the hospital since its services were growing so fast that trained technicians were needed in every department. At the same time, the Department of Human Services came under fire for being an "octopus" agency. Many people advocated cutting the sales tax back to 1 percent, or separating DHS into several agencies to allocate funds more efficiently. With expenditures under fire, Mr. Lloyd Rader, DHS director, decided to subcontract housekeeping services at the hospital. This would free 50 to 60 positions for technicians that had previously been taken by housekeepers. He assigned Mr. Jim Thompson, supervisor of OCMH accounts payable, to design and administrate a contract. Mr. Thompson was a retired naval officer with extensive contract-writing experience. He had not previously been involved with housekeeping of any sort.

---

[4] This is measured in square feet. The largest children's hospital in terms of bed count is in Toronto.

Mr. Thompson and Mr. Kelly Roach, the hospital's executive housekeeper, prepared specifications for the contract. Mr. Roach, who had worked for a contract-cleaning firm before DHS took over OCMH, said, "With all the state benefits and insurance programs, the cost of having in-house employees was almost twice what a contract cleaner would have charged. If the hospital could get equal coverage at half the cost, at the same time they allocated their 'allowed body count' to expand more critical areas of patient care, there wasn't any reason not to subcontract." Mr. Roach had supervised the housekeeping department through the early construction on the hospital. The 49 people in the department manned two shifts, cleaning patient areas from 7:30 A.M. to 3:30 P.M. and office areas from 4:30 P.M. to 12:30 A.M. The department had to contend with 50 percent turnover annually, and with constant dust and dirt caused by the construction. The work was complicated by unlimited visiting privileges and parents who roomed-in with their children. Despite Mr. Roach's efforts to keep the hospital clean, services were unsatisfactory at times.

Keeping his experience in mind, the contract was written so that only a large company could bid. The contract specified, among other things, that the head housekeeper be a certified executive housekeeper or have equivalent experience at a similar hospital, and that all equipment brought into the hospital be new. Mom-and-pop cleaning services could not afford to meet this provision, as the capital outlay necessary for the equipment was in the neighborhood of $180,000. Also, few people could claim equivalent experience at a similar hospital, since there were only about 100 other children's hospitals in the country. Only large contract companies could provide an executive housekeeper with equivalent experience.

THE HOUSEKEEPING CONTRACT

When the Department of Human Services took over Children's Hospital, the department's director, Mr. Lloyd Rader, took the project on as his pet project. Mr. Rader had been DHS director since 1955, and was familiar with the problems at the hospital through his work on crippled children's programs. Even before the department took control of the institution, DHS employees worked closely with the admitting personnel at the hospital to ensure that patients who were eligible for state and federal aid applied for it. Thus, when renovation began on the facility, Mr. Rader took an active interest in the progress and plans. He was in the hospital for meetings about twice a week.

As OCMH grew, the aesthetic conditions worsened. In an attempt to get better services from the contractors, every year the contract was awarded to a new company. Service had been contracted to Servicemaster and AMSCO in alternating years. Neither company had proven satisfactory.

The Current Contract

The housekeeping contract ran from July 1 to June 30. Servicemaster had won the contract that was in effect in early 1985. The company had been plagued by personnel problems during the first six months of the contract, notably personality conflicts between Mr. Thompson and first one then another female executive housekeeper. These conflicts made it difficult for the executive housekeepers to exercise authority over their people and made the job conditions very unpleasant for the workers. A male executive housekeeper was installed in late December, by which time conditions had deteriorated significantly. The workers had little morale and turnover was high. Construction on the building and the growing number of people visiting the hospital each day aggravated the conditions. "Once they saw litter on the floor, the public would assume it was all right to put trash there. If we could ever get the floors clean, everyone would be reluctant to be the first one to make it dirty," Mr. Roach said.

Several times on visits to OCMH, Mr. Rader had found very dirty conditions, such as dirty diapers on clinic floors, or litter in the halls. After these visits, attempts were made to prevent litter. Conditions did not improve. After one visit in January 1985, during which the hospital was particularly dirty, Mr. Rader approved hiring several women as "hostesses" to keep the clinic waiting areas picked up. A job description is in Exhibit 3. These women were supplementary housekeeping personnel, but were on the DHS payroll and were under the supervision of nursing services.

As Mr. Thompson was responsible for the administration of the housekeeping contract, the lack of satisfactory services was blamed on him. He patrolled the hospital every day, checking conditions of different wards at different times of the day. Any unsatisfactory conditions were reported to the housekeeping switchboard operator, who in turn relayed the information to a housekeeper to remedy the situation. Often, however, the condition was never rectified. Mr. Thompson did not know if this was due to the operator not relaying the message or because the worker did not do his job.

The hospital's condition was of particular concern for three reasons. First, if the hospital could not meet some minimal aesthetic conditions it might lose its accreditation by the American Hospital Association. Second, a dirty hospital might signal an increase in the level of infection in the hospital. Fortunately, for the previous few years, the level of nosocomial infection had remained at a relatively

---

EXHIBIT 3

Hostess

General Function
Under direct supervision from the head nurse of the clinic or inpatient area to which they are assigned, will maintain an orderly appearance of waiting areas and provide location information to visitors. Working hours will vary according to unit hours.

Samples of Work Performed
1. Keep litter picked up out of waiting areas.
2. Maintain furniture in an orderly fashion.
3. Wash chairs on a routine basis, empty trash, and general housekeeping duties.
4. Help families and visitors locate cafeteria, brown bag room, public telephones, and hospital bus stop.
5. Also may assist mothers with children.
6. Will call housekeeping if specific needs require their attention. Maintain a log of the time housekeeping was called and the time assistance was received. If any problems arise they should contact their head nurse.

Minimum Qualifications
1. Completion of the 10th grade.
2. Ability to follow oral and written instructions/direction and to establish and maintain effective working relationships with others; all as evidenced by an investigation and/or interview.

Clinic Hostesses

Duties
1. Keep magazines and books straightened and thrown away if torn.
2. Keep ashtrays emptied, cups and wrappers thrown away.
3. Empty trash cans as needed.
4. Periodically clean waiting room chairs.
5. Periodically check restrooms in areas and call housekeeping if they need attention.
6. Tactfully request that people do not smoke beyond waiting room area and that they use available ashtrays.
7. Wipe up liquids on floor as accidents occur or call housekeeping to do so, depending on size of accident.
8. Be gracious and helpful to patients and parents, especially to mothers having difficulty managing several small children, carrying packages, etc.
9. Report to triage nurse or head nurse in area when patients need assistance beyond what she can give.
10. Obtain extra disposable diapers, warm bottles, or obtain additional formula (when mother runs out, probably need to check with nurse regarding formula).
11. Need to be able to give directions frequently, to snackbar, cafeteria, restrooms, public telephone, etc.
12. Keep triage nurse or charge nurse informed if any patient or parent appears to be unduly upset or emotional for whatever reason.
13. Help make waiting more pleasant when clinics are so busy that an extended waiting period occurs.

SOURCE: Department personnel files.

---

constant level. No significant difference in infection levels existed between AMSCO's contract tenure, which had expired June 30, 1984, and Servicemasters', which had begun July 1, 1984. AMSCO's performance, although unsatisfactory, was considered by most of the hospital staff to have been superior to that of Servicemaster.

The situation was of special concern because of the recent loss of sovereign immunity, and a decision by DHS to self-insure the hospital. Until 1980, OCMH was protected from malpractice claims because it was part of a state agency (DHS). As a general rule of case law, the government is immune from lawsuits. However, in 1980, in *Herschel* v. *University Hospital*, DHS lost its right to sovereign immunity for the operation of its hospitals. This meant if a citizen had a claim against the state while they were a patient at OCMH, they could resort to legal action for recompense.

Since 1980, 39 claims had been filed against OCMH and the two sister hospitals that were also part of the University of Oklahoma Health Sciences Center, one third of which involved claims for nosocomial infection. One of the 39 lawsuits resulted in a loss to the hospital of $1.2 million. Another resulted in a loss of $85,000. In the year 1982 alone, 11 lawsuits were filed, totaling almost $60 million. Of these, four were won outright by the hospital and resulted in no claim paid, two were settled for a total of $55,000, and the rest were still pending resolution. The $55,000 loss figure in 1982 is similar to the national average for a hospital the size of OCMH. Statistics indicate the probability of a multimillion dollar judgment over the course of five years is about 1 in 20.

In spite of the lawsuits being filed, officials of DHS decided to self-insure the hospital. A quote obtained in 1983 for traditional malpractice insurance was almost $532,000. This provided liability insurance for one year, with limits of $2 million per lawsuit, and $4 million in total claims paid out. This included general liability, premises liability to cover slips and falls, and protection for directors and executives against such activities as negligent contracting. Coverage with higher limits is extremely expensive.

The factors insurance companies consider in determining rates include the size of the hospital, the nature of the patient mix, the hospital's loss record, the scope of services, the cost of insurance in the area, and the rate of nosocomial infection. Large hospitals, those with large surgical practices, and those with large ambulatory care practices are at greater risk for lawsuits, especially for single claims for more than $2 million.

Because of the extraordinary costs involved in malpractice insurance, DHS decided to self-insure, and follow a concerted effort of risk management. This involved two steps: hiring patient representatives and strong emphasis on environmental health. Patient representatives dealt with families during or soon after admission. They solved many claims on the spot, usually through adjustment of charges. The emphasis on environmental health involved carefully monitoring the rate of nosocomial infection. The program also included training programs for professional and nonprofessional staff, to reinforce actions necessary to maintain an aseptic environment.

Ms. Wilson's Report

Ms. Wilson reviewed the contract and identified the key provisions that had to be met in order for the hospital to meet accreditation standards. Excerpts from the contract are in Appendix A. She felt Servicemaster had not complied with the task and frequency schedule in the contract. They had been reluctant to comply with unscheduled activities such as spill cleanups. Frequently, Servicemaster employees were seen eating or smoking on the job. Often they were not trained as they should have been and thus did not perform their tasks according to the contract. Mr. Thompson had not enforced the contract provision that Servicemaster employees have uniforms or that the executive housekeeper and Mr. Thompson make weekly inspections of the hospital. Mr. Thompson had made weekly inspections on his own and relayed problems to housekeeping by phone. Thus, he had very few written records of problems that had not been corrected. He had not received any summary reports from housekeeping explaining the resolution of problems he had called to their attention.

Servicemaster had requested that lockers be installed so that their employees could store their personal belongings, and that additional space be allotted on some floors for the storage of equipment and supplies. OCMH had not complied with these contract provisions. Even considering these breaches of the contract, the service received was below the minimum acceptable level.

Ms. Wilson wondered what the cost of in-house personnel would be. A call to the personnel office netted the information that housekeepers would be ranked as custodial workers or housekeepers, according to the work they did. Base salaries are shown in Table 1. She knew Classifications II and III were supervisors, and that Class I workers required immediate supervision. Custodial workers cleaned office areas. Housekeepers cleaned living quarters. An executive housekeeper could be hired for about $35,000 a year.

In addition to the base salary, each employee of the state had three weeks paid vacation the first year, four weeks after 5 years, five weeks after 10 years and six weeks after 15 years. A maximum of three weeks paid sick leave was allowed each year and could be accumulated to a maximum of 72 days. Other benefits included 14 percent of the gross salary for pension, $67 per month for health and life insurance, 3.1 percent of base salary per year for state unemployment insurance, and 7.15 percent of the first $43,800 a year for social security. All these benefits were paid by the Department of Human Services at no cost to the employee.

The OCMH contract called for 187,200 worker production hours, 2,080 hours for an executive housekeeper, 6,240 hours for shift supervisors, and 18,720 hours for production supervisors. This translated in

---

TABLE 1 Base Salaries for Housekeeping
Personnel per Month

Custodial	*I*	*II*	*III*
Salary	$602	$610	$632
Housekeeping	*I*	*II*	*III*
Salary	$653	$734	$864

40-hour weeks into 1 executive housekeeper, 3 shift supervisors, 9 worker supervisors, and 90 workers. To figure the number of housekeepers needed for the hospital, Ms. Wilson knew a rule of thumb allowed 15,000 square feet per worker. Another rule of thumb allowed 20 beds per maid per day.

With these factors before her, her knowledge of the human factors involved in housekeeping, and her knowledge of the malpractice risks created in a septic environment, Ms. Wilson looked critically at the alternatives and wondered what to recommend to Mr. Rader.

APPENDIX A Oklahoma Children's Memorial Hospital: Housekeeping Contract Excerpts

---

Section I
General

1.01 Scope
A. The work covered in these specifications consists of furnishing all management supervision, housekeeping employees, housekeeping supplies, and equipment necessary for accomplishment of complete housekeeping services. All regular housekeeping employees will be on the contractor's payroll. Work shall be accomplished in accordance with the procedures and standards outlined here.
C. The task and frequency schedule indicates the minimum acceptable service frequencies; however, it will be the contractor's responsibility to effect immediate intensified cleaning procedures . . . in those areas in which visible appearances do not meet with the approval of the administration.
E. Unscheduled activities such as spill cleanups will be performed immediately upon request without additional charge.

1.02 Superintendence by Contractor
A. The contractor will assign an executive housekeeper and three (3) assistant executive housekeepers to serve in full-time duty residence in the hospital for the purpose of supervising and training contractor's housekeeping employees.
B. Executive housekeeper: Prior to the contract effective date, this individual will be required to have completed:
  1. A recognized publicly offered executive housekeeper course which is endorsed by the National Executive Housekeepers Association, or
  2. A formal executive housekeeper course or in-service management program. A copy of the contractor's course will be appended to the bid proposal for evaluation of adequacy.

APPENDIX A *(continued)*

1.03 Personnel Qualifications and Sanitation
A. Contractor will employ only qualified operators and competent workers who are proficient in performing housekeeping services. . . .
C. Eating or smoking by housekeeping personnel while on their performance of duties will not be permitted.

1.05 Personnel Uniforms
A. All housekeeping employees . . . will wear a uniform.

1.06 Personnel Training
A. All housekeeping service personnel must be specifically trained . . . first, intensive training and secondly . . . regularly scheduled refresher training. . . .

1.08 Inspections
A. Daily: The administrator and/or his immediate staff will accomplish daily random inspections. . . . All examples of incomplete or defective work requiring corrective action will be conveyed to the contractor's executive housekeeper.
B. Weekly: The administrator . . . and the contractor's executive housekeeper will accomplish scheduled weekly inspections. . . .
C. A brief summary report of each weekly inspection be furnished to the administration.

1.10 Safety and Fire Prevention
Cleaning shall be accomplished such that at no time shall it be necessary for personnel or patients to cross a wet surface to gain access to other parts of the area. . . .

1.12 Housekeeping Services Administration and Storage Space
The hospital will provide adequate, secure space for storage of supplies and equipment belonging to the contractor.

1.13 Employee Facilities
The hospital will provide lockers for employee use. . . .

Section II
Definitions of Housekeeping Tasks

2.01 Floor Sweeping
No dust shall be allowed to remain in corners, behind radiators, space heaters, doors, or under furniture. . . .

2.03 Damp Mopping
Mop water shall be changed at least one time per hour.

2.22 Trash/Waste Removal
E. All large containers will be steam cleaned or thoroughly washed and scrubbed to remove soil every day.

Results Desired:
While the foregoing definitions of *tasks* are intended to produce a "minimal acceptable" level of performance, the contractor is encouraged to expend all possible effort to deliver "optimal achievable" RESULTS at acceptable economic levels. The introduction of new and improved supplies, equipment, and procedures shall not be unreasonably opposed.

APPENDIX A *(continued)*

Section III
Task and Frequency Schedule

Section II task and frequency schedules are on the next four pages as follows:

Task and frequency code index
Task and minimum frequency chart 2.01–2.09
Task and minimum frequency chart 2.11–2.18
Task and minimum frequency chart 2.19–2.20

Surgery: Terminal cleaning only—Daily
Machine scrub floors—Weekly
Thoroughly clean walls—weekly

Gift Shop: On-call basis—usually floors once a week.

Public Areas: Check six times daily and cleaned as needed.

Section III
Task and Frequency

Task and Frequency Code Index

R—Monday–Friday	M—Monthly
NR—Friday–Monday	2M—Twice monthly
D—Daily	M/2—Every two months
W—Once weekly	M/3—Quarterly
2W—Twice weekly	M/4—Every 4 months
3W—3 times weekly	M/6—Semiannually
4W—4 times weekly	Y—Annually
5W—5 times weekly	AR—AR (as required)*
6W—6 times weekly	WV—When vacant

* The technical provisions of the Task and Frequency Chart that are annotated with a cleaning frequency of ''AR'' (as required) shall be cleaned as frequently as necessary to maintain a maximum state of aseptic cleanliness and a maximum state of aesthetic or visual cleanliness in all other areas of the health care facility.

Task and Minimum Frequency Chart

Room/Area/Building Designation	2.01 Floor Sweeping	2.02 Wet Mopping Floor Scrubbing	2.03 Damp Mopping	2.04 Spot Cleaning Floors	2.05 Floor Finish Removal (Stripping)	2.06 Application of Floor Finish	2.07 Floor Finishing Buffing Spray Buffing	2.08 Carpet Maintenance Vacuuming	2.09 Carpet Maintenance Spot Cleaning
Patient rooms	D	AR	D	AR	M/6	AR	W		
Corridor—patient	D	AR	D	AR	M/6	AR	D		
Utility—treatment	D	AR	D	AR	M/6	AR	W		
Examination rooms, etc.	D	AR	D	AR	M/6	AR	W		
Nurses & Drs. station	D	AR	2D	AR	M/6/AR	AR	D		
Public areas—corridors	AR	M	2D	AR	M/6	AR	D		
Nursery—neonate	2D	AR	5W	AR	M/6	AR	W		
Offices	2W/AR	AR	D	AR	M/6	AR	3W	5W/AR	AR
X-ray, lab, emergency	D	AR	D	AR	M/6	AR	3W		
Pharmacy—inhalation therapy	D	AR	D	AR	M/6	AR	3W		
Cafeteria	D	AR	D	AR	M/6	AR	D		
Dining areas	AR	AR	AR	AR	M/6	AR	D		
All clinics	5W/AR	AR	5W	AR	M/3	AR	D	5W/AR	AR
Stairways	D	AR	D	AR	M/6	AR	D		
Elevators	D	AR	D	AR	M/6	AR	D		
Tunnels, elevated walkways		W		AR					
Entrances	D	W	D	AR		AR	D		
Other departments	D	AR	D	AR	M/6	AR	W		
OR—cir	D	W	D	AR	M/6	AR	W		
Locker rooms, lounges	D	M	D	AR		AR	D		
Public restrooms	AR	AR	AR	AR	M/6	AR			
Necropsy area	D	AR	D						

Room/Area/Building Designation	2.10 Carpet Maintenance Shampooing	2.11 Carpet Maintenance Antistatic Application	2.12 Spot Cleaning	2.13 Wall Cleaning	2.14 Wheelchair and Stretcher Cart Cleaning	2.15 Window Cleaning	2.16 Glass Cleaning Miscellaneous	2.17 Damp Wipe Ledges	2.18 Metal Surface Cleaning
Patient rooms			AR	M/6	W	M/3	AR	D	AR
Corridor—patient			AR	M/6	W	M/3	AR	D	AR
Utility—treatment			AR	M/6	W	M/3	AR	D	AR
Examination rooms, etc.			AR	M/6		M/3	AR	D	AR
Nurses & Drs. station			AR	M/6		M/3	AR	D	AR
Public areas—corridors			AR	M/6		M/3	AR	D	AR
Nursery—neonate			AR	M/6	W	M	AR	D	AR
Offices	M/6/AR	AR	AR	M/6		M/3	AR	5W/AR	AR

Room/Area/Building Designation	2.19 Ceiling Maintenance	2.20 Light Fixture Cleaning	2.21 Cleaning Furniture Cabinets and TVs	2.22 Trash/Waste Removal	2.23 Dispensing Servicing	2.24 Artificial Plant and Flower Cleaning	2.25 Ceramic Metal Utility Cleaning	2.26 Duct/Louver/Door/Grill Cleaning	2.27 Soiled Linen Removal	2.28 Drape and Curtain Cleaning
Patient rooms	AR	M/6	D	D	D		D	D	AR	AR
Corridor—patient	AR	M/6	D	D	D	AR	D	D		AR
Utility—treatment	AR	M/6	D	D	D		D	D		AR
Examination rooms, etc.	AR	M/6	D	D	D	AR	D	D		AR
Nurses & Drs. station	AR	M/6	D	D	D/AR	AR	D	D	AR	AR
Public areas—corridors	AR	M/6	D	AR	2D	AR	D	D	AR	AR
Nursery—neonate		M/6	D	D	D	AR	5W/AR	D	AR	AR
Offices	AR	M/6	5W/AR	D	D	AR	D	D	AR	AR
X-ray, lab, emergency	AR	M/6				AR		D		AR
Pharmacy—inhalation therapy	AR	M/6				AR				AR
Cafeteria		M/6						D		
Dining areas	AR	M/6	D	AR		AR		D	AR	AR
All clinics	AR	M/6		AR	5W/AR	AR	5/W	5/W	AR	AR
Stairways	AR	M/6		AR			5W/AR	5/W		
Elevators	AR	M/6		AR			5W/AR	D		
Tunnels, elevated walkways	AR	M/6		D		AR				
Entrances	AR	M/6	D	AR	D	AR	D	D	AR	AR
Other departments	AR	M/6	D	AR	D	AR	D	D	AR	AR
OR—cir	AR	M/6	D	D	AR		D	D	AR	
Locker rooms, lounges	AR	W		AR	AR		AR	AR	AR	
Public restrooms	AR	M/6		AR	AR		D	D	D	AR
Necropsy area	AR	M/6		D	AR		D	D	D	

APPENDIX A *(concluded)*

Section IV
Special Services

4.01 Initial Cleaning

Upon cleaning each area for the first time, as identified on the task and frequency schedule . . . the contractor shall remove all residual and accumulated dirt and soil even though such dirt and soil may have been in existence prior to the effective date of the contract.

4.09 Patient Unit Checkout Cleaning

A. 3. Under normal conditions, renovation must begin within fifteen (15) minutes after notice and housekeeping personnel will complete the work as rapidly as possible.

B. This service includes:
1. Damp wiping mattresses and pillows.
2. Damp wiping the entire bed frame and bed rails, exterior and interior surfaces of all other patient room furniture and televisions.
3. Clean closets.
4. Restroom cleanliness will be checked and the necessary cleaning operations performed.
5. Dispensers will be checked and refilled if necessary.
6. Wastebaskets emptied and cleaned.
7. Walls, cabinets, and glass surfaces spot cleaned.
8. Floors will be swept or wet mopped.
9. Damp-wipe all fixtures.
10. All furniture will be neatly arranged in the room.
11. All utilities will be checked and a report made if repairs are needed.
12. Place patient admission kit in bedside stand.

This service shall include removing all bed linens and towels from the room, and remaking the bed upon completion of cleaning duties.

Section V
Supplies and Equipment

A. General

5.01 Hospital housekeeping tools shall not be transferred between use areas.

5.14 All material used in the hospital will effectively contribute to the reduction of hospital sepsis, decreased noise level, and a general neat and clean appearance.

H. Equipment

The contractor shall furnish all equipment for accomplishment of all work specified in these technical provisions.

5.28 All wheeled and movable equipment must be equipped with protective nonmarking rubber bumpers or guards . . . to prevent damaging the building structure or other objects. . . . Equipment with improper bumpers or guards will be removed from service immediately.

5.31 Equipment Submittals

Under no circumstances will any type of used equipment be introduced into the hospital.

SOURCE: Department of Human Services housekeeping contract.

21.   East Alabama Medical Center: Educational Services Department

"At the present level of operation our department will not attain its goals for the current year," reflected the director of the educational services department at East Alabama Medical Center. The cutback in the department staff was beginning to have its effect.

In July 1983, the hospital had signed a two-year management contract with National Healthcare, Inc., a hospital management firm in the Southeast. An initial program to freeze hiring had resulted in the allied health instructor position remaining unfilled. East Alabama Medical Center was facing the cost crunch that was affecting the entire health care industry.

HEALTH CARE INDUSTRY

According to the 1985 *U.S. Industrial Outlook,* hospital care is the largest sector in the health care industry and experienced a 5.7 percent increase in expenditures over 1983. Increased hospital use accounts for much of this increase. Between 1965 and 1981, the average hospital stay decreased from 7.8 days to 7.6 days, while the number of hospital admissions rose from 26.5 million to 36.5 million. Outpatient visits increased from 92.6 million to over 206.7 million in the same time period.

The average daily charge for hospital care went from $40 in 1965 up to $284 in 1981. That is an annual average increase of 13 percent. The average charge for an inpatient stay experienced a 12 percent annual average increase from $354 to $2,167 during this period. Expenditures further increased as hospital laboratory tests went from 2.2 billion tests in 1972 to over 6 billion in 1977.

Of the 6,900 hospitals in the United States, 5,800 were classified as community hospitals. Community hospitals' inpatient care accounted for 73 percent of total hospital expenditure, while their outpatient care contributed an additional 12 percent. From 1972 until 1982, the average expense per inpatient stay went from $729 to $2,493,

This case was prepared by Clinton H. LeNoir, Jr., of the Auburn Technical Assistance Center, Auburn University, Alabama.

respectively. This expense was about $2,898 in the second quarter of 1984.

With the implementation of medicare's prospective payment system for hospital inpatient services, an attempt is being made to encourage greater efficiency. The federal government's Health Care Financing Administration has fixed payments for illness in advance and linked them to diagnostic related groups. Under this system hospitals that operate efficiently are expected to benefit from treating medicare patients, while the hospitals that do not operate efficiently are expected to lose money.[1]

EAST ALABAMA MEDICAL CENTER

The East Alabama Medical Center (EAMC) began in 1952 as Lee County hospital with 81 beds. EAMC offers the most modern medical resources in this six-county area of East Central Alabama. It has undergone constant expansion and renovation over the years and is currently licensed for 334 beds. During 1983, EAMC operated with 190 beds. It is presently operating with 220 while the expansion project continues.

The hospital employs over 900 people on a full- and part-time basis. There are over 65 physicians on the medical staff representing almost all specialty areas. The nursing staff has experienced a 44 percent increase in the past year to accommodate the current expansion of the hospital.

MANAGEMENT OF EAMC

The hospital is directed by a nine-member volunteer board of directors, as EAMC is a nonprofit institution. The hospital is operated by a management team illustrated in the organization chart in Exhibit 1.

The board of directors, in the middle of a $9 million expansion program and faced with increased cost, signed a two-year contract with National Healthcare, Inc. The revenues had remained constant and were not keeping pace with costs. In addition, there had been no new services added and no new markets tapped. Under the contract, National Healthcare, Inc. would provide the management expertise to carry out the policies set by the board of directors of EAMC.

---

[1] Contractual agencies (i.e., Blue Cross–Blue Shield, medicare, medicade, etc.) reimburse the hospital for services rendered to their clients. These reimbursements are made on an agreed-upon schedule and amount. At year-end these accounts are audited and any additional reimbursements due the hospital or any overpayments made to the hospital become retroactive settlements.

EXHIBIT 1 Organization Chart

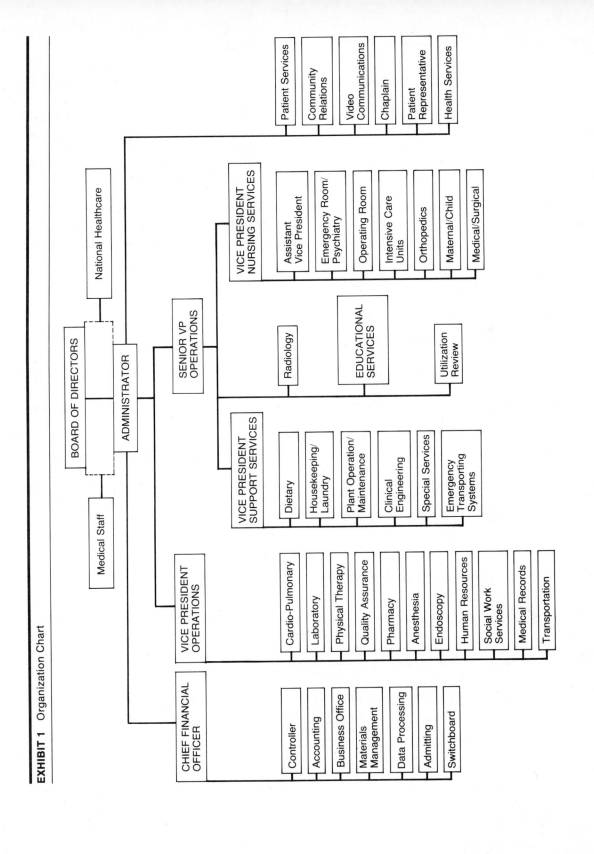

The decision to contract with National Healthcare, Inc. was made because of (1) the firm's record with not-for-profit hospitals; (2) the availability of management backup provided by the firm; and (3) the board's desire to incorporate a new philosophy and more aggressive management style in the administration of the hospital.

The previous philosophy had been one of maintaining the current level of service to the current market. The new philosophy is one of providing competitive medical care, while operating on a sound financial basis. The results have been (1) a change to a favorable financial position; (2) new services such as increased outpatient services; and (3) new markets as illustrated by the name change from a county hospital to a regional hospital.

FINANCIAL CONDITION OF EAMC

EAMC is operating under a revenue/cost squeeze that has been affecting much of the industry for the past several years. One of the primary concerns of the new management group is a strong financial position. The hospital is completing a $9 million expansion program, plus the board is looking toward improved services and expanded markets in the future. In order to handle these challenges EAMC must have a solid financial base.

Numerous changes have taken place since the new management group arrived. The initial results are reflected in the financial statements in Exhibit 2. The year ended in 1983 was prior to National Healthcare, Inc. managing the operations. The year ending 1984 is following a full year of management by National Healthcare, Inc.

EDUCATIONAL SERVICES DEPARTMENT

The educational services department began with two professional staff members and a grant from the Veterans Administration to provide continuing medical education for physicians, nurses, and allied health professionals at EAMC. Within three years EAMC was awarded a three-year, nonrenewable grant from the VA to establish a regional educational center to provide medical education on an outreach basis to 13 area hospitals in 8 counties. Three additional professional staff members were added to the department at this time.

The regional educational center enjoyed three years of progressive continuing education, while receiving grant funding each year. The funding program ended during the period when hospitals began

EXHIBIT 2

EAST ALABAMA MEDICAL CENTER
Balance Sheet

	1984		1983	
Assets				
Current assets				
Cash and certificates of deposit.		$ 247,736		$ 224,315
Accounts receivable:				
Patients	$10,309,001		$ 7,827,591	
Less: Allowance for uncollectibles.	3,137,527		2,422,821	
	7,171,474		5,404,770	
Contractual agencies—retroactive				
settlements	264,807		1,142,268	
Other	129,210	7,565,491	101,220	6,648,258
Inventories.		754,900		442,417
Prepaid expenses		167,962		145,061
Total current assets		$ 8,736,089		$ 7,460,051
Other Assets				
Board-designated investments		6,079,147		416,739
Trustee-restricted investments		6,045,667		12,869,640
Accrued interest		154,250		572,816
Deferred financing costs		306,287		312,441
Property, plant and equipment, at cost				
Land	$ 60,409		$ 60,409	
Land improvements	503,712		503,712	
Buildings	10,678,949		7,478,915	
Fixed equipment	7,287,220		5,594,577	
Major movable equipment	7,636,642		6,683,215	
Minor equipment.	69,239		69,239	
Total	$26,236,171		$20,390,067	
Less: Accumulated depreciation.	8,371,074		7,109,569	
Total	$17,865,097		$13,280,498	
Construction work in progress	8,614,416		6,126,527	
Net property, plant and equipment		26,479,513		19,407,025
Total other assets		$39,064,864		$33,578,661
Total assets		$47,800,953		$41,038,712
Liabilities and Fund Balance				
Current liabilities				
Bank overdraft		$ 692,938		$ 524,355
Accounts payable		1,189,380		925,885
Accrued payroll		326,950		365,687
Accrued vacation compensation.		179,323		183,020
Payroll taxes		210,295		63,329
Accrued pension		26,800		40,744
Retroactive settlements due contractual				
agencies.		519,283		–0–
Advances from contractual agencies		324,000		114,000
Current maturities of long-term debt.		748,255		209,271
Total current liabilities		$ 4,217,224		$ 2,426,291

EXHIBIT 2 *(concluded)*

	1984		1983	
Other liabilities				
Current bond maturities	$ 13,000		$ 13,000	
Tax bond anticipations notes	2,500,000		2,500,000	
Accrued interest payable	273,709		289,854	
Payable to contractors	881,309		880,876	
Total other liabilities		3,668,018		3,683,730
Long-term debt				
Revenue bonds, Less:				
Unamortized discount of $845,482 and $884,193 for 1984 and 1983, respectively.	$25,154,518		$25,115,807	
Hospital Tax Anticipation Bonds	41,000		54,000	
Notes payable	3,722,933		1,213,724	
Total	$28,918,451		$26,383,531	
Less: Current maturities	761,255		222,271	
Total long-term debt		28,157,196		26,161,260
Deferred reimbursement—contractual agencies*		932,666		1,084,283
Fund balance		10,825,849		7,683,148
Total liabilities and fund balance		$47,800,953		$41,038,712

EAST ALABAMA MEDICAL CENTER
Statement of Revenues and Expenses

	1984		1983	
Revenues				
Patient revenue				
Inpatient routine	$11,396,760		$10,137,819	
Inpatient ancillary	20,709,866		14,712,484	
Outpatient	4,320,540		3,373,308	
Total patient revenue	$36,427,166		$28,223,611	
Less: Deduction from revenue	11,151,786		8,517,831	
Net patient revenue		$25,275,380		$19,705,780
Other operation revenue		379,073		549,828
Total operating revenue		$25,654,453		$20,255,608
Expenses				
Operating expenses				
Service departments	$ 8,211,540		$ 7,246,448	
Earning departments	12,081,150		11,753,050	
Provision for depreciation	1,372,897		1,331,486	
Interest and amortization	2,216,931		1,635,195	
Total operating expense		23,882,518		21,966,179
Income (loss) from operations		$ 1,771,935		$ (1,710,571)
Nonoperating revenue		1,370,766		842,932
Excess of revenue over (under) expenses before extraordinary item		$ 3,142,701		$ (867,639)
Extraordinary item-gain on extinguishment of debt less deferred cost reimbursement $1,102,500		–0–		798,307
Excess of revenue over (under) expenses		$ 3,142,701		$ (69,332)

dealing with the high-cost inflationary spiral of the late 1970s and early 1980s. This increased cost resulted in a sharp drop in outside attendance from other hospitals. An attempt was made to continue the regional educational center, but without the grant to support the programs and the inability of area hospitals to absorb some of the costs of the programs in the form of fees, changes had to be made.

The educational services department was established and the total focus of the department was as an internal continuing education program for the EAMC staff. This is not to say that some programs were not open to area professionals, because the department still provided continuing education opportunities in the area of nursing. The scope of the total program did not have the regional focus as its main objective, however.

The philosophy of the department (Exhibit 3) clearly spells out the department's current role. The program should be directed to all employees and staff members of the hospital, with the ultimate goal of improved patient care.

The staff consists of (a) the director (Exhibit 4), an RN, who also serves as an educational coordinator 50 percent of the time; (b) two educational coordinators (Exhibit 5), RNs; (c) one patient educator (Exhibit 6), an RN; (d) one clinical coordinator (Exhibit 7), an RN, part time; and (e) the department secretary (Exhibit 8). The job descriptions are current and define the expectations of each department member. Each staff member is highly qualified and has been on the staff for several years, with the exception of the patient educator, who joined the department this year.

The director is reviewing the first five months of the year. The department has been busy and productive, yet she feels they are not progressing as well as they should to accomplish all the goals established for the current year. The goals were set this year just as they had been in the past. The director met with the department members to review the preceding year and to outline the program for the coming year. The goals were then approved by the senior vice president of operations.

A review of the goals of the previous year (Exhibit 9) and the current year's goals (Exhibit 10) indicate that her suspicions are correct. The previous year's goals had been 90 percent attained with the remaining 10 percent carried forward. It is not unusual to have a program carry over from the previous year. The current year, however, was not progressing quite as well. She projects the completion of less than 60 percent of the current goals.

Further review reveals that the majority of the staff has been involved with nursing programs. Only the community programs (e.g., Lamaze classes), physicians' conferences, and the new patient education program have been conducted. Even so, the community programs

EXHIBIT 3 Educational Services Department Philosophy

It is inherent that any comprehensive educational program prior to implementation incorporate a basic philosophical foundation upon which to rest. Basic philosophical beliefs give permanent program structure, serve as a consistent guide in all learning experiences, subsequent program evaluations, and provide future program direction.

As a public health care institution, the East Alabama Medical Center exists for the purpose of providing quality health care to the population it serves. Therefore, the ultimate responsibility of all the institution's employees, staff, and departments is to constantly strive to offer patients excellent health care services and the utmost in personal consideration. It is believed that the priority responsibility of the training and continuing education program, provided all departments of the institution, should be that of coordinating and servicing educational experiences and activities conducive to improved patient care. It is thought that a comprehensive educational program of learning experiences and training activities, made available for all employees, staff, and departments, should assume responsibility to better prepare each individual for their important health service role. Opportunity for optimum personal skill and/or knowledge acquirement should be provided for employees and staff. Professionally licensed staff members must also be able to attain some approved continuing education credit required of them by external professional licensing boards and organizations. Improved patient care is the principal emphasis of the continuing education program.

It is also important from the outset that the educational program consider it a responsibility to develop among all employees and staff an ever-increasing understanding of each individual's and department's contribution and value to the total health care program. Though duties, roles, and responsibilities are different, each individual and department make a valuable contribution to the total health care program provided by the institution. The hospital is truly a valid full-time human service organization and as such it is imperative that commitment be made to consistently improve human relations, communication, and understanding among its employees.

A training and continuing education program, from its inception, should involve maximum employee and professional staff participation. Local institution written policy, administration guidance, and external organization and board mandates will dictate to some degree educational plans, procedures, and requirements. However, the majority of kind and scope of learning experiences and training activities should be decided and evaluated in terms of effectiveness by employees and professional staff based upon individual and department needs and requirements.

Finally, it is believed that the educational program presented should provide meaningful learning experiences and be scheduled as conveniently as possible to insure maximum participation. A superior teaching staff is available within the institution and this outstanding source of skilled and learned talent should be utilized completely. Moreover, an effort should be made to determine the availability of and to seek and secure the more cognizant and highly trained professionals and skilled technicians to participate in the educational program. Educational training and learning experiences, well founded in their origin, preparation, and presented by the instructor who is interested, skilled, and knowledgeable, are believed the basis to achieve a successful educational program.

have not been promoted as in the past. They are well established in the community and are requested without much publicity.

To date none of the allied health areas such as pharmacy or lab technology has been addressed in the current department programs. To compound the situation, for the remainder of the year the hospital has experienced an increase in the nursing staff of 44 percent, up from 202 to 291. This unusual increase is part of the hospital expansion

---

EXHIBIT 4 Director of Educational Services Department: Job Description

---

1. *Job Summary*

   The director coordinates the planning, development, implementation, and evaluation of education programs and in-services conducive to improved patient care for East Alabama Medical Center patients, the public, and employees.

2. *Education*

   Graduate of an accredited school of nursing, or college or university.

3. *Experience*

   Three years teaching experience preferably in a health care setting. Training or experience in hospital procedure, routines, and policies desirable.

4. *Mental Demands*

   Requires ability to communicate and listen in order to spot and solve problems; consideration, initiative, and judgment for reviewing and analyzing educational needs and problems while working independently; attentiveness and critical thinking in developing programs; empathy, patience, and diplomacy in dealing with others; potential to be a facilitator in order to integrate the goals and activities of the educational services department with overall goals of East Alabama Medical Center; ability to organize materials and time; be able to teach and facilitate group learning; be instinctive in understanding the environment and ethics of the institution; willingness to be an advocate of the institution; ability to motivate.

5. *Responsibility for Supervision*

   The director is responsible for the supervision of the education department employees, provides coordination of the planning, development, implementation, and evaluation of the hospitalwide education program. The director performs supervisory functions without intermediate supervisors and reports to the senior vice president.

6. *Contact with Others*

   Requires frequent contacts with many people at different levels inside and outside the hospital to coordinate continuing education, in-service, patient and community education. Devotes large amounts of time to intermittent contacts with many people at all levels to assess needs, formulate plans, write objectives, obtain CEUs from appropriate agencies, research content, implement learning experience, and evaluate programs. Serves on appropriate hospital, community, and professional committees.

7. *Effect of Error*

   Work evaluated by formal written methods, performance appraisals, verbal feedback, and peer review. Errors could result in loss of credibility for the department and poor professional and public image, and ultimately errors in the direct delivery of patient care.

8. *Physical Demands*

   Work requires sitting, standing, and walking throughout the working day, frequently standing for long hours teaching in the classroom. The ability to lift, push, and pull equipment and carts and the manual dexterity to operate various types of audio-visual equipment required. Requires good vision and communication skills. Fatigue resulting from mental stress in dealing with numerous demands, rapidly changing situations, and a wide variety of personalities not unusual. Workload and working hours inconsistent requiring flexibility in availability. Some traveling required.

9. *Working Conditions*

   Works in an office and classroom setting most of the day.

EXHIBIT 5 Educational Coordinator: Job Description

---

1. *Job Summary*

   The educational coordinator is directly involved with the planning, development, implementation, and evaluation of educational programs, in addition to planning and implementing orientation for new nursing service employees at EAMC.

2. *Education*

   Graduate of an accredited school of nursing, registered professional nurse, currently licensed with the state of Alabama Board of Nursing.

3. *Experience*

   A minimum of three years clinical experience in a hospital setting.

4. *Mental Demands*

   Communication and listening skills; ability to solve problems; organizational abilities; ability to identify educational needs and the initiative to plan and implement appropriate programs or in-services to meet those needs; ability to work independently and with others within and outside the department; understand the principles of learning and be able to effectively teach others; motivated to maintain the high standards of the department and the institution.

5. *Responsibility for Supervision*

   None.

6. *Contact with Others*

   Requires frequent contact with many people at different levels inside and outside the hospital; must be able to communicate effectively with others in order to assess needs, plan, and implement educational activities, and evaluate outcomes; communication with outside agencies frequently required; serves an appropriate hospital, community, and professional committees and organizations.

7. *Effects of Errors*

   Work evaluated by the department director in the form of written performance appraisals and verbal communication. Errors could result in loss of credibility for the department, poor professional and public image, and possible errors in the actual delivery of patient care.

8. *Physical Demands*

   Work requires sitting, standing, and walking throughout the working day, frequently standing for long hours teaching in the classroom. The ability to lift, push, and pull equipment and carts and the manual dexterity to operate various types of audiovisual equipment required. Requires good vision and communication skills. Fatigue resulting from mental stress in dealing with numerous demands, rapidly changing situations, and a wide variety of personalities not unusual. Workload and working hours inconsistent, requiring flexibility in availability. Some traveling is required.

9. *Working Conditions*

   Works in an office and a classroom setting most of the day.

---

currently underway. It also means the resources of the department will be heavily involved with the orientation program for the new nurses.

To further complicate matters, the department secretary is planning to leave to return to school. This means an inexperienced replacement. The director knows that the updating of physician's con-

---

EXHIBIT 6   Patient Educator: Job Description

---

1. *Education*

   Graduate of an accredited school of nursing. Registered in the state of Alabama.

2. *Experience*

   Two years of hospital-based clinical experience preferred. Previous teaching experience desirable.

3. *Mental Demands*

   Requires ability to communicate and listen in order to spot and solve problems; consideration, initiative, and judgment for reviewing and analyzing educational needs and problems while working independently; attentiveness and critical thinking in developing programs; empathy, patience, and diplomacy in dealing with others; potential to be a facilitator in order to integrate the goals and activities of the educational services department with overall goals of East Alabama Medical Center; ability to organize materials and time; be able to teach and facilitate group learning; be instinctive in understanding the environment and ethics of the institution; ability to motivate.

4. *Responsibility for Supervision*

   The patient educator reports directly to the director of the educational services department.

5. *Contact with Others*

   Requires frequent contacts with many people at different levels inside and outside the hospital to coordinate patient education services within the hospital. Devotes large amounts of time to intermittent contacts with many people at all levels to assess needs, formulate plans, write objectives, research content, implement learning experience, and evaluate programs. Serves on appropriate hospital, community, and professional committees.

6. *Effect of Error*

   Work evaluated by formal written methods, performance appraisals, verbal feedback, peer review, and statistical data. Errors could result in poor patient response to treatment, decreased credibility for the educator, and poor professional and public image.

7. *Physical Demands*

   Work requires sitting, standing, and walking throughout the working day, frequently standing for long hours teaching in the classroom. The ability to lift, push, and pull equipment and carts and the manual dexterity to operate various types of audiovisual equipment required. Requires good vision and communication skills. Fatigue resulting from mental stress in dealing with numerous demands, rapidly changing situations, and a wide variety of personalities not unusual. Workload and working hours inconsistent, requiring flexibility in availability. Some traveling is required.

8. *Working Conditions*

   Works in an office, classroom setting, and patient care areas.

---

ference records are eight months behind and the educational program records have not been updated for the past six months. These records are maintained manually by the secretary. The director has discussed temporary help with the secretary to bring these records up to date. There has been some discussion also about getting a personal com-

EXHIBIT 7 Clinical Coordinator: Job Description

1. *Job Summary*

   The clinical coordinator is a member of the educational services department, under the direction and supervision of the director of the educational services department, human resources director, and the nursing services director. This is a part-time position consisting of approximately 20 hours per week or less.

2. *Primary Duties*
   a. Responsible for orientation of all students using East Alabama Medical Center clinical facilities.
   b. Meet periodically with instructors or appointed personnel from the various schools to assure that educational objectives are being met.
   c. Scheduling of students in the various clinical areas of East Alabama Medical Center.
   d. Meet periodically with supervisors from the various clinical areas to discuss any problem areas concerning students, instructors, etc.
   e. Responsible for scheduling times for name badges to be made.
   f. Responsible for providing feedback to the various faculties concerning students' work at East Alabama Medical Center.
   g. Responsible for making sure contracts are kept current.
   h. Responsible for maintaining lines of communication with our scholarship nurses.
   i. Assist with recruiting of nurses when needed.

EXHIBIT 8 Department Secretary: Job Description

1. *Summary of Duties*

   Performs secretarial and general office work to relieve the RN instructors and educational consultants of administrative and clerical details; assists in carrying out responsibilities of the educational services department as directed by the director of educational services.

2. *Primary Duties*

   Type and route correspondence for RN instructors and allied health instructor. Design, type, xerox, and mail brochures and flyers for educational programs. Type and xerox handout material for educational programs. Prepare name tags and folders for educational programs. Type, xerox, and mail program records and certificates. Keep registration for regularly scheduled educational programs. Type, xerox, and route weekly educational calendars to hospital department heads. Responsible for Tuesday morning physicians' conference: type, xerox, and route memorandums, schedule speakers, set up audiovisual equipment, maintain records. Prepare news releases for community programs. Prepare monthly schedules for dietary and housekeeping departments. Submit program approval forms and records for nursing, radiology, pharmacy, and medical records program. Control checkout system for audiovisual software, equipment, books, etc. Control correspondence, receiving, and shipping of all rented or loaned audiovisual software. Prepare slides as requested by the director. Maintain continuous listing of programs conducted. Prepare, xerox, and route monthly "program update" sheets. Assist with registration, breaks, and lunches at special programs and conferences. Responsible for maintaining orderliness of paper supplies located in graphics department. Other typing, xeroxing, and filing, etc. as requested.

EXHIBIT 8 *(concluded)*

3. *Periodical or Occasional Duties*

Assist with programs held outside the hospital. Type special brochures for other departments. Set up films, videotapes, etc. for other departments. Attend special meetings and record minutes. Assist with EMT functions. Be present at Tuesday morning physicians' conferences. Run errands outside the hospital for the department. Plan and organize educational programs for secretarial and clerical workers. Attend educational programs in the evening.

4. *Job Relationships*

Workers supervised: None. Supervised by educational services department director.

5. *Machines, Tools, and Materials*

Standard office equipment and supplies, primarily a typewriter, Xerox machine, videotape player, Sony videocamera, 16 millimeter projector, and 35 millimeter carousel.

6. *Education, Training, and Experience*

Minimum requirements are graduation from high school including courses in English, typing, business writing, and some mathematics. Either commercial training, one year secretarial experience, or related college courses preferred. Posthigh school degree desirable. Courses in medical terminology desirable.

7. *Worker Traits*

Aptitudes: Verbal ability is needed to communicate with the general public and department heads in planning and implementing educational programs. Clerical perception is needed to verify educational records and information for reports. Motor coordination is needed for typing forms. Manual dexterity is need for sorting, summarizing, and filing records.

Interests: A preference for business contacts, typing, writing, and keeping records. A preference for routine, concrete, and organized activities.

Temperaments: Versatile; work involves a variety of duties to be done for the director and three nurse/staff instructors. Communicates with the general public, doctors, and department heads while discussing educational programs.

Physical demands and working conditions: Work is sedentary, requiring some lifting and moving of audiovisual equipment, books, and files. Reaches for, handles, and fingers records, reports, and typewriter. Walks through the hospital at least once a week issuing weekly calendars to department heads and nurse stations. Must observe strict personal hygiene habits.

---

puter in the department to computerize some of the records to help in the clerical area. The director also knows that the secretary is the "operating hub" of the department. She deals with practically every call or caller to the department and greatly facilitates a smooth-running department.

As the director surveys her findings, she considers the management policy that allows no overtime in the department. Overtime will not help, she thinks, as the staff performs very creative, high energy, and self-starting functions in the identification and development of programs to improve staff performance; hence, overtime might not be productive. Besides, many programs are held in the evening in order

EXHIBIT 9 Educational Services Department: Goals for 1982–83

1. Offer community programs for the public on a regular basis—four to six programs this year.
2. Have the closed-circuit TV system in operation.
3. Have monthly unit conference in each area.
4. Hospitalwide monthly movies.
5. Continue monthly registered nurse (RN), licensed practical nurse (LPN), cardiopulmonary resuscitation (CPR), and nurse aid training program (NATP).
6. Continue biannual RN state board review, LPN IV therapy, hospitalwide CPR.
7. Offer a critical care course for EAMC employees biannually.
8. Offer five all-day regional workshops.
9. Develop a comprehensive in-house diabetic patient education program.
10. Continue to offer pediatric group preparation program weekly.
11. Develop and begin the quality assurance "quality investigator team."
12. Continue the current individualized orientation program as revised in June and evaluate next June.
13. Continue to plan and implement in-service programs on all new equipment, materials, and procedures as needed.
14. Continue to offer 30 hours to hospital and community pharmacist.
15. Sponsor or cosponsor two advanced cardiac life support (ACLS) courses per year.
16. Cosponsor one advanced trauma life support (ATLS) per year.
17. Sponsor one regionwide program for department heads and supervisors.
18. Continue prenatal and Lamaze, increasing Lamaze to three classes per six week period.
19. Continue to provide support to physicians' continuing medical education (CME) program.
20. Continue monthly CPR for the public.
21. Host one basic cardiac life support (BCLS) instructor course.
22. Provide clinical coordination for students of educational institutions.
23. Assist when possible in recruiting and retention activities.
24. Support and coordinate emergency medical technician (EMT) training for basic and intermediate-level students.
25. Schedule a planning session for regional in-service coordinators to determine the continuing education needs of the regional hospitals.
26. To provide increased opportunities for in-service and continuing education programs for allied health personnel.
27. To review Joint Commission on Accreditation of Hospitals (JCAH) education standards for all departments and provide opportunities for the fulfillment of those standards.
28. To develop a system of documentation of educational records that would be easily and quickly accessible.
29. To serve as liaison to community health care providers in areas where coordination of services and awareness of services could be enhanced.
30. Host one continuing education conference for hospital educators.

EXHIBIT 10   Educational Services Department: Goals for 1983–84

1. Offer community programs for public on wellness—four to six programs this year.
2. Continue to offer pediatric group preparation program weekly.
3. Continue prenatal, Lamaze, Lamaze refresher, C-section birth, and early pregnancy classes.
4. Continue monthly CPR for the public.
5. Offering sibling preparation classes quarterly.*
6. To participate, when possible, in health related community functions.
7. Have the closed-circuit TV system in operation.
8. Develop a comprehensive in-house diabetic patient education program.
9. Offer monthly unit conferences in each area as needed.
10. Offer hospitalwide monthly brown bag luncheons with presentations on health and fitness.*
11. Continue to plan and implement in-service programs on all new equipment, materials, and procedures as needed.
12. To review JCAH education standards for all departments and provide opportunities for the fulfillment of those standards.
13. Cosponsor ATLS as requested.
14. Continue to provide support to physicians' CME program.
15. Continue monthly RN, LPN continuing education programs.
16. Continue biannual RN state board review, LPN IV therapy, hospitalwide CPR.
17. Offer a critical care course for East Alabama Medical Center employees at least biannually, or more often as required by nursing services.
18. Offer five all-day regional workshops.
19. Continue to offer 30 hours to hospital and community pharmacists.
20. Sponsor one ACLS course per year.
21. Cosponsor with administration, hospitalwide program for department heads and supervisors as indicated.
22. Sponsor one BCLS instructor course.
23. Support and coordinate EMT training for basic and intermediate-level students.
24. Schedule a planning session for regional in-service coordinators to determine the continuing education needs of the regional hospitals.
25. Develop a system of documentation of educational records that would be easily and quickly accessible.
26. Host one continuing education conference for hospital educators.
27. Offer a statewide nursing assistant (NA) conference.
28. Offer statewide secretary/unit secretary conference.*
29. Actively participate in appropriate professional organizations Alabama Society for Health, Education, and Training (AlaSHET).
30. Obtain appropriate continuing education units (CEU) approval for nursing and allied health programs.
31. Plan and implement continuing education programs as requested by radiology.
32. Continue development of continuing education for medical records personnel.
33. Assist in planning and developing bimonthly continuing education programs for medical technologists.
34. Offer hospitalwide medical terminology course quarterly.*
35. Offer NA training program and unit secretary course as needed.
36. Continue the current individual orientation program as revised in June and evaluate next June.
37. Assist when possible in recruiting and retention activities.
38. Provide clinical coordination for students of educational institutions.

* New program.

to meet with staff that are off duty and to serve the needs of the community.

With this on her mind, she cannot help thinking of the meeting she had recently with the senior vice president of operations where they had discussed the addition of a marketing function in the educational services department.

The Aviation Segment

22.   Beech Aircraft Corporation

As 1979 drew to a close, Mrs. Beech, the company's cofounder, knew she would be reporting record earnings for the seventh straight year. Olive Ann Beech and her nephew Frank Hedrick had directed the company since the death of her husband Walter H. Beech in 1950. Both Beech and Hedrick had participated in merger discussions for the past five years. To some, the question seemed to be not "Should Beech merge?" but "With whom?" Accordingly, Beech had contracted with a New York investment banker to do a study of merger possibilities. More than a dozen potential partners were to be considered and the firm was to recommend the best candidate for merger with Beech. The name Beech had always stood for quality. How could the company plan a future which would maintain its identity as a producer of high-quality commercial and military aircraft, achieve a 15 percent sales growth every year, and continue the development of new aircraft and aerospace technologies?

COMPANY HISTORY

Walter Beech, who cofounded Beech Aircraft Corporation with his wife, was born on a farm near Pulaski, Tennessee, on January 30, 1891. Even as a child, Beech was mechanically inclined. Beech's interest in airplanes led to his first solo flight in an old Curtiss pusher biplane in 1914. In World War I, he served three years as an army pilot, flight instructor, and engineer. With this experience, he became an exhibition pilot in 1920. He further increased his aeronautical knowledge, coming up with many ideas for improved aircraft design and construction. In 1923, Beech moved to Wichita to accept a job with Swallow Airplane Corporation. A year later, he formed his own aircraft company, Travel Air Manufacturing. By 1929, Travel Air was the world's largest commercial producer of both monoplanes and biplanes[1] which

This case received a "Best Case Award" at the 1981 Case Research Association meeting in Atlanta. The development of the case was supported in part by the University of Kansas Fund for Instructional Improvement and the School of Business. The case was prepared by Professor Marilyn L. Taylor of the University of Kansas. The collaboration of Michael Neuburger of Beech Aircraft Corporation and Carolyn Patterson, Brian Kaufman, and Teresa Wolfe is gratefully acknowledged.
    [1] A monoplane has one pair of wings. A biplane has wings at two different levels, usually one above and one below the fuselage.

were known for their superior quality. As the depression deepened, sales in the aircraft industry fell. This led to a merger of Travel Air and Curtis-Wright. Beech's responsibilities in the new company were mainly executive and he had little involvement in design and construction. Since his new duties were inconsistent with his personal goals, he resigned in 1931. In 1932, Walter and Olive Ann Beech cofounded Beech Aircraft in Wichita.

A long-time resident of Wichita commented on the Beeches' contributions to the company.

> Mrs. Beech was a source of strength and stability for the company. She put the organization together . . . (he was) the inventive genius; she was the organizational aspect of the company.

The Beeches formulated the company objective "to design and build a five-place biplane having the interior luxury and passenger comfort of a fine sedan, a top speed of 200 mph or better, a landing speed no higher than 60 mph, a nonstop range close to 1,000 miles, and easy controllability and sound aerodynamic characteristics. [7] The first Beech biplane flew on November 4, 1932. Design improvements were added and by 1934, the Beechcraft B17L was ready for full-fledged production. Business was brisk and production doubled so that 18 Model 17 planes were built during the year. Development work was initiated on a Model 18 plane, and it made its maiden flight in 1937.

In 1936, Beech Aircraft Company was succeeded by Beech Aircraft Corporation. The reorganization was purely a financial move increasing capitalization from $25,000 to more than $100,000 and creating a base for growth. Beech Aircraft Corporation prospered throughout the 1930s and Walter Beech realized one of his goals— sales exceeding $1 million. As the Axis powers gained strength, Beech went into the production of hospital transports and bombardiers and navigator trainers for the government. During World War II, except for priority orders, all commercial production was curtailed, as the company went into full support of the war effort. By the end of the war, the company had produced 7,400 airplanes for defense.

In 1943, the company organized a subsidiary to dispose of surplus and obsolete materials resulting from war production. Although the subsidiary was dissolved when the surplus was depleted, this move was a unique idea in the industry and demonstrated the innovativeness of management. At the end of the war, Beech went back into commercial production. By the end of the 1940s, the Beechcraft line included an eight-place deluxe Model 18 and the start of the famous Bonanza line with Model 35. The Bonanza plane immediately had a 1,500-plane order backlog. In 1950, Mrs. Beech took control of the company when Walter died.

Operations were expanded to include leased plants at a former air base in Liberal, Kansas. The company added many models in the 1950s, including the world's first executive jet airplane, the MS760 "Paris," the Beechcraft Twin-Bonanza and Beechcraft Travel Air. The first flight of a Beechcraft missile target was successfully completed in 1955.

In the 1960s, many milestones were passed. Beech expanded its product line in 1962 to include the Model 23 Musketeer, the Model 65 Queen Air, the Model 60 Duke and the 99 Airliner. The U.S. Navy accepted the Beechcraft supersonic missile target in 1963. In 1964, Beech introduced the turboprop engine into its corporate series by bringing the Model 90 King Air to the market.

The 1970s were prosperous years for Beechcraft. The first Beech Aero Club was initiated in 1974, and this idea spread widely. Beech won many defense contracts over competitors. In the closing years of the 1970s, Beech introduced the executive flight plan to boost sales to companies. Beech also recorded its first sale to the Republic of China in over 30 years and international backlog was at an all-time high. The company had been a subcontractor for the other major companies since 1944. Included in subcontracts in the late 1970s were parts for McDonnell Douglas' F-4 and F-15s and a $13 million subcontract for the space shuttle program for Rockwell.

The key to the company's growth was the breadth of its product line (Exhibit 1). The Beech line included small single-engine planes like the Sierra and Sundowner; the larger, more widely known Bonanza line; the multiengine Duke and Baron series; and the larger Queen Air. The King Air line, consisting of turboprop aircraft, represented the top of Beech's line. These commercial sales plus military sales gave Beech a record sales level of $527 million in 1978, and a net income of $35 million (Exhibits 2, 3, 4, and 5).

In 1979, Beech had one of the highest market shares in the general aviation industry. The company was second in terms of dollar volume and third in number of aircraft sold. Major competitors were Cessna and Piper. C. A. Rembleske, vice president of engineering, echoed the company philosophy:

> We don't care about *most*, just better airplanes and customer service support. Beech has always prided itself in setting the pace.

COMPANY OPERATIONS

In 1978, Beech's facilities included the main plant and general offices in Wichita; a company-owned plant plus engineering and research and development facilities in Boulder, Colorado; and two leased facilities in Liberal and Salina, Kansas. The Wichita site had complete manufacturing facilities (which included over 1,000 acres of land) and

EXHIBIT 1 Cessna, Beechcraft, and Piper Product Lines

Price 1975	Model	Engine (single)	Recommended Flight Range	Maximum Cruise Speed
CESSNA				
Two-seaters:				
$ 17,995	152	110 hp Lycoming	403 miles	127 mph
19,000	152 Aerobat	110 hp Lycoming	662 miles	126 mph
Four-seaters:				
$ 23,495	Skyhawk	160 hp Lycoming	558 miles	174 mph
—	R172E	210 hp Continental	1010 miles	152 mph
31,595	R172HawkXP	195 hp Continental	662 miles	153 mph
49,975	Cardinal Classic	180 by Lycoming	772 miles	160 mph
43,950	Cardinal RG	200 hp Lycoming	823 miles	180 mph
Agricultural:				
$ 43,950	AG Wagon (one-seater)	300 hp Continental	370 miles	151 mph
49,650	AG Truck (one-seater)	300 hp Continental	295 miles	121 mph
49,400	AG Carryall (2-6 seater)	300 hp Continental	565 miles	148 mph
Five- to eight-seaters:				
$ 48,750	Stationair 6	300 hp Continental	702 miles	180 mph
54,750	Turbo Stationair 6	310 hp Turbo-chg. Con.	662 miles	192 mph
54,950	Stationair 7	300 hp Continental	449 miles	173 mph
61,500	Turbo Stationair 7	310 hp Turbo-chg. Con.	604 miles	196 mph
63,950	Centurion	310 hp Continental	1226 miles	202 mph
123,500	310	Two flat-six engines	1303 miles	238 mph
69,900	Skymaster	Two 210 hp Continental	—	—
—	Skylane	—	—	—
34,950	Skywagon 180	One 230 hp Continental	835 miles	192 mph
198,000	340A	Two 310 hp Continental	1322 miles	281 mph
	402	Two 300 hp Continental	1243 miles	264 mph
Eight- to thirteen-seaters:				
$ 257,000	414A Chancellor	Two 310 hp Continental	1316 miles	275 mph
316,000	421C	Two 375 hp Continental	1440 miles	297 mph
280,000	Titan	Two 375 hp Continental	1749 miles	267 mph
850,000	Conquest (turboprop)	Two Garrett-Aires	1490 miles	340 mph
1,150,000	Citation I (turbofan)	Two Pratt & Whitney	1532 miles	403 mph
1,395,000	Citation II (turbofan)	Two Pratt & Whitney	1968 miles	420 mph
—	Citation III	Two Pratt & Whitney	2170 miles	540 mph
BEECHCRAFT				
Two- to five-seaters:				
$ 31,750	Sundowner 180 C23	180 hp Lycoming	687 miles	123 kn.
26,300	Sport 150 B19	150 hp Lycoming	747 miles	110 kn.
43,850	Sierra 200	200 hp Lycoming	790 miles	142 kn.
72,575	Bonanza	285 hp Continental	824 miles	182 kn.
91,850	Duchess 76	Two 180 hp Lycoming	818 miles	197 mph
115,500	Baron (up to $216,850)	Two 260 hp Continental	1044 miles	231 mph
279,500	Duke B60	Two 380 hp Lycoming	1203 miles	283 mph
Six- to twelve-seaters:				
309,500	Queen Air	Two 380 hp Lycoming	1102 miles	248 mph
561,500	King Air (turboprop)	Two 550 hp Pratt & W.	1295 miles	287 mph
Up to seventeen-seaters:				
937,000	B99 Airliner (turboprop)	Two 680 hp Pratt & W.	1456 miles	276 mph
825,000	King Air 100 (turboprop)	Two 680 hp Pratt & W.	1395 miles	270 mph
1,065,000	Super King Air 200 (turboprop)	Two 850 hp Pratt & W.	1370 miles	333 mph

EXHIBIT 1 *(concluded)*

Price 1975	Model	Engine (single)	Recommended Flight Range	Maximum Cruise Speed
PIPER				
Two-seaters:				
$ 21,750	Super Cub	150 hp Lycoming	460 miles	153 mph
15,840	Tomahawk	112 hp Lycoming	402 miles	109 kn.
Four- to eight-seaters:				
$ 118,250	Aztec F Turbo	Two 250 hp Lycoming	1317 miles	253 mph
22,360	Warrior II	160 hp Lycoming	674 miles	176 mph
27,510	Archer II	180 hp Lycoming	679 miles	171 mph
40,650	Arrow III	200 hp Lycoming	1047 miles	214 mph
—	Dakota	235 hp Lycoming	801 miles	170 mph
43,860	Cherokee Six ($47,910)	260 hp Lycoming (300)	806 miles	180 mph
58,990	Lance II	260 hp Lycoming	900 miles	217 mph
193,000	Navajo (turbo-charged)	Two 310 hp Lycoming	1002 miles	261 mph
219,560	Chieftain (turbo-charged)	Two 350 hp Lycoming	869 miles	271 mph
519,500	Cheyenne I (turboprop)	Two 500 hp Pratt & W.	1133 miles	265 mph
532,300	Cheyenne II (turboprop)	Two 620 hp Pratt & W.	1589 miles	326 mph
91,000	Seneca II	Two 200 hp Continental	902 miles	225 mph
—	Cheyenne III (11-seater)	Two 680 hp Pratt & W.	2452 miles	283 mph
Agricultural:				
$ 38,220	Pawnee D-235	235 hp Lycoming	290 miles	150 mph
54,760	Brave ($73,170)	300 hp Lycoming (375)	360 miles	149 mph
—	Tomahawk	552 hp Lycoming	552 miles	150 mph

EXHIBIT 2 Beech Aircraft Corporation Consolidated Balance Sheets

	September 30	
	1978	1977
Assets		
Current assets		
Cash.	$ 7,457,183	$ 2,883,889
Marketable securities—at cost (approximate market)	8,539,891	6,433,248
Trade notes and accounts receivable:		
Installment receivables, less allowances for losses and unearned finance charges	47,130,979	40,034,408
United States government and prime contractors.	11,742,846	6,503,490
Other, less allowances of $336,197 in 1978 and $329,848 in 1977	9,690,911	7,541,834
	$ 68,564,736	$ 54,079,732
Inventories.	142,149,846	124,940,146
Prepaid expenses.	1,202,940	715,556
Total current assets.	$227,914,596	$189,052,571
Investments in securities—at cost (approximate market)	$ 19,440,229	$ 17,269,666
Other assets	494,102	393,206

EXHIBIT 2 *(concluded)*

	September 30	
	1978	1977
Property, plant, and equipment		
Land.	$ 1,700,000	$ 1,700,000
Buildings and improvements	18,846,625	18,392,506
Machinery and equipment.	36,121,196	32,244,029
	$ 56,667,821	$ 52,336,535
Less allowances for depreciation	(37,888,849)	(34,897,728)
	$ 18,778,972	$ 17,438,807
	$266,627,899	$224,154,250

	September 30	
	1978	1977

Liabilities and Stockholders' Equity

	1978	1977
Current liabilities		
Notes payable to banks	$ 4,766,560	$ 4,719,887
Trade accounts payable.	37,654,035	31,046,598
Payroll and payroll deductions	12,411,763	8,899,833
Accrued expenses	7,076,851	5,408,840
Customer deposits	6,114,273	14,956,650
Federal and state income taxes (including deferred tax of $2,936,000 in 1978 and $1,849,000 in 1977)	17,107,770	10,051,601
Current portion of long-term debt	212,554	205,192
Total current liabilities	$ 85,343,806	$ 75,288,601
Long-term debt.	$ 24,096,940	$ 33,486,953
Deferred income taxes	2,200,000	
Reserves for insurance claims.	8,919,246	6,059,388
Stockholders' equity		
Common stock, par value $1 a share: Authorized 15,000,000 shares; issued 1978—12,097,392 incl. 688,356 in treasury	$ 12,097,392	
1977—7,528,081 incl. 446,116 in treasury.		$ 7,528,081
Additional paid-in capital	$ 30,122,432	$ 20,683,932
Retained earnings	107,892,250	85,027,416
Less cost of common stock in treasury	(4,044,167)	(3,920,121)
	$146,067,907	$109,319,308
Commitments and contingent liabilities	$266,627,899	$224,154,250

SOURCE: 1978 *Annual Report,* Beech Aircraft Corporation.

a flying field. All of the metal work along with most final assembly work was done at this plant because it was the only one with the necessary equipment. Portions of some models were shipped to Wichita from the other plants to be incorporated into Wichita-assembled aircraft, which were then thoroughly flight tested before being sold. All of the leased plants were former air force military bases. The Schilling Airbase in Salina, Kansas, a 582,000-square-feet area which

EXHIBIT 3 Beech Aircraft Corporation Consolidated Statements of Income and Retained Earnings

	Years Ended September 30	
	1978	*1977*
Net sales	$527,510,511	$417,419,646
Other income	8,434,525	6,353,498
	$535,945,036	$423,773,144
Costs and expenses		
Wages, materials, and other costs	$396,122,481	$317,909,910
Selling, general, and administrative expenses . . .	48,184,146	40,435,377
Interest	3,264,442	3,455,903
Depreciation	3,751,244	3,354,028
Taxes, other than income taxes	11,693,847	8,847,425
	$463,016,160	$374,002,643
Income before income taxes	$ 72,928,876	$ 49,770,501
Federal and state income tax provision	$ 37,408,000	$ 24,288,000
Net income	$ 35,520,876	$ 25,482,501
Retained earnings at beginning of year	85,027,416	66,563,113
	$120,548,292	$ 92,045,614
Less:		
Cash dividends paid: 1978—$.76 a share	$ 8,383,192	
1977—$.65 a share		$ 7,018,198
Market value of common stock issued as 2%		
stock dividend.	4,101,308	
Cash payment in lieu of fractional shares	171,542	
	$ 12,656,042	$ 7,018,198
Retained earnings at end of year	$107,892,250	$ 85,027,416
Earnings per share		
Primary	$3.14	$2.32
Fully diluted.	$2.83	$2.08
Source:		
Primary	$3.14	$2.32
Fully diluted.	$2.83	$2.08

SOURCE: 1978 *Annual Report,* Beech Aircraft Corporation.

had been leased since 1966, produced the twin-engine pressurized Baron, the Duke, and wings for most Beech airplanes. The leased base in Liberal, Kansas, produced the smaller aircraft of the Beech line such as the Skipper, Sundowner, Sierra, and tail surfaces for other aircraft. This 113,000-square-feet facility ran test flights and delivered the planes that it produced. In February 1979, Beech leased a base in Selma, Alabama, where the King Air 200 was modified into a surveillance aircraft. This site was also suited for the construction of commuter planes. Beech had also leased a plant in Newton, Kansas, in order to expand operations. Beech's other owned facility, in Boulder, Colorado, consisted of 111,000 square feet of plant and office space.

EXHIBIT 4 Consolidated Statements of Changes in Financial Position

	Years Ended September 30	
	1978	*1977*
Source of funds		
From operations:		
Net income for the year.	$35,520,876	$25,482,501
Expenses not requiring use of working capital:		
Depreciation.	3,751,244	3,354,028
Increase in reserves for insurance claims . . .	2,859,858	565,251
Deferred income taxes	2,200,000	
Total from operations.	$44,331,978	$29,401,780
Proceeds from long-term debt	—	2,930,000
Disposals of property, plant, and equipment	192,032	515,209
Issuance of common stock under stock option		
plans	812,740	1,358,688
Issuance of common stock for debenture		
conversions	9,093,763	168,383
	$54,430,513	$34,374,060
Application of funds		
Increase in working capital	$28,806,820	$18,649,868
Additions to property, plant, and equipment	5,283,441	7,710,319
Increase in investments.	2,170,563	220,076
Reductions of long-term debt.	9,390,013	728,165
Cash dividends paid	8,383,192	7,018,198
Cash payments in lieu of fractional shares in		
connection with stock dividend	171,542	
Cost of common stock purchased for treasury . . .	124,046	
Increase in other assets.	100,896	47,434
	$54,430,513	$34,374,060
Changes in components of working capital		
Increase (decrease) in current assets:		
Cash	$ 4,573,294	$ (1,900,101)
Marketable securities.	2,106,643	6,193,630
Trade notes and accounts receivable	14,485,004	11,287,510
Inventories.	17,209,700	18,895,628
Prepaid expenses	487,384	20,529
	$38,862,025	$34,497,196
Decrease (increase) in current liabilities:		
Notes payable	$ (46,673)	$ 1,745,497
Trade accounts payable	(6,607,437)	(5,660,538)
Payroll and payroll deductions	(3,511,930)	228,698
Accrued expenses	(1,668,011)	(1,446,653)
Customer deposits	8,842,377	(7,310,767)
Federal and state income taxes	(7,056,169)	(3,382,459)
Current portion of long-term debt	(7,362)	(21,106)
	(10,055,205)	(15,847,328)
Increase in working capital	$28,806,820	$18,649,868

SOURCE: 1978 *Annual Report,* Beech Aircraft Corporation.

EXHIBIT 5   Five Years in Review (dollars in thousands—except per share data)

	Fiscal Years Ended September 30:				
	1978	*1977*	*1976*	*1975*	*1974*
Summary of operations					
Net sales	$527,511	$417,420	$346,926	$267,149	$241,603
Commercial	414,692	328,530	291,300	246,924	219,260
Defense/aerospace	112,819	88,890	55,626	20,225	22,343
Wages, materials, and other costs	396,122	317,910	264,309	198,114	186,488
Interest expense	3,264	3,456	4,135	4,818	4,257
Cash dividends paid	8,383	7,018	5,369	4,432	3,614
Cash dividends per share*	.76	.65	.50	.42	.33
Taxes on income	37,408	24,288	18,017	13,784	9,687
Net income	35,521	25,483	20,361	15,612	12,479
Net income as a percent of sales	6.7%	6.1%	5.9%	5.8%	5.2%
Earnings per share†					
Primary	3.14	2.32	1.88	1.46	1.15
Fully diluted	2.83	2.08	1.69	1.33	1.06
Financial position					
Working capital	$142,571	$113,764	$ 95,114	$ 81,532	$ 66,376
Plant and equipment, net after depreciation	18,779	17,439	13,598	12,747	11,658
Stockholders' equity	146,068	109,319	89,328	73,786	62,864
Stockholders' equity per share‡	13.13	10.09	8.34	6.93	5.82
Other information					
Number of employees at September 30	10,395	9,076	8,216	7,747	7,580
Total salaries and wages	129,760	104,692	93,947	84,468	71,063
Expenditures for fixed assets	5,283	7,710	4,617	4,412	2,766
Depreciation	3,751	3,354	3,239	2,992	2,627
Taxes levied on company	49,102	33,135	26,014	21,124	15,992
Taxes levied on company per share‡	4.41	3.06	2.43	1.98	1.48
Shares outstanding (less treasury stock) at year end (in thousands)	11,409	7,082	6,965	6,836	6,790

* Based on rate paid and adjusted for the stock dividends and split.

† Primary and fully diluted earnings per share have been adjusted for the 3 for 2 stock split in 1978; one percent stock dividends in 1975, 1976; two percent stock dividend 1978 and the 1 percent stock dividend paid November 17, 1978.

‡ Based on average outstanding shares and adjusted for the stock dividends and split.

SOURCE: 1978 *Annual Report,* Beech Aircraft Corporation.

Research and development at the Boulder facility had accelerated with the use of the computer in designing products. The Boulder plant also manufactured aircraft related products. [10]

The manufacturing and assembling of airplanes had become increasingly automated. By the 1970s, shop orders were computerized and the parts were machine produced. A quality control inspector examined each lot to check for flaws. Beech used an expensive procedure, chemical milling, to reinforce stress points on the parts. The process included applying latex rubber cement to areas of the stress points. Chemical baths reduced the metal weight where the thickness was not needed. The process, though expensive, reduced excess metal weight unlike the design which most competitors used. The parts were then sent through an automatic electrostatic painting process, which accommodated 10,000 parts/hour. From here, the parts were ready for assembly. Nearly all parts for airplanes, except for engines, brakes, avionics, and certain other components, are produced by Beech, Turbine engines for turboprop Beechcraft are manufactured by Pratt-Whitney and Garrett, while Continental and Lycoming produce engines for the piston-engine models.

Some of the satellite plants did subassemblies which were integrated into the final product in the assembly-line operation at Wichita. In the assembly process of a plane at Wichita, the bottom of the plane was structured first, and then the cabin and top added. The airplanes were physically moved from one workstation to the next twice a day. The plant used three shifts: the first shift did most of the production and assembly; the second shift completed the work the first shift could not finish; and the third shift was mainly for security and maintenance.

The company had good employee relations. In fact, the only work stoppage in the entire history of the company occurred in 1969. Beech's employees—numbering over 10,000—were provided with benefits including a company-supported retirement income program, group insurance plans with life, medical, and dental benefits, a hospitalization program, a credit union, an employees' club offering hobby and recreational activities, a cafeteria and activity center, and a built-in cost of living pay increase in their contract. When the 1969 strike was settled, all employees returned to work. The company was not in a good financial position at the time and there was no backlog of work. One long-term employee recalled some executives urging Mrs. Beech not to recall the employees. He stated that Mrs. Beech would not hear of a layoff. She reportedly said, "In spite of the strike, I won't have us laying off people just before Thanksgiving and Christmas."

Beech stresses employee relations. Building quality airplanes requires high degrees of skill and experience. Good employee relations contribute to the low employee turnover required to develop an experienced workforce. In 1979 about 40 percent of Beech's employees had been with the company 10 years or more and 25 percent for over 15 years [1]. "Many families have more than one generation working here," said a longtime employee.

The labor market in the Wichita area in 1978 and 1979 was very tight, as was available space for plant expansion. The Wichita unemployment rate was about 2.5 percent compared to a national average of 7–9 percent. Beech had approached the capacity ceiling in Wichita and had thus been forced to expand company operations into other cities and states. The plant established in Selma, Alabama, was located there primarily because of the area's good labor market and enthusiastic community support. The quality control procedures that Beech employed ensured that all products from the Sundowner to the

King Air were of high quality, regardless of where they were produced and assembled.

PRODUCTS

Beech products consisted mainly of airplanes for the general aviation industry. This industry consisted of four major market segments: business planes, commuter planes, personal planes, and defense aerospace aircraft. Of the four, Beech relied most heavily on the business market. Said Rembleske:

> The personal airplane is a business tool. The time loss is significant to executives. With air to ground telephones and such, executives can work while they're flying!

The business market was the largest segment of the general aviation market and accounted for about 55 percent of the mileage. The business market was also less cynical than the personal plane market. [4] Beech's prices in this market were higher than the industry average, but this factor had not affected sales because of Beech's reputation for quality and the planes' higher-than-average resale value.

Over 40 percent of Beech's total sales volume in 1978 was attributed to the King Air turboprop models. Beech held about 53 percent of the U.S. turboprop market. The King Air turboprop models, sold primarily for companies, all had pressurized cabins. Their seating capacity ranged from 6 to 15 seats, and the maximum cruise speed ranged from 256 to 305 mph. The maximum flight range on a King Air was from 1,474 to 1,870 miles, and its price range was between $560,000 and $1,110,000.

Beech did not produce any pure jet aircraft for the business market. In 1975, it stopped marketing Britain's Hawker Siddeley after having sold 64 jets since the program's initiation in 1970. In 1979, Beech had no plans to develop a jet of its own because it saw greater opportunities in the turboprop—mostly because of greater fuel efficiency. Also, a jet was not compatible with the current design, building, and marketing of the turboprop. Regarding turboprop, Rembleske said,

> The turboprop airplane meets the travel requirements of most corporations in that it provides the speed, comfort, reliability, and economy demanded for the vast majority of business trips.

The personal or owner-flown market segment made up the other main component of Beech's general aviation commercial sales. This segment, which consisted entirely of piston-powered engines, could be divided into two subdivisions: the single-engine planes and the multiengine. The single-engine planes were used almost solely for personal use with the exception of the Bonanzas which were used for some business flying. In 1977, these planes accounted for about 15 percent of the company's commercial sales dollars and held about 8.8 percent of the single-engine market share. [4] Sales of these planes were somewhat related to the state of the economy.

The single-engine models were the Beechcraft Sport, Sundowner, Sierra, and Bonanza series. Their seating capacity ranged from two to six seats; the maximum cruise speed ranged from 127 to 209 mph; and the maximum flight range went from 687 to 790 miles. The price range fell between $35,000 and $100,000. [2] A two-seater Skipper model was expected to be certified in January 1979 for delivery early in the spring. This model was intended to be competitive with Cessna's Model 152 and 152 Aerobat, and Piper's Super Cub and Tomahawk. The Skipper was intended to replace the Sport.

The multiengine, piston-powered planes are used for personal and business flying. In 1977, these planes accounted for about 25 percent of Beech's commercial sales dollars and held about 17 percent of the multiengine general aviation market. [4] Many buyers of these aircraft move up into more expensive Beech planes after owning these smaller Beech planes. The twin-engine models were the Duchess, Baron series, and Duke series. Their seating capacity ranged from four to six seats; the maximum cruise speed ranged from 191 to 275 mph; and the maximum flight range went from 898 to 1,517 miles. The price range fell between $90,000 and $315,000.

Beech saw good possibilities for expansion in the commuter market. In 1979, only 420 cities were served by the airlines and many companies were moving away from metropolitan areas. Beech first entered the commuter market in 1965 with the sale of the 10-place Queen Air to Chicago Commuter Airlines. Sales to other commuter lines followed. In 1969, Beech made its first sale of the 15-place Model 99 to the commuter airline market. Beech planned in 1978 to divisionalize the company as part of the larger effort to pursue this market more vigorously. A separate division would market these commuter planes. Beech was designing a 19-passenger turboprop for the commuter market. Beech had been in the commuter market with a 15-seater 99 Airliner model. The 99 Airliner was refined and reintroduced to the market in 1981 as the Commuter 99.

The final Beech product class, defense-aerospace, accounted for about 22 percent of sales. [4] Major sales included the C-12 cargo transports for the army, navy, air force, and marines; single- and multiengine trainers for the navy; and flight simulators for the navy. Besides aircraft, Beech also made missile targets for the military and did major subcontract work for McDonnel Douglas and Bell Helicopter. In addition, the company had a $13 million production subcontract from Rockwell International and the space shuttle program. Defense aerospace contracts in 1978 totaled $122,430,000.

Included in commercial sales were international sales which reached $112,007,911 in fiscal 1978, a 61 percent increase over 1977. About half of these sales were military planes to foreign governments. Beech sold planes to over 130 countries, including the 1979 sales to the republic of China. To avoid currency problems in the international market, Beech's policy required all payments to be made in U.S. dollars. In addition, planes to non-U.S. buyers were not delivered until full payment was received. Even with this strictly enforced foreign policy and Beech's higher prices, international sales continued to increase. Primary reasons for this consistent growth were Beech's reputation for quality aircraft and its emphasis on after-sale support. Beech had improved field service capability through company incentive programs and had increased the number of service technicians.

In 1978, Beech had fewer aircraft models available than Cessna and Piper, but production of the Skipper, twin-engine Duchess model, and introduction of additional King Air models decreased the gap.

MARKETING

Beech planes were manufactured to order for the end customer or distributor. The buyer had options on the plane's seating arrangement, its technical equipment, and its decor. "Give the customer what he wants" was Beech's key to developing versatile customer aircraft which could be adapted to the needs of many buyers.

Domestic Marketing

Domestic marketing was conducted through 21 corporate aviation centers, 17 of which were wholly owned. Twelve wholly owned distributorships accounted for about 24 percent of domestic sales in 1977. The company's franchise organization consisted of three types. Corporate Aviation Centers handled the full line of aircraft, but concentrated on turboprop planes; Executive Aviation Centers concentrated on Bonanzas, Barons, and Dukes; Aero Centers were concerned with smaller aircraft, with most operating a Beech Aero Club. There were about 175 franchises in the United States and plans called for this number to increase to 500. [6]

In mid-1978, the marketing department developed an experimental, innovative executive flight plan for some of the 60 executive aviation centers. [3] This plan allowed businessmen to contract with

Beech franchisees for blocks of flight time on an annual basis. Beech had three goals it hoped to achieve through implementation of this plan. First, it hoped to increase executive center cash flows and aircraft utilization. Franchisees could not afford to have aircraft sitting around idle, especially since inventory was so costly. Second, as the businessmen's companies grew, these customers would hopefully want to purchase their own airplane—a Beechcraft, of course. Beech's prospective customer list was made up of businesses not currently using business aircraft. Third, the program was used to train salespersons. [3] Beech expected to expand this program, if it continued to be as successful, as initial indications suggested.

Aero Centers had an established program similar to the experimental EFP. Members of the 120 aero clubs paid monthly dues and were able to take flying lessons or rent planes from aero centers [4]. The planes used for these clubs were usually the smaller aircraft, such as Skippers and Sundowners, but also included Sierras, Duchesses, some Bonanzas, and Barons. The purpose of the program was to keep new pilots actively engaged in flying until such time as they could justify ownership of a Beechcraft. Almost all of the aero centers participated in this program.

Beech had integrated forward into establishing their own retail outlets for a number of reasons. The main reason was to create a strong position in the general aviation market, thereby increasing sales and profit potential. Other reasons for outlet ownership included enhancing the company's ability to learn about their products firsthand, and putting Beech's sales and marketing philosophies to work. The company had established dealerships where it found a potentially strong market and good physical facilities available. There had been increased marketing support from the factory, including retail outlet assistance in recruiting badly needed sales personnel. The company had also instituted a program where one of its representatives visited a sales outlet, instituted a program for job interviews, and then assisted the franchisee in employee selection, all at company expense. Beech was considering extending this program to help recruit service technicians who were in short supply.

In 1978, Beech's advertising expenditures grew 49 percent from the previous year to a high of $4.8 million. The reason for this increase was more advertising emphasis; more sales promotions; greater participation in coop advertising; and inflation. Brewer, an advertising agency located in Kansas City, handled all of Beech's domestic advertising. The company's objective in advertising, according to Vice President Neuburger, was "advertising is addressed to the type of buyers the firm wants to attract." The advertising theme has consistently been "We are not the cheapest, but we are the best." Attempts were made to relate the Beech name with quality, speed, dependability, and comfort.

In planning the advertising programs. Brewer asked each distributor what models they would like to emphasize and in what magazines. Beech advertised in numerous aviation magazines such as *Aviation Weekly* and *Intervia,* and also placed ads in *The Wall Street Journal, Time,* and *Fortune.* Some advertisements included a coupon which could be returned to the company as a request for additional information. The follow-up on these coupons was estimated to have generated approximately $27 million in retail sales in the first 11 months of fiscal 1978. More importantly, 75 percent of these sales were to first-time buyers of aircraft. Beech had also run ads on the theme "America the Beautiful," which showed America's beautiful countryside being viewed from a Beechcraft plane. In addition, the company had spent some advertising dollars on civic causes, such as promoting free enterprise.

One factor of concern in Beech's marketing approach was that Beech had few smaller planes on the market. Marketing Vice President Roy McGregor stated that, "There's habit buying in aircraft, just like anything else. If you get in a Beech when you buy your first airplane, chances are much better that we will get you in a King Air someday." [6] However, in this segment, Beech would compete head on with the established lines of Cessna and Piper.

The commuter market presented a different challenge. Beech had a strong competitive position in the commuter market with both its twin-engine piston and twin-engine turboprop models. Beech's ability to compete effectively in the commuter market could, however, be challenged by introduction of new models or more aggressive marketing by Cessna, Piper, or other aircraft manufacturers.

International Marketing

As indicated in Exhibit 6, Beech had divided its international markets into seven regions. There were no company-owned distributorships outside the United States and, in fact, the foreign distributors entered into only one-year contracts with Beech. Despite this short contract length, however, many of the dealers had been associated with Beech for more than 15 years. The stability of these associations indicate the dealer loyalty which Beech had developed. Beech selected its dealers carefully. Each distributor was encouraged to carry the full product line and Beech supported its dealers through service arrangements and advertising.

One of Beech's goals domestically, as well as internationally, was to have complete service support for the Beechcraft owner. The com-

EXHIBIT 6 Beech Aircraft Corporation Regions

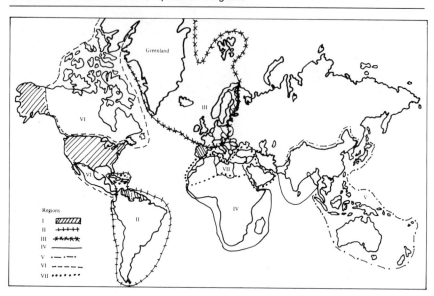

pany had established many service facilities around the world. To assist these field locations, Beech provided training and maintained a customer service organization staffed mainly by engineers who were multilingual and who could provide answers and assistance to inquiries involving the service and operation of their products.

The Beechcraft product improvement committee published service instructions and publication changes, and kept in touch with desired product improvements through constant monitoring of customer feedback and field service records.

Advertising was also done overseas. Beech placed advertisements in many international publications. These ads carried the same basic quality theme that was used domestically. Michael Neuburger related a story illustrating this internationally known quality image. He said, "I was with a customer in Germany when his phone rang. A competitor was on the other end of the line and was offering to sell his company's plane at cost to the German businessman. My customer's reply was, 'No, thank you. I drive a Mercedes. I fly a Beech.'"

CRYOGENICS

One of the company's engineers remarked, "Technological advances are evolutionary, not revolutionary."

In the late 1970s, research and development efforts at Beech were geared to improvements in aircraft performance, subsonic and supersonic missile target systems, and cryogenic systems for space use.[2] Beech was a pioneer in cryogenics and had conducted cryogenic research, development, and production since 1954. The cryogenic systems produced by Beech supplied hydrogen and oxygen for fuel cell power plants and breathing oxygen systems for NASA manned Gemini, Apollo, and Skylab space missions. In 1979, Beech was under contract to design and produce the power reactant storage systems for the NASA space shuttle Orbiter.

Cryogenic technology includes the systems in which gases are cooled, liquified, and stored in specially built tanks which keep the liquified gas at $-420°$ F, until such time as the gas is used. In 1979, members of Beech management were excited over commercial application of the cryogenic technology. Beech had developed an automobile powered solely by liquid methane, a primary constituent of natural gas. Methane is a commonly occurring natural fuel that burns cleaner than gasoline. Methane can be produced a number of ways, even from garbage or manure.

Beech estimated that converting the nation's 10 million fleet-operated motor vehicles to LNG would reduce gasoline consumption by the equivalent of 1.25 million barrels of oil per day. Mike Neuburger and R. G. Oestreicher envisioned a snowballing effect for cryogenics.

"The total technology system is what Beech has," said Oestreicher. He was referring to the process of LNG liquefaction, storage, transport, service stations, and automotive fuel systems.

Further experimentation in cryogenics, however, would require a substantial capital investment. One knowledgeable member of the engineering industry stated that an investment of $18 million would purchase only a minimal amount of the equipment required for experimentation.

FINANCE

Beech's strong financial position (Exhibits 2, 3, 4, and 5) made it an attractive merger candidate. Sales ($527 million in 1978) had more than doubled since 1974. During this same time, net income as a percentage of sales increased from 5.2 percent to 6.7 percent. As of September 30, 1978, the company had only $24 million in long-term debt, with about $200,000 of this amount maturing each year until 1993. Given this strong financial position, the board of directors voted to raise the annual cash dividend to $0.92 per share, up $0.12 from 1977. The increase was the eighth since 1973. Dividends were paid on a quarterly basis and the company had paid 122 consecutive divi-

---

[2] During the late 1940s, hydrogen and helium liquifiers were first commercially developed. This began a new era of cryogenics. (Data taken from G. G. Haselden, *Cryogenic Fundamentals*, Academic Press, 1971, p. 4.)

dends. The company held about $20 million in short-term investments and because of its overall position, Wey Kenny, assistant treasurer, asserted, "We could buy a company or have a stock exchange . . . and (we) could be the surviving company in a merger. . . . Also, if needed we have enough credit in banks to borrow any needed funds." The firm's 1979 credit line was $23 million, but Kenny felt that it could easily be extended. The large cash flows that Beech's success had generated had made the treasury department an important administrative function. The treasury department's main responsibility was to manage the company's assets. Another important treasury responsibility was the management of Beech's cash flow. Whenever Beech finalized a contract, the treasury department in conjunction with the product manager, established a timetable. This was done to help the treasury department plan its cash flow picture. The department also kept track of the contract's progress. The system had been effective and the company had never experienced any major cash flow problems.

About 20 percent of Beech common stock was held by employees—mainly the management staff. The Beech family had about another 15 percent of the shares. The remaining 65 percent of the common stock was spread out over about 11,000 shareholders which were mostly comprised of institutions such as pension funds and mutual funds. Beech did not have to worry about a takeover by these institutions because any institution holding more than 10 percent of a company's stock must register with the Security Exchange Commission and state whether the ownership is for investment or takeover purposes. The 20 percent management ownership was a result of a stock option plan implemented in 1957. Beech felt that this program provided an incentive to various levels of management.

MANAGEMENT

In 1979, Beech was headed by President Frank Hedrick, age 69. Hedrick was a respected figure in the general aviation industry. He was well known for spearheading Beech's responsiveness to changing market demands, including the decisions to concentrate on turboprop technology, to pursue the business market aggressively and, more recently, to establish the company more firmly in the commuter market. The company's success could also be attributed to the management below Hedrick and to the influential board of directors, chaired by his aunt, Mrs. Beech. The board of directors consisted of Beech's top management plus several respected businessmen. Most members were involved in community affairs and/or served on committees affecting the aircraft industry. Involvement with the industry was essential in Beech's efforts to keep track of environmental changes. (See Exhibit 7 for background on key executives.)

EXHIBIT 7 Key Executives

Name	Age	Years with Beech (as officer)	Current Positions	Education (college)
O. A. Beech	76	47 (35)	Chm. of Board, dir.	Wichita, KS—Business College
Frank E. Hedrick*	69	34 (15)	President, dir.	No college
E. C. Burns†	58	15 (8)	Group VP, dir.	University of Kansas—Industrial Management
James N. Lew	63	26	Senior VP-Engr., dir.	Curtiss-Wright School of Aeronautics (graduate)
M. G. Neuburger	64	23 (8)	Senior VP-Intn'l., dir.	University of Munich (Germany)—JD (law)
Leddy L. Greever	66	23	VP & Corp. Dir., dir.	No college
Seymour Colman	62	9 (4)	Senior VP-operations	Chicago-Kent College of Law—JD
Harold W. Deets	58	7 (1)	VP-material	Southwestern-Business—BA
Glenn Ehling	57	4	VP-manufacturing	No college
George D. Rodgers	46	2	VP-domestic comm. mkt.	Duke University, BA; Columbia University, MA
William G. Rutherford	59	1	VP-gov't. relations	San Bernardino Valley College, Kelsey Jenny Business College (attended)
E. C. Nikkel	61	7	VP-aerospace programs	Southwestern Institute of Technology—Business Administration
John A. Pike	48	4	VP-research & develop.	University of Colorado, BS and MS—Aeronautical Engineering
C. A. Rembleske	59	4	VP-engineering	Aeronautical University of Chicago—Aeronautical Engineering
Austin Rising	61	17	VP	New York University, BA
Stewart Ayton	62	2	VP	Beacom College—Accounting and Finance—BA

* Nephew of O. A. Beech.
† Nephew of Walter H. Beech.
( ) Active on indicated number of aviation-related committees.

A concern had arisen, however, over Beech's future management. In the late 1970s, four of Beech's top executives were lost to the company because of death or illness. At least one of these employees was not replaced, but rather, managers who had reported to him began reporting directly to Hedrick.

Mrs. Beech's view on management manpower planning within the company was, "We have very qualified people in lower management who could move up to top positions—otherwise they would not be working here." Mrs. Beech's statement about her employees' abilities to move up in the organization was based, in part, on the management manpower reserve chart system which began in the 1970s. These charts, prepared by officers, executive managers, and other management representatives who report to a member of the executive management group, were used to identify and monitor executive talent in the organization. Information on the chart included name, age, and rating on the employee's promotability as well as a rating on his/her competence.

The key management program was also developed to assist high-potential employees in preparing for future middle- and upper-management positions. Candidates for this program were selected on the basis of their performance within the company, their eligibility for promotion, and their commitment to self-development. Employees were recommended by their immediate superiors for the key management program. Normally, key management employees had the prospect of at least 10 years' future service at Beech. In addition to assessment by supervisory, executive, and personnel, the key management program candidates were asked for their own personal assessment of their abilities and potential as well as input into the individualized plan of career development.

The attitude of management toward Beech employees was characterized by J. L. Sheldon, manager of personnel placement, "At Beech, memos go from individual to individual, not title to title. . . . This whole organization is alive, it's dynamic!"

MERGER

Beech had held discussions with several companies about possible mergers. However, none of these talks progressed beyond the preliminary discussion stage. The qualities that Beech looked for in a merger prospect were the company's goods or products, the company's compatability with the general aviation industry, the company's technological base, the company's continuing research and development efforts, and the financial situation of the company. Basically, Beech wanted to find a company that would offer the possibility for an interchange of personnel, knowledge, and abilities. Beech did not want to merge with a company with products that would put Beech in competition with other aviation supplier companies. Potential merger possibilities in 1979 were General Dynamics Corporation, Raytheon Company, and Sperry Corporation.

General Dynamics Corporation, based in St. Louis, Missouri, mainly developed and produced military and commercial aircraft, space systems, and tactical missiles. The company was also engaged in shipbuilding and produced a variety of other products. In 1978, sales of military aircraft accounted for 31.1 percent of sales, tactical missiles 13.2 percent, marine 29.4 percent, telecommunications 5.7 percent, and the rest divided up in other areas. The F-16 jet fighter was an example of one product included in aircraft production. In 1978, General Dynamics had net sales of $3,205,205,000 and a net loss of $48,088,000 incurred because of a settlement with the navy on a program which caused a total loss of $359 million. In previous years, however, net income had grown steadily from $2.5 million in 1969 to $103 million in 1977. Growth was primarily internal with a few acquisitions. In 1978, General Dynamics' debt totaled $82,534,000, and total assets were $1,778,723,000.

Raytheon Company, based in Lexington, Massachusetts, was a conglomerate with many products dealing with electronics. In 1978, electronics accounted for 56.6 percent of sales, energy sources 23.7 percent, major appliances 12.3 percent, and other 7.4 percent. U.S. government end-use business was 37 percent of sales. The company's subsidiaries included Amana Refrigeration, Inc.; Seismograph Service Corporation; Machlett Laboratories, Inc.; and United Engineers and Constructors, Inc. The company was known for its strong research and development work, particularly in electronics. Sales for 1978 were $3,239,302,000, with net income of $150,034,000. This net income figure has been growing steadily from the $35 million in 1969. Long-term debt was $76,060,000 and total assets stood at $2,060,945,000. Acquisitions and mergers accounted for much of the company's growth. [5]

Sperry Corporation was a company with a worldwide business. In 1978, computer systems and equipment accounted for 49 percent of their sales; farm equipment, 20 percent; guidance and control equipment, 16 percent; fluid power equipment, 10 percent; and other, 4 percent. The guidance and control equipment consisted of avionic and radar gear for airplanes ranging from those used in general aviation to gear used in large commercial airliners. Sperry was one of many avionic producers for the general aviation industry. Sperry's sales for 1978 were $3,649,487,000 and their net income was $176,619,000. Long-term debt totaled $496,112,000 and total assets were $3,286,610. Income had grown steadily from the 1970 level of $81 million. Sperry had experienced significant internal growth. The company's acquisitions, particularly in the computer field, provided additional growth. [8, 11]

REFERENCES

1. *A Pocketful of Facts.* Prepared by the editorial staff of Beechcraft Corporation. Wichita, Kansas: McCormick Armstrong Company, 1978.

2. *A Tradition of Excellence.* Prepared by the editorial staff of Beechcraft Corporation. Wichita, Kansas: McCormick Armstrong Company, 1978.

3. "Beech Planning Expansion in Wake of Record Sales." *Aviation Week & Space Technology.* October 23, 1978, pp. 20–21.

4. "Beech Aircraft—Its Earnings in Sharp Climb." Ed. Steven S. Anreder. *Barrons.* May 15, 1979, p. 39.

5. Bulban, E. J. "Beech Moves Toward Merger." *Aviation Week & Space Technology.* April 8, 1979, p. 78.

6. "General Aviation: Beech's Choice." *Forbes.* April 17, 1978, pp. 93–94.

7. McDaniel, William. *History of Beech.* 2d ed. Wichita, Kansas: McCormick Armstrong Company, 1976, pp. 13–14.

8. *Moody's Industrial Manual.* New York, N.Y.: Moody's Investor's Services, Inc., 1979, p. 1412. (Annual.) An extensive listing of corporations listed on the NYSE and ASE listing their financial reports and current financial status.

9. *Public Relations.* Prepared by the editorial staff of Beechcraft Corporation. Wichita, Kansas: McCormick Armstrong Company, 1978.

10. Securities and Exchange Commission. Form *10-K.* Washington, D.C.: U.S. Government Printing Office, 1978.

11. *Standard & Poor's Corporation Records.* New York, New York: Standard & Poor's Corporation, 1979, p. 1336. (Semiannual.)

23. Texas Air Corps

Frank Lorenzo, chairman and chief executive officer of Texas Air Corporation (TAC), once said that "by 1990 there will be only six (6) major airlines in the United States. I intend to own one of them."[1] Since coming to the Houston-based carrier at the age of 30 in late 1971, most of his efforts have been directed toward that goal. By December 1980, Texas Air could boast of an operation which generated almost $300 million in revenue on an asset base of almost $400 million, employed 3,500 people, and produced profits in seven of the nine years under Lorenzo's control. These are significant accomplishments for a carrier which 11 years earlier was on the brink of bankruptcy.

THE PRE-LORENZO YEARS: 1947–1971

Trans Texas Airways (TTA), the forerunner of Texas International (TXIA) and Texas Air Corporation (TAC), began official operations on Saturday, October 11, 1947. It was a rather inauspicious start. R. Earl McKaughan mortgaged everything he owned to purchase two World War II surplus DC-3 aircraft. Each had seating capacity for 21 passengers. Trans Texas employed 96 people and its route structure included eight Texas cities: San Angelo, Brownwood, Fort Worth, Dallas (Love Field), Palestine, Houston (Hobby), Victoria, and San Antonio. Due to its size, the nature of the airline industry, governmental regulation, and its regional nature, Trans Texas was beseiged by problems from its infancy. Even its airline code letter, TTA, bore the brunt of many remarks such as Tinker Toy Airlines, Tree Top Airways, and Try Try Again.

To really appreciate TTA's position during the pre-Lorenzo years, one must first recognize the regulated condition of the industry. In most business activities, profits are realized by outperforming the competitors. Tactics such as producing a superior product, obtaining patents and better management potential, or reducing costs could be

---

This case was prepared by Tim Singleton and Robert McGlashan of the University of Houston at Clear Lake City.

[1] Author unlisted, "The Great Texas Air War," *Texas Monthly*, November 1975, p. 97.

effectively employed. Prior to deregulation in 1978, the Civil Aeronautics Board (CAB) strictly controlled activities within the airline
business. Basically, the industry had two types of companies, the
trunk or cross-country carriers, and the local or intrastate feeder
lines.

The trunk carriers were essentially government franchised by the
CAB, thus almost guaranteed to make money. Losses occurred due to
mismanagement and overzealous acquisition plans for aircraft rather
than market forces. The real competition among the trunk carriers
took place in the offices of the Civil Aeronautics Board rather than the
marketplace. The CAB's major purpose was to control the airline industry through approval of new routes, a process which could take as
long as 30 months. The degree of control was remarkable.[2]

1. Sixteen trunk carriers were chartered by the CAB in 1938.
2. By 1975, 11 of these were still operating; the remaining 5
    disappeared through merger.
3. None of the original 16 had ever been bankrupt.

Life for the local or so-called feeder lines, such as Trans Texas,
which were not as regulated by the CAB, was radically different. They
were "created to lose money, to fly the routes where passengers
ain't."[3] With the aid of government subsidies which decreased each
year, the feeder lines were relegated to service small cities such as
Jonesboro, Arkansas; Big Spring, Texas; and the like. Of the original
19 local airlines authorized in 1945, all but 10 were lost through bankruptcy by 1975.

In spite of these conditions, a fleet of aging aircraft, and a route
structure composed primarily of small Texas towns, Trans Texas Airways registered revenue growth and modest profits until 1966 when a
group of "Minnesota investors" purchased the airline. They immediately embarked upon an ill-conceived expansion program from an
already highly leveraged financial base. This expansion program included additional routes into more unprofitable cities and purchase of
the Tropicana Hotel in Las Vegas. Net income fell dramatically and a
revolving door of presidents followed. The small Texas airline did not
have a profitable month from 1966 to 1972. By 1971, Texas International, as it became known in 1969, was $20 million in debt and facing
bankruptcy. Its stock, which was traded in the over-the-counter market, fell from $20.25 per share in 1969 to $3.50 per share by 1971. It
was then that Frank Lorenzo entered the TI picture.

---

[2] Author unlisted, "The Great Texas Air War," *Texas Monthly*, November, 1975,
p. 92.

[3] Ibid., p. 90.

FRANCISCO A. LORENZO: ENTREPRENEUR

"My aim is to build the most successful, low-fare airline in the United States."[4] Francisco A. Lorenzo is an enigma, publicly quiet and unassuming, yet an energetic and highly ambitious individual. Lorenzo has been described in many terms; a pure entrepreneur, a listener rather than a talker, the maverick of the airways. He seems to be highly regarded in financial circles both in the United States and abroad, but viewed with apprehension by his peers within the industry. When reminded that Wall Street investors had highly acclaimed his financial dealings, his reply was typically modest. "People think we're financial geniuses when all we do is add."[5]

Frank Lorenzo was not unfamiliar with the airline industry. Born in 1940 in Queens, New York, to a beauty shop owner, he is a licensed pilot. By the age of 23, his academic credits included a degree in finance from Columbia University and an MBA from Harvard. Prior to forming Jet Capital, Inc., with fellow Harvard classmate Robert Carney, Frank Lorenzo worked for three years in the financial departments of both Eastern and Trans World Airlines. The latter has been a successful conduit for many of Texas Air Corporation's top executives.

Lorenzo seems to feel most comfortable when surrounded by highly talented professionals and is willing to gamble on creative ideas. Carl R. Pohlad, an investment banker and director at Texas Air, describes him as "the initiator who sets the tone (of the board) and provides the broad perspectives."[6] However, Pohlad quickly adds that the company is by no means "a one-man show."

Jet Capital, Inc. (formerly Lorenzo-Carney Enterprises) was and still is Lorenzo's investment base. He and Carney launched the highly speculative financial venture in 1966 with the expressed intention of leasing airplanes. However, the underlying implications were clear; Lorenzo wanted an airline. The more official intent was expressed in Jet Capital's charter "to provide a meaningful platform for successful participation in the exciting but beleaguered field of air transportation."[7] They were thwarted by Allegheny in the first acquisition attempt, Mohawk Airlines. Unsuccessful in this effort, Jet Capital shifted gears and acted as a consulting firm to airlines for large New York banks. It was a time when many investment contacts were made on Wall Street, within the industry, and abroad.

---

[4] Author unlisted, "Texas International's Quiet Pilot," *Business Week*, July 30, 1979, p. 78.

[5] Ibid., p. 80.

[6] Author unlisted, "Who Are the TI Whiz Kids?" *The TI Flyer*, May 1979, p. 21.

[7] Author unlisted, "The Great Texas Air War," *Texas Monthly*, November 1975, p. 94.

THE EARLY YEARS: 1971–1974

By the spring of 1971, Texas International was a financial shambles. Losses were running over $1 million a month. Employee morale was low and creditors were about to foreclose and liquidate the carrier. These events were viewed as an opportunity by Lorenzo. The Chase Manhattan Bank of New York retained Jet Capital for a $15,000 per month fee to help Texas International out of their dilemma. The Lorenzo-Carney management team went to work. One year later, Frank Lorenzo, at the age of 31, was president and chief executive officer and Robert Carney was chief financial officer of TI. Together, either directly or through ownership of Jet Capital, they controlled 49 percent of TI's voting stock. The results of their work were dramatic. The carrier's net loss for 1972 was $1.707 million versus a loss of $7.416 million the year before and total debt (current and long term) was reduced by $24.123 million.

The airline industry had caught the first glimpse of Lorenzo's wizardry of debt leverage at work. He worked out a $35 million debt restructuring plan with the Chase Manhattan Bank. This was no small feat considering TI's financial condition. In addition, through reinvesting the $180,000 in consultants' fees and $60,000 in "finder's fees" from Chase for arranging the new loans, he was able to leverage the Jet Capital venture to provide an additional capital infusion of $1.150 million into Texas International.

Lorenzo's expertise went to work in other areas as well. A management housecleaning ensued which formed the nucleus of his new team. Expense reduction areas were identified and plans implemented. The Tropicana operation, a severe drain on profits, was sold. More lucrative routes to large cities such as Denver, Albuquerque, and Mexico City were obtained. The groundwork to replace the aging Convair aircraft with more fuel efficient McDonnell Douglass DC-9s was laid. Productivity improvements were implemented. Route structures were put to the pencil. These were thoroughly analyzed in an attempt to reduce Texas International's dependence on federal subsidies. Through "creative scheduling," service to many of the small marginal cities which plagued profits was discontinued.

Once again, the tactics produced positive results. In 1973, Lorenzo's first full year, the carrier produced a $121,000 profit, its first in eight years. By 1974, passenger load factor and yield per revenue passenger mile, key profit criteria in the industry, had risen to 50.4 percent and .0981 from 47.2 percent and .0796 in 1971. In the process, profits of $257,000 in 1974 more than doubled 1973 levels.

THE STRIKE: DECEMBER 1, 1974–APRIL 3, 1975

Frank Lorenzo was in his element. Eight years had passed since the formation of Jet Capital and he was finally building his airline. In spite of fierce competition from the major trunks and smaller regional carriers such as Southwest, his handpicked management team had turned a company from bankruptcy to a profit-generating enterprise in just two short years. However, the storm clouds of change were brewing.

If Lorenzo has a weakness, it is his relationship with Texas International unions. The Texas carrier has some of the toughest in the industry with which to deal:

A. ALEA—Airline Employees Association (1968–1980) (clerical/secretarial).
B. Teamsters—1980 to present (clerical).
C. ALPA—Airline Pilots Association (pilots, stewards, and stewardesses).
D. IAM—International Association of Machinists (mechanics).

The friction has always centered around the unions' versus Lorenzo's perception of how the company should be operated in order to allow it to compete within the industry. Pay and benefits have always been competitive and are seldom the root issues involved. On December 1, 1974, the carrier's union personnel walked out in a bitterly contested four-month strike which curtailed the momentum gained in the previous two years.

A lawyer representing the union employees expressed resentment concerning the changes made by Lorenzo with the following interview in *Texas Monthly Magazine* in 1975:

> Management had to weather the strike to keep the company afloat. It's the easiest thing in the world to avoid a strike, all you have to do is give in. It's harder to make the necessary judgment of what the company can sustain in the long run.

Numerous small issues were involved. However, each side used these merely as negotiating chips. The major areas of concern could be boiled down to two key points of difference.

1. Management's contention that they had the right to hire part-time help in lieu of later furloughing full-time employees in order to handle peak traffic periods.
2. Management's contention that they had the right to have employees work split shifts at premium pay in order to operate the unique flight scheduling requirements at the smaller stations.

On the surface, it may seem that the strike issues were not critical. However, underlying currents of mistrust had grown in the early Lorenzo years. The unions, especially ALEA, viewed these actions as attempts to usurp their authority and weaken them. They had become very apprehensive about the constant changes taking place within the company. Lorenzo, on the other hand, felt that Texas International's survival was at stake. He firmly believed that unless such actions were adopted, the feeder airlines would not be able to compete against the major trunk lines and Southwest Airlines, a nonunion very aggressive regional carrier.

Both sides dug in for the mini-war which followed. It is fair to point out that there was sharp disagreement among union members about the major issues. Management's hand was further strengthened when 19 percent of the membership refused to honor the picket lines and worked systemwide during the strike. This enraged the prounion faction and deep bitterness and resentment persisted for a long period after the strike had ended. By April 3, 1975, the unions had exhausted their resources and settled for essentially the same package offered in December 1974. The end was welcomed by both sides. The airline had been kept afloat primarily because of a package called mutual aid, which was unique to the airline industry. Mutual aid was a fund, contributed to by all airlines based upon revenues. Its purpose was to provide capital to maintain skeleton operations during labor difficulties. Shortly after settlement of the Texas International strike, mutual aid was found to be unconstitutional.

Financially, the strike was devastating to Texas International. The net loss for 1975 was $4,249,000 versus income in 1974 of $257,000. More importantly, it had allowed Southwest Airlines to entrench itself as the number one carrier into "The Valley," a group of very lucrative vacation/business routes into the McAllen-Harlingen-Brownsville areas of Texas. Heretofore, these stations represented some of the most profitable in the TI system. The corporate intrigue and courtroom dealings which followed between Texas International and Braniff against Southwest could fill volumes and was referred to as "The Great Texas Air War." The litigation portion came to an end when Braniff and TI were found guilty of conspiracy and antitrust violations against Southwest.

On the union front, ALEA, the clerical union, became the real loser. It was the one which initiated the strike and from whom most of the "scab-labor" came. For all practical purposes, it was broken and wielded considerably less influence. In 1980, its membership voted to have it replaced by the Teamsters to handle contract negotiations.

The concurrent forces of the strike, hints of deregulation, the antitrust suit, and recession produced a dismal atmosphere at Texas International. Both morale and profits had reached their lowest ebb under Lorenzo. He needed a gimmick to infuse increased revenue and purpose. It was found in the "Fly for Peanuts" marketing program.

The advantages of the strike concessions were the key ingredients. Lorenzo's management team began a route-by-route analysis of revenues versus costs, an almost unheard of practice in the industry prior to its adoption at TI. The major thrust of the "peanuts campaign" was to attract a new class of traveler, one who would normally drive or take trains and buses. The economics were clear. It requires nearly as much in operating costs to fly a jet 20 percent full as it does at 60 percent. TI opted for higher load factors by reducing prices. The results of this innovative marketing ploy were phenomenal. Load factors increased to 53.6 percent in 1976, 57.7 percent in 1977, and 60 percent in 1978. Net income for the same period was $3.479 million, $8.238 million, and $13.151 million. By 1978, Texas International ranked fourth in terms of traffic among the regional lines, experienced 39 consecutive months of record earnings and was heralded as the fasted growing regional airline in the United States. The infusion of profits allowed it to continue its upgrading to a strictly jet fleet and petition the Civil Aeronautics Board for permission to carry its "peanut fares" into 23 new markets. Some of the more lucrative included Las Vegas, Baltimore, Kansas City, Salt Lake City, and the Mexican resort communities of Cancun, Cozumel, and Merida.

Such expansionist moves were viewed with suspicion by the large trunks such as Delta, Eastern, Continental, Allegheny (U.S. Air), North Central (Republic), and National. Industrywide fare discounting ensued but they found it difficult to compete against Texas International's cost structure, said to be near the lowest in the industry. TI responded to these competitive threats by reducing prices further. In the highly contested Houston-Baltimore routes, its fares were 50 percent below those charged by Delta on certain late evening flights. By late 1978, "peanuts fares" accounted for 34 percent of all seats sold.

The mood in Washington toward the airline industry was beginning to change. A more consumerist congress applauded the fare discounting methods employed by the regionals. By the end of 1978, the regulatory environment which stabilized the industry and strangled competition for so many years was being phased out. The major trunks found themselves in a crucial position. Their cost structures could not compete and the regionals were aggressively pursuing their best routes.

PEANUTS AND PREACQUISITION

Either by design or happenstance, Lorenzo had prepared his airline for the deregulatory environment more than any other large regional or major trunk airline. As airlines were still reeling under the effects of the new government regulations and discount fares, Lorenzo took both Wall Street and the industry by surprise. After secretly obtaining major European and South American financial agreements, he announced that Texas International owned 9.2 percent of National's stock and was intent on merger.

Possessing attractive Sun Belt routes, a relatively debt-free balance sheet, and a grossly underpriced stock, National was a plum ready to be picked. Other large trunk carriers immediately joined in the bidding. Pam Am desired the domestic routes to complement its international network. Air Florida submitted a plan to liquidate National so that it could buy its planes. Eastern wanted merger so that National's western routes would provide it access to the West Coast. Eastern's proposal came under severe antitrust scrutiny due to the natural competitive nature of Eastern and National on the eastern seaboard and Florida. While recommendations as to what to do about National were bantered about, Lorenzo methodically increased Texas International's holdings of National to 24.5 percent before it was frozen. By April of 1979, the contestants had been whittled down to Texas International and Pan Am. Bidding had reached $40 per share.

Publicly, Lorenzo was confident and wore his gambler's mask. Internally, things were much different. National's board rejected TI and highly favored Pan Am as their "white knight." In addition, the burden of $400,000 per month in interest charges was beginning to take its toll on profitability. Lorenzo realized his airline probably could not afford the hostile merger attempt and set the stage for one of his patented financial gambles. In mid-May he insinuated in a speech before a group of Wall Street analysts that the book value of National's assets was at least $76 per share rather than the $46.50 indicated by National's board. It was a risk that paid off. Pan Am promptly offered $50 per share which Lorenzo accepted. The after-tax profit realized by Texas International was said to be around $46–$50 million. TI's stock was selling at 11 times earnings.

The industry was still guessing where Lorenzo would strike next. It didn't take long. On September 13, 1978, Texas International announced that it had acquired 4 percent of TWA's 16 million shares of stock. Trans World Corporation, the holding company for such diverse ventures as the airline, the Hilton Hotel chain, and Century 21 Real Estate, was almost four times Texas International's size and announced on September 19 that it would fight the takeover attempt.

Through complex lending agreements and commitments by Lorenzo to liquidate or sell off the nonairline related ventures, he seemed to have adequate financing leverage. Robert J. Joedicke, an analyst from Lehman Bros. remarked:

> Financing such an acquisition would be attractive to lenders primarily because of the reputation of Lorenzo and Texas International. When you have a track record such as his, a lot of people will back you a second time around.

Though hostile toward merger, Trans World Corporation opted to meet with Lorenzo personally rather than fight him in the press. Both factions were very familiar with one another. Some of Texas International's top management had been recruited from the larger airline, Lorenzo had once worked at TWA, and all parties were familiar with his financial dealings. After a series of meetings, Lorenzo, for whatever reason, decided not to press merger talks further. It is said that Texas International realized approximately $6 million in profits from the sale of TWA stock. It is interesting to note that Continental stock, once mentioned as a possible TI acquisition, fell to $12 per share during the merger talks.

"MR. PEANUT" MEETS NATIONAL AND TWA

Primarily due to the sale of National stock, profits in 1979 rose to over $41 million dollars. Only $6.5 million came from operations, down almost $9 million from the year before. The primary factors for decreased earnings from operations were a 68 percent increase in fuel costs and a 30 percent increase in other expenses. Revenues were up only 30 percent to offset these increases. Passenger load factor of 62.1 percent had reached an all-time high and yield per passenger mile had decreased slightly.

The company had began to utilize its windfall from Pan Am. Contracts were negotiated to purchase 20 used DC-9-30 aircraft, now the standard for the TI fleet. The highly acclaimed peanuts program was expanded. New "stations" such as St. Louis, Tulsa, and Guadelajara were added to the system. Six marginal cities were dropped and the airline operated without a dollar in federal subsidies for the first time since inception. During the period, a common stock dividend ($.04 per share) was paid for the first time in history.

By late 1979, Lorenzo's seven-year tenure had produced an airline whose book value assets totaled over $319 million of which approximately $141 million consisted of cash and short-term investments which could be utilized for another merger attempt, expansion, or both. To manage such an asset portfolio the carrier decided to reorganize. In March of 1980, it formed a holding company in the name of Texas Air Corp. In Lorenzo's own words:

> The holding company structure will permit greater business and financial flexibility. For example, the company would be able to raise funds on either the credit of the holding company, the airline, or any subsidiary. We may find it easier to pursue diversification should we find it advisable to enter into either regulated or nonregulated business activities without necessarily being under the jurisdiction of the Federal Aviation Act.[8]

With the formation of the holding company concept in 1980, Texas International was transformed into a subsidiary. In the face of a reces-

---

[8] Author unlisted, "Trans World to Fight Takeover," *Aviation Week & Space Technology*, September 24, 1979, p. 25.

sionary environment during 1980, the airline decided to change some fundamental strategic directions.

1. Greater emphasis would be placed on the business traveler who is affected less by a changing economic environment. Efforts were made to raise the ratio to a 60–40 mix in favor of business travel. Prior to that time, the carrier had near the reverse.
2. Consolidate the two major hubs, Dallas/Fort Worth and Houston. Route expansions would spring from those points only.
3. Reestablish ties with travel agents to expand their marketing network rather than relying solely on incoming calls to their reservation center.

MORE PEANUTS, "TAC," AND NEW YORK AIR 1979–1980

In short, 1980 was a year of consolidation. However, the company remained committed to expansion. Houston's Intercontinental Airport is the 8th busiest in the United States and 20th in the world according to the Airport Operator's Council International. In June of 1980, Texas Air Corporation announced that 15 of the 26 new gates added upon completion of Terminal C would belong to the airline. The other 11 were reserved by Continental. At the time of the announcement, Texas Air was operating 59 flights from five gates in Terminal A at Houston Intercontinental.

Financial and operating data for Texas Air Corporation for the years 1971–1980 is shown in Appendix A.

In January of 1980, a falling out occurred between Lorenzo and part of his management team concerning among many things the new "Peanuts Payola" marketing plan. The result was the resignation of some key personnel: Dave Burr, president of Texas International and a member of TAC's board; Jerry Gitner, senior vice president of marketing and planning; and Bob McAdoo, controller and vice president of information systems. The group left with other Texas Air management personnel to form People Express, a low-cost "commuter line" between New York and Washington. To add insult to injury, Melrose Dause, Lorenzo's ex-administrative assistant, was named president of the newly formed venture. She may be the first woman in the United States to hold such a position.

Not to be outdone, Lorenzo announced his version of Peoples' Express, New York Air, on September 12, 1980. The newly formed subsidiary was formed when $24 million and six DC-9-30s from Texas International's fleet was provided by Texas Air. A public offering of stock was made to raise additional capital. However, Texas Air maintains about an 80 percent interest in New York Air.

New York Air's system is planned to ultimately span 15 cities in 7 states and the District of Columbia. The hub is planned to be the New York/Newark area with no destination requiring more than two hours in flight time. Cities listed in its initial filing included Detroit, Boston, Newark, Albany, Buffalo, Rochester, Syracuse, New York City, Cincinnati, Cleveland, Columbus, Dayton, and Pittsburgh. The airline competes directly with Eastern, the entrenched shuttle system master in the area. Through creative advertising programs such as requiring passengers to take the New York Oath ("to never ever again fly the Eastern shuttle") before receiving the discount fares, the airline has become the darling of the press. Dubbed "Son of Shuttle" by the New York City media, its passenger load factor has been in the 65–70 percent range.

The venture has not been without its detractors. Being a nonunion subsidiary of Texas Air has caused an uproar from ALPA, Texas International's pilots union. They claim that their contract forbids the use of nonunion pilots and that New York Air is in violation. Lorenzo contends that their contract is with Texas International and that New York Air is a subsidiary of Texas Air, not TI. Therefore, he sees no justification in their complaints. The issue is crucial in that if TAC wins, a new nonunion precedent will be established in a highly unionized industry.

THE ATTEMPT TO ACQUIRE CONTINENTAL 1980–1981

Western and Continental were very near a corporate marriage when Frank Lorenzo announced in early 1981 that Texas International (i.e., not Texas Air) had acquired 9.4 percent of Continental's stock and intended a takeover. Western negotiations terminated and the Los Angeles-based carrier was in the fight of its life. On February 9, 1981, Lorenzo announced a tender offer for 4.3 million shares of Continental stock (48 percent of the outstanding stock) for $13 per share, a quote which bore a 25 percent premium over the price at which Continental closed on February 5. In a carefully worded statement to Continental shareholders, Texas International reminded them of some facts about the proposed Western merger.

1. There was no guarantee that the merger would either equal or exceed TI's cash offer.
2. The combined loss for Continental and Western in 1980 was $52.7 million.
3. The combination would have produced a net loss of $1.94 per share on Continental stock versus the 64 cents per share actually recorded.

4. The combination would have $321.2 million in debt coming due within the next five years.

5. The proposed company would have a total long-term debt structure of over $763.8 million, a 132 percent increase over current levels.

Almost 4.3 million Continental shares were tendered to TI within four days.

By the first week of April, Continental was desperate. It proposed a $185 million ESOP[9] offering in which employees would be able to buy the airline and effectively dilute the ownership of existing shareholders, including Texas International, by 50 percent. The battle has raged for months. In late June of 1981, the New York Stock Exchange ruled that it would delist Continental if the ESOP plan was implemented. The California Commission of Corporations, the first governmental authority to issue an option, ruled that Continental could not issue the additional 15 million ESOP shares without a vote from shareholders and employees. In addition, it acted to neutralize Texas International's voting power by allowing it to vote only in the same proportion as the remaining small investors.

---

[9] Employee stock option plan.

APPENDIX A   Texas Air Corporation Financial and Operating Data 1971–1980 ($ thousands except for share data)

	1980	1979	1978	1977	1976	1975	1974	1973	1972	1971
Summary of operations										
Passenger revenues	$ 266,837	$ 213,218	$ 158,185	$ 122,038	$ 102,051	$ 60,595	$ 74,431	$ 62,758	$ 58,181	$ 56,203
Other revenues	24,659	20,943	22,007	22,749	18,342	18,529	17,345	14,547	14,907	13,788
Total operating revenues	291,496	234,161	180,192	144,787	120,383	79,123	91,776	77,305	73,088	69,991
Total operating expenses	284,949	218,825	164,118	132,623	114,375	79,833	87,711	73,618	70,348	71,591
Operating income (loss)	6,547	15,336	16,074	12,164	6,018	(710)	4,065	3,687	2,740	(1,600)
Interest and debt expense—net	19,650	15,092	6,656	4,305	3,496	3,510	4,267	4,128	4,324	4,821
Other (income) expense—net	(20,402)	(48,051)	(3,733)	(379)	(957)	29	(459)	(562)	(63)	156
Provision for income taxes	2,630	6,900	5,174	1,034	822	—	43	13	—	—
	$ 1,878	$ (26,059)	$ 8,097	$ 4,960	$ 3,361	$ 3,539	$ 3,851	$ 3,579	$ 4,261	$ 4,977
Income (loss) from continuing operations	$ 4,669	$ 41,395	$ 7,977	$ 7,204	$ 2,657	$ (4,249)	$ 214	$ 108	$ (1,521)	$ (6,577)
Income (loss) from Tropicana Hotel	—	—	5,174	1,034	—	—	—	—	199	—
Extraordinary items	—	—	—	—	822	—	43	13	(305)	(839)
Net income (loss)	$ 4,669	$ 41,395	$ 13,151	$ 8,238	$ 3,479	$ (4,249)	$ 257	$ 121	$ (1,707)	$ (7,416)
Earnings (loss) per common and common equivalent share	$ .64	$ 5.88	$ 2.17	$ 1.52	$ .70	$ (3.48)	$ .02	$ (.03)	$ (1.42)	$ (6.19)
Earnings (loss) per common share assuming full dilution	.64	4.84	2.05	1.52	.70	(3.48)	.02	(.03)	(1.42)	(6.19)
Financial information (at year-end)										
Current assets	$ 196,169	$ 156,927	$ 39,785	$ 37,266	$ 27,287	$ 21,457	$ 18,846	$ 19,127	$ 18,793	$ 16,216
Current liabilities	82,871	68,452	44,578	44,433	33,401	30,301	26,160	23,698	21,748	36,726
Working capital (deficit)	113,298	88,475	(4,793)	(7,167)	(6,114)	(8,844)	(7,314)	(4,571)	(2,955)	(20,510)
Net investment in flight equipment	158,062	143,824	83,592	55,661	43,723	46,856	47,790	46,262	52,152	56,604
Total assets	386,428	319,201	194,855	108,796	78,868	73,575	73,998	80,076	75,307	78,946
Total long-term debt	217,790	175,295	113,213	61,610	49,966	50,302	51,739	56,548	55,476	64,621
Net worth (deficit)	89,903	81,218	40,784	11,749	4,267	760	4,932	4,573	5,214	(7,527)
Common Stock price range	14 3/4-6 3/8	13 5/8-7 1/2	16 3/8-7 3/8	8-2 1/8	3 5/8-1 5/8	2 3/4-1 1/4	3 7/8-1	4 3/4-1 7/8	7-4	8-3 1/2
General statistics*										
Employees at year-end	3,500	3,400	3,000	2,600	2,300	2,150	2,000	2,153	2,019	2,089
In scheduled service for the year:										
Passengers boarded	3,970,197	4,073,019	3,699,079	3,002,913	2,397,256	1,515,196	2,116,605	2,045,933	2,160,928	2,220,515
Revenue passenger miles (000s)	2,241,586	2,186,297	1,560,553	1,167,059	946,756	580,269	758,949	681,904	686,353	705,853
Available seat miles (000s)	3,898,422	3,523,128	2,601,677	2,022,907	1,767,488	1,167,349	1,506,193	1,484,787	1,374,167	1,494,642
Passenger load factor	57.5%	62.1%	60.0%	57.7%	53.6%	49.7%	50.4%	45.9%	49.9%	47.2%
Break-even load factor	55.8%	57.6%	55.0%	53.9%	51.9%	53.3%	50.1%	45.5%	51.5%	52.7%
Average fare	$ 67.10	$ 52.35	$ 42.76	$ 40.64	$ 42.57	$ 39.99	$ 35.17	$ 30.67	$ 26.92	$ 25.31
Yield per revenue passenger mile	$ .1189	$ .0975	$ .1014	$ .1046	$ .1078	$ .1044	$ .0981	$ .0920	$ .0848	$ .0796

* Texas International only.

24. The Eastern Saga

I have it on good authority that Delta is buying Eastern. Eastern is buying Pan Am. Pan Am is really going after United now that it has all of United's cash, and American's Bob Crandall who has been devilishly silent all along, is getting ready to make a tender offer for the whole industry once he reaches agreement with his pilots. Furthermore, I spoke to Frank Lorenzo this morning and he assured me his next targets are Peru and Bolivia, which he plans to merge into the first low-cost country. (Maldutis, *Business Week*, March 10, 1986, p. 107.)

Eastern Airlines, led by former astronaut Frank Borman, had experienced during the first quarter of 1986, the most volatile period in its history. The drama was reflected in most of the major newspapers:

January 7, 1986—Eastern's Labor Talks Face Growing Pressure—Eastern will have to reach agreements with its three major unions by the end of February. Eastern's management is under pressure to win concessions in order to meet requirements set by lenders to keep the carrier out of default. (*New York Times*, January 7, 1986, p. D1.)

January 8, 1986—Eastern Strike Date Delayed—Eastern's flight attendants revised the mid-January strike deadline to coincide with a February 28 default deadline set by the airline's creditors. (*New York Times*, January 8, 1986, p. D4.)

January 22, 1986—Eastern's Battle Over Wages—Wayne A. Yeoman, senior vice president of finance at Eastern, gave a presentation this week which emphasized the point that labor was the only place to gain cost reductions. Charles E. Bryan, president of District 100 of the International Association of Machinists and Aerospace Workers, stated, "that's what they have been saying for the past 10 years." (*New York Times*, January 22, 1986, p. D1.)

February 20, 1986—Eastern in Reversal, Says Pilots' Strike Would Force Airline to Suspend Flights—Eastern said that it intends to shut down the airline if its pilots go on strike next week, reversing its previous position

---

This case was written in the spring of 1986 by University of Houston-Clear Lake MBA candidates T. T. Asim, D. R. Kostyal, P. G. Merta and P. E. Stanton under the supervision of Timothy Singleton. Permission to use this case must be obtained from Timothy Singleton.

that it would fly through a possible strike. (*The Wall Street Journal,* February 20, 1986, p. 4.)

February 23, 1986—Eastern's Choice: Chapter 11?—Julius Maldutis, senior airline analyst for Salomon Brothers, Inc., a major Wall Street investment banking firm, predicted that if Eastern's pilots go on strike, a Chapter 11 filing is a "distinct possibility." (*Houston Post,* February 23, 1986, p. E2.)

February 24, 1986—Texas Air Bid Studied by Eastern—Mr. Charles E. Bryan, the president of the largest union at Eastern and also an Eastern director, said that the board was considering a takeover offer by the Texas Air Corporation's chairman, Frank Lorenzo. He also stated that his union would not open its contract to negotiate concessions, and instead was willing to take its chances with Frank Lorenzo. (*New York Times,* February 24, 1986, p. D1.)

February 25, 1986—Unions Accept Sale of Eastern—Labor unions grudgingly accepted Eastern's decision to sell out to Houston-based Texas Air Corp. Charles Bryan of the IAM accused Eastern of "complicity designed to destroy the unions." The pilots' union called the sale to Texas Air "a bad decision by the board of directors." (*Houston Post,* February 25, 1986, p. C1.)

February 26, 1986—Texas Air's Past Draws Rumors of Rival Offers—Pan American World Airways was said to be studying a possible bid for Eastern. Another possible suitor mentioned was Delta Airlines. Frank Borman thinks the terms of the Texas Air pact make it completely impossible to subvert the agreement that is in place. (*The Wall Street Journal,* February 26, 1986, p. 4.)

February 27, 1986—Strike Threatened at Eastern—The flight attendants' union renewed its threat yesterday to strike Eastern on Saturday. Analysts said that a strike could conceivably jeopardize the Texas Air deal because of technical default on its loans. (*New York Times,* February 27, 1986, p. D5.)

March 3, 1986—Eastern Airlines Attendants Get Three-Year Contract— Eastern reached an agreement with its flight attendants on a three-year contract which calls for 20 percent pay cuts. Federal mediator Harry Bickford stated, "Each time we reached a crucial point, something came up to complicate it." (*The Wall Street Journal,* March 3, 1986, p. 4.)

March 5, 1986—Pay Cuts Will Save Eastern $300 Million—Eastern said the pay cuts extracted from the pilots, flight attendants, and nonunion employees will save $300 million in labor costs. The company is still seeking wage concessions from its machinists' union, whose contract expires in 1987. Eastern management said it was confident that senior lenders would "act soon to lift the declaration of technical default imposed on the carrier at midnight Friday, February 28." (*Houston Post*, March 5, 1986, p. C1.)

March 6, 1986—Eastern Plans to Add Flights, Recall Workers—Eastern said Wednesday it was planning a 6 percent increase in flights, and will recall furloughed flight attendants. In addition, the board approved redemption of the "poison pill" share purchase redemption rights it issued to its common stockholders. (*Houston Post*, March 6, 1986, p. C1.)

March 9, 1986—Eastern-Texas Air Merger Draws Fire—Sen. Howard Metzenbaum wrote Transportation Secretary Elizabeth Dole, urging her to disapprove the proposed Texas Air-Eastern merger. He said that the merged company would control 73 percent of the New York-Boston market and 78 percent of the New York-Washington market. (*Houston Post*, March 9, 1986, p. C1.)

March 15, 1986—U.S. Seeks Record $9.5 Million Fine Against Eastern—The Federal Aviation Administration is seeking a record $9.5 million fine for Eastern's alleged failure to carry out inspections and repairs and to comply with maintenance procedures. This follows a March 7 FAA notification that they were prepared to suspend Eastern's operating certificate unless a written commitment to comply with all government regulations was received by March 14. (*Houston Post*, March 15, 1986, p. A1.)

THE HISTORY OF EASTERN AIRLINES

Company Background

Eastern Airlines has what is considered by many to be a colorful and exciting history. In 1926 the U.S. Post Office invited competitive bids to transport mail between New York and Atlanta. Harold Pitcairn, who operated out of a barn near Philadelphia, submitted the winning bid of $3 per pound. With the contract as security, Pitcairn was able to build a series of biplanes, and recruit World War I pilots and barnstormers.

In late 1927, before Pitcairn had even inaugurated the service, the post office awarded him a 595-mile extension between Atlanta and Miami. The service officially began on May 1, 1928. On July 10, 1929—less than four months before the stock market crash—Pitcairn sold his airline to North American Aviation for $2.5 million. Clement Keys, North American's founder, promptly changed the name of Pitcairn Aviation to Eastern Air Transport. Passenger service was introduced in 1930, utilizing the safe and comfortable Custiss Condors. (Kelly, p. 231.)

In 1933, General Motors bought outright control of North American, and installed Captain Eddie Rickenbacker, the World War I flying ace, as general manager of Eastern Air Transport. Profane and aggressive, Rickenbacker drove his people hard, but progress was slow and painful. By 1938, North American prospered as a manufacturer of airplanes. The prospect of increasing business for military aircraft in Europe and the presence of legal restrictions here at home led General Motors to put Eastern on the auction block. A group of investors including Laurence Rockefeller, swung a deal, and set Rickenbacker up as president of the now-independent Eastern Airlines.

Rickenbacker's first emphasis was on safety—and after safety was economy. His objective was to fly the most planes, with the greatest capacity, and with the least cost. In the 1940s, Eastern had little competition on most of the routes it flew, and passengers had to live with its growing reputation for lost baggage, late departures, and poor treatment. When competition entered the picture, Eastern's business dropped off alarmingly. Delta Airlines provided some of Eastern's stiffest competition, particularly in the eastern United States.

In the 1950s, Eastern, along with other airlines, was scrambling to enter the jet age in commercial aviation. Rickenbacker was aware that Eastern would have to keep abreast of technological change; otherwise, it would face ruinous competition on some of its most important routes. Many factors had to be weighed. Boeing and Douglas aircraft companies were designing turbojet airplanes, but at a cost of at least $4.5 million each. Commercial jet technology was as yet unproven, even though military jets had been operating for years. Lockheed provided another option that was open to airlines in that transitional time—the turboprop engine, which used both a propeller and a gas turbine. Such an engine was considerably lighter than a piston engine of equal power, and was capable of much greater speed, though not as fast as a jet engine. Plans for the Lockheed L-188 Electra, utilizing four turboprop engines, were announced in 1955, at a projected cost of $1.8 million each. (Lewis, p. 268.) Rickenbacker felt that the jet engine would only be superior on extremely long flights, and that the turboprop would be more economical and efficient on Eastern's route system. Rickenbacker ordered 40 Electras—more than any other airline—to fly routes in the Northeast. Delta, Eastern's major competitor, decided to pin its hopes on the Douglas DC-8 jetliner, which could not be delivered before late 1959. Delta's decision was to later prove fortunate.

On January 12, 1959, Eastern put its first Electra into service on its run from New York to Miami. A series of Electra accidents occurred, and the resulting unfavorable publicity severely handicapped all airlines using them. The Civil Aeronautics Board imposed speed restrictions on all remaining Electras in service, which resulted in mounting operating costs. (Kelly, p. 239.) As one of the principal airlines involved in the development and use of the Electra, Eastern suffered greatly from this turn of events. It was clear that turboprop airplanes could not compete in the public eye with the speed and smoothness of jet aircraft. By the early 1960s, the Electra was already obsolete. (Lewis, p. 271.)

In spite of all these difficulties, Eddie Rickenbacker remained CEO until 1963. Floyd Hall of TWA left his position of general manager to join Eastern in 1963 as president and CEO. He had worked his way through the ranks at TWA, starting there as a pilot. He led a new management team which guided Eastern back to profitability and growth. By 1972 Eastern had become one of the Big Four domestic airlines along with United, TWA, and American.

Business travel accounted for a substantial amount of revenue. In an effort to develop the market for vacation travel, Eastern launched a joint program to promote Walt Disney World in Florida and a series of TV ads showing its travel-planning services. These strategies were part of a campaign titled "Eastern—the Wings of Man." (Wyckoff, p. 89.)

THE AIRLINE INDUSTRY

The U.S. domestic airline industry was born in the early 1900s with foundations in the carrying of mail and passengers on a limited basis. As flight technology improved, the need for a comprehensive system of air transportation to serve commerce, national defense, and the U.S. Postal Service was manifested. As with railroads and trucking, it was felt that competitive forces of our capitalistic economy alone would not provide for effective development of an air transport system. With the objective of providing balanced coordinated growth of an air transportation system in the best public interest, the Civil Aeronautics Act of 1938 was born.

The initiation of economic regulation similar to that of public utilities, the act was designed to "promote adequate, economical, and efficient service by air carriers at reasonable charges, without unjust discriminations, undue preferences or advantages, or unfair competitive practices." (Congressional Declaration of Policy, sec. 2(c).) Administration of the act was to be performed by the Civil Aeronautics Board (CAB). The CAB was given broad regulatory powers in the areas of setting fares, approving entry to the industry, structuring routes, and supervision of mergers.

In the 40-year period that followed, growth of the domestic air transportation system was staggering. Major airlines, such as Delta, American, and United increased individual route mile capacities from approximately 5,000 to the 50,000 mile range. Passengers carried increased from 1 million in 1938 to 267 million in 1978. Increases in technology supported this growth. For example, equipment was improved from a 21-seat Douglas propeller-driven DC-3 to the 400-seat

Boeing 747 with a 6,000 mile range. The airline industry became one of the nation's major industries, employing over 300,000 in 1978.

Despite the positive aspects of industry growth under the CAB, studies were performed as early as 1951 questioning the necessity of strict airline regulation. (Keyes, 1951.) As the years passed, strict government control over airlines came under increased scrutiny. Under regulation, CAB restrictions on fares and routes were said to cause a high level of industry seat overcapacity. The "cost-plus" pricing technique employed by the CAB led to operational inefficiency and high costs. This combined with fare increases associated with a recession and the 1973 oil embargo and a general distrust of government regulation in the 1970s led to the first deregulation bill in 1975. The CAB itself stated: "(Regulation) is not justified by the underlying cost and demand characteristics of commercial air transportation. . . . The industry is naturally competitive." (*Civil Aeronautics Board Report,* 1975).

These massive shifts in public policy led to the passage of the Airline Deregulation Act of 1978. The focus of the act was on improvements in efficiency, innovation, and service through competition. In the phased execution of the act, restrictions to industry entry and routes serve were to be removed by 1981. Control over fares was to be phased out by the end of 1982. By 1985, the CAB itself would be phased out. It was planned that removal of burdensome CAB restrictions was to act as a catalyst for strategic business change in the industry.

In the tumultuous years that followed 1978, airline management teams were confronted with some of the greatest challenges ever. With a scramble to retain viability in the new environment, massive route restructuring took place. Large (trunk) carriers moved into one another's territories to exploit perceived new opportunities. A rash of new entrant carriers moved in on abandoned and reduced-frequency routes. In the period from 1978 to 1983, entrants and local carriers displaced 10 percent of the large carriers' market share. During this period, the number of interstate carriers increased from 36 to 123 with a contrasting note of 34 bankruptcies and 69 airlines ceasing operations. Clearly, structural equilibrium was being sought.

Deregulation spawned a variety of innovative operating concepts. One is the hub-and-spoke concept. Using this arrangement, a carrier establishes one or more "hub cities," where most of its routes converge to provide a multiplier effect on the number of point-to-point routes available (Exhibit 1). In addition to reducing the amount of competition at the hub cities, this concept also allows for more effective equipment utilization by "feeding" the hub with short-range equipment and "deploying" the hub using large-capacity aircraft on long-range routes. The market fragmentation that resulted increased

EXHIBIT 1

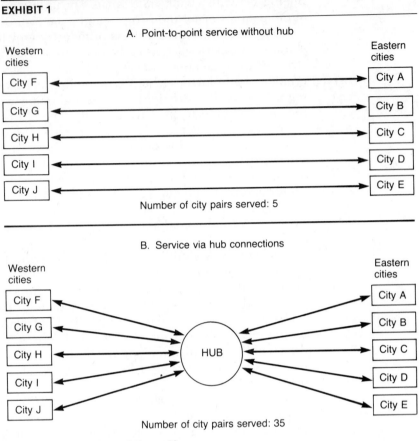

A. Point-to-point service without hub

Western cities

Eastern cities

City F → City A
City G → City B
City H → City C
City I → City D
City J → City E

Number of city pairs served: 5

B. Service via hub connections

Western cities

Eastern cities

City F
City G
City H
City I
City J

HUB

City A
City B
City C
City D
City E

Number of city pairs served: 35

SOURCE: *Airline Deregulation*, p. 83.

the need for smaller airliners. (*Aviation Week and Space Technology,* March 10, 1986, p. 203.)

The removal of fare regulation and the mass of low-cost new entrants created heated price competition on heavily traveled routes. Majors usually responded by matching an entrant's fare on routes that were of value to them. Controversy existed over the ultimate effect on consumers due to the fact that cheaper fares were evident on heavily traveled, competitive routes. On marginal routes, fares had increased sharply. Overall indications relative to service and convenience offered to the flying public were that more passengers were receiving improved service than the number experiencing deteriorated service.

With all factors taken into account, the overall effects of deregulation seem to be positive. Severe competitive financial pressures have caused belt tightening of inefficient carriers in the push for lower operating costs. Flights have been modernized with new fuel-efficient equipment, and lower labor costs are emerging as a result of pressures by new entrants. The service of air transportation is now available to a wider range of the general public with low, no-frill fares.

AIRLINE SAFETY

One of the principal concerns to many airline passengers during the transition to a deregulated environment is the level of safety. One of the most common factors cited by the flying public is the effect austerity programs might have on safety. Is less money being devoted to maintenance? Can pilots with less experience handle emergency situations as well as highly tenured ones? What is the effect of entrants flying used, high-time equipment?

The literature responds to these items in two ways. First, deregulation involved removing of regulation in economic areas. Basic crew and maintenance certification processes were not changed. Second, a look at actual safety records reveals an increase in airline safety since deregulation. For large transport aircraft, the fatal accident rate per 100,000 flight hours has decreased 32 percent, when comparing 1975–1979 to 1980–1984. In commuter airlines, a 56 percent decline has been experienced. Most agree that deregulation has not had an adverse effect on safety.

In March of 1986, a $9.5 million fine was proposed against Eastern by the FAA for alleged safety and bookkeeping violations. A previously undisclosed threat to shut down the carrier was lifted. A total of 78,372 individual violations were cited during the three month "blue-ribbon" inspection. (*Houston Post*, March 15, 1986, p. A1.) One of the most serious violations involved a landing gear prone to collapse on landing. It was not being replaced as required on an entire fleet of B-727s. On one aircraft, an actual collapse did occur during a landing.

The $9.5 million fine was due by March 20, 1986. Eastern has the option to appeal the case to the National Transportation Safety Board if it fails to reach an agreement with the FAA.

THE BORMAN ERA

Frank Borman was an officer in the United States Air Force for more than 20 years before he joined Eastern in 1969 as a special adviser. He was born in Gary, Indiana, graduated from West Point, took his commission in the newly formed air force, and saw service in a bomber squadron in the Philippines.

Borman later received a master's degree in aeronautical engineering, and returned to West Point to teach. His teaching career was interrupted in 1962 when he was picked to be an astronaut in the Gemini program. Three years later, he orbited the earth in Gemini 7, and in 1968, was one of three to orbit the moon in Apollo 8 on Christmas Eve.

Once at Eastern, Borman quickly assumed power and responsibility. The following table outlines his career path at Eastern. (Eastern Airlines, Form 10-K, p. 7.)

Date	Promoted to:
July 1970	Vice president
January 1971	Senior vice president—operations group
July 1974	Executive vice president—general operations manager
July 1974	Elected to board of directors
June 1974	President and chief operating officer
January 1976	President and CEO
December 1976	Chairman of the board, president, and CEO

In December 1976, when Borman took over for Floyd Hall as chairman and CEO, Eastern was facing severe problems.

- The airline was badly overstaffed, with employees bound by restrictive work rules.
- It had a crushing long-term debt—the result of buying too many L-1011 airplanes.
- Floyd Hall had maintained separate corporate offices in New York and Miami, which he later conceded was a mistake. (*Business Week*, December 22, 1975, p. 40.)
- Over the years Eastern had developed a reputation for late arrivals and departures, discourteous employees, and terrible food.
- The airline industry was soon to become deregulated, and the ground rules for competition would change. Eastern appeared on almost everybody's list of airlines that would fold.

In May of 1975, Frank Borman became president of Eastern. In his new position, Borman inherited several formidable challenges. He was greeted by operations which incurred a $95.6 million loss by the end of 1975. Behind this loss was a troubled cost element that represented 43 percent of revenues—labor. Its work force of over 38,000 was almost 60 percent unionized. The largest representation was by the International Association of Machinists (IAM), accounting for 12,000 employees in mechanical and ground service positions. Pilots and flight attendants were represented by the Air Line Pilots Association (ALPA) and the Transport Workers Union (TWU), respectively. For years, a strong adversarial relationship existed between Eastern management and the unions. The staunch union members earned a reputation in the industry for contract enforcement to the letter, even

A Chronology of Eastern's Recent Milestones

1975	Frank Borman becomes president. A $95.6 million loss.
1976	Borman becomes chairman. A $39.1 million profit.
1978	Airline industry is deregulated. Eastern debt grows with fleet modernization. Fare wars begin.
1979	A $57.6 million profit. Fourth consecutive profitable year.
1980	A $17.4 million loss (the first of 5 consecutive years). Debt continues to rise, $2.24 billion at year-end.
1983	A $183.7 million record loss. Borman threatens labor with bankruptcy and later retreats. Temporary peace with labor.
1985	January, Borman unilaterally extends wage cuts—retreats and restores full pay. A $73.8 million profit in first 9 months. Fare wars intensify. Profits turn to loss in fourth quarter—$6.3 million profit for the year.
1986	Debt rises to $2.5 billion. Consultants recommend drastic pay cuts or Chapter 11. 1,010 flight attendants laid off. 20% pay cuts for flight attendants. Machinists refuse 20% pay cuts. Pilots accept 20% pay cuts. Eastern agrees to be bought by Texas Air. $9.5 million fine levied for safety violations.

SOURCES: *The Wall Street Journal*, February 25, 1986, p. 1; and *Houston Post*, March 15, 1986, p. A1.

if it meant the company losing money. Stories circulated the industry, such as several mechanics standing around during a maintenance task, waiting for a designated electrician to replace a small terminal or light bulb before proceeding.

VARIABLE EARNINGS PROGRAM (VEP)

This program was instituted in 1975 by Eastern management in order to combat the financial losses in excess of $100 million. Under this program, employees would return 3.5 percent of their wages each year, but would receive a share of profits in any year in which net earnings exceeded 2 percent of gross revenues. Once the net wage losses were in millions, unions accused Eastern of maliciously manipulating the reportable profits below 2 percent of gross revenues in order to keep the unions from sharing the profits. This development angered the unions and solidified their position against Eastern management. Borman, during this period of distrust and confusion, made the following statement to the press:

> Employee cooperation is a key to productivity, which, in turn, is one of the few available weapons against inflation and runaway costs. Participation of personnel in the carrier's corporate interests through stock ownership and variable earnings program will generate the productivity needed to compete effectively. (Kuttner, 1985, pp. 96–98.)

In 1976, Frank Borman became chairman of Eastern. During this year, Eastern turned a profit of $39.1 million. From management's perspective, things at Eastern were improving. Temporary relief from burdensome wages were realized from VEP. (Note that this also involved a pay freeze.) Borman began to form long-term strategies for future profitability. One area of concentration was on upgrading the existing fleet then predominated by fuel-thirsty B-727 and DC-9 equipment with new technology, high-bypass turbofan equipment. In mid-1977, Borman committed $10 million to the trial lease of four new technology Airbus Industrie A-300s with an eventual plan to purchase 50. (*Aviation Week and Space Technology*, May 16, 1977, p. 30.) For increased efficiency, Borman planned a 10-hour per day utilization of the A-300s (some 30 percent more than the next-highest A-300 utilization in the industry).

In 1978, the Airline Deregulation Act ravaged the airline industry. With deregulation as an added incentive for long-term austerity, Borman forged ahead with the acquisition of new fuel-efficient equipment at a fast pace. This decision was at the cost of a marked increase in Eastern's long-term debt.

To maintain its position on the East Coast corridor and other heavily traveled routes, Eastern engaged in intense fare competition which translated into reduced revenues. In addition, Eastern's high labor costs and low productivity became totally out of line with competitive trends brewing at new entrant carriers. Despite this adversity, Eastern continued to make a profit through the end of 1979.

Also brewing at the time was increased distrust between Eastern management and the IAM work force. By 1979, the VEP program had accounted for some $100 million in wage losses. After inspection of the company's books, the IAM accused Eastern of tampering with the figures to keep reportable profits below the 2 percent level that triggered the profit-sharing mechanism—a claim that was never substantiated. Increased union militance resulted. To counter, management added fuel to the fire by adding a layer of first-line supervision to displace responsibility of unionized head mechanics.

Charles Bryan

In 1979, District 100 of the IAM elected a new, more militant president, Charles Bryan. Bryan had coined VEP as the "Veritable Extortion Plan," because he was convinced the union had accepted Borman's plan out of ignorance. When the IAM's contract expired in 1981, bargaining stretched clear into 1983. To avert a threatened strike, Borman reversed a final offer to the union and granted a 17 percent increase over three years. Borman referred to the ratified contract as a "rape." (Kuttner, 1985, p. 93.)

In 1984, as part of a wage concessions pact, Bryan was elected to Eastern's board of directors. During the 1984–1985 union contract negotiations, mistrust was building up between the unions and Eastern. In mid-April 1985, the IAM disapproved the initial proposal. Bryan blamed the defeat on several factors. Since Bryan was considered to be a newcomer in the IAM, anti-Bryan strongholds voted against the proposal in order to embarrass him. On a second ratification vote in May 1985, the contract passed by a two-to-one margin.

During the IAM first-quarter 1986 negotiations, Bryan had offered a 15 percent cut, but only under the condition that Frank Borman resign. Eastern would probably have never been offered for sale to Texas Air Corporation had Bryan not insisted on Borman's departure. "Charlie has this competitive relationship with Frank. He ended up deciding that the devil he didn't know was better than the devil he knew," stated an Eastern board member. (*Business Week*, March 10, 1986, p. 106.)

Nineteen eighty marked the first of five consecutive years of losses. Eastern lost $17.4 million in 1980, $65.9 million in 1981, $74.9 million in 1982, and $183.7 million in 1983. Despite the increasing losses, Borman continued his push for new equipment. In 1982, for example, 27 Boeing 757s were ordered. After this purchase, Eastern's long-term debt exceeded $2 billion, or more than 63 percent of assets. Interest expenses were consuming almost 5 percent of revenues, compared with .6 percent at Delta, one of Eastern's major competitors.

By the summer of 1983, the financial picture continued to worsen. In response to creditors' demands to restructure debt, Borman called emergency meetings with the unions, demanding a 20 percent pay cut to avert financial collapse. In a videotaped message to all employees shown one day after Continental Airlines' Chapter 11 filing, Borman offered these choices:

1. Go out of business "a-la-Braniff."
2. File for protection "a-la-Continental," or
3. Reduce labor costs drastically. (Kuttner, 1985, p. 93.)

Following analysis of the company's books, the unions accepted an average wage reduction of 18 percent for a period of one year. "In return, Eastern gave its employees 25 percent of its common stock (12 million shares), to be held in trust until 1986, plus a new junior-preferred security that is convertible to three million shares of Eastern common. This new stock has a liquidation preference of $260 million, so that employees will be compensated for most of their first-year wage concessions in the event of bankruptcy." (Kuttner, 1985, p. 94.)

The new agreement reduced losses and returned Eastern to profitability by the third quarter of 1984. The first quarter of 1985 boasted a profit of $107.4 million. These earnings translated into profit sharing averaging $1,500 per employee.

Also in the new agreement were provisions to give back large amounts of operational responsibility to the ranks previously assigned to supervisors. The atmosphere that resulted was one of model cooperation between labor and management, which laid a foundation for massive productivity gains. Pride seemed to pervade the work force.

This temporary labor management utopia was quickly torn down when Borman, under pressure from creditors, told labor that he could not restore wage cuts after the previously agreed upon one-year date. With a new IAM contract due on December 31, 1984, and no agreement in sight, Eastern slipped into technical default of its loan obligations. In response, Borman unilaterally extended the one year 18 percent pay cuts for all unions into 1985. The IAM immediately began litigation based on a violation of the Railway Labor Act for failure to return contractually guaranteed wage restorations. In true Borman tradition, talk of Chapter 11 again began to surface.

The unrest spread outside of the boardroom when travel agents became nervous of Chapter 11, and began to cancel bookings. Suppliers and airlines in interline ticket agreements also began to fear Chapter 11 proceedings of Eastern. To deal with this self-inflicted crisis, Borman rescinded the unilateral pay cuts, ceased Chapter 11 threats, and resumed negotiations with the IAM.

On a second ratification vote in May of 1985, a new contract was approved by a margin of two-to-one. Basic provisions included a 5 percent restoration of the 18 percent pay cut and a two-tier wage scale. Also included was a profit-sharing plan.

POWER SHARING

The unions decided to agree on wage concessions demanded by Borman in order to keep the airline viable. In return for the wage concessions, unions were granted:

- A large block of company stock.
- Seats on the board of directors.
- Profit-sharing program.
- Increased union responsibility on the shop floor.

As a result of the wage concessions, Eastern saved approximately $300 million and provided its employees with 25 percent of Eastern's common stock (12 million shares). Eastern returned to profitability in the third quarter of 1984, while the employees averaged $2,000 in

1985 profit sharing. The principle of power sharing rather than profit sharing was a revolutionary development. The unions became involved in analyzing financial data, corporate planning, fare structures, and supervising the shop floor. The routine supervisory responsibilities of completing flight forms, certifying flight weight, verifying attendance, and communication also became an integral part of their daily responsibility. The unions were finally involved in all levels of management. "There is a genuine working together, a whole new cooperative spirit," says Joseph Leonard, the chief operating officer of Eastern. (Kuttner, 1985, p. 97.) He recalled a classic occurrence where the collaboration between management and union was indeed at its apex. Evidently, Eastern management was confronted with the decision of laying off some of its employees in Houston because of severe competition from Continental. Upon unions' recommendations, Eastern managed to develop an overnight freight service routed through Houston with passenger seats at cheap prices to complement this service. This project was dubbed the "Moonlight Express." There was no reduction in force.

The trend toward lower labor cost is expected to continue in the 1980s. The established airlines are vigorously reducing labor cost in order to remain competitive with the new entrants and low-cost airlines. Operators like New York Air and Continental experienced labor costs in the neighborhood of 20 percent of operating costs. By contrast, Eastern's labor cost was approximately 35 percent of total operating costs in late 1984. (Kuttner, 1985, p. 98.) Unlike fuel costs, labor cost can be controlled by means of wage concessions and reduction in labor force. Industry analysts predict that for airlines to compete effectively, the lucrative wage contracts will have to be abandoned.

MOONLIGHT EXPRESS

In early 1985, Eastern announced that on April 1, it would offer cut-rate seats to passengers willing to fly at night on flights devoted primarily to moving freight. Labeled the "Moonlight Express," the service would cover a 10-city network with a hub in Houston. For $98 one way, a passenger could fly from coast to coast, or fly to and from Houston for $49 one way. (*Aviation Week and Space Technology*, March 5, 1985, p. 75.)

Eastern was able to arrange a contract with CF AirFreight of Palo Alto, California, to lease belly space on seven of Eastern's Airbus Industrie A300 jets for three years for the purpose of overnight delivery of freight covering the United States. Under the terms of the agreement, CF AirFreight was paying enough for the freight service to cover the costs of the flights. (*The Wall Street Journal*, July 22, 1985, p. 5.)

For Eastern, the contract was an excellent deal. Since the flights were in the middle of the night, Eastern made money from planes that would otherwise be idle. Because the freight revenue covered the costs, passenger fares were almost all profit. Eastern and Pan Am were the only U.S. airlines that operated Airbus Industrie A300 jets, whose unusually large cargo areas and relatively low operating costs make such a service possible. Therefore, Eastern had only one likely competitor in the future.

In exchange for discount fares, passengers would have to accept spartan service, an overnight flight, and a 90-minute stay in Houston. The schedule was timed to permit freight deliveries by noon. What Eastern set out to do was to duplicate what People Express had proven—there is a large segment of the population totally motivated by price, rather than convenience. By July 1985, the venture was already one of Eastern's most successful operations. The load factor, or percentage of available seats occupied, had averaged 92 percent, and reservations were running so strong that Eastern virtually stopped advertising the service. The service was expected to produce an operating profit of $25 million to $35 million during its first year. (*Aviation Week and Space Technology*, March 5, 1985, p. 75.)

On August 1, 1985, Eastern expanded its service to include a flight between Newark, New Jersey, and Los Angeles by way of Chicago. Houston would continue as the hub for existing service. By late August, the airline announced its plans to expand to fifteen cities, allowing passengers to fly coast to coast for $119. People Express, for example, charged $149 for a one-way fare on the same route. Eastern was also planning to add five more cities to the service by the end of 1985.

FINANCE

Eastern Airlines made the strategic decision to modernize its aging fleet in the late 1970s. Its competitiveness had been badly damaged by rising fuel prices, and it was decided to modernize by purchasing more fuel-efficient planes. This decision was based upon a projected fuel price of above $2 a gallon.

Two major orders were placed for 21 Boeing 757s and 23 Airbus Industrie A300s. The total price tag was $1.42 billion. (*New York Times*, February 27, 1986, p. D5.) As of December 31, 1985, substantially all of the owned flight equipment was mortgaged as collateral for the promissory notes under an indenture of mortgage. This indenture contains covenants relating to level of leverage, level of net worth, and amount of specific financing that may be accomplished.

In May 1980, Eastern entered into the 1980 Bank Credit Agreement with a number of major banks. This agreement provided for a standby commitment to lend $400 million to the company, subject to certain conditions relating to compliance of certain financial tests for level of financial leverage, stockholder equity, and subordinated indebtedness. (*Eastern Airlines, Form 10-K,* filed May 28, 1985.)

Deregulation rocked Eastern, and its impact was even more severe when interest costs and fuel costs failed to follow the company's projections. Eastern's income/(losses) follow:

	Annual Income/Loss ($ millions)	*Cumulative Loss ($ millions)*
1980	$ 17.4 loss	$ 17.4 loss
1981	65.9 loss	83.3 loss
1982	74.9 loss	158.2 loss
1983	183.7 loss	341.9 loss
1984	37.9 loss	379.8 loss
1985*	6.3 gain	373.5 loss

* Includes $67.5 million fourth-quarter loss.

Deregulation spawned vigorous competition and increased use of discount fares to gain market share. Also, low-cost carriers entered the market, and cut fares to Florida and many of Eastern's key markets. (*Houston Post,* February 25, 1986, p. C4.)

The 60 Eastern lenders threatened in late 1985 to put the company in technical default if it did not lower costs significantly by February 28, 1986. (*The Wall Street Journal,* January 24, 1986, p. 1.) Faced with this ultimatum, the Eastern management decided to extract $400 million to $500 million in permanent savings from its three unions. Wayne A. Yeoman, senior vice president of finance, stated in January 1986, that as the following chart illustrates, wage concessions were necessary.

*Salary/Wages Cost per Seat Mile**		*Other Operating Expense Cost per Seat Mile**	
Delta	3.44 cents	Piedmont	4.91 cents
Eastern	3.21	Eastern	4.74
United	3.04	Delta	4.70
American	2.87	United	4.63
Piedmont	2.85	American	4.51
Western	2.26	Western	4.30
Southwest	1.74	Continental	4.29
Continental	1.33	Southwest	3.85
People Express	0.68	People Express	3.46

* January–September 1985.

He stated that the airline's other expenses were not much higher than other carriers except for wages. (*New York Times*, January 22, 1986, p. D1.)

Eastern weathered similar battles in 1983 and 1985, when it won sweeping wage concessions. The company long had been preparing financially for its first quarter 1986 stand against unions by accumulating $417 million cash as of December 31, 1985. Yeoman stated "that money could disappear in a hurry." (*The Wall Street Journal*, January 24, 1986, p. 1.)

Another major expense being incurred by Eastern was that of interest paid to service the debt acquired in fleet modernization.

1980	$109.8 million
1981	141.2
1982	178.3
1983	236.0
1984	277.5

The financing on the loans was arranged by Yeoman, who joined Eastern in September 1972 as staff vice president-development planning, and served in that capacity until April 1974. He served as vice president-development planning from April 1974 to January 1976, as vice president-finance from February 1976 to November 1977, when he became senior vice president-finance. Prior to joining Eastern, Yeoman was an officer of the U.S. Air Force for 26 years, retiring as brigadier general. (Eastern Airlines, Form 10-K, filed May 28, 1985.)

Eastern Air Lines, Inc.: Financial and Statistical Summary

Balance Sheet*	1984	1983	1982
Assets:			
Current assets	$ 889.1	$ 847.7	$ 712.8
Operating property and equipment, net	2,796.3	2,805.2	2,419.0
Other assets	84.0	104.8	93.1
Total assets	$ 3,769.4	$ 3,757.7	$ 3,224.9
Liabilities:			
Current liabilities	$ 966.3	$ 897.0	$ 774.8
Current obligations—capital leases	71.0	67.6	73.6
Long-term debt	1,428.9	1,515.2	1,053.6
Long-term obligations—capital leases	861.9	803.8	857.3
Deferred credits and other long-term liabilities	115.9	157.4	70.7
Total liabilities	3,444.0	3,441.0	2,830.0
Redeemable preferred stock	140.0	139.8	139.6

Eastern Air Lines, Inc.: Financial and Statistical Summary

Balance Sheet*	1984	1983	1982
Common/nonredeemable preferred stock and retained earnings (deficit):			
Common stock.	43.5	35.9	24.9
Non-redeemable preferred stock	53.6	46.8	—
Capital in excess of par value.	396.0	380.9	333.1
Earnings (deficit) retained for use in the business	(324.0)	(285.8)	(101.8)
Employee stock to be issued	17.2	—	—
Treasury stock as a reduction.	(0.9)	(0.9)	(0.9)
Total Common/Nonredeemable Preferred Stock and retained earnings (deficit)	185.4	176.9	255.3
Total liabilities, capital stock, and retained earnings (deficit)	$ 3,769.4	$ 3,757.7	$ 3,224.9

Statement of Income*			
Operating revenues:			
Passenger	$ 3,989.3	$ 3,608.3	$ 3,406.0
Cargo, incidental and other.	374.6	333.8	363.2
Total operating revenues	4,363.9	3,942.1	3,769.2
Operating expenses:			
Expenses excluding depreciation and amortization.	3,886.6	3,772.1	3,563.1
Depreciation and amortization	287.7	270.1	224.9
Total operating expenses.	4,174.3	4,042.2	3,788.0
Operating profit (loss)	189.6	(100.1)	(18.8)
Interest expense	(277.5)	(236.0)	(178.3)
Other nonoperating income and (expense)—net	50.0	152.4	122.2
(Provision for) reduction in income taxes	—	—	—
Income (loss) before extraordinary item	(37.9)	(183.7)	(74.9)
Extraordinary item	—	—	—
Cumulative effect of a change in accounting principle . . .	—	—	—
Net income (loss)	$ (37.9)	$ (183.7)	$ (74.9)
Earnings per average share of Common Stock:			
Income (loss) before extraordinary item	$ (1.53)	$ (7.19)	$ (3.82)
Net income (loss)	$ (1.53)	$ (7.19)	$ (3.82)
Operating statistics:			
Revenue plane miles*	325.7	302.7	290.5
Available seat miles*	51,648.4	48,020.9	46,143.8
Revenue passenger miles*	29,408.7	28,328.7	26,140.1
Passenger load factor	56.94%	58.99%	56.65%
Revenue passengers carried*	37.9	36.8	35.0
Available ton miles*	6,248.4	5,749.4	5,504.4
Revenue ton miles*.	3,359.2	3,193.5	2,959.7
Weight load factor	53.76%	55.54%	53.77%
Percent performance.	98.58%	98.62%	98.74%
Yield per revenue passenger mile	13.53¢	12.71¢	13.00¢
Yield per revenue ton mile	124.98¢	118.72¢	121.16¢
Total operating expenses per available seat mile.	8.08¢	8.42¢	8.21¢
Total operating expenses per revenue passenger mile . . .	14.19¢	14.27¢	14.49¢
Total operating expenses per available ton mile	66.81¢	70.31¢	68.82¢
Total operating expenses per revenue ton mile	124.26¢	126.58¢	127.99¢
Aircraft utilization—hours per day.	8:53	8:35	8:23
Number of personnel employed at year-end	38,400	37,100	39,200

* All amounts in millions.
SOURCE: 1984 Eastern Air Lines, Inc., *Annual Report.*

Eastern Air Lines, Inc.: Statement of Changes in Financial Position (all amounts in thousands)

	Year Ended December 31		
	1984	1983	1982
Funds provided by:			
Net loss	$ (37,927)	$(183,667)	$ (74,927)
Depreciation and amortization—operations	287,657	270,073	224,882
Depreciation and amortization—other	13,970	13,612	12,487
Foreign currency transactions	885	(138)	(66)
Charge for employee stock under 1984 Wage Investment Program, net	46,696	—	—
Funds provided from operations	311,281	99,880	162,376
Proceeds from issuance of $3.00 Cumulative Convertible Junior Preferred Stock, net of expenses	—	46,732	—
Proceeds from issuance of Common Stock, net of expenses	—	76,453	—
Proceeds from issuance of Series C Equipment Trust Certificates	—	153,761	15,544
Long-term debt financing	107,706	413,911	294,682
Termination of capital leases (excluding gains of zero, zero, and $59)	—	5,046	160
Proceeds from sale of equipment (excluding gains (loss) of $6,328, ($2,944) and $32,676)	18,389	37,877	35,548
Increase in long-time obligations under capital leases	127,822	18,002	84,715
Cash advances returned on leased equipment	—	—	25,049
Working capital components	151,902	44,915	78,790
Total funds provided	717,100	896,577	696,864
Funds applied for:			
Flight and ground equipment purchases and advances	163,645	668,163	387,503
Capital lease additions	130,763	21,242	77,378
Notes payable retired or maturing within one year	191,418	115,654	81,869
Acquisition of Latin American routes of Braniff	—	—	29,265
Decrease (increase) in deferred credits and other long-term liabilities	42,098	(84,733)	(36,974)
Obligations under capital leases maturing within one year	69,738	71,011	71,840
Cash dividends on Preferred Stock	—	17,685	19,780
Other—net	(1,179)	23,846	23,336
Working capital components	26,380	(31,910)	(11,482)
Total funds applied	622,863	800,958	642,515
Increase in cash and short-term investments	94,237	95,619	54,349
Cash and short-term investments at January 1	266,231	170,612	116,263
Cash and short-term investments at December 31	$360,468	$ 266,231	$170,612
Summary of changes in working capital:			
Funds provided:			
Accounts receivable	$ 57,732	$ (21,828)	$ (9,896)
Notes payable	38,327	50,429	6,090
Current obligations—capital leases	3,397	(5,991)	9,269
Unearned transportation revenues	52,446	22,305	73,327
	151,902	44,915	78,790
Funds applied:			
Materials and supplies	3,264	(4,953)	(3,939)
Prepaid expenses and other current assets	1,628	22,435	8,898
Accounts payable and accrued liabilities	21,488	(49,392)	(16,441)
	26,380	(31,910)	(11,482)
Net (decrease) in working capital, excluding cash and short-term investments	(125,522)	(76,825)	(90,272)
Increase in cash and short-term investments	94,237	95,619	54,349
Net (decrease) increase in working capital	$ (31,285)	$ 18,794	$ (35,923)

SOURCE: 1984 Eastern Air Lines, Inc., *Annual Report*.

Eastern Air Lines, Inc.: Statement of Operations and Earnings (Deficit) Retained for Use in the Business

	Year Ended December 31		
	1984	*1983*	*1982*
Operating revenues:			
Passenger	$3,989,283	$3,608,321	$3,406,009
Cargo	208,866	182,869	180,022
Incidental and other revenues	165,749	150,944	183,206
Total operating revenues	4,363,898	3,942,134	3,769,237
Operating expenses:			
Salaries, wages, and benefits	1,539,760	1,573,816	1,386,257
Aircraft fuel	1,003,556	980,227	1,032,935
Aircraft maintenance materials and repairs	110,168	101,637	96,330
Rentals and landing fees	185,053	163,917	154,090
Passenger food and supplies	172,657	151,401	136,116
Commissions	295,504	255,451	220,467
Advertising and promotional	90,090	91,762	81,144
Depreciation and amortization	287,657	270,073	224,882
Other operating expenses	489,822	453,957	455,796
Total operating expenses	4,174,267	4,042,241	3,788,017
Operating profit (loss)	189,631	(100,107)	(18,780)
Nonoperating income and (expense):			
Interest income	41,743	35,982	27,784
Interest expense (net of interest capitalized in the amounts of $9,650, $13,948 and $18,320)	(277,471)	(235,999)	(178,274)
Profit (loss) on sale of equipment	6,328	(2,944)	32,735
Gain on sale of tax benefits	—	121,439	51,279
Other, net	1,842	(2,038)	10,329
Total	(227,558)	(83,560)	(56,147)
Loss before income taxes	(37,927)	(183,667)	(74,927)
Income taxes	—	—	—
Net loss	(37,927)	(183,667)	(74,927)
Earnings (deficit) retained for use in the business:			
Balance at beginning of year	(285,781)	(101,877)	(26,737)
Amortization of excess of redemption value of Redeemable Preferred Stock over carrying value	(259)	(237)	(213)
Cash dividends—Preferred Stock, net of zero, $17,685 and $19,780 charged to capital in excess of par value	—	—	—
Balance at end of year	$ (323,967)	$ (285,781)	$ (101,877)
Net loss per common share	$ (1.53)	$ (7.19)	$ (3.82)

SOURCE: 1984 Eastern Air Lines, Inc., *Annual Report.*

Long-Term Debt (long-term debt [including current maturities] follows [in millions])

	December 31	
	1984	*1983*
Nonsubordinated:		
Banks		
Promissory notes due 1990–1991	$ 125.0	$ 125.0
Institutional		
6%–8¼% promissory notes due 1985–1993	58.8	73.4
Export credit		
6%–9⅛% promissory notes due 1985–1994	517.5	554.7
Manufacturers		
Senior obligations due 1985–1986.	41.9	56.8
16⅛% secured equipment certificates,		
Series C, due 2002	169.8	169.3
Other		
6½%–18% installment and other purchase		
obligations due 1985–1995	140.4	146.3
Total nonsubordinated	$1,053.4	$1,125.5
Subordinated:		
Manufacturers subordinated notes due 1985–1993	$ 130.3	$ 128.0
9¼% manufacturers subordinated notes due 1989–1998 . .	171.4	169.1
4¾% convertible subordinated debentures due		
October 1, 1993; convertible into Common Stock at		
$34 per share, callable	12.8	12.8
5% convertible subordinated debentures due		
November 1, 1992; convertible into Common Stock at		
$50 per share, callable	30.3	30.3
5% convertible subordinated debentures due		
September 30, 2008; convertible into Common Stock at		
$16 per share, callable	19.5	—
11½% convertible subordinated debentures due		
June 15, 1999; convertible into Common Stock at		
$16 per share, callable	150.0	150.0
11¾% convertible subordinated debentures due		
November 1, 2005; convertible into Common Stock at		
$13 per share, callable	32.7	32.7
Total subordinated	547.0	522.9
Total long-term debt (including current maturities)	1,600.4	1,648.4
Less current maturities	171.5	133.2
Total long-term debt	$1,428.9	$1,515.2

SOURCE: 1984 Eastern Air Lines, Inc., *Annual Report.*

Total Airlines versus Eastern Airlines

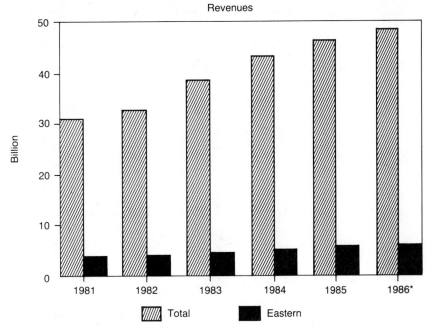

Revenues

* 1986 estimate per Value Line, Inc.

Total Airlines versus Eastern Airlines

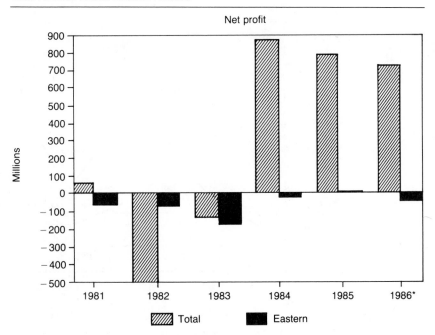

Net profit

* 1986 estimate per Value Line, Inc.

Eastern Airlines

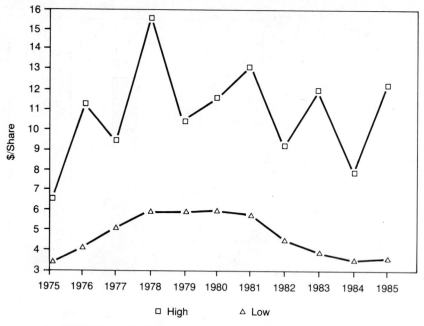

SOURCE: 1/3/1986 Value Line, Inc., p. 258.

Total Airlines versus Eastern Airlines

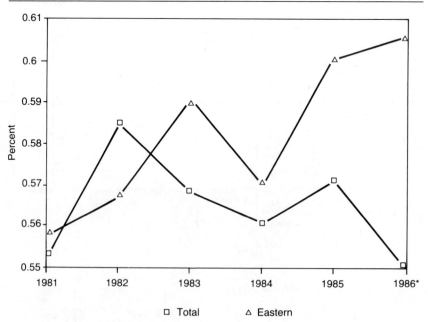

* 1986 estimate per Value Line, Inc.

APPENDIX A Principal Executive Officers of the Company

Name	Title	Age as of December 31, 1985
Frank Borman	Chairman of the board and CEO	57
Joseph B. Leonard	President and chief operating officer	42
Thomas R. Buttion	Senior vice president—airline operations	60
Jerry Cosley	Senior vice president—corporate communications	50
Jack W. Johnson	Senior vice president—human resources	50
Richard Magurno	Senior vice president—legal affairs and secretary	42
John E. Hurst, Jr.	Senior vice president—technical support services	57
Wayne A. Yeoman	Senior vice president—finance	62
David B. Kunstler	Senior vice president—planning	51
John W. Nelson	Senior vice president—marketing	43
Donald P. Martin	Senior vice president—operations coordinator	49
Jose I. Smith	Senior vice president—sales and service	45

Frank Borman joined the company in 1969.

Joseph Leonard joined the company in 1984, and was promoted to president in 1985. Prior to joining, he was a vice president at American Airlines and a manager at Northwest Orient Airlines.

Thomas Buttion joined the company in 1949 as a pilot, and was promoted to vice president in 1974. He retired on January 1, 1986.

Jerry Cosley joined the company in 1985, and was vice president–corporate communications at TWA.

Jack Johnson joined the company in 1983, after serving 23 years with the B. F. Goodrich Company.

Richard Magurno joined the company in 1970 as an attorney, and became a vice president in 1980.

John Hurst joined the company in 1971 as a vice president.

Wayne Yeoman joined the company in 1972 after serving 26 years in the air force, retiring as brigadier general.

David Kunstler joined Eastern in 1963, and has served in various marketing positions.

John Nelson became a senior vice president in 1985.

Donald Martin became a senior vice president in 1985.

Jose Smith became a senior vice president in 1985.

SOURCES: Eastern Airlines, Inc., Form 10-K, filed May 28, 1985, pp. 7–8, *The Wall Street Journal*, September 25, 1985, p. 39, and based on a conversation with Eastern Airlines Public Relations Office on April 7, 1986.

APPENDIX B Board of Directors December 31, 1985

Harry H. Bassett (67), a director since 1968, is a commercial banker.

Thomas Hale Boggs, Jr. (44) has served as a director since 1983, and is a senior law partner.

Frank Borman (57) has served as a director since 1974. He is also a director of Cameron Iron Works, Home Depot, and Southern Bell.

Charles E. Bryan (52) has served since 1984, and is a labor union leader with the International Association of Machinists and Aerospace Workers.

Robert V. Callahan (40) has served as a director since 1984, and is a union leader with the Transport Workers Union of America.

Peter O. Crisp (53) has served since 1980, and is a business executive.

James A. Elkins, Jr. (67) has served since 1959, and is a commercial banker.

Karl Eller (67) has been a director since 1978, and is a media consultant, and is chairman of the board of Circle K Corp.

John T. Fallon (62) has served since 1977, and is a real estate executive.

Robert D. Lund (66) has served since 1983, and is a retired executive of General Motors.

Enrique Madero (58) has been a director since 1979, and is a mining executive in Mexico.

Thomas O. Paine (64) has served since 1981, and is currently a consulting executive.

Wesley W. Posvar (60) has served since 1972, and is president of the University of Pittsburgh.

Willie C. Robinson (51) has served since 1982, and is a college administrator.

Julian Scheer (60) was elected in 1979, and is an executive with the LTV Corp. of Dallas.

Arthur R. Taylor (50) has served since 1983, and is chairman of a private investment company.

Thomas R. Williams (57) has served since 1981, and has been engaged in commercial banking.

David W. Wallace (62) was elected in 1985, and is the retired chairman of Bangor Punta Corporation.

Elmer L. Ward, Jr. (51) was elected in 1985, and is chairman of Palm Beach, Inc.

Joseph B. Leonard (42) was elected in 1985, and is also the president and chief operating officer of the company.

Wayne A. Yeoman (62) was elected in 1985, and is also senior vice president for finance for the company.

SOURCES: Eastern Airlines, Inc., Form 10-K, filed May 28, 1985, pp. 29–31; and *The Wall Street Journal*, September 25, 1985, p. 39.

REFERENCES—PERIODICALS

Airline Executive

"GAO Report on Deregulation," January 1986, p. 8.

"Inching Toward Health," January 1986, pp. 4–5.

Aviation Week and Space Technology

"U.S. Airlines Predict Profitability Will Continue for Third Year," March 10, 1986, pp. 203–209.

"FAA Begins Reorganization of Airline Inspection System," January 27, 1986, pp. 30–31.

"Transports' Long Haul to Profits," November 11, 1985, p. 11.

"Changing Airline System Prompts Safety Concerns," November 11, 1985, pp. 108–117.

"Competition Leads to Better Passenger Service," November 11, 1985, p. 185.

"Eastern Airlines Foresees Need for 50 Airbus-Type Aircraft," May 16, 1977, p. 30.

"Eastern Records First-Quarter Net Profit," April 22, 1985, p. 36.

"Eastern Faces Default on Loan Term," May 2, 1985, p. 38.

"Eastern to Pare Payroll by 1,600," April 18, 1985, pp. 32–33.

"Eastern, Freight Carrier Plan Passenger Service," March 5, 1985, p. 75.

Business Week

"Can Frank Borman Make Eastern Take Off?" December 22, 1975, pp. 40–44.

"Frank Lorenzo, High Flier," March 10, 1986, pp. 104–107.

Eastern Airlines

Eastern Airlines, Inc. 1984 *Annual Report,* pp. 14, 15, 18, 19.

Securities and Exchange Commission Form 10-K as amended by Form B filed May 28, 1985. Eastern Airlines, Inc. for the fiscal year ended December 31, 1984, p. 8.

Financial Times

"It Was Texas Air or Bust for Eastern," February 25, 1986, p. 27.

Fortune

"Eastern Airlines on the Brink," October 17, 1983, 102–112.

Harvard Business Review

Kuttner, Robert. "Sharing Power at Eastern Airlines," November/December 1985, vol. 63, pp. 91–101.

Houston Post

"Eastern's Choice: Chapter 11?" February 23, 1986, pp. E1–E2.

"Unions Accept Sale of Eastern," February 25, 1986, p. C1.

"No Santa Claus, Lorenzo Says," February 26, 1986, p. E1.

"Eastern Strike Threatens Sale to Texas Air," February 27, 1986, pp. C1–C2.

"Pay Cuts Will Save Eastern $300 Million," March 5, 1986, p. C1.

"Eastern Plans to Add Flights, Recall Workers," March 6, 1986, p. C1.

"Eastern-Texas Air Merger Draws Fire," March 9, 1986, p. C1.

Industry Surveys—*Aerospace and Air Transport*

"Profit Improvement Continuing," December 6, 1984, pp. A28–A33.

"Some Nationals Prospering under Deregulation," December 6, 1984, pp. A34–A35.

"Moderate Improvement Seen for Major Airlines," December 6, 1984, pp. A38–A40.

New York Times

"Eastern's Labor Talks Force Growing Pressure," January 7, 1986, pp. D1, D7.

"Eastern Strike Date Delayed," January 8, 1986, p. D4.

"Eastern's Battle over Wages," January 22, 1986, pp. D1, D5.

"Texas Air Bid Studied by Eastern," February 24, 1986, pp. D1, D4.

"Strike Threatened at Eastern," February 27, 1986, p. D5.

"A Split Decision on Borman," February 27, 1986, pp. D1, D5.

"Unionist Says Eastern Acted to Shield Borman," February 27, 1986, p. D5.

Report on Airline Service, Civil Aeronautics Board, September 1984, p. 44.

Travel Weekly

"Airline Bankruptcies Since Deregulation," January 10, 1985, p. 33.

Value Line

"Eastern Airlines," January 3, 1986, p. 258.

The Wall Street Journal

"Eastern Airlines Rebounds from the Brink," September 10, 1985, p. 6.

"Eastern Airlines Is in Yet Another Crisis that it Should Survive," January 24, 1986, 1, p. 12.

"Eastern in Reversal, Says Pilots' Strike Would Force Airline to Suspend Flights," February 20, 1986, p. 4.

"Texas Air Pact Draws Rumors of Rival Offers," February 20, 1986, p. 4.

"Eastern Air's Changes Aid Delta Now, But Longer Term Problems are Likely," February 26, 1986, p. 4.

"Eastern Attendants Get 3-Year Contract," March 3, 1986, 4.

"Eastern Air's Borman Badly Underestimated Obduracy of Old Foe," February 25, 1986, p. 1.

"Eastern Air Overnight Cut-Rate Service Proves Successful, Surprising Skeptics," July 22, 1985, p. 5.

"Eastern Air, in Bid to Get More Votes, Adjourns Meeting," June 26, 1985, p. 19.

REFERENCES—BOOKS

Biographical Data: Frank Borman. NASA: Lyndon B. Johnson Space Center.

Brenner, Melvin A. et al. *Airline Deregulation.* Eno Foundation for Transportation, Inc. Westport, Conn.: 1985.

Kelly, Charles J., Jr. *The Sky's the Limit: The History of the Airlines.* New York: Arno Press, 1972.

Keyes, Lucille. *Federal Control of Entries into Air Transportation.* Cambridge, Mass.: Harvard University Press, 1951.

Lewis, W. David, and Wesley Phillips Newton. *Delta: The History of an Airline.* Athens, Ga.: University of Georgia Press, 1979.

Wyckoff, D. Daryl, and David H. Maister. *The Domestic Airline Industry.* Lexington, Mass.: Lexington Books, 1977.

Financial Organizations

25. Brookfield Bank and Trust

David Fraser, executive vice president of Brookfield Bank and Trust (a state-chartered, independent bank), was reviewing the bank's current situation. Until two months previous, Brookfield had been the only bank in town. That situation changed with the opening of the First National Bank of Brookfield in July 1979.

Events had happened quickly since the application for chartering of the new bank was approved nearly two years prior. The president of the new bank, Charles Moore, resigned as executive vice president of Brookfield Bank and Trust in August 1978, giving 30 days notice. He was well respected and widely known in the community and had been with Brookfield for 17 years. Moore's resignation was followed by others. In October 1978, an individual who had been vice president and loan officer at Brookfield resigned to join a bank in another city, but six months later joined First National as vice president and loan officer. He had six years experience with Brookfield, and a good following in the community. A woman who had been with Brookfield for 12 years resigned her position as vice president and cashier in December 1978 to join the new bank in a similar capacity. She was married to a local businessman and also was well known and respected in the community. The resignations of the three officers were followed by those of three clerical personnel. They also joined the new bank, and it was Fraser's opinion they did so out of friendship for Moore and the other former Brookfield employees. To the best of Fraser's knowledge, salaries in the two banks are comparable for similar positions.

DEMOGRAPHIC INFORMATION

Brookfield was a city of about 16,500 population, located in one of the southern states on the Gulf Coast. In the immediate 60–70 square mile area surrounding Brookfield, there was a population of about 90,000 in several incorporated and unincorporated communities. Brookfield, one of the oldest communities in this area, was largely self-supporting. Within approximately a 25-mile radius from Brookfield, there was a population of some 550,000.

This case was prepared by Robert McGlashan and William V. Rice of the University of Houston at Clear Lake City.

The primary industries in the area were fishing, nrimping, truck farming, shipping, chemical production, and oil refining. There was also a major government installation located nearby which employs several thousand people.

In addition to First National, there were 8 other banks within a 10-mile radius of Brookfield, and a total of 20 within a 15-mile radius.

LOCATION AND FACILITIES

Brookfield Bank and Trust had been doing business at the same location since its opening in 1956. It was located on Center Street, the main thoroughfare in town, and about one and one-half miles from an interstate highway. The original bank building occupied about 3,500 square feet. As a result of several additions, the building in 1979 included 20,000 square feet of floor space, which included a community room added in the latest expansion.

According to Fraser, the recent expansion was overdue. The lobby was crowded and the drive-in facilities were awkward. Traffic often overflowed into the street. The current facility included an 11-lane motor bank, night depository, and automatic teller machine. There was also a large message sign in front of the bank.

In the past, some of the bank building space had been rented to an insurance business, savings and loan association, and an attorney. In 1979, the banking operations utilized the entire building. Fraser felt that parking was adequate and the available floor space was sufficient to handle a substantial increase in growth for several years.

ORGANIZATION AND PERSONNEL

The present organization chart is shown in Exhibit 1. The years of experience in banking for each of the 13 officers is also shown. The members of the board of directors and their business interests are shown in Exhibit 2. The membership of the board was quite stable.

John Duncan, president, was majority stockholder in the bank, a member of the board of directors, and chairman of the executive committee of the board. He also was majority stockholder in three other area banks and owner of three insurance agencies in the immediate vicinity. In 1979, Duncan was 74 years of age, had 40 years experience in banking and insurance and, according to Fraser, was a hard-driving and demanding individual. Duncan made daily visits to all four banks to discuss operations and policy matters with bank officers. Fraser also stated that, while Duncan expected much from the people in his organization, he rewarded work well done. Duncan, a lifelong resident of Brookfield, was well known in the area.

EXHIBIT 1 Organization Chart of the Bank Showing Number of Years of Banking Experience

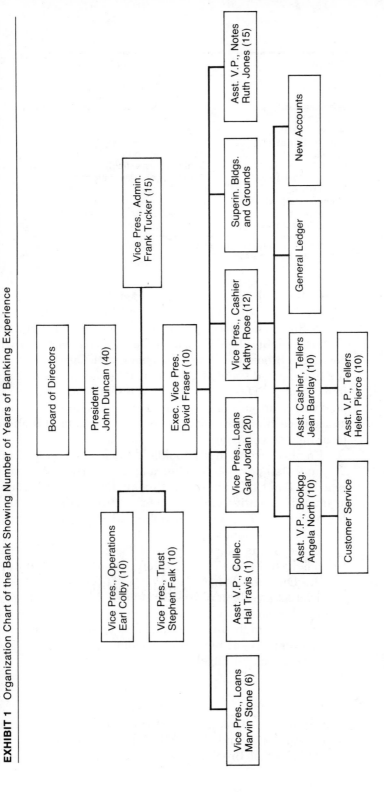

SOURCE: **As described by management personnel to case writer. Number in parentheses shows number of years of banking experience.**

EXHIBIT 2   Brookfield Bank and Trust Board of Directors

Name	Business Interest
John Duncan*	Banking and insurance (Brookfield)
Jack Bowen	Real estate
James Carson*	Physician
Charles Duncan†	Insurance
Louise Elliott	Retired bank officer (Brookfield)
David Fraser*	Banking (Brookfield)
George Morris	Construction, raw materials
Thomas Roberts	Retired grocer
Michael Stafford	Director, government agency
Ed Williams	Business advisory service
Frank Tucker (Advisory)	Banking (Brookfield)

* Member, executive committee, of which John Duncan is chairman.
† John Duncan's son.

Of the 13 bank officers, the oldest is 58. The three workers who replaced the individuals who moved to First National were Fraser, Kathy Rose, and Gary Jordan. Fraser came to Brookfield from City Federal, another bank in which Duncan is a majority owner. Prior to coming to Brookfield, Fraser had been with City for two years. Prior to the time he had spent at City, he had been in banking for seven years in a city about 200 miles away in the same state. He had been associated with Duncan's banks prior to that time. Rose previously had been assistant cashier at Brookfield. Jordan's previous affiliation was with a local finance company.

Frank Tucker joined Brookfield Bank and Trust in March 1978, in a central staff position for Duncan's banks. He had come from a bank in a city about 180 miles from Brookfield in the same state. He served as interim executive vice president of Brookfield Bank and Trust from September 1, 1978, until November 1, 1980. Fraser assumed the executive vice president's spot at that time.

Three of the officers—Colby, Tucker, and Falk—had offices at Brookfield Bank and Trust but they had central staff duties for all four of John Duncan's banks.

There were 60 employees at Brookfield Bank and Trust. Turnover among clerical personnel was about 30–40 percent per year. Fraser believed the high turnover was due to the transient nature of the population in the communities surrounding Brookfield and to a lesser extent in Brookfield itself.

OPERATIONS

The Brookfield Bank and Trust's original objective was to serve the local community, and in 1979 this objective remained in effect. Fraser pointed out that Brookfield was a liberal, consumer-oriented institu-

EXHIBIT 3 Deposits of Brookfield Bank and Trust
(in millions)

Year	Total Deposits	Public Funds Deposits
1965	$ 8.4	$3.0
1966	10.6	2.4
1967	12.7	4.3
1968	14.2	3.6
1969	16.0	4.7
1970	19.8	7.1
1971	20.3	5.6
1972	24.0	9.0
1973	22.7	6.0
1974	25.3	7.9
1975	27.4	7.2
1976	31.4	7.6
1977	33.3	6.7
1978	35.3	6.8
1979 (August)	38.9	8.6

tion, but that it was becoming increasingly difficult to make small, consumer-type loans. Loans less than $1,000, he observed, were just not economically feasible. Frank Tucker commented that Brookfield's previous executive vice president had operated under loan policies which were too loose and which had resulted in many bad loans. As a matter of fact, Tucker stated that bank personnel recently had to spend a good deal of time cleaning up some loans and repossessing goods in many of these instances. Tucker also commented that he was one of two officers in the bank who were authorized to make commercial loans.

The bank's deposits grew gradually from its inception in 1956 to 1965 and then began to rise more rapidly. The deposits at the end of year for 1965–1978, and for August 31, 1979, are shown in Exhibit 3.

The drop in total deposits from 1972 to 1973 was caused, according to Fraser, by a reduction in employment at the government installation in the area.

Ninety percent of the public funds deposited with the bank come from the local school district. The school district placed its funds on the basis of a biannual bid and Brookfield had had these funds since the bank opened. Through a working agreement, Brookfield kept only about one third of these funds. The rest was redeposited in other area banks.

The services offered by Brookfield were typical of most banks. The bank offered automatic funds transfers from savings to checking accounts, a 24-hour teller drive-through banking, trust services, and Saturday banking. On Saturday and after 2 P.M. on weekdays, a "minibank" operated in the lobby. The minibank allowed new customers to

open accounts after regular bank hours. The regular banking hours
were:

Lobby
Monday through Thursday 9 A.M.–2 P.M.
Friday: 9 A.M.–5:30 P.M.

Drive-in Facilities
Monday through Friday: 8 A.M.–5:30 P.M.
Saturday: 8 A.M.–12 noon

As far as marketing was concerned, Fraser observed that the bank had
no marketing program as such. Advertising emphasized convenience
as the primary basis why customers should do business with the bank.

The bank started an employee of the month program in February
1979. Employees voted on one of their members as the employee of
the month. The individual selected received a free meal and a trip to a
hair stylist. Fraser felt the program had been well received by the
employees.

THE NEW BANK IN TOWN

The First National Bank of Brookfield employed 12 people and had $3
million in deposits on August 31, 1979. It was also located on Center
Street, but about two miles from Brookfield Bank and Trust and on the
opposite side of the interstate highway.

First National had three drive-in lanes and its hours of operation
were the same as Brookfield Bank and Trust except that it remained
open until 6 P.M. on Friday. The services it offered were similar to
those of Brookfield except that there was no automatic teller and no
minibank operation.

David Fraser knew he had lost some old customers to First National and believed this was due, in part at least, to their faith in the
officers of the new bank. He felt that in order for a person to do
business with a certain bank, it was necessary to trust either banks in
general or the particular officials of that bank. He felt this explained
why some people had moved their accounts. He also stated the accounts lost were not large ones.

The question in Fraser's mind was how First National would affect his bank's performance in the future. What problems might arise
which had not existed before? What areas of the bank's operations
might be affected most? Then there was the task of deciding what to
do once the problems, if any, were identified.

26. First National Bank of Fayetteville

George Shelton, president of the First National Bank of Fayetteville, Arkansas, was feeling harassed this morning. He had already received three requests for bank contributions to "worthy" projects, and it was only 10:15 A.M. While the public relations director had the responsibility for receiving requests for contributions, each solicitor was convinced that his cause deserved special attention and had asked for the president specifically.

THE PROBLEM

The first caller was the secretary of the local chamber of commerce. The national chamber had organized a project to develop educational materials on the American free-enterprise system for use in the public schools and was seeking funding. He was hoping for a contribution of at least $300. The president had hardly hung up when his secretary buzzed to tell him that his old friend on the University of Arkansas coaching staff was on the line. After preliminary pleasantries, the coach broached the subject of the great need for lighting for the university football stadium. Lighting would make possible more practice time, permit night games, and make the stadium more suitable for national television. The already great contribution of the University of Arkansas athletic program to the economy of Fayetteville would be enhanced by the lighting. The coach mentioned that the "other" bank had pledged $2,000. As the president's secretary brought in his morning cup of coffee, she told him that the administrator of the Washington Regional Medical Center was waiting to see him. He knew that the Medical Center was conducting a drive to equip a cancer treatment unit so that patients could receive outpatient care without having to travel to distant cities. As expected, the administrator asked for bank support, suggesting that $2,500 might be appropriate. He pointed out that 50 percent matching would be available from the federal government. It seemed to the president that the community

---

This case was prepared by Thomas R. McKinnon of the University of Arkansas, Fayetteville, Arkansas.

EXHIBIT 1 Statement of Income and Expense

	Annual Total 1978	Annual Total 1979
Income		
Interest on loans	$6,256,922.52	$ 7,358,706.36
Bond interest taxable.	910,866.26	7,787,334.71
Bond interest nontaxable	1,185,958.53	1,346,959.71
Other income	563,577.79	819,093.91
Total income.	$8,917,325.10	$11,312,094.69
Expenses		
Salaries and payroll taxes. . . .	1,743,952.65	1,970,513.70
Interest paid	4,288,661.28	6,321,126.61
Building and equipment	380,625.97	526,184.46
Other expenses	1,139,638.77	1,367,231.85
Total operating expenses . . .	$7,552,878.67	$10,185,056.62
Total operating expenses before taxes	$1,364,446.43	$ 1,127,038.07
Income taxes accrued before security gains	(75,943.00)	(130,663.00)
Net operating income.	$1,440,389.43	$ 1,252,554.01
Securities gains $30,857.83	($3,058.53)	
Applicable income taxes 14,812.00	None	
Securities gains net	16,045.83	(3,058.53)
Net income	1,456,435.26	1,254,612.54
Earnings per share	29.13	25.09

had almost forgotten that the bank was a profit-making institution and looked on it as a soft touch for any financial campaign.

Thinking of profits reminded the president that net income, and therefore earnings per share for 1979, were down from 1978 (Exhibit 1). The primary reason for the decline was that the interest received on loans had not kept pace with the cost of money because of the state usury ceiling. Arkansas has a constitutional interest ceiling on all loans of 10 percent with the substantial penalty of forfeiture of principle and interest for violators. The prime rate had already passed 18 percent nationwide and the cost of money to the bank had increased proportionally. National banks had received some relief with the federal banking regulation allowing national banks to charge 1 percent over the discount rate, which now was at 11 percent. Also, a new federal law allowed up to 5 percent above the discount rate for agricultural and commercial loans over $25,000. These provisions gave some relief, but the pinch was still being felt. A proposed constitutional amendment to remove the interest ceiling had twice failed to gain voter approval in recent years, and the issue would be on the ballot again in November 1980. Perhaps a moratorium on all contributions would impress the public with the squeeze banks were feeling and maybe voters would remove, or at least make more flexible, the stringent constitutional limitations.

PAST PRACTICES

The First National Bank has a long tradition of practicing social responsibility in Fayetteville. While George's father was president, the bank was instrumental in setting up an industrial park so that orderly growth could take place. The voters had three times voted down bond issues to finance the park, so the town fathers acted directly to establish it with the two Fayetteville banks' financing. The industrial park was highly successful and what the bank perceived as a public contribution turned out to be a profit-making venture.

On a later occasion, when it was apparent that the only hotel in downtown Fayetteville was closing, the First National Bank participated in a consortium that bought stock of the hotel to keep it going. The bank did all right again when it sold the stock, and the hotel is still in business.

More recently, the bank became concerned with the deterioration of downtown Fayetteville. Like so many other towns, large and small businesses were leaving downtown for shopping centers in outlying areas. Not only was the character and charm of the city giving way to urban sprawl, but the major shopping center was developing outside the Fayetteville School District so that local schools were losing tax revenues. When one important attraction to downtown, the federal offices, was about to be moved, the First National Bank participated in a group that bought land in the area for a new federal building. The land was exchanged for the old federal building in the town square which later was made into an attractive restaurant. Not only was the federal office retained, but county offices and others also decided to forego moves. Currently, the bank is participating in a community development corporation to develop the south side of the square, an area of largely abandoned retail stores. These developments, along with new financial buildings, a University of Arkansas continuing education center, and a new hotel, seem to have reversed the trend, and downtown Fayetteville is being revitalized.

George was proud of the First National Bank's role in these developments and would see that it would be continued. After all, what is good for the community is good for the bank, and his bank had done very well. However, these requests would have to be considered individually and in relation to other donations (see Exhibit 2).

EXHIBIT 2 1979 Contributions to Date

Washington Regional Medical Center	$ 5,000.00
Boy Scout Expo	100.00
Young Life	1,200.00
SAE Fight Night	50.00
NWA Charity Horseshow	25.00
Community Concert	100.00
City Hospital	200.00
American Cancer Society	100.00
Salvation Army	1,100.00
Fayetteville Youth Center	100.00
Boy Scouts	1,500.00
The New School	1,100.00
4-H Club	350.00
Christmas Seals	75.00
Prairie Grove Industrial Park	1,000.00
Arkansas State Council on Economic Education	500.00
Square Flowers	1,500.00
United Fund	4,000.00
University of Arkansas	5,000.00
Razorback Fund Club	1,600.00
Razorback Fund (Basketball)	700.00
Football Tickets	1,327.00
	$38,777.00

PROCEDURE AND CRITERIA FOR DECISIONMAKING

The bank's process of determining how to respond to a request was very informal. For requests up to $250 or $300, the public relations director usually made an independent decision. For requests of about $300 to $2,500, the public relations director, the president, and the chairman of the board met to make the determination. When a solicitation exceeded $2,500, the executive committee made the decision.

The criteria used were even more informal. A proposal was evaluated generally on the basis of what good it would do for the community and the bank. More specifically, projects with more local impact were given preference over regional, state, or national impacts. Also, whether matching funds would multiply the effects of their contribution was considered. Realistically, it had to be admitted that regular customers of the bank were given preferences. Since Fayetteville is education-centered, with the University of Arkansas its major industry, proposals to enhance education generally and the university specifically were given special consideration. Finally, the First National Bank had to keep up with its competition and this meant matching contributions made by the other major bank and the larger savings and loan institutions. In fact, they often conferred with each other on their giving to community projects.

THE IMMEDIATE DECISION

Since the three requests were generally in the category to be considered by the public relations director, the chairman, and the president, George had his secretary call the others and a meeting was arranged for that afternoon. Eating lunch alone at his desk, George wondered how the meeting would go. Perhaps the time had come to consider just what the bank's social responsibilities were. Certainly the impacts on stockholders, employees, and customers should be considered along with the general community. George was not even sure at this point how he would vote on the three proposals.

27. The Farmers Bank

THE MEETING

Late Friday afternoon, November 3, 1984, John Wade, president of the Farmers Bank, Inc. sat in his office contemplating the bank's present predicament and wondering what his next step should be. John had just returned from a meeting with the FDIC and state banking department where he had been informed that the bank needed to enter into some corrective action in certain areas of concern. These areas were the lending and collection policies and procedures of the bank, its loan-loss reserve, its capital, and its compliance with federal and state statutes, rules, and regulations (Exhibit 1).

BACKGROUND

The Farmers Bank was established in 1901. Being established around the turn of the century and located in rural southeastern United States, the bank's roots are deeply embedded in agriculture. In fact the bank's logo, a cotton boll, is symbolic of the bank being established through agriculture needs. During the early years most loans were agriculture in nature and many were made on the basis of a farmer's name or "worth," and little or no collateral was required. In years of crop failure the bank, if possible, carried the farmer through these hard times. To a certain degree this philosophy still holds today, although modified by various federal and state regulations. Also, a large percentage of current loans continue to be agriculture oriented.

The Farmers Bank is located in a small community of approximately 30,000 persons, its clientele consisting of the usual small town businessmen, consumers, several small industries, a college with an enrollment of about 6,500, and area farmers. Approximately one third of its loans are crop production loans. However, many of the numerous local-owned businesses are highly dependent upon the farm population. The local saying is "As the farmers go so goes the community." John, an outsider, came to the bank as president in 1980. Prior to John's arrival the bank had a consistent history of paying what was

This case was prepared by Emit B. Deal, Georgia Southern College, Department of Economics, Statesboro, Georgia.

EXHIBIT 1   President's Report Annual Meeting, March 28, 1985

1984 was a challenging and difficult year for many banks, with problems ranging from narrowing spreads to increasing nonperforming loans. Your bank experienced another disappointing year performancewise, more so than in 1983. The losses we experienced during both years were a result of loan losses.

As a part owner of the Farmers Bank you look to us for solutions, not problems. What does your bank plan to do to offset this continued downward trend in earnings? We have an obligation to our customers to provide and maintain the service to which they are entitled. Equally important is an obligation to you, our shareholders, to assure that your investment is protected and that you are fairly rewarded. Certainly we intend to fulfill that dual responsibility.

For the year 1984 total deposits increased $6.93 million and net loans increased $2.5 million. We are particularly pleased with our increase in demand deposits from $13.4 million in 1983 to $16.6 million at year-end 1984. Today the Farmers Bank offers more than 60 services from 24-hour banking and investor's choice checking to trust services, IRA plans, and OptionLine—a new line of credit that was introduced last fall.

We are particularly pleased with the reception of OptionLine in our marketplace. Many of our loan customers have found it to be a convenient alternative to the traditional way of borrowing money. OptionLine allows customers to write their own loan using a special check with repayment based on a revolving schedule according to the outstanding balance. Usage of our SIBIL 24-hour teller showed consistent increases during 1984 and this activity is another indication that consumers are becoming much more convenience oriented. The assets in our trust division have shown a steady growth and this division is important to the overall success of our bank.

So much for the past. I am sure you are interested in the future of your bank.

The key forces shaping the banking industry in the years immediately ahead are:

1. Deregulation of interest rates on deposit;
2. Increased competition from outside the banking industry; and
3. Interstate banking.

Taken together these forces imply that banking is more complex and challenging than existed in the past. Excellence will be more quickly rewarded and the lack of excellence will be more quickly punished.

The success of a bank is largely determined by its customers—a statement as true today as it was yesterday and one that will grow in importance in the face of increased competition and deregulation.

Our concerns must be more than just doing things right. . . . We must be sure that we are doing the right things.

Banking in America remains safe and sound, and the system is threatened more by rumors of bank problems than by actual failures. Public confidence is banking's greatest asset. The recently retired chairman of Citicorp was asked the question, "What is your view on the future of small banks in the United States in light of CitiBank and other major bank invasions of their traditional territories?"

His answer, I quote, "I think the small bank in the small town is probably the most secure business in the world."

Now, I want to be straightforward and discuss the condition of the bank at the present time and our plans for the future.

As most of your know, after an examination by the FDIC in the fall of 1984, the bank agreed to enter into a plan of corrective action with the FDIC and the state banking department to address areas of concern in the bank's operations. These areas were the lending and collection policies and procedures of the bank, its loan-loss reserve, its capital, and its compliance with federal and state statutes, rules and regulations. The plan of corrective action was dated January 24, 1985, with its effective date established to be February 25, 1985. Under the corrective action plan, the bank has agreed to:

1. Increase its level of capital to 8 percent of its assets.
2. Take steps to maintain and adhere to its written loan policy.

EXHIBIT 1 *(concluded)*

---

3. Closely supervise its lending and collection personnel, and to monitor the extension of credit to customers of the bank.

4. Eliminate from our books by collection, charge-offs, or other proper entries, 100 percent of all assets or portions of assets classified "loss" and 50 percent of all assets or portion of assets classified "doubtful" as of October 26, 1984.

5. Sixty days from effective date, submit to the regional director and the commissioners specific plans and proposals to effect reduction and/or collection of any lines of credit which are considered classified by the FDIC as of October 26, 1984.

6. One hundred twenty days from effective date, the bank shall establish an effective system of loan documentation and shall correct and/or eliminate all technical exceptions as of October 26, 1984.

7. One hundred eighty days from effective date, reduce the remaining total of all assets classified "substandard" and "doubtful" as of October 26, 1984, by $1,600,000.

8. Three hundred sixty days from the effective date of the order, reduce assets classified "substandard" and "doubtful" as of October 26, 1984, by another $1,600,000.

9. Five hundred forty days from the effective date of the order, reduce assets classified "substandard" and "doubtful" as of October 26, 1984, by another $1,500,000.

I see 1985 as a year to rebuild that firm foundation of your bank. We will experience further loan losses as we enforce our collection procedures, but certainly not to the extent of the last few years. We are preparing for additional loan losses by making a monthly provision to the reserve for loan losses. After taking into consideration all we must do this year to strengthen the bank, I am forecasting a modest profit for 1985. I am trying to be realistic and we need your help and support. We will keep you informed of our progress with a midyear report.

Although 1985 will be one of increased challenges, we enter the year with both determination and dedication. We are grateful for the continued support of our customers, shareholders, and directors. The truly outstanding effort and dedication of the Farmers Bank employees during this period provides confidence as we face the challenges ahead. I ask each of you to share with us that confidence and the belief that our restructuring is a good change for the times.

---

considered a good return on one's investment. Also net income and earnings per share had been steadily increasing (Table 10). In fact the Farmers Bank declared its highest dividend at the end of John's first year.

The bank's financial data for 1980 through 1984 is shown in Tables 1 through 10. Reference to the tables and the letter from John Wade (Exhibit 2) will reveal an enlightening picture of the bank's present and past financial situation.

Although not shown in the data, over 60 percent of the loan charge-offs were farm loans. John asked himself, why so many farm loan charge-offs? In reflection he came up with several reasons. First, farming is highly dependent upon the weather and in the 1980s it was unfavorable for farming. Second, interest rates paid by farmers were high during the 1980s. Third, the overall economy was sluggish. Last,

TABLE 1

Comparative Statement of Condition
December 31, 1984, 1983, 1982, 1981, and 1980

	1984	1983	1982	1981	1980
Assets:					
Cash and due from depository institutions	$ 5,325,406	$ 3,999,120	$ 3,497,762	$ 3,467,153	$ 3,150,318
Interest-bearing deposit with banks	250,000	250,000	—	—	—
U.S. Treasury securities (Note 5)	5,352,723	2,740,146	1,639,255	1,886,470	1,883,590
Obligations of other U.S. government agencies and corporations	7,590,516	4,269,665	1,012,746	747,173	389,052
Obligations of states and political subdivisions in the United States (Note 5)	9,601,031	10,251,489	10,275,685	10,071,293	9,964,934
Corporate stock	—	—	—	—	25,000
Federal funds sold and securities purchased under agreements to resell	6,510,000	8,975,000	5,723,663	3,171,067	3,740,000
Loans (net of unearned income) (Note 5)	51,214,205	48,757,571	49,681,455	52,667,157	49,478,648
Less: Allowance for possible loan losses (Note 7)	(850,000)	(850,000)	(750,000)	(655,000)	(850,000)
Loans, net	50,364,205	47,907,571	48,931,455	52,012,157	48,628,648
Bank premises, furniture and fixtures and other assets representing bank premises (Note 8)	1,999,741	2,047,928	2,131,515	1,599,420	1,136,777
Other real estate	304,036	1,123,437	155,481	—	—
Other assets	2,511,121	3,574,593	2,199,270	2,101,428	1,575,964
Total assets	$89,808,779	$84,538,949	$75,567,832	$75,056,161	$70,494,283
Liabilities:					
Deposits:					
Demand deposits	$16,649,400	$13,449,681	$14,330,658	$15,818,369	$17,511,006
Savings deposits	10,057,483	9,581,087	14,882,767	9,368,270	4,674,993
Time deposits	56,851,433	53,219,097	37,005,218	40,968,379	40,378,083
Total deposits	83,558,316	76,249,865	66,218,643	66,155,018	62,564,082
Federal funds purchased and securities sold under agreements to repurchase	—	—	215,488	344,161	—
Interest-bearing demand notes (note balance) issued to the U.S. Treasury	—	—	379,990	146,461	286,602
Other liabilities	1,013,400	1,391,197	902,041	811,650	688,399
Total liabilities	$84,571,716	$77,641,062	$67,716,162	$67,457,290	$63,539,083
Equity Capital:					
Common stock, $10.00 par value, authorized 200,000 shares; outstanding 190,000 shares (Note 4)	1,900,000	1,900,000	1,900,000	1,900,000	1,900,000
Surplus	2,800,000	2,800,000	2,800,000	2,800,000	2,800,000
Undivided profits	537,063	2,197,887	3,151,670	3,198,871	2,855,200
Total equity capital	5,237,063	6,897,887	7,851,670	7,598,871	6,955,200
Total liabilities and equity capital	$89,808,779	$84,538,949	$75,567,832	$75,056,161	$70,494,283

TABLE 2

Comparative Statement of (Loss) Income
December 31, 1980, 1981, 1982, 1983, and 1984

	1984	1983	1982	1981	1980
Interest income:					
Interest and fees on loans.	$ 7,290,609	$7,968,012	$8,537,405	$7,959,462	$6,275,837
Interest on balances with depository institutions	28,085	1,765	—	—	—
Income on federal funds sold and securities purchased under agreements to resell	620,977	455,011	246,224	395,588	439,777
Interest on investment securities:					
U.S. Treasury securities.	512,625	173,226	239,396	207,640	176,278
Other U.S. government agencies.	671,243	399,031	104,854	98,157	31,306
Obligations of states and political subdivisions in the United States	690,699	735,242	660,794	591,265	541,722
Total interest income	9,814,238	9,732,287	9,788,673	9,252,112	7,464,920
Interest expense:					
Interest on time certificates of deposit of $100,000 or more	1,540,148	1,411,562	2,102,882	2,460,362	2,495,413
Interest on other deposits.	4,764,512	4,129,877	3,744,607	3,392,443	1,721,968
Interest on federal funds purchased and securities sold under agreements to repurchase	—	—	102,128	92,638	214
Interest on demand notes (note balances) issued to the U.S. Treasury	—	4,087	44,774	37,661	25,823
Total interest expense	6,304,660	5,545,526	5,994,391	5,983,104	4,243,418
Net interest income.	3,509,578	4,186,761	3,794,282	3,269,008	3,221,402
Provision for loan losses (Note 7)	3,799,979	3,953,492	1,366,364	417,086	341,238
Net interest income after provision for loan losses	(290,401)	233,269	2,427,918	2,851,922	2,880,264
Other operating income:					
Income from fiduciary activities	45,658	27,945	17,648	9,477	—
Service charges on deposit accounts	487,946	464,087	438,881	472,232	393,022
Other service charges, commissions, and fees	76,367	97,177	69,942	62,394	60,886
Other	82,383	63,060	29,121	24,932	20,541
Total other operating income	692,354	652,269	555,592	569,035	474,449
Other operating expenses:					
Salaries and employee benefits (Notes 2 and 3).	1,431,115	1,364,093	1,277,801	1,148,226	1,004,978
Net occupancy expense of bank premises	311,698	304,891	311,703	269,974	211,539
Furniture and equipment expense	364,135	366,638	330,127	331,406	106,679
Other	778,147	698,817	721,076	576,174	563,956
Total other operating expenses	2,885,095	2,734,439	2,640,707	2,325,780	1,887,152
(Loss) Income before income taxes	(2,483,142)	(1,848,901)	342,803	1,095,177	1,467,561
Applicable income taxes (Note 9)	(822,318)	(1,151,135)	(166,496)	191,425	413,111
Net (loss) income.	$(1,660,824)	$ (697,766)	$ 509,299	$ 903,752	$1,054,450
(Loss) Earnings per common share (Note 4)	$ (8.74)	$ (3.67)	$ 2.68	$ 4.76	$ 5.55

TABLE 3

Comparative Statement of Changes in Financial Position
Years Ended December 31, 1984, 1983, 1982, 1981, and 1980

	1984	1983	1982	1981	1980
Funds provided by:					
Net income	$(1,660,824)	$ (801,783)	$ 509,299	$ 903,752	$1,054,450
Depreciation	158,270	147,281	129,242	109,721	111,196
Provision for loan losses	3,799,980	3,953,492	1,366,364	417,086	341,238
Deferred income taxes		337,077	(31,571)	154,450	5,704
Provided from operations	2,297,426	3,636,067	1,973,334	1,585,009	1,512,588
Increase in:					
Deposits	7,308,451	10,031,222	63,625	3,590,936	5,337,867
Federal funds purchased and securities sold under agreements to repurchase	—	—	—	344,161	—
Other liabilities	—	264,086	31,411	94,418	—
Interest bearing demand notes issued to the U.S. Treasury	—	—	233,529	—	—
Decrease in:					
Loans	—	—	1,714,338	—	—
Other real estate	819,401	—	74,708	—	—
Cash and due from banks	—	—	—	—	425,530
Other assets	1,063,472	—	—	—	—
Federal funds sold and securities purchased under agreements to resell	3,165,000	—	—	568,933	—
Total	$14,653,750	$13,931,375	$4,090,945	$6,183,457	$7,275,985
Funds applied to:					
Cash dividends	—	$ 152,000	$ 256,500	$ 256,500	$ 237,500
Accrual for compensated absences through December 31, 1980	—	—	—	3,581	—
Increase in:					
Cash and due from banks	$ 1,926,286	151,358	30,609	316,835	507,193
Securities	5,982,970	4,332,614	223,750	442,359	25,000
Federal funds sold and securities sold under agreements to resell	—	3,251,337	2,552,596	—	5,963,473
Loans	6,256,614	2,929,608	661,337	3,800,594	39,710
Fixed assets	110,082	63,694	—	572,365	—
Other real estate	—	967,956	—	—	—
Other assets	—	1,487,330	—	—	—
Other—net	—	—	237,480	651,081	211,600
Decrease in:					
Interest-bearing demand notes issued to the U.S. Treasury	—	379,990	—	—	—
Federal funds purchased and securities sold under agreements to repurchase	—	—	—	140,142	96,587
Other liabilities	377,798	215,488	128,673	—	194,922
Total	$14,653,750	$13,931,375	$4,090,945	$6,183,457	$7,275,985

TABLE 4

Reconciliation of Capital Accounts
December 31, 1984, 1983, 1982, 1981, and 1980

	1984	1983	1982	1981	1980
Balance, beginning of year. . . .	$6,897,887	$7,851,670	$7,598,871	$6,955,200	$6,138,250
Addition:					
Transferred (to) from statement of income, as restated for 1983	(1,660,824)	(801,783)	509,299	903,752	1,054,450
Deduction:					
Accrual for compensated absences through December 31, 1980— net of tax effect	—	—	—	3,581	—
Cash dividends declared ($.00 per share in 1984, $.80 per share in 1983, $1.35 per share in 1982 and 1981, and $1.25 per share in 1980 (Note 4)	—	152,000	256,500	256,500	237,500
Balance, end of year.	$5,237,063	$6,897,887	$7,851,670	$7,598,871	$6,955,200

See Notes in Financial Statements, Table 9.

TABLE 5

Reconciliation of Allowance for Loan Losses
December 31, 1984, 1983, 1982, 1981, and 1980

	1984	1983	1982	1981	1980
Balance, beginning of year	$ 850,000	$ 750,000	$ 655,000	$ 850,000	$ 750,000
Additions:					
Recoveries credited to these reserves	265,078	437,818	113,580	32,446	11,818
Transferred from operating income.	3,799,979	3,953,492	1,366,364	417,086	341,238
Total additions	4,065,057	4,391,310	1,479,944	449,532	353,056
Deduction:					
Loan charge-offs	4,065,057	4,291,310	1,384,944	644,532	253,056
Total deductions	4,065,057	4,291,310	1,384,944	644,532	253,056
Balance, end of year	$ 850,000	$ 850,000	$ 750,000	$ 655,000	$ 850,000

TABLE 6 Note 5—Securities

(The following summary presents the par value, book value, and approximate value of investment securities at December 31, 1984, and 1983)

Type and Maturity Grouping	Principal Amount	Book Value	Approximate Market Value
December 31, 1984:			
U.S. Treasury securities:			
One year or less.	$ 3,867,500	$ 3,841,139	$ 3,868,398
Over one year through five years	1,554,750	1,511,584	1,510,980
Total	5,422,250	5,352,723	5,379,378
Obligations of other U.S. government agencies and corporations:			
One year or less.	4,900,000	4,145,386	4,235,381
Over one year through five years	3,415,000	3,445,130	3,503,361
Total	8,315,000	7,590,516	7,738,742
Obligations of states and political subdivisions:			
One year or less.	1,120,000	1,120,868	1,113,067
Over one year through five years	4,985,000	4,901,336	4,715,755
Over five years through ten years.	2,995,000	2,954,712	2,519,473
Over ten years.	625,000	624,115	481,996
Total	9,725,000	9,601,031	8,830,291
Total	$23,462,250	$22,544,270	$21,948,411

	Principal Amount	Book Value	Approximate Market Value
December 31, 1983:			
U.S. Treasury securities:			
One year or less.	$ 500,000	$ 501,333	$ 502,750
Over one year through five years	2,170,000	2,163,127	2,133,959
Over five years through ten years.	76,000	75,686	69,279
Total	2,746,000	2,740,146	2,705,988
Obligations of other U.S. government agencies and corporations:			
One year or less.	3,900,000	3,885,436	3,842,524
Over one year through five years	350,000	384,229	375,375
Total	4,250,000	4,269,665	4,217,899
Obligations of states and political subdivisions:			
One year or less.	985,000	986,781	979,471
Over one year through five years	4,845,000	4,763,063	4,576,287
Over five years through ten years.	3,500,000	3,414,672	2,995,962
Over ten years.	1,090,000	1,086,973	814,014
Total	10,420,000	10,251,489	9,365,734
Total	$17,416,000	$17,261,300	$16,289,621

(As of December 31, 1984, and 1983, securities with a par value of $6,695,000 and $5,521,000, respectively, were pledged to secure customers' deposits.)

TABLE 6 *(continued)*

Type and Maturity Grouping	Principal Amount	Book Value	Approximate Market Value
December 31, 1982:			
U.S. Treasury securities:			
One year or less.	$ 700,000	$ 699,984	$ 701,313
Over one year through five years	610,000	604,017	626,791
Over five years through ten years.	336,000	335,254	313,527
Total	1,646,000	1,639,255	1,641,631
Obligations of other U.S. government agencies and corporations:			
One year or less.	600,000	569,935	589,630
Over one year through five years	450,000	442,811	451,906
Total	1,050,000	1,012,746	1,041,536
Obligations of states and political subdivisions:			
One year or less.	1,020,000	1,016,293	1,005,798
Over one year through five years	4,405,000	4,353,926	4,234,762
Over five years through ten years.	3,445,000	3,342,575	3,059,737
Over ten years.	1,580,000	1,563,891	1,188,780
Total	10,450,000	10,276,685	9,489,077
Total	$13,146,000	$12,928,686	$12,172,244

(As of December 31, 1983, and 1982, securities with a par value of $5,521,000 and $6,177,500, respectively, were pledged to secure customers' deposits.)

	Principal Amount	Book Value	Approximate Market Value
December 31, 1981:			
U.S. Treasury securities:			
One year or less.	$ 650,000	$ 649,638	$ 644,500
Over one year through five years	910,000	901,706	871,806
Over five years through ten years.	336,000	335,126	258,551
Total	1,896,000	1,886,470	1,774,857
Obligations of other U.S. government agencies and corporations:			
One year or less.	800,000	747,173	764,042
Total	800,000	747,173	764,042
Obligations of states and political subdivisions:			
One year or less.	1,180,000	1,180,459	1,150,262
Over one year through five years	3,330,000	3,313,078	2,809,711
Over five years through ten years.	3,665,000	3,528,219	2,467,688
Over ten years.	2,065,000	2,049,537	2,049,537
Total	10,240,000	10,071,293	8,477,198
Total	$12,936,000	$12,704,936	$11,016,097

TABLE 6 *(concluded)*

Type and Maturity Grouping	Principal Amount	Book Value	Approximate Market Value
December 31, 1980:			
U.S. Treasury securities:			
One year or less.	$ 350,000	$ 350,065	$ 348,250
Over one year through five years	1,210,000	1,198,527	1,157,674
Over five years through ten years.	336,000	334,998	273,453
Total	1,896,000	1,883,590	1,779,377
Obligations of other U.S. government agencies and corporations:			
One year or less.	200,000	189,052	193,636
Over one year through five years	200,000	200,000	183,250
Total	400,000	389,052	376,886
Obligations of states and political subdivisions:			
One year or less.	960,000	959,677	938,982
Over one year through five years	3,655,000	3,651,378	3,299,605
Over five years through ten years.	2,875,000	2,812,890	2,310,732
Over ten years.	2,570,000	2,540,989	1,900,936
Total	10,060,000	9,964,934	8,450,255
Total	$12,356,000	$12,237,576	$10,606,518

(As of December 31, 1981, and 1980, securities with a par value of $8,115,000 and $7,610,000, respectively, were pledged to secure customers' deposits.)

TABLE 7 Note 6—Loans

The following summary reflects the classification of loans at December 31, 1984, 1983, 1982, 1981, and 1980:

	1984	1983	1982	1981	1980
Real estate loans	$11,684,215	$16,639,898	$18,995,342	$21,734,818	$22,401,495
Loans to financial institutions	—	—	5,000	5,000	—
Commercial, farm, and industrial loans. . . .	26,589,267	20,826,088	22,232,188	22,045,903	20,160,503
Loans to individuals for household, family and other consumer expenditures	13,501,220	12,507,511	10,345,757	10,804,264	8,556,098
All other loans	305,989	464,600	312,760	357,805	327,721
Total	52,080,691	50,438,097	51,891,047	54,947,790	51,445,817
Allowance for possible loan losses.	850,000	850,000	750,000	655,000	850,000
Unearned interest.	866,486	1,680,526	2,209,592	2,280,633	1,967,169
Net loans.	$50,364,205	$47,907,571	$48,931,455	$52,012,157	$48,628,648

The largest aggregate amount of loans outstanding to officers, directors and principal security holders and associates during the years ended December 31, 1984, 1983, 1982, 1981, and 1980 were $2,159,521, $1,726,057, $2,252,437, $1,512,710, and $1,846,561, respectively.

TABLE 8   Note 7—Allowance for Loan Losses

The determination of the balance of the allowance for loan losses has been determined by management in light of past loan loss experience and evaluation of potential loss in the current loan portfolio. It reflects an amount which, in management's judgment, is adequate to provide for potential loan losses.

All of the allowance for loan losses at December 31, 1984, 1983, 1982, 1981, and 1980 constituted valuation reserve and was available in full to absorb future losses.

Note 8—Bank Premises, Equipment, and Depreciation

	Cost	Accumulated Depreciation	Book Value
December 31, 1984:			
Land.	$ 187,465	—	$ 187,465
Bank premises	1,780,243	$ 589,162	1,191,081
Equipment	1,246,623	625,428	621,195
Total.	$3,214,331	$1,214,590	$1,999,741
December 31, 1983:			
Land.	202,465	—	202,465
Bank premises	1,808,192	567,799	1,240,393
Equipment	1,225,628	620,558	605,070
Total.	$3,236,285	$1,188,357	$2,047,928
December 31, 1982:			
Land.	202,465	—	202,465
Bank premises	1,795,655	504,348	1,291,307
Equipment	1,174,471	536,728	637,743
Total.	$3,172,591	$1,041,076	$2,131,515
December 31, 1981:			
Land.	202,465	—	202,465
Bank premises	1,460,223	473,000	987,223
Equipment	902,054	492,322	409,732
Total.	$2,564,742	$ 965,322	$1,599,420
December 31, 1980:			
Land.	202,465	—	202,465
Bank premises	1,194,855	419,623	775,232
Equipment	599,183	440,103	159,080
Total.	$1,996,503	$ 859,726	$1,136,777

Provision for depreciation of $158,270 in 1984, $147,201 in 1983, $129,242 in 1982, $109,721 in 1981, and $111,196 in 1980 is included in operating expenses.

TABLE 9   Note 9—Income Taxes

Total income tax expense for 1984, 1983, 1982, 1981, and 1980 is less than the amount compared by applying the statutory federal income tax rate to income before income taxes. The reasons for this difference are as follows:

	1984		1983		1982		1981		1980	
	Amount	Percent of Pretax Income	Amount	Percent of Pretax Income	Amount	Percent of Pretax Income	Amount	Percent of Pretax Income	Amount	Percent of Pretax Income
Income tax at statutory rate	$(1,142,245)	(46.0)%	$ (850,494)	(46.0)%	$ 157,689	46.0%	$ 503,781	46.0%	$ 675,078	46.0%
Surtax exemption	57,750	2.3	—	—	—	—	(19,250)	1.8	(19,250)	1.3
Net	(1,084,495)	(43.7)	(850,494)	(46.0)	157,689	46.0	484,531	44.2	655,828	44.7
Increase (decrease) in taxes:										
Interest on state and municipal obligations	(326,616)	(13.1)	(294,355)	(15.9)	(297,830)	(86.9)	(263,747)	(24.0)	(240,191)	(16.4)
Investment tax credit, net of recapture	(10,518)	(.4)	(5,381)	(.3)	(27,426)	(8.0)	(29,445)	(2.7)	(4,060)	(.3)
Interest to carry tax-exempt securities	8,079	.3	—	—	—	—	—	—	—	—
Loss carry forward	603,234	24.3	—		—		—		—	
Credit carry forwards	110,979	4.5	—		—		—		—	
Deferred taxes offset by net operating loss carry forward in excess of current year net deferred taxes	(123,379)	(5.0)	—		—		—		—	
Other, net	398	—	(905)	(.1)	1,071	.3	86	—	1,534	.1
Income tax	$ (822,318)	(33.1)%	$(1,151,135)	(63.3)%	$(166,496)	(48.6)%	$(191,425)	(17.5)%	$(413,111)	(28.1)%

The components of income taxes (credits) are as follows:

	1984	1983	1982	1981	1980
Income taxes currently payable	$(698,939)	$(1,488,212)	$(134,925)	$ 36,975	$407,407
Deferred income taxes applicable to:					
Transfer to allowance for loan losses	578,390	264,734	(43,700)	89,700	(30,543)
Accretion of bond discount	33,568	30,133	24,084	23,157	17,282
Accreted discount on matured bonds	(16,197)	(25,490)	(14,903)	(17,895)	(16,183)
Depreciation deducted for tax purposes in excess of depreciation on books	58,208	56,505	49,799	23,571	—
Interest on past due loans not recorded as income	(458)	20,610	(39,471)	—	—
Contributions in excess of tax limitation	(8,998)	(10,561)	(8,813)	—	—
Other, net	2,244	1,146	1,433	823	54
Deferred taxes offset by net operating loss carry forward	(770,136)	—	—	—	—
Change in accounting method from cash to accrual	—	—	—	35,094	35,094
Total income tax	$(822,318)	$(1,151,135)	$(166,496)	$191,425	$413,111

TABLE 10 Five-Year Comparison of Selected Financial Data

		Years Ended December 31,						
	1984	1983	1982	1981	1980	1979	1978	1977
Operating income	$10,506,593	$10,253,374	$10,344,265	$ 9,821,147	$ 7,939,369	$6,529,814	$5,202,550	$4,382,377
Operating expenses	12,989,735	12,233,457	10,001,462	8,725,970	6,471,808	5,050,342	4,021,874	3,386,512
Income (loss) before income taxes and securities gains (losses)	(2,483,142)	(1,980,083)	342,803	1,095,177	1,467,561	1,479,472	1,180,676	995,865
Applicable income taxes	(822,318)	(1,178,300)	(166,496)	191,425	413,111	439,458	341,624	296,329
Net income (loss)	$ (1,660,824)	$ (801,783)	$ 509,299	$ 903,752	$ 1,054,450	$1,023,123	$ 839,052	$ 700,218
(Loss) earnings per common share	$ (8.74)	$ (4.22)	$ 2.68	$ 4.76	$ 5.55	$ –0–	$ –0–	$ –0–
Net assets (at year-end)	$89,808,779	$84,538,949	$75,567,832	$75,056,161	$70,494,283	$ –0–	$ –0–	$ –0–
Annual cash dividends per common share	$ .00	$ .80	$ 1.35	$ 1.35	$ 1.25	$ 5.38	$ 4.42	$ 3.69

EXHIBIT 2

Dear Dr. Deal:

This letter is in reference to your question concerning the bank's current financial problems. The problems which the bank is now facing are the cumulation of several factors over an extended period of time. In fact, by the time the problems were revealed in the annual report they were several years old and well on the way to being solved. Since our financial problems were primarily in farming, perhaps the following narrative will help clarify why the problems occurred and why they were so slow in coming to the surface.

The late 1960s and early to mid-1970s were profitable years for farmers. Interest rates, prices, and growing conditions were favorable and it was good period for agriculture. Farmers were expanding by buying additional land, new equipment, etc.; land and equipment were increasing in value, so farmers had no difficulty in obtaining sufficient collateral for these purchases. Then in 1978 the unexpected, a drought, left most farmers with a large financial loss. Many agriculture loans were partially paid, interest paid only, or interest paid by renewal. No one expected a prolonged period of financial disaster for farming. However, it happened as the bad weather continued, crop prices decreased, interest rates increased, and land and equipment values declined. This persisted through the remainder of the 1970s, the early 1980s, and to some degree today. Why didn't we call these loans in immediately? Remember the local saying, "As the farmers go so goes the community." Thus, the bank was trying to keep the farming segment of the community alive, in the belief that each year a turnaround in their financial situation would occur. In this interim time period the collateral value declined to such a degree that to foreclose would result in a loss. This gave rise to the dilemma; to continue carrying the farmers in hopes that they could eventually pay out, or foreclose and accept a financial loss. The dilemma was solved by the FDIC and a state banking department audit requiring the bank to write off certain loans. Up to this time a paper profit was being shown. As you can see it's a rather complex problem originating in the 1970s.

If I can be of further assistance let me know.

Sincerely,

John Wade, President

---

many farmers had purchased equipment and land during the more prosperous years and were caught with payments during the 1980s when bad weather, high interest, and sluggish economy occurred. He thought, why didn't the loan charge-offs occur earlier in the 1980s? Again, a little investigation revealed that the bad loans, especially to farmers, were carried by renewal for several years. The bank's philosophy was that the farmers would have a good year and be able to pay off whereas if the bank foreclosed the bank stood to recover only a portion of the loan. This was due to deflated land and equipment values so that the collateral was not adequate for most of the loans. Therefore foreclosing was not a desirable alternative. In addition, foreclosing would have hurt other segments of the local economy (Exhibit 2).

THE PROBLEM

In 1980 John thought he was being given the reins of a vigorous, profitable, rapidly growing financial institution. In fact his previous banking experience had been primarily public relations. How was he going to solve the major problems facing the Farmers Bank?

28. Dixie National Bank

The Dixie National Bank[1] was located in a growing industrial southern city. In addition to its large industrial and commercial lending activities, it still attempts to service the credit needs of the agricultural area surrounding the city. As it became predominantly a "city" bank, it lost touch with agricultural borrowers and increasingly was forced to make these loans through its correspondent banks located not only in the state but throughout the South. While the Dixie National Bank is not particularly noted as a "progressive" bank, it is quite aggressive and competes fiercely with other banks in the city for deposits and good loan accounts. Since it acts as a "correspondent" it feels that solicitation of deposits from large national companies with southern operations fits naturally into its activities. Despite the rapid growth of the industrial community in recent years and the declining importance of the agricultural and rural community, the Dixie National Bank still feels strong ties to the rural area and its economic and financial problems.

Howells Cobb is a typical product of his state. He grew up in a small rural county seat and was graduated from the state university and its law school. Tiring of the struggle to establish a legal practice in his home town, he was glad to accept a position in a bank in the large metropolitan area as an executive trainee. He advanced rapidly and in 1958 he switched banks, taking a position as vice president of the Dixie National Bank with the responsibility of control over agricultural loans.

Because of Dixie's strong development of correspondent banking, credit files are often built up on borrowers who are not direct customers of the bank. The bank had built up such a file on the L. Flaire Enterprises because there had been an increasing number of inquiries from all over the South concerning the credit worthiness of this company.

Leroy Flaire is almost a prototype of the American ideal. He is a completely self-made man who from obscure beginnings had created single-handedly the largest chicken hatchery in the world. Despite his unkempt appearance, his poor speech, and an almost complete

---

This case was prepared by R. R. Dince, University of Georgia.

[1] All names in this case are disguised.

EXHIBIT 1 Broiler Production in Selected States, 1955–1958 (number produced—000 omitted)

	1955	1956	1957	1958
North Carolina	72,936	94,087	106,352	134,185
Georgia.	177,642	222,780	261,000	292,119
Alabama	57,764	82,085	103,875	130,024
Mississippi	37,486	52,855	66,597	85,424
Arkansas	76,954	99,271	110,191	133,331
Delaware	69,820	85,699	93,537	94,250
Maryland	58,367	67,033	74,288	86,209
Indiana	32,368	38,518	42,370	44,912
California.	48,516	52,397	43,490	47,839
Total for 22 states . . .	959,681	1,192,822	1,303,397	1,496,864

SOURCE: Agricultural Marketing Service, United States Department of Agriculture.

lack of formal education, Flaire is known by the industry as the greatest hatchery man in the business.[2] Hatcheries under his management reputedly had higher hatch proportions than industry averages and he was known to have improved broiler chicken breeding strains through his own breeding experiments.

One of the most rapidly growing agricultural industries in the United States, particularly in the South, has been the broiler industry. (See Exhibit 1.) The basis of the growth can be traced to the fact that broiler meat is relatively inexpensive in comparison to other meats. Using sound managerial techniques, the production of broilers is somewhat like a factory, not like other types of farming. Because broiler raising resembles factory production, the industry has tended to locate in areas of abundant farm labor and marginal farms. Since it is a labor-intensive industry requiring year-round labor, with land quality having no bearing on production, the southern piedmont has emerged as a natural area for growth. Because of relatively low labor costs, it is more economical to ship small grains from the Midwest into the South to be processed into feed than it would be to raise the chickens nearer the cheaper grain areas.

The one important factor concerning the poultry industry—any phase of the industry—is that it requires huge sums of working capital; chickens must be produced in large quantities to keep costs down. This problem of raising capital to finance the relatively short production cycle has plagued the industry from its inception, particularly as competition between individual producers and producing areas has lowered prices and profits. The industry has reacted to lower profits

---

[2] Poultry husbandry is an exacting science generally under the control of university-trained scientific research personnel. The goal in breeding has been to create a broiler chicken which will produce high quality meat at the lowest possible feed conversion ratio.

by intensifying the drive for lower costs through even greater production, in this way increasing the need for credit.

So far as a hatchery is concerned, its need for financing arises from two sources. First, often it is asked to extend trade credit on the sale of its baby chicks. While this credit is supposed to be turned over in 30 days, often the hatchery has to wait until the chicks have been raised to marketable size before receiving payment. If the hatchery is not a custom hatchery—processing someone else's eggs—then an additional and more important need for credit arises out of the necessity for maintaining its own laying flocks. In order to have highly productive laying flocks, it must always have flocks being raised in preparedness to replace existing flocks. Typically these birds are financed in two ways. As pullets and cockerels, the feed and chick costs are financed by giving notes secured by the birds themselves. These notes are replaced with new notes when the birds reach laying size to cover the feed costs necessary to maintain the flocks while they are laying for the hatchery. The general rule of thumb is that credit should not exceed the meat value of the breeding flocks, approximately $1.25 per bird.

It seemed that there had been an unusually large number of requests from depositors and correspondent banks in the spring of 1959 concerning the credit standing of the Flaire Enterprises. So far as Cobb knew there was little reason to believe that any significant change either in the Flaire companies or the problems of the poultry industry itself warranted any change in the bank's advice. Almost uniformly, he counseled banks and others to be extremely wary about extending too much unsecured credit to Flaire or any of his enterprises unless proper security for the loan could be secured. While Flaire did not file any specific credit information with Dun and Bradstreet or other credit agencies, credit reports were generally derogatory but not specific. The major point to be drawn from the credit report was that Flaire with his many companies, while a dominant factor in the industry, was generally known as a slow payer—though no one had ever actually lost any money on a Flaire receivable.

It was just after Cobb had answered a credit inquiry in July 1959 regarding Flaire that the Dixie National Bank was asked by its correspondent bank in Winton to participate in a loan to one of the Flaire companies. Cobb, while reluctant to make such a loan, felt that at least he had to receive and discuss the credit application. An appointment was made for Cobb to meet with Winton bank officers and Flaire. At the meeting, Cobb was introduced to Flaire, Mr. Joyce, who had just been named president of the major Flaire companies, and to Mr. Pine, who had joined the companies with Joyce and was now vice president and treasurer. Considering that he and his bank had formed a rather adverse surface opinion of Flaire, Cobb questioned the trio of company officers closely to get a clearer picture of the size and scope of their operations. Cobb knew Flaire to be the largest hatchery operator in the world, but he did not know the complete scope of the operations.

Flaire presented the facts of the operation. There were three major Flaire companies. The three major companies were not the apex of a pyramid, but they were merely the largest companies in the Flaire group. Flaire, Inc., was a completely separate operation; it was the most recently founded company and was devoted solely to the hatching of Leghorn laying hens. Flaire's Hatchery actually was the center of the broiler hatching business; in essence it was the production unit. Winton Hatcheries did little or no hatching; this corporation owned the laying flocks and produced the eggs used by Flaire's Hatchery and other hatchery units. The 24 or more smaller corporations were not all producers of hatching eggs or hatchery units. Many of them were sales corporations owning almost no assets and transacting little except book transactions for other Flaire corporations. As the sales effort grew, the smaller operations were founded to feed the expanding market. However, the major reason separate entities were formed for each new expansion apparently stemmed from an attempt to get an income tax advantage by dividing up the total business in such a way that no single corporation would show more than $25,000 profit.

It is not exactly clear how rapidly the Flaire complex grew, but by the beginning of 1959 consolidated sales were in excess of $10 million. From the several hundred dollars of borrowed capital, Flaire now controlled corporations which had total assets of over $10 million with an estimated net worth of over $2 million. He controlled over 2 million chickens[3] and was producing over 140 million baby chicks a year. While there were several hundred employees of all the organizations and each hatchery had a manager, the whole operation was under the control of Flaire and his major assistant Joseph Prince. In order to expand output as rapidly as possible with minimum working capital, a maximum use of credit of every type was necessary.

In his questioning of Flaire, Cobb asked for some financial information. Flaire handed him a balance sheet dated March 31, 1959, and said that this covered the corporation that desired to make the loan (see Exhibit 2). Cobb asked to see a consolidated statement, but he was told that the accountants had not yet pulled one but that he would receive a copy when it was available. Cobb questioned Flaire further on the various items and found that Flaire used heavily the sale leaseback technique. All vehicles used by the corporation were leased—

---

[3] Breeding flocks. Breeder hens have a useful laying life of seven months after reaching maturity; therefore new flocks (now productive) must always be ready to replace inefficient flocks.

EXHIBIT 2 Flaire's Hatchery, Inc.
Statement of Financial Condition* March 31, 1959 (cents omitted)

Assets

Current assets		
Cash on hand in bank		$ 4,044
Accounts and notes receivable		
Customers	$449,414	
Related companies	431,937	
	$881,351	
Deduct: Provision for doubtful accounts . . .	30,955	850,396
Inventory—Eggs		17,790
Total current assets		$ 872,230
Officers and employees accounts receivable . .		343,049
Cash value life insurance		3,600
Buildings and equipment—net.		101,460
Other assets		
Receivables from old partnerships and proprietorships controlled by L. A. Flaire— liquidating	$205,334	
Other miscellaneous assets	8,333	213,667
Total assets.		$1,534,007

Liabilities and Capital

Current liabilities		
Accounts and notes payable		
Banks		$ 123,234
Trade.		107,416
Related companies		1,042,450
Payroll taxes		1,020
Accrued expense		317
Total current liabilities.		$1,274,438
Capital stock	$216,500	
Retained earnings		
Balance—September 30, 1958	$28,259	
Net income for six months ending March 31, 1959	14,810	43,069
		259,569
Total capital and liabilities.		$1,534,007

* Not certified.

these included officers' cars, chick buses, and four light planes. Flaire had over 200 incubators in use; while payments had been completed on some of them, incubator lease payments annually were running in excess of $250,000. Almost all of the incubator leases were taken out personally by Flaire; the payments on the leases, however, were made by the hatcheries either directly or indirectly. The huge buildup in breeding flocks needed to service the incubator space available required Flaire to enter into agreement with farmers who had capital available whereby the Flaire companies leased farms and the equipment necessary to maintain large breeder flocks.

EXHIBIT 3

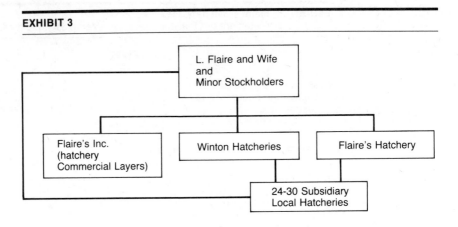

Over the years, Flaire had built up an organization which produced a substantial portion of the total hatch of broiler eggs in the United States. Flaire in running his business occupied himself solely with the problems of output and sales, leaving much of the internal financial operations to a $100-a-week bookkeeper. He admitted that in his drive to expand he had ignored the internal organization of his business. In building up his production and sales effort, Flaire formed well over two dozen subsidiary corporations located in various poultry production centers. Flaire owned all or almost all of the stock in the subsidiary corporations, but several of the subsidiaries were in great part owned by the three master corporations (see Exhibit 3).

Flaire had to leave the meeting early saying that he had to fly to Texas to supervise the beginning of a new hatchery. Cobb continued his discussion with Joyce and Pine. Frankly, he was quite interested in their role in the business and how they had become chief officers of the consolidated Flaire Enterprises. Joyce explained that he had been brought into the Flaire picture in February by a group of Flaire's major creditors led by the Hooker Corporation, a large national feed company. The worsening poultry and egg market, compounded by the confused state of Flaire's corporate and personal affairs had prompted these creditors to insist that Flaire bring in some outside management help. Joyce and his staff, acting as consultants, submitted a report in May. After the report was rendered. Flaire voluntarily stepped down as chief executive officer, becoming operations manager, and with the approval of his creditors named Joyce and Pine as the new top management. The major function of the new management team was to make the management report effective. A condensed version of the report follows.

THE MANAGEMENT REPORT

The following six general observations are made:

1. No integrated policy in force for the business as a whole.
2. Functions not clearly segregated and authorities and responsibilities not clearly established or delegated.
3. Decisions made on basis of tax savings without paying attention to effect on operations, organization, and costs of production.
4. Horizontal expansion carried on without analysis of markets. Vertical expansion carried on without appraisal of costs.
5. Necessity of disposing of perishable product has the effect of producing an emergency attitude in the organization. Marketing not orderly.
6. There is little evidence that the operation is assuming the proper responsibility for leadership in the industry.

Corporate and Department Organization

It is recommended that the complex of corporations be merged into one unified corporation, unless an evaluation of tax savings versus intangible and tangible operating costs prove tax savings devices worthwhile. It is recommended that personal proprietorship in the complex be abandoned. The present division of functions, duties, and responsibilities is vague, resulting in top management having to make decisions which should properly be made at the departmental level. These departments have not been established nor have clear lines of communication and authority been laid down.

Sales

Broiler chick sales should be under the control of the individual hatchery managers except for the separate operation of Flaire, Inc. It is recommended that chick sales and hatchery operations be clearly separated. Sales territories should be established and competition between hatcheries should be eliminated. Excess eggs, culls, and cracks sales should be taken away from individual salesmen and should be turned over to a sales department.

Hatchery Operations

Hatcheries would become more efficient if more attention were paid to operations rather than sales. Costs would fall and hatchability percentages would rise. Hatcheries should not determine their own production but should do so in accordance with a sales projection.

Farm and Flock Operations

There should be a separate department controlling and coordinating this important activity. This department would control size of flocks on the basis of the now nonexistent sales forecast of chicks.

Employee Relations

A formal personnel department should be organized to determine salary schedules, conditions of employment, job evaluation, job description, and fringe benefits.

Finance

The accounting and internal controls systems is under revision, but it cannot be accomplished until corporate reorganization along the lines in the report have been completed. The objective of the finance department is to provide an adequate accounting system which can provide accurate current operating results and statements of financial condition, on the basis of which budgeting and financial planning can be put into effect. None of these goals are now being accomplished.

CONCLUDING REMARKS

All further expansion, either horizontally or vertically, should be abandoned until the organization of the business is rationalized. It is further recommended that an expert management consultant be hired and given the authority to put into effect the plan outlined in the report. Further, a controller with cost accounting experience and experience in negotiating long- and short-term loans should be hired immediately.

After looking over the management report and listening to explanations from Joyce and Pine, Cobb felt relieved concerning the affairs of the Flaire Enterprises since the rather loose administration of Flaire himself was to be replaced with "rational" management. With a little more interest, he asked Joyce exactly how much credit Flaire's Hatchery wanted. At this point, the representative of the correspondent bank interrupted to explain that this particular credit was to be like many others his bank had made to Flaire. The initial credit line was to be $250,000 split evenly between the two banks. The loans were to be made in the form of discounted notes arising out of Flaire's Hatchery's shipping baby breeding chicks to contract farmers. Farmers sign the notes for the chicks and Flaire's Hatchery endorses them, making them two-name paper. When the chicks reach the age of approximately 12 weeks they are shifted from the first contract farmer to another who raises the birds until they are laying age and then cages them and sells the eggs under contract to one of the Flaire hatcheries. When the pullets and cockerels are shifted, the old note is paid off and a new one written by the succeeding contract farmer and again endorsed by the Flaire's Hatchery. The second note, which runs for nine months, covers most of the useful laying life of the hen and is to be written in the amount of a dollar a bird. At maximum size, the bird would weigh six to eight pounds and would have a rough collateral value as meat of at least $1.44. (The Winton banker pointed out here that hens rarely sold for less than $0.24 a pound live.)

Cobb said before leaving the meeting that he would be happy to present the information to his board but that he could not commit the Dixie National at this time. The officer of the Winton bank accompanied Cobb out of the room and privately urged him to make the loan. He pointed out that his area was dependent on the poultry industry and Flaire was one of the most important people in the industry. He further argued that the Dixie should make every effort to help the rural areas, particularly in situations where its correspondents wanted to make loans. When Cobb expressed his doubts about Flaire personally, the Winton bank man answered quickly, "Well, we have never lost a dime with him—and don't forget Flaire's is the largest hatchery in the world. Besides, nobody has ever lost anything on a loan collateralled by a chicken." Cobb, impressed by the correspondent's fervor, said he would think it over but he could not make a decision until either Flaire or Joyce sent him a consolidated statement which would show the condition of the other Flaire companies.

The next morning Cobb received a telephone call from Gordon Cotler, vice president in charge of poultry feed sales for the Hooker Corporation. He told Cobb that Flaire had called him before leaving town and had suggested that Cotler get in touch with the Dixie National Bank regarding the proposed loan. Cotler outlined his company's relationship with Flaire. The Hooker Corporation had been seeking methods of expanding its sales in the South when Flaire made a proposition to use Hooker feed exclusively in areas where Hooker could supply it on competitive terms. Considering the number of chickens under Flaire's control, this amounted to a market of approximately 60,000 tons of feed a year. Figuring conservatively, this would mean an annual volume of sales of at least $4,500,000. Cotler reminded Cobb that Flaire was the largest and most successful hatchery operation in the United States and the Hooker Corporation was happy to service this customer and provide the various Flaire companies with a total credit line of $1 million. Then Cobb asked Cotler if his company thought so much of Flaire's ability, why had Hooker led the group of creditors in insisting that a management study be made; and when it was completed, why had Hooker forced Flaire to appoint outsiders to top executive positions in his own company. Cotler answered by saying that the Flaire companies were so tangled up in intercompany transfers and relationships that the appointment of skilled executives would give Flaire more time to devote to hatchery and breeder flock operations. Cotler pointed out that southern banks should be in the forefront of promoting the economic development of the South. He added, "Listen, if he's good enough for us to sink a million bucks into, why are you dragging your feet?" Cobb remained noncommittal and said that his hands were tied in the matter and that he would have to take the loan up with the bank's executive vice president and the loan committee. In any case, he said that he couldn't do a thing until he received more detailed financial information. Cobb reminded Cotler that he couldn't check the credit of every small farmer who put his name on a note, and added, "Maybe the Winton bank could, but so far as I'm concerned, the whole thing depends on Flaire's current credit standing."

The next morning Cobb went in and talked the Flaire situation over with his executive vice president, Dennis Craig. Cobb pointed out that so far he had little inclination to make the loan. Craig listened sympathetically and then said that this "little loan" had certainly stirred up a lot of interest. He commented that he had received a call from the president of the Winton bank asking about the Dixie's decision. Craig then rather pointedly reminded Cobb that the Hooker Corporation maintained large deposit balances in both the Dixie National Bank and the Winton Bank. He made no further comment.

About a week later, Cobb received three statements from Pine of the Flaire companies (see Exhibit 4). In his letter Pine said that the income statements were still in the process of being worked up and the accountant could not promise a definite date. Pine called attention to the fact that while the statements of the three companies were not certified they were prepared by an outside auditing firm.

EXHIBIT 4   Winton Hatcheries, Inc.
Statement of Financial Condition, June 30, 1959

Assets

Current assets		
Cash on hand in bank		$ 125,658.72
Accounts receivable		
Customers.	$ 800,163.11	
Related companies.	3,067,887.15	
	$3,868,050.26	
Less: Provision for doubtful accounts	80,016.31	3,788,033.95
Inventory		2,568,356.83
Total current assets		$6,482,049.50

EXHIBIT 4 *(continued)*

Officers' and employers accounts		
L. A. Flaire.	$ 36,974.65	
Payments made on equipment, charged to		
L. A. Flaire during fiscal year	47,987.45	84,962.10
Cash value life insurance.		3,600.00
Fixed assets—net		14,209.05
Other assets		
Accounts receivable due from old partnerships		
and proprietorships controlled by L. A.		
Flaire—liquidating	$ 295,608.15	
Investment—Flaire's Breeder Farm, Inc..	1,054,716.86	
Deposit	425.00	1,350,750.01
Total		$7,935,570.66

Liabilities and Capital

Current liabilities		
Accounts payable		
Outside creditors.	$2,956,142.88	
Related companies.	1,268,584.19	$4,224,727.07
Notes payable		1,825,973.23
Accrued expenses		6,285.00
Total current liabilities		$6,056,985.30
Capital		
Capital stock issued	$ 65,000.00	
Less: Treasury stock	20,478.67	
Capital stock outstanding.	$ 44,521.33	
Retained earnings	$1,834,064.03	$1,878,585.36
Total		$7,935,570.66

Flaire's Hatchery, Inc.
Statement of Financial Condition
June 30, 1959

Assets

Current assets			
Cash on hand and in bank			$ 3,667.54
Accounts and notes receivable			
Customers.	$ 374,774.23		
Related companies	215,841.98		
Notes receivable	196,127.62		
	$ 786,743.83		
Less:			
Provision for doubtful accounts . . $230,302.27			
Notes receivable discounted . . . 125,614.47	355,916.74		430,827.09
Inventory			14,905.14
Total current assets			$ 449,399.77

EXHIBIT 4 *(concluded)*

Officers and employees		
L. A. Flaire.	$ 241,338.42	
Undistributed expenditures for		
various Flaire companies		
charged to L. A. Flaire during		
fiscal year	275,363.47	516,701.89
Fixed assets—at cost less		
accumulated depreciation		114,830.57
Other assets		
Receivables from old		
partnerships and		
proprietorships controlled by		
L. A. Flaire—liquidating.	$ 196,297.43	
Deposits and prepaid expenses . .	8,426.18	
Cash value of life insurance. . . .	3,600.00	208,323.61
Total		$1,308,535.29

Liabilities and Capital

Current liabilities		
Bank overdraft		6,070.66
Accounts payable		
Outside creditors.	151,385.75	
Related companies	1,101,240.71	1,252,626.46
Notes payable		811.92
Accrued expenses		800.46
Total current liabilities		$1,260,309.50
Capital		
Capital stock outstanding.	216,500.00	
Retained earnings (deficit)	(168,274.21)	48,275.79
Total		$1,308,535.29

Assets

Current assets			
Cash on hand and in bank			$ 23,596.26
Accounts and notes receivable			
Customers.		$ 821,356.88	
Related companies		1,013.80	
Other		34,575.74	
		$ 856,946.42	
Less			
Notes receivable discounted . .	$594,028.14		
Reserve for bad debts	50,264.00	644,292.14	212,654.28
Inventory			500,016.17
Total current assets			$ 736,266.71
Officers and employees accounts . .			16,642.78
Fixed assets—net			4,704.26
Subscription to Capital Stock			1,000.00
Total			$ 758,613.75

EXHIBIT 5 Georgia Chick Prices 1958 and 1959* (broilers, price per pound, North Georgia)

	1958			1959		
	Broilers (price per 100 chicks)	Layers	Live Broilers (price per pound)	Broilers	Layers	Live Broilers (price per pound)
January	13.5	38.0	17.1	8.8	38.0	14.6
February	14.0	40.0	19.0	9.2	41.0	15.1
March	14.0	40.0	21.0	8.3	41.0	15.5
April	14.2	40.0	19.2	6.7	40.0	15.8
May	13.8	40.0	20.0	7.2	40.0	14.9
June	13.8	38.0	20.0	8.7	39.0	14.5
July	12.4	38.0	19.8	8.8	39.0	15.5
August	10.7	37.0	17.0			
September	11.0	37.0	15.6			
October	11.0	38.0	15.2			
November	11.0	38.0	16.1			
December	11.0	38.0	14.2			

* There were 325 million chicks produced in Georgia in 1959 and 2.4 billion in the United States.

SOURCE: Agricultural Marketing Service, U.S. Department of Agriculture, *Agricultural Prices* (monthly, 1958–59).

That afternoon Cobb was called out of town on important bank business. He gave the new information to Craig and ventured the opinion that he was still not sold on the idea, particularly in view of the state of the market for broilers and eggs (see Exhibit 5). Craig thanked him and said that the loan committee would discuss the matter that week.

29.   First Columbia Bank

It was the early 1980s, and Robert S. ("Bob") Balk reflected on his 25 years in financial service. His area of expertise, the savings and loan industry, had seen problems of disintermediation in the 1960s and 1970s. Later, in 1980 and 1982, the depository deregulation legislation had presented a contrast of challenges and opportunities to the industry. Balk had taken early retirement from the presidency of an old and respected S&L association operating in the Augusta, Georgia, metropolitan area. Since he was only in his mid-50s and not ready for permanent retirement, he had become active in financial consulting. Now Balk faced a major career decision about an entrepreneurial opportunity in the rapidly changing, deregulated financial services arena.

THE FINANCIAL SERVICES INDUSTRY AND REGULATION

The S&L industry traditionally is composed of voluntary mutual benefit associations that gather interest-bearing deposits from the general public and invest these funds in long-term fixed rate mortgage loans. If federally chartered, the associations are regulated by the Federal Home Loan Bank board. Deposits are insured by the Federal Savings and Loan Insurance Corporation. State-chartered associations, with varied arrangements for depositor insurance, also operate in the industry. Historically, earnings of S&L associations depended upon the difference between interest earned on mortgage loans and interest paid on deposits.

Current regulation of federally chartered S&Ls extends from the separation of S&L and commercial bank financing and investing activities of the 1930s. Extension of Regulation Q interest rate ceilings and provision for a rate advantage to S&Ls was intended to provide a stable supply of funds for home mortgages. But abnormally high market interest rates in the 1960s and 1970s, coupled with the development of nonregulated financial instruments such as money market funds, led to substantial disintermediation and financial disaster for many S&Ls.

This case and the accompanying teaching notes were written by Otha L. Gray and Harry G. McAlum, professors in the Division of Business Administration, Lander College, Greenwood, South Carolina. All rights are reserved.

EXHIBIT 1 Major Provisions of the Depository Institutions Deregulation and Monetary Control Act of 1980 and the Depository Institutions Act of 1982

The 1980 Act

1. Permits NOW accounts nationwide.
2. Increases deposit insurance ceiling to $100,000.
3. Expands thrift powers to include consumer loans.
4. Provides for uniform reserve requirements on transaction accounts at all depository institutions.
5. Gives all depository institutions access to the Federal Reserve Bank discount window.
6. Sets up the Depository Institutions Deregulation Committee.
7. Phases out interest-rate ceilings on all deposits.

The 1982 Act

1. Gives deposit insurance agencies new powers and methods for handling problem institutions.
2. Creates money market deposit accounts.
3. Expands thrift powers in areas of consumer and commercial lending.

With the passage of the Depository Institutions Deregulation and Monetary Control Act of 1980 and the Depository Institutions Act of 1982 (known as the Garn–St. Germain Act), a new set of competitive rules developed for both S&Ls and commercial banks. The major provisions of the legislation are stated in Exhibit 1.

The effect of these acts was to eliminate the distinction between banks and "thrifts." The environment changed suddenly: Fierce competition caused deposits to flow into S&Ls, which in turn invested these funds to cover the higher interest rates being paid to attract the deposits. An expansion of consumer and commercial lending became an available strategy for S&L managers. Part of this expansion concerned secondary mortgages—a natural investment opportunity that followed the S&L development of the mortgage banking business. The rapidly developing market for loan portfolios to be sold to GNMA, FNMA, FHLMC, and conventional lenders such as pension funds and insurance companies, offered S&Ls the opportunity to earn substantial profits. In the past, interest rate ceilings and a single market (residential mortgage lending) had limited profit opportunities.

In Georgia, the regulatory climate was favorable for a state-chartered S&L association. Under Georgia law, an S&L is required to invest 50 percent of lendable funds in residentially related mortgage loans, including construction, apartments, and loans resold. Then, up to 50 percent of lendable funds may be invested in any loans or investments authorized for a commercial bank. The new depository checking accounts and the recently authorized capital stock ownership permitted for a Georgia state-chartered S&L made S&Ls (in the eyes of the public) the equivalent of commercial banks.

BACKGROUND OF THE NEW INSTITUTION

Against the backdrop of the rapidly changing financial services industry, Balk and some of his business associates planned the establishment of the new depository financial institution. Balk himself was the "man on the scene" with the experience and ability to take advantage of the changing environment and emerging opportunities for the financial services industry. He enjoyed the confidence of his business and professional friends, who later became investors in First Columbia.

The timing seemed right for a new financial enterprise. Besides the federal deregulatory legislation of 1980 and 1982, changes in the state financial scene favored the new institution. Georgia regulatory bodies had recently authorized state-chartered Georgia S&Ls to raise capital by issuing common stock to the public. Moreover, the Georgia banking laws, which allow branching beyond their county of domicile by purchase only, do not apply to S&L institutions. Close votes in the 1984 and 1985 Georgia legislative sessions prevented statewide branching by commercial banks. And this action gave the new depository financial institution a head start on the competition in the proposed market area of Columbia County.

Equally as important as the changing regulatory environment was the economic vitality of the proposed market area. Since 1970, the Augusta, Georgia, metro SMSA had sustained stable and substantial rates of economic growth, which accelerated in the 1980s environment. Columbia County led in the SMSA in terms of population increase and residential housing units.

INITIAL ORGANIZATION

A small group of interested investors selected Balk to provide the organizational leadership to secure regulatory authorization for the establishment of a new depository financial institution. As its president and chief executive officer, he would provide the managerial direction in the new institution.

A small local financial institution, especially one in the formation stage, has limited access to capital markets. Initial operating capital of $1,500,000 would be raised by the directors of the S&L association. They would sell stock on a "best efforts" basis without compensation to anyone. The organizational plan was to form a holding company that would wholly own a single, subsidiary, financial depository institution. The holding company structure would permit greater flexibility in raising capital and could engage in operating activities not allowed a depository institution. Thus, the parent holding company could raise capital as needed through additional stock issues to augment the capital base of the depository subsidiary institution. Through some form of debt financing, the holding company might raise capital funds for the needs of the depository institution and for other operations of the holding company.

A key decision in the organizational plan was to organize the operating depository institution as a capital stock S&L association under Georgia law. Of the initial capital raised by the holding company stock offering, $1.5 million was to be invested in 100 percent of the capital stock of the S&L to provide the initial equity capital base for the depository institution.

The choice of the S&L organizational form was logical, given Balk's managerial experience in the S&L industry and the prevailing financial climate. Although either a federal or a state charter was an option, a state-chartered S&L form is less regulated. Regulation is through a single regulatory authority, the Georgia Department of Banking and Finance. Also, a state-chartered S&L under Georgia law has virtually the same investment powers as a commercial bank. Furthermore, state chartering allowed participation in a state insurance fund, sponsored by the Georgia Department of Banking and Finance. Thus, management chose to participate in the Georgia Credit Union Deposit Insurance Corporation (GDIC), rather than the Federal Savings and Loan Insurance Corporation (FSLIC).

FEASIBILITY STUDY

A major part of the regulatory approval process for a new state-chartered financial institution is the preparation of an economic feasibility study to be submitted in support of the application. The study must demonstrate the community's need for the new institution and show that the proposed institution is capable of making a profit in a reasonable period of time. Accordingly, a consultant who was a professor of finance at a nearby university prepared a study of the proposed association's primary service area for submission to the state department of banking and finance. The study analyzed the economic and demographic characteristics of Columbia County and the primary service area, the characteristics of the deposit and loan market in the area, and the profit potential of the proposed association. The study, which comprised 84 pages and 38 tables of data, concluded:

> All measures of economic conditions evaluated indicate that the Columbia market is experiencing above-average growth compared to surrounding counties and areas and state averages. These include population growth, household formation, housing unit growth, income growth, income levels, retail sales growth, and business and commercial development. Projections for the 1980s are similarly optimistic. This rapid growth translates into very favorable financial market conditions. Existing insti-

tutions are experiencing above-average growth and satisfactory profitability. By all indications the market can easily support the entry of a new financial institution. Indeed, the economic conditions are very positive for the formation and entry of a new institution.

The study cited Columbia County as the most rapidly growing area in the Augusta metropolitan region and as an area that ranks high in growth relative to the state as a whole. All indications were that the solid growth trends are likely to continue in the foreseeable future. Deposit growth has been high and loan demand is strong in the area. Additionally, a forecast of the proposed institution's income and expense suggests that a profit can be expected early in the life of the institution.

THE PROPOSED PRIMARY MARKET AREA

A critical element influencing the approval of the operating charter by the department of banking and finance and the later success of the operation was the selection of the primary service area and the location of business offices. The proposed site for transaction of business was 4109 Columbia Road, Martinez, Georgia. This site is in the eastern edge of Columbia County, adjacent to the Richmond County line on the western side of the greater Augusta, Georgia, metro area. The business offices will be located in a new strip shopping center anchored by a major Kroger supermarket. This site is situated between two major traffic arteries serving the residential suburbs and provides primary access to the commercial, financial, professional, medical, and industrial sectors of metropolitan Augusta.

The contiguous unincorporated sections of Martinez and Evans in Columbia County are predominantly residential and retail suburban shopping areas. The population of the greater Augusta metro area is approximately 385,000. About 40 to 50 percent of the population of 45,000 of Columbia County live in the Martinez and Evans suburban areas. An equivalent proportion of the commercial business activity in Columbia County is concentrated in the area.

The adjacent county of Richmond, largest in the Augusta metro area, has a well-developed system of financial institutions. There are four national banks with 49 offices and three federally chartered S&L associations with 17 offices, suggesting a well-established branch network in Richmond County. Each of these institutions operates statewide through some parent or holding company affiliation. However, under applicable state law, banks cannot expand across county lines into Columbia County except by acquisition of an existing Columbia County bank. Federal S&Ls are not similarly restricted by state law from branch expansion across county lines. At the date of the formation of First Columbia, only two S&L offices were located in the

EXHIBIT 2 Map of Columbia County, Georgia: Primary Market Area

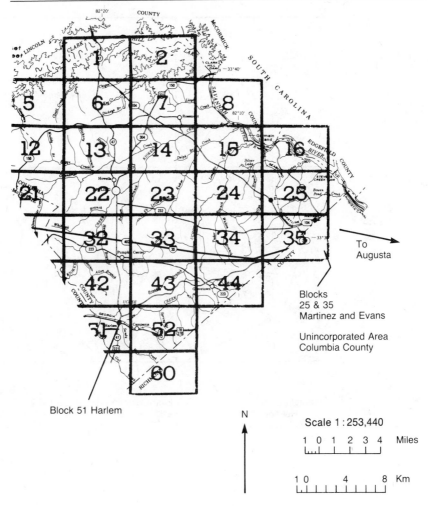

To
Augusta

Blocks
25 & 35
Martinez and Evans

Unincorporated Area
Columbia County

Block 51 Harlem

N

Scale 1 : 253,440

1 0 1 2 3 4   Miles

1 0   4   8 Km

county. Both offices were within one mile of each other and of the proposed main business offices of First Columbia in the densely populated Martinez area. One locally owned commercial bank is located in the proposed primary service area of Martinez. Only one other commercial bank operates in the county. It is 15 miles distant in the village of Harlem, on the west side of the predominantly rural county. Exhibits 2 and 3 show the geographic relationships of the market area and competitive institutions. In Columbia County, the ratio of population to the number of S&L offices and bank offices exceeds the state-wide average.

EXHIBIT 3 Competition in the Primary Service Area

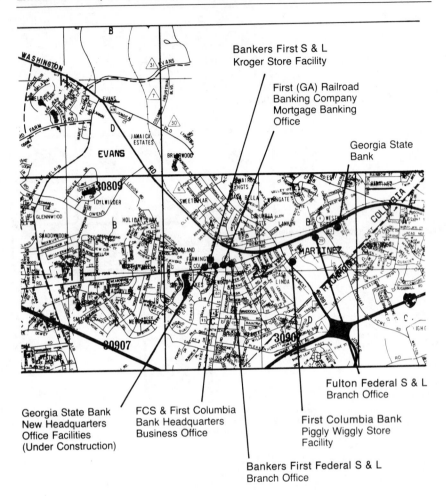

INITIAL OPERATING PROJECTIONS

The proposed association will be a new enterprise in a very competitive industry. As with any new business, it has no operating history on which to base estimates of its future prospects. Management projects that the association will incur a loss in its first year of operation and that it will become profitable in the second year. Operating projections for the first three years of full-service operations are based on the following assumptions:

	First Year	Second Year	Third Year
Deposits	$4,000,000	$8,000,000	$12,000,000
Total revenues	737,784	1,474,545	2,143,475
Pretax income (capital loss)	(172,433)	134,233	333,324

Even though S&L deposits in Columbia County increased by more than 400 percent to $31 million from 1977 to 1981, there was no assurance that the association could attain these projections.

All earnings of the holding company and the association are expected to be retained for several years to expand the association's capital base. The earnings retention will support deposit growth and preclude dividend payments for several years, even if the total operations are profitable.

If the association does not become profitable in its second year of operation, the holding company may raise additional funds through another public stock offering. Alternatively, if the association's operating prospects appear favorable at the time, the holding company may borrow and contribute the proceeds to the association as additional capital. But the association must be able to sustain any loss by passing sufficient earnings to the holding company to service the holding company debt. Future borrowing decisions will have to take into consideration the financing of the main business office complex of First Columbia with tax-exempt industrial revenue bonds issued through the Columbia County Industrial Authority. The bonds are held as investment by the Trust Company of Augusta, a major correspondent bank which also provides check clearing and data processing services to First Columbia.

CHANGES IN ORGANIZATIONAL FORM

Savings and Loan/Bank Charter

The association was organized under the laws of the state of Georgia on May 16, 1983, and opened its doors to the public on June 20, 1984. However, dark clouds already loomed on the horizon. The experience of state-chartered S&L associations and state depository insurance funds, notably the Ohio and Maryland situations, cast a bad light on the proposed Georgia insurance fund (GDIC). An alternative was needed. The Federal Savings and Loan Insurance Corporation (FSLIC) did not want to take on additional state-chartered business. Fortunately, First Columbia met the technical definition of *bank* for purposes of federal law and thus could apply for membership in the Federal Reserve system and automatically qualify for Federal Deposit Insurance Corporation (FDIC) coverage without incurring supervision by the FDIC. Under these circumstances, management logically sought conversion to full-bank status since differences under Georgia law between a chartered S&L and a bank were minimal. On July 1, 1985, articles of amendment were issued by the secretary of state of Georgia to convert the association from an S&L to a banking institution and to change its name to First Columbia *Bank*.

Holding Company

FCS Financial Corporation (the holding company) was incorporated under the laws of the state of Georgia on April 27, 1983, to operate as an S&L holding company and to purchase 100 percent of the issued and outstanding stock of First Columbia S&L Association. Concurrently with the conversion to bank status, the holding company filed an application with the Federal Reserve Board to become a bank holding company pursuant to the Bank Holding Company Act of 1956 as amended. The application was approved on May 29, 1985.

President Balk indicated that changing organizational form required a minimum of paperwork and took only about 60 days to accomplish without interruption to operations. Retention of the initial name First Columbia, without any emphasis of the S&L form, minimized public visibility of the change to full bank status. The most positive and public notice was the erection of a sign and advertisement of FDIC coverage of deposits for the bank.

Thus, at the end of the first year of operations, First Columbia became a full service state-chartered commercial bank, but lacked trust powers. It operated as a single subsidiary of FCS Financial Corporation. All financial operations from June 1984 through June 1985 were conducted as S&L activities; as of July 1, 1985, operations were conducted through First Columbia as a full-service bank. Banking services were described as follows:

> The bank offers personal and business checking accounts, negotiable order of withdrawal NOW) accounts, savings accounts, money market checking accounts, various types of certificates of deposit, commercial loans, consumer/installment loans, real estate loans, and safe deposit boxes, and provides such services as banking by mail, drive-in teller, night depository, money orders, utility bill payment, bond coupon redemptions, cashier and travelers checks, direct deposit of social security funds, wire transfers, mortgage collection, and automatic teller services (ATMs). The bank also offers individual retirement accounts.

SUPERVISION AND REGULATION

The holding company and bank operate in a highly regulated environment. Business activities are closely supervised by a number of federal regulatory agencies, including the Federal Reserve Board and the Georgia Department of Banking and Finance.

A bank holding company is generally prohibited from acquiring control of any company which is not a bank, from engaging in any business other than that of banking or managing and controlling. However, certain activities closely related to banking have been identified by the Federal Reserve Board as permissible for bank holding companies. Such activities include operating a mortgage banking business and arranging real estate equity financing, of particular interest to FCS, First Columbia's parent holding company.

As a state bank, First Columbia is subject to the supervision of the Georgia Department of Banking and Finance and, to a limited extent, the Federal Reserve Bank of Atlanta and the Federal Reserve Board. With respect to expansion, the bank may establish branches only within the geographical limits of Columbia County, Georgia, except through the acquisition of banks located in other counties. It may open loan production offices outside Columbia County. The bank is subject to the Georgia banking and usury laws restricting the amount of interest which it may charge in making loans or other extensions of credit. In addition, the bank, as a subsidiary of the holding company, is subject to restrictions under federal law in dealing with the holding company and other affiliates, if any.

ORGANIZATION AND MANAGEMENT

Balk indicated that the management of First Columbia does not have a formal management process; the experienced management and operating personnel "just opened the doors and went to work without a lot of detailed planning." In reality, a great deal of planning preceded implementation. The organization structure for the holding company and bank is reflected in Exhibit 4.

At present, a nine-member board of directors for the holding company and bank meets on all appropriate matters and writes separate sets of minutes. Future expansion probably will lead to separate boards of directors. The holding company and the bank will have separate concerns, necessitating a separate board for each.

Balk said that a significant degree of delegation is practiced in the management from the board down to the operating level of the bank. For example, the board delegates loan approval authority; then at monthly meetings, the board reviews the loan decisions to see that established policies have been followed. The same operational policy

EXHIBIT 4   Organization Chart for FCS Financial Corporation & First Columbia Bank

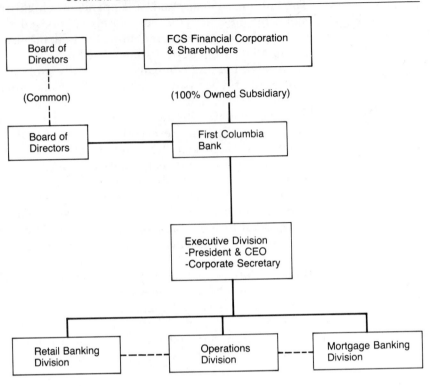

is followed in the bank with specific authority delegated to make investment and lending decisions.

Investment and lending authority criteria and limits are defined in a formal policy manual approved by the board. The policy manual contains a mission statement and a statement of institutional objectives (see Exhibits 5 and 6).

EXHIBIT 5   First Columbia Mission Statement

First Columbia Savings and Loan Association has been created by FCS Financial Corporation to provide a complete range of financial services to the individual and business residents of the trade area in the vicinity of Martinez, Georgia. First Columbia will always strive for the highest possible quality of service, unquestioned integrity, and community support, all to be provided in a warm and friendly manner.

First Columbia must be operated with sound business principles that will reward the investors in FCS Financial Corporation with a generous and profitable return on their investment.

EXHIBIT 6 First Columbia Institutional Objectives

External Policy Goals

The primary external objective of First Columbia Savings and Loan is to establish, maintain, and enhance our public image as a high-quality, friendly place to provide a complete banking business. Our reputation and a high level of public confidence is extremely important.

Internal Policy Goals

Our internal objective is to establish a sound asset portfolio that will return approximately 20 percent on stockholders' equity so we can retain sufficient earnings to maintain a capital to assets ratio of about 7.5 percent. These goals can only be attained if our return on average assets is approximately 1.5 percent.

This objective might be constrained somewhat by long-term customer considerations as well as requirements of liquidity, flexibility, and risk. We approach the objective, mindful of the constraints, through tight control of noninterest expenses and close management of our total asset portfolio. We will attempt to maintain a liquidity position between 15 and 25 percent, which is the minimum that prudent management or the regulatory authorities will allow. Investment trade-offs between liquidity and profitability are unavoidable, and these trade-offs between liquidity and profitability should be resolved toward a more liquid position to achieve our desired asset flexibility.

The funds remaining after we have achieved our liquidity and investment positions will be used to make consumer, commercial, and real estate loans which will at all times be in excess of 50 percent of our total portfolio. These loans will be supported only as absolutely necessary by purchases of federal funds.

GOALS AND GUIDELINES

Long-range plans and objectives are summarized as general goals. These goals are:

1. To preserve the integrity and safety of the deposit base and the capital base of the bank.
2. To attain and sustain a strong level of earnings as further protection for our depositors and to assure an appropriate return to our stockholders on their investment.
3. To be an asset to our community within our capacity to be responsive to the needs of the community.

Profitability for First Columbia is to be achieved through good management planning. Guidelines include the establishment of a solid customer base through customer services and marketing, control of interest spread through asset/liability management, and control of noninterest expenses through management controls. As part of the profit planning, First Columbia has established loan and deposit pricing policies that are competitive in the marketplace, yet allow sufficient interest spread to meet profit goals.

Other guidelines set forth in the manual consider criteria related to deposit policy; asset and liability management and strategy; profit planning; liquidity, capital, and dividend management; investment policy; general loan policy and guidelines; and lending administration (with specific dollar lending authority of banking officers). Provision for board review of investment and lending decisions is detailed. An internal bank investment committee reviews and presents monthly reports to the board. The policy manual is very thorough and is updated as changes are approved, particularly in the investment and lending policies.

The initial organization of First Columbia included the preparation of a detailed set of pro forma financials for five years. Detailed operating financial budgets are prepared on a six-month basis and compared with actual achievements. A review of the key elements of the pro forma financials indicates a significant degree of accuracy in predicting the bottom line profitability from operations in the second year. Deposits and gross revenues far exceeded expectations.

REVIEW OF OPERATIONS

Staffing

At First Columbia, recruitment for key positions was enhanced by advancement opportunities and by the security of working for a locally owned and managed institution. The area statewide banks, on the other hand, faced the potential of statewide and interstate merger activity—with the very real possibility of a reduction in managerial positions. Taking advantage of the situation, Balk sought to hire the best trained people away from other financial institutions. (Needless to say, the managers of these financial institutions were not pleased to see their highly qualified personnel leave to join the competition!) As a result of his "head hunter" strategy, Balk recruited one of the best branch managers of a major bank in the metro area as his vice president for retail banking. First employed by First Columbia at only 32 years of age, this very able manager later became senior vice president of the bank. In addition, experienced management and technical staff were recruited for the real estate lending operation and additional personnel were sought to expand the bank's profitable mortgage activities.

Competition

Competitors in the area have responded aggressively. Augusta-based Bankers First Federal S&L established additional branches and automatic teller machines (ATMs) in shopping centers in the primary service area of First Columbia. Additionally, Bankers First extended hours of drive-in teller service to 8 P.M. weeknights and until 2 P.M.

Saturdays in a major branch location within one block of First Columbia. In the Kroger supermarket facilities in the shopping center complex adjacent to First Columbia offices, Bankers First offered complete consumer deposit/checking services. Extended hours and an ATM also were available there.

Georgia State Bank, the most competitive local Columbia County full-service commercial bank, is located only one mile from First Columbia's offices. This bank responded by starting construction of a new headquarters building, which will be adjacent to the shopping center complex now occupied by First Columbia and the Kroger supermarket housing Bankers First. Additionally, the Georgia Railroad Bank and Trust Company, with a 55 percent share of the retail banking market in the Augusta metro area and a major component of First Railroad and Banking Company (the fifth largest banking system holding company in Georgia), positioned itself for future banking opportunities. In an adjacent shopping center complex less than one block from the growing competitive activity, Georgia Railroad opened a loan production facility for real estate mortgages—a response that apparently anticipated statewide banking authorization by the Georgia legislature. Georgia Railroad envisioned expansion into the rapidly growing Columbia County area of Martinez and Evans.

The management of First Columbia was keenly aware of the growing competition for consumer deposits and banking services. They responded by opening a consumer banking facility in a new Piggly Wiggly supermarket in another major shopping complex being built within a mile of the concentrated competition. To match the competition, First Columbia offered extended hours of service on weeknights and Saturdays (see Exhibit 7).

REVIEW OF FINANCIAL OPERATIONS

According to President Balk, First Columbia's primary sources of income are consumer depository services and consumer loans. Real estate mortgage lending conducted primarily as a mortgage banking activity for the secondary market generates substantial revenue in the form of fees. Construction loans and commercial loans also contribute to interest earnings.

First Columbia offers very competitive depository checking account services, including lower minimum balances, check clearing fees, and the opportunity to earn interest on checking account balances. The interest structure on its savings accounts is one of the most competitive in the Augusta metro banking market. The positive results of these operating policies is shown in the growth of deposits during the first full year of banking operations.

First Columbia's lending activity emphasizes consumer install-

---

EXHIBIT 7   Competition in Retail Banking

First Columbia Comes in First

Bank X	*First Columbia*	*Bank Y*
$500 minimum balance	$200 MINIMUM BALANCE	$300 minimum balance
Pays 5¼% interest	PAYS 5¼% INTEREST	Pays no interest
	UNLIMITED CHECKS	
Below $500	BELOW $200	Below $300
$3 per month	$5 FLAT FEE	$2 per month
$.20 per check	NO PER CHECK CHARGE	$.22 per check

Bank Where You Live—First Columbia—Your Hometown Bank
4109 Columbia Road & Piggly Wiggly Branch on Bobby Jones Expressway

First
Columbia
Bank

Banking Hours at Piggly Wiggly Branch

Monday, Tuesday, & Wednesday—10 A.M. to 6 P.M.
Thursday & Friday—10 A.M. to 8 P.M.
Saturday—10 A.M. to 4 P.M.
Closed Sunday

---

ment loans, nonamortizing commercial loans, real estate construction loans, and long-term real estate mortgage loans with adjustable rates. Balk's prior S&L experience convinced him to provide in long-term fixed rate mortgage loans for an adjustment of interest rates when substantial changes occur in the market.

Restructuring of operations and staffing with experienced personnel permitted a positive response to substantial growth in real estate mortgage lending demand and created the need for more space. The real estate lending operations were then moved from the main banking facilities into separate quarters in a nearby commercial and professional complex. Incidentally, this new location was adjacent to a major competitor's subsidiary mortgage banking operation headquarters.

The mortgage banking activity is currently conducted under the commercial bank structure. Balk indicated that all long-term real estate mortgage loans are made against prior commitments and that the bank is not at risk. Since these loans will be financed only temporarily by the bank during processing, there will be a 100 percent rollover of investment. Given such liquidity, he has been able to convince bank regulatory authorities to count loans in process for resale as a part of the bank's asset base for liquidity computation.

Balk noted that this real estate mortgage banking activity provides the opportunity to earn three types of income. An origination fee is received from the residential borrower, a gain on points is earned on the long-term financing, and a placement fee is received from the sale of servicing rights to some loan servicing organization. First Columbia's management adopted an initial policy of not servicing long-term real estate mortgage loans. Servicing would require a larger organization, additional experienced personnel, and a data processing system, all of which are not feasible at the present state of organizational development.

According to President Balk, the real estate mortgage banking activity has the potential to generate more revenue than do the consumer service activities. However, to take full advantage of the opportunities in real estate mortgage banking, additional capital must be raised. Plans for raising additional capital are being developed. Simultaneously, merger/acquisition possibilities are being explored with an existing mortgage banking operation. Such an expansion would represent significant development for FCS and First Columbia Bank.

FINANCIAL ANALYSIS

Asset/Liability Management

The objective of the bank is to manage assets and liabilities to provide a satisfactory consistent level of profitability within the framework of established cash, loan investment, borrowing, and capital policies. Certain officers of the bank are responsible for developing and monitoring policies and procedures that are designed to ensure acceptable composition of the asset/liability mix. The overall philosophy of management is to support asset growth primarily through the growth of deposits of all categories made by individuals, partnerships, and corporations. Managers of the bank seek to invest the largest portion of bank assets in commercial, consumer, and real estate loans.

The bank's asset/liability mix is monitored on a daily basis. A monthly report that reflects interest-sensitive assets and interest-sensitive liabilities is presented to the board of directors. The objective of this policy is to control interest-sensitive assets and liabilities so as to minimize the impact of substantial movements in interest rates on the bank's earnings.

Exhibit 8 presents an analysis of the net interest of the bank for the year ending June 30, 1985, and for the three months ending September 30, 1985, with respect to each major category of interest-earning asset and interest-bearing liability.

Deposits

The bank offers a wide range of commercial and consumer deposit accounts, including noninterest-bearing checking accounts, money

EXHIBIT 8 Analysis of Net Interest Earnings

Assets	Year Ended June 30, 1985			Three Months Ended September 30, 1985
	Average Amount	Interest Earned	Average Yield	Average Yield
Interest-earning deposits	$1,490,339	$126,288	8.5%	8.4%
Taxable securities	511,094	63,072	12.3	11.0
Federal funds sold	603,500	61,656	10.2	11.9
Net loans	3,833,753	510,060	13.3	13.3
Total earning assets	$6,438,686	$761,076	11.8%	12.2%

Liabilities	Average Amount	Interest Earned	Average Rate Paid	Average Rate Paid
Interest-bearing deposits	$5,130,834	$437,172	8.5%	8.6%
Interest spread			3.3%	3.6%

market checking accounts (consumer and commercial), negotiable order of withdrawal accounts, individual retirement accounts, time certificates of deposit, and regular savings accounts. The bank pays competitive interest rates on time and savings deposits. In addition, the bank utilizes a service charge fee schedule that is competitive with other financial institutions in the market area, covering such matters as maintenance fees on checking accounts, per item processing fees on checking accounts, and returned check charges.

Exhibit 9 presents, for the periods indicated, the average amount of and average rate paid on each of the deposit categories which are in excess of 10 percent of average total deposits, and time deposits outstanding of $100,000 or more by maturity.

Investments

Investment securities comprised only a small portion of the bank's assets at September 30, 1985, with loans constituting the bulk of assets. The bank's investment policy is to invest primarily in obligations of the United States or its agencies or obligations guaranteed as to principal and interest by the United States or its agencies. The bank also enters into federal funds transactions with its principal correspondent banks and acts as a net seller of such funds.

The maturity structure of investments is important in the management of the asset/liability mix and the opportunity for repricing of investments upon market interest rate shifts.

Exhibit 10 presents, for the period indicated, the book value of the bank's investment. Also indicated is the amount of investments due in one year or less, one to five years, and over five years.

EXHIBIT 9 Average Amount and Average Rate Paid on Deposits: Amounts Outstanding of Time Deposits of $100,000 or More by Maturity

	Average Amount (Average Rate Paid)	
Deposit Category	Year Ended June 30, 1985	Three Months Ended September 30, 1985
Noninterest-bearing demand deposits	$ 830,173	$1,597,214
Interest-bearing demand deposits	2,130,104	4,841,648
	(7.86%)	(6.88%)
Savings deposits	172,908	484,799
	(5.5%)	(5.5%)
Time deposits	3,233,099	7,151,006
	(10.92%)	(9.76%)

Amounts Outstanding of Time Deposits of $100,000 or More and Respective Maturities*

Period Ended	3 Months or Less	3–6 Months	6–12 Months	Over 12 Months	Total
June 30, 1985	$ 300,000	$310,000	$1,121,000	$400,000	$2,131,000
September 30, 1985	1,331,000	504,000	311,000	500,000	2,646,000

* The maturity structure of liabilities is of extreme importance in management of interest-sensitive liabilities.

Loan Portfolio

The bank's loan department is comprised of a real estate division and a retail division. The real estate division consists of first mortgage residential loans sold in the secondary market. The retail division consists of consumer, commercial, and land development loans. With respect to residential and commercial real estate conversion loans, the bank sells participations to other financial institutions since these loans occasionally exceed the bank's lending limit.

The bank currently sells all of its residential real estate loan portfolio in the secondary market. On September 30, 1985, residential loans for resale comprised approximately 28 percent of the bank's total real estate (commercial and residential) loan portfolio.

Exhibit 11 presents various categories of loans contained in the

---

EXHIBIT 10 Investments at Book Value by Maturity

Investment Category	Year Ended June 30, 1985	Three Months Ended September 30, 1985
Obligations of U.S. Treasury and agencies:	$596,212 (total)	$2,022,496 (total)
0–1 years	596,212	559,664
1–5 years	–0–	1,462,832
Over 5 years	–0–	–0–
Federal Reserve Bank stock	45,000	45,000

EXHIBIT 11   Outstanding Loans by Category

Type of Loan	Year Ended June 30, 1985	Three Months Ended September 30, 1985
Domestic:		
1. Commercial, financial, and agricultural*	$1,203,129	$ 1,968,732
2. Real estate—construction*	1,307,525	2,697,096
3. Real estate—mortgage	3,651,883	3,545,817
4. Installment loans	2,685,789	3,484,531
Total (net of allowance)	$8,817,247	$11,646,932

* These loan amounts are due in one year or less.

bank's loan portfolio for the periods indicated and the total amount of all loans for such periods.

Loan Loss Experience

The accrual of interest is discontinued on a loan when management determines that collection of interest is doubtful upon consideration of economic and business factors affecting collection efforts. At June 30 and September 30, 1985, the amount of loans accounted for on nonaccrual basis amounted to $17,352. There were no amounts of accruing loans past due 90 days or more as to principal or interest.

An analysis of the bank's loss experience shows a provision of $30,979 charged to operations for the year ending June 30, 1985, and $18,265 additional charge to operations for the three-month period ending September 30, 1985. Pursuant to a formula, the bank has been making additions to the allowance by charges to operating income on a monthly basis, with the goal of building to an allowance of 1 percent of total loans (excluding loans for resale) over a period of time. To date, the bank has not allocated the allowance to particular categories of loans. At the present time, management of the bank is unable to estimate accurately the anticipated amount of charge-offs by category during its next year of operations.

Consolidated Financial Statements

Consolidated financial statements of the holding company and bank are available for several periods and dates in Exhibits 12 A–F. Separate statements for the bank and holding company are not available. The primary assets of the holding company are the 100 percent investment in the bank and the physical facilities for the banking offices financed through an external loan of $800,000 with the Columbia County Industrial Development Authority. The bank holds title to about $100,000 of furniture and fixtures for operations. Thus, with

EXHIBIT 12A

**FCS FINANCIAL CORPORATION
AND SUBSIDIARY
FIRST COLUMBIA BANK
Consolidated Balance Sheets**

	June 30 1984	June 30 1985	September 30 1985	December 30 1985
Assets				
Cash and due from banks	$1,587,489	$ 1,425,279	$ 878,207	$ 351,947
Interest-bearing deposits in banks*	*	398,270	1,000,000	1,100,000
Investment securities (Note 2)	119,667	596,212	2,022,497	2,017,390
Federal funds sold	0	1,200,000	200,000	1,800,000
Loans, less allowance for loan losses (Note 3)	73,568	8,817,347	11,646,932	11,304,480
Office buildings, equipment, and leasehold improvements, net	880,461	944,018	945,857	940,695
Other assets	148,339	295,957	378,329	343,577
	$2,809,524	$13,677,083	$17,071,822	$17,858,089
Liabilities and Stockholders' Equity				
Deposits:				
Demand	$ 98,543	$ 1,139,520	$ 1,564,027	$ 1,049,721
Interest-bearing demand	63,050	3,587,874	4,861,093	4,788,081
Savings	177,967	415,120	522,977	536,848
Time, $100,000 and over	0	2,131,146	2,645,858	3,059,815
Other time	50,399	4,072,520	4,894,430	5,903,400
	$ 339,560	$11,346,180	$14,488,385	$15,337,865
Federal income taxes	2,760	0	0	0
Bonds payable (Note 7)	800,000	800,000	800,000	773,334
Accrued interest and other liabilities	101,145	161,520	289,478	252,918
	$1,293,864	$12,307,700	$15,577,863	$16,364,117
Commitments and Contingent Liabilities (Note 8)				
Stockholders' equity:				
Common stock, par value $1; 1,000,000 shares authorized; 156,750, and 172,750 shares outstanding	$ 150,000	$ 156,750	$ 172,750	$ 172,750
Surplus	1,350,000	1,410,750	1,554,750	1,554,750
Accumulated (deficit) earnings	15,660	(198,117)	(233,541)	(233,528)
Total stockholders' equity	$1,515,660	$ 1,369,383	$ 1,493,959	$ 1,493,972
	$3,809,524	$13,677,083	$17,071,822	$17,858,089

* Opened for business to public, June 20, 1984.

working capital in the holding company, the separate assets would approximate $1 million when computing bank ratios of liquidity and capital adequacy.

President Balk reviewed the consolidated financial statements, constituting primarily bank operations. He indicated that a single full

---

EXHIBIT 12B

FSC FINANCIAL CORPORATION
AND SUBSIDIARY
Consolidated Statements of Income

	Months Ended December 31 1984	Year Ended June 30 1985	Three Months Ended September 30 1985	Six Months Ended December 31 1985
Interest income				
Interest and fees on loans	$ 183,760	$ 733,196	$423,809	$ 866,809
Interest on U.S. Treasury securities and obligations of U.S. government agencies	28,755	63,082	36,177	81,557
Interest on federal funds sold.	75,921	108,887	30,590	49,108
Interest on deposits in banks	30,594	79,070	20,161	50,884
	$ 319,030	$1,024,235	$510,737	$1,048,358
Interest expense				
Interest on deposits	141,328	$ 444,743	$254,115	$ 535,545
Interest on other debt	32,455	59,883	12,210	24,568
	$ 173,783	$ 504,626	$266,325	$ 560,113
Net interest income	145,247	$ 519,609	$244,412	$ 488,245
Provision for loan losses	13,996	30,979	18,265	31,663
Net interest income after provision for loan losses	$ 131,251	$ 488,630	$226,147	$ 456,582
Other income				
Service charges on deposits	11,435	$ 38,203	$ 19,348	$ 40,524
Other	11,378	23,306	7,837	8,549
	$ 22,813	$ 61,509	$ 27,185	$ 49,073
Other expense				
Salaries and employee benefits	197,134	$ 421,272	$188,521	$ 316,716
Equipment and occupancy expense. . .	35,826	74,935	23,780	52,174
Other operating expenses	127,166	267,709	84,455	172,176
	$ 360,126	$ 763,916	$288,756	$ 541,066
Net (loss)	$(206,062)	$ (213,777)	$ (35,424)	$ (35,411)
Net (loss) per share of Common Stock . .	$ (1.37)	$ (1.42)	$ (.21)	$ (.21)

---

year of audited financial statements showing deficit operations did not provide sufficient data to permit traditional ROA or ROI analysis of earnings to assets and equity. The financial statements showed that the first fiscal year ending June 30, 1984, covered operations from only the opening date of June 20, 1984. A small net interest income was reported due to interest earning by the holding company on funds invested pending the beginning of depository operations by First Columbia. As initially projected, there was an operating deficit for the first full fiscal year of operations ending June 30, 1985. Although de-

EXHIBIT 12C

FCS FINANCIAL CORPORATION
AND SUBSIDIARY
FIRST COLUMBIA BANK
Consolidated Statements of Changes in Financial Position

	Six Months December 31 1984	Year Ended June 30 1985	Six Months December 31 1985
Financial resources provided			
Operations			
Net (loss)	$ (206,062)	$ (213,777)	$ (35,411)
Net (loss)	35,648	44,738	36,490
Provision for loan losses	13,996	30,979	31,663
Total resources provided by (used in) operations	$ (156,418)	$ (138,060)	$ (32,742)
Proceeds from sale of common stock	—	67,500	160,000
Increase in:			
Deposits	5,452,373	10,956,221	3,991,685
Accrued interest and other liabilities	—	57,615	91,398
Reduction in cash and due from banks	—	550,818	1,073,332
	$5,295,955	$11,494,094	$5,349,157
Financial resources applied			
Increase in:			
Cash and due from banks	$ 83,349	$ 786,878	$ —
Interest-bearing deposits in banks	800,000	—	701,730
Investment securities	459,843	476,545	1,421,178
Federal funds sold	—	1,200,000	600,000
Loans, net	3,813,423	8,774,758	2,518,796
Other assets	8,047	147,618	61,486
Reduction in bonds payable. . . .	—	—	26,666
Purchases of bank premises and equipment	107,969	108,295	19,301
Reduction in accrued interest and other liabilities	23,324	—	—
	$5,295,955	$11,494,094	$5,349,157

posit levels, interest revenues from bank operations, and fees from real estate mortgage lending activities were growing, the bank still was not operating at a profit. Comparing the results of operations for the three months ending September 30, 1985, and the six months ending December 31, 1985, shows substantial progress toward profitability. Unaudited information provided by Balk for the six months ending June 30, 1986, indicated gross revenue of $1,573,536, net earnings before taxes of $173,751, total deposits of $23,375,177, and total

FCS FINANCIAL CORPORATION
AND SUBSIDIARY
FIRST COLUMBIA BANK
Consolidated Statement of Changes in Stockholders' Equity

Fiscal Year-End June 30, 1985
Three Months Ended September 30, 1985
Six Months Ended December 31, 1985

| | Common Stock | | | | |
	Shares	Par Value	Surplus	Accumulated Deficit	Total
Balance, June 30, 1984	$150,000	$150,000	$1,350,000	$ 15,660	$1,515,660
Net (loss)				(213,777)	(213,777)
Sale of 6,750 shares of Common Stock	6,750	6,750	60,750	—	67,500
Balance, June 30, 1985	$156,750	$156,750	$1,410,750	$(198,117)	$1,369,383
Net (loss) three months ended September 30, 1985 (unaudited) . .				(35,424)	(35,424)
Sale of 16,000 shares Common Stock .	16,000	16,000	144,000	—	160,000
Balance, September 30, 1985 (unaudited)	$172,750	$172,750	$1,554,750	$(233,541)	$1,493,959
Net (loss) six months ended December 31, 1985				(35,411)	(35,411)
Balance, December 31, 1985				$(233,528)	$1,493,972

EXHIBIT 12E   Selected Notes to Consolidated Financial Statements

---

Note 2.   Investment Securities

Carrying amount and approximate values of investment securities are summarized as follows:

	June 30, 1985		September 30, 1985 (unaudited)	
	Carrying Amount	Approximate Market Value	Carrying Amount	Approximate Market Value
U.S. Treasury securities	$596,212	$607,700	$ 299,219	$ 308,100
Obligations of other U.S. government agencies	—	—	1,723,278	1,715,675
	$596,212	$607,700	$2,022,497	$2,023,775

Note 3.   Loans

Loans consisted of the following:

	June 30, 1985	September 30, 1985 (unaudited)
Real estate loans	$3,651,883	$ 3,545,817
Construction loans.	1,307,525	2,697,096
Commercial and personal loans—noninstallment . . .	1,203,129	1,968,732
Installment loans	2,685,789	3,484,531
	$8,848,326	$11,696,176
Allowance for loans losses	30,979	49,244
Loans, net.	$8,817,347	$11,646,932

Loans on which the accrual of interest has been discontinued or reduced amounted to $17,352 at June 30, 1985, and September 30, 1985 (unaudited).

---

capital of $2,109,301. It is expected that cumulative profitability (i.e., accumulated profits above accumulated losses) will be achieved in the quarter following June 30, 1986.

ADDITIONAL CAPITAL NEEDS

Capital Adequacy/Liquidity

Financial standards imposed by regulatory authorities were reviewed by President Balk. Banking regulations of the Federal Reserve Board and FDIC require that the bank maintain a minimum ratio of capital to assets. In addition, federal banking regulations require the bank to maintain an amount of liquid assets equal to at least 20 percent of deposit liabilities. On September 30, 1985, the board of directors determined that the bank's 7.75 percent ratio of capital to assets was less than desirable for a small growing financial institution such as First Columbia. Although the bank's liquidity position is enhanced by the issuance of capital stock and the operation of the mortgage banking

EXHIBIT 12F Selected Notes to Consolidated Financial Statements

Note: Bonds payable

The corporation borrowed $800,000 from the Development Authority of Columbia County, Georgia, through the issuance of industrial development revenue bonds which were subsequently sold to the Trust Company Bank of Augusta. The principal of these bonds is payable in 60 equal quarterly installments plus accrued interest, with the first installment due on October 1, 1985, and subsequent installments due on each January 1, April 1, July 1, October 1 thereafter. The bonds bear interest on the unpaid principal balance equal to 64 percent of prime, not to exceed 11 percent per annum or to be less than 6 percent per annum.

Maturities of bonds payable for each of the five years succeeding June 30, 1985, and September 30, 1985 (unaudited) are as follows:

June 30 and September 30	Bonds Payable
1986	$ 40,000
1987	53,333
1988	53,333
1989	53,333
1990	53,333
Thereafter	546,668
	$800,000

Note 8: Commitments and contingencies

In the normal course of business there are loan commitments that are not reflected in the financial statements. These include commitments to extend credit and letters of credit.

Commitments to extend credit totaled $2,426,510 and $1,535,980 at June 30, 1985, and September 30, 1985 (unaudited), respectively.

The bank does not anticipate any material losses as a result of the commitments and contingent liabilities.

The nature of the business of the bank is such that it ordinarily results in a certain amount of litigation. In the opinion of management and counsel for the bank, there is no litigation in which the outcome will have a material effect on the financial statements.

activity as a secondary market activity, more capital was needed to support the growth potential of First Columbia. The board must immediately address the issue of raising additional capital.

Alternatives

The board projected the amount of funds needed to support the bank's growth, liquidity, capital ratio, and the expanded real estate mortgage banking operation to be in the range of $1,600,000 to $2,000,000. Traditional sources of capital are earnings, debt, and stock issue. For a new organization still in the deficit operating, expansion of capital through the generation and retention of bank earnings is obviously not feasible. Additionally, debt as a source of capital for holding company expansion is limited by the existing loan outstanding used to finance the construction of the bank's business offices.

The board explored the third option to raise capital. Additional stock could be sold by directors of the holding company, thereby minimizing expenses. The board determined that a stock offering of $1,875,000 would provide net proceeds of $1,831,000 after estimated expenses of $44,000. The proceeds could provide $600,000 to acquire additional stock of the bank and thereby increase its invested capital. In addition, $1 million would be available for the holding company to invest in organizing or acquiring a mortgage banking subsidiary. The balance of $231,000 would be available for additional working capital as needed. The initial offering of the holding company common stock had been priced at $10 per share for 150,000 shares to raise the desired amount. There is no public market for the existing common stock of the holding company, and there can be assurance to potential investors that such an established market will develop after the stock issue. Without any record of earnings and no existing market, the pricing of the stock issue will be purely arbitrary.

It is essential to consider the potential dilution effects the stock issue might have on shareholders and to develop a consolidated pro forma financial statement showing the equity position of the holding company after the proposed stock issue.

30. Southern Federal Savings and Loan Association

(A)

Southern Federal Savings and Loan Association grew from $15 million to over $160 million in assets between 1960 and 1980. In July 1980, the association's officers were taking steps to introduce new services and activities allowed by the Depository Institutions Deregulation and Monetary Act of 1980. In commenting on Southern Federal's approach to these changes, Mr. Knight, the chief executive officer, explained:

> Realizing that tremendous changes are going on in the banking world and the world of finance, we can't just sit here and say that we're going to be able to survive in the foreseeable future by operating just like we have in the past. I don't think we can do it. I've been telling our people for a year and a half that we're just not going to get the money in like we have; the game has changed. When they loosened up and went with CDs, that was the beginning of a great, great change in this business. Now with deregulation, it's a totally new ballgame!

THE IMPACT OF DEREGULATION

Savings and loan associations are not unfamiliar with changing regulations. Between 1968 and 1977, regulatory changes came with increasing regularity—everything from truth-in-lending to equal rights as shown in Table 1.

New regulatory changes, however, open up competition between financial institutions. President Carter signed the 1980 Depository Institutions Deregulation and Monetary Control Act into law on March 31, 1980, after four years of efforts by bankers to equalize competition in, to update, and to reform the financial industry. The new law included major provisions covering (1) expanded Federal Reserve Board management of the monetary system, (2) the phaseout of interest ceilings on deposits, (3) permanent authority for financial services of automatic transfers, remote service units and share drafts, and ex-

---

This case was prepared by William R. Boulton and James A. Verbrugge, University of Georgia.

TABLE 1 Federal Legislation Affecting Savings Association Mortgage Lending

Item	Year	Item	Year
Truth-in-Lending Act	1958	Home Mortgage Disclosure Act	1975
Fair Housing Act	1968	Amendments to the Real Estate	
Fair Credit Reporting Act	1970	Settlement Procedure Act	1976
Flood Disaster Protection Act	1973	Amendments to the Equal	
Real Estate Settlement		Credit Opportunity Act	1976
Procedures Act	1973	Amendments to the Flood	
Equal Credit Opportunity Act	1974	Disaster Protection Act	1976
Amendments to the		Consumer Leasing Act	1976
Truth-in-Lending Act	1974	Community Reinvestment Act	1977
Fair Credit Billing Act	1974		

SOURCE: U.S. League of Savings Associations.

---

tension of NOW accounts nationwide, (4) expanded powers, especially in the areas of consumer credit and trusts, for S&Ls and federal MSBs, (5) a federal override of state usury laws, and (6) simplified disclosure requirements for truth-in-lending. Some key aspects of this deregulation include the following:

Regulation Q. Controls on interest rate ceilings will be phased out by March 31, 1986. The rate of the phaseout will be determined by a newly formed deregulation committee, composed of the Treasury, the Fed, FDIC,[1] FHLBB,[2] and FCUA,[3] to reach market rates as soon as feasible. The new law suggests an annual 25 percent phaseout through March 1983 and 50 percent annual phaseouts thereafter. Thrifts retain their 25 percent rate differential during the phaseout.

Federal Reserve controls. The Fed's control over the monetary system is expanded to all depository institutions for all transaction accounts and for all nonpersonal time deposits. Fed members will be phased into the new requirements by 1984, while nonmember and nonbank depository institutions will be brought under the requirements by 1988. The law will (1) reduce current reserve requirements for all Fed members, (2) require reserves for NOW accounts beginning December 31, 1980, (3) provide all depository institutions access to the Fed's discount window, and (4) require all nonmember and nonbank institutions to transmit required reserves to the Fed by March 31, 1988.

State usury laws. State usury laws for home mortgage loans, including mobile homes, are set aside as of April 1, 1980, unless reimposed by state action by April 1, 1983. All business and agricultural

---

[1] Federal Deposit Insurance Corporation.

[2] Federal Home Loan Bank Board.

[3] Federal Credit Union Administration.

EXHIBIT 1 Southern Federal Savings and Loan Association Statement of Condition for Southern Federal, 1973–1979 (thousands of $)

	1979	1978	1977	1976	1975	1974	1973
Assets							
Mortgage loans and contracts*	$130,154	$119,327	$105,577	$ 84,055	$75,809	$65,480	$55,485
VA guaranteed	2,651	2,581	2,374	1,911	1,762	1,585	1,229
FHA-HUD	302	437	259	111	270	191	199
Conventional	126,445	116,000	100,723	81,825	71,597	61,881	54,042
Other loans*	5,067	3,727	3,078	2,050	1,070	926	745
Serviced by savings accounts	3,528	2,291	1,841	1,049	510	569	472
Unsecured property improvement	1,062	1,045	399	599	350	174	110
	0	0	0	0	0	0	0
Mobile home	502	249	222	201	194	162	155
Unsecured education	99	91	71	179	0	10	0
Other	19,534	17,842	18,026	16,112	12,842	7,034	9,051
Cash and investment securities*	549	163	637	329	288	335	410
Cash and demand deposits eligible for liquidity	17,195	14,923	13,807	14,154	11,496	6,159	8,098
Investment securities eligible for liquidity	1,002	923	734	630	554	467	400
FHLB stock	0	54	0	0	0	0	0
Real estate owned*	1,708	1,515	1,424	1,225	1,207	1,086	713
Fixed assets (net)							
Mortgage backed securities and mortgage participation guaranteed by federal agencies	3,536	5,869	2,757	3,129	1,471	1,022	0
Total assets*	$160,475	$146,607	$129,263	$106,343	$90,720	$75,858	$66,290

* Indicates subtotal or total.

EXHIBIT 1 *(concluded)*

	1979	1978	1977	1976	1975	1974	1973
Liabilities							
Savings accounts*	$145,775	$131,595	$115,980	$ 97,182	$80,991	$65,804	$59,041
Earning in excess of regular rate	119,951	101,484	85,981	68,969	54,936	42,589	55,459
Accounts greater than $100,000	4,474	719	388	616	N.C.	N.C.	N.C.
Accounts less than $100,000	115,477	100,765	85,593	68,352	N.C.	N.C.	N.C.
Earning at or below regular rate	25,822	30,111	51,999	23,214	26,055	23,215	25,581
Borrowed money*	1,215	2,522	1,945	730	730	730	0
FHLB advances	1,215	730	730	730	730	730	0
Other	0	1,792	1,215	0	0	0	0
Debentures	0	0	0	0	0	0	0
Loans in process	1,204	2,215	2,452	1,200	2,128	481	1,626
Specific reserves	15	14	6	4	3	2	0
Deferred credits	860	1,018	781	672	606	365	320
Total liabilities*	$150,649	$158,005	$121,684	$100,208	$84,762	$68,494	$61,521
Net worth							
Permanent stock and paid-in surplus	$ 0	$ 0	$ 0	$ 0	$ 0	$ 0	$ 0
General reserves	4,916	4,916	4,190	3,554	3,454	3,304	2,954
Other reserves	0	0	0	0	0	0	0
Surplus and undivided profits	4,910	3,686	3,389	3,086	2,505	2,061	1,814
Total net worth*	$ 9,825	$ 8,602	$ 7,579	$ 6,640	$ 5,959	$ 5,364	$ 4,768
Total liabilities and net worth*	$160,475	$146,607	$129,263	$106,848	$90,720	$75,358	$66,290

loans over $25,000 can also be made for up to 5 percent over the discount rate plus surcharge of the Fed's regional bank. All federally insured institutions are allowed to lend at up to 1 percent over the discount rate.

Truth-in-Lending. Financial regulators are allowed to order repayments to customers for Truth-in-Lending violations where the pattern finance charges on APRs since January 1, 1977, have been inaccurately disclosed beyond 25 percent of the exact figure (within certain provisions and limited creditor civil liability).

Provisions for thrifts and CUs. S&Ls and federal mutual savings banks are allowed to add services and credit unions are freed from their 12 percent interest ceiling for loans. Federally insured S&Ls can (1) operate remote service units, (2) offer NOW accounts effective December 13, 1980, (3) offer lines of credit, consumer loans, and credit cards, (4) offer mortgage loans of unlimited amounts, and (5) lend to customers without geographic restrictions. S&Ls can invest up to 20 percent of assets in consumer loans, commercial paper, and corporate debt securities. Credit unions are allowed to offer share drafts and raise the interest limit on loans to 15 percent. Savings and loan associations were now allowed to broaden their services, thereby competing more directly with other financial institutions. With regard to these changes, Jack Pope, vice president of Southern Federal, commented:

> Since I've been with Southern Federal, we've never had so many significant changes at one time. With the suddenness in which deregulation is coming, the advantage is shifting to the commercial banks because they already have the branches and have a head start. It will take S&Ls a long time to catch up.

HISTORY AND BACKGROUND OF SOUTHERN FEDERAL

Southern Federal Savings and Loan Association was incorporated in 1929 as the Mutual Building and Loan Association. The association didn't really get going until the 1930s when it became a federal association. In 1935, its name was changed to the Southern Federal Savings and Loan Association, commonly known as Southern Federal.

Since Southern Federal's beginning, it has had four presidents serving the periods 1929–1931, 1931–1943, 1943–1964, and 1964 to the present. Long tenures became the tradition; Mr. Knight was currently serving his 16th year as president and chief executive officer.

Between 1960 and 1970, Southern Federal more than doubled its assets from $15 to $39 million. By 1978, assets increased to over 10 times the 1960 level reaching $160 million. As shown in Southern Federal's financial statements (Exhibits 1 and 2), the association more than doubled in size during the past five years. Exhibits 3 and 4 show

EXHIBIT 2 Southern Federal Savings and Loan Association Income and Expenses for Southern Federal, 1973–1979 (thousands of $)

	1979	1978	1977	1976	1975	1974	1973
Gross operating income							
Interest*.	$13,296	$10,965	$9,081	$7,646	$6,230	$5,155	$4,339
On mortgage loans	11,080	9,139	7,427	6,303	5,378	4,527	3,689
On investment securities							
and deposits	1,488	1,235	1,163	1,090	778	559	605
On other loans	417	342	242	158	74	69	45
On mortgage participation,							
mortgage-backed							
securities	311	249	249	95	—	—	—
Fee income	392	482	613	328	318	253	257
Other	130	101	49	49	48	58	44
Total*	$13,818	$11,548	$9,743	$8,023	$6,596	$5,466	$4,640
Operating expense							
Compensation and other							
benefits	$ 854	$ 853	$ 708	$ 593	$ 496	$ 436	$ 337
Office occupancy	299	283	250	221	188	139	153
Advertising	68	73	72	65	70	47	64
Other	$ 351	$ 353	$ 304	$ 257	$ 196	$ 168	$ 153
Total*	$ 1,572	$ 1,562	$1,334	$1,136	$ 950	$ 790	$ 707
Cost of funds							
Interest on savings accounts							
certificates	$ 8,605	$ 6,695	$5,396	$4,509	$3,500	$2,589	$1,913
Interest on savings accounts							
passbooks	1,551	1,682	1,612	1,450	1,289	1,218	1,138
Interest on borrowed money . .	103	86	65	58	55	0	0
Total*	$10,259	$ 8,463	$7,073	$6,017	$4,844	$3,807	$3,051
Nonoperating income	$ 13	$ 1	$ 20	$ 84	$ 7	$ 4	$ 1
Nonoperating expense.	239	3	3	3	8	41	1
Income taxes: federal and							
state*	538	499	414	264	207	220	252
Net income*	$ 1,223	$ 1,023	$ 939	$ 688	$ 595	$ 611	$ 631

* Indicates subtotal or total.

comparative financial statements for all FSLIC-insured savings and loan associations in the industry. During this time, the nature of Southern Federal's business also continued to change. James Redding, Jr., Southern Federal's executive vice president, explained how different the loan side of the business had become.

When I first came here, they had all their notes printed with 5½ percent like it was always going to be 5½ percent interest. We were probably paying 4 percent on savings back in the 1960s. We continued that for a good while and did some FHA and VA loans. Our loans were primarily residential, though we would make a church loan or rental property loan.

As both the lending and savings aspects changed, they added the 90 percent loan so you could lend 90 percent of the value. Later on, residential loans went to 95 percent where you only needed five percent down.

EXHIBIT 3 Southern Federal Savings and Loan Association Assets, Liabilities, and Net Worth: All Associations in State, 1973–1979 (thousands of $)

	1979	1978	1977	1976	1975	1974	1973
Assets							
Mortgage loans and contracts*	$ 8,699,063	$8,036,401	$7,179,452	$6,278,727	$5,493,408	$4,918,079	$4,566,741
VA guaranteed	85,370	87,206	87,374	87,105	86,452	87,099	89,145
FHA-HUD	51,100	52,631	56,094	59,403	64,616	72,034	75,989
Conventional	8,527,492	7,864,218	7,002,309	6,106,816	5,331,931	4,754,501	4,398,996
Other loans*	333,137	224,177	108,951	184,043	173,087	174,427	176,552
Secured by savings accounts	231,737	154,938	107,364	54,656	67,505	60,955	57,711
Unsecured property improvement	35,350	29,727	28,207	29,041	23,851	17,352	10,081
Mobile home	31,572	33,753	50,254	56,205	68,714	84,707	97,645
Unsecured education	18,235	14,146	12,113	11,673	11,254	10,410	9,697
Other	15,544	11,613	11,033	2,470	1,763	1,003	1,118
Cash and investment securities*	367,047	780,363	665,256	617,046	538,490	424,675	393,773
Cash and demand deposits eligible for liquidity	58,967	43,501	48,650	54,473	57,708	55,115	50,249
Investment securities eligible for liquidity	459,612	626,210	535,631	494,384	417,366	303,353	285,282
FHLB stock	76,213	67,509	58,628	55,595	51,102	50,954	45,183
All other	72,255	43,143	22,346	14,596	12,314	16,253	15,059
Real estate owned*	19,034	27,395	43,922	53,895	38,784	8,976	1,225
Acquired by foreclosure	18,541	26,955	43,557	52,722	38,174	8,735	1,477
Other	192	440	440	1,171	610	240	448
Fixed assets (net)	148,136	144,453	139,392	133,867	124,349	109,255	92,570
Mortgage backed securities and mortgage participation guaranteed by federal agencies	109,404	111,178	84,977	35,557	48,098	18,352	14,119
Other assets*	75,855	71,103	69,357	57,424	64,920	62,652	46,950
Total assets*	$10,235,312	$9,377,944	$8,372,119	$7,356,655	$6,470,620	5,713,000	$5,291,945

EXHIBIT 3 *(concluded)*

	1979	1978	1977	1976	1975	1974	1973
Liabilities and net worth							
Borrowed money*	698,532	606,983	461,445	375,934	499,888	551,187	487,364
FHLB advances	420,520	535,446	388,228	347,506	427,725	518,715	464,294
Other	62,004	55,537	57,218	11,728	6,165	16,442	7,270
Debentures	16,000	16,000	16,000	16,000	16,000	16,000	16,000
Loans in process	157,304	146,334	138,383	93,381	74,254	51,979	83,388
Specific reserves	1,687	2,020	3,701	3,915	4,863	2,174	1,308
Deferred credits	36,726	31,167	39,150	30,924	74,161	63,976	68,311
Other liabilities	98,022	63,037	44,789	57,159	32,644	31,110	29,498
Total liabilities*	$ 9,637,119	$8,347,939	$7,206,502	$6,935,066	$6,080,746	$5,540,832	$4,347,822
Net worth							
Permanent stock and paid-in surplus	$ 0	$ 0	$ 0	$ 0	$ 0	$ 0	$ 0
General reserves	383,419	345,338	300,530	259,258	239,369	216,196	199,141
Other reserves	2,070	2,073	2,008	2,107	2,267	1,929	3,050
Surplus and undivided profits	212,704	182,593	162,976	149,907	148,057	153,384	141,936
Total net worth*	$ 598,194	$ 530,005	$ 465,563	$ 421,271	$ 389,373	$ 372,208	$ 344,127
Total liabilities and net worth*	$10,235,312	$9,377,944	$8,372,119	$7,356,655	$6,470,620	$5,713,040	$5,291,948

* Indicates subtotal or total.

EXHIBIT 4 Southern Federal Savings and Loan Association Income and Expense All Associations in State, 1973–1979 (thousands of $)

	1979	1978	1977	1976	1975	1974	1973
Gross operating income							
Interest	$813,770	$692,693	$589,169	$509,808	$444,546	$404,456	$353,722
On mortgage loans	711,757	623,474	537,436	462,036	399,388	359,259	218,179
On investment securities and deposits	78,441	51,726	36,792	34,982	33,695	33,439	24,754
Other	23,572	17,494	14,941	12,791	11,463	11,857	10,788
Fees and discounts on loans	37,264	36,232	36,173	30,305	25,307	20,389	23,777
All other	27,443	23,263	19,375	17,581	8,213	6,685	6,517
Total*	878,477	752,188	644,717	557,695	478,065	431,530	384,016
Operating expense							
Compensation and other benefits	61,514	54,814	49,129	43,565	39,742	37,032	31,786
Office occupancy	12,970	11,646	11,142	10,335	9,151	7,868	6,863
Advertising	8,981	6,942	6,189	6,340	6,751	7,788	7,650
Other	44,594	39,484	37,244	34,774	26,205	22,138	18,679
Total*	128,058	112,885	103,705	95,015	81,848	74,827	64,979
Cost of funds							
Interest on savings accounts	598,089	503,829	444,433	383,828	323,782	273,710	228,231
Interest on borrowed money	58,853	42,775	27,026	30,027	35,623	40,928	27,577
Total*	656,942	545,604	471,458	413,855	359,405	314,637	255,808
Nonoperating income	6,043	4,653	5,946	5,145	4,271	4,746	4,169
Nonoperating expense	5,162	5,809	8,263	8,935	11,446	6,610	4,094
Income taxes*	25,699	26,479	18,681	12,100	8,594	10,864	16,027
Federal	25,645	26,441	18,618	12,019	8,514	10,864	15,990
State, local, and other	54	38	63	81	81	0	37
Net income*	$ 68,658	$ 65,064	$ 48,556	$ 32,933	$ 21,043	$ 29,338	$ 47,277

* Indicates subtotal or total.

Then we got into land development—you know, financing subdivisions and lot development. Then they liberalized the amounts you could lend on apartment and commercial properties as a percent of total assets. They added student loans. I think property improvement loans came since I've been here. The wobbly boxes—mobile homes—we never have done much of that.

At one point in time, they added nursing homes. You know, we had no need for nursing homes in 1960 because folks were kept at home, but the welfare state and mobility of people have changed. We financed the first one out here, the Heritage. They financed it for 6½ percent. We charged 6 percent on residential so we stuck them with another half of a percent.

The condominium concept came, and we made the first condominium loan in town, about nine years ago. There were 44 units, and it took three years from the day they broke ground until they finished and sold them out.

Exhibit 5 shows Southern Federal's mortgage loan composition from 1973 through 1979.

Redding also explained how the savings side of business changed.

Going back to the savings end, we now go for the jumbo accounts. We bid on university money, state money, city money, county money, and individual's money of $100,000 or more.

Of course, we've come up with various certificates. It used to be just a passbook. Now you've got the 90-day notice account passbook; the one-year CD and 30-month CD; and the six-month, $10,000 money market certificate. We still sell a four, a six, and an eight year if somebody wants it. We can go up to 10 years with a 30-month CD—we go 3 years on the stated rate and shave it off after 3 years. It's 9½ percent on the money market and 9¼ percent after 3 years for a 10-year one, compounded daily. It used to be that we paid semiannually, then we started paying quarterly; compounding daily; and now we pay it monthly if you have a sizable account.

Exhibit 1 provides a detailed breakdown of Southern Federal's mix of savings and loan business.

Not only did Southern Federal's savings and loan activities change, but their base of operations also grew rapidly through the establishment of new branches as seen in Exhibit 6. Redding explained their approach to branching.

We've been out at Eastside Mall for about 10 years. It was a matter of feeling like that was a good area out there. The banks were branching so we followed the banks out there, and that's turned out to be a good spot.

We went out and set up another branch on South Rim Road Mall, and that's been a mediocre spot. We then started looking outside South County—looked at about six neighboring counties. I went to the county courthouses and looked at the mortgage loan records. To the south of here, about 90 percent of the mortgage activity was Farm Home Administration. I noticed a good bit of activity in counties west of us and, after

EXHIBIT 5 Southern Federal Savings and Loan Association Southern Federal's Mortgage Loan Composition, 1973–1979 (thousands of $)

	Total Mortgage Loans, Including Mortgage Participations*	Total Insured Loans (VA, FHA, HUD)	Total Conventional Loans	Mortgage Participations, Mortgage-Backed Securities	Total Single-Family Loans	Total Multifamily Loans	Other RE, Improved RE, Land Loans, Other
1979	$133,670	$2,933	$126,443	$5,536	$100,607	$14,753	$14,016
1978	123,196	3,018	116,000	3,869	88,147	13,771	17,100
1977	100,334	2,633	100,723	2,757	79,861	11,719	11,776
1976	87,165	2,022	81,825	3,130	65,096	9,051	9,699
1975	75,280	2,032	71,597	1,471	56,160	8,275	9,193
1974	64,501	1,574	61,881	1,021	47,033	7,765	8,656
1973	55,483	1,428	54,042	0	40,405	7,497	7,568
Percentage							
1979	100.0	.022	.946	.026	.753	.110	.105
1978	100.0	.024	.942	.031	.716	.112	.139
1977	100.0	.025	.947	.026	.751	.110	.111
1976	100.0	.023	.939	.036	.747	.104	.111
1975	100.0	.027	.951	.020	.746	.110	.122
1974	100.0	.024	.959	.016	.729	.120	.134
1973	100.0	.022	.974	.000	.728	.135	.136

* Individual loan types will not add to total mortgage loans because some loans appear in several categories.

EXHIBIT 6 Southern Federal Savings and Loan Association: Deposits by Branch Office 1971–1979 (thousands of $)

	Main Office	Eastside Mall	South Rim Mall	Lake County	River County	Total
1979	$94,028	$26,112	$9,471	$8,875	$3,335	$141,821
1978	90,437	22,149	7,322	6,656	2,160	128,724
1977	83,448	17,673	5,060	4,450	886	111,517
1976	75,653	13,193	2,763	3,828	—	95,437
1975	65,016	10,663	1,257	1,282	—	78,218
1974	57,568	6,408	—	—	—	63,976
1973	53,866	2,664	—	—	—	56,530
1972	47,251	—	—	—	—	47,251
1971	58,382	—	—	—	—	38,382

studying the population growth and a few other demographics, selected Lakeview in Lake County. It was a good spot as far as loan volume and sales. We went to the River County, just south of us, because we heard someone else was going out there. It's been sort of a stepchild—it's out there and doing about four million. I don't think you can get profitable until you reach six or seven million.

We then started questioning whether we were going to put in a computer with all these new things coming up, changes and running out of space. This building (the main office) was designed for $50 million in business and leisurely living—so we had to chop around on it until it began looking choppy. We thought about adding on, or raising the roof, or going downstairs or into the parking lot. We decided we would go out on North Highway with an operations office; then we decided to put a branch in it while we were there. The branch then kind of became the tail that wagged the dog—and it's a real nice branch. We sent a lady out there who had a big following in savings, and she's done real well so far—it's just amazing. I think the location is good on the bypass. You can come around town now on the new bypass in just no time. It's given a lot of convenience to that spot. We have space out there with a big basement, if we ever put in a computer.

In addition to the development of its branches, Southern Federal also completed a recent merger with the Building and Loan Association of North County. In discussing the merger's background, Redding explained:

We decided we wanted to play the big game. We'd been talking to the president of North County B&L and dealing with his people for a good 10 years. It started when two associations wanted to move into the neighboring county and we both objected. At that time, someone suggested that North County B&L wasn't going to survive and rubbed his feathers the wrong way.

Since that time, we kept an eye on North County's operation. Two years ago, they decided they could merge with us. It took a year and a half to finally get it consummated. That was a lot of work. The Home Loan

TABLE 2 Private Housing Starts, by Regions

Region	Number of Units				Percentage Distribution			
	1975	1976	1977	1978*	1975	1976	1977	1978*
Northeast	149,200	169,200	201,600	200,000	12.9%	11.0%	10.1%	9.9%
North Central	294,000	400,100	464,600	449,500	25.3	26.0	23.4	22.3
South	442,100	568,500	783,100	824,100	38.1	37.0	39.4	40.8
West	275,100	399,600	537,900	544,900	23.7	26.0	27.1	27.0
Entire U.S.	1,160,400	1,537,500	1,987,100	2,018,500	100.0%	100.0%	100.0%	100.0%

* Preliminary.
Note: Components may not add to totals due to rounding.
SOURCE: Bureau of the Census.

Bank was mighty slow, and we finally got some outside help. In the meantime, we had to worry with the thing up there, trying to get the salaries the same as ours—that's a big problem with a merger. You either have it too low or too high—kind of like the farmers, either too wet or too dry. That was the last state-chartered association and it was a $14 million dollar outfit.

THE SOUTHERN COUNTY FINANCIAL MARKET

Southern County, located 65 miles from a major southern metropolitan center, is part of the rapidly growing Sunbelt and continues to attract new families. Housing starts in the South represented over 40 percent of all housing starts in the U.S. as shown in Table 2.

South County lies just below the foothills of a scenic mountain range and was the site of one of the state's major educational institutions. Its social and cultural attractions to families of wealth were evident by the fine federal-style homes and grand mansions with massive columns and beautiful formal gardens.

While South County was one of the smallest in the state, it was in the top 7 percent of counties in population with over 80,000 residents. The city dominated the county with 55,000 residents and was the major retail center, drawing over 300,000 residents into its trading area. Over 100 manufacturers and processors employed over 10,000 persons, while four industrial parks continued to attract new industry. The university, with over 18,000 students, provided over 9,000 full- and part-time jobs.

Continued growth in South County can be seen by the deposit base growth in Exhibit 7. For example, deposits grew from $261 million in 1975, to $380 million in 1979, a 46 percent increase over the period. The two savings and loan associations accounted for nearly 50 percent of the total, having grown 68 percent since 1975. The four area banks increased by only 27 percent during this period.

EXHIBIT 7 Southern Federal Savings and Loan Association: Summary of Deposits in Commercial Banks and S&L Associations in South County, 1974–1979 (thousands of $)

	Total Bank Time and Savings Deposits	Total Bank Deposits	Total S&L Deposits	Deposits in Commercial Banks						
				Total Bank and S&L Deposits	Demand Deposits	Public Demand Deposits	Savings Deposits	Other Time Deposits	Public Time and Savings	All Other
1979	$95,234	$192,886	$187,631	$380,517	$75,349	$17,360	$25,603	$55,047	$14,584	$4,943
1978	80,535	179,942	175,523	355,465	69,263	25,265	25,153	42,848	12,534	4,879
1977	76,329	160,390	156,011	316,401	61,908	17,405	23,443	38,053	14,833	4,748
1976	72,917	150,843	123,219	283,062	58,282	14,997	19,715	42,664	10,540	4,647
1975	77,128	150,159	111,000	261,159	56,307	10,156	16,667	37,097	23,364	6,568
1974	54,521	151,609	93,487	245,096	54,364	56,901	14,310	40,211	0	5,823

	Savings & Loan Associations		Commercial Banks	
	Number of Associations	Number of Offices	Number of Banks	Number of Offices
1980	2	6	4	14
1979	2	5	4	15
1978	2	5	4	10
1977	2	5	4	10
1976	2	5	3	9
1975	2	5	3	9
1974	2	4	3	9

Southern Federal Savings and Loan is the largest financial institution in the area, with over $130 million in deposits in 1979—a 34 percent share of the deposit market. The Republic Bank held a 23 percent market share ($87 million); followed by the First National Bank with 19 percent ($74 million); and First Federal Savings and Loan with 15 percent ($58 million). First American Bank held only 7 percent of the market ($26.6 million); followed by a new 1977 entry, South Bank and Trust, which held only 1 percent ($5.5 million) in deposits by 1979.

Exhibit 8 shows a breakdown of all the financial institutions in South County. By 1979, they had all branched beyond the downtown shopping area into the new shopping malls—Eastside Mall, South Rim Mall, and Westgate Plaza. New branches were recently opened by First American and South Bank on the major throughway passing Eastside Mall. In fact, major growth was expected to occur beyond the Eastside Mall area as a regional shopping mall was to be built just beyond South County.

First National Bank had long-established branches across from Eastside Mall, in Westgate Plaza, and University Avenue; but all these branches appeared to be losing business and be marginal operations. Republic Bank, the South County branch of a multibillion dollar regional bank, had growing locations downtown (near the university), on the street leading from downtown into the North Highway, in the Eastside Mall, and in South Rim Mall. Southern Federal S&L had one

EXHIBIT 8 Southern Federal Savings and Loan Association Summary of Deposits for Commercial Banks and S&L Associations in South County by Branch, 1974–1979 (thousands of $)

First National Bank

	Downtown	Eastside Mall	Westgate Plaza	University Avenue	Total
1979	64,685	3,979	2,798	2,048	73,510
1978	64,398	3,815	2,758	1,992	72,943
1977	51,172	4,599	3,300	2,400	61,471
1976	25,842	14,357	11,485	5,745	57,427
1975	38,012	5,231	12,747	4,300	60,340
1974	55,442	11,623	9,168	4,758	60,991

Republic Bank

	Downtown	North Highway	Eastside Mall	South Rim Mall	University Extention	Total
1979	54,819	14,317	14,317	6,615	0	87,158
1978	51,197	8,841	12,033	4,744	0	76,815
1977	49,455	7,947	11,134	3,990	0	72,526
1976	50,658	7,704	9,825	3,215	—	71,402
1975	49,989	6,953	9,761	3,263	—	69,966
1974	52,711	6,404	8,884	2,404	—	70,403

EXHIBIT 8 *(concluded)*

First American Bank

	Downtown	Metropolitan Highway	Total
1979	26,628	108	26,636
1978	26,008	—	26,008
1977	24,055	—	24,053
1976	22,014	—	22,014
1975	19,853	—	19,853
1974	20,215	—	20,215

South Bank & Trust

	Main	Metropolitan Highway	Total
1979	5,079	403	5,482
1978	4,176	—	4,176
1977	2,358	—	2,338
1976	—	—	—
1975	—	—	—
1974	—	—	—

Southern Federal Savings & Loan

	Main	Eastside Mall	South Rim Mall	Total
1979	94,028	26,112	9,471	129,611
1978	90,437	22,149	7,322	119,908
1977	83,448	17,673	5,060	106,181
1976	75,655	13,193	2,763	91,609
1975	65,016	10,663	1,257	76,956
1974	57,568	6,408	—	63,976

First Federal Savings & Loan

	Main	Westgate Mall	Total
1979	52,600	5,419	58,019
1978	51,390	4,225	55,615
1977	44,953	4,877	59,830
1976	38,310	3,600	41,610
1975	32,785	1,279	34,064
1974	29,242	269	29,511

---

branch in Westgate Plaza. First American Bank had just opened its first branch across from South Bank and Trust on the main highway out of town, as mentioned previously.

Southern Federal's growth in the financial community had not been accidental. "Personally, I like to play the offense rather than the defense," explained Knight. "I guess I'm lazy—I think its easier." Adding new services had been part of their offense. Redding explained:

We haven't gone overboard though. We've been in on a conservative basis: land development, condos, commercials, lot loans. A fella can buy a lot and we'll finance it, pay it out in five years.

MANAGING THE INVESTMENT PORTFOLIO

The loan committee at Southern Federal includes Knight, Redding, and Bob Thompson. In describing their processing of loan applications, Redding explained:

Surprisingly, the branches are kind of like laundry pickup stations. You leave the laundry there and it's brought down to the main office and washed. Branches are primarily for savings. They seldom take loan applications, except for North County. Folks come down to the main office to make loan applications. I guess they know that's where the answer is going to come from anyway, and that's the way we operate; we bring them all in here for the loan committee meeting once or twice a week.

We don't have any schedule here; we look at the calendar and set every third Tuesday or fourth Wednesday. We're only meeting once a week now with the loan volume off. We don't set a fixed schedule, but maybe that's wrong and we'll have to do that as we get bigger. I think the lending operation is just a kind of bull session. We have Bob Thompson in charge of the mortgage loan department and taking applications. Occasionally, I'll take an application too.

When Redding was asked why Southern Federal had done so well with its loan portfolio in limiting bad loans, he replied:

Well, I guess inflation has saved most of us. I'd hate to be thrust in the business of making loans with no inflation. I don't know if we could survive or not. But then I think South County has been protected from the economic ups and downs with the university and the technical school here. It's been pretty steady. We haven't been hit hard. Although, as we get more industrialized, things like that will affect us more.

We're lending on about 80 percent residential property. Everybody has to have a house; a house is just basic, and this has been growing.

But during the recent escalation of home mortgage rates, Southern Federal pulled out of the residential market. Knight explained:

It worries us if we have to pull out of the mortgage business. In the 16 years that I've been here, we've only pulled out of mortgage lending one time, and that was in recent times with the escalation of interest rates. You would come in and make an application to us, and we would quote you a fair rate, but before we could get your loan processed and closed, we would be paying more for the money than the rate we quoted you. Well, it didn't take me too long to realize that we were playing a losing game here. So we said, "Until the dust settles, so to speak, we are going to pull out of mortgage lending. We've got the money, but we don't know what to quote you unless we quote a rate that is going to insult you. So right now we're just not going to make any quotes." So we pulled out for about eight weeks, because it didn't make any sense.

We were taking that money and matching up six-month money markets; we were paying 14 percent—we were probably getting 16 percent on like terms through channels we could invest in. Now we got through that and we got back in and there was a backlog of loans. So we've been just as active as we could be for about the last eight weeks.

Regarding Southern Federal's success in its commercial loan involvement, Knight further explained:

We're going to be aggressive and go after business, but when it doesn't look like it's good business, we're going to back off. James Redding, who at times acts kind of radical, is really a conservative when it comes down to money and the way it goes out of here. After appraising one project, he said, "They don't have enough income-producing units. There is no way this thing can go!" Since that was a friend of mine, we dodged it by saying, "At this time, we don't believe we can appraise it for enough money to generate what you are asking for it." We didn't do it.

On big loans, like the local Holiday Inn, we felt that for our size we should sell half that loan. We also participated in another Holiday Inn because we could get a 90 percent guarantee from Farmer's Home Administration. I think that's being aggressive in getting out and getting loans but, at the same time, we feel fairly secure.

But we miss them. If you don't occasionally make a mistake, you're probably not making enough loans. You're ultraconservative I'd say. Now hopefully that mistake will be in the realm where it takes time on somebody's part to work it out and wouldn't be a loss to the association. For example, you can have some problems when you make loans that depend on one person. Those are the kind where I say, "Well, we're going into business with this one." You don't want to make too many of those.

Redding commented on some of the loans they had missed:

We were offered all the new motels that came into town. The only one we took was the Holiday Inn. About six motels and 550 beds were added after we made that loan. Several have already sold out under duress or been foreclosed.

We never could understand the big apartment complexes either. They would come in here with the MAI appraisals that look good, projected rents that weren't in the market, with 100 percent financing, and about every one of them went under. We make apartment loans, but we never could get the big ones because we couldn't bid low enough. Everyone was foreclosed or sold under duress.

We did the Cambridge development and they came over here with that Riverbend East—gonna build about 70 homes and had them priced more than the Cambridge and we'd been struggling with Cambridge for more than three years; it wasn't a struggle, but it was slow. They were projecting 3,500 more people, and I was about to believe all that stuff. Riverbend East went under. We just got outbid.

We stick to the smaller units and we try to stick with the one or two-house builders. It's like the paint contractor who was in here this morning. He said, "If I do a million dollars in paint work, I make $120,000. If I do half a million in paint work, I make $135,000. I just lose control." These guys can handle two houses, but when they get more—they get six—they just can't handle it; stealing material and laying down on the job.

In addition to Southern Federal's success in making loans, the association had also maintained fairly high levels of liquidity. Redding commented:

Our liquidity has been as low as 10 or 12 percent and once got up to about 20 percent. Some folks are used to operating at 7 or 8 percent but we have just never got comfortable with that.

When asked about Southern Federal's current liquidity level, Knight commented:

It depends on whether you look at net or gross liquidity. Gross involves money we owe on escrow, taxes, etc. It was 16.6 percent as of last Friday and Saturday on gross. It was 15.96 percent on net. It's conservative in one sense and it's just been good business. It made us a lot of money when interest rates got up to 17 and 18 percent. That's one way we stayed in the black, so we're pretty close to it all the time. Now we'd like to get that money out except—if we could get it out on RRMs, I'd be ready to shove it on out.

It concerns me when I see people putting their money in six-month CDs, and I'm letting that money go out for 25 or 29 years. It concerns me. How do I know but what this government of ours, in all their wisdom, is not going to come out with something else? They're not going to do it with the full intent of doing it, but we might lose several million dollars to Merrill Lynch or whoever, and how do I cover that? What do I do? They'll say, "Well, if you're in bad enough shape, you can borrow from the Federal Home Loan Bank on our terms."

As part of Southern Federal's liquidity management strategy, Redding also used the Home Loan Bank. He explained:

We use advances—those inner-city advances—those subsidized deals. We borrowed when money got scarce back during the last crunch. We borrowed from the Home Loan Bank. We owe two million right now in reverse repos which is another way of borrowing, but instead of selling stuff to cover the withdrawal of those Jumbos, we just borrow on a reverse repo and handle it that way. It's easy and we get a little better rate. Just pick up the phone and call them and make the deal.

You know, if you go sell something, you're not going to get the deal because they have to find somebody else in there who will do it. They just work on a closer margin with the reverse repo. We only use it on a short-term basis for dividend payments or when something unexpected comes up.

In explaining the current investment strategy, Redding continued:

> It was a management decision to keep liquidity high in order to cover our money market certificate rates which were high. Now we've jumped out and bought a little over one million in participations. The fact is that I'm going up to Rocky Mount on Monday to look over what they've got.
>
> I tried standbys but found out long ago that they weren't very good. You see, for $1 million, you could get a $10,000 commitment fee for a six-month standby at 10½ percent on a Ginny Mae. It was an insurance hedge by people putting together packages of Ginny Maes. They would give the builder a commitment at 10 percent and if things didn't work out and rates went to 11 percent, everyone was happy and they would stick me with 10½ percent when rates were 11 percent. If it went to 10½ percent or lower, they wouldn't put it to me, and I would make my 1 percent or $10,000. Well that looked good and I did that a few times with half a million or so. But then I realized that you couldn't plan your liquidity management, not knowing if someone was going to call on you or not to fund these things. So I quit.
>
> Some S&Ls and pension funds got to buying them. Twenty-five million at 1 percent is $250,000. Well, $250,000 commitment fees for an association of $35 million would be .7 percent. That's what most of them netted, if that, so the profit picture looked good with descending mortgage rates. Then the damn market turned over the last two years and the standbys were being put to them. They caught one or two in Georgia. One association of about $25 million committed $20 million. The pension fund in Houston got caught. All these hustlers were selling this stuff. I learned early that wasn't the way to go.
>
> We bought Ginny Maes. I bought a package of Ginny Mae Mobile Homes the other day at 11½ percent, if it pays out on the average of six years—or whatever the life of them. But I just try to match up the liquidity.

When asked about the nature of Southern Federal's deposit structure, Redding explained:

> We've been going after money market certificates, but, of course, this last month has turned around. The six-month money market was about 38 percent or $66 million. Two-and-a-half-year money markets were 7 percent and growing. The 7½ percent CD is about 20 percent and decreasing. The regular passbook is about 14 percent and dropping.
>
> We've been caught like everyone else, borrow short and lend long. But if the trend continues, we'll probably work out of it by the end of the year.

PLANNING FOR DEREGULATION

To continue its leading role in their financial community, Southern Federal planned to adjust to the changing environment, as Redding explained:

> If it's going to be like it was in the old days, taking in savings and lending it out on houses, then you have to have the most attractive sav-

ings account in town or else they'll leave it somewhere where they can get other services and a checking account. So when they take off the differential, we're going to have to make ourselves just as attractive as the next place.

You have things like nice tellers, friendly people, pretty buildings, and good locations; but still you've got to have the services available. This is what we're just forced to do. It seems like looking at the future we just have no choice. We put in lock boxes at two branches; travelers checks for whatever good that was; money orders; we transfer money by phone for big accounts. What else can we offer? The NOW accounts, automobile loans, and consumer "help momma get the icebox financed" loans. But we'll be staying away from the commercial end of it.

But it's going to take a hell of a lot more people. I don't see how we'll be able to make money unless that consumer lending lets you really stick them. Had a quote this morning though. We quoted 17 percent APR, Republic was 14, the First National was, I think, 13. So we're out of the market. We thought we were entitled to that much on a smaller loan, but we're not; maybe we're making too much.

Hours of operation is another question. At North County we're closed on Wednesday afternoon and open Saturday morning. It's just five days a week here. We close at four. Most of the banks are open on Saturday mornings. Whether we'll have to change to that for some branches in South County at some point in time is another question.

Southern Federal was also considering RRMs—rollover rate mortgages. Knight explained:

I'm just wondering if these 12 percent loans we're putting on the books today are good loans. We're getting top interest rates right now because loan activity is very good. We've done well in the last six or eight weeks. It's been hot. But is that a good loan for the association 10 or 15 years down the road with almost universally expected 10 percent annual inflation for the decade of the '80s? If that's true, that's a poor loan to be putting on the books today.

But I don't think it will be easy to sell RRMs. People don't like to change—I want a fixed rate and know what it's going to be for the next 25 or 29 years, because you all might change something and I don't trust the government—I hear all these things. And from the standpoint of competition. First Investors is in the secondary mortgage business and that's what they do. I assume they will stay with fixed rates as long as they can sell them, so how do you combat that? We don't want to switch all our business over to First Investors. Republic will probably do about the same thing because they're strong in the secondary mortgage business. I don't think we'll be too concerned about First Federal.

LOOKING AT THE FUTURE

With continued deregulation and competition in the South County area, Southern Federal was concerned about its future actions. Redding explained:

Well, we worry about the competition with banks. That's the main thing once you take all the differential off. We're twice as big as the First National and the Republic—I think they run about half our size. I don't know what's going to happen when we get into the NOW account business. We'll soon be $200 million in assets. That ought to be something we can work with. We have a net worth of $10 or $11 million. With branches around us, we can pretty much do anything, but it's going to take a lot of people and a lot of scurrying about and a lot of expense.

We've talked about going into metropolitan areas, but getting it done is just too much right now. You just wonder about the logistics of it, or the ability to compete over there, or the cost of start-up in that high rent area. I don't know. One county has had a lot of racial problems, and nobody is moving down there—we'd move up into the growth area.

I looked at the operating statements of some of the S&Ls, wondering if any of them were getting tired and wanting to merge. I've toyed with the idea of just doing it from a mortgage banking standpoint, opening something over there.

Expansion of Southern Federal's branch operations would probably not be necessary in the near future. Knight explained:

The North Highway branch turns out to be a great location. It has shifted our business from Eastside Mall and downtown and that is what we wanted. We had been having trouble waiting on the numbers of people we had in the manner in which we liked to wait on them. After looking at alternatives for two years, it was decided that, even though we didn't need another branch, another branch located in the right place would take pressure off this office and Eastside Mall. They had a constant stream of cars and would probably need another drive-in window. That's not necessary now.

A savings and loan association near Lakeview had just approached Southern Federal regarding possible merger. Knight explained:

The future of this association doesn't promise as much as it did in North County, because North County is more of a growth county than the Lake County area has been. I don't see how it is going to pick up all that much.

This association got anxious when they ran out of money. They haven't made a loan since last fall. But they had made a million dollars in loans in the previous year which had drained them. That's the problem.

It's a nice building; an old brick bank building that you feel good about. You won't have to go build an office. I think I'll let the board help decide this one. It's not one I'm going to jump up and down and crack my heels for.

I think that with NOW accounts and consumer loans, it could give us another office. That would give us a circle in the northeast part of the state.

Redding and Knight had also discussed the possibility of going public. With regard to taking Southern Federal public, Redding picked up a copy of a savings and loan magazine advertisement and explained:

> We've discussed going public and I've cut out this ad: "If an S&L goes public, it needs Schroders!" Well, I thought I'd write that fat fellow there and see what he had to say. You know, it's pro and con. I talked to an outfit in the Orlando area—they're just going public. He said the key people got a five-year contract so, if somebody wanted to take them over they'd have to take them over with a five-year contract. Whether he's speaking the truth or not, I don't know.
>
> If you put a lot of effort in here, you feel like you ought to be able to take some of it with you. A mutual doesn't have that. You can go federal, but it takes a year and a half or two years. I'm thinking of converting back to state when they get the state laws changed and it might be a heck of a lot easier to go stock with a state law.

Knight continued:

> We're going to look at the stock form a little bit here. I think it has some promise. But it's not going to be me—somebody else is going to have to do that. It's going to be a lot of work to get into that. I think Redding is more or less fascinated by it. It has some dangers in it. If you get into that, you'll have a lot of people to deal with; they'll come in here and shake their finger at you and have the right to do it.

(B)

Southern Federal Savings and Loan Association's offices were gearing up to offer consumer loans, NOW accounts, and renegotiable rate mortgages (RRMs) which were now allowed by the Depository Institutions Deregulation and Monetary Control Act of 1980. By July of 1980 steps to introduce these new products were well underway. Mr. Knight, the chief executive officer, explained:

> We'll get into consumer loans as early as September 1 or 15—whenever we can gear up and get in. We're trying hard to get in just as soon as possible because we know it will affect all our branch offices—all branch managers and at least one other person have got to be trained and familiar with them. That's a big job. But we need to get on with it just as quickly as possible because NOW accounts are coming January 1, and we don't want two things of this magnitude slapping us at the same time. If we can get into consumer lending in September, then we'll have a little bit of time to get feeling comfortable with that before starting to feel uncomfortable when NOW accounts go.

SOUTHERN FEDERAL'S MANAGEMENT

Mr. Knight was in his 16th year as president of Southern Federal. He had not grown up in this business but had become president of Southern Federal after selling his poultry business. In describing how he became involved, Knight explained:

> I sold out my interests in the poultry business on February 1, 1962, became mayor of the city on January 1, 1964, and came over here in December 1964. My predecessor had reached retirement age, but they didn't give him until the first of January as was customary. There was some internal conflict. I replaced him on the 11th of December. That didn't set well with him, but I didn't have anything to do with it. I wasn't an applicant for the job.
>
> I didn't seek the job and didn't particularly want it, but one of the directors came by and asked me if I'd consider filling in for an interim time. I assumed he was talking from January on. I said, "Well, I hadn't thought about it, but I might be interested," because the position as mayor was supposed to be a part-time job. After that, four directors fell in behind me; they said, "We'd just like to have you fill in." So I've been filling in since 1964, but my filling-in time is about up, because I turned 65 on June 17. I don't know what my relationship will be after January 1.

James Redding, Southern Federal's second in command, also came from the outside in 1960. Prior to joining Southern Federal, he had been in the real estate and insurance business and had been helping the association part time. He explained:

> I was helping them out part time with problems they were having in the appraising and construction end of the business, and decided to try it full time. I did the appraising and developed inspection sheets for builders to use in drawing money for construction loans. I worked on that end of it and later just sort of became general flunky around here.

A copy of Southern Federal's current organization structure was not readily available to Jack Pope, vice president and the one to develop such charts. He explained:

> I've done some sketches of the organization chart, but passed them on to Redding and didn't keep a copy. We've talked about it. We know how it works, or at least the department heads know.

Exhibit 9 shows the organization chart which Pope drafted for the writer. Knight commented on the development of the organization.

> There was no organization 16 years ago. We were small by comparison. But we are a whole lot larger, so we have had to departmentalize. We had to gear up for that. We had to employ people. Besides Redding and Billings, assistant in mortgage loans, I've employed everyone in frontline management. They are more or less the type of people that I like on my side.

In discussing the actual structure of Southern Federal, Knight continued:

EXHIBIT 9   Southern Federal Savings and Loan Association Organization Chart—August 4, 1980

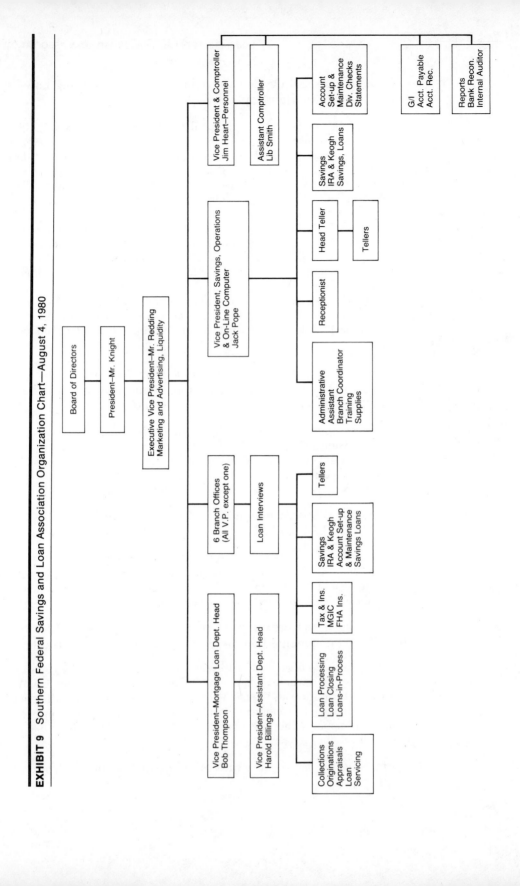

The direct line is myself, James Redding, and Jack Pope. After that you break down into various departments. Bob Thompson is mortgage loan officer. Jim Heart is controller.

I'm the managing officer and the president and the chairman of the board, but after January 1, if I stay I'd probably like to take a little different role—back off just a little bit—and let James and Jack and those folks really run the association and I act more in a policy and advisory capacity. If the board is willing to do that, I'd like to do it, because I'm not a retirement-type person.

With regard to the key positions at Southern Federal, Jack Pope explained the concept.

I took an ideal S&L organization chart and tried to compare it to what we once had. I think that may have assisted in the decision to reorganize our loan department and put someone in control. The loan department had been split up between Thompson, Billings, and Heart into loan originations, loan processing, and taxes and insurance so that one person was in charge. Now Bob Thompson is department head. Harold Billings is responsible for closings and handling loans in process.

Jim Heart was put in charge of accounting. Elizabeth Smith had reported to me in accounting. Jim didn't have any training as controller, but it was felt he could do the job, and he has. I didn't think Elizabeth was particularly pleased at first, but it has worked out well. Jim is also responsible for new employee and personnel interviews and keeps EEOC and affirmative action records in order. He has little to do with daily personnel operations except in his own department.

My duties are in operations. I have responsibility for tellers and savings counselors. I have a branch coordinator working for me now. I'm responsible for the on-line computer service, so I write the procedures or make any changes when we change the system. Supplies and purchases also come under my jurisdiction. Someone else is responsible for custodial services.

The new branch coordinator position has responsibility for branch communication and training. Knight explained the branch coordinator's role.

We just promoted one of the girls who has a lot of talent and ability to branch coordinator. From that respect, she has no supervisory jurisdiction over a branch manager, but she is really coordinating personnel. If someone doesn't show and the manager doesn't think he can operate, he calls her; and we get somebody on the road to help out. The same for supplies. When you get six branches, you just can't do it from your hip pocket. You have to have some plan of handling things.

THE BOARD OF DIRECTORS

Southern Federal's board of directors significantly changed since Knight joined the association. He explained the early structure.

> When I came over here, the average age of the board was about 70. We had one that was 90. Another that was 80. Several in the 70s—they were the young guys. I was just a babe in the woods. That had to be changed. You may think that's no trouble, but it is.
>
> We set limits of 70. When I reach 70, I'm off the board and that's the way it ought to be. We finally agreed that if they served three years, from the time we made that agreement, that was fair and they would become emeritus members and leave the board. It just takes time to do those things.

In describing the current membership of the board, Knight continued:

> We have the director of campus planning, who has been here a long time. The university football coach also represents another area of thinking as a director. We also have the owner of a downtown retail men's store, and a fine doctor and surgeon who has a good financial mind. We have the controller for a local textile plant, and an ex-government official that now heads up the university research lab. We then have myself, Redding, the president of North County B&L, and one of our retired executives that know the business.

Southern Federal's board of directors held meetings on the second Tuesday of every month. Knight explained the role of his board members.

> We have an agenda which includes basic items that are required, then gets into new business and things that need to be brought to the board's attention.
>
> Two of the members, Redding and myself, serve as members of the loan committee. We provide a written report from the loan committee and the board acts on that. The director of campus planning is a good board member who takes the time to read the information we send him. So I usually ask if he has any comments on the loan committee meeting's minutes. If he sees one he doesn't understand, he'll ask a question. We may give our reasons for that particular loan and the interest rate charged, or whatever attracted his attention.
>
> The controller over at the textile mill has a real good financial mind. I usually ask him for comments on the financial statement that's prepared by Jim Heart. He's sharp enough that if he sees an unusual figure, it flags him and he'll put a circle around it. So we get into things that he doesn't understand or needs clarification. Sometimes he'll understand it, but he'll do it for the benefit of the other board members. That kind of takes care of the nuts and bolts.

Redding commented further on their board's involvement.

> Our board is made up of a pretty knowledgeable group of folks here in town. They set the policy and the tone of what we're going to do. For what services we offer, I think they take most of the recommendations that management makes.
>
> They turned us down on a logo one time. We've got to get us a logo. I was talking to our advertising man the other day about getting one. We

had about three logos and they turned them all down. You have to get some uniformity in advertising as you get bigger. We're working on that in sort of a hit and miss way.

They were quite active in the designing, planning, and style ideas for the North Highway branch. Quite active. But they're not like down at South Bank and Trust—they're down there all the time. Of course, South Bank, and Trust almost lost all the money they had down there too.

They weren't active in the North County merger, but of course, participated in some group meetings and gave the green light to see if we could go ahead and affect it. That was a chore and we don't have all the strings tied together yet.

They had a discussion of consumer loans last meeting. Bob Thompson was also at the last meeting talking about the rollover rate mortgage, explaining that. We had one meeting on NOW accounts; they said go ahead on those two things.

SOUTHERN FEDERAL'S MANAGEMENT PHILOSOPHY

Southern Federal has become a leading institution in the community. This had not always been the case, as Knight explained:

When I came here we had several problems that I perceived. One was that we were really an organization that survived or prospered or declined based on its participation in the community. If you don't participate in the community, I don't know how the community is going to participate with you. The way that they participate with us is to put their savings and their loans here. But the association was really just withdrawn. It wasn't outgoing. It took no real part, for instance, in the United Way or in supporting those things that make a good community. It did not actually suggest that the officers of the association join the civic clubs and take part. These are things that I believe you've got to do if you're going to be successful in your operation and have the name and image out there all the time.

We gave just a little token to financial drives. Today we are the largest financial institution in South County, given the fact that Republic is a branch and the chain could swallow us up many times; but one-on-one, we're larger. We try to give a leading gift. I think we have to.

Besides attempting to have a meaningful leadership role in the community, Southern Federal also attempted to maintain a good working environment for its employees, as Jack Pope explained.

We have a good working environment—somewhat relaxed. We don't push people. We assign a job and expect it to be completed in a reasonable period of time. Most people like that.

This atmosphere did not mean that employees lived a "life of ease," as Knight pointed out.

One thing that Jack Pope places a lot of emphasis on is encouraging employees to take advantage of the courses that we pay for which are furnished by the U.S. League's financial education section. They are constantly involved in courses.

This is part of our merit program—to be qualified for a position, you must have passed satisfactorily those courses to make you qualified for that position. Now if it comes down to two people going for the same position, the one who had qualified his or herself in the best manner— and, if it came down to a fine line, had the best grades—would probably be the one to get that position, everything else being equal. Most of these people will make As and A+s. When these girls go after something, they usually work at it and do a good job.

Southern Federal also had been able to attract and keep good people. With regard to their low employee turnover, Knight explained:

Generally speaking, we don't have much turnover. We have always had a great esprit de corps. We have tried to encourage that with fringe benefits, uniforms, family get-togethers, etc. So far we've screened our employees pretty darn good. We've been lucky. We've had some misfits, but I think they realized they were and eventually worked out.

Now First National Bank works on a different concept. They employ a lot of students and have a lot of turnover. They kind of accept that turn- over, and I think it costs them too. We'd rather have continuity and have you see the same person when you come in here—if it's possible.

In commenting on the loss of several employees earlier in the year, Knight explained:

Gosh, we took a siege here about three months ago and we lost them bam, bam, bam, just like that. And we're losing another next Tuesday. You just can't help it—she used to work for this dentist. That joker is now going to also have an office here and he remembered and made an offer she couldn't turn down. He offered her $2,500 more than we are paying here. She's a good employee and we hate to lose her, but there is no way we can keep her without destroying the whole scale. You lose some like that reluctantly.

Redding also expressed his feelings about the recent turnover.

We had the quitting bug come through here about a year ago, and everyone got to quitting. And then we'll have the baby bug come by here, and it'll bite a bunch of them. And then we'll have the hysterectomy bug—that's broken out here now—but it seems to come like that.

James Redding had primary responsibility for managing short- term investments. In commenting on the process, Redding explained:

I handle the investments, but go through the executive committee, which meets once a month, to get approval. It takes two signatures— Knight is generally the one to sign and approve the transaction.

As Redding turned and pointed to the large calendar scheduling board on the wall behind his desk, he explained:

Right now you see a lot of yellow stuff—that's short term to match up with the six-month stuff that's been feasting on us. I made an error because I didn't move quickly enough to go out long. Then we have a lot of Jumbo CDs and we have to keep up with that too. We have six or seven million of those, I guess. It will vary from four million to eight million. We got into bidding on the university and got them more money. They were kind of getting low balled a little bit. We got the first one we bid on.

EMPLOYEE COMPENSATION AND INCENTIVES

Along with having a good work environment, Southern Federal had also attempted to provide competitive salary and benefits for its employees. Pope explained:

We try to be competitive on salary with the banks around here and benefits are on top of that. We have not had a great deal of turnover except for earlier this year. Usually the bank people come to us for jobs because they hear good things about us.

All employees with over six months employment in the association participate in Southern Federal's profit sharing. Knight explained the system:

We have profit sharing—I guess you would call it that. There is no setting aside and waiting 10 years. We have a little formula and Redding works it up, that for the last two years has, generally speaking, amounted to between 10 and 14 percent of salary. How long you have been here and how much you are making is all tied into it. If you've been here less than six months you're gonna get a ham. If you've been here over six months, you're gonna get your pro rata.

We take a fixed percentage of income which we're adding to net worth. It's about a 50 percent deal. I believe it behooves us to treat the employees well and try to have people who are willing and ready to wait on people when they come through our doors and make the person want to come back. Most of our people go out of their way.

The association also provided employee uniforms and other benefits, as Redding explained:

Many years ago we put in a dress code. We gave the ladies dresses. They got to squabbling about the thing here the other day so we put it to a vote and they voted 34 to 4 to keep the dresses.

We also furnish meals here. We have a dining room downstairs. The branch personnel get $1.75 a day to buy their cokes and soup. Here it's free cokes, free coffee, free doughnuts, free lunch, free uniforms. Whether we should put that in a paycheck and forget about it, I don't know; but I like it this way.

We provide hospital insurance, retirement, all of that—not for the dependents, but we have life insurance tied in with their retirement and hospitalization.

SOUTHERN FEDERAL'S MANAGEMENT CONTROL AND INFORMATION SYSTEMS

Southern Federal did not set formal goals and objectives for the association. Knight explained about the absence of objectives.

> We just haven't set any objective over here that we're trying to reach. I'll tell you, we would have missed them so far. I told the board at the first of the year that we would be lucky if we were in the black for the year. Well, we made so much money in the first four months on penalties that they said, "What are you talking about?" I said, "Just wait. It's coming." It came, but now, again, we're turning it back the other way. Our projections don't look all that bad for the rest of the year, if we can hold it. It's very upsetting. There is no real way to keep up with it.
>
> There just doesn't seem to be any way to cope with some of the things we encounter. Suppose that last January we had set up some goals and objectives. We would have missed them for various reasons. We would have missed it on income for four months. We had the best income we've ever had because we were collecting penalties. I wasn't smart enough to look ahead and say we were going to collect penalties, because I didn't even know we were going to be levying penalties. It's not from lack of thought or desire to do it that way; it just seems beyond our control. Everybody else seems to be controlling what you can do. The only thing we can do is operate as best we can with what they give us to operate with, and try to better our performance. This is what we tell our employees, "We have to do better than we did last year," and we try to tell them various ways to do it.
>
> No, we don't set goals, except that we try to do better each year than we did the year before. It's a relative thing. We're working against ourselves to do better. I don't know how you can set goals with the Federal Home Loan Board and with policies, now, of the DIDC committee. You could set some goals, but you don't have the ability to meet them. They're changing things so fast. Now, if they ever settle down, it may be different.

Redding commented further:

> We don't have any formal goals. We don't belong to the Rotary Club. I guess subconsciously we'd like to be the biggest one in the state, try to build up our deposits, get savings. We look at it and, if it looks like the loan volume is off and we got money and feel the economy is better, we'll have our advertising man go after the loans, start working with the real estate people, try to be competitive with rates, and scheme as best we can. We would like to get 1 percent net, but we haven't done it. We're on profit sharing here and everyone participates—its not going to be as good a year as it has been.

Southern Federal's savings operations had been installed on NCR's time-sharing system which allowed management to trace savings throughout the day. Jack Pope explained:

When we first started using the NCR system, Redding used to come in every hour to find out how savings and withdrawals were coming. We found that you couldn't tell how you were doing until late afternoon because it fluctuates so much from hour to hour.

Besides tracking their savings operations, management also tracks the association's overall performance. Knight, as he picked up a summary of branch profit performance, explained:

I can show you expenses and income from each branch. Of course, some of it's hard to come by exactly, but we can come within sight of it, and that's all you really need to know. The total accounting picture is accurate. River County, for instance, has a little branch out there. It's not a profitable situation. It's slowly growing.

We keep strict accounting on each branch. We separate them so I can look at my records and tell you how each one of them is doing. I can look at my daily record and tell you what each one of them is doing in savings. It is good to know how much you're receiving. You certainly don't want to put more money into an area than you're taking in. It varies. This month, Lakeview's having a real good month on savings.

North Highway is the leading branch on savings and has been ever since Mary Defoe went out there. That's the way I knew it would happen, because she really has a good rapport with people that save with us.

Redding further explained:

We have an annual budget—keep up with it and track variances monthly. It's done by hand. We have a Wang upstairs, but don't use it. The damn thing takes a chauffeur and we don't have one.

Jack Pope commented on the reason Southern Federal had the Wang computer.

We bought the Wang because we were going to put our loan-processing records on the computer. We bought that system because we thought it would be easy to adapt the software—but when we got our lawyers involved and we couldn't decide what format was legal, etc. It's been a year and a half and we still don't use it.

Management had also planned to have a more extensive computer facility in the future. Knight explained:

I was ready to buy a computer about two years ago, but Jack Pope, the operations officer, and Jim Heart, the controller, both felt like it would be money that could be better spent somewhere else. They felt we could stay on NCR until we reached about $250 million. Well, with NOW accounts coming in, I think that timetable is going to be changed.

The North Highway office was designed—the floor, wiring, and everything is ready to go—to set the computer and everything that goes with it in there. That will go into the basement out there—it's a good place because the temperature won't change as much and it's easy to keep it cool which is better for the computer.

Pope also commented on their planning system.

> We have looked at several models, but haven't decided on one yet. We do some hand calculations, or what ifs, of existing figures. But it isn't done with much depth.

With regard to keeping in touch with the critical operations of the association, Redding looked at the papers covering his desk and responded:

> Gosh, I don't know. You see how tidy my desk is! I guess Knight and I talk and we talk with the other people in the departments, listen to all sorts of rumors, talk to other people in the business—other associations. We watch our profit picture—it looks gloomy right now though. The monkey market rates being what they are, it'll be October before we really get rid of the bad stuff.
>
> I think we've done a pretty good job in spite of the fact that we're not organized. We're not highly structured. I'm just now getting around, after 20 years, to getting some little plan for the janitor. This has become a problem, now, on how to keep the darn branches cleaned up. That thing out on North Highway has weeds everywhere. We have about three acres out there. We ought to have had better sense. We had to paint the Eastside Mall Branch because it wasn't quite so clear—you see we throw a little competition in there. Get them competing with each other. South Rim and Lakeview, they're about the same size—I pick on them to ask them why they're not doing so well.

With Southern Federal's first priority being entrance into the consumer loan business, there was a need to recruit a new manager. James Redding, executive vice president, was concerned about the kind of person they were going to need. He explained:

> Now facing us is the consumer loan which we'll be getting into by September. That will entail adding someone who is knowledgeable of consumer lending which will include automobile loans, signature loans, 90-day loans, or anything oriented to family financing. We want someone who will charge enough. We might get someone from one of these short-loan places. I used to be in the short-loan business. I'm the secretary and treasurer for Equitable's loan company. We took it over. We had a manager and I supervised it from afar. Our motto was, "Consolidate all your little bills into one huge staggering debt." That's from the lending end.

With the rapid introduction of consumer lending activities, Southern Federal also had to prepare employees to handle them. Redding continued:

> That's a problem in going into consumer lending. You're going to have to do it in the branches and what do they know about consumer lending? Nothing! So you're going to have to get that trained. Whether they do one automobile a day, or a week, or an hour, we're going to have to give them responsibility and work from there. Jack Pope is reviewing that.

Of course with consumer lending, you're going to have to be able to give customers answers in 10 minutes or an hour—so we're also going to have to change our approval process.

(C)

In late September 1980, Robert Reese heard that Southern Federal had decided to enter the consumer loan market. He had become disenchanted with his current position since the diversified financial company that he worked for had been acquired by a Gulf and Western subsidiary in July 1979. The new management wanted to take advantage of the high-interest charge "short-loan" business. This would mean that Reese would have to give up much of the floor plan and second mortgage business that he had developed over the years. After a chance meeting with James Redding, Jr., Southern Federal's executive vice president, he was offered the new position as manager of consumer credit. He started work the next month (see attached resume).

Reese was given an office in the basement of Southern Federal's main office. He started by hiring a secretary. He explained:

I hadn't realized when I accepted the job how big a job it was. We don't have anyone who knows anything about consumer credit but me. I tried meeting with people from the branches to begin educating them about the new service, but found that I was over their heads. I had to define and explain terms which I thought were common knowledge.

I've been working night and day to put together a loan manual and training materials. We haven't even had time to get furniture in here or hire an assistant. We have only a month before we start making loans.

In discussing the needs for training branch personnel in making consumer loans, Reese continued:

I had expected that branch managers would have been making decisions before now, but that has not been the case. It turns out that all decisions until now were made at this office. Now we have the job of teaching these people how to make decisions about giving customer loans on the spot. It will really be a change in the way they've been expected to perform.

I don't want to use a loan appraisal form because its fairness has to be documented, but I need to train them to make good decisions that use experience already known to the industry.

In commenting on the proposed consumer loan product line to be offered, Reese explained:

We're going to allow each branch to approve unsecured loans up to $5,000 and secured loans up to $8,000 on their own authority. This authority will be good for such loans as signature and collateral loans, em-

Resume of Robert C. Reese
September 1980

143 Clifton Drive
Macon, GA 39393
Residence Telephone   555-2187

BIRTH: Born January 28, 1937
                       Raised in Macon, Georgia

EDUCATION: Graduated from Macon High School.

MARITAL STATUS: Married—two children. One married and one in col-
                       lege.

EXPERIENCE: Served in U.S. Marine Corp from 7-54 until 7-57.

                       Employed with Independent Life and Accident Insur-
                       ance Company 8-57 until 8-58. (Debit insurance
                       sales.)

                       Employed with Georgia Loan Company, a privately
                       owned company in Macon, Georgia, from 8-58 until
                       9-59.

                       Employed by Home Credit Company from 9-59 until
                       2-63, leaving this company to further my education in
                       the field of the finance business by accepting a posi-
                       tion with Motor Contract Company 3-1-63 to the
                       present.

                       Motor Contract Company was a very diversified finan-
                       cial company dealing in the field of new and used
                       cars, wholesale floor plan, purchasing conditional
                       sales contracts, making loans of all types, first and
                       second real estate mortgages, and loans under the
                       Georgia Industrial Loan Act. On July 1, 1979, Motor
                       Contract Company was sold to Associated Financial
                       Services Company of North America, a Gulf & West-
                       ern Corporation.

HOBBIES: Football and golf.
                       Member of Chapelwood Methodist Church.
                       Member of the Macon Country Club.

ployer loans, recreation vehicle, mobile home and auto loans, marine product loans, and furniture and household goods loans. The loan manual will spell out the details of each kind of loan.

In talking about the future of consumer loans, Reese commented:

If this grows the way I expect, we'll need 20 or 30 people in this department over the next several years. This space won't be nearly large enough to handle this business. I haven't had a chance to talk with Redding or Knight, so I don't really know what they expect this business to do. It's more than just another product.

31. Bankers First

INTRODUCTION

As he sat at his desk and reviewed recent performance, H. M. "Monty" Osteen, the chief executive officer of the Bankers First Federal Savings and Loan Association, felt considerable pride at the company's progress in recent years. After four years of very hard work, Bankers First had arrived at the end of 1986 as an expansion-minded, marketable, and profitable company.

Bankers First started small—very small. When attorney William M. Lester began the People's Building and Loan Association in 1925, it consisted of a single desk in a small second-floor office in the Masonic Building. Mr. Lester wrote the association's first loan for $1,625.

The association later named the First Federal Savings and Loan Association became a federal mutual savings and loan association and conducted its operations in the Augusta, Georgia, area. Its business consisted primarily of attracting deposits from the general public and originating and investing in loans secured by liens on residential and other real estate and to a lesser extent, other types of loans.

OSTEEN

Bankers First Chairman Osteen has a reputation for cockiness unsurpassed by the bosses at other thrifts. He has been described as having the mind of an economist and the soul of a politician. In his 40s, Osteen, a native of Anderson, South Carolina, has a master's degree in economics from the University of South Carolina.

At 28, working for First National Bank of Atlanta, he managed a research department that pioneered the use of computers to analyze tax strategies, credit risks, municipal bond prices, balance sheets, and investment portfolios. Osteen got his picture in *Time* magazine, and First Atlanta got profits from selling the services to other banks.

First Railroad Bank of Augusta hired him in 1973 to handle mergers and acquisitions for its new holding company. He rose to third in command, responsible for daily operations. He left First Railroad for

This case was prepared by Otha Gray and Harry McAlum of Lander College.

535

Bankers First, then called First Federal, in 1981, because he wanted to run his own show.

By and large Osteen's plans have fulfilled his reputation for cockiness. "Remember, he is in an industry where a lot of the other managements are not alert, not bright, not energetic," says Bradford M. Johnson, an analyst for Johnson, Lane, Space, Smith & Co. "So by comparison, he is someone who seems cocky."

When he came to Bankers First the company was in the same interest rate bind as other thrifts and most of their loans were at a fixed rate. Osteen had winced every time he passed the interest rate signs in the lobby. The bank was paying 17 percent and lending at 12 percent. In 1982 Bankers First Corporation posted a $3.2 million loss. In the first six months of 1986 the corporation's net earnings were $3.35 million.

INDUSTRY BACKGROUND

The operations of savings and loan associations usually are significantly influenced by general economic conditions, by the related monetary and fiscal policies of the federal government, and by the policies of financial institution regulatory authorities. Deposit flows and costs of funds are influenced by a number of factors including interest rates on competing investments and general market rates of interest. Lending activities are affected by a number of factors including demand, interest rates, the supply of housing, and the availability of funds. The earnings of a savings and loan association had depended primarily on the difference between its income from lending activities and to a lesser extent, its investment activities, and the interest cost of its deposits and borrowings.

In the beginning of the 1980s changes in federal legislation significantly affected the operation of federally chartered savings and loan associations. The most significant legislative changes were contained in the Depository Institutions Deregulation and Monetary Act of 1980 and the Garn-St. Germain Depository Institutions Act of 1982.

During 1979—especially after the fed's drastic money-tightening moves of October of that year—serious financial problems were faced by most of the country's thrifts. During the first several weeks of 1980, the situation worsened. The inflation rate increased and interest rates continued to move up to record levels. There was increasing concern about the financial safety of much of the thrift industry. In a near-crisis environment of the first three months of 1980 Congress tried to design a bill that would not only meet the emergency needs of the crisis but also set the stage for the economic health and growth of the nation's financial services institutions during the decade of the 1980s and beyond. The bill was passed by Congress and signed into law by President Carter on March 31, 1980.

The Depository Act provided, among other things, for the phased elimination over a six-year period of the system of federal regulations limiting the rates of interest which federally insured savings and loan associations, commercial banks, and institutions were allowed to pay on deposits. The Depository Institutions Deregulation Committee (the DIDC) eliminated the interest rate differential between commercial banks and savings and loan associations on certain types of accounts including deposits with maturities of 31 days or more. The act also authorized the issuance of negotiable order of withdrawal (NOW) accounts, which are deposits similar to interest-bearing checking accounts, and it expanded the lending, investment, and certain other powers of federally chartered savings and loans associations.

This piece of legislation is considered one of the most significant, far-reaching, and revolutionary changes that had occurred in the financial industries in this country since the depression of the 1930s. The larger and more aggressive of the S&Ls welcomed the new act because it unleashed them to compete more effectively. It gave them a much broader range of "competitive tools" with which to work. Many of the smaller thrifts had been satisfied with their niche as it existed before and had no desire to offer transaction accounts. But under the new rules of the game, all financial institutions were more or less forced into this new situation of more aggressive competition. Their survival depends on how effectively they can cope with this new environment.

The Depository Institutions Act of 1982 is popularly known as the Garn-St. Germain Act after its sponsors. This act further accelerated the deregulation of federal interest rate limitations on savings accounts by directing the DIDC to authorize a new insured deposit account with terms intended to be directly competitive with money market funds. In addition, the act required that interest rate differentials between federally insured commercial banks and savings and loan associations for all categories of accounts be eliminated on January 1, 1984. The act also provided expanded powers for federal savings and loan associations in areas such as consumer and corporate equipment leasing, unsecured commercial and consumer lending, and commercial real estate.

Most of the thrift industry enthusiastically supported the Garn-St. Germain Act. Bankers on the other hand were quite opposed to some of the provisions granting new commercial lending and deposit powers to the thrifts. It was recognized that most of the S&Ls were not yet "tooled up" to take advantage of the new powers. Throughout 1983 most of the thrifts kept on doing what they had been doing in the past. A few moved rapidly to take advantage of their new powers.

An ultimate result of the new legislation may be to speed the consolidation of small thrifts and banks into larger financial services units and ultimately bring an end to the distinctions between banks and thrifts.

POLICY FORMULATION

Osteen has long been a firm believer in effective strategic planning. He brought in outside consultants to work with his key management people in forging a strategic framework.

BANKERS FIRST'S BELIEFS, MISSION, AND POLICIES

Beliefs

We believe there are certain transcending values which together create an environment that enables us to achieve all successes, individually and corporately: faith in God, the family, the democratic form of government, and the free-enterprise system.

We believe we should provide our customers with highest quality service and products in our marketplace, at a fair price, in an atmosphere of integrity and trust.

We believe our employees are our most valuable asset and that they should be provided an environment in which they can achieve their fullest potential and that reward should be commensurate with performance.

We believe we must provide our stockholders with a superior rate of return on their investment.

We believe that we should promote community well-being and development through our active responsible involvement individually and corporately.

We believe we must not be restrained by tradition or that which is familiar.

We believe that we can be the best at what we do.

Mission

To be a leading regional banking corporation of entrepreneurial business units providing superior financial products and related services differentiated by market demand.

Policies

1. We will appropriately capitalize each business unit separately.

2. Capital investments, acquisitions, and mergers will be evaluated on a discounted cash-flow basis, based on an acceptable return on investment, considering the risk involved.

3. In order to maximize profits with minimum risks (exposure) we will adhere to the following:
   a. We will not have more than 115 percent of our deposits in loans, excluding residential loans held for sale.
   b. The level of "risk" assets will not exceed 40 percent of total assets.
   c. Substandard assets less reserves for loan losses will not exceed 1.5 percent of total assets.

4. We will maintain and continually update a long-range strategic plan.

5. The profitability of any new product or service will be determined before implementation and will be evaluated periodically for continuation.

6. We will subscribe to the principle of participative management in that decisions will be made at the lowest level possible within relatively autonomous responsibility centers.

7. Management will encourage an entrepreneurial approach to our business in terms of creativity, innovation, and personal leadership.

8. We will operate on a basis where decisions are made in the best long-term interests of the total corporation despite possible implications to a business unit or an employee.

9. The holding company will not allow the merger/acquisitions process to disrupt the personnel policies and procedures which are the prerogative of the management of the affiliates.

10. We will maintain the necessary, adequate, and comprehensive programs for the development of the human resources necessary to provide for management succession, and whenever possible will promote from within.

11. We reserve the right not to do business with persons or organizations whose character, reputation, or obvious intent do not reflect positively on the public image on Bankers First or which are in direct conflict with the mission, policies, and/or objectives of Bankers First.

POLICY IMPLEMENTATION

Company Restructuring

Osteen changed the name from First Federal to Bankers First. Bankers First still isn't a bank. It is a savings and loan holding company, but a S&L that purposely looks more and more like a bank each month. Call Bankers First a thrift and its executives clear their throats and say even our name identifies us as a banking organization. Osteen has remarked that a traditional thrift is a regulatory dinosaur. He sees his thrift as the only way left to build a statewide banking network.

In September 1983 Bankers First converted to a federally chartered stock savings and loan association as part of a holding company structure. The company became publicly owned when it sold 2,300,000 shares of common stock at 7⅜ per share. The initial issue was sold to account holders, borrower members and directors, officers and employees of Bankers First, as well as to the general public. The company's common stock is traded in the over-the-counter market and is quoted on the NASDAQ National Market System under the symbol BNKF.

Supported by market research the company sharpened its focus on its retail market. The company designed a range of new deposit and checking accounts and in 1985 alone attracted 11,000 new deposit accounts. The company added branch locations, installed automatic teller machines in key locations including 7-Eleven convenience stores and opened full-service banking centers in Kroger supermarkets.

There have been gloomy predictions of bankers setting themselves up for financial disaster by issuing long-term fixed rate loans at today's low rates. This not the case at Bankers First, said Victor Mills, president of Bankers First. Years ago, it was true many savings and loans and some banks held onto the mortgage loans they issued. The institutions which held long-term loans at low interest rates suffered when the rates increased. The cost of the money they borrowed increased and the interest they paid depositors increased, while their funds were tied up in a low-interest mortgage. Today financial institutions merely originate and service their mortgages, selling their loans in the secondary market. The homeowner probably never knows that his loan has been sold because he will still deal with his local banker to make payment. Secondary market investors include insurance companies, pension funds, and government agencies. Savings and loans at one time held a lot of their loans because it was the only investment they were allowed. Deregulation changed that.

Mills said Bankers First set down a policy four years ago governing the management of its mortgage loan portfolio. The policy prohibits placing loans in the thrift's portfolio that don't provide for interest rate adjustment within five years, preferably within three years. Bankers First also began to sell off the fixed rate loans already in its portfolio. Four years ago in 1982, 80 percent of the loans in its portfolio were fixed rate loans. Mills said today fixed rate loans make up less than 14 percent of the thrift's total assets.

Bankers first paid the price to realign its assets and liabilities according to its policy. In 1982, it sold almost $8 million of fixed rate loans at a loss of $2,475 million.

Bankers First has concentrated on building a mixed portfolio. They have focused on short-term loans with adjusting interest rates. Corporate loans and construction loans that are tied to the base lending rate and short-term consumer loans are kept in the Bankers First portfolio, Mills said. Bankers First also took another action to protect itself from an "interest rate gap" by extending the maturity date of its liabilities. More than 35 percent of the thrift's total liabilities provide for maturities and interest rate adjustments in two or more years.

Marketing

To remake its image, Bankers First has embarked on an ambitious marketing campaign. Osteen has doubled his marketing budget over the last three years to about $1.4 million. Osteen selected for a marketing man not a financier but a retailer. He got John R. Richter, a 35-year-old marketing manager from Sears. Richter markets himself by saying that he brought Levi's into Sears stores and put Cheryl Tiegs into them. He has remarked that there wasn't any difference between marketing women's garments and marketing finance.

Since arriving in Augusta in August of 1985, Richter's stunts have included a balloon race that he managed to tie in with both Augusta's 250th anniversary and the Statue of Liberty renovation. His newspaper ads are hard hitting and give the phone numbers of competing banks, inviting readers to compare checking account fees. Instead of promoting Bankers First with a slender model, he brought Henry Kissinger to Augusta at a healthy fee. Kissinger inaugurated the Bankers First Business Development Council with a lecture on the art of negotiating. The invitations were like gold.

Expansion

In September 1986 Bankers First completed the purchase of Athens Federal Savings Bank in Athens, Georgia. The acquisition was valued at $33.6 million. Bankers First had offered about $25 a share for the more than 1.36 million shares outstanding of Athens Federal.

The combined assets of Bankers First and Athens Federal would total $1.1 billion, making Bankers First the fourth largest savings bank in the state. Osteen said the acquisition will enable Bankers First to handle larger types of credit and to expand its operations geographically.

Analysts have generally applauded the match of Athens' traditional savings and mortgage operation, dominant in its market, with Bankers First's construction and development financing.

Thrift industry regulations allow thrifts to establish branches anywhere in state, regardless of where they are based. Commercial banks cannot establish branches across county lines except in contiguous counties that have more than 250,000 people. Why does Osteen want to build a statewide network through acquisitions, which cost much more than it would to start a branch office? "We hope to go into markets with institutions that have established substantial market share," he said. Athens Federal has a 30 percent market share in its total market area.

The Athens Federal purchase will be a model for future Bankers First acquisitions, Osteen said. Athens Federal will retain its name and management, and will operate independently rather than as a Bankers First branch.

The Athens Federal purchase did not dilute Bankers First's book value per share nor its earnings per share because of Bankers First's strong market position and because its stock has been so well received.

At the time of the acquisition Bankers First had 13 branch offices and 29 automated teller machines in Augusta, 2 Savannah branches, and 12 loan production offices throughout Georgia and South Carolina. Athens Federal operates 10 branch offices and 5 automated teller machines in Athens and surrounding northeast Georgia communities.

In early December 1986, Bankers First announced that it was acquiring Southeast Federal Savings Bank, a $220 million asset company headquartered in Rossville, Georgia, a bedroom community of Chattanooga, Tennessee. Southeast was a mutual company, so Bankers First will assume 100 percent of its shares in exchange for a capital infusion of $6.5 million.

Bankers First will not have a change in its nominal book value as a result of the acquisition, but will experience a 35 cents a share decline in tangible net worth. Adjustments in the final accounting for its earlier acquisition, Athens Federal, will increase goodwill about $1.5 million.

The impact on earnings is expected to be as much as 40 cents a share annually. The acquisition is expected to be finalized in early 1987.

Diversification

On February 27, 1986, Bankers First announced the creation of Bankers First Mortgage Service Company as a separate subsidiary. The mortgage service company had previously operated as a division of Bankers First.

The mortgage service company issues payment books, pays insurance and taxes out of escrow, sends yearly statements, and forecloses on defaulted mortgages. The company does all the modifications on adjustable rate mortgages.

Bob G. Taylor, executive vice president and chief operating officer of the newly formed subsidiary, said Bankers First was making a $300,000 investment in equipment and computer software. With the added capacity the company can offer its services nationwide. Taylor said the company will both purchase servicing rights and try to originate servicing on a contract basis. Taylor said his company will be able to offer their services at a lower cost than many others because it owns the necessary equipment and doesn't have to pay an access charge to use the needed software, as many service companies do. Taylor said the company has the capacity to service 80,000 to 100,000 loans on its present system and within four years hopes to be the largest mortgage service company in the Southeast.

On April 17, 1986, Bankers First announced the formation of a data processing subsidiary to take advantage of increased third-party data processing opportunities for financial institutions. The new subsidiary will be known as Bankers First Data Processing and previously operated as a division of Bankers First. The division, which employs 22, was established at an investment of $2 million.

The company will concentrate at first on servicing small to medium-sized S&Ls in the Southeast. They have targeted about 200 institutions in their initial plans. The company will focus on a "turnkey approach" to provide ancillary services to smaller institutions who otherwise wouldn't have these kind of capabilities.

Long-term plans for the subsidiary are to build the subsidiary's revenue to $8 million by 1990 and to expand its market to include other types of financial institutions within the next three to five years. The company has signed its first customer and several other agreements are pending, announced Larry DeMeyers, president and chief executive officer of the subsidiary.

Through its subsidiary, Bankers First Real Estate Development Corporation, the company has been active in various real estate developments. As of 1985 the real estate subsidiary owned 235 acres of undeveloped land and five developed lots located 11 miles west of Augusta in Columbia County. They also owned 17 acres within the city limits of Augusta, Georgia, as well as other lots in Columbia County.

The real estate development corporation was also a 50 percent participant in Jones Creek. This venture owns 520 acres on which a golf course and residential and commercial building sites are being developed. The venture acquired 205 acres from the real estate development corporation.

Another subsidiary corporation, Goshen-Woodward Developers, Inc. owns 18 acres of undeveloped land and a number of developed lots located approximately 13 miles south of Augusta in Richmond County.

In 1985 the company organized Bankers First Life Insurance Company under the laws of Arizona. The company was capitalized with $150,000 in June 1985. The life insurance company plans to act only as a reinsurer. Under Georgia law the company will insure only credit life and credit health and accident risks.

Corporate Headquarters

In January 1986 Bankers First opened the Lafayette Center, the focal point of the company's $7.5 million downtown renovation project and the largest restoration project approved by the state Historic Preservation Agency. Bankers First decided it wanted to keep the main office downtown because it would aid in revitalization. The center includes several buildings in the 900 block of Broad Street. Five buildings have been certified as historic structures, and range in age from the 1836 Mercantile building to the 1921 YMCA building.

The development is anchored by the old YMCA building at 945 Broad Street. The top three floors house Bankers First executive offices. The name Lafayette was chosen because the Marquis de Lafayette stayed in the Planters Hotel—later the site of the YMCA—when he visited Augusta in 1825. Renovations of the 52,000-square-foot structure cost an estimated $4.2 million. A covered skywalk was built to connect the Bankers First building on Broad Street to the Lafayette Center. Adjoining buildings house the data processing and support departments as well as the company's first retail banking office and two condominiums for overnight guests of Bankers First.

The renovations were financed through a combination of federal grants, tax-free industrial bonds, and a partnership of private investors who will lease the building back to tenants.

The Georgia Trust for Historic Preservation, Inc. recognized the Bankers First project with an award for an outstanding rehabilitation project of a nonresidential structure. The trust said it hoped the project will serve as an inspiration for others, showing the viability of old structures in the future life of downtowns.

Corporate Citizenship

In addition to their efforts in downtown rehabilitation, the company has offered continued community support in education and fine arts, and a dependable presence in civic and sporting events. The company has provided support and financial assistance for projects ranging from ballet and symphony performances to senior citizens olympics.

EXHIBIT A

**BANKERS FIRST FEDERAL SAVINGS
AND LOAN ASSOCIATION AND SUBSIDIARIES
Consolidated Statements of Financial Condition**
($ thousands)

Assets

	June 30, 1982	June 30, 1983	December 31, 1983 (unaudited)
Cash and amounts due from depository institutions	$ 3,665	$ 5,894	$ 8,543
Interest-bearing deposits in other banks.	35,601	22,739	25,949
Unsecured loans to commercial banks for federal funds, at cost	—	300	—
Investment securities, at amortized cost (market value, $10,504, $10,229, and $13,204 at June 30, 1982, and 1983, and December 31, 1983 (unaudited), respectively)—(Note 1).	10,487	10,360	13,245
Loans receivable, net (Notes 2, 3, 5, 6, and 7)	320,072	394,199	393,823
Premises and equipment (Note 3).	4,455	4,779	6,367
Real estate owned (Note 4).	2,437	2,769	2,891
Federal Home Loan Bank stock (Note 7).	2,334	2,547	2,547
Accrued interest receivable.	3,329	4,693	5,090
Other assets (Notes 2, 8 and 11)	2,123	1,007	1,155
Total	$384,503	$449,287	$459,610

Liabilities, Deferred Income, and Retained Earnings

Deposits (Note 5).	$317,763	$372,450	$380,517
Repurchase agreements (Note 6)	13,201	8,392	14,640
Advance payments by borrowers for taxes and insurance.	1,783	1,981	1,365
Deferred federal income taxes (Note 8)	1,794	1,673	1,943
Other liabilities (Note 8)	4,883	5,820	8,700
Federal Home Loan Bank advances (Note 7).	26,970	39,850	33,160
Other borrowings (Notes 3 and 4).	622	1,572	1,370
Total liabilities	367,016	431,738	441,695
Deferred income.	953	1,504	1,466
Retained earnings (Notes 10 and 11):			
Restricted	11,147	11,147	11,147
Unrestricted	5,387	4,898	5,302
Total retained earnings.	16,534	16,045	16,449
Commitments (Notes 2 and 9).			
Total	$384,503	$449,287	$459,610

Personnel Development

In late 1985 Bankers First started a teller certification program which they called the First Club Program. The goal of the program is to give tellers increased responsibility and job satisfaction.

Arthur J. Gay, senior vice president of Bankers First, said the

EXHIBIT B

BANKERS FIRST FEDERAL SAVINGS
AND LOAN ASSOCIATION AND SUBSIDIARIES
Consolidated Statements of Earnings (Loss)
($ thousands)

	Years Ended June 30,			Six Months Ended December 31,	
	1981	1982	1983	1982	1983
				(unaudited)	
Interest income:					
Interest and fees on loans	$27,795	$34,414	$42,431	$19,899	$23,671
Other interest income	3,479	4,681	5,083	2,897	1,626
Total interest income	31,274	39,095	47,514	22,796	25,279
Interest expense:					
Interest on deposits (Note 5)	26,429	33,836	37,601	18,923	19,204
Interest on repurchase agreements	—	1,003	1,367	1,088	570
Interest on Federal Home Loan Bank advances on other borrowings	1,692	2,647	5,310	2,288	2,229
Total interest expense	28,121	37,486	44,278	22,299	22,003
Net interest income	3,153	1,609	3,236	497	3,294
Provision for loan losses	—	11	639	122	382
Net interest income after provision for loan losses.	3,153	1,598	2,597	375	2,912
Other income:					
Fees and service charges	1,366	1,581	2,457	1,035	1,553
Federal Home Loan Bank stock dividend.	107	214	271	119	141
Gain (loss) on sale of loans.	—	(2,475)	1,579	263	771
Gain on sale of investment securities . . .	9	12	73	25	—
Profit on sale of real estate.	310	170	137	7	111
Other	174	139	193	51	141
	1,966	(359)	4,710	1,500	2,717
Other expense:					
Salaries and employee benefits	2,356	2,831	4,117	1,862	2,673
Net occupancy expense of premises . . .	604	933	1,182	528	692
Advertising and promotion	316	457	557	222	292
Other operating	1,055	1,383	1,886	865	1,114
	4,331	5,604	7,742	3,477	4,771
Earnings (loss) before income tax benefit (expense)	788	(4,365)	(435)	(1,602)	858
Income tax benefit (expense)—(Note 8) . . .	(107)	1,137	(54)	381	(454)
Net earnings (loss).	$ 681	$ (3,228)	$ (489)	$ (1,221)	404

EXHIBIT C

**BANKERS FIRST FEDERAL SAVINGS
AND LOAN ASSOCIATION AND SUBSIDIARIES**
Consolidated Statements of Changes in Financial Position
($ thousands)

	Years Ended June 30,			Six Months Ended December 31,	
	1981	1982	1983	1982	1983
				(unaudited)	
Sources of funds:					
Operations:					
Net earnings (loss)	$ 681	$ (3,228)	$ (489)	$ (1,221)	$ 404
Noncash charges (credits):					
Interest credited to savings deposits	17,186	24,984	29,734	15,121	14,696
Depreciation	234	317	338	167	187
Income taxes payable (receivable)	(108)	(1,835)	175	(456)	184
Deferred tax (benefit) expense	215	698	(121)	75	270
Accrued interest receivable	(758)	145	(1,364)	(569)	(397)
Amortization of deferred income	(197)	(193)	(516)	(201)	(483)
Provision for loan losses	—	11	639	122	382
Other, net	19	(123)	(212)	(856)	(616)
Funds provided by operations	17,272	20,776	28,184	12,182	14,627
Loan collections	37,149	46,561	72,765	24,525	78,210
Net increase in deposits	9,000	—	24,953	4,057	—
Net increase in repurchase agreements	—	13,201	—	—	6,248
Decrease in cash and investments . .	5,080	—	10,460	2,666	—
Advances from Federal Home Loan Bank and other borrowings	4,201	9,221	22,100	23,027	—
Cost of loan participations and whole loans sold	—	7,918	81,593	19,459	43,918
Proceeds from sale of real estate owned	632	416	502	37	174
Increase in other liabilities	448	4,404	762	—	2,696
Other, net	142	107	2,440	1,793	479
	$73,924	$102,604	$243,759	$87,746	$146,352
Use of funds:					
Investment in loans	$61,871	$59,299	$134,271	$48,474	$112,723
Net decrease in deposits	—	1,840	—	—	6,629
Net decrease in repurchase agreements	—	—	4,810	2,517	—
Repayment of Federal Home Loan Bank advances and other borrowings	3,640	1,160	8,270	690	6,892
Purchase of participations in loans . .	7,787	17,296	95,471	35,558	9,889
Investment in Federal Home Loan Bank stock	52	170	213	57	—
Purchase of premises and equipment	495	587	724	310	1,775
Real estate development costs	79	30	—	—	—
Increase in cash and investments . . .	—	22,222	—	—	8,444
Decrease in other liabilities	—	—	—	140	—
	$73,924	$102,604	$243,759	$87,746	$146,352

EXHIBIT D

Consolidated Statements of Financial Condition
BANKERS FIRST CORPORATION AND SUBSIDIARIES
($ thousands)

	December 31, 1985	December 31, 1984	June 30, 1984
Assets			
Cash and amounts due from depository institutions	$ 21,344	$ 12,810	$ 10,317
Interest-bearing deposits in other banks.	20,798	28,315	25,727
Federal funds sold, at cost	2,715	880	150
Investment securities, at amortized cost (market value $385, $10,719, and $11,727 at December 31, 1985 and 1984 and June 30, 1984, respectively) — (Note 2)	333	10,699	11,831
Loans receivable, net (Notes 3, 6, 7, and 8)	565,699	453,037	411,581
Premises and equipment (Notes 4 and 8)	20,563	10,735	9,762
Real estate acquired by foreclosure	3,152	992	1,110
Real estate held for development and sale.	2,078	1,013	1,903
Investment in and loans to partnership (Note 5)	6,073	1,705	—
Federal Home Loan Bank stock, at cost (Note 8)	4,212	2,762	2,762
Accrued interest receivable.	6,420	5,698	5,217
Other assets	4,153	1,456	725
Total	$657,540	$530,102	$481,085
Liabilities, Deferred Income, and Stockholders' Equity			
Deposits (Note 7).	$461,041	$405,160	$378,821
Repurchase agreements (Note 6)	15,669	28,375	21,290
Advance payments by borrowers for taxes and insurance.	2,146	1,850	2,313
Other borrowings (Note 8)	97,220	44,680	34,874
Deferred income taxes (Note 9)	3,196	2,750	2,381
Other liabilities (Notes 9 and 10)	12,374	11,699	7,816
Total liabilities	$591,646	$494,514	447,495
Deferred income	2,608	2,280	1,610
Stockholders' equity (Notes 10 and 11):			
Common Stock, $.01 par value; authorized 12,500,000 shares; issued 4,386,297 shares at December 31, 1985, and 2,300,000 shares at December 31, 1984, and June 30, 1984.	44	23	23
Serial Preferred Stock, $.01 par value; authorized 7,500,000 shares; none outstanding.	—	—	—
Additional paid-in capital	42,542	14,875	14,875
Retained earnings (substantially restricted)	22,650	18,410	17,082
Amounts receivable to purchase stock from the Employee Stock Ownership Plan (Note 10)	(1,950)	—	—
Total stockholders' equity	63,286	33,308	31,980
Commitments (Notes 3, 4, 10, and 15)			
Total	$657,540	$530,102	$481,085

EXHIBIT E

Consolidated Statements of Earnings (Loss)
BANKERS FIRST CORPORATION AND SUBSIDIARIES
($ thousands)

	Year Ended Dec. 31, 1985	Six Months Ended Dec. 31, 1984	Years Ended June 30, 1984	1983
Interest income:				
Interest on loans.	$60,719	$27,081	$47,262	$42,431
Other interest income	2,443	1,853	3,953	5,083
Total interest income.	63,162	28,934	51,215	47,514
Interest expense:				
Interest on deposits (Note 7)	39,479	19,469	38,110	37,601
Interest on repurchase agreements	1,149	1,254	1,314	1,367
Interest on other borrowings	6,707	2,110	4,389	5,310
Total interest expense	47,335	22,833	43,813	44,278
Net interest income	15,827	6,101	7,402	3,236
Provision for loan losses	1,136	455	552	639
Net interest income after provision for loan losses.	14,691	5,646	6,850	2,597
Other income:				
Loan origination fees	3,567	1,319	2,546	2,136
Other fees and service charges	2,243	537	824	321
Dividends on Federal Home Loan Bank stock	388	195	291	271
Gain on sale of loans (Note 3)	3,520	709	1,061	1,579
Gain on sale of investment securities	283	165	—	73
Profit on sale of real estate.	400	289	517	137
Other	714	203	379	193
Total other income.	11,115	3,417	5,618	4,710
Other expense:				
Salaries and employee benefits.	9,842	3,747	5,782	4,117
Net occupancy expense of premises	3,708	1,350	1,775	1,182
Advertising and promotion	830	260	547	557
FSLIC insurance premiums.	878	159	299	264
Other operating	4,045	1,603	2,267	1,622
Total other expense	19,303	7,119	10,670	7,742
Earnings (loss) before income tax expense and extraordinary item.	6,503	1,944	1,798	(435)
Income tax expense (Note 9)	2,263	777	761	54
Net earnings (loss) before extraordinary item.	4,240	1,167	1,037	(489)
Extraordinary item (net of deferred income tax expense of $79) (Note 14).	—	161	—	—
Net earnings (loss).	$ 4,240	$ 1,328	$ 1,037	$ (489)
Earnings per share (Note 13):				
Net earnings before extraordinary item	$ 1.30	$ .51	N/A	N/A
Extraordinary item	—	.07	N/A	N/A
Net earnings.	$ 1.30	.58	N/A	N/A

Consolidated Statements of Changes in Financial Position
BANKERS FIRST CORPORATION AND SUBSIDIARIES
($ thousands)

	Year Ended Dec. 31, 1985	Six Months Ended Dec. 31, 1984	Years Ended June 30, 1984	Years Ended June 30, 1983
Sources of funds:				
Operations:				
Net earnings (loss) before extraordinary item.	$ 4,240	$ 1,167	$ 1,037	$ (489)
Noncash charges (credits):				
Interest credited to savings deposits . .	24,212	15,590	27,409	29,734
Depreciation.	1,384	442	491	338
Income taxes payable	(457)	487	53	175
Deferred tax expense (benefit)	446	369	708	(121)
Accrued interest receivable.	(628)	(481)	(524)	(1,364)
Amortization of deferred income	(1,569)	(543)	(1,093)	(516)
Provision for loan losses	1,136	455	552	639
Other, net	(758)	(157)	(160)	(212)
Funds provided by operations exclusive of extraordinary item.	28,006	17,329	28,473	28,184
Extraordinary item, net of related income taxes	—	161	—	—
Loan collections.	209,856	75,425	168,822	72,765
Net proceeds from sale of common stock	25,688	—	14,898	—
Net increase in deposits	4,653	10,749	—	24,953
Net increase in repurchase agreements . . .	14,310	7,085	12,898	—
Decrease in cash and investments	9,436	—	—	10,460
Proceeds from other borrowings	79,376	10,000	2,421	22,100
Cost of loan participations and whole loans sold	167,003	51,103	98,225	81,593
Proceeds from sale of real estate	2,796	729	1,171	502
Other, net	—	3,851	2,523	3,202
	$541,124	$176,432	$329,431	$243,759
Uses of funds:				
Investment in loans	$475,189	$163,712	$245,620	$134,271
Net decrease in deposits	—	—	21,038	—
Net decrease in repurchase agreements. . . .	—	—	—	4,810
Repayment of other borrowings	27,050	194	8,969	8,270
Purchase of participations in loans	12,643	4,727	39,361	95,471
Investment in and loans to partnership . . .	4,368	1,705	—	—
Investment in Federal Home Loan Bank stock	1,450	—	215	213
Purchase of premises and equipment	9,767	1,415	5,496	724
Increase in cash and investments	—	4,679	8,732	—
Other, net	3,283	—	—	—
Acquisition of Southeastern Mortgage Corporation:				
Loans receivable.	2,715	—	—	—
Capitalized servicing	1,316	—	—	—
Premises and equipment	1,445	—	—	—
Other assets.	2,484	—	—	—
Borrowings	(214)	—	—	—
Other liabilities	(372)	—	—	—
	$541,124	$176,432	$329,431	$243,759

EXHIBIT G Yield and Cost of Funds Data

| | At December 31, | | At June 30, | |
	1985	1984	1984	1983
End of period				
Weighted average:				
Yield on loan portfolio	11.14%	12.29%	12.38%	11.83%
Yield on total investments	8.28	8.72	10.96	9.64
Yield on all interest-earning assets	11.02	11.88	12.11	11.65
Rate on deposits	8.73	9.99	9.86	10.24
Rate on repurchase agreements	6.95	7.83	9.87	8.90
Rate on FHLB advances and other borrowings	9.48	11.79	12.11	11.47
Rate on all interest-bearing liabilities	8.85	10.03	10.04	10.33
Interest rate spread*	2.17	1.85	2.07	1.32
Net interest margin†	2.45	2.16	2.49	1.47

| | For the Twelve Months Ended December 31, | | For the Years Ended June 30, | |
	1985	1984	1984	1983
For the period				
Weighted average:				
Yield on loan portfolio	11.89%	12.19%	11.94%	11.47%
Yield on total investments	8.96	10.51	9.97	10.26
Yield on all interest-earning assets	11.75	12.04	11.76	11.33
Rate on deposits	9.16	10.02	10.26	10.96
Rate on repurchase agreements	6.69	9.23	8.84	11.13
Rate on FHLB advances and other borrowings	10.60	12.14	11.78	11.59
Rate on all interest-bearing liabilities	9.25	10.15	10.34	11.03
Interest rate spread*	2.50	1.89	1.42	.30
Net interest margin†	2.93	2.24	1.70	.77

* Yield on all interest-earning assets less rate on all interest-bearing liabilities.
† Net interest income divided by average interest-earning assets.

Certain Significant Ratios

| | At or for the Twelve Months Ended December 31, | | At or for the Years Ended June 30, | |
	1985	1984	1984	1983
Return on assets[a]	.72%	.40%	.22%	(.11)%
Return on equity[b]	9.21	7.26	5.49	(3.06)
Equity-to-assets ratio[c]	7.84	5.58	4.12	3.73
Fixed-rate loans as a percentage of total assets[d]	21.29	33.90	42.14	54.90
Delinquent loans as a percentage of total loans[e]	3.44	1.88	1.61	1.43
Allowances for loan losses as a percentage of total loans[f]	.43	.42	.39	.28
Net charge-offs as a percentage of total loans[g]	.110	.037	.013	.009
Noninterest income as a percentage of total income[h]	14.96	10.33	9.89	9.02
General and administrative expenses as a percentage of total income[i]	25.99	21.28	18.77	14.82

[a] Net earnings (loss) divided by average total assets.
[b] Net earnings (loss) divided by average net worth.
[c] Average net worth divided by average total assets.
[d] Fixed-rate loans and GNMA, FHLMC, and FNMA participation certificates divided by total assets at period end.
[e] Loans 30 or more days past due divided by total loans at period end.
[f] Allowances for loan losses divided by total loans at period end.
[g] Losses charged to allowances less recoveries divided by total loans at period end.
[h] All noninterest income divided by interest income plus noninterest income for the period.
[i] All noninterest expense, except for provision for loan losses and income taxes, divided by interest income plus noninterest income for the period.

EXHIBIT H

Selected Consolidated Financial Data
BANKERS FIRST CORPORATION AND SUBSIDIARIES

The following tables set forth certain consolidated financial information concerning the company and its subsidiaries at the dates or for the periods indicated. (Dollars in thousands except per share amounts.) These tables are only a summary and should be read in conjunction with the more complete information contained in this *Annual Report*.

	As of December 31,		As of June 30,			
	1985	1984	1984	1983	1982	1981
Balance sheet data						
Total assets	$657,540	$530,102	$481,085	$449,287	$384,503	$337,987
Loans receivable, net	565,699	453,037	411,581	394,199	320,072	297,808
Total investments*	23,846	39,894	37,708	33,399	46,088	25,415
Deposits	461,041	405,160	378,821	372,450	317,763	294,163
Borrowings:						
FHLB advances	84,240	42,240	32,240	39,850	26,970	18,570
Repurchase agreements	15,669	28,375	21,290	8,392	13,201	—
Other borrowings	12,980	2,440	2,634	1,572	622	777
Stockholders' equity	63,286	33,308	31,980	16,045	16,534	19,762
Stockholders' equity per share	14.43	14.48	13.90	—†	—†	—†

	Year Ended December 31, 1985	Twelve Months Ended Dec. 31, 1984 (unaudited)	Year Ended June 30,			
			1984	1983	1982	1981
Income statement data						
Interest income on loans	$60,719	$50,672	$47,262	$42,431	$34,414	$27,795
Other interest income	2,443	4,180	3,953	5,083	4,681	3,479
Interest expense	(47,335)	(44,643)	(43,813)	(44,278)	(37,486)	(28,121)
Net interest income	15,827	10,209	7,402	3,236	1,609	3,153
Provision for loan losses	(1,136)	(625)	(552)	(639)	(11)	—
Fees and services charges	5,810	3,673	3,370	2,457	1,581	1,366
Gain (loss) on sale of loans	3,520	999	1,061	1,579	(2,475)	—
Other income	1,785	1,646	1,187	674	535	600
General and administrative expenses	(19,303)	(13,018)	(10,670)	(7,742)	(5,604)	(4,331)
Income tax benefit (expense)	(2,263)	(1,084)	(761)	(54)	1,137	(107)
Net earnings (loss) before extraordinary item	4,240	1,800	1,037	(489)	(3,228)	681
Extraordinary item, net of taxes	—	161	—	—	—	—
Net earnings (loss)	$ 4,240	$ 1,961	$ 1,037	$ (489)	$ (3,228)	681
Net earnings per share	$ 1.30	—†	—†	—†	—†	—†

* Includes interest-bearing deposits in banks, federal funds, and investment securities.
† Bankers First converted from mutual to stock form on April 27, 1984; therefore, stockholders' equity per share and earnings per share are not presented for periods prior to conversion.

company recognizes that we have our tellers on the line meeting the public more often than any other group, including management and that more than 80 percent of customer contact is made by the teller. Because many customers form an impression of the company through teller contact, management decided that increased knowledge and responsibility of tellers was essential. A survey conducted of the company's tellers found that many tellers wanted increased responsibility and challenge from their jobs.

Tellers must qualify for the program based on customer service, job performance, and referrals by an appropriate Bankers First official. The three-level program takes 20 to 26 months to complete. The program includes hands-on experiences in various departments of Bankers First, instruction in a classroom-type environment, and self-study workbooks.

Tellers completing all levels of the program should be able to make decisions that formerly had to be made by supervisors one and two management levels above the tellers, Gay said. Employees completing each phase of the program are compensated through cash bonuses, service pins, and promotions.

BANKERS FIRST COMMON STOCK

The company's common stock is listed on NASDAQ under the symbol BNKF. Prices quoted for the stock are reported in the NASDAQ over-the-counter national market section of *The Wall Street Journal*.

The common stock was first traded on April 24, 1984. The stock began trading on the national market on October 1, 1985.

| | Price Range (in dollars) | |
	Low	High
1984	6¼	10
1985	9⅞	17½
1986	13¾	19

32.   Banking in a World of Change

Old stories are the best stories. People tell them because they reveal some important truth. A young banker asks an old banker, "What is your philosophy of banking?" The old banker answers, "I believe in the 3-6-3 rule, young man. Pay 3 percent—lend at 6 percent—go play golf at three." Bankers hate this story because before 1972, it was almost totally accurate. Banks operated under a huge government umbrella which limited where banks could be and how much they could pay their deposit customers. In return, competition was rigidly limited and a reasonably able bank manager could make substantial profits. A really aggressive banker could make even larger profits by exploiting the fact that the government insured the depositors against risk.

All of this describes American banking before deregulation. But the same government that made the high profits possible and removed the risk from banking also created a new inflationary environment which destroyed the old protected world. Nonbanks found that they could effectively compete with banks. The 13 largest American banks found that they could evade all domestic restrictions and compete in a totally unfettered overseas world. For example, Citibank, the largest American bank, despite its aggressive domestic growth, is a bank with 65 percent of its assets overseas.

The average American lives in a world of change—change occurring so rapidly that it is hard to assimilate it all. In the banking world, the most important change has been the growth of the power and strength of the major regional banks. Banks are no longer Atlanta banks or Jacksonville banks. Now through interstate compacts, banks in Florida, Georgia, North and South Carolina, and Tennessee can merge and become one bank. The recent merger between Sun Banks of Florida, the Trust Company of Georgia, and now the Third National of Nashville is the perfect example. The Citizens and Southern has merged with its namesake in South Carolina and Landmark of Florida. Only the Bank of the South remains unaffiliated in Atlanta. All of this is only the beginning of a long list of mergers that will occur in the South, New England, the Midwest, and now finally California. Thirty-four states now permit some form of interstate banking. Six states

---

This case was prepared by Robert R. Dince, Professor of Finance, University of Georgia and former Deputy Comptroller of the Currency, U.S. Treasury.

permit unlimited entry provided that the incoming bank buys an existing bank in the state. Most of the other states have legislation which restricts banking mergers across state lines to a designated state list. Permission is granted on a reciprocal basis.

No other nation in the world has as complicated a banking system as the United States. We have over 14,800 chartered insured banks (plus thousands of savings institutions). One federal agency, the Comptroller of the Currency, U.S Treasury, charters national banks, and 50 states also can charter new state banks. Two other federal agencies, the Federal Reserve and the Federal Deposit Insurance Corporation also regulate banking.

But deregulation and persistent specialized economic problems have raised fundamental questions about the safety of the American depository system. Bank failures are at record highs (since the Great Depression); 96 this year, 120 in 1985. The usual procedure is for the FDIC to arrange a takeover by another bank. But sometimes the troubled bank is too large and state and federal laws are too restrictive. In other cases, the government attempts to keep the bank alive using whatever means are available.

The whole question of risk to the depositor must be raised. As long as the deposit is kept under $100,000 the depositor is absolutely guaranteed. (For a married couple $300,000; $100,000 in his name, $100,000 in her name, and $100,000 in joint name.) But in a few smaller banks recently, deposits *greater* than $100,000 have not been paid off. In the case of the Continental Illinois Bank of Chicago, all deposits including foreign deposits were guaranteed. There is a moral to the story and that is that insurance over the $100,000 limit is strictly a matter of governmental policy and not some form of an implied contract.

Profit on Average Assets at FDIC-Insured Banks

Asset Size	1981	1982	1983	1984	1985
Less than $300 million	1.08%	0.97%	0.87%	0.82%	0.68%
$300–$1,000 million	0.89	0.80	0.79	0.87	0.71
More than $1 billion	0.64	0.61	0.54	0.53	0.60
All banks	0.80	0.73	0.66	0.64	0.63

SOURCE: Federal Deposit Insurance Corporation.

The table in the text shows the profitability of American banking in recent years. Deregulation has dealt a heavy blow to small banks. The table further shows why interstate banking is both inevitable and beneficial. Deregulation has meant that the market and not the government tells the bank what to pay depositors. Deregulation has also meant that banks have been permitted to offer the community a wider menu of products—sometimes with disastrous results. The table shows that smaller banks are 37 percent less profitable than they were five years ago and that large banks have not suffered. The profit numbers do not break down between the 13 huge international banks like Citibank, Bank of America, Chase, Security Pacific, etc., and just ordinary large regional banks like Wachovia or Southeastern. Some of the really large banks, because of their heavy involvement in international finance, have had rocky times. For example, the Bank of America had to write off $684 million of loans in 1986. The profitable banks are the regional banks like Sun Trust or Barnett. These banks can do most of the things the large banks can do but they are still tied to local markets and a local deposit base.

But this raises a crucial question: Just how local should a banking market be? Up until quite recently, some of the best regional banks in the United States were located in Texas and Oklahoma. In 1986 the largest bank in Oklahoma has gone under and some of the big Texas banks are staggering badly. A bank to survive and prosper should be able to meet the community's legitimate credit needs. But suppose the community gets sick, what happens to the community bank with the area's deposits? Banks all over the United States are in trouble. At last count, 1,411 banks are known to be on the FDIC's potential problem list. Where the local community is in trouble, the bank is in trouble—agricultural areas, old smokestack communities, oil-producing areas. You cannot remove the risk of failure by combining one Texas bank with another Texas bank.

One of the problems that American banks are being forced to meet is competition from foreign banks. For example, there are roughly 20 foreign banks in Atlanta plus a large number of out-of-state banks that maintain offices in the Atlanta community. What is the Sumitomo Bank doing in Atlanta and the Banco do Brasil or Barclay's? One thing the foreign banks are doing is lending one dollar out of every five to American and foreign firms doing business in the United States. Most of these foreign banks do not need American brick and mortar branches to service their customers; they can secure their funds in the huge $2 trillion eurodollar market. International banks buy funds in this market when and where they need them and for as long as they need them. These funds exist completely outside the United States and for all intents and purposes out of the control of the American monetary and banking authorities.

What all this means is that banks must compete with foreign banks and even more important they must compete with all the players in the new financial services industry. They must compete when profits are eroding and 1,411 banks are in serious trouble. The solution to this problem does not lie within the traditional local community bank.

Suppose you headed an Oklahoma community bank being run in the usual conservative manner. You have not made any speculative "oil patch loans"—loans to developers on unproven or overvalued reserves. But as the price of oil has fallen to less than $20 a barrel, even good oil loans have not generated enough cash flow to pay expenses and service existing debt. Workers get laid off. Good installment loans go into arrears. Construction loans go sour. Lines of credit extended to retail merchants cannot be paid as agreed.

The well-run community bank suddenly finds itself with too many nonperforming loans and it is in serious trouble. It makes little difference how well run the bank is or how well the bank is examined by federal or state authorities. Banks operating in stricken communities are seriously impacted by local economic conditions beyond their control.

The classic financial prescription against this kind of trouble is diversification. Diversification across state lines. Diversification—previously impossible due to restrictive state and federal laws—is the only way to provide the solution. Even now, Texas banks cannot be saved until the Texas legislature makes it legal for a non-Texas bank to buy a Texas bank. Wachovia going into Atlanta or the C&S going to Florida, or the Sun Trust going to Tennessee is the only way to reduce risk in the American banking system. It will not eliminate risk but it will reduce it. And all of this can be accomplished without any government money.

Interstate banking is not only beneficial, it is necessary. The government can neither afford all the insurance it offers nor can it prop up another big bank. Consolidation and diversification seems to be the only solution.

There is a very special problem concerning the financial stability and future of the thrift industry. Thrifts are depository institutions whose defined traditional mission is to be a community depository for savings and a source of loans for home ownership. Unfortunately for the traditionally managed thrift, the wild swings in interest rates over the last 20 years exposed these institutions to unexpected and unparalleled risks.

Return on Assets: Insured Savings and Loan Associations, 1983–1986 (September 30)

	1983	1984	1985	1986
Over $1 billion	0.36%	0.23%	0.53%	0.37%
$500–1 billion	0.33	0.15	0.40	−0.11
$250–500 million	0.26	0.27	0.32	−0.02
$100–$250 million	0.19	0.23	0.23	−0.26

As the figures show, the savings and loan industry profits are considerably lower than banks. And the fall in interest rates has not cured the problems for the smaller institutions. Losses have returned in 1986 to plague the smaller institutions.

Going back to our old banking joke, even if interest rates go to 12 or even 22 percent (they did in 1982), most banks will not get in serious trouble. If the bank has to pay 12 percent for money, the typical loan comes due in six months or a year and the borrower will have to pay the current interest rate when the loan is renewed.

But a savings and loan is not that lucky. Suppose Joe and Mary Bush buy a $75,000 home in 1978 and borrow $65,000 for 30 years at 8 percent interest. They will pay $476.95 for 360 months. As long as the cost of money is no greater than 6½ percent, the S&L will be profitable. But by 1980 long-term interest rates were 11 percent and by 1982 they were 13 percent. The S&L to survive has to pay a going market interest to savers or risk an outflow of funds to competitors. But that good old loan to the Bushes is paying only 8 percent. How many "Bush" loans they have made determines how long the S&L can survive. Suppose that 60 percent of their assets earn 8 percent and 40 percent earn 12 percent; they earn 9.6 overall. But their deposits cost 10 percent and it costs 1 percent to run the institution. The institution has a negative cash flow of 1.4 percent on assets. This is "savings and loan" disease.

Obviously the only way to cure the disease is to raise the yield on assets. It is impossible to lower the cost of money because this is determined by the market. But old mortgages can only be sold with disastrous results. The Bush mortgage in 1982 would be worth no more than $45,284 in a 12 percent market in 1983. (Its book value assuming 60 payments would be $61,795.) You can see how sick this S&L is since 60 percent of its assets have a market value 27 percent less than book. That is a lot more than its capital position. This institution is already insolvent but the government is going to turn a blind eye until the negative cash flow erodes the net worth.

So the solution is to let the S&L sell its new loans as fast as they make them, passing the risk to another buyer. Or another solution is to charge the Bushes a variable rate—something the Bushes hate, thus passing the risk to the borrower. Another solution is to let this very limited-function S&L with a set of very limited skills get out and hustle for new car and boat loans and make loans to real estate developers. Diversification is the ticket for thrifts as well as banks, but new business means new risks and possibly large loan losses.

In 1987, over 200 S&Ls remain on the endangered list and the government insurance fund is itself insolvent. Making home loans is not the simple business we once thought. Hopefully the problems of banks and thrifts will become less severe as they both diversify to create a new financial service industry.

International Business Activities

33.   Windward Islands Aloe, Inc.

This evening, as he hoisted his pleasantly tired legs onto the bannister of his modest house, reached for his lime punch, and gazed out across his shimmering aloe fields to the Caribbean Sea and Martinique beyond, Marshall "Barney" Barnard knew he had more to do than just relax. He had to decide whether or not to risk investing more of his and his wife's money in Windward Islands Aloe, Inc., money that they could not afford to lose.

Barney had always been one to follow his own drummer. While still in his teens, he had followed the example of his fellow New Englander Jack Kerouac and had taken to the roads—traveled a lot and worked when he had to. Finally, he settled down in the Florida Panhandle, raised a family with his wife Loe, and with her as an equal partner ran a number of reasonably successful businesses: an organic farm, a family style restaurant, and a stained glass manufacturing operation. Loe was an artist and her paintings, along with some real estate deals, provided the little extra that made life comfortable.

Barney smiled as the first swallow of the cool refreshing punch slid down his welcoming throat.

"It was the dabbling in real estate that got me here, for better or worse," he mused.

The past decade in Florida had been an excellent time to buy and sell undeveloped farmland in Florida. Barney, in a small way, had made some tidy profits through this type of venture.

Through these real estate deals, he had met Bill Nelson, a Florida agribusiness entrepreneur, who also handled real estate on the side. Barney and Bill had been partners in a couple of deals and along the way became close friends. It was Bill who convinced Barney and Loe not only to become junior partners in Windward Islands Aloe, but also to come to Dominica, in the eastern Caribbean, and manage the operation.

In early 1983, Bill had returned from an OPIC[1] investment promotion mission to the Caribbean with an inordinately high level of en-

---

This case was prepared by William Naumes and Kevin Kane as the basis for class discussion, and is not designed as a description of effective or ineffective administrative decision making. All rights reserved to the authors; 1986.

[1] Overseas Private Investment Corporation—A U.S. government agency that promotes overseas investments by United States and issues risk insurance for appropriation of company assets by foreign governments.

thusiasm for one country, Dominica. He had gone to Dominica to look at the prospect of taking over a lime plantation and juice extraction factory that had been sold to the government by Rose's Lime Juices Ltd., a British Company. That project proved not to be feasible. Rose's had built a white elephant of a processing unit, far too large and expensive to operate for the island's limited supply of limes.

However, Bill had been greatly impressed by the government's interest in attracting foreign investors. The prime minister, a successful lawyer and businesswoman herself, had spent many hours with the members of the mission, discussing opportunities and concerns, and assuring them that her government would promptly expedite all the required investment paperwork. Then Kenny Alleyne, the managing director of the government investment promotion organization, the Industrial Development Corporation (IDC), had taken over and very competently handled the nuts and bolts parts of the visits; discussions of corporate and individual tax holidays, duty-free import of production equipment and materials for reexport, tours of agricultural and industrial sites around the island, etc. All in all, Bill felt that the climate for agribusiness investments in Dominica was excellent, even if his initial interest, the lime juice factory, did not pan out.

Subsequently, while in Dominica, he had been introduced to a potentially better investment opportunity, aloe vera, by Andrew Proctor, IDC's PDAP[2] adviser. Aloe vera, Nelson learned, is a cactus plant whose liquid pulp's moisturizing properties have long been known by medicinal healers and burn specialists. Only recently had the commercial possibilities of aloe vera become evident. Now demand was exploding as aloe vera was being introduced as an ingredient in suntan lotion, skin-care products, shampoos, and health tonics, to name a few. Almost all commercially grown aloe was presently produced in the Rio Grande River Valley of Texas and Mexico. However, expansion of production there was limited by other crops, the fear of frost, and a competitive labor market. Both Nelson and Proctor felt that Dominica was well positioned to be a competitive aloe producer. The southern part of the island had a suitable climate and soil, there was no danger of frost, and a ready supply of trained agricultural workers were available for U.S. 50 cents per hour (compared to the U.S. $3–$4 an hour rate in the Rio Grande Valley). Further, with the IDC's assistance, Nelson had identified a partially abandoned lime estate suitable for aloe production that was available for purchase.

---

[2] Private Development Assistance Project—A U.S. Agency for International Development (USAID) program implemented by Coopers & Lybrand for the purpose of promoting foreign investment in the eastern Caribbean; part of the Reagan administration's Caribbean Basis Initiative (CBI).

All of Nelson's agribusiness contacts in Florida were enthusiastic about aloe's potential and gradually Barney and Loe became interested in the project. Their children were all grown and the idea of a new business in an exotic location was very appealing.

After a trip to Dominica with Nelson later in the year, Barney's interest grew to excitement. Bill was right; the government and the IDC were very helpful, working capital could be provided through the local development bank, and the land and labor requirements were available. Marshall quickly went about assembling a cadre of investors, a specialty of his, and plans were set in motion to launch Windward Island Aloe, Inc. With Kenny Alleyne of the IDC and Peter Wright, the PDAP successor of Andrew Proctor handling the in-country preparations, things moved quickly. By early 1984, the Barnards had arrived in Dominica to develop the estate.

Now in the middle of 1985, taking another sip of his punch, Barney knew that he and Loe would not regret it even if the project collapsed. It had been a wonderful year and a half, something they would not have wanted to miss. And there in front of him, in the evening light, was the result of their efforts—60 acres of 600,000 aloe plants, well on their way to the first cuttings.

"Now I can laugh about them, but there had been some difficult times," Barney mused.

He remembered the first night he slept on the estate, when like a fool, he drank water from an abandoned cistern. By morning, wracked with fever, chills, and vomiting, he not only thought he was dying, he hoped it would come soon. It took weeks to fully regain his strength.

Then there was the time the rust bucket of a ship they had chartered to bring aloe plants down from Haiti broke down and had to be towed into Fort de France, Martinique. The French authorities were demanding hundreds of thousands of francs[3] for towing fees, repairs, and port charges. Meanwhile, the aloe plants were wilting in the steamy hold of the ship. If the Dominican government had not intervened, all would have been lost. Likewise, if the estate workers and nearby Soufriere villagers had not worked around the clock to get the plants off the ship by whale boat, and up the road on every pickup truck available, and immediately planted, all would have been lost anyway.

"Sacre Dieu!" Barney chuckled in his best Creole, "That was a time."

Now, however, the problem was a different one. They were just about out of money and the first returns might still be a year away. The accounts were kept in Florida, but Barney knew the situation all too

---

[3] At the time $1 U.S. = 8.5 Francs.

well. To date, about $250,000 had been invested in the project. Most of the money came from stateside investors, but about $50,000 was from a local bank financed at 13 percent interest. Barney felt that another $20,000 was required for further capital investment. It was to be used to build a primary processing shed. Also, working capital requirements for labor, materials, and management expenses would average about EC $7,000[4] per month for the next year. There might also be additional working capital needed for expenses incurred in the U.S. part of the operations.

Barney had a good working relationship with the manager of the Development Bank. He reminded Barney of the shrewd country bankers back in the Florida Panhandle for whom financial projections were nice, but the character of the man across the table and what he was willing to transfer from his wallet to the project were much more important. Since Bill Nelson, increasingly occupied by other entrepreneurial projects, was taking more time than expected in raising the second level of investment capital, Barney knew he would very soon have to secure an agreement with the Development Bank for additional working capital. And Barney knew the manager was going to require an increased equity investment. A logical amount would be the U.S. $20,000 required to build the primary processing shed. If the project was not going to grind down to an irreversible halt, Barney was going to have to provide the required $20,000. He and Loe could draw down that much from their account in Florida. That would expose them to added risks, however, due to another investment with which they were involved.

Six months before coming to Dominica, Barney and Bill Nelson had secured financing to purchase a 100-acre farm. They had anticipated a quick turnaround for the property as it was perfect for a thoroughbred stud or country gentleman's farm. Initially there were a number of interested buyers. One of them had, in fact, kept them within a week of closing for about six months before backing out. By then, farm prices had begun to fall and they were now stuck with heavy monthly payments with no ready prospects for a buyer. To draw down $20,000 would leave Barney and Loe in a potentially precarious position.

Both Loe and he felt the aloe project had a good chance of success. The landed price for a 45-gallon drum of aloe in the United States was U.S. $50 and the price was if anything, expected to rise in the short term. His direct production, processing, and shipping costs were not likely to exceed U.S. $22 per barrel. With each of the 600,000 plants

---

[4] EC $2.68 = U.S. $1—For the last seven years the eastern Caribbean (EC) dollar has been tied to the U.S. dollar. There is now pressure from banana exporters to Britain and the tourist industry to devalue because of the overvalued U.S. dollar.

on the 60 developed acres yielding 16 ounces of pulp each year, less a 2.5–5 percent loss and wastage factor, good profits were likely even in the initial stages. Later, another 25 acres could be developed, and the small farms in the area could be assisted in developing their own plots. They also were experimenting with papaya, sorrel (a flowering plant used to produce a popular West Indian juice), and tropical sheep production on the excess land available on the plantation.

Not that there still were not worries. In some way it was like *Don't Stop the Carnival.*[5] Of paramount concern was the processing operation, an area in which neither Barney nor Loe had much experience. Barney would do the primary processing and stabilizing on the estate. The government lime factory had promised to gear up for the secondary processing and homogenizing. Barney also knew he could get training for his workers from the local skill program.[6] None of the government activities had been finalized yet, however.

Bill Nelson, in an effort to tap into the exploding market, had begun shipping trial shipments of aloe processed from wild plants from Haiti. While quarantine inspectors had passed the shipments in Miami, they had been rejected in Texas, the major end-processing center. The Texas quarantine inspectors said the levels of active impurities were too high, but Nelson suspected local industry pressure, to protect the local crop.

The processing operations could also suffer from lack of spare parts or shortages of the stabilizing compound. Dominica was definitely at the end of the transport supply line; even freighted items often took two to three weeks to arrive.

Barney knew he got along well with his workers. They liked the way he had designed the task system so that as soon as they had completed their assignment they could go home. They also appreciated the fact that they were allowed to maintain gardens in various nooks and crannies of the estate. This was a very valuable "nonwage benefit" in a land-scarce district. Still, Barney knew that unions were very strong in Dominica and organizers were already talking to his workers. He did not think he could maintain the high levels of productivity he presently had with his relaxed informal style of management if he had to negotiate details of working conditions with a professional union organizer. "Besides," thought Barney, "most of the unions are associated with political parties, and if there are two things I cannot claim any understanding of here, it is politics and cricket. I suppose I should think more about politics even though everyone assumes the

---

[5] Herman Wouk's humorous account of trying to run a hotel in the U.S. Virgin Islands.

[6] A job-training program jointly funded and operated by USAID, the Dominican government, and the Organization of American States (OAS).

prime minister is a shoo-in for another five-year term. After all, this electorate is the party's strongest and most of my friends are as pro free enterprise as I am. That certainly does not appear to be the case with her 'leftist' opponents."[7]

By now darkness had descended, the chattering Colibiri, the birds after whom the estate had been named, had returned to their nests, and the twinkling lights of Martinique could be seen in the distance. The aroma of simmering mountain chicken wafted up from the kitchen, reminding Barney that he had considered the situation long enough. He knew Loe's position; the project had the feel of a winner and now Dominica was home. She wanted to stay, but as always the decision would have to be a mutually agreeable one. If he thought the risk was too great, they could return to Florida and develop some prospects there.

Tomorrow he would have to decide.

---

[7] Politics in the English-speaking West Indies are usually personalized, passionate, and democratic. In the context, the term *leftist* varies in definition by place and time. At the time in Dominica, it referred to individuals sympathetic to the ideals of the New Jewel Movement in Grenada, the disastrous end of which had occurred a few months earlier. It was commonly assumed that leftist leaders not only had ties to the New Jewel Movement, but also with Cuba and Libya. It was allowed that the leftists saw state, not private ownership, as the primary vehicle for economic development—unlike 1980, when the traditional and radical left-of-center group campaigned independently and allowed the prime minister's party to win 17 of 21 parliamentary seats despite less than 50 percent of the vote. The opposition in Dominica had united for the upcoming election. Most observers felt that the prime minister's party would win the election as a result of the trauma produced by Grenada and an impressive development program, however.

34. Marketing in Carma Developers Ltd. (Revised)

On July 30, 1979, Rudy Janzen, executive vice president of Carma Developers Ltd. of Calgary, Alberta, had just returned from a board of directors meeting. The directors had recommended that Carma's use of outside marketing consulting firms be reviewed. Although Rudy couldn't quite "put his finger on it," he suspected that given Carma's rapidly expanding operations, the time had come to reexamine the entire role of marketing in Carma. Rudy thought that the next directors' meeting in September would be a good time to present a plan to more directly address market issues and strategy development at Carma.

BACKGROUND INFORMATION: CARMA

In 1958 in Calgary, the city itself was the prime land developer and the major source of serviced lots. Demand for lots, fueled by the growth of Calgary's petroleum industry, placed such pressure on the city that small builders would literally line up at city hall when a lot or two was offered for sale. The only other source of serviced lots in Calgary was two large builder-developers. These companies first selected lots for themselves and then sold the few remaining lots to small builders.

During 1958, Mr. Bennett, Mr. Roy Wilson, and Mr. Howard Ross approached Calgary's small builders to form an organization to develop lots. The men convinced 40 of Calgary's small builders to become shareholders in a new builder-owned development company. Over $260,000 was raised and Carma Developers Ltd. was formed as a private corporation. Mr. Joe Combe, the first employee hired by Carma Developers Ltd. was currently the CEO of the firm.

In the following 14 years, Carma developed 10 low-density (sin-

This case was prepared by James B. Graham, associate professor, with the assistance of Denise E. Paluck, research assistant, and Michael Fuller, lecturer, for the sole purpose of providing material for class discussion. Any use or duplication of the material in this case is prohibited except with the written consent of the faculty. Copyright © 1979, The University of Calgary.

gle-family and duplex) communities in Calgary, ranging in size from 100 to 2,800 lots.

CARMA'S GROWTH (1972–1979)

In 1972, Carma became a public corporation. During that same year, divisional offices were opened in Edmonton, Alberta, and Vancouver, B.C. In 1973, Carma opened another divisional office in Hamilton, Ontario. In 1974, Carma expanded its operations into Prince George, B.C.

In 1975, a new division, the Industrial, Commercial, and Investment Division (ICI), was created to develop and manage revenue-producing properties.

By 1976, 90 percent of Carma's total sales revenue was derived from the Alberta operations. In 1977, Carma began expansion into the U.S. market by opening a divisional office in Houston, Texas. Between 1972 and 1977, Carma produced over 10,000 single-family and duplex lots, surpassing its total production over its previous 14 years as a private company.

In 1978, Carma opened another divisional office in Seattle, Washington, acquired land in Sacramento, California, and a shopping center in Denver, Colorado. Low-density housing lot sales for 1978 totaled 2,188, a new high for one year's operations. Selected elements of Carma's financial growth are shown in Exhibit 1.

SALES METHODS

In the North American development industry, developers typically sell their serviced lots to independent builders or to builders owned by them. Carma is unique in that most of its shareholders are builders.

Carma is organized geographically with each region referred to as a marketing pool (e.g., Calgary, Edmonton, and Hamilton each constituted a separate marketing pool). Builder-shareholders are required to buy separate marketing contracts for each of the marketing pools in which they plan to buy lots. Each applicant for a marketing contract must:

a. Be an active homebuilder.
b. Agree to acquire building lots for the purpose of building, not for speculation by resale.
c. Be approved by Carma's board of directors (this approval involves a credit check).
d. Hold a specified minimum number of Carma common shares (this minimum is agreed upon by Carma and each builder when the contract is granted).

EXHIBIT 1 Summary of Carma Developers Ltd. Performance

Five-Year History	1978	1977	1976	1975	1974
Financial highlights (thousands of dollars)					
Revenue	$ 104,620	$ 62,100	$ 57,755	$ 39,487	$ 24,889
Net income	21,949	11,410	10,429	7,266	3,871
Funds from operations	36,996	17,357	10,173	10,920	4,959
Dividends	3,085	1,762	1,091	267	162
Per common share*					
Net income—basic	$ 1.95	$ 1.04	$ 0.96	$ 0.70	$ 0.40
fully diluted	1.93	1.03	0.94	0.69	0.34
Funds from operations	3.31	1.58	0.93	1.06	0.51
Dividends	0.48	0.16	0.10	0.025	0.017
Book value	5.58	3.88	3.02	2.18	1.51
Market price range	4.15–10.75	2.75–4.63	2.13–3.00	1.31–2.44	1.17–2.36
Other statistics (thousands of dollars except shares and employees)					
Land	$ 159,854	$ 127,599	$ 94,091	$ 74,779	$ 49,175
Rental properties	28,984	5,157	—	—	—
Total assets	281,258	179,011	127,373	103,423	64,825
Appraisal increment	222,557	160,604	157,719	113,029	70,418
Long-term debt	128,681	84,637	45,317	54,518	31,645
Shareholders' equity	66,495	47,798	33,054	23,282	14,672
Common shares outstanding*					
Actual	11,052,140	11,039,280	10,959,136	10,678,884	9,710,012
Weighted average	11,048,589	11,013,614	10,912,996	10,297,484	9,696,576
Number of employees	87	61	53	39	24

* Adjusted for the three-for-two split in September 1975, the two-for-one split November 1976, and the two-for-one split in November 1978.

SOURCE: 1978 Annual Report.

As of June 1979, Carma had individual marketing contracts with 39 builder-shareholders in Calgary, 28 in Edmonton, 28 in Surrey-Delta (Vancouver), 19 in Mapleridge (Vancouver), 19 in Vancouver Centre, and 24 in Hamilton. A contract similar to the standard marketing contract was used in the United States.

A marketing contract gives a builder-shareholder the right to purchase a defined percentage of the residential lots developed by Carma in each marketing pool in which a contract has been granted. The percentage is prorated to the number of Carma shares registered to the builder-shareholder in that particular market pool.

The right to purchase specific lots in a marketing pool is distributed among builder-shareholders by means of a "lot draw." Builders appear in person at the lot draw and pick numbers from a hat to determine the order in which they will select lots. Half of the lots are selected, based on the order established by the numbers drawn, then the order of lot selection is reversed and the second half of the lots are made available.[1] A builder who selects a lot has the option of purchasing the lot or "horse trading" his option to purchase with another builder for a lot that more closely meets his firm's needs.

To encourage the orderly build-out of a new community, Carma's board of directors may give an annual volume rebate of up to 5 percent of total dollar purchases to builder-shareholders who promptly obtain building permits and start construction. In all other respects, the terms of sale of the lots to all builders is the same.

At present, Nu-West Development Corporation Ltd.[2] is the largest builder-shareholder, holding 48.8 percent of Carma's shares. The next largest builder-shareholder (3.6 percent) is Britannia Homes Ltd. Carma's directors and senior officers own a further 11.8 percent, with the remaining share capital held by other builder-shareholders and the public.

LAND DIVISION AND DISTRICT ADVISORY BOARDS

Carma is a geographically decentralized company (see Exhibit 2). Regional land division managers, with the assistance of district managers, are responsible for the assembly, subdivision, servicing, and

---

[1] For example, assume that XYZ Company has the right to purchase 5 percent of any lots offered in Calgary's marketing pool. Five hundred twenty lots in Beddington Heights are offered for sale. XYZ's manager draws number 1 from the hat. Of the 260 (520 × .5) lots first offered, XYZ can select his 13 (260 × .05) first. As the remaining 260 lots are offered for sale, XYZ will have last choice of 13 lots. Because Carma's builder-shareholders cater to many market segments, it is likely that XYZ will be able to trade the lots least desirable for its purposes with another builder.

[2] Nu-West is Calgary's largest builder, and also handles some of its own land development.

EXHIBIT 2 Approximate Organization Structure of Carma Developers—June 1979

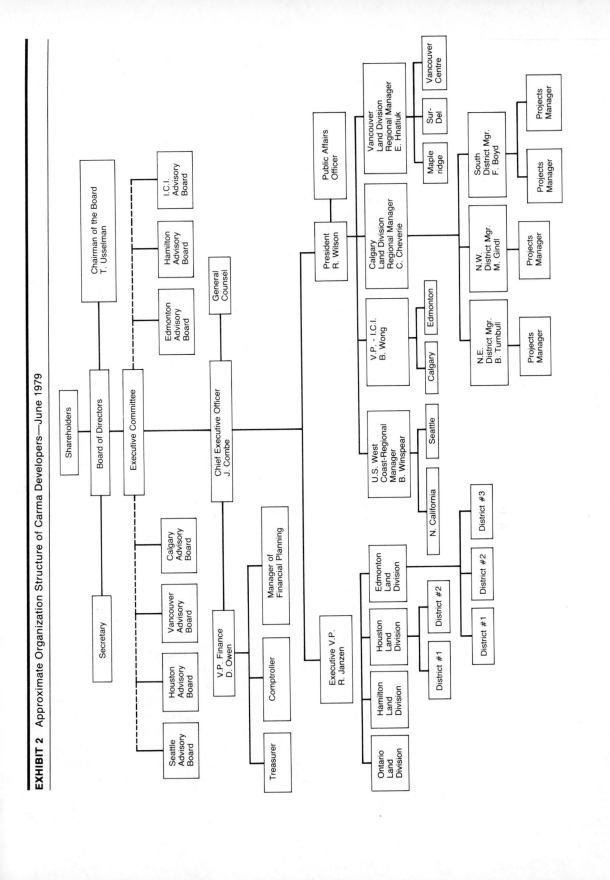

sale of residential land in their region. Each regional manager has specific authority to:

1. Purchase land and execute land transfers with a value of up to $50,000.
2. Alter the purchase price of larger land acquisitions (already approved by the board of directors) by an amount not to exceed 5 percent).
3. Select and train divisional staff, and monitor the employee benefit system.
4. Prepare a one to five-year strategy plan for the division.
5. Enter into land-servicing contracts.
6. Appoint consultants from an approved list for engineering and planning.
7. Plan the land use and control the development of each of the projects being developed.

The decisions of the project manager are under the control of the divisional advisory board (DAB). This board, of up to 10 members, is composed of representatives of local builder-shareholders elected yearly by builders holding marketing contracts in the area, a lawyer, and Carma management (including divisional management, the president, chief executive officer (CEO) or chairman of the board).

Each DAB provides advice to divisional management for decisions regarding land acquisition, the timing and form of land development, and the marketing of land. Each DAB may make recommendations to management concerning:

1. Land purchases and sales of undeveloped land.
2. Expected market demand and the planning of new communities, including street layout, lot sizing, architectural guidelines, merchandising, and promotion.
3. The price and terms of sale of developed land.

Divisional advisory boards are Carma's principle source of market information. The local members of the DAB are active in the geographic area and usually have good experience-based knowledge of local markets. However, Rudy Janzen expressed concern over the lack of sophisticated marketing expertise on the part of the builder-shareholders. With a few notable exceptions, such as Nu-West, the builder-shareholders like Carma Developers did not have marketing departments. As a result, Carma did not have a source of professional marketing expertise available to them, except through the use of consultants. This had not been a concern up to this time, however, since Carma's main problem had been finding managers who could move projects through the complicated political process involved in producing building lots in a market where the demand was greater than the supply.

INCENTIVE SYSTEM

One of the factors in Carma's success is its incentive system. Incentives are based on performance measured against the established performance levels for each profit center in the company. The annual profit targets are developed as part of the normal budget process each fall. These budgets are set in a series of negotiations with upper management. The chief executive officer is paid a percentage of profits no matter what the performance level, so his motivation is always to achieve higher levels of earnings. The corporate philosophy is that profits are used to increase retained earnings on the balance sheet. This is a key factor in keeping a reasonable debt-to-equity ratio for financing new growth.

The performance levels are labeled ordinary, good, great, and wow. Typically, a project manager has his incentive based 15 percent on overall corporate targets, 15 percent on personal goals (not dollar oriented) and 70 percent on yearly performance in his profit center. The remuneration at the good level is approximately 10 percent to 15 percent of his salary; great is 15 percent to 25 percent of his salary; and wow is 25 percent to 35 percent of his salary. The employee earns 1 percent of all earnings beyond the wow level of performance. Carma's base salaries are slightly above the industry average so that the total compensation package makes employees some of the highest paid in the industry.

Support staff are paid a percentage of their salary based on the performance of their bosses' profit center. The bonus ranged from 4 percent for good to 12 percent for wow. There is no open-ended performance incentive beyond wow for the support staff.

CARMA'S COMPETITION

In Calgary, Carma has three major competitors: Daon Development Corporation, Genstar Ltd., and Nu-West Development Corporation.

Daon Development is a Vancouver-based company with offices in Calgary, Edmonton, Washington, Oregon, Texas, and California. Daon supplies serviced residential lots to over 30 independent home builders. Daon entered the Calgary market in 1973 by developing a northeast Calgary residential community called The Properties. The Properties is a large development on relatively flat land and lot prices are below the Calgary average. As of July 1979, one of Daon's major residential projects is Project 16 in southeast Calgary. The first phase of Project 16 (651 acres) is under construction.

Daon is also involved in developing industrial parks, retail shopping centers, and downtown office buildings. Daon is constructing Horizon Industrial Estates, a 350-acre industrial park. The park is located on Barlow Trail in northeast Calgary in the same vicinity as Carma's Deerfoot Business Center.

Genstar Ltd., based in Montreal, has over 300 offices in North America and overseas. Genstar is highly diversified with 40 operating divisions engaged in marine services, the manufacture of building materials, construction, cement manufacturing, housing and land development, financial services, and investment. In Calgary, Genstar is best known to home buyers through its building companies Engineered Homes and Keith Construction. These builders were noted for medium-priced homes located in well-planned Genstar developments, offering special features such as golf courses and artificial lakes. Nu-West also develops, owns, and manages industrial parks, shopping centers, and small office complexes.

Residential land developed by Nu-West is either sold to outside builders or used by Nu-West's building subsidiaries Nu-West Homes and Cairns Homes.

As of July 1979, a large volume of lots were in various stages in the development process awaiting city approval. Of these lots, about 29 percent are owned by Carma and Nu-West, 23 percent by Genstar, and 15 percent by Daon.

DEVELOPING A RESIDENTIAL AREA

The development of a residential area in Canada is a long and costly process (see Exhibit 3).

For example, in Calgary the development process begins with the purchase of raw land that is either annexed or forecasted to be annexed by the city. Annexation places land under the administrative control of the city. The rate of development following annexation is dependent on market demand, city approval, and the financial ability of the city to provide trunk servicing. Annexation allows the municipality to control the direction and extent of urbanization and reduce land costs by increasing the supply of developable land.

In Calgary, the next stage of development is the creation of an area structure plan, which establishes the most appropriate form of development for a new area. Major elements of the area structure plan are: population density; broad land-use categories, such as residential, industrial, or commercial; public facilities, such as schools, libraries, or recreational projects; transportation requirements, including bus, truck, and pedestrian routes; and parks. The area structure plan is prepared by the city, with input provided by public hearings and submissions by businesspeople, builders, and developers. It must be approved by the city council.

Using the area structure plan as a starting point, Carma produces an outline plan detailing street and lane patterns, utility layouts, re-

EXHIBIT 3   The Development
Process in Calgary*

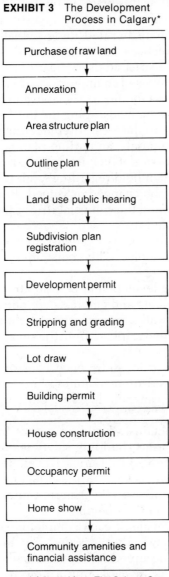

* Adapted from The Calgary General Municipal Plan, Table 4.1.1 "Local Plans and Permits," Planning Department, The City of Calgary, 1978.

serve dedications,[3] specific location of major land uses, street names, and lot lines.

---

[3] Ten percent of the total land in the development area must be "donated" as community reserve. An additional 30 percent must be used for streets and lanes.

Carma's involvement at this stage is intense. The possibility of historic and archaeological sites must be investigated. Land with a slope of 15 degrees or more is ruled undevelopable unless Carma obtains permission and finances restructuring of the land. Carma management meets with its district advisory board to establish architectural guidelines for the proposed community. Architectural guidelines establish the design criteria for the size, shape, and finishing material used on homes, as well as the landscaping the builder must provide if the firm is to build homes in the area. After meeting with city officials to obtain feedback on proposals, an outline plan is submitted to the Calgary Planning Commission (CPC) for approval.

A public hearing is then held regarding land use. At the hearing, designated land uses can be changed or vetoed. Primary issues here are housing mix, density, and the compatability of the planned development with adjoining land uses.

The next development stage is the registration of a plan of subdivision with the land titles office. This registration formally classifies the land.

Carma then obtains a development permit. Stripping and grading of the land begins. Financing and contracts are obtained for the construction of streets, sidewalks, sewers, street lighting, underground power lines, and park landscaping. Construction of streets, etc. is started.

Carma usually holds a lot draw once construction has begun. Unique features of the area are marketed to builder-shareholders by the district manager. This can include giving builders a bus tour of the area.

Next, each builder obtains a building permit by submitting detailed construction blueprints, building safety features, and a list of materials. These are approved by Carma Developers to ensure that architectural guidelines are met and by the chief building inspector to ensure the home will comply with the Alberta Uniform Building Standards Act. Construction can then begin.

A final inspection is made of each completed site by a building inspector and an occupancy permit is issued. The finished homes are then ready to be sold or occupied if they have been "presold."

Carma assists builders in marketing a new residential area by sponsoring home shows. The sponsorship may include making lots available for home shows, advertising to show, and planning special promotions to attract crowds. Carma provides community amenities such as parks, golf courses, and bicycle paths.

Carma communities that are already complete can receive capital assistance from Carma for the construction of community facilities such as recreation centers and/or swimming pools. Sports programs in Carma communities also receive donations from the company.

In total, between 40 and 70 government agencies and departments have veto power over any new land development. Each draft of the outline plan alone requires 68 copies to be forwarded to the city of Calgary. The entire approval process, including annexation, ranges from 3 to 10 years in length. This is the case for most metropolitan Canadian cities. Mr. Janzen believes that one of the main reasons for Carma's success was the ability of Carma's managers to deal with the politics and bureaucracy involved in the development process.

MARKETING AT CARMA

Carma does not have a marketing or marketing research division. Most market information was obtained from the members of the divisional advisory boards or consultants. The type of outside consulting reports that Carma commissions vary considerably, as three recent reports show.

The first report, prepared by a small Calgary consulting firm, was a simple reanalysis of Statistics Canada data on Edmonton's population growth, other demographic changes, and home purchases. The second report by California-based Richard Clasky and Associates outlined a marketing strategy for one of Edmonton's satellite communities. The recommendations were based on 2,400 household surveys on occupant lifestyles and preferences. The third study was being conducted by the IBI Group for Rudy Janzen to form the basis for a marketing information system.

The IBI Group identified five different types of decisions and information collection.

1. The entry/exit—The decisions are long-range decisions on land purchase or sale. The information collected came from secondary sources, such as Statistics Canada, and could be used to project long-term demand for housing. Currently, decisions were based on the experience of operations personnel.
2. Production targets—The decisions are made one to three years in advance of homes sales and cover what type of lot and what style of subdivision to build. Project managers needed to know which land to develop, how much inventory to carry, how much to charge for lots, and for what type of housing to plan. The manager currently relies on his experienced builders and the DAB for this information.
3. Product, lotting, and pricing—These decisions, made with one year of home sales, are similar to the production target decisions but are more detailed, and address the needs of specific target markets. The project managers, through these decisions, determine the detailed structure of the subdivi-

sions, including both the overall layout of the subdivision and the specifics of lot location, etc. Information is currently derived from outside consultants, the DABs, and the experience of the project managers.

4. Community design—The major decisions are the establishment of development guidelines. These decisions are those regarding the specifics of community features such as parks or recreation facilities, architectural guidelines, road design, planning entrance ways, etc. The information needed includes the consumer segments to be addressed, competitive offerings, and changing consumer preferences. Sources of information used include some consumer research, information from the DABs, and the experience of managers.

5. Sales and merchandising—These decisions, made at the time of home sales, center on advertising, show home organization and signage in the final presentation of the finished product. The information needed includes, again, consumer tastes, competitive offerings, and consumer perceptions of advertising. The firm does use advertising agencies, but most decisions are made by the project managers, based on their past experience.

Mr. Janzen wondered how he should proceed with the marketing information study. He was concerned that the past experience of his managers would not be sufficient in the future as competition increased in the markets served by Carma Developers. The construction business has always been cyclical. The major markets serviced by Carma had grown steadily since 1972 based on the continued growth of the oil industry. Mr. Janzen expressed concern that things could change quickly and the lack of a coordinated marketing strategy could "hit you over the head like a two by four." There had not been much incentive to be concerned over the implications of consumer preferences on the operations of the firm since the demand for homes had been greater than the developer's ability to supply lots. He wondered what recommendations he should make to his board at the September meeting.

Can this company, located in the piney woods of East Texas, continue to compete with the onslaught of foreign competition? Or are they, as numerous other American manufacturers, riding a dinosaur? Can Ed Stanley and his two brothers make this third-generation operation a fourth-generation one? Can they keep manipulating their product mix and finding those specialty niches that will insure the economic survival of their 200 employees? These, as well as other important strategic questions, will have to be decided in the near future.

COMPANY HISTORY

The 20th Century Glove Company relocated from Chicago shortly after World War II to the small community of Atlanta, Texas. Approximately 150 employees made cotton and leather gloves for the automotive industry. Fifteen percent of their production was sold to the consumer rack-jobbing trade in the local area. The remainder of the production was sold directly to Ford, Chrysler, and General Motors for use in their assembly plants.

Jerome Laden was the first owner/manager and held that position until the mid-1950s. Walter F. Frank then became the general manager and operated the company until Homer F. Stanley purchased substantial stock in 1958. At that time Maurice E. Stanley was named sales manager and vice president and assumed the sales and marketing responsibilities. Walter F. Frank was president of the company and responsible for production and financial matters.

When Mr. Frank resigned in 1963, Maurice E. Stanley purchased controlling interest, changed the company name to Guard-Line, and was named president and chief operating officer. Just prior to this, the major automotive contracts were lost to foreign competition. Guard-Line sales were then made to several safety and welding supply distributors. All types of work gloves were being made: welders, leather palm, drivers, terry, and some full cotton. The employment level at that time was approximately 20.

After the death of Maurice E. Stanley in early 1967, his oldest son Edward R. Stanley, age 22, assumed responsibility as president and

This case was prepared by James L. Harbin of East Texas State University, Texarkana, in cooperation with Edward R. Stanley, president of Guard-Line.

chief operating officer of the company. There were approximately 25 employees with annual sales of $350,000. The company operated in a 10,000-square-foot building.

The primary goods being manufactured at that time were welding gloves, leather jackets, capesleeves, bibs, aprons, and asbestos gloves. The company sold their products to a master wholesaler, who sold to a distributor, who sold to the ultimate consumer.

In 1968, the company joined the National Welding Supply Association, a trade organization for welding supply distributors. It was felt that greater market penetration could be obtained by exhibiting the product line at regional and national meetings. There were approximately 750 distributor members at the time.

The company produced the first million dollar annual sales in 1971. Additional wholesale distributors were also added, allowing the company to expand sales into the northeastern states. In the early 1970s, an additional 10,000 square feet of manufacturing space was added.

The Spartan Cap Manufacturing Company was purchased in 1973. This Houston, Texas, operation manufactured headwear for various welding and industrial users. Dennis J. Stanley, Ed's brother, joined the company as vice president and sales manager for the Houston operation. Approximately 3,000 square feet of manufacturing space, 15 employees, and $200,000 in sales were added to Guard-Line as a result of this acquisition.

Less than a year later the headwear operation was moved to Atlanta, Texas. Guard-Line purchased a building directly across the street from its main plant to house this activity.

Improved safety products from Japan, Korea, and the Far East began to have an impact in the U.S. market in 1973–74. In order to meet the competition of lower-priced goods, Guard-Line started importing certain textiles and raw materials from Japan and Korea.

Although the general market was slow in the mid 1970s, Guard-Line won several sizable contracts to provide arctic-type welders' gloves and protective clothing for the Alaskan Pipeline project. Approximately $300,000 in sales were generated as a direct result.

The Blue Blazer line of welding gloves and clothing was introduced in 1975 largely through advertising in national trade magazines. This high-quality bright blue line with excellent eye appeal helped Guard-Line expand their wholesale distribution. They were now supplying four of the five leading wholesale welding and safety supply companies in the country. Manufacturer's agents were also utilized to reach some areas of the U.S. market.

The company added Firestop clothing (100 percent cotton, flame resistant) to its product line in 1976. Leather and cotton combination work and drivers'-type gloves were also added to the product line.

EXHIBIT 1 Guard-Line Sales

Year	Sales (in millions)	Year	Sales (in millions)
1967	$ 350	1977	$4,600
1968	400	1978	5,400
1969	500	1979	6,100
1970	700	1980	6,200
1971	1,000	1981	6,800
1972	2,000	1982	4,700
1973	2,500	1983	4,200
1974	3,000	1984	6,200
1975	3,300	1985	8,000
1976	3,600	1986	9,500

Guard-Line's sales were particularly strong during the 1978–81 period. Total glove production in all factories exceeded 8,000 pairs per day by 1981. Reasons for the strong sales were a strong economy and the employment of a direct field representative to work expressly with the distributors. The product line was exhibited at two major welding and safety conventions (Philadelphia and Houston) in 1980.

As a result of heavy customer back-order sales, the company opened a welding glove plant in Antlers, Oklahoma. This addition of 4,000 square feet and 50 employees produced a popular line of high-quality gloves.

A business trip to South America was made by Ed Stanley in early 1979. Caracus, Venezuela, Bogata, Columbia, Lima, Peru, and several other cities were visited in search of cattle-hide, split-leather raw material, cotton, and finished industrial safety products. An industrial rainwear and PVC-coated glove plant was also toured but it was felt the quality and pricing were substandard for the American market. Ed felt that the economic condition of South America at that time was such that it would be very difficult to import raw materials and finished products.

Automotive and steel industry cutbacks in production began at Guard-Line in 1982. The Antlers, Oklahoma, facility was closed only one year after it was opened. The other manufacturing units were rescheduled for three and four workdays per week. The employment level at Guard-Line dropped to 120. Sales revenues dropped 40 percent from the previous year (see Exhibits 1 and 2).

It was obvious too that imported industrial gloves were gaining a larger market position particularly for price-conscious consumers. Mainland China had recently started producing industrial consumer goods with extremely competitive pricing. But more important, Chinese quality, materials, and workmanship equaled those of Japan, Korea, and other Far East countries.

In the past, management at Guard-Line had taken the position

EXHIBIT 2 Number of Guard-Line Employees

Year	Number	Year	Number	Year	Number
1967	25	1975	125	1981	250
1970	35	1976	150	1982	150
1971	45	1977	180	1983	135
1972	55	1978	190	1984	175
1973	80	1979	200	1985	185
1974	100	1980	220	1986	200

that imported goods would only supplement its product lines. At this point, Guard-Line purchased imported gloves through jobbers and agents.

It was agreed, rather reluctantly, that someone should tour mainland China to select a manufacturer for direct importing. A successful 10-day trip was made in late 1982 by Ed Stanley, and orders were placed with two reputable manufacturers. The goods were designed by the company bearing the FTC welding and work glove logo. National advertising was implemented and the program proved to be an immediate success.

A new distribution and sales approach was implemented by management whereby master wholesale distribution was to be diluted. It was felt inadequate market penetration was being obtained since master distributors handled as many as 100 product lines. One particular client purchased up to 25 percent of the company's production in sales. Further, the sag in the economy forced one master distributor out of business and the company suffered heavy financial and marketplace losses.

Guard-Line's largest competitor, Racine Glove Company, in Rio, Wisconsin, was forced into bankruptcy after 50 years of continuous operation. Other smaller manufacturers/competitors also closed as a result of the diminishing industrial market. This caused an upswing in demand for Guard-Line, however, and the Antlers, Oklahoma, facility was reopened.

The company undertook several moves in 1984–85.

1. Thirty manufacturers' agents were employed for direct solicitation to safety supply distributors throughout the country.
2. A new improved product catalog was distributed.
3. A second trip to mainland China resulted in a third supplier.

THE CURRENT GUARD-LINE SITUATION

Guard-Line's primary market lies in the industrial sector. Examples include steel, automotive, heavy industry, metal fabrication, welding, cutting, hand, foot, and body protection for high-heat applications, and various equipment and area protective products.

Guard-Line currently sells to more than 2,000 safety and industrial supply wholesale distributors throughout the United States and Canada. Sales of the company's products are handled by over 40 commissioned manufacturer's agents.

Guard-Line practices a participative, hands-on style of management. All three brothers have bachelor's degrees in business. Ed Stanley has just started an MBA degree at a local university.

The company does not have a formal quality control program, but they do have regular meetings through which employees can have direct input to their own jobs and productivity.

The average age of Guard-Line employees is 40. The average tenure is seven years. There are six employees with over 25 years of service.

The average 1986 wage rate is $6 an hour. Almost all production employees work on a piece-rate system, with many of them earning up to $9 an hour. It has always been a nonunion company and doesn't expect that to change in the future.

The company is a closely held family operation. The widow of Maurice Stanley is the chief stockholder, while Ed and his two brothers hold the remaining shares. The board of directors consists entirely of the family members.

The cut-sew-trim manufacturing industry is one of America's oldest. Most companies in this industry, Guard-Line included, still utilize old technology. It is an industry which is highly labor intensive. There also exist few patents for this industry's products. Companies have to maintain large inventories in order to fill unexpected rush orders.

Management at Guard-Line takes pride in their philosophy of attempting to provide security for its employees. Until 1981, there wasn't a layoff. They have even worked four-day weeks in the past in order to retain employees.

The Stanleys still reserve the Guard-Line label only for those products that are made domestically. These lines also carry the "made in the USA" logo. A different label is used for all imported safety products (see Exhibits 3, 4, 5, and 6).

THE GUARD-LINE CHINA CONNECTION

When Guard-Line first started considering an importer, it secured almost a hundred names of possible sources. The list included organizations from such countries as Japan, Mexico, Taiwan, Peru, Korea, and China. After a trip to Mexico and Peru, and a careful consideration of Korea and Japan, it was decided that Ed should make a trip to Hong

EXHIBIT 3 Guard-Line, Inc. Table of Organization

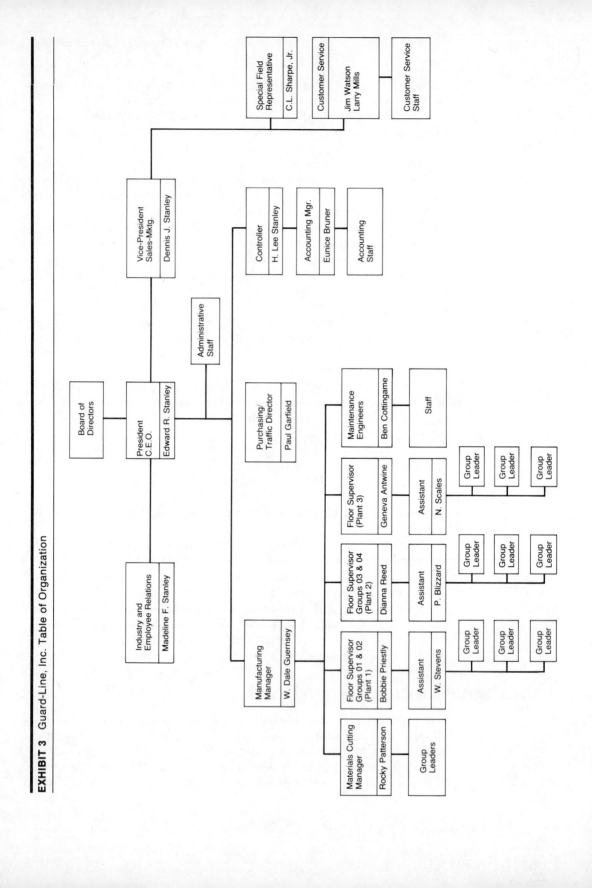

EXHIBIT 4 Percent of Guard-Line's Sales by Product Group

Group	Current Percent of Total (of sales dollars)	Five Years Ago	Five Years from Now
1. Heat fabric gloves and mittens	12.0	15.0	8.0
2. Full leather protective gloves, hand pads, and mittens	35.0	55.0	20.0
3. Protective apparel and accessories	25.0	25.0	20.0
4. Protective headwear and accessories	8.0	5.0	8.0
5. Resale items (special fabrics and other products purchased for resale, from domestic suppliers)	3.0	—	4.0
6. Imported gloves and other hand protectors	17.0	—	40.0
	100.0	100.0	100.0

EXHIBIT 5 Comparative Cost Information: Imported versus Domestic-Made Welding Gloves (full leather guantlet-type welding gloves, with liners, cost per dozen pair)

	Import Cost Data	Domestic Cost Data
Leather	$11.18	$25.92
Cotton lining	1.11	2.25
Thread	.39	.80
Other direct materials	1.22	5.50
Total, direct materials	$13.90	$34.57
Direct labor	2.25	12.25
DL & DM	$16.15	$46.82
Manufacturing markup	4.04 (20% margin)	25.75 (35% margin)
Net sell price	$20.19 (FOB cost)	$72.57
Duty (15%)	$ 3.03	—
Ocean freight	$ .72	—
Other import expenses (2.5%)	$ .51	—
Inland freight	$ .48	—
Net landed cost	$24.93	$72.57

Recap:

Landed cost	= $ 2.08/pair	Sell price	= $ 6.05/pair
Sell price	= $ 3.50/pair		$ 6.05/pair
Gross profit	= $ 1.42/pair		$ 2.15/pair
	$17.04/dozen		$25.75/dozen

Ratio to obtain same dollar profit per dozen:
$1.50 to $1.00
18 pairs imports to 12 pairs domestics

EXHIBIT 6 Typical Costs and Income of a U.S. Cut-Sew-Trim Manufacturing Firm (January 1987)

Direct labor	18.0%
Direct materials	47.0
Subtotal	65.0%
Operating expenses	15.0
Factories overhead	12.0
Pretax operating income	8.0
Net income after applicable income taxes	5.0
Gross operating margins = DL + DM + FO =	23.0
Direct labor add-ons	
Social security	7.15%
Health insurance	5.5
PSRT	5.0
SUT	8.9
FUT	.08
Holiday and vacation	7.0
Total	33.63
Example:	
Average factory worker hourly rate	$5.75
Direct labor add-ons plus 33.6 =	1.93
Total	$7.68

Kong to investigate further what appeared to be the best source for their imported products.

Ed secured the names of 12 agents in Hong Kong who might be able to supply Guard-Line with its needs. This trip took place in the summer of 1982. After talking with all 12 agents, an agent by the name of Stephen Chan was chosen.

Stephen was a well-qualified, well-educated executive with many connections in both Hong Kong and mainland China. He had previously been a banker, and had the equivalent of an MBA and CPA from a well-known school in London. But what really sealed the deal was the personal chemistry between Stephen and Ed. Even today, most of their ongoing business relationship is based on handshakes and oral agreements.

Stephen is the owner-manager of Yinglun Gloves. He has three factories: two in Canton, China, with 400 workers in 20,000 square feet of buildings, and one in Hong Kong with 20 workers in 4,000 square feet. Although a limited amount of Guard-Line's orders are made in the Hong Kong factory, the bulk is performed in Canton. The prime reason for this is the difference in labor cost in mainland China and Hong Kong. In China, the average monthly income for piece-rate workers working for foreign companies is $70 (for other workers, the rate ranges between $14 to $35). In Hong Kong the average monthly income for this type of work is approximately $500.

Ed continues to make at least one trip a year to Hong Kong and Stephen usually makes one trip a year to Atlanta, Texas. These trips have been mutually beneficial to both parties. Ed, who is continually amazed at the primitiveness of Stephen's factories, particularly the two in mainland China, often shares his knowledge of glove-making techniques with individual workers and managers. Stephen, with his experience in international banking, has shared his expertise with Guard-Line on various banking transactions necessary to conduct business with foreign companies. In fact, Guard-Line has changed its international financing arrangement from a local banking company to a Houston bank. This has shortened, somewhat, a lengthy process and provided some economies of scale.

Although they are in contact at least weekly, via telephone and telex, Ed has recognized the need to increase the number of trips to Hong Kong to three or four a year. A major limiting factor, though, is the amount of time it takes combined with the cost.

The association with Yinglun Gloves has not been without its problems. For one thing, from the time an order is first placed with Yinglun until actual delivery in the hands of the final customer in the United States is typically four months or more. That greatly complicates the planning process. It also hampers the quick delivery ability that so often is called for by the end consumer (see Exhibit 7).

Also, there have been some quality problems with gloves from the Canton plants. These are often not detected until the gloves are in the hands of the user. It greatly adds to the cost if Guard-Line has to physically inspect each glove in each box that they receive from Yinglun.

There have been a few times when Ed found that Stephen was "gouging" on the price. Another time he found Yinglun selling gloves to a domestic Guard-Line competitor. But these problems, for the most part, have been resolved to both parties' satisfaction. Ed characterizes it as a relationship that has experienced a few bumps along the way, but one that is getting smoother as time goes by. The players are getting to know each other better.

The Hong Kong government remains committed to free trade, and the market is open to all suppliers with few import or export restrictions. With China's growing openness to foreign trade, Hong Kong has continued to play a key role as an entry port for China trade.

ED STANLEY'S PERSPECTIVE OF THE SITUATION

For a long period of time, and even somewhat today, we here at Guard-Line believed in "apple pie, motherhood, and no Toyotas in the parking lot." But we have found out that we are the "rednecks" and we're the ones up against the wall. The bottom line in our battle is the imported cost versus the domestic cost. Our average wage here is $6 per hour (not

EXHIBIT 7 Guard-Line's Process to Import Foreign Goods

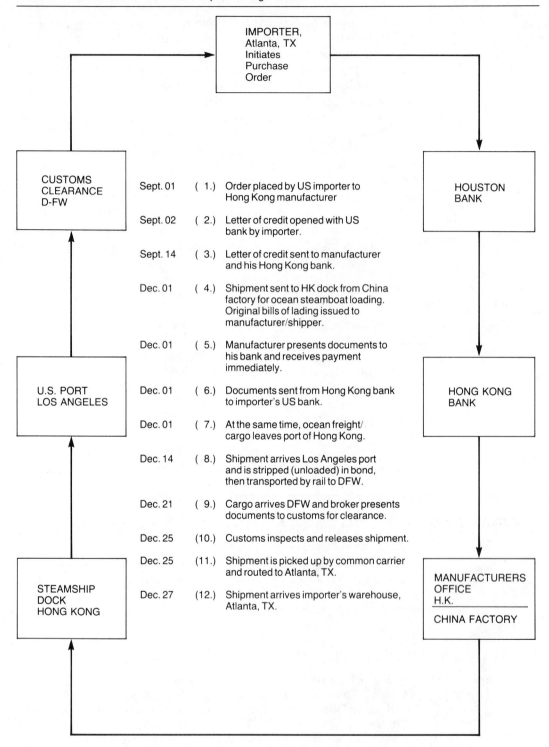

Sept. 01	(1.)	Order placed by US importer to Hong Kong manufacturer	
Sept. 02	(2.)	Letter of credit opened with US bank by importer.	
Sept. 14	(3.)	Letter of credit sent to manufacturer and his Hong Kong bank.	
Dec. 01	(4.)	Shipment sent to HK dock from China factory for ocean steamboat loading. Original bills of lading issued to manufacturer/shipper.	
Dec. 01	(5.)	Manufacturer presents documents to his bank and receives payment immediately.	
Dec. 01	(6.)	Documents sent from Hong Kong bank to importer's US bank.	
Dec. 01	(7.)	At the same time, ocean freight/cargo leaves port of Hong Kong.	
Dec. 14	(8.)	Shipment arrives Los Angeles port and is stripped (unloaded) in bond, then transported by rail to DFW.	
Dec. 21	(9.)	Cargo arrives DFW and broker presents documents to customs for clearance.	
Dec. 25	(10.)	Customs inspects and releases shipment.	
Dec. 25	(11.)	Shipment is picked up by common carrier and routed to Atlanta, TX.	
Dec. 27	(12.)	Shipment arrives importer's warehouse, Atlanta, TX.	

Boxes in diagram:

IMPORTER, Atlanta, TX Initiates Purchase Order

CUSTOMS CLEARANCE D-FW

HOUSTON BANK

U.S. PORT LOS ANGELES

HONG KONG BANK

STEAMSHIP DOCK HONG KONG

MANUFACTURERS OFFICE H.K.

CHINA FACTORY

counting the indirect labor costs). In China they pay 26 cents an hour, or about $2 a day. So one can see quite readily the type of problem we are facing.

I come from the old school of management: where we paid the employees on Fridays, paid the suppliers at the end of the month, and what was left over at the end of the year was profit. And in the past few years the profit margin has been getting smaller and smaller. We used to make 12 percent net profit on sales, now we are lucky to make 2 percent. Of course the volume is larger now. Another problem is that we now have to sell one and one half pairs of imported gloves to make the same profit margin we make on a pair of domestic gloves.

It all started several years ago when we began hearing such things from our customers as "Geez guys, we want to buy from you, and are willing to pay a premium for American goods. Maybe as much as 10 percent to 20 percent; but we're talking 50 percent difference in price here. Plus, the quality is just as good."

In order to compete, we started looking at a greater variety of products. Let me give you a sampling of some of the things we have considered doing in the past few months and years.

1. We are looking more and more at rack jobbing—an area which has not interested us in the past. There is a large convenience chain in the local area that we could do business with.
2. We've looked at making bandannas as a small addition to our business. Willie Nelson's fame helped popularize those items. In fact we sold 500,000 to a Florida discounter recently, but that was small change compared to what we really need.
3. Another thing we have looked at making is curtains for X rays, but that is a very complex product.
4. We have also looked at making work aprons—such as denim cotton ones for NAP. Nail aprons are another possibility.
5. We have looked at making hard hats, and making breathing apparatus for various dangerous jobs.
6. Another small item is making chaps for cowboys and rodeo riders. These are some very fashionable and useful garments.
7. Another thing we have looked at is making packages which hold in heat. One such package involved a discussion between Guard-Line and Domino's Pizza for a package to hold their pizzas, but again we found it cost us 50 percent more than what they were currently paying for their packaging.
8. We have also looked at exporting to other countries. But so far the difficulty of doing that is almost insurmountable.
9. We have never had a government contract, but have talked to TVA. So that represents another possibility.
10. We have also looked at such things as sunglasses, blue jeans, jewelry, and many others. But really that is not our business. If we are to survive maybe we should "stick to the knitting" as Tom Peters quotes.

EXHIBIT 8 Average Annual Percentage Change in Unit Labor Costs Measured in National Currencies and in U.S. Dollars (1980–84)

	National Currency	U.S. Dollars
United States	2.1	2.1
Canada	6.4	3.9
Japan	−1.0	−2.7
Italy	14.0	−4.1
Norway	6.7	−5.8
Denmark	6.5	−8.1
Germany	1.7	−8.2
France	8.3	−9.5
Netherlands	.6	−9.9
United Kingdom	3.3	−10.2
Sweden	4.5	−12.3
Belgium	1.6	−14.2

So you can see that we have considered many other products, some of which we are just beginning to manufacture, others we are still a ways off either in terms of perfecting or getting the cost down or the profit up.

The items which have really enabled Guard-Line to stay in business are the specialty items. These items carry a high profit, but also mean lower volume. A good example of this would be the lead curtains for X rays. The high-volume, low-profit items have just about all gone to the importers.

We still manufacture some high-volume items. In fact, we are a heck of a lot more productive than our China connection. Here we have giant presses that stamp out 20 plus gloves on a single template, we have conveyor belts, and some of the best sewing machines available. The factory in China has 20 people with 20 scissors cutting out gloves. Our operation is over 25 percent more productive than Yinglun's.

We are either the number one or the number two firm in the industry. Our being in the South with a low overhead is a major contributing factor to our ranking. But we also outsold and outproduced those in the East and the North.

Five years ago there were approximately 25 U.S. companies producing 90 percent of the market. Today there are about 12 left, and they are producing somewhere between 10 and 30 percent of the market.

There is tremendous pressure in our industry today. In addition to the importers, there is a shrinking industrial market out there. Robots do not wear welding gloves or jackets.

The variety of products needed to fit various safety standards has boomed recently. In the 1950s we made 2 or 3 products, five years ago we made 100 or 200. Today there are over 1,000 possible products that we can and do produce.

Of course, I could get a mini-warehouse and a station wagon and become a job shopper, peddling gloves and other safety equipment from overseas. But one of the big reasons I wouldn't want to do that is that I

EXHIBIT 9 Annual Percent Changes in Manufacturing Productivity, 12 Countries, 1960–84

Year	United States	Canada	Japan	France	Germany	Italy	United Kingdom	Belgium	Denmark	Netherlands	Norway	Sweden	Eleven Foreign Countries (Weighted)*
Output per hour:													
1960–84	2.4	3.4	8.3	5.7	4.9	5.5	3.5	7.1	5.6	6.6	4.7	3.6	5.5
1960–73	2.8	4.5	10.6	6.7	5.9	6.9	4.4	7.0	6.4	7.6	6.6	4.5	6.9
1973–84	2.1	1.6	5.9	4.6	3.4	3.8	2.3	6.2	3.5	4.6	2.8	2.3	3.8
1973–80	1.7	2.0	5.9	4.9	3.9	3.5	1.2	6.4	4.5	5.2	2.2	2.0	3.9
1981	2.2	2.0	3.7	3.9	2.1	3.5	6.2	6.9	1.6	2.7	-.4	.4	3.4
1982	2.2	-2.8	6.1	6.1	1.6	2.0	4.5	4.7	-.7	2.4	3.0	2.7	2.8
1983	6.6	6.4	5.4	4.2	6.1	2.4	7.3	6.8	3.5	5.3	7.7	5.6	5.7
1984	4.9	3.7	7.0	5.7	4.6	6.6	4.7	4.6	.8	10.5	5.7	2.0	5.5

* A trade-weighted average of the 11 foreign countries. See description of weights in text.
Note: Rates of change computed from the least squares trend of the logarithms of the index numbers. Index numbers for the data are available from the authors.

EXHIBIT 10 Annual Percent Changes in Hourly Compensation and Unit Labor Costs in Manufacturing, 12 Countries, 1960–84

Year	United States	Canada	Japan	France	Germany	Italy	United Kingdom	Belgium	Denmark	Netherlands	Norway	Sweden	Eleven Foreign Countries (Weighted)*
Hourly compensation:													
1960–84	7.2	9.2	13.6	12.7	9.7	16.8	13.6	11.9	12.3	12.8	12.0	11.6	12.1
1960–73	5.0	6.4	14.5	9.5	9.8	12.3	8.6	10.4	10.7	11.8	12.6	9.8	10.5
1973–84	8.9	11.0	8.2	14.9	7.7	19.3	16.0	10.5	10.7	11.0	8.2	11.3	11.1
1973–80	9.5	11.7	10.7	15.7	8.9	19.9	19.4	12.6	12.9	12.9	10.4	12.8	12.8
1981	9.6	16.0	7.6	15.4	7.0	23.1	13.5	10.8	11.1	10.1	4.5	11.6	11.6
1982	8.5	10.3	5.2	17.9	5.0	20.4	9.3	5.0	5.0	7.7	6.9	9.3	8.8
1983	3.6	7.3	3.0	12.1	5.7	16.7	7.5	8.0	8.1	8.2	4.9	11.1	6.8
1984	3.7	1.4	2.9	8.4	3.7	10.8	7.2	6.3	6.4	5.5	5.6	7.0	4.6
Unit labor costs:													
1960–84	4.7	5.6	4.9	6.7	4.6	10.7	9.8	4.8	6.8	5.0	7.3	7.7	6.2
1960–73	2.2	1.8	3.6	2.6	3.7	5.1	4.1	3.4	5.1	4.7	6.0	5.1	3.3
1973–84	6.6	9.2	2.2	9.8	4.2	15.0	13.4	4.3	7.3	3.4	5.4	8.8	7.0
1973–80	7.6	9.5	4.5	10.2	4.8	15.9	17.9	6.2	8.0	5.0	8.2	10.7	8.6
1981	7.3	13.7	3.7	11.1	4.9	18.9	6.9	3.9	8.3	1.8	4.9	11.2	7.9
1982	6.2	13.5	-.8	11.2	3.4	18.1	4.6	.3	8.5	4.3	3.9	6.4	5.8
1983	-2.8	.8	-2.3	7.6	-.4	14.0	.2	1.2	4.5	-.4	-2.8	5.2	1.0
1984	-1.2	-2.2	-3.9	2.6	-.9	3.9	2.4	1.7	4.6	-4.4	-.1	5.0	-.8
Unit labor costs in U.S. dollars:													
1960–84	4.7	4.9	7.5	5.7	8.1	7.0	7.0	6.1	6.1	6.6	7.3	8.8	6.7
1960–73	2.2	1.9	5.0	2.4	6.1	5.4	2.6	4.4	4.5	5.0	6.0	6.0	4.0
1973–84	6.6	6.3	4.5	4.3	4.4	4.8	9.2	1.3	1.6	2.6	2.9	5.9	5.3
1973–80	7.6	6.4	9.5	11.3	11.3	9.5	16.1	11.8	11.3	9.7	10.6	12.7	10.3
1981	7.3	10.9	6.1	-13.8	-15.6	-10.7	-6.9	-13.5	-18.0	-14.5	-18.8	-4.4	-3.3
1982	6.2	10.2	-12.1	-8.1	-4.1	-.7	-9.7	-15.8	-18.9	-7.3	-2.9	-5.4	-5.4
1983	-2.8	1.0	2.5	-7.1	-5.3	1.6	-13.1	-9.0	-9.3	-4.7	6.8	-7.0	-3.3
1984	-1.2	-7.0	-3.8	-10.5	-11.0	-10.1	-9.7	-5.0	-9.9	-7.6	-15.0	-6.1	-7.9

* A trade-weighted average of the 11 foreign countries. See description of weights in text.
Note: Rates of change computed from the least squares trend of the logarithms of the index numbers. Index numbers for the data are available from the authors.

EXHIBIT 11 U.S. Merchandise Trade

$ Billion, f.a.s./c.i.f. annual rates

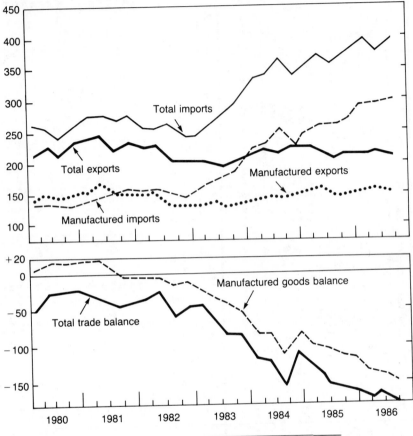

	Exports f.a.s.	Imports Customs	Imports c.i.f.	Balance f.a.s./c.i.f.
	(billions of dollars, annual rates)			
Total trade				
1985 annual	213.1	345.3	361.6	−148.5
1985: III	201.4	338.4	354.7	−153.4
IV	209.3	356.7	372.8	−163.5
1986: I	214.6	371.5	388.5	−173.9
II	217.9	363.2	379.7	−161.8
III	211.3	369.2	387.0	−175.7
Manufacturers trade				
1985 annual	150.7	246.8	258.2	−107.5
1985: III	143.2	244.4	256.0	−112.9
IV	145.1	253.9	265.1	−120.0
1986: I	153.2	272.1	283.8	−130.6
II	154.8	276.8	288.0	−133.2
III	150.0	286.3	298.3	−148.3

EXHIBIT 11   *(concluded)*

	Exports f.a.s.	Imports Customs	Imports c.i.f.	Balance f.a.s./c.i.f.
(billions of dollars, annual rates)				
Agricultural trade				
1985 annual	29.6	20.0	22.0	7.6
1985: III	23.0	18.4	20.3	2.7
IV	31.5	19.4	21.3	10.2
1986: I	30.0	22.7	24.8	5.2
II	23.1	21.7	23.6	−0.5
III	22.4	20.1	21.9	0.5

Note: Commodity values do not add to U.S. trade totals because of omission of miscellaneous products.

Quarterly data are not seasonally adjusted unless noted. All values in current dollars. f.a.s.—Free alongside ship. c.i.f.—Cost, insurance, and freight.

EXHIBIT 12   Composition of U.S. Merchandise Trade

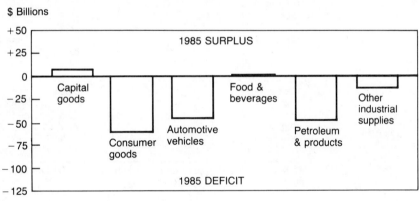

	Exports f.a.s.	Imports c.i.f.	Balance f.a.s./c.i.f.
(billions of dollars, annual rates)			
Capital goods			
1985 annual	73.9	67.3	6.6
1985: III	69.7	66.1	3.6
IV	72.1	67.6	4.5
1986: I	75.7	77.4	−1.7
II	75.2	77.8	−2.6
III	76.0	79.9	−3.9
Consumer goods			
1985 annual	12.6	72.5	−59.5
1985: III	12.2	76.4	−64.2
IV	12.2	76.0	−63.8
1986: I	13.2	76.9	−63.7
II	13.9	76.6	−62.7
III	13.9	90.0	−76.1

EXHIBIT 12 *(concluded)*

	Exports f.a.s.	Imports c.i.f.	Balance f.a.s./c.i.f.
	(billions of dollars, annual rates)		
Automotive vehicles and parts			
1985 annual	22.9	68.9	−46.0
1985: III	21.0	64.7	−43.7
IV	21.9	73.6	−51.7
1986: I	22.9	77.5	−54.6
II	24.6	83.6	−59.0
III	18.8	77.5	−58.7
Food and beverage			
1985 annual	24.0	23.9	0.1
1985: III	20.3	22.7	−2.4
IV	25.1	23.9	1.2
1986: I	24.8	26.4	−1.6
II	19.2	26.9	−7.7
III	20.4	26.0	−5.6
Petroleum and products			
1985 annual	5.0	52.6	−47.6
1985: III	4.8	49.9	−45.1
IV	6.1	58.4	−52.3
1986: I	4.9	49.4	−44.5
II	3.5	32.8	−29.3
III	3.2	34.8	−31.6
Other industrial supplies			
1985 annual	53.5	66.9	−13.4
1985: III	52.7	65.4	−12.7
IV	51.8	63.6	−11.8
1986: I	51.8	71.1	−19.3
II	52.4	73.6	−21.2
III	54.1	70.3	−16.2

Note: Commodity values do not add to U.S. trade totals because of omission of miscellaneous products.

Quarterly data are not seasonally adjusted unless noted. All values in current dollars. f.a.s.—Free alongside ship. c.i.f.—Cost, insurance, and freight.

EXHIBIT 13 U.S. Merchandise Trade by Area

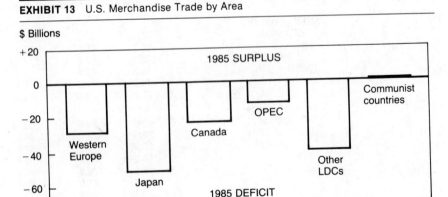

EXHIBIT 13   *(concluded)*

	Exports f.a.s.	Imports c.i.f.	Balance f.a.s./c.i.f.
	(billions of dollars, annual rates)		
Western Europe			
1985 annual	56.8	84.2	−27.4
1985: III	51.3	80.9	−29.6
IV	58.1	89.4	−31.3
1986: I	62.9	93.6	−30.7
II	59.2	95.9	−36.7
III	58.1	91.8	−33.7
Japan			
1985 annual	22.6	72.4	−49.8
1985: III	22.1	72.9	−50.8
IV	22.3	73.5	−51.2
1986: I	22.3	83.6	−61.3
II	30.0	83.5	−53.5
III	28.9	86.2	−57.3
Canada			
1985 annual	47.3	69.4	−22.2
1985: III	45.0	64.6	−19.6
IV	44.2	71.3	−27.0
1986: I	45.8	69.4	−23.6
II	46.8	70.3	−23.5
III	41.5	65.5	−24.0
OPEC			
1985 annual	12.5	24.1	−11.6
1985: III	12.6	23.5	−10.9
IV	12.1	28.2	−16.1
1986: I	11.1	26.5	−15.4
II	11.2	18.9	−7.7
III	10.3	20.8	−10.5
Other developing countries			
1985 annual	59.2	99.0	−39.8
1985: III	56.0	99.7	−43.7
IV	57.6	98.0	−40.3
1986: I	57.1	101.4	−44.3
II	58.5	98.4	−39.9
III	61.1	108.3	−47.2
Communist countries			
1985 annual	7.1	6.3	0.7
1985: III	5.6	6.3	−0.7
IV	8.0	6.5	1.4
1986: I	7.1	7.5	−0.4
II	5.5	6.8	−1.3
III	3.8	7.9	−4.1

Note: Areas are not intended to add to U.S. trade totals.

Quarterly data are not seasonally adjusted unless noted. All values in current dollars. f.a.s.—Free alongside ship. c.i.f.—Cost, insurance, and freight.

would lose control. I have 20 years experience in this industry. That's a heck of a lot of knowledge. I know how to both make and sell gloves.

Where can a company, management, and/or employees complain to about these type problems? I suppose Washington and our representative would be a place to start. Provided there is an answer, the problem is that it would entail a long-term solution and what we have here is a short-term crisis.

This was something that I thought maybe our sons and grandsons would enjoy and continue. We have a lot of family to support here—my family, my 2 brothers, plus 200 employee families. Our payroll turns an average of seven times. That means a lot to a local community.

What do I do? Become a hero to a lot of folks? The future really scares me. We are stumbling around looking for a direction to go in the future (see Exhibits 8–13).

36. Case Apparel Company, Inc.

Barry Case, plant manager of Case Apparel, sat behind his desk, his head resting on his interlocked fingers and his eyes fixed on the ceiling of his office. He and Sam Case, his father and president of Case Apparel, had just returned from their accountant's office with bad news (see Exhibits 1 and 2). Barry knew that Case Apparel was having problems, but he had not realized how serious those problems were. He did know that if he ever hoped to become president of Case Apparel he needed to think of something, and soon.

HISTORY OF CASE APPAREL

In 1953 Sam Case, a manufacturing manager for Memorial Apparel Corporation, decided to start his own company. By early 1954, he had located a large vacant warehouse in Radford, Virginia, and opened his operations under the name Sam Case Apparel Company, Inc., commonly known as Case Apparel.

Case never aspired to be a complete line manufacturer or to have his own line. Rather, he chose to operate as a private label sewer for other lines and to specialize in women's blouses and shirts. This strategy was reasonably successful and employment expanded from 20 to 50 people in several years. (Current employment is 24 with equipment available for 32 should business expand.) As employment expanded, the pressure to unionize grew, but Case Apparel was able to stave off organizing attempts by paying better-than-average wages and benefits. Over the years costs and competition increased. Equipment became worn or obsolete, and the company was hard pressed to achieve its goals of high quality and high production. And, like others in the U.S. apparel industry, Case Apparel was rocked by inexpensive foreign imports.

This case was written by McRae C. Banks of Mississippi State University and Edgar R. McGreevy of the Department of Management and Marketing, Radford University, Radford, Virginia. Former Radford University students Ray Fadool, Tom Harman, Shelly Roof, Benny Snuffer, and Jerome Wimmer collected the data. The facts presented are accurate, but names, places, and financial data have been changed.

EXHIBIT 1

SAM CASE APPAREL COMPANY, INC.
Income Statements

	1984	1983	1982	1981	1980
Sales	$513,397	$591,715	$610,706	$612,126	$501,853
Cost of goods sold					
Labor	265,442	306,231	299,687	288,779	252,116
Materials	36,089	39,445	40,600	40,470	33,298
Total cost of goods sold	301,531	345,676	340,287	329,249	285,414
Gross profit	211,866	246,039	270,419	282,877	216,439
Expenses:					
Salaries	64,778	61,246	57,998	53,722	52,860
Advertising	3,409	4,495	3,300	2,928	2,378
Bad debts	11,202	10,114	6,049	7,822	8,087
Donations and contributions	487	450	400	200	200
Dues and subscriptions	633	633	600	500	500
Utilities	50,166	57,875	56,638	50,293	44,239
Bank charges	30	50	25	25	25
Insurance	15,099	15,099	14,300	12,438	10,941
Interest	0	0	0	0	0
Taxes and licenses	25,814	29,780	29,144	25,958	22,833
Office supplies	2,435	2,500	2,300	1,950	2,200
Postage	974	1,200	1,000	857	932
Repairs	43,834	44,951	32,993	21,631	30,920
Miscellaneous	487	532	500	278	423
Depreciation	8,839	9,074	7,681	9,460	3,513
Rent	18,000	18,000	15,000	15,000	15,000
Pension and benefits	24,840	28,657	26,394	22,172	19,503
Total expenses	271,027	284,656	254,322	225,234	214,554
Net income (loss)	$ (59,161)	$ (38,617)	$ 16,097	$ 57,643	$ 1,885

THE INDUSTRY

Apparel manufacturing is a fragmented industry with more than 15,000 domestic producers who have approximately 15,000 plants in 50 states. Fragmentation is due primarily to low entry and exit barriers; little capital is required. Despite low capital requirements, many new entrants are undercapitalized. As a result, one out of every six firms enters bankruptcy each year.

Many new entrants are private label sewers. This type of manufacturer furnishes labor and equipment to sew garments to contracted specifications. In some cases, the contract includes cutting fabric into component pieces which are then sewn together elsewhere. Often the contractor provides materials, patterns, and special trim or accessories.

Apparel manufacturing is labor intensive. Although more than one half of all firms in the industry have fewer than 50 employees, total employment for the industry is 1.3 million. Of these, 85 percent are

EXHIBIT 2

	1984	1983	1982	1981	1980
Balance Sheet					
Current assets:					
Cash	$ 20,857	$ 34,094	$ 26,857	$ 25,753	$ 21,361
Accounts receivable	66,542	67,250	88,322	86,539	63,593
Inventory	33,134	69,223	81,500	97,407	98,282
Total current assets	120,533	170,567	196,679	209,699	183,236
Office furniture and fixtures	3,853	3,853	3,853	3,853	1,480
Equipment	107,460	107,460	105,844	75,724	40,736
Accumulated depreciation	(63,732)	(54,893)	(45,819)	(38,138)	(28,678)
Total assets	$168,114	$226,987	$260,557	$251,138	$196,774
Current liabilities					
Accounts payable	7,422	7,387	3,356	9,590	8,177
Taxes payable.	4,046	3,793	2,777	3,221	7,913
Total current liabilities	11,468	11,180	6,133	12,811	16,090
Paid-in capital.	150,000	150,000	150,000	150,000	150,000
Retained earnings	6,646	65,807	104,424	88,327	30,684
Total liabilities and equity	$168,114	$226,987	$260,557	$251,138	$196,774

production workers, compared to 69 percent for all manufacturers. Approximately 81 percent are women, 27 percent are minorities, and 50 percent are unionized. Wages average $5.20 per hour, 43 percent below the average wage for all other manufacturing workers.

The labor intensive nature of the industry hampers technological development. Unless there is a large labor force or few garment styles, frequent production changes are required. Often, only larger firms can realize enough labor savings to warrant investing in the latest technology in garment manufacturing. Recent advances in the industry include lasers to cut garment parts, computer-aided pattern design, and programmable sewing machines. Japan, on the forefront of technological application, has invested $60 million in apparel automation research, hoping to develop a largely robotized factory.

Competition in the industry is fierce. Not only do domestic firms compete against each other, but they compete against foreign companies as well. The effect has been low price increases, resulting in generally low profits.

FOREIGN COMPETITION

Imported apparel has become a major issue of our time. Though textile protectionism dates to 1816, quotas on textiles and apparel were devised by the Roosevelt administration in 1935 and have been in effect continuously since 1958. The present quota system is administered under the Multi-Fiber Agreement (MFA), a series of bilateral agreements between the United States and 34 other nations. Enacted in 1974 and due to expire in 1986, the MFA sets quotas on 600 specific apparel items. However, because quotas are established by item and country, they can be easily circumvented.

Three common methods for circumventing quotas are "island hopping," transhipping, and product changes. The first involves moving operations from one country to another when import quotas from the first country are filled. The second, transhipping, involves shipping goods from a country which has satisfied its quota to a country which has not satisfied its quota, and then shipping the goods to the United States. Product changes take advantage of specific item quotas. If, for instance, the quota for cotton sweaters is reached, production is changed to cotton and silk sweaters.

Attempting to minimize transhipping, U.S. Customs adopted the Rules of Origin, effective October 31, 1984, which stated that goods imported from a country must have been made in that country. While the ruling was well intended, the backlash was immediate. Hong Kong boycotted U.S. cigarettes, worth $135 million in U.S. exports, and China delayed two million metric tons of grain purchases.

Within the United States, debate rages over the most appropriate manner of handling the apparel trade imbalance (in 1984, imports totaled $14.3 billion while exports were only $1 billion). Legislators from apparel-producing states are concerned because of the large number of jobs involved; apparel manufacturing employs more workers than are employed in the automobile, chemical, or steel industries. While quotas have been somewhat accepted in the past, that is less true today. Not only do exporting nations have reciprocal power to limit imports of U.S. goods, but U.S. retailers are lobbying vigorously against existing and future quotas.

Many economists argue that the quota program is nothing more than a U.S. subsidy. The nation, by awarding quotas to specific countries for specific products, creates a tradable commodity in quota trade rights, for which there is a strong market. So long as the price to purchase the right, manufacture the garment, and tranship the finished merchandise is less than the selling price, a profit can be made.

A complicating factor in the import quotas argument is the need to determine at what level competition exists. Many view the competition as occurring between U.S. and foreign manufacturers. Because of low labor costs overseas (only 10 cents an hour in Bangladesh and $1.18 an hour in Hong Kong), U.S. companies cannot compete effectively without quota protection. Others believe that U.S. apparel manufacturers are competing against other U.S. apparel manufacturers with higher wages, causing wage escalation in less productive industries. If one expands this argument to encompass international markets, sufficient allocation of productive capability becomes even more important. In other words, if U.S. industry A is more productive than U.S. industry B and it is also more productive than industry A in another country, we should export product A and import product B, even if U.S. industry B is more productive than foreign industry B. The result, of course, is unemployment in U.S. industry B, which in this case is apparel manufacturing. The solution to this situation, it is argued, is a tariff surcharge which will generate funds for retraining U.S. industry B workers to work in industry A.

Of course, this argument does not imply that U.S. apparel manufacturers are not responding to the competitive challenge. At present, favorable import treatment is awarded to U.S. apparel manufacturers who ship garment pieces made from domestic fabric to foreign operations which sew the finished garments. Duty is paid only on the value added by sewing the garment.

UNIONS

Two unions, the Amalgamated Clothing Workers of America (ACWA) and the International Ladies Garment Workers Union (ILGWU), dominate domestic apparel manufacturing. The ACWA is the AFL-CIO union in the men's clothing industry, boasting 380,000 members in 640 locals. Formed in 1924, the ACWA pioneered engineering and modernization assistance for manufacturers, union-owned banks and housing, insurance plans, and educational and cultural activities. The ILGWU, also an AFL-CIO affiliate, occupies a similar role in the women's clothing industry and has 250,000 members. The ILGWU, like the ACWA, was a prime mover in union assistance to employers and members, and also pioneered impartial arbitration in collective bargaining and union political action.

CASE APPAREL OPERATIONS

As a private label sewer, Case Apparel, unlike company-owned plants, makes products to order. Orders differ considerably in terms of processing requirements, materials required, processing time, and processing sequence and setups. Another complicating factor is the difficulty in establishing firm production schedules because the private label sewer serves primarily as a means of expanding production capacity without investing large amounts of capital. Because of these inherent difficulties, scheduling and controlling production in apparel plants is fairly complex. Production schedulers are constantly faced with the need to decide how to distribute the workload among work centers and what job processing sequence to use.

Case Apparel is a medium-sized manufacturing plant which produces women's blouses and knit shirts. There are approximately 25,000 square feet of floor space at the plant. The cutting room operations occupy the entire second floor, which is about 12,500 square feet of floor space, while the first floor is devoted to office space, finished goods storage, and production. The plant has 25 operating sewing machines, 5 steam presses, several hand-operated irons, and eight hanger racks for final inspection and tagging.

PHYSICAL PLANT

The red brick building that houses the plant was built in 1923 and is not particularly attractive. A recent visitor to the plant remarked that it has a "1933 sweatshop appearance." The plant sits on a side street in Radford in a residential neighborhood near Radford University. Two blocks away is a Burlington Industries plant which manufactures textiles and Russell Apparel Corporation, an apparel contract sewer.

Case Apparel has attempted to modernize bit by bit rather than in large chunks. By paying cash for equipment and using a pay-as-you-go system, the company keeps its debts low. All equipment functions, but some of the older machinery is in constant danger of breaking down. When possible, old equipment is replaced with newer used equipment that has been purchased at auction (see Exhibit 3).

PRODUCTION

Cutting is the first phase in Case Apparel's production process. Contracting companies provide large rolls of patterns, which are rolled over several layers of fabric. Various sizes are printed on each roll, and each pattern is numbered for easy identification after cutting. Small pieces are cut by using a press with an appropriately sized die which is punched through the fabric. Larger pieces are cut with an electric saw similar to a jigsaw. Finally, pieces are sorted by color and size, bundled, and numbered for later processing (see Exhibit 4).

Phase two in making a garment is known as joining. The initial process consists of steam pressing a lining into the collar, cuffs, and button panels. Linings are made of a plastic fabric which adheres only to one side of the fabric. Temperatures of 280 to 300 degrees are required for adhesion, and temperature control is crucial to the process. With too little heat, the lining will not stick to the fabric; with too much heat, the lining will shrink and bunch, making the piece unfit for production. Next, garments are assembled by sewing machine operators whose machines sew thousands of stitches per minute. The blouses are sewn by sections which consist of cuffs, sleeves, two collars, a strip for button holes, pocket components, and ruffling or other trim. Any embroidering is also completed at this point. Front and back

EXHIBIT 3 First Floor Front

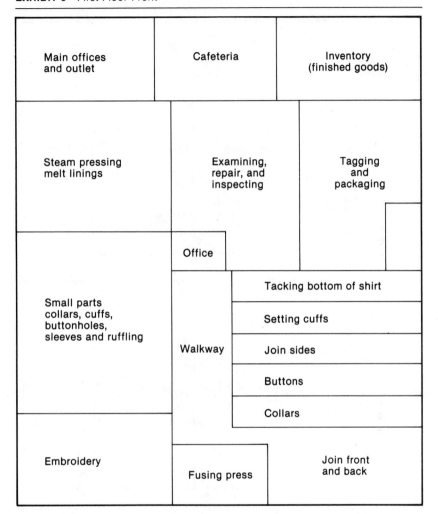

panels of the blouse are then sewn together at the shoulders. Next the collars are attached and the buttons are sewn on. Then the blouse is joined at the sides, and the last two joining procedures are setting the cuffs and tacking the bottom of the garment.

In phase three, the garments are moved to an examining and repairing area where they are checked for major flaws. The blouses are put on hangers and buttoned to see if the holes and buttons match, and any loose threads are clipped. Blouses are ironed and steam pressed to eliminate wrinkles. Final inspection and spot removing are usually performed by one of the senior employees. Once the blouse is approved by the inspector, it can be readied for shipment.

EXHIBIT 4 Second Floor

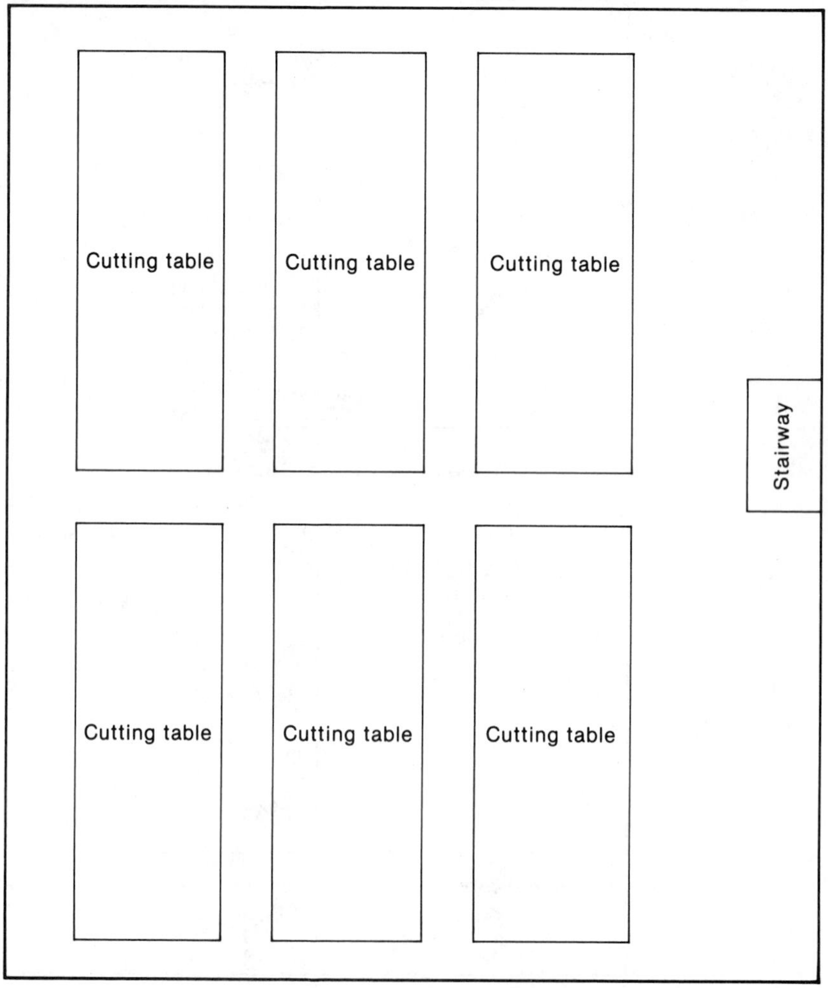

Cutting table	Cutting table	Cutting table
Cutting table	Cutting table	Cutting table

Stairway

Preparing a garment for shipment involves tacking on the designer label, attaching the price tag, and pinning the blouse. The garments can be shipped on a hanger or folded, pinned, and inserted into a plastic package.

The production process is monitored by means of Gantt charts and lot number tags. The charts are situated in several strategic places throughout the plant and updated periodically to let employees and managers know if they are on target for meeting their daily quotas. If not, the managers can react quickly by balancing the line. Lot number tags are used to eliminate mixing designs and sizes and to determine the number of pieces produced by each employee.

Direct labor accrues on a per-piece basis. Each employee is guaranteed a minimum of $3.35 per hour; some workers, depending on their jobs, earn as much as $6.70 an hour. A standard rate of pay per operation has been established, but it may be varied when inferior fabric is provided.

Terms of credit extended to the client are net 10 after the garment has been shipped. The client pays all shipping costs for raw and finished goods. Turnover in producing the merchandise from cutting to final product is estimated at five weeks to allow for delays in shipment and production.

At present, Case Apparel has no long-term debt. New equipment is purchased on a cash basis, despite the availability of a line of credit.

MARKETING

Case Apparel markets to two distinct types of customers: large companies which wish to offer private label merchandise to their customers and individual end users who come into the Case Apparel outlet shop. The outlet shop comprises a very small percentage of the company's sales. It offers seconds and overruns to the public and is staffed on a rotating basis by several employees. A nominal amount of advertising is undertaken, usually in the form of local newspaper ads. Other forms of advertising are the Yellow Pages and periodic direct mail flyers sent throughout the New River Valley area.

Promotion of the manufacturing operations is handled by Sam Case. He initiates most contacts, although occasionally a firm will contact Case Apparel to have certain items made. Case Apparel has long had a reputation for high-quality merchandise at low cost; recently, however, its ability to compete on cost has been threatened by foreign competition. In the past Case Apparel has enjoyed favorable relations with such companies as Junior House, Ship & Shore, and Lands End.

MANAGEMENT AND EMPLOYEE RELATIONS

Barry Case, the plant manager, is a 1979 graduate of Radford University. He has a bachelor of science in management and has attended several Radford University Management Center programs and workshops on productivity improvement and employee motivation. He has been with Case Apparel full time since graduation but has worked part time with the company since his youth.

Two key supervisors report to Barry. Marlene Metzger supervises cutting operations as head cutter. She has been with Case Apparel since her graduation from Radford High School in 1963 and has handled every production job in the plant. As head cutter, she is responsible for laying out fabric and patterns and making sure that pieces are cut, bundled, tagged, and sent to joining. If material defects exist, Marlene calls them to Barry's attention and he decides whether to return the material or to add a defective materials surcharge to the contract price.

Monica Shuman supervises joining operations. An expert seamstress, Monica has been with Case Apparel since her daughter graduated from high school in 1972. Like Marlene, Monica has performed every production job and can assist operators who have problems. Though she still does some sewing, Monica is primarily responsible for implementing Barry's monthly production schedule while making daily and sometimes hourly adjustments to ensure that production is kept at a high level.

Low productivity is a major problem at Case Apparel. With the exception of Sam Case, Barry Case, and a maintenance man, all employees of the company are women. Sam believes that most of the women, who work to supplement family income or to have something to do outside of the house, have little interest in performing at high levels. Additionally, the work itself is perceived as monotonous and unchallenging.

A concomitant problem is low employee morale. As mentioned previously, Case Apparel pays its employees by the piece. The more pieces a worker produces, the more she earns. While piecework rewards each employee according to her ability to produce, this method of payment has long been associated with the sweatshop. Other negative factors which contribute to employee dissatisfaction are equipment down time for repair, defective materials, and absences. Recently, increases in equipment down time and absences have aggravated problems in scheduling, production efficiency, and morale.

Pressure from employees and the ILGWU to organize the shop is an additional difficulty. The company has resisted this effort in the past, maintaining that its wages are higher than the ILGWU contract and its benefits are comparable. Furthermore, employees do not have to pay union dues and thus take home more pay. Employees are divided on ILGWU membership, although more are in favor of organizing than ever before. Employees appear to resent the work situation, rather than the pay, judging from the comments of one worker.

"Money ain't worth beans if a person is too tired to go out and spend it," June Jarrett said. "The way they drive us at this place, it's a disgrace."

When asked why she stays at Case, Jarrett replied, "Where the heck else is someone like me gonna get a job? The only thing I know is sewing. Same as these other women!"

BARRY'S EFFORTS

In an effort to overcome motivation problems, Barry has placed around the plant large Gantt charts, which are updated hourly. By glancing at the charts, employees can estimate their progress. He has also posted a variety of motivational signs, which ask the employees to "strive for quality" and "whistle while you work."

Barry earnestly wants to improve his management skills and to be able to make more meaningful recommendations to his father. Recently, he read *In Search of Excellence* and has implemented one management strategy by walking about the plant. Also, he has reviewed current materials from Radford University courses in international business and business policy. His review has alerted him to such concepts as comparative advantage and absolute advantage, to manufacturing and marketing requirements for entry into foreign markets, and to the importance of environmental assessment and a market screening process.

EPILOGUE

Barry began jotting down a few notes he thought might help him to establish a framework for his plan. First, he needed to define the business and, with the help of past plans, determine the purpose and objectives of Case Apparel. Next, he wanted to conduct a situation audit so that he could determine the strengths and weaknesses of the company. From his environmental assessment, he could determine both its opportunities and liabilities. He hoped, by combining these steps, to develop a variety of alternative strategies for Case Apparel.

Barry discussed his thoughts with his father and, over the next several days, worked on his analysis. The facts revealed that the problems facing Case Apparel were serious and required immediate attention. Barry and Sam agreed that the situation required the objectivity of an outside consulting group.

The Industrial Segment

37. Carlton Shipyard, Inc.

Tom Carlton, founder and owner of Carlton Shipyard, found himself in a new and unenviable position. The shipyard that he had built from nothing into a $60 million business had been forced into Chapter 11 bankruptcy. And Carlton and his staff had to develop a plan, acceptable to the bankruptcy judge and major creditors, to make the company solvent again. Carlton also had to meet with the unsecured creditors to explain to them their position and options.

HISTORY OF CARLTON SHIPYARD

Carlton, a middle-aged entrepreneur, had been associated with shipyards most of his life. He had worked at several shipyards in a number of different positions and had learned as much as he could about ship repair and drydock operation. In 1972 he formed Carlton Shipyard as a private corporation with all of the stock in his name. The company leased land on the intracoastal waterway near Jacksonville, Florida, and began repairing small craft, minesweepers, and auxiliary ships. Working almost exclusively on small U.S. Navy vessels that needed minor repairs, the company acquired a reputation for excellent work completed on time and at a reasonable price.

Because of the company's good reputation and competitive bids, CSI was awarded larger navy contracts as well as some civilian jobs. In 1974 the corporate offices were moved to larger quarters in Jacksonville, and the original facility was closed. Production shops were established at the new site, permitting the company to undertake major repair work on both government and commercial ships. A facility was also established at the U.S. Navy base, and CSI became the first prime contractor to have an on-base facility with the capability to respond to SupShipJax (supervisor of shipbuilding, Jacksonville) repair demands.

The close proximity of this facility to the waterfront permitted CSI to move personnel to the work site quickly for emergency and routine repairs. Critical repair equipment and materials were stocked on site. CSI developed the first quality assurance program to be implemented by a commercial shipyard in the Jacksonville area. The company drafted a quality assurance manual and submitted it to SupShips for approval. The document was approved by SupShips in September 1974 and has become the standard for private sector, small shipyard quality assurance programs. The manual has been regularly revised and updated to meet more stringent quality assurance requirements.

RELOCATION OF FACILITIES

When CSI's corporate headquarters were moved in 1974, the company also leased several piers and surrounding land on St. Johns River. This facility has been used for major overhauls, conversions, modernizations, and repairs to ships of the U.S. Navy, Coast Guard, Military Sealift Command, and the commercial fleet. The facility at the naval base was expanded and improved to allow CSI to do more complex work and to expedite emergency repairs to surface combatant and auxiliary ships.

In 1977, CSI purchased a large tract of land and pier facilities in Jacksonville and established the present St. Johns River site. The corporate offices were moved to this new location. Warehouses, production shops, and administrative offices were constructed and expanded to complete the ship-repair facility as it exists today. The expansion included a complete material handling and warehouse area for government and contractor-furnished materials that meets stringent government criteria for covered and secure storage.

In 1982, CSI established a repair facility at Cape Canaveral, Florida. Most of the repair work undertaken at this facility involved ships of the Military Sealift Command. The Cape Canaveral facility successfully completed single contracts in excess of $1 million, and the facility could be expanded if necessary. Also in 1982, CSI established temporary facilities at the U.S. Naval Submarine Base at Kings Bay, Georgia, to repair the USS *Oak Ridge* service craft and the work barges supporting the Trident Submarine Base.

EXPANSION

When CSI moved to its current location, it began to expand and add services needed for larger jobs. An in-house engineering and design capability was established. The planning/estimating and purchasing departments were moved to the new location. CSI's accounting department, in conjunction with its management information department, established a computerized purchasing system that allowed bulk buying and distribution of costs to single items or projects. This system, which used a Burroughs 1900 computer, made CSI the first commercial shipyard repair facility in the area with this computerized capability. Additionally, CSI acquired new equipment, machinery, special tools, shop assets, and qualified personnel and managers to support all existing and new demands for ship repair, overhaul, and conversion.

OPERATIONS

When Carlton founded CSI, the company worked only on small military and commercial vessels. Through expansion and relocation, however, CSI became capable of repairing ships of almost any size. The company did not compete with very large companies like the Newport News Shipyard, but it could compete effectively with other yards its own size. Revenues in 1984 totaled more than $63 million, and quality work earned CSI the Small Business of the Year award in 1982 for firms in the Southeast. (Shipyards with fewer than 1,000 employees are considered to be small.) CSI received National Safety Council awards for each year from 1981 to 1984.

ORGANIZATION

When CSI was a small struggling shipyard, Carlton was the only individual in the company with managerial and decision-making responsibilities. A typical entrepreneur, he believed that only he was capable of making the shipyard a success. As the company grew, Carlton realized that he needed a capable management team to help him operate the shipyard profitably. He also felt the need for advice and policy assistance from persons who were not connected with the shipyard. Accordingly, he established a board of directors composed primarily of well-known local businessmen. The company was organized along functional lines (see Exhibit 1) with supervisors and managers responsible for different aspects of the shipyard's operation. Carlton found that he was able to make the transition from entrepreneur to manager.

PROJECT TEAMS

Carlton was not satisfied with CSI's growth from its Jacksonville facility, so he developed mobile teams which could go anywhere in the world to repair ships. CSI also leased facilities in other East Coast cities to work on navy ships for short periods of time. In 1975 and 1976 CSI leased a repair facility at the Brooklyn Navy Yard to repair navy and Military Sealift Command ships. This facility was closed in 1976, when the company leased a facility at the ex-U.S. Navy Shipyard, South Boston Annex, to work on commercial and navy ships. This

---

EXHIBIT 1

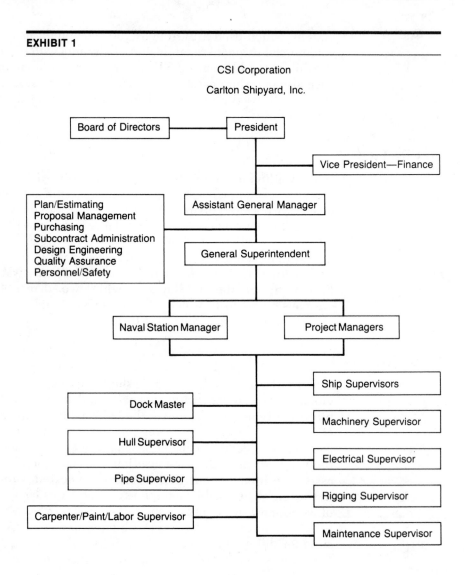

CSI Corporation

Carlton Shipyard, Inc.

facility was closed in 1978 because of high overhead costs and a depressed market.

In 1975, CSI deployed a team of production and supervisory personnel to Holy Loch, Scotland, to do major repairs on the USS *Los Alamos*. The company maintained a facility and team at Holy Loch through 1983 to work on various navy ships. In 1977, CSI deployed another team of workers and supervisors to La Madalena, Italy. This team repaired the USS *Howard W. Gilmore* and several surface combat ships of the U.S. Navy's Sixth Feet. Other project teams have been profitably deployed to other parts of the world to do temporary work for the U.S. Navy.

CONTRACTING JOBS

When the navy needs repair or conversion work done, it calls for technical and management proposals from all interested shipyards. The navy reviews the proposals it receives to determine which ship-yards are qualified to do the work. Then the navy opens the fixed-price bids from those yards that are qualified.

Most of CSI's contracts are secured through competitive bidding. CSI's planning/estimating department determines how much a given job will cost the company. After an exacting process which requires estimates of competitors' prices and cost estimates for materials, per-sonnel, and hundreds of different activities, the department arrives at a bid. The sealed bid is submitted in competition with 5 to 12 other shipyards. CSI has been low bidder about 20 to 30 percent of the time.

Once a company wins a government contract, it is expected to do the original specified work at the agreed-upon price. However, if the shipyard is asked to do additional work, it can request more funds from the government. For example, at the end of 1982, CSI claimed that added work requested by the government cost the company an additional $4,773,770. After review and negotiation, the navy agreed to pay CSI $3,040,499 more than the original contract. The difference was written off by the company as a loss.

PERSONNEL

Like most shipyards, CSI retains a permanent core of employees and augments its work force when it bids successfully for new contracts. The company employs a core of 150 hourly workers and has employed as many as 600 workers on a temporary basis. The temporary workers are hired from other shipyards which are completing contracts or from companies which use similarly skilled employees. Retired navy per-sonnel are used as temporary employees when the demand for work-ers cannot be met from traditional sources. Temporary employees receive the same benefits as do permanent workers; however, since most contracts are for less than one year, temporary employees do not benefit from vacation provisions or retirement plans. Temporary em-ployees do receive health insurance. There are no unions at CSI, mainly because the company pays well and offers relatively generous benefits.

FINANCES

CSI's income from contracts is recorded on the percentage-of-comple-tion method, which means that contract costs incurred during the period are expensed. Percentage complete is determined as the ratio of current costs to estimated total costs when the final results of the

EXHIBIT 2

CARLTON SHIPYARD, INC.
Balance Sheet
September 30, 1982, 1983, and 1984*

Assets

	1984	1983	1982
Current assets			
Cash	$ 4,256,041	$ 1,043,740	$ 360,076
Accounts receivable	10,428,413	9,499,447	9,692,037
Notes receivable	102,669		674,905
Other receivables.	1,590,753	811,394	
Income tax refund receivable		1,898,117	
Insurance proceeds receivable		683,350	
Costs and estimated earnings in excess of billings	485,730	1,284,209	785,091
Advances and other amounts due from related companies.			435,428
Inventory of supplies	624,748		109,368
Prepaid expenses.	356,698	215,831	417,584
Total current assets.	$17,845,052	$15,436,088	$12,474,489
Assets held for sale.	7,049,247	14,074,741	
Fixed assets			
Land and land improvements	$ 295,698	$ 286,023	$ 830,552
Buildings and improvements	1,467,668	1,425,481	1,394,829
Leasehold improvements	983,018	873,036	325,227
Machinery and equipment.	2,198,361	1,117,928	1,035,647
Automotive equipment	273,274	262,031	256,973
Boats, barges, and piers	483,539	483,279	586,572
Office furniture and equipment	489,374	436,440	350,553
Drydock	5,239,580		9,325,190
	$11,430,512	$ 4,884,218	$14,105,543
Less accumulated depreciation	3,218,250	1,554,725	1,121,466
Net fixed assets	8,212,262	3,329,493	12,984,007
Other assets			
Receivables	$ 42,737	$ 786,022	$ 354,367
Cash surrender value of officer's life insurance	98,169		90,305
Land held as investment	347,522	347,522	
Unamortized loan cost	299,948	402,067	67,757
Other	388,882	393,179	
Total other assets	1,177,258	1,928,790	441,542
Total assets	$34,283,819	$34,769,112	$25,970,995

* 1983 and 1984 are consolidated figures for CSI and NJS

contract can be estimated. Revenue recognized is the percentage complete times the contract price. Revisions in cost and profit estimates during the period of construction are reflected in the accounting period in which the facts causing revision become known. When estimates indicate a probable ultimate loss on a contract, the full amount of the loss is expensed (see Exhibits 2 and 3 for pertinent financial information).

EXHIBIT 2 *(concluded)*

	Liabilities 1984	1983	1982
Current liabilities			
Notes payable		$ 1,380,956	$ 1,227,405
Current installment of notes payable	$ 1,651,539		1,212,223
Accounts payable-trade.	9,494,026	5,568,277	1,285,591
Accounts payable-other.			1,030,815
Billings in excess of costs and estimated earnings	356,808	349,196	148,667
Accrued costs to complete contracts	412,357		73,433
Accrued salaries payable	569,948	618,021	423,947
Accrued retirement payable-current	10,754		28,656
Accrued interest payable	337,141	620,188	
Other accrued expenses	666,956	949,014	478,728
Deferred income taxes payable			2,052,024
Income taxes payable.			1,425,090
Accrued state income taxes. . . .		64,261	
Total current liabilities	13,499,529	9,549,913	9,386,579
Noncurrent liabilities			
Notes payable	15,339,325	16,914,465	9,631,192
Accrued expenses	249,166	272,203	247,766
Accrued retirement payable. . . .	10,000		36,266
Deferred income taxes	2,022,048	3,445,414	
Total noncurrent liabilities . .	17,620,539	20,632,082	9,915,224
Stockholders' equity			
Common stock (3,000,000 shares authorized; issued 410,000 shares of par value of $1). . . .			410,000
Retained earnings (deficit)	(2,208,989)	(785,623)	6,342,290
			6,752,290
Less treasury stock (78,394 shares at cost)			83,098
Total stockholders' equity.	3,163,751	4,587,117	6,669,192
Common stock-Class A (no par, 20,000,000 shares authorized 6,501,000 shares issued)	5,372,742	5,372,740	
Common stock-Class B (10,000,000 shares authorized, none issued)			
Total liabilities and stockholders' equity	$34,283,819	$34,769,112	$25,970,995

Since CSI could not be paid for repairs until the work was well underway, it needed a line of credit which would enable the company to pay its expenses as they were incurred. Short-term loans constituted the bulk of the company's debt until 1982. In that year the company decided to increase significantly its capability to work on large ships, so it purchased a new drydock for $9,325,190. The pur-

EXHIBIT 3

CARLTON SHIPYARD, INC.
Statement of Income and Retained Earnings
Year Ended September 30, 1982, 1983, and 1984*

	1984	1983	1982
Operating income			
Income from ship repairs	$63,235,703	$41,445,509	$43,890,275
Cost of contracts:			
Labor	15,320,703	6,753,283	5,932,872
Materials.	6,374,810	5,515,617	7,550,891
Subcontractors.	21,531,705	14,239,435	14,007,604
Other direct costs	838,150	826,371	1,058,490
Direct costs to complete job . .			90,083
Total cost of contracts	44,065,280	27,334,706	28,639,940
Gross profit on contracts . . .	19,170,423	14,110,803	15,250,335
Indirect ship repair costs	13,936,670	11,042,543	7,774,962
Income before expenses . . .	5,233,753	3,068,260	7,475,373
Operating expenses			
	5,781,545	7,305,061	3,809,585
Net operating income (loss)	(547,792)	(4,236,801)	3,665,788
Other income (expense)			
Interest income.	153,067	97,490	43,516
Insurance proceeds from loss			
of use of drydock.		3,750,000	
Gain on sale of assets and			
involuntary conversion	14,932	95,267	968,009
Loss on abandoned assets			(239,782)
Other income	137,521	539,250	284,138
Interest expense	(2,604,459)	(2,353,136)	(756,344)
Total other income	(2,298,939)	2,128,871	299,537
Net income (loss) before			
taxes	(2,846,731)	(2,107,930)	3,965,325
Income tax (expense) benefit . . .	1,423,366	1,322,307	(1,542,345)
Cumulative effect of a change			
in accounting principle			33,602
Net income (loss).	(1,423,365)	(785,623)	2,456,582
Retained earnings, beginning			
of year.	(785,624)	6,342,290 †	3,885,708
Retained earnings, end of year . . .	$ (2,208,989)	$ (785,624)	$ 6,342,290

* 1983 and 1984 figures are for CSI and NJS.
† Retained earnings restated after the firm declared bankruptcy.

chase of the drydock, which was to be built in Germany and towed to Jacksonville, was financed by Third State Bank at an interest of prime rate plus 1 percent. Third State Bank also provided CSI with a revolving line of credit of approximately $1 million, also at prime plus 1 percent.

The drydock was severely damaged in transit and was not used until April 1983. CSI filed a loss claim with its insurance carrier and received $5,245,000 for damages and $3,750,000 for loss of use. The cost (basis) of the drydock was reduced by the amounts of the proceeds from damages, and the proceeds for loss of use were reflected in the statement of operations. Costs related to the repair of the drydock approximated $700,000 and were capitalized.

ACQUISITION AND REORGANIZATION

Acquisition

When CSI put its new drydock into operation, it was finally able to accommodate most of the navy and commercial ships in the Jacksonville area. However, Carlton still wanted his company to expand and to be capable of working on any size vessel on the East Coast. In 1982 he learned that a major manufacturing company wanted to sell its shipyard and concentrate on its primary business. New Jersey Shipyard (NJS) had two facilities in New Jersey, one (Site A) across the river from New York, N.Y., and the other (Site B) a few miles south of the first facility. The purchase price was less than $2 million. Carlton believed that the land alone was worth the purchase price and decided to purchase both facilities.

On February 15, 1983, CSI purchased NJS for $9,365,000, using a leveraged buyout plan. In order to pay for the new shipyard, Carlton borrowed $10 million from the following sources: $7 million from Lawyers Insurance and Annuity Association of America, secured with stock warrants to purchase 545,220 shares of Class B nonvoting common stock; $3 million from Southern Life Insurance Company, secured with stock warrants to purchase 155,777 shares of Class B nonvoting common stock; and $2 million from Southeastern National Life Insurance Company, secured with 133,666 shares of Class B nonvoting common stock.

The secured notes, payable with warrants of $7 million, $3 million, and $2 million, are due on December 31, 1992. Interest at 14 percent is payable semiannually on the last day of June and December. Contingent interest, due 120 days after year-end, is based on the daily average principal balance of the notes at a rate of 2.5 percent if annual gross profit on contracts is between $18 and $27 million, or 3 percent if such gross profit exceeds $27 million. The notes are collateralized by receivables, inventory, property, and equipment. The notes contain certain restrictive covenants relating to maintenance of working capital and tangible net worth and ratios of current assets to current liabilities. Additional restrictions pertain to net tangible assets plus long-term lease assets to secured funded debt plus long-term lease obligations. In addition to the term loan, CSI established a line of credit with several banks of $6,500,000.

Using borrowed funds, Carlton had expanded facilities from one small drydock to an additional six drydocks in one year. Before the

EXHIBIT 4

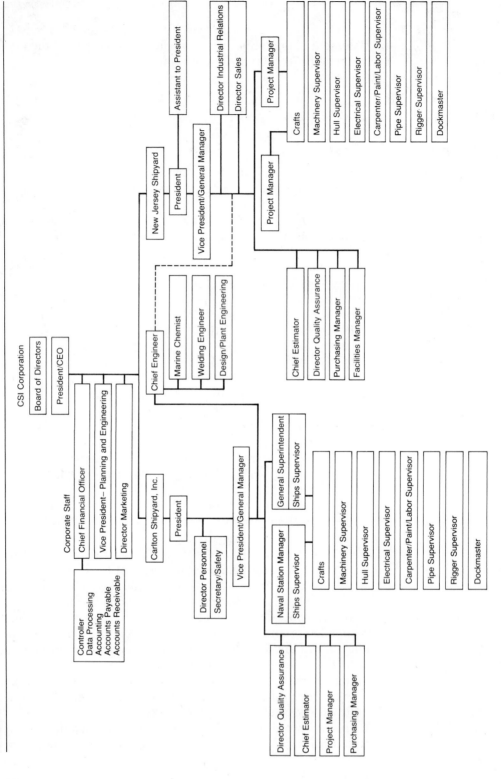

acquisition, he could repair 2 ships at his shipyard piers; now, he could repair 10 ships simultaneously.

Reorganization

A corporate reorganization was undertaken in order to facilitate the acquisition of NJS by CSI. The first step in the reorganization was the formation of a holding company, CSI Corporation (CSIC), which became the parent corporation of both Carlton Shipyard, Inc., and New Jersey Shipyard. Since Carlton owned all of the stock of both shipyards, he merely transferred the stock to the holding company. Once the reorganization was complete, redundant positions and activities were eliminated as a cost-cutting measure. The organizational chart (see Exhibit 4) shows, for example, that the chief engineer and his staff were located in Jacksonville but also provided services to the New Jersey site. Because business was not very successful at NJS, Site A was closed 18 months after acquisition and all operations were diverted to Site B.

CHAPTER 11 BANKRUPTCY

The acquisition of NJS did not enhance CSIC's profit for 1983 or 1984. In fact, CSIC lost $785,623 in 1983, and $1,423,366 in 1984, despite more than a $20 million increase in revenues in 1984. In 1984 Third State Bank, one of CSIC's principal lenders, declared that the company had not maintained its required ratios and the bank called its loans. Without Third State Bank's line of credit, CSIC was unable to pay its expenses. Therefore, on August 13, 1984, the company filed for protection from its creditors under the provisions of Chapter 11 of the Federal Bankruptcy Act. CSIC's accountants stated that the effects, if any, on the classification of assets and the classification and amount of liabilities on the accompanying balance sheet due to the filing for protection under Chapter 11 were not determinable.

The realization and the classification of the company's assets and the classification and the liquidation of its liabilities are dependent upon (1) selling certain fixed assets, (2) operating the company successfully under the protection of Chapter 11, and (3) obtaining sufficient working capital and lines of credit for continuance of operations in the future without the protection of Chapter 11. The company is trying to sell its Site A facility to a group of developers interested in building condominiums on the land. CSIC is also trying to sell drydocks, machinery, equipment, buildings, and some inventory valued at $14,074,741 to satisfy the claims of some of its secured creditors.

CSIC has had to make some operational changes as a result of its Chapter 11 filing. The company must make monthly financial reports to the bankruptcy officials, and its access to additional capital has been limited. Directors of the company resigned their positions when they realized that they could be held responsible for CSIC's financial problems. CSIC cannot bid on some contracts for the Military Sealift Command because that agency requires contractors to be bonded on large jobs (CSIC cannot be bonded in its current condition). Carlton believes that CSI and NJS have lost some navy and civilian business because of the bankruptcy action. However, he estimates that revenues for 1985 will approximate $50 million.

REQUIRED ACTION

CSIC must develop a detailed plan showing how it intends to rectify its financial condition and return to profitable operations. Two recent actions initiated by CSIC could solve the company's financial crisis. The first is a $250 million lawsuit filed by CSIC against certain secured creditors alleging wrongful action in accordance with the provisions of the financing agreements. This case has not been resolved; however, Carlton believes that both parties could reach an out-of-court settlement as part of an overall agreement on reorganization. The other action is the attempted sale of Site A in New Jersey and certain drydocks, land, and equipment. If these assets are sold for the asking price, CSIC will attempt to negotiate a reorganization plan with its creditors and emerge from Chapter 11 as a viable concern. Carlton's immediate responsibility is to develop a plan showing how and when the company will return to profitability.

38. Western Kentucky Steel

Irv Hastings, treasurer of Western Kentucky Steel Company, was examining the various sources of funds available to finance the first phase of the company's capital expansion. The president of Western Kentucky Steel, Lloyd Hodges, wanted a report on the advantages and disadvantages of each type of financing and Hasting's recommendation. Hodges wished to have the report by late February 1971—within approximately three weeks.

THE COMPANY

Western Kentucky Steel Company was located in Paducah, Kentucky, situated in the far western portion of the state, approximately equidistant from St. Louis and Memphis. The company was founded in 1913 as Paducah Steel and in 1937 changed its name to Western Kentucky Steel. The firm produced steel with open hearth furnaces until the mid-1950s, when it converted to the electric furnace due to superior operating efficiencies associated with the latter and the declining cost of scrap. Most of the firm's output was composed of low-carbon steel, although some high-carbon items were manufactured. For the most part, the company marketed its output in Kentucky, Illinois, Indiana, Missouri, and Tennessee.

The company produced a varied combination of products, mostly falling into two groupings. Hot rolled products comprised approximately 6 percent of Western Kentucky's dollar output and 75 percent as measured by tonnage. Among the most important goods in this grouping were reinforcing bar, structural shapes, flats, and angles, with structural shapes showing the most rapid growth during the last five years. The other grouping consisted of wire products which accounted for 35 percent of the firm's dollar output and 20 percent of tonnage. Among the most important products in this grouping were nails, bright wire, welded reinforcing mesh, and high carbon spring wire. The latter two items had shown extraordinary growth over the last two years. The remaining 5 percent of the company's dollar sales and tonnage consisted of miscellaneous items (see Exhibit 1, Exhibit 2, and Exhibit 3).

This case was prepared by Harry R. Kuniansky, Georgia State University.

EXHIBIT 1 Western Kentucky Steel Company Comparative Balance Sheets ($ thousands)

	1968	1969	1970
Current assets			
Cash	$ 4,071	$ 4,543	$ 3,732
Accounts receivable, net	16,100	17,516	19,936
Inventory	37,499	38,533	38,766
Prepayments	704	911	491
Total current assets	$ 58,374	$ 61,503	$ 62,925
Long-term assets			
Land	$ 1,820	$ 1,820	$ 1,820
Buildings	37,517	37,615	38,223
Machinery and equipment	117,751	121,275	128,006
Less: Accumulated depreciation	(55,888)	(61,905)	(68,285)
Note receivable	1,355	1,316	1,138
Total long-term assets	$102,555	$100,121	$100,902
Total assets	$160,929	$161,624	$163,827
Current liabilities			
Accounts payable	$ 12,747	$ 8,425	$ 10,038
Accruals except taxes	3,378	2,910	3,066
Taxes payable	871	1,390	1,219
Current maturity of long-term debt	2,356	2,293	3,200
Total current liabilities	$ 19,352	$ 15,018	$ 17,523
Long-term debt*	$ 30,191	$ 34,054	$ 31,622
Stockholders' investment			
Common stock, $3 par, 4,000,000 shares authorized, 860,000 shares issued . . .	$ 2,580	$ 2,580	$ 2,580
Paid-in capital	23,898	23,898	23,898
Retained earnings	84,908	86,074	88,204
Total capital	$111,386	$112,552	$114,682
Total liabilities and capital	$160,929	$161,624	$163,827

* The company's long-term debt at December 31, 1970 is presented below:

6½% notes due in 1980 minimum of $2,200,000 payable annually. Prepayments not to exceed $1,100,000 in any one year	$21,622
6¾% notes maturing 198_ payment of $1,000,000 per year, first payment 1971	10,000
	$31,622
Current maturities of long-term debt	3,200
	34,822

THE INDUSTRIAL ENVIRONMENT

Historically, the steel industry was oligopolistic in nature. There were a few major producers such as United States Steel and Bethlehem, and the major producers tended to initiate price changes. Generally, Western Kentucky followed the price movements of the large firms. Only

EXHIBIT 2 Western Kentucky Steel Company Comparative Income Statements ($ thousands)

	1968	1969	1970
Net sales.	$165,218	$164,931	$173,554
Cost of goods sold (excluding depreciation).	137,648	137,959	142,979
Selling and administrative expenses.	12,928	12,603	13,556
Depreciation	5,093	6,017	6,380
Other (income) expense	(317)	211	(108)
Net income before interest and taxes	$ 9,866	$ 8,141	$ 10,747
Interest	2,144	2,391	2,291
Federal income taxes.	4,077	3,036	4,262
Net income after tax	$ 3,645	$ 2,714	$ 4,194
Earnings per share.	$ 4.24	$ 3.16	$ 4.88
Cash dividends per share	$ 1.80	$ 1.80	$ 2.40

in very rare instances did it deviate from this pattern and the price variance was usually achieved through freight absorption. However, in the last five years the company faced a new source of competition, the so-called mini-mills. The mini-mills produced a limited number of products in only the most popular sizes. Very often they utilized non-union labor and the great majority of them used a new steel-making process called continuous casting.[1] For these reasons, the mini-mills were able to produce steel at a lower cost than Western Kentucky. The

EXHIBIT 3 Western Kentucky Steel Company Selected Operating Data ($ thousands)

Year	Net Sales	Earnings Before Interest and Taxes	Depreciation Charges	Interest Charges
1961	$ 80,617	$ 3,967	$2,422	900
1962	91,393	5,986	2,520	945
1963	96,582	6,529	2,569	1,800
1964*	90,043	3,010	3,378	1,800
1965	135,064	10,235	3,479	1,800
1966	150,910	11,771	3,819	1,873
1967	180,586	13,543	4,498	2,018
1968	165,218	9,866	5,093	2,144
1969*	164,931	8,141	6,017	2,391
1970	173,554	10,747	6,380	2,291

* Strike for two months.

---

[1] Continuous casting—the casting of semifinished shapes that eliminates the ingot and primary mill stages of rolled steel production, with the expectation of reducing production costs.

average price of these mills was between 15 to 25 percent below that of the company. Western Kentucky's policy was to price its products in line with those of the large steel companies, and generally to ignore the prices of the mini-mills. At present, the company believed it could compete with the mini-mills by emphasizing its ability to assure continuity of supply for its customers and by offering a wide range of sizes in all products. Whether this nonprice type of competition would be successful, or whether the firm would have to cut prices to meet those of the mini-mills, was uncertain.

In addition to competition from the mini-mills, foreign steel, notably from Japan and West Germany, posed a competitive challenge to all the steel industry. The industry was attempting to gain some relief from Congress in the forms of quotas and higher tariffs, but had met with little success. The foreign pressure had been especially intense on several of the firm's products, notably reinforcing bar and wire goods. However, there was a possibility of some relief from Japanese imports as a result of the voluntary quota system imposed by Japan. Since this quota was based on tonnage and not dollars, it was possible that imports would shift to steel products with a higher dollar markup, such as special alloy and stainless steel goods. Such a shift would benefit Western Kentucky as the company produced very few of these goods. Regardless of the import situation, the company's management believed that modernization of its facilities and aggressive marketing procedures would enable it to meet foreign competition.

THE INVESTMENT DECISION

Western Kentucky's first phase expansion was estimated to require about $20 million in external funds. Most of the expenditures were for an electric furnace and supplementary equipment. Vigorous debates were held about what project the company should invest in. Some production executives preferred to install a continuous casting system. They believed this type of installation was necessary if the company was to compete effectively with the mini-mills. On the other hand, some marketing officers argued that the new funds should be expended toward the development of a plastics operation in order to diversify somewhat the firm's activities. They pointed out that the firm was highly cyclical and that the plastics operation could lend more stability to the firm's sales. Although the debate was resolved in favor of the electric furnace, the idea of diversification was received quite enthusiastically by all top management. The consensus among top management was that some sort of diversification should be effected within the next three years and that external financing would be necessary. Estimates of outside requirements for the diversification project ranged from $10 million to $15 million.

EXHIBIT 3A Western Kentucky Steel
Company Estimated
Future EBITS*
($ thousands)

Year	High	Low	Median
1971	12,400	11,600	11,900
1972	14,600	12,300	13,000
1973	16,400	12,400	15,000
1974	17,000	11,500	14,000
1975	18,600	14,000	16,000
1976	19,400	14,600	16,900

* Estimations made by seven members
of the board of directors and eight operating
officers. The estimations assume no steel
strike.

In calculations involving after-tax earnings, the firm has assumed a tax rate of 48
percent.

The addition of the electric furnace was estimated to increase
earnings before interest and taxes by an additional $1,750,000 to
$2,250,000 in 1972. The new equipment would generate very little
earnings in 1971 as the furnace was not expected to become operative
until the latter part of the year. Exhibit 3A provides the range of
future estimations from 1971 through 1976 and, except for 1971, as-

EXHIBIT 4 Capital Structures of Selected Steel Companies Between 1963 and
1969 ($ millions)

Steel Company	Type of Capital	1963	1965	1967	1969
United States	Long-term debt*	$ 770	$ 705	$1,200	$1,434
	Preferred stock	360	360	0	0
	Common equity	3,379	3,624	3,220	3,432
		$4,509	$4,689	$4,420	$4,866
Bethlehem	Long-term debt	$ 128	$ 240	$ 370	$ 418
	Preferred stock	93	0	0	0
	Common equity	1,667	2,609	1,857	2,024
		$1,888	$2,849	$2,227	$2,442
Inland	Long-term debt	$ 186	$ 169	$ 202	$ 240
	Common equity	578	658	708	774
		$ 764	$ 827	$ 910	$1,014
CF&I	Long-term debt	$ 64	$ 49	$ 37	$ 51
	Preferred stock	7	5	0	0
	Common equity	112	130	141	161
		$ 183	$ 184	$ 178	$ 212
Granite City	Long-term debt	$ 63	$ 90	$ 148	$ 137
	Common equity	107	117	121	112
		$ 170	$ 207	$ 269	$ 249

* Represented by funded debt and excluding deferred credits and other long-term liabilities.

EXHIBIT 5 Western Kentucky Steel Company Selected Financial Data

Year	Common Stock Price Range		Number of Shares Traded (in thousands)	Earnings Per Share	Dividends Per Share
	High	Low			
1961	$47¾	$37⅝	155	$5.17	$2.60
1962	42½	37⅛	255	4.24	2.60
1963	44⅛	33½	305	5.50	2.60
1964	54½	39	300	2.37*	1.60
1965	88⅝	41⅞	190	6.83	3.00
1966	73¾	51⅜	180	6.10	3.00
1967	73½	48¼	217	6.78	3.40
1968	57½	30⅝	225	4.24	2.80
1969	47⅞	33⅛	205	3.16*	1.80
1970	55½	34	262	4.88	2.40

* Strike for two months.

sumes the installation of the new furnace and excludes any diversification projects.

THE FINANCING DECISION

Hastings believed that three financing alternatives were feasible for the company: (1) finance with common stock, (2) sell debenture bonds, and (3) issue a convertible preferred stock. Accordingly, Hastings explored each of the three alternatives. From preliminary discussions with an underwriting firm in St. Louis, Hastings learned that a common stock offering would net the company $50 a share. The common stock was currently selling in the over-the-counter market at $54. Hastings believed the figure $50 per share to be a reasonable one, in light of the overall weakness in the new issues market. Of course, he realized that stock market conditions might change during the next three months and this would cause the offering price to vary accordingly. Although a common stock sale would increase the number of outstanding shares approximately 45 percent, the underwriters assured management that this would not pose a control problem for the company.

The debenture bond issue would be for $21,240,000, the additional $1,240,000 being necessary to cover underwriting fees. The bonds would mature in 20 years and be callable after 5 years. A sinking fund provision required no payments for the first two years, with annual installments of $1,180,000 beginning in 1973 and continuing for the following 18 years. The interest rate would be in the neighborhood of 8 percent and the bonds would sell at par. The following restrictive covenants would likely be imposed on Western Kentucky Steel Company.

EXHIBIT 6 Western Kentucky Steel Company Industrial Production of Ingots and Steel for Casting 1950–1969 ($ thousands)

Year	Ingots	Year	Ingots
1950	96,836	1960	99,282
1951	105,200	1961	98,014
1952	93,168	1962	98,328
1953	111,610	1963	109,261
1954	88,312	1964	127,076
1955	117,036	1965	131,462
1956	115,216	1966	134,101
1957	112,715	1967	127,213
1958	85,255	1968	131,462
1959	93,446	1969	141,262

1. Maintenance of a current ratio of at least 2.5 to 1.
2. Prohibition of any additional senior long-term debt including long-term bank notes payable.
3. Restriction of cash dividends to 50 percent of cumulative earnings per share, unless approval was received from the trustee.

The preferred stock issue would carry a 7 percent rate and would sell for $100 par. It would be cumulative, nonparticipating, and convertible to 1.5 shares of common stock. The convertible feature would become operative in 1973. Underwriting fees were estimated at $1,500,000. The issue was callable in 1976 at $102.

The board of directors believed that the target payout ratio should be between 35 and 45 percent of earnings. Although the board wished to avoid cutting dividends per share, they realized the difficulties of this policy in a cyclical company such as Western Kentucky. Accordingly, they were more likely to stress a target payout ratio rather than a stable dividend per share.

39. Raybo, Inc.: The Selling of a Small Manufacturing Company

As Messrs. Smiley and Pere convened their annual state of the company meeting in January 1986, both knew they stood at a crossroads. Their interests were shifting away from running a manufacturing business, and they were beginning to position affairs and finances to support a new phase of their lives in which more time could be devoted to family, travel, and honing their golf games. While both agreed that time was right to sell Raybo, neither man felt comfortable determining a reasonable price for the company. They decided to enlist the assistance of an objective third party—Venture Brokers, a firm specializing in the valuation and sale of privately held manufacturing businesses. The information summarized in the following sections was compiled by Smiley, Pere, and Venture Brokers, and represents the substantive data used to value the company.

COMPANY BACKGROUND

History

Raybo, Inc. was established in 1967 by the company's founders R. P. Smiley and R. W. Pere. Prior to that time, Smiley was employed by a vehicle lamp manufacturer that purchased lenses from Pere's plastics manufacturing company. Prompted by a change in management, Smiley left to start his own company. He approached Pere and together they purchased a small metal fabricating company that became Raybo, Inc. Initially Raybo operated out of space in Pere's plastics factory. As the company grew, Smiley and Pere acquired and moved Raybo into the adjacent facility that it now occupies.

Products

Raybo produces exterior and interior lighting systems for speciality service vehicles, primarily school buses, ambulances, and fire trucks. The company's extensive product line consists of stop, stop-tail, marker, warning, flood, and dome lamps, as well as accessory equip-

---

This case was prepared by Wendy W. Guda and Michael Lubatkin of the University of Connecticut, Storrs.

ment, all in a wide range of sizes, styles, and colors. These lighting systems are designed to increase vehicle presence, which reduces accidents and saves lives and property.

In developing its product line, Raybo has created several unique products. In the ambulance market, Raybo sells the only dome light available for an engineered installation. This product solidly positions Raybo into a market in which 12,000 new ambulances, each requiring approximately 7 dome lights, are built annually.

Raybo's patented alternately operating flasher controls warning lights on specialty service vehicles. It is unique because it is totally moisture sealed. The product has had only moderate market success even though the company has shown that it has a lower cost over the life of the vehicle because it is trouble free. The product has not yet been aggressively marketed and there has been recent outbreak of price competition among competitors' products. Raybo management, however, feels that their product has significant potential because of its distinctive feature. Research is nearly completed on a second patented product, a warning light controller for the eight-light system on school buses. This product is expected to be ready for market in fiscal 1987.

Raybo also provides its customer base with replacement lamps. One area with proven potential is replacement lamps for school buses. Federal regulations dictate that once a lamp is placed on a school bus as original equipment, any replacements must meet identical specifications. This means that any replacement of lighting equipment, whether a complete lamp assembly or a single part (such as a lens), must meet the original equipment's specifications as a unit. If a change in equipment occurs, an independent testing lab must certify that the replacement lamp complies.

Since Raybo's school bus lamps differ from its competition, it is unlikely that anyone would replace any part of Raybo's lamps with a competitor's product. Since 10 years is the estimated life of a school bus, capturing the original equipment sales to the school bus manufacturers creates a long-term and profitable replacement market for Raybo's products.

Providing replacement parts is especially critical during recessionary times. When new vehicle equipment purchases are down, the existing aging fleets require greater numbers of replacement parts.

Marketing

Raybo's mission is to produce lighting products that meet specialty service vehicle safety needs. The company enters one market segment at a time, assesses the market's needs, and then develops a utilitarian, high-quality lighting system to meet those needs. This approach has given the company a dominant position in its selected markets and has committed clients to long-term relationships for new and replacement parts.

Raybo's primary markets in the vehicle-lighting industry are school buses, ambulances, and fire trucks. While the total vehicle lighting industry has annual sales in excess of $100 million, the markets that Raybo serves total approximately $6 million to $7 million dollars. Raybo estimates that in its niche it has captured 85 percent of the school bus, 80 percent of the ambulance, and 10–15 percent of the fire truck markets.

Over the years, a shakeout has occurred in the markets that Raybo serves, particularly for the manufacturers of fire trucks and ambulances. Of the 70 customers that the company serviced five years ago, only 30 remain today. These customers are bigger, financially solid, and firmly established. As a result, Raybo's bad debt write-off has dropped significantly. (Management felt that the acceptance of the bad-debt losses in prior years was part of the investment necessary to develop the company's ambulance and fire truck business to its present level.)

Raybo sells principally to the United States and Canada with some exports through distributors to Central and South America and Europe. Eleven customers account for 98 percent of the school bus business while 30 customers make up 90 percent of the ambulance and fire truck business. Although Raybo sells to a relatively small number of large customers, it sells many products to different divisions of the same corporation. There are some 300 other accounts in the aftermarkets. The company's sales breakdown is as follows:

60%	School bus body builders
25	Ambulance and fire truck builders
15	Parts replacement aftermarkets
100%	

Exhibit 1 shows the fiscal 1985 sales breakdown by major account groups.

Because Raybo produces an extensive line of lighting products for its markets, customers often buy Raybo products exclusively. Pere emphasizes: "There is no competitor that produces substantially the same product line as Raybo, Inc. For example, in the school bus lighting market, Raybo has one competitor that produces only the belt-line lights, tail lights, and marker lights. We have two competitors that only produce turn signals, marker lights, flashing lights, and dome lights." Pere also indicates that other competitors would not enter the market. "Since the market segment dominated by Raybo is relatively

EXHIBIT 1 Raybo, Inc.: Sales Breakdown by Account Groups

Top five accounts	$715,843		
	642,787		
	213,020		
	209,012		
	96,120		
		$1,876,782	59.0%
Second top five	80,464		
	70,562		
	55,527		
	45,794		
	42,517		
		294,864	9.3
All others		1,004,115	31.7
Totals		$3,175,761	100.0%

small, it is unlikely that any competitor would be willing to commit the tooling and development investments that would be required to compete effectively with our entire product line. This means that we should never lose an entire large account at any one time."

GROWTH POTENTIAL

Lighting equipment sales tend to follow specialty vehicle production which is, in turn, affected by population changes. Of particular interest to Raybo is that after many years of decline in school-aged children, there is now upward movement. The trends indicate that not only is the number of busing age schoolchildren (primarily kindergarten through eighth grade) on the rise, but also that per-pupil transportation cost is increasing nationwide. Not reflected in this increased spending is the fact that school districts are consolidating, and consolidation of school districts requires greater numbers of school buses.

The general aging of the population and the continuing trend to move away from population centers will create a need for more emergency vehicles, such as ambulances and fire equipment. With U.S. health expenditures on the rise and increased competition among health care institutions, there will be increased purchases of modern equipment to provide better services at a competitive cost. "Also, a new competitor," explains Smiley, "is entering the health care market—the private hospital. These hospitals that run for profit must fill beds, so more vehicles will be required to attract and transport critically ill patients. Something else to consider is that as the population ages, there is less of a chance that people will vote for decreases in health care expenditures."

Raybo is considering a careful entry into a new market segment in vehicle lighting. Smiley has identified the need for a safety light package for public utility vehicles. This "work field light package" is in the final design stages and could be on the market within three years.

The company employs 27 full- and part-time people. Eighteen full-time people work in the factory, and six people are employed full time in management and administrative functions. The three part-time employees perform miscellaneous office functions.

THE ORGANIZATION: THE OWNERS

R. P. Smiley

Mr. Smiley serves as the company's president and CEO and has held that position since the company's inception 18 years ago. With formal education in engineering and business, Smiley began his career working for a local metal products company as a salesman and engineer. He is 56 years old and has been involved in designing, manufacturing, and selling vehicle lighting throughout his career.

Smiley owns 51 percent of the corporation stock. He retains responsibility for establishing the broad marketing direction of the company and reviewing the reports submitted to him by the management group. In recent years, Smiley has delegated most of his operational responsibilities (including most customer contact) to his management group. He estimates that he now spends only 15 hours per week with matters pertaining to the company.

R. W. Pere

Mr. Pere owns the remaining 49 percent of the corporate stock. At the age of 57, he serves in a management support and engineering backup capacity. His formal education includes a degree in industrial engineering and most of his background has been in the management of plastic manufacturing. He is the former president of a thermal-plastics injecting molding company and a metal fabricating company, both sold in the mid-1970s. He currently owns a company providing plastic product sales and design services, and he is involved in several plastics and real estate development ventures. He does not deal with the daily operation of Raybo, but he is in touch with the management group on a regular basis.

THE ORGANIZATION: THE MANAGEMENT GROUP

Aside from Messrs. Smiley and Pere, Raybo employs 25 people: 4 in management, 18 in manufacturing, and 3 in part-time office administration positions. The management group is responsible for Raybo's daily operation. Each of the managers has a knowledge of multiple company functions, a necessity in a company of Raybo's size. The management team is aware of the owners' intent to sell the company, and each person has indicated that they wish to remain with the company after the sale. The following is a brief description of the management group, and an organization chart is presented as Exhibit 2.

Name	Responsibility	Service	Age
Terry Oswald	General Manager	9	33
William Weill	Manufacturing Manager	14	50
Beth M. Nickle	Manufacturing Foreman	7	37
Melvin Geck	Materials Manager	5	32

Terry Oswald

As general manager, Mr. Oswald now performs most of the administrative functions that were initially handled by Smiley. His major responsibilities include product engineering, management of accounts receivable, accounts payable, data processing, preparation of monthly statements for the owners, and preparation of data necessary for the annual audit. In addition, Oswald has regular customer contact. He reports to Smiley.

William Weill

Mr. Weill manages the manufacturing facility which includes machinery and equipment, tools and dies, molds, productivity methods, and quality control. In addition, he also has regular customer contact in keeping with his production responsibilities. Weill reports to Oswald.

Beth M. Nickle

Ms. Nickle schedules production, supervises the factory work force, and is responsible for all shipping and receiving activities. Nickle reports to Weill.

Melvin Geck

As material control manager, Mr. Geck is responsible for all phases of purchasing. He and Nickle work closely to ensure a smooth production cycle. He has regular customer and vendor contacts, and he reports to Oswald.

EXHIBIT 2 Rabo, Inc. Organization Chart

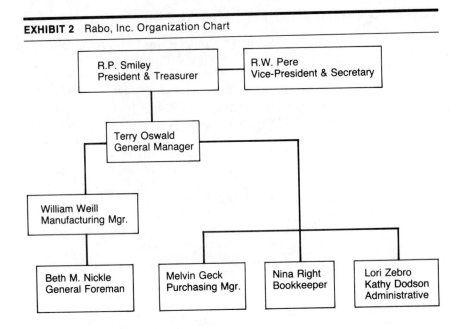

GENERAL OPERATIONS

Factory Employees

The factory workers belong to the United Rubber Workers Union with which the company has an excellent relationship. Production employees have been cross-trained to do a variety of jobs. Employee benefits are believed to be equal or superior to those offered by similar employers in the area. These benefits include medical, dental, optical, and life insurance. The company also provides its union employees with a pension plan.

Production

Raybo's production and manufacturing functions can be classified as follows:

1. Stamping (broadcast category)
2. Cleaning
3. Painting
4. Riveting
5. Spot welding

   6. Assembly
      a. Wire harness and subassemblies
      b. Finish product
   7. Material handling
   8. Setup
   9. Maintenance
  10. Shipping and receiving

Stamping utilizes single- and double-crank presses ranging from 5 to 60 tons capacity. The majority of these are in the 40 to 60-ton range. Most of the product line has been retooled to produce a finished part from coiled stock feeding through progressive dies. A few lower volume items are produced in successive dies in separate presses. The older tooling has been retained for backup purposes, but has generally been written off the books.

Cleaning is done in a Detrex degreaser. Painting is performed by the dip method and baking in a continuous conveyorized oven.

Assembly is accomplished with air screwdrivers, spot welding, riveting, and various clinching methods through the use of jigs and fixtures.

All lamp assemblies require the use of wire assemblies. The production process for wire assemblies involves cutting and stripping wire cable and attaching various solderless terminals and connectors. A new highly automated machine was recently placed into production to accomplish this work. It is expected to greatly reduce setup and production times, as well as provide quality improvements.

PROPERTY, PLANT, AND EQUIPMENT

Management strives to have a state-of-the-art production facility and to have both plant and equipment sufficient to accommodate expected future production increases. For example, Raybo recently invested a quarter of a million dollars in new manufacturing equipment, tools, dies, jigs, and leasehold improvements to reduce production costs and expand capacity. While sales have grown during this time, the investments have resulted in a greater than 25 percent reduction of manufacturing work force and considerably improved profitability.

In addition, new tool and equipment designs and regularly scheduled maintenance programs have held maintenance costs constant with increased production activity. Management now feels that production could be increased fourfold without significant purchases of additional equipment.

Raybo leases 46,918 square feet of a 144,000-square-foot building owned by Pere and Smiley. This leased space is sufficient to accommodate growth for the foreseeable future. On March 1, 1983, Raybo

---

EXHIBIT 3   Fixed Asset Summary:
Estimated Market/
Replacement Value

Leasehold improvements	$ 34,750
Machinery	442,558
Industrial trucks	12,450
Molds and tools	635,030
General plant equipment	15,275
Office furniture and fixtures	10,000
Business machines	58,950
Total	$1,290,013

---

exercised its lease option and entered into a new 10-year lease for the space it now uses at a cost of $3,900 per month. The lease contains an escalation of rent clause in the amount of 4 percent annually over the life of the lease. The physical plant has a monitored sprinkling system throughout and is well maintained by the company.

Considering the escalation of like-kind machinery and equipment prices in conjunction with the depreciation of these assets for the company's accounting and tax purposes, much of Raybo's machinery, dies, tools and jigs, injection molds, furniture, and office equipment have values far greater than their book values. Management conservatively estimates the replacement value of these assets to be $1.3 million and independent appraisals support this view. A listing of the estimated market or replacement value of Raybo's fixed assets is included in Exhibit 3.

CAPITAL STRUCTURE

The balance sheet showing the position of Raybo, Inc. at the fiscal year-end (January 31) for 1986, 1985, and 1984 can be seen in Exhibit 4. All financial statements of this corporation are subject to a certified audit annually. According to management, this is not a common practice for companies of Raybo's size, but was adopted at Pere's suggestion. "After putting all the numbers together so that your financial status is known," indicates Pere, "a certified audit is not that much more time consuming or costly. Besides, it gives the figures much more weight when dealing with major suppliers and financial institutions."

In general, cash balances are minimal as cash is used to the benefit of the owners. Inventories are valued at the lower of cost (first-in, first-out basis) or market. Property, plant, and equipment are depreciated on a straight-line method based on useful lives. Part of the accounts receivables ($113,078) represents advanced operating capital

EXHIBIT 4

RAYBO, INC.
Balance Sheet
Years Ending January 31

Assets

	1986	1985	1984
Current assets			
Cash	$ 1,459	$ 6,249	$ 5,475
Accounts receivables.	543,910	481,810	412,292
Inventory	263,598	209,649	216,777
Income tax receivable	0	0	6,685
Prepaid expenses	33,491	9,877	10,607
Total current assets	$ 842,458	$ 707,585	$ 651,836
Plant and equipment			
Equipment and autos.	$ 141,541	$ 193,584	$ 197,211
Machinery	237,465	166,154	170,604
Tools, dies, and jigs	243,520	218,212	290,208
Office equipment.	81,989	37,966	83,493
Leasehold improvements	40,126	36,110	72,394
	744,641	652,026	813,910
Less: Accumulated depreciation. . . .	317,824	269,206	416,978
Net plant and equipment	$ 426,817	$ 382,820	$ 396,932
Other assets			
Patents, net of amortization.	$ 12,392	$ 14,727	$ 17,063
Deposits.	4,013	4,346	4,821
Surrender value of life insurance . . .	92,452	75,233	56,819
Total other assets	$ 108,857	$ 94,306	$ 78,703
Total	$1,378,132	$1,184,711	$1,127,471

Liabilities

	1986	1985	1984
Current liabilities			
Current portion installment notes . . .	$ 0	$ 0	$ 923
Current maturity of long term debt . .	45,000	45,000	45,000
Current portion capital leases.	21,805	46,276	39,707
Accounts payable	231,336	186,749	267,165
Accrued expenses and taxes	65,814	75,180	64,150
Accrued Federal income tax	37,613	30,495	0
Total current liabilities	$ 401,568	$ 383,700	$ 416,945
Long-term liabilities			
Obligations under capital leases. . . .	$ 100,498	$ 89,851	$ 125,597
Long-term debt	3,750	48,750	97,500
Total long-term liabilities	$ 104,248	$ 138,601	$ 223,097
Deferred federal income tax.	$ 67,713	$ 51,003	$ 24,990
Total liabilities	$ 573,529	$ 573,304	$ 665,032
Stockholders' equity			
Common Stock (250 shares)	$ 2,500	$ 2,500	$ 2,500
Contributed capital.	24,594	24,594	24,594
Retained earnings	777,509	584,313	435,345
Total stockholders' equity.	$ 804,603	$ 611,407	$ 462,439
Total	$1,378,132	$1,184,711	$1,127,471

EXHIBIT 5 Statement of Earnings and Retained Earnings

	1986	1985	1984
Sales	$3,829,097	$3,175,761	$2,821,056
COGS			
Materials, labor, overhead	$2,330,417	$1,903,050	$1,539,842
Manufacturing expenses	501,351	466,719	404,976
	2,831,768	2,369,769	1,944,818
Less overstatement of overhead	255,952	252,316	39,464
	2,575,816	2,117,453	1,905,354
Gross margin	$1,253,282	$1,058,308	$ 915,702
Selling and administrative expenses:			
Selling expenses.	$ 97,405	$ 87,422	$ 90,104
Administrative expenses	790,475	691,663	635,148
	887,880	779,085	725,252
Net operating income	$ 365,402	$ 279,223	$ 190,450
Other income and (expense)			
Misc. income	$ 2,148	$ 1,393	$ 1,242
Gain on sale of property			
and equipment	0	6,500	0
Bad debt	(2,700)	(500)	(12,860)
Interest expense.	(34,137)	(42,991)	(48,453)
Misc. expense	(5,708)	(4,391)	(6,733)
	(40,397)	(39,989)	(66,804)
Pretax earnings	$ 325,005	$ 239,234	$ 123,646
Federal income tax			
Current	$ 109,348	$ 59,503	$ 14,020
Deferred	16,710	26,013	14,809
	126,058	85,516	28,829
Net earnings.	$ 198,946	$ 153,718	$ 94,817

Changes in Retained Earnings

Retained earnings, beginning.	$ 584,313	$ 435,345	$ 344,778
Net earnings.	198,946	153,718	94,817
Dividends (250 shares)	(5,750)	(4,750)	(4,250)
Retained earnings, ending	$ 777,509	$ 584,313	$ 435,345

in the form of noninterest receivables to affiliated entities which have some of the same individuals as shareholders/partners. The company is the owner and beneficiary of life insurance policies on Smiley and Pere with a face value of $705,000.

Two patents registered in the name of R. P. Smiley and Terry Oswald are assigned to Raybo, Inc. They are approximately three years old. These patents are recorded at cost and amortized over 10 years.

EXHIBIT 6   Statements of Changes in Financial Position

	1986	1985	1984
Funds provided by:			
Net earnings	$198,946	$153,718	$ 94,817
Depreciation and amortization expense . .	76,805	94,656	81,758
Total from operations.	275,751	248,374	176,575
Decrease (increase) in deposits	333	475	(1,237)
Increase in deferred income taxes	16,710	26,013	14,809
	$292,794	$274,862	$190,147
Funds used for:			
Purchase of plant and equipment, net . . .	$118,467	$ 78,208	$186,836
Purchase of patents	0	0.	1,900
Increase in cash surrender value			
of life insurance	17,219	18,414	16,109
Decrease (increase) in L-T-D	34,353	84,496	(26,857)
Dividends paid	5,750	4,750	4,250
	175,789	185,868	182,238
Increase in working capital	$117,005	$ 88,994	$ 7,909
Changes in working capital:			
Increase (decrease) in current assets:			
Cash.	$ (4,790)	$ 774	$ (13,465)
Accounts receivable	62,100	69,518	47,120
Inventory.	53,949	(7,128)	22,958
Income tax receivable.	0	(6,685)	(1,205)
Prepaid expenses.	23,614	(730)	2,828
	$134,873	$55,749	$ 58,236
Increase (decrease) in current liabilities:			
Current portion			
notes payable, L-T-D	$ (24,471)	$ 5,646	$ 21,031
Accounts payable.	44,587	(80,416)	32,447
Accrued expenses and taxes	(9,366)	11,030	(3,151)
Accrued FIT	7,118	30,495	0
	17,868	(33,245)	50,327
Increase in working capital	$117,005	$ 88,994	$ 7,909

FINANCIAL PERFORMANCE

The earnings statement and the change in financial position statement for the most recent three fiscal years are presented in Exhibits 5 and 6. The company utilizes a full absorption accounting system. Standard costs are conservatively established as of February 1 and sales and production activity recorded during 13 four-week periods each year. Each order is followed through production and reviewed regularly for favorable or unfavorable variances, volume changes, purchasing efficiencies, and pricing levels. Since all standard costs (material, labor, and overhead) are determined at the beginning of the fiscal year, a variance adjustment is made at the end of each fiscal period to the cost

EXHIBIT 7 Historical Sales and Income (000s omitted)

	1986	1985	1984	1983	1982
Sales.	$3,829	$3,176	$2,821	$2,418	$2,258
Cogs	2,576	2,118	1,908	1,573	1,576
Gross margin	1,253	1,058	913	845	682
S&A expense	888	779	725	655	559
Net operating income . . .	365	279	188	190	123
Other income (expense) . . .	(40)	(39)	(67)	(66)	(64)
Pretax earnings	325	240	121	124	59
Taxes	126	86	29	31	6
Net income	$ 199	$ 154	$ 92	$ 93	$ 53

of goods sold. This annual variance adjustment can be seen in Exhibit 6.

Exhibit 7 summarizes the company's historical sales and income for the most recent five years. Smiley comments: "When industry sales for lighting equipment declined during the recession in 1982 and 1983, Raybo held its own and improved profitability."

Exhibit 8 presents management's projections of sales and income for the next six years (1986–1991), as developed in January 1985. These forecasts reflect only Raybo's current product line, with sales growth based on growth in public school transportation, health expenditures, and trends in public and private school populations. These forecasts do not reflect Raybo's entry into the public utility market, the demographic effects of consolidation of school districts, decentralization to smaller communities, replacement of aged fleets, etc. The forecasts are believed to be conservative, representing the "most likely" operating results given the identifiable variables. For reference, the projection used for fiscal 1986 (created in January 1985) is shown so that it can be compared to 1986 actual sales and income results shown in Exhibit 7.

EXHIBIT 8 Projected Sales and Income as of January 1985 (000s omitted)

	1986	1987	1988	1989	1990	1991
Sales	$3,656	$4,204	$4,960	$6,051	$7,684	$9,758
Cogs	2,419	2,808	3,324	4,054	5,147	6,538
Gross margin	1,237	1,396	1,636	1,997	2,537	3,220
S&A expense.	841	883	995	1,255	1,559	2,049
Net operating income.	396	513	641	742	978	1,171
Other income (expense)	(37)	(38)	(44)	(46)	(45)	(50)
Pretax earnings `.	359	475	597	696	933	1,121
Taxes*.	145	198	254	300	409	495
Net income	$ 214	$ 277	$ 343	$ 396	$ 524	$ 626

* Taxes assume 1984 rates.

EXHIBIT 9 Robert Morris Associates' 1984 Annual Statement Studies (percentages)

	SIC 3561*	SIC 3714†
Assets		
Cash and equivalents	7.0	7.4
Accounts and notes receivables	27.6	26.3
Inventory	28.6	28.6
Other current assets	2.0	3.1
Total current assets	65.2	65.4
Fixed assets—net	25.8	25.6
Intangibles—net	1.1	0.9
Other noncurrent assets	7.9	8.1
Total assets	100.0	100.0
Liabilities and net worth		
Notes payable (short term)	8.4	9.3
Current maturity L-T-D	2.7	2.7
Accounts and notes payable (trade)	17.3	13.7
Accrued expenses	8.0	7.3
Other current liabilities	3.3	5.8
Total current liabilities	39.7	38.8
Long-term debt	16.1	16.3
Other noncurrent liabilities	2.3	2.6
Net worth	42.0	42.2
Total liabilities and net worth	100.0	100.0
Income data		
Net sales	100.0	100.0
Cost of sales	75.3	69.5
Gross profit	24.7	30.5
Operating expenses	19.0	27.2
Operating profit	5.7	3.2
All other expenses (net)	1.6	1.3
Profit before taxes	4.1	1.9

* SIC 3561: Manufacturers—General Industrial Machinery & Equipment.

† SIC 3714: Manufacturers—motor Vehicle Parts and Accessories. (192 and 93 companies represented, asset size—Exhibit 7.)

ADDITIONAL INFORMATION

In addition to compiling information directly from Raybo, Venture Brokers researched comparable companies and possible acquisition scenarios. Robert Morris Associates' annual statement studies covering companies similar to Raybo in product type and size are provided in Exhibits 9 and 10. While Raybo does not fall precisely into a standard industry classification, management feels that SIC 3561, manufacturers, general industrial machinery and equipment, and SIC 3714, manufacturers, motor vehicle parts and accessories, provide the clos-

EXHIBIT 10 Robert Morris Associates' 1984 Annual Statement Studies: Ratio Analyses

Ratios	SIC 3561*	SIC 3714†
Current ratio		
Upper quartile	2.6	2
Median	1.7	1.6
Lower quartile	1.3	1.3
Quick		
Upper quartile	1.4	1.2
Median	0.9	0.8
Lower quartile	0.6	0.6
Cost of sales/inventory		
Upper quartile	6.3	8.7
Median	3.9	5.6
Lower quartile	2.8	3.5
Sales/average receivables		
Upper quartile	8.3	9.6
Median	6.5	7.5
Lower quartile	5.2	5.9
Sales/average total assets		
Upper quartile	2.2	2.7
Median	1.6	1.9
Lower quartile	1.2	1.5
Sales/working capital		
Upper quartile	3.8	4.9
Median	6.3	9.5
Lower quartile	11.8	18.4
EBIT/interest		
Upper quartile	5.8	8.8
Median	2.5	3.4
Lower quartile	0.8	1.3
Percent pretax profit/net worth		
Upper quartile	27.0	40.8
Median	11.1	18.7
Lower quartile	−0.7	6.8
Percent pretax profit/total assets		
Upper quartile	9.6	14.0
Median	5.1	7.6
Lower quartile	−0.6	1.7

* SIC 3561: Manufacturers—General Industrial Machinery & Equipment.

† SIC 3714: Manufacturers—Motor Vehicle Parts and Accessories (192 and 93 companies represented, asset size $1–10MM).

est associations. (Since Raybo's fiscal year ends in January, financial comparisons are made using the previous year's RMA figures.)

Research was conducted into the company's accounts to ascertain the owners' costs to Raybo. Exhibit 11 indicates the historical owners' compensation (1982–1986), as well as the projected compensation (1987–1991).

Both the owners and Venture Brokers realize that Raybo would be acquired in one of two ways. Either individuals would purchase the

EXHIBIT 11   Raybo, Inc. Owners' Compensation

Historical	1982	$272,000
	1983	342,000
	1984	359,000
	1985	375,000
	1986	390,000
Projected	1987	$410,000
	1988	430,000
	1989	451,000
	1990	474,000
	1991	498,000

company to run themselves as the owners/managers, much as Smiley and Pere have done, or an established firm would acquire the company as a subsidiary. Venture Brokers' initial studies indicate that if an existing company were to acquire Raybo as a subsidiary, it would have to hire a CEO to replace Smiley and Pere. The annual compensation for such an individual is estimated to be $75,000.

40. The Standard Candy Company (Goo Goo)

As Jimmy Spradley walked through his modern manufacturing plant, past the boiling cauldrons of confections, he summed up his company's situation this way:

> We're a growth oriented company. We've got very good quality candy being made here and we're going to keep it that way. Our Goo Goos have been in existence since 1912 and are the mainstay product of the company—that's because people love them and associate them with the Old South. We use the same ingredients now as we did back then, only now technology gives us a helping hand. Our Goo Goo Supreme is fast becoming a favorite, too. We've got other quality candy like the King Leo Stick Candy that has been around for generations, and new products as well, but the Goo Goo is the best loved. Our major decision now is whether to become well known nationally and compete with the big boys or to remain regional and increase sales in already established territories. Either way, we're going to grow. I can guarantee it.

HISTORY OF THE STANDARD CANDY COMPANY

The Standard Candy Company was established in 1901 by Howell H. Campbell, Sr. At that time, the company occupied a large, three-story building in the heart of Nashville. The "candyworks" was characterized by tall windows and the heavy scent of confections as 50-pound blocks of chocolate were melted down in the factory's huge vats.

Responsibility for managing the business was inherited by Campbell's son Howell H. Campbell, Jr., in 1946 and although the company had earned a reputation in the region for manufacturing some of the best candy, Mr. Campbell was content to fill orders for his regular customers and any new customers who sought his candy. On the other hand, in 1968 Mr. Campbell arranged for the Goo Goo cluster to be advertised on the radio in a slot that had previously been occupied by Prince Albert Tobacco. Other than this action, Mr. Campbell did not aggressively pursue an expansion of sales.

This case was prepared by Marie Rock, MBA, Ed.M.; and by Walter Greene, Ph.D., to be used as a basis for class discussion.

Indeed, when the business was sold in 1974, the new owners James Fischer and Jimmy Miller also did not make any dramatic changes to the direction of the business, which was "to manufacture and sell good, quality candy." However, a physical change implemented by the new owners was to move the operation to a new, one-story, windowless plant in an office park near the city's airport in 1979.

By 1982, the potential of the small company had attracted two new investors. Jim Spradley and his son Jimmy Spradley exercised their option to purchase 50 percent of the business and to become active in management. Jimmy Spradley, in his mid-20s and fresh out of graduate business school at the University of Chicago, moved into the president's position, with responsibility for developing and managing marketing aspects of the business. Jim Spradley assumed responsibility for production and James Fischer retained his board chairmanship. The company's 85-person work force, with a typical range of 20–25 years of service per person, remained stable throughout these management transitions. In another change, the company instituted a new product line centered around its famous Goo Goo cluster.

PRODUCTS

The Goo Goo Cluster

This product became a regional favorite, and recently, a novelty item in specialty stores. Introduced in 1912, the Goo Goo cluster rapidly developed anecdotes about how it came to be named. One account is that it was earned during a contest for a descriptive name. A different story lends a personal touch, claiming that when Howell Campbell, Sr., handed the gooey cluster to his small son, the child's first reaction to the cluster was "goo, goo." However, Howell Campbell, Jr. asserts that his father was discussing the naming of the candy with fellow passengers during his streetcar ride to work one morning when a schoolteacher suggested the name. Since 1968, the candy cluster also has been associated with Nashville's Grand Ole Opry, which is aired over the radio. During these broadcasts was heard the familiar exclamation: "Go and get a Goo Goo! It's gooooood!!" Although many people believe that "Goo Goo" is the three capital letters of the Grand Ole Opry name, spoken twice, the Grand Ole Opry was not in existence in 1912.

The delectable ingredients of the cookie-shaped confection were mixed and cooked in the plant's kitchen. Here, men worked over industrial-sized copper kettles, artfully adjusting measured amounts of corn syrup from taps, mixing in a variety of vegetable oils and powdered egg whites, and finally heating the concoction until it was hot enough to flow into a machine that discharged creamy, nougat centers about the diameter of a baseball onto large trays coated with cornstarch.

In the production room, women efficiently assembled the final product as they flipped the centers into molds placed on a moving belt. This belt then conveyed the partly filled molds to beneath a bellowing machine with two pipes, one that dropped a certain amount of factory-roasted Georgia peanuts onto the nougat center, and the other that "enrobed" the cluster with a steaming sweet milk chocolate. There were two such machines in the plant, each of which could produce 200 clusters per minute in an eight-hour workday.

According to Jimmy Spradley, the cost of making the clusters varied, but generally direct costs of a gross of Goo Goos met a target of 60 percent of the price; indirect costs, such as selling and administrative expenses, and a profit margin made up the residual of the target figure. In the past, sales of the regular Goo Goo have accounted for 48 percent of the company's total sales, while sales of the Goo Goo Supreme have accounted for 12 percent.

The Goo Goo Supreme

The Goo Goo Supreme was launched in 1982 and quickly became a favorite of consumers who enjoyed the flavor of pecans over that of peanuts. The production process remained the same, with the exception of the substitute nut. In the company's most recent year, 2 million Goo Goo Supreme's were sold; this is in contrast to sales of 26 million regular Goo Goos. The Spradleys have considered expanding the line to include a nut log confection.

Other Confections

In addition to the Goo Goos, Standard Candy Company also manufactured the King Leo Stick Candy in four flavors: clove, lemon, peppermint, and vanilla. The company typically sold approximately 1.6 million pounds of stick candy per annum, reaping one dollar per pound in revenues.

Nujoy Candies were bagged in hard and soft varieties and included Haystacks, Love Cremes, Peanut Butter Crisps, Peppermint Pillows, Assorted Pillows, and Candy Bowl Mix. Their revenue yield was similar to that of the stick candies.

PRICING

The prices of the various products fell in line with those of the company's competitors. Jimmy Spradley described the pricing policy this way:

We are price followers, not price leaders. We hope to be able to aggressively compete with the leaders someday. But right now we are a small company and when commodity prices fluctuate, we can't help but be affected by it. As the cost of materials increases, our profit margins decrease. The major manufacturers are able to make price shifts much quicker than Standard Candy, so in the short run we hurt, but eventually we are able to make that price shift and our margins increase over the long run.

Recently, price discounts were offered to wholesalers and retailers as an added incentive. Although national confectioners used such discounts for a number of years, this was Standard Candy's first attempt to increase sales through this method.

DISTRIBUTION

In previous years, Standard Candy's products were not available outside of a 200-mile radius from Nashville. However, the products were recently available in 23 states, from Texas and Florida in the South to Michigan in the North. Plans were developed to concentrate regional sales to within a 700-mile radius of Nashville and to continue regional and nonregional sales in various outlets. The products were sold through the following outlets:

Dollar General Stores

Major grocery chains

Grocery coop buying offices

Wholesale grocery companies

Convenience stores

Discount houses

Discount grocery stores

Bloomingdale's retail stores

Marshall Field's retail stores

Retailers generally carried the Goo Goo as a novelty southern item in their stores, and Dollar General Stores carried the item in over 800 of its outlets. In addition to such typical outlets, the Goo Goo cluster developed popularity with many visitors to the Opryland theme park in Nashville.

Shipping restricted distribution of the Goo Goo cluster to those areas that could be reached by refrigerated truck. Refrigeration is required for any milk chocolate product, since this ingredient melts at 92 degrees Fahrenheit. John Tippitt, traffic manager for the company, offered this assessment of the transportation problem:

We would never be able to ship abroad. We're really restricted by the melting factor. I suppose there might be a way, someday. Right now we're looking into shipping to new areas, like Chicago and Detroit.

PROMOTION

The business relied upon word of mouth and limited advertising to promote the Goo Goo cluster. No advertising funds were expended for the King Leo Stick Candies nor the Nujoy Candies. The radio slot during the Grand Ole Opry broadcast was the only media advertising used by the company, although several articles in local, regional, and national magazines provided publicity for the Goo Goo.

Even though price discounts were offered, Standard Candy Company often faced stiff competition for shelf space for its products. Jimmy Spradley commented:

More often than not, our Goo Goos have wound up on the bottom shelf. We've placed a high priority on getting better shelf location in the retail stores, but you know, it's all complicated by the number of new product entrants into the market. They seem to be growing every day.

FINANCIAL CONSIDERATIONS

The move to the modern plant on Massman Drive marked the beginning of a series of financial problems for the business. First, moving the entire company to the expensive new facility required plant operations to be halted during a four-month period that extended through the Halloween and Christmas seasons. Next, 40 percent of the peanut crop was destroyed by a severe drought and an industrywide price war began shortly after Standard Candy Company increased its product prices in stores. Then, the prime lending rate rose and affected the company's ability to manage its debt. These rapidly accumulated financial troubles brought the business to the brink of bankruptcy in 1982. It was at that time that the Spradleys assumed half of the company's liabilities, while acquiring a 50 percent interest in the business.

Since then, the company has made a concerted effort to increase its financial stability. Certain controls were instituted to monitor the economic environment and the company's finances. Jimmy Spradley explained some of the changes.

We monitor the commodity prices very closely now and we look for price shifts from our competition. You have to realize that the largest manufacturers often start price wars between themselves, each trying to increase their share of the market. So we watch for that.

We also watch our cash flow. Our collection cycle is under 30 days and our payable cycle is under 20 days. Of course, we take all the discounts we can get.

THE COMPANY'S FUTURE

Jimmy Spradley sat back in his comfortable armchair and speculated on the future of Standard Candy Company:

As I mentioned, we do have some problems: there are more and more competitors for finite shelf space, and commodities, competition, and cash need constant surveillance. That's just the nature of the industry, and it's becoming more risky.

Oh, I know that we've had some rough times in the past, but things are looking up. Sales of our Goo Goos are increasing, even though we sometimes take an order that barely cover the manufacturing overhead. We intend to keep increasing our sales too. We're not looking to capture a particular market share—we just want to sell all the candy that we can. I think the Goo Goo has a shot at becoming a top 20 candy, something you find in all the 7-Elevens, K marts, and Woolworths. This may mean that the Goo Goo eventually loses its snob appeal in the specialty stores, but right now profit lies with the masses.

EXHIBIT 1 Simplified Balance Sheets

STANDARD CANDY COMPANY, INC.
Nashville, Tennessee

	1982 (unaudited)	1983	1984	1985
Assets				
Total current assets	$ 428,906.8	$ 735,393.9	$1,019,553.3	$2,592,427.6
Total fixed assets	1,990,014.7	2,103,906.9	2,084,788.4	2,975,576.1
Total other assets	146,523.6	140,500.9	137,791.2	128,455.6
Total assets.	$2,565,445.1	$2,979,801.7	$3,242,132.9	$5,696,459.3
Liabilities				
Total current liabilities.	$ 822,372.9	$ 680,372.3	$1,001,433.3	$2,415,258.7
Total long-term liabilities	1,784,876.3	1,886,740.8	1,770,522.8	2,742,460.9
Total liabilities	$2,607,249.2	$2,567,113.1	$2,771,956.1	$5,157,719.6
Equity				
Capital stock	$ 45,000.0	$ 45,000.0	$ 45,000.0	$ 45,000.0
Retained earnings, prior years . . .	106,260.3	(89,562.8)	190,818.7	369,335.5
Current period earnings	(193,064.4)	457,251.4	234,358.1	124,404.2
Total equity.	$ (41,804.1)	$ 412,688.6	$ 470,176.8	$ 538,739.7
Total liabilities and equity	$2,565,445.1	$2,979,801.7	$3,242,132.9	$5,696,459.3
Net sales	$2,793,887.0	$5,562,797.6	$7,542,895.3	$8,796,425.0
Net income before taxes.	(193,064.4)	475,251.5	411,193.9	213,122.4
Net income after taxes			234,358.1	124,404.0
Current ratio	0.5	1.1	1.0	1.1
Fixed assets utilization	1.4	2.6	3.6	3.0
Total assets turnover	1.1	1.9	2.3	1.5
Debt ratio.	1.0	0.9	0.9	0.9
Basic earning power ratio	(0.1)	0.2	0.1	0.0
Return on equity	(4.6)	1.2	0.5	0.2
Profit margin on sales*			0.0	0.0

* This ratio uses income after taxes only in its numerator.

EXHIBIT 2 Comparative Statement

STANDARD CANDY COMPANY, INC.
Nashville, Tennessee
Comparative Statement of Income and Expense for the
Fiscal Years Ending June 30

	1982	1983	1984	1985	1985 Percent
Sales	$2,793,887.0	$5,562,797.6	$7,542,895.3	$8,796,425.0	104.6
Less returns and allowances	0.0	81,963.3	140,934.4	198,009.2	2.4
	$2,793,887.0	$5,480,834.2	$7,401,960.9	$8,598,415.8	102.2
Less customer discounts	52,537.5	140,364.5	198,788.2	188,572.7	2.2
Net sales	$2,741,349.6	$5,340,469.7	$7,203,172.7	$8,409,843.1	100.0
Cost of goods sold					
Ingredients and packaging*	$ 0.0	$2,589,020.7	$3,713,795.1	$4,245,804.6	50.5
Direct labor	330,068.9	517,896.9	661,123.6	825,701.0	9.8
Manufacturing overhead	1,806,130.5	572,101.8	710,086.3	1,125,431.9	13.4
Total cost of goods sold	$2,136,199.4	$3,679,019.6	$5,085,005.0	$6,196,937.6	73.7
Gross earnings	$ 605,150.2	$1,661,450.2	$2,118,167.7	$2,212,905.5	26.3
Operating expenses					
Selling expenses	$ 328,098.5	$ 724,046.1	$1,106,342.8	$1,326,680.1	15.8
Administrative expenses	159,016.7	214,139.8	258,738.5	378.291.5	4.5
Total operating expenses	$ 487,115.2	$ 938,185.9	$1,365,081.3	$1,704,971.5	20.3
Earnings from operations	$ 118,035.0	$ 723,264.2	$ 753,086.4	$ 507,933.9	6.0
Other income	0.0	0.0	76,046.1	144,514.3	1.7
Net other expenses	311,099.4	266,012.7	417,938.6	439,325.8	5.2
Net earnings before taxes	$ (193,064.4)	$ 457,251.5	$ 411,193.9	$ 213,122.4	2.5
Provision for taxes			176,835.8	88,718.4	1.0
Net earnings after taxes			$ 234,358.1	$ 124,404.0	1.5

* Included in manufacturing overhead in 1982.

EXHIBIT 3   17 Percent Target Sales Increase

STANDARD CANDY COMPANY, INC.
Nashville, Tennessee
Pro Forma Income Statement
For the Fiscal Years Ending on June 30

	1985	*Base Year* 1986	1987	1988
Sales	$8,796,425.00	$10,291,817.25	$12,041,426.18	$14,088,468.63
Less returns and allowance*	198,009.20	231,670.76	271,054.79	317,134.11
	$8,598,415.80	$10,060,146.49	$11,770,371.39	$13,771,334.52
Less customer discounts*	188,572.70	220,630.06	258,137.17	302,020.49
Net sales*	$8,409,843.10	$ 9,839,516.43	$11,512,234.22	$13,469,314.04
Cost of goods sold*				
Ingredients and packaging	$4,245,804.60	$ 4,967,591.38	$ 5,812,081.92	$ 6,800,135.84
Direct labor	825,701.00	966,070.17	1,130,302.10	1,322,453.46
Manufacturing overhead	1,125,431.90	1,316,755.32	1,540,603.73	1,802,506.36
Total cost of goods sold	$6,196,937.60	$ 7,250,416.87	$ 8,482,987.74	$ 9,925,095.66
Gross earnings*	$2,212,905.50	$ 2,589,099.55	$ 3,029,246.48	$ 3,544,218.38
Operating expenses*				
Selling expenses.	$1,326,680.10	$ 1,552,215.72	$ 1,816,092.39	$ 2,124,828.10
Administrative expenses	378,291.50	442,601.05	517,843.23	605,876.58
Total operating expenses.	$1,704,971.50	$ 1,994,816.77	$ 2,333,935.62	$ 2,730,704.68
Earnings from operations*	$ 507,933.90	$ 594,282.78	$ 695,310.85	$ 813,513.70
Other income	144,514.30	144,514.30	144,514.30	144,514.30
Net other expenses	439,325.80	439,325.80	439,325.80	439,325.80
Net earnings before taxes (EBIT)	$ 213,122.40	$ 299,471.28	$ 400,499.35	$ 518,702.20
Provision for taxes.	88,718.40	149,735.64	200,249.68	259,351.10
Net earnings after taxes	$ 124,404.00	$ 149,735.64	$ 200,249.68	$ 259,351.10

Assumptions:
1. Certain variables are tied directly to sales and are indicated by *.
2. The current level of most balance sheet items are optimal for the current sales level.
3. An increase in sales will approximate that of '84–'85. 1.17 times the previous year.
4. Beginning in 1986, all taxes will amount to 50 percent of EBIT.
5. Other income and other expenses remain constant.

EXHIBIT 4 20 Percent Target Sales Increase

STANDARD CANDY COMPANY, INC.
Nashville, Tennessee
Pro Forma Income Statement
For the Fiscal Years Ending June 30

	1985	Base Year 1986	1987	1988
Sales.	$8,796,425.0	$10,555,710.0	$12,666,852.0	$15,200,222.4
Less returns and allowance*.	198,009.2	237,611.0	285,133.2	342.159.9
	$8,598,415.8	$10,318,099.0	$12,381,718.8	$14,858,062.5
Less customer discounts*.	188,572.7	226,287.2	271,544.7	325,853.6
Net sales*	$8,409,843.1	$10,091,811.7	$12,110,174.1	$14,532,208.9
Cost of goods sold*				
Ingredients and packaging	$4,245,804.6	$ 5,094,965.5	$ 6,113,958.6	$ 7,336,750.3
Direct labor.	825,701.0	990,841.2	1,189,009.4	1,426,811.3
Manufacturing overhead.	1,125,431.9	1,350,518.3	1,620,621.9	1,944,746.3
Total cost of goods sold.	$6,196,937.6	$ 7,436,325.0	$ 8,923,590.0	$10,708,308.0
Gross earnings*.	$2,212,905.5	$ 2,655,486.7	$ 3,186,584.1	$ 3,823,900.9
Operating expenses*				
Selling expenses	$1,326,680.1	$ 1,592,016.1	$ 1,910,419.3	$ 2,292,503.2
Administrative expenses.	378,291.5	453,949.8	544,739.8	653,687.7
Total operating expenses	$1,704,971.5	$ 2,045,965.9	$ 2,455,159.1	$ 2,946,190.9
Earnings from operations*.	$ 507,933.9	$ 609,520.8	$ 731,425.0	$ 877,710.0
Other income	144,514.3	144,514.3	144,514.3	144,514.3
Net other expenses	439,325.8	439,325.8	439,325.8	439,325.8
Net earnings before taxes (EBIT).	$ 213,122.40	$ 314,709.3	$ 436,613.5	$ 582,898.5
Provision for taxes; EBIT	88,718.4	157,354.6	218,306.7	291,449.2
Net earnings after taxes	$ 124,404.0	$ 157,354.6	$ 218,306.7	$ 291,449.2

Assumptions:
1. Certain variables are tied directly to sales and are indicated by ∗.
2. The current level of most balance sheet items are optimal for the current sales level.
3. An increase in sales will be a new target of 20 percent or 1.2 times the previous year.
4. Beginning in 1986, all taxes will amount to 50 percent of EBIT.
5. Other income and other expenses remain constant.

EXHIBIT 5 Top Ten Best Selling Candies in the United States

Five of the 10 by Mars Inc. ⎫
The other 5 by Hershey   ⎬ make up 70 percent share of the market

#1 is Snickers by Mars Inc.

Hershey Products	Mars Products
Hershey's Kisses	Snickers
Big Block	M&M candies
Reese's Peanut Butter Cups	Mars
Hershey Milk Chocolate	Milky Way
Hershey Almond	3 Musketeers

SOURCE: Hershey Foods is in bitter war with Mars to dominate the $8 billion/year
U.S. candy market. *Fortune*, July 8, 1985, pp. 52.

EXHIBIT 6 Prices of Commodities

(Note: The prices are average figure for that particular year.)

Commodity	1984	1983	1982	1981	1980
Cocoa[a]	126.2	108.2	92.4	108.5	135.4
Milk	13.42[b]	13.57	13.59	13.80	13.00
	13.60[c]	13.70	13.80	14.00	13.20
Peanuts[d]	24.1	25.1	26.9	25.1	20.6
Sugar	21.74[e]	22.04	19.92	19.73	30.11
	5.21[f]	8.46	8.40	16.89	28.66

[a] Spot cocoa bean prices (ACCRA) in New York in cents/lb.
[b] Average price received by U.S. farmers for all milk in $/cents.
[c] Farm price of milk eligible for fluid market.
[d] Average price received by producers in United States for peanuts in the shell in cents/lb.
[e] Raw sugar N.Y. spot price in cents/lb.
[f] Spot raw sugar international sugar agreement world price in cents/lb.
SOURCE: 1985 CRB Commodity Year Book.

EXHIBIT 7 Top Ten Candy Companies in the United States

1. Mars, Inc.
2. M&M/Mars
3. Hershey Foods Corporation
4. Beatrice Companies—International Food
5. Hershey Chocolate—PA.
6. Grace WR—General business
7. Life Savers Inc.
8. Brach & Sons
9. Nabisco US—confectioner
10. Russell Stover Candies Inc.

SOURCE: Ward's Business Directory, Vol. 1, Largest U.S. Companies, 25th Anniversary Edition, 1986.

The Technical Side

41. Colby Electronics

Gauntlet Associates
1319 Fox Avenue
Upperville, California

Colby Electronics
1010 West Second St.
Smithton, Iowa

Dear Mr. Colby:

Any company that has been able to survive our volatile economy for 47 years has certainly performed well in a significant number of areas.

With the very rapid downturn in our economy in the first quarter of 1982, and the devastating agricultural panic in the first quarter of 1986, it is a miracle any business venture is still surviving.

Therefore, Colby Electronics, like many other midwestern businesses, was in a survival mode when Gauntlet Associates began its analytical review in 1986.

What follows is a stipulation of our review. If any of our recommendations are predicated on information we erroneously interpreted, we apologize.

Sincerely,

Alfred P. Troan
Senior Partner

/sb

This case was prepared by Eugene Nini of the University of Texas, Permian Basin, Odessa, Texas.

FINDINGS

I. ORGANIZATION:
   A. *Structure:* Colby Electronics has a structure which consists of a president and four division managers.
      1. President: Jason Colby is the president and overall leader of the organization. He is the final decision maker on all facets of the business as a whole and all business functions in each division.
      2. Division managers: Each of the Colby sons is responsible for their division's operation even though all are complimentary to each of the other divisions to some degree.
         a. Commercial Division   Jeff Colby
         b. Retail Division   Miles Colby
         c. Service and Repair Division   Adam Colby
         d. Auto Stereo Division   Fallon Colby
   B. *Organizational Climate:* As a result of Colby Electronics economic crisis we found an organization in a very dysfunctional mode causing the organization to function very unsynergistically. We found a leader being forced to perform tasks he had no inclination to perform, nor were the tools available to him which would enable him to perform his tasks in an efficient manner.

      When a firm has a severe working capital shortage it demands precedent over all other functions. In fact, if the proper tools are not available to manage the shortage properly, a severe cash crunch will cause the entire organization to function improperly.

      In addition, the atmosphere at Colby Electronics was further affected by the tumultuous relationship between the division managers; the leader and some division managers; some division managers and employees; and some employees and other employees. It is not unusual for the political environment of a business organization to become imbalanced in the climate we found at Colby Electronics. The ostensible cause of the turmoil is a working capital shortage. However, we believe other factors were the root cause.

      We found that each of the division managers were held responsible for their division (as they should be) but they did not seem to have the authority necessary to function semiautonomously and definitely did not have the tools needed to manage effectively and efficiently.

In our opinion, only a very small and uncomplicated firm or a firm operating in an economic "boom" could survive in the leadership environment we found.

It is considered common knowledge that entrepreneurial genius and professional operational management is a rare and unusual combination found in leaders. In fact, from a personality profile standpoint, it seems rather ludicrous to expect a truly creative risk taker to assume the mantel of operational leadership in an environment which demands rigorous planning, sophisticated controlling procedures, and constant follow-up.

II. ACCOUNTING: *Overview.* While the effect of accounting considerations on any particular function, transaction, or area of business operation may vary from firm to firm, this section is aimed at giving both the owner and managers of Colby Electronics and their professional accounting staff a broad overview of generally accepted accounting principles and practices as we feel should normally apply under consistently applied standards.

Accordingly, this section attempts to identify for the owner and managers, with a basic knowledge and understanding, the important accounting tools and concepts that are missing from the system and the resultant gaps which are occurring in monitoring, managing, controlling, and financing the business.

To accomplish this task with clarity we have chosen to break the findings into four subcatagories dealing with important interrelationships in the summary.

A. *System Effectiveness:* The accounting system in general has had little attention over the past several years and is viewed as bothersome or erroneous by top management in all divisions.

1. Accuracy: Little if any demand is evident for accurate decision-making information resulting in the absence of investigation and follow-up where system controls have failed to achieve desired objectives or identify internal or external constraints as they may from time to time affect the business. This is most apparent in the purchasing and inventory control functions and we suspect is rooted in a lack of confidence by management in knowing where they actually are financially.

2. Timeliness: Generally a function of the demands placed on the accounting department for information needed for decision making, timely preparation, and presentation of current financial data is most indicative

of top management's attitude toward the accounting information system. In Colby Electronics' case critical information to the current decision-making environment is being withheld for as long as 90 or more days, rendering the information useless. Priorities have been set by subordinate personnel whose accountability is nonexistent in the final analysis. The overall perception and nature of delays in the system have *now* become acceptable indicating a low-value attitude in key organizational positions where critical operational decisions are made.

3. Adequacy: The impact that relevant information may have on a decision is a function of content as well as timing. Report generation including but not limited to variance analysis, job status, commission reports, inventory on hand, and current profit and loss statements are not utilized throughout the Colby Electronics' organization forcing seat-of-the-pants decisions generating "what-do-you-know" results.

B. *Budgeting Process:* Planning, although based on the most thorough deliberations of management, loses much of its potential value if not followed with prompt feedback from the operating levels of management. Comparison of planned performance with actual results by department or cost center highlights problem areas where corrective action is needed. Responsibility accounting is the description given to the process of comparison and control at each appropriate level of organizational structure. Moreover, it is facilitated with a plan that is geared to the actual level of operations of the period resulting in the preparation of what is called a flexible budget. The following key elements of the flexible budget are *missing* from Colby Electronics' program.

1. *The formalization of the plan for profit* which contains an evaluation of available resources, evaluates past experiences, and projects future earnings potential within organizational objectives and constraints.

2. *The organization for action* which quantifies the opportunities over the relevant range, prepares forms and procedures, and establishes a comprehensive budget for each division and for the company as a whole.

3. *The administration of actual performance* establishing benchmarks of progress and responsibility of personnel for attaining objectives.

4. *The measurement of actual with planned results* utilizing (currently nonexistent) accounting techniques to compare actual performance.

5. *The necessary formalized system for correcting and improving* operating and financial practices for the next period.

An example of inadequate budgetary control is evident in the findings concerning the inventory system at Colby Electronics.

a. Inventories are not physically counted and reconciled to the books each year.

b. There is no centralized control over inventories.

c. There are no formal company policies and procedures for handling and accounting for inventories.

d. Perpetual inventory records are not maintained for expensive or hard-to-get products.

e. Appropriate requisitions are not required to transfer out of control stores.

f. There is not adequate control over, and reporting of slow moving items, obsolete items, overstocks, or scrap.

g. There are no effective safeguards against theft or pilferage.

h. Inventory valuation methods are inconsistent from one period to the next.

i. Inventory turnover analysis is inappropriate.

C. *Cost Accumulation System:* An internally oriented tool of management which categorizes and evaluates the subcomponents of the income statement is commonly known as cost accounting or managerial accounting. This section highlights the subsystems of job process or job order costing as they apply to Colby Electronics.

Three key areas of cost accounting which were found to be ineffective or nonexistent are covered separately and include:

1. Cost determination required primarily in inventory costing.

2. Cost control featuring the comparison of budgeted costs with actual cost by cost center, resulting in shown variances from planned performance and thus stimulating corrective action by the appropriate level of management.

3. Cost analysis, to assist in decision making by answering the many "what if" types of managerial questions.

    a. Cost Determination: Although inventory is cited as the primary target in the determination function, all aspects of the cost-of-goods-sold statement are subject to evaluation within these parameters. Accordingly, additional weaknesses noted include the following:

        (1) Misallocation of costs.

        (2) Ineffective labor reporting system:

            (*a*) Hours.

            (*b*) Efficiency measurement.

            (*c*) Feedback controls for the bid process.

    b. Cost Control: Notwithstanding the aforementioned weaknesses, variances from any formal or informal budget or target are not adequately investigated nor do they invoke any discernible response from management.

        (1) Proper forms for reporting do not exist for operational activities.

        (2) Variances for various categories of costs are not reported.

        (3) Cost responsibility is not clearly defined in most cases.

        (4) General attitude reflects inattention to detail assuming that the solution is to sell more.

    c. Cost Analysis: The shortcomings mentioned above inhibit even the evaluation of this section of the report. However, we must mention that the decision-making process rests on a three-legged stool of analysis, design, and implementation and the eliminating of one leg will slowly result in the eventual failure of the predictive properties essential to organizational success.

D. *Management Information Systems:* Although many definitions have been advanced for management information systems, specifically defined (for purposes of Colby Electronics), it is a system intended to serve management in its basic functions of organizing, planning, staffing, directing, and controlling.

It is appropriate to draw upon an analogy which relates the relative importance and illustrates common dysfunctions of the information system.

Comparing the information system to the nervous system of the body facilitates this relationship. Moreover, the basic functions of the organization identified above may be compared accurately to the parts or processes which occur within a healthy organism.

Thus the overall control and coordination of an organization relies on a carefully designed and implemented management information system which matches closely the structure and flow patterns within the organization. Colby Electronics system interface is poor and has resulted in the following weaknesses:

1. The organizational structure varies regularly changing lines of authority, areas of responsibility, and perceptions of accountability.
2. The data-gathering system is haphazard and without formal definition.
3. While some well-structured reports are available in various forms, they are not utilized effectively.
4. The lack of desire to share top-management responsibilities with division heads has stopped the flow of information from the top down. (It should be remembered that managers can't give what they don't get.)
5. Manual processing of the largest part of Colby Electronics' information has created severe bottlenecks in many key information links, e.g., between departments or across divisional lines.

In short, Colby Electronics has outgrown its current informal, centrally managed information system and the price for continuing unchanged has been confusion, insecurity, inefficiency, ineffectiveness, loss of control, and complacency.

III. OPERATIONS: *Overview.* Although the structure, climate, and efficiencies of the executive levels of management are of vital importance to the success of any business entity, the means by which the successes are measured are the structural, relational, and communicational efficiencies of the operational levels of management.

Accordingly, this section attempts to identify the managerial concepts and practices which were either in need of improvement, in need of replacement, or in need of establishment.

A. *Findings:* Structure. In theory, the operational levels of Colby Electronics' management were established; however, in reality, operational management has been nonexistent. Due to a lack of the necessary financial information being made available to the division managers and due to the lack of authority to make decisions, no real supervision has existed. The operational managers are those who are supposed to be responsible for planning, organizing, directing, and controlling the day-to-day operations. In addition, they should be the managers who convert the policies and goals of the organization into reality. Since the organization's policies, procedures, and goals need establishment, sense of direction and relationship within the organization also need establishing. These structural problems have caused inefficiencies to develop within Colby Electronics' organization.

B. *Relationships:* One of the factors affecting the operational efficiencies of Colby Electronics is the relations not only within each separate division but between each division manager. The relations between each division manager and his own employees were found to be good overall with one minor exception with the retail sales division and a few labor law relations problems. The relations between each division manager were found to be very poor. The only interaction which has taken place between division has been when conflicts arise. Each manager feels that they are alone in their work, that they virtually have no one to talk to and no one to go to when they need help with their activities. They also feel that they are each responsible for the results of their own division, but are each unaware of their division's results. In addition, personality conflicts have also created work related problems, and to a certain degree, age has caused some relational problems. One of the biggest conflicts found was the relationship of *the sales division versus the technical division* which entails communication inefficiencies.

C. *Communication:* Although some communication occurs on a daily basis between each division manager and his own employees, and occasionally just between division managers, vast improvements are needed. In short, effective communication requires: (1) the ability to be alert to what is going on, (2) the ability to transmit ideas effectively to others in the organization, and (3) the ability to absorb ideas communicated by others in the organization. Pertaining to the above three requirements, the following three respective situations were found at Colby Electronics:

1. Each division manager is sometimes unaware of what is going on in his own division.

2. None of the division managers have been successful in transmitting their own ideas to others in the organization which affect their own operations nor have they been able to transmit their own ideas which affect others' operations.

3. Finally, no division appears to be willing to absorb ideas communicated by other divisions. Also, none of the divisions have bulletin boards or suggestion boxes for employees and written "before and after" sales communication is nonexistent. All of these communication problems have added to the inefficient operations.

D. *Efficiency:* Although each division manager is highly qualified in their own technical aspect of the business, each needs improvement concerning the managerial aspect of their business. At the present time, structural, relational, and communicational inefficiencies exist. In addition, inefficiencies are evident in the quality and service of each division's employees and pay scales appear to be high considering the present status of the local economy. Also found were inefficiencies concerning product knowledge, pricing, promotion, planning, budgeting, forecasting, organizing, directing, and controlling.

IV. COMPANY'S FINANCIAL POSITION: *Overview.* The financial indicator of the efficiency of any organization is displayed in the presentation of what is termed "financial statements" which includes but is not limited to the balance sheet and the income statement.

Accordingly, this section attempts to identify the components of Colby Electronics' balance sheet and income statement and to disclose and analyze the company's financial position and organizational efficiencies.

A. *Findings:* Balance Sheet: The purpose of the balance sheet is to show the financial condition of an entity as of a particular date. The balance sheet consists of assets, which are the resources of the firm; liabilities, which are the debts of the firm; and stockholders' equity, which is the owners' interest in the firm. Exhibit B of this report contains Colby Electronics' balance sheet for various periods in a spreadsheet format.

1. Assets: Assets are probable future economic benefits obtained or controlled by a particular entity as a result of past transactions or events. Assets are divided into two major categories, current and noncurrent (fixed assets).

a. Current: Current assets are assets:

    (1) In the form of cash.

    (2) That will normally be realized in cash.

    (3) That conserve the use of cash during the operating cycle of a firm or for one year, whichever is longer.

b. Noncurrent or fixed assets take longer than a year to be converted to cash or to conserve cash in the long run. For Colby Electronics' purposes, the noncurrent assets have been spread between three categories:

    (1) Fixed assets, which consist of equipment, autos, and leasehold improvements.

    (2) Noncurrent receivables, which consist of advances to employees and accounts receivable, other.

    (3) Prepaid and deferred expenses.

    Reviewing the noncurrent receivables category, it can be seen that an exorbitant amount of cash has been provided to employees. It should also be noted that in order to evaluate book value versus market value, an entire list of equipment and autos must be compiled and then updated market values maintained in order to make decisions concerning the sale or acquisition of these items. To my knowledge, a market valuation does not exist. Further, it appears that all of the corporation's assets have been pledged as collateral.

2. Liabilities: Liabilities are probable future sacrifices of economic benefits arising from present obligations of a particular entity to transfer assets or provide services to other entities in the future as a result of past transactions or events. Liabilities are classified as either current or long term.

a. Current: Current liabilities are those that require meeting the obligation within one year or operating cycle. Colby Electronics' current liabilities have been spread into six categories:

    (1) Floor plan notes payable, secured by specific inventory.

    (2) Notes payable: Banks which includes Commerce National Bank and the FDIC.

    (3) Current maturities. Long-term debt, which has

been spread on the interim statement to include all bank debt due to maturity dates.

(4) Accounts payable—trade.

(5) Accrued expenses.

(6) Layaways.

Although all liabilities are listed as current, and although negotiations have been attempted with the FDIC, it appears no formal debt restructure has been approved.

b. Noncurrent: Noncurrent liabilities are those due in a period exceeding one year or one operating cycle, whichever is longer. At the present time, Colby Electronics is not reporting any long-term liabilities. It should also be mentioned that the collateral position of the financial institutions is unclear at this point due to the questionable market value of the remaining pledged assets.

c. Stockholders' equity: The stockholders' equity is the residual ownership interest in the assets of an entity that remains after deducting its liabilities. It is divided into two basic categories: capital (including stock and paid-in-capital, and retained earnings. Colby Electronics' capital consists of $1 par value common stock of which 500,000 shares have been authorized and 25,000 shares have been issued and are presently outstanding. Jason Colby presently owns all of the issued stock. The second basic category of stockholders' equity, retained earnings, are the undistributed earnings of the corporation; that is, the net income for all past periods minus the dividends (both cash and stock) that have been paid. Colby Electronics' retained earnings figure is negative, due to four consecutive unprofitable years which began in 1983.

B. *Income Statement:* An income statement is a summary of revenues and expenses and gains and losses ending with new income or new loss for a particular period of time. Exhibit C of this report contains Colby Electronics' income statement for various periods in a spreadsheet format.

1. Sales or revenues: Sales represent revenue on goods or services sold to a customer. Colby Electronics' revenues appear to be adequately accounted for and appear to be relatively stable.

2. Cost of goods sold: This item indicates the cost of goods that were sold to produce the sales. For a retailing firm this will be equal to beginning inventory plus purchases, minus ending inventory.

Due to the lack of the physical inventory process, doubts concerning the accuracy of this figure exist. In addition, no consideration has been given to direct labor cost which affects not only the cost of goods sold but should also assist in determining the sales price of the products. In all the Colby Electronics' divisions, true and accurate costs are not known; consequently, adequately profitable gross profit margins have not been established.

3. Operating expenses: Operating expenses consist of two types: selling and administrative. These are expenses not specifically identifiable with or assigned to production. Selling expenses, resulting from the company's effort to create sales, include advertising, *salespeople's commissions*, depreciation on sales equipment, sales supplies used, etc. Administrative expenses relate to the general administration of the company's operation. They include office salaries, insurance, depreciation on office equipment, telephone, etc. Also included are bad debts expense, and costs difficult to allocate. For spreading purposes, Colby Electronics' interest expense has been separated for analysis purposes. In addition, depreciation and amortization expenses have been separated in order to calculate the company's cash flow.

4. Cash flow: A simplified definition of cash flow is net income plus noncash expenditures. This calculation determines the amount of cash supposedly available after operations. However, this calculation in reality measures the amount of cash available to spend on acquiring resources, reducing debts, and continuing the operations of the firm. A more complete cash flow statement is attached to this report as Exhibit D which, when combined with the ratio analysis provides an effective management tool. Due to the inadequacies of the firm's inventory control system and lack of financial reporting procedures, no breakeven analysis will be prepared at this time.

C. *Ratio Analysis:* Planning is the key to the financial manager's success. Financial plans may take many forms, but any good plan must be related to the firm's existing strengths and weaknesses. The strengths must be understood if they are to be used to proper advantage, and the weaknesses must be recognized if corrective action is to be taken. The financial manager can plan his future financial requirements in accordance with forecasting and budgeting procedures, but his plan must begin with financial analysis. Ratio analysis, a form of financial analysis, employs financial data taken from the firm's balance sheet and income statement and then transforms the data into formulas or ratios. These ratios are fractions expressed in percent or times and consist of several types; liquidity, leverage, activity, and profitability. Exhibit E of this report contains some of the calculated ratios used in Colby Electronics' financial analysis.

1. Liquidity: Liquidity ratios measure the firm's ability to meet its maturing short-term obligations and the relative balance sheet data assists in determining the amount of working capital generated by operations and in forecasting the amount of future working capital requirements. Two commonly used liquidity ratios are the current ratio and the quick ratio. The current ratio indicates the extent to which the claims of short-term creditors are covered by assets that are expected to be converted to cash in a period roughly corresponding to the maturity of the claims. The quick ratio measures the firm's ability to pay off short-term obligations without relying on the sale of inventory. In both instances, Colby Electronics' liquidity ratios appear to be below the industry's average. The company's liquidity position has drastically declined since 1982, yet has partially stabilized since 1983. Considering inventory levels have increased significantly year after year, while cash balances have decreased, and while sales have remained fairly stable, Colby Electronics' liquidity position is extremely poor. Moreover, the company apparently has invested an exorbitant amount of cash in inventory, indicating managerial inefficiencies.

2. Leverage: Leverage ratios measure the extent to which the firm has been financed by debt and measures the funds supplied by owners as compared with the financing by creditors. Firms with low leverage ratios have less risk of loss when the economy is in a downturn, but they also have lower expected returns when the economy booms. Conversely, firms with high leverage ratios run the risk of large losses but also have a chance of gaining high profits. The ratio which measures the per-

centage of total funds provided by creditors is the total debt to total assets ratio. The times interest earned or interest coverage ratio measures the extent to which earnings can decline without resultant financial embarrassment to the firm because of inability to meet annual interest costs. Again in both instances, Colby Electronics does not compare favorably to the industry standard.

3. Activity: Activity ratios measure how effectively the firm is using its resources. These ratios all involve comparisons between the level of sales and the investment in various asset accounts. They presume that proper balance should exist between sales and the various asset accounts. The inventory turnover ratio measures how many times within the reporting period that the total volume of inventory has sold. The average collection period or accounts receivable turnover measures how many days it takes to convert sales into cash. The ratio of sales to fixed assets measures the turnover of plant and equipment. The total assets turnover ratio measures the turnover of all the firm's assets. The important point that the activity ratios indicate is that either Colby Electronics' inventory levels are extremely too high to support the level of sales, and/or sales have to increase either by volume or quantity in order for the firm to survive.

4. Profitability: Profitability is the net result of a large number of policies and decisions. Therefore, the profitability ratios measure how effectively the firm is being managed. The profit margin on sales provides the profit per dollar of sales. The ratio of net profit to total assets measures the return on total investment. The ratio of net profit after taxes to net worth measures the rate of return on the stockholders' investment. Colby Electronics' managerial inefficiencies are best measured by the profitability ratios. These ratios further indicate that the company's profit margins are inadequate, that neither sales nor cost of goods sold nor operating expenses are properly managed, nor are the assets properly managed.

V. PERSONAL FINANCIAL POSITION: *Overview:* Due to the relative simplicity of Mr. Colby's personal financial statement, a detailed analysis will not be prepared. Virtually all of his assets are encumbered, and he has executed personal guarantees giving added security to several vendors/creditors. Some guarantees are limited and some are unlimited. His net worth amounts to approximately $260,000, and his contingent liabilities amount to approximately $1,150,000.

EXHIBIT A

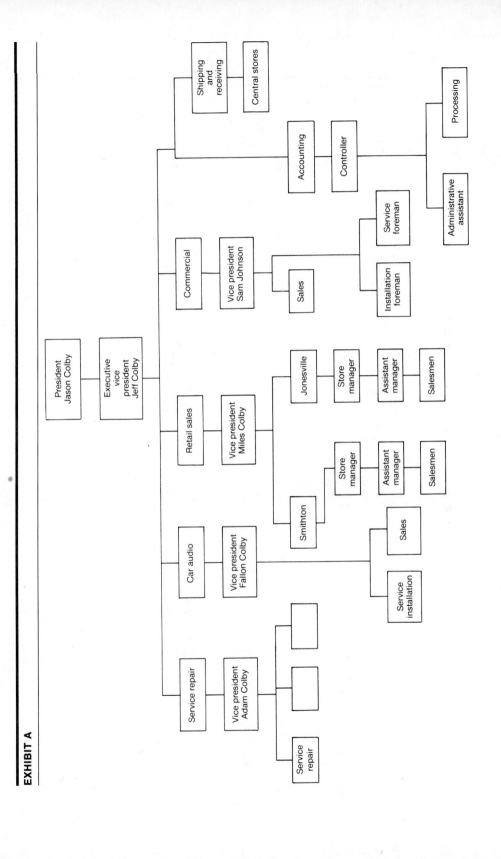

EXHIBIT B   Colby Enterprises Balance Sheet

	4-30-86	Percent
Cash	$ 0	0%
Marketable securities	0	0
Accounts receivable trade	94,554	7
Accounts receivable other	14,546	1
Accounts receivable-Emp	78,674	6
Inventory	1,065,575	78
Total current assets	1,253,349	92
Gross fixed assets	625,556	46
Less: Accumulated depreciation	530,824	39
Net fixed assets	94,732	7
Nonmarket securities	0	0
Noncurrent receivables	0	0
Prepaid and deferred expenses	7,700	1
Deposits	12,100	1
Intangibles	0	0
Total noncurrent assets	114,532	8
Total assets	$1,367,881	100%
Book overdraft	$ 17,965	1%
Floor plan payable	269,874	20
Notes payable banks	0	0
Current Mty LTD	683,404	50
Accounts payable, trade	483,306	35
Accounts payable, other	0	0
Accruals and miscellaneous	192,231	14
Layaways	10,085	1
Income tax liability	0	0
Total current liabilities	1,656,915	121
Long-term debt—banks	0	0
Long-term debt	0	0
Deferred taxes	0	0
Total long-term liabilities	0	0
Total liabilities	1,656,915	121
Deferred income	0	0
Subordinated debt	0	0
Preferred stock	0	0
Common stock	25,000	2
Capital surplus	0	0
Retained earnings	(314,034)	−23
Treasury stock	0	0
Total capital funds	(289,034)	−21
Total liabilities and capital funds	$1,367,881	100%

EXHIBIT C Colby Enterprises Income Statement

Income Statement as of:	5-31-82	Percent	5-31-83	Percent	5-31-84	Percent	5-31-85	Percent
Net sales/revenue	$4,525	100%	$4,126	100%	$4,121	100%	$4,414	100%
Cost of sales	2,657	59	2,191	53	2,553	62	2,920	66
Gross profit	1,868	41	1,935	47	1,568	38	1,494	34
Depreciation and amortization	102	2	152	4	129	3	105	2
Other operating expenses	1,620	36	2,010	49	1,479	36	1,452	33
Total operating expense	1,722	38	2,162	52	1,608	39	1,557	35
Operating profit	146	3	(227)	−6	(40)	−1	(63)	−1
Other expense	0	0	0	0	0	0	0	0
Other income	0	0	14	0	0	0	11	0
Profit before interest and tax	146	3	(213)	−5	66	2	(74)	−2
Interest expense	46	1	93	2	26	1	104	2
Profit before tax and extra	100	2	(306)	−7	98	2	(178)	−4
Income taxes	11	0	(73)	−2	(72)	−2	0	0
Profit before extra items	89	2	(233)	−6	(72)	0	(178)	−4
Net profit	$89	2	($233)	−6	($72)	−2	($178)	−4
Funds from operations	$191	2	($81)	−6	$57	−2	($73)	−4

Reconciliation of Capital Funds

	5-31-82	5-31-83	5-31-84	5-31-85
Capital funds—beginning	85	262	1	(71)
Plus: Net profit	89	(233)	(72)	(178)
Restatement of retained earnings	88	(28)	0	0
Rounding adjustment	0	0	0	0
Less: Dividends	0	0	0	(1)
Capital funds—ending	262	1	(71)	(250)

EXHIBIT D Colby Enterprises Cash Flow Statement

For the Period Ended:	5-31-82	5-31-83	5-31-84	5-31-85
Net income	89	(233)	(72)	(178)
Depreciation and amortization	102	152	129	105
Deferred income taxes	0	0	0	0
Funds from operations	191	(81)	57	(73)
Accounts receivables (Incr.)/Decr.		(29)	35	57
Inventories (Incr.)/Decr.		(108)	(237)	9
Prepaid expenses (Incr.)/Decr.		7	(9)	6
Other current assets (Incr.)/Decr.		0	0	0
Accounts payable Incr./(Decr.)		206	39	(50)
Income taxes payable Incr./(Decr.)		0	0	0
Accruals and miscellaneous Incr./(Decr.)		(87)	43	75
Other current liabilities Incr./(Decr.)		(31)	1	(13)
Net operating capital (Incr.)/Decr.	—	(42)	(128)	84
Net cash throw-off (deficit)	—	(123)	(71)	11
Capital expenditures—net		(176)	110	(14)
Dividends		(0)	(0)	(0)
Other sources/(uses)	—	(37)	(69)	28
Excess (deficit) cash before financing activities	—	(336)	(30)	25
Notes payable—banks Incr./(Decr.)		764	60	(73)
Long-term debt Incr./(Decr.)		(485)	(40)	7
Subordinated debt Incr./(Decr.)		0	0	0
Capital accounts Incr./(Decr.)	—	0	0	0
Financing activities—net cash provided/(used)	—	279	20	(66)
Change in cash and marketable securities	—	(57)	(10)	(41)
Change in cash-balance sheet		(85)	(10)	(42)
Unexplained difference		28	0	1
Analyst's initials:		WMM		

EXHIBIT E Colby Enterprises Financial Analysis

	4-30-86
Earnings/profitability	
Return on equity	24.3%
Return on assets	−3.4%
Return on sales	−1.7%
Return on investment	−5.1%
Interest coverage	(2.0)
Cash flow/CMLTD	.0
Net profit + depreciation/funded debt	0.0
Liquidity:	
Working capital	($403,566)
Current ratio	0.8
Quick ratio	0.1
Working capital turnover	(11.2)
Inventory to working capital	(2.6)
Accounts receivable turn (days)	8
Inventory turnover (days)	133
Conversion cycle (days)	140
Accounts payable turn (days)	60
Capital position:	
Tangible net worth	($289,034)
Net fixed assets/Tangible net worth	(0.3)
Total debt/Tangible net worth	(5.7)
Funded debt/Capital funds	(3.4)
Total debt/Total net worth	(5.7)
Total debt/Total assets	1.2

42. Biotech, Inc.

HISTORY OF THE FIRM

As Dr. Edward Williams enjoyed his morning coffee in the den of his newly purchased condo on the fashionable Chicago lakefront, he reflected on where his life had taken him over the last decade and a half. In 1971, armed with a BS in biology, he found himself with a job which included such glamorous duties as cleaning monkey cages, keeping track of white mice, and picking up fresh blood at the airport in the middle of the night. Although glamorous, the job didn't pay much, so he had to take an extra job tending bar at the American Legion to supplement his income. One thing that Edward Williams wasn't afraid of was hard work.

The hard work paid off. A distinguished immunologist, Dr. Charles Maxwell, recognized Edward's talents, and began what amounted to an on-the-job training program for him. Edward was involved in research projects, coauthored scholarly articles and papers, and even took a sabbatical abroad—all with only an undergraduate degree. Eventually he became manager of one of the nation's most prestigious university immunology laboratories under the direction of Dr. Maxwell.

While managing the laboratory, he met and became friends with two other laboratory employees—Dorothy Mays and Leanne Jacobson. Like Edward, neither Dorothy nor Leanne had doctorate degrees, but both had learned a great deal and had become valuable members of the research team at the laboratory.

After several years of managing the lab, Edward decided that his advancement required that he get a Ph.D.—his "union card" he called it. Thus, he went back to school (while still working full time) and completed his Ph.D. in biology. Now with his degree, he thought that his career would take off. But he found that lab management didn't change much after he finished school. Ph.D.s and M.D.s were still just as hard to manage, the phone rang just as much, the pa-

This case was prepared by W. Edward Stead, John Garner Stead, and M. Blaine McCormick III, Management and Marketing Department, East Tennessee State University, Johnson City, Tennessee.

perwork was piled just as deep, and the sales reps were still knocking on the door.

He wanted more. He wanted more freedom and independence, and he wanted to be financially rewarded for all his hard work. He wanted to be captain of his own ship. Many ideas ran through his head. He considered taking a vice presidency of a new biotechnology firm located in another metropolitan area, but decided against it. He even talked about using his culinary skills to open a restaurant. But science was his first love, and it was science that he chose to pursue.

In March of 1982, Edward, along with Dorothy and Leanne, who were also dissatisfied with their jobs at the lab and wanted more excitement, challenge, and reward from their careers, started a new firm—Biotech, Inc. The purpose of the firm was to produce high-quality antibodies for both research and commercial use in the rapidly emerging field of biotechnology. The firm also wanted to support monoclonal antibody research efforts. Excitement was running high as Edward and his partners anticipated great opportunities.

The opportunities were there, but taking advantage of them wasn't easy. They had to conduct business out of their homes. None of the partners could afford to quit their jobs at the lab, so they all held full-time jobs while they tried to make a go of the business in the evenings and on weekends. They had to perform all the tasks themselves, including injecting and bleeding goats, producing and marketing antibodies, and keeping the books. Eventually they brought in a fourth partner to handle marketing for the firm, but this relationship didn't work out and was eventually dissolved.

What they needed most was money. This became very frustrating for Edward. He knew that he had a good idea, and he knew that he could make it work, but someone had to have some faith in him—faith backed up by a healthy checkbook. He looked into many opportunities, and several seemed on the verge of succeeding only to fail. Then, while working in the university lab, Edward was introduced to Franklin Carroll.

Franklin Carroll, an attorney with an MBA, had sources of seed capital and was searching for a high-tech firm in which to invest. His plans for such an investment were quite specific. Once he found the right firm, he wanted to find the necessary seed capital to get the firm off the ground. He then wanted to get involved in managing the firm in its early stages with the goal of developing a firm that would become attractive to venture capitalists. Once the firm found the necessary venture capital and grew sufficiently, the next step was to go public with the company. In his search for the right firm, he asked a friend one day if there were any new biotechnology firms springing up in the area. The friend introduced him to Charles Maxwell who introduced him to Edward Williams. This appeared to be a match made in heaven.

Over the next several months, things began to happen for Biotech. Edward and Franklin decided that $50,000 in initial seed capital would get them started. Franklin found three outside investors willing to invest the $50,000 in return for a 25 percent interest in the company, which the working principals can buy back for $150,000. Biotech was off and running with a quality product in an industry so new that no one could even define it well much less guess its ultimate potential. Dorothy and Leanne had wanted excitement and challenge in their careers. Well, it seemed like they were going to get their wish.

The time came when Edward could no longer keep his job in Dr. Maxwell's laboratory and do his work at Biotech. When he informed Dr. Maxwell of his decision to resign from the lab, Dr. Maxwell gave him a one-year leave of absence to pursue his new career. Immediately after Edward took leave, Biotech moved into its first commercial location.

Edward and Franklin began to devise a marketing strategy. Both had contacts in the Northeast—Franklin through his classmates and Edward through his relationships with research institutions. They took a three-week marketing trip through Pennsylvania, New York, and Delaware. Although they didn't sell a lot of antibodies, they made many contacts and learned a great deal about the market. They decided that they were credible and that they indeed had a chance to make it in this business. They also decided that they could not manage all of the marketing and distribution of their products on their own. They needed a national distributor, and it so happened that one of Franklin's classmates was employed by one of the largest scientific products distributors in the nation.

Franklin and Edward negotiated with the national distributor, and the negotiations were quite a success. The distributor agreed to purchase $100,000 worth of antibodies over the next six months. They also paid $35,000 to have an impressive, slick cover, color brochure produced for Biotech presenting the firm's products, staff, and production processes. In return for the brochure and the purchase order, Biotech agreed to sell its products to the distributor at a 30 percent discount and give the distributor exclusive distribution rights in the United States. Franklin Carroll probably put the importance of this agreement most succinctly when he said, "This $100,000 purchase order, along with the original $50,000 in seed capital, put Biotech in business."

THE INDUSTRY

Edward Williams' career had been quite exciting. His growth as a professional scientist was virtually paralleled by the birth and development of the now-burgeoning biotechnology industry. He began to reflect on how that industry had developed and changed, and he began to wonder where it was going.

Although biotechnology research has existed in laboratories for some time, the development and growth of a viable biomedical/genetics industry was restricted for years by the inefficiencies surrounding the production of antibodies. Antibodies, which are essentially proteins produced by the body's immune system in response to foreign or invading substances (antigens), are some of the basic materials studied and used in immunology research and genetic engineering. Historically, antibody production has been an inefficient process primarily because antibody-producing cells could be grown in vitro (in cultures outside the body) for only a short time. With no efficient means of producing antibodies for research and commercial operations, the growth of the field was quite limited [4;16].

The development of "hybridoma technology" changed all that. In 1975, Dr. Georges Kohler and Dr. Cesar Milstein first reported their Nobel Prize-winning research on the hybridoma method of producing immortal antibody-producing cell lines. This method is essentially an in vitro cloning process in which antibody-producing cells are fused with cancerous cells. The resulting "hybridoma" produces an unlimited supply of highly specific "monoclonal antibodies." Thus, hybridoma technology has allowed for the efficient production in vitro of pure highly specific monoclonal antibodies which can be cultured indefinitely or frozen for later use [4;16].

The result of hybridoma technology on biomedical research has been far-reaching. One research group referred to the discovery as "one of the most important methodological advances in biomedicine . . . which has opened completely new possibilities for basic and applied medical research" [16, p.1]. It has had significant impacts on the research and treatment of several cancers, the diagnosis of hepatitis B and streptococcal infections, and the study of heart disease, multiple sclerosis, organ transplantation, allergies, kidney disease, lupus, and rheumatoid arthritis [16]. Approximately $10 billion annually is currently being spent on biomedical research [1].

Hybridoma technology is a major factor in the growth of the biomedical/genetics industry [11;17]. Currently, the industry consists of over 200 firms with Genentech, Inc., and Cetus, Inc., both of California, being the leaders in financial strength and product innovation [17]. Although many of the firms in the industry have been unprofitable, the focus of the industry is now making the all-important transition from the research laboratory to the marketplace. This transition is expected to have a major impact on the profit potential and stock performance of the firms in the industry during the second half of the 1980s [5;11;17]. Further, many of the major pharmaceutical companies who have thus far stayed out of the biomedical/genetics industry because of its early stage of development and low profitability are now getting in the industry. Eli Lilly recently acquired Hybritech and Bristol Myers has announced its intention to make a bid for Genetic Systems. These moves seem to validate the current high public valuation of biotechnology firms. They also signal a strong movement toward a more mature phase for the industry where the focus on product development is being replaced by a focus on bringing profitable products to market [11;17].

This transition will likely lead to a market shakeout by 1987 or 1988 [17]. According to analysts, the industry will continue to see consolidations, mergers, and acquisitions for three reasons. First, outside sources of funding are disappearing. Second, many firms have fallen behind in their business plans; and third, many firms are experiencing a management transition from the founding scientists to professional managers [15].

Because of the ability of monoclonal antibodies to recognize foreign invaders in the body, the most rapidly growing commercial use of monoclonal antibodies is in diagnostic kits to detect such conditions as pregnancy, hepatitis B, certain cancers, drug abuse, and sexually transmitted viruses such as herpes and AIDS [4;16;17]. The worldwide sales of monoclonal antibody-based diagnostic kits has expanded tremendously and is expected to continue to expand in the future. Sales in this market segment grew from less than $30 million in 1983 to $207 million in 1985 and are expected to reach $1.7 billion by 1990 [11;17].

Many types of firms have appeared in the growing biomedical/genetics industry. Several of these new firms specialize in supplying various antibody products to the large firms such as Genentech and Cetus which in turn use those products in both research and commercial undertakings. Biotech is one such firm.

Essentially, these supply firms purify and isolate selected antibodies and supply them to other firms for evaluation of monoclonal antibodies by hybridoma technology. The supply firms use laboratory animals such as goats and mice in the production of the antibodies. Each antibody product must have a specific molecular configuration to work properly. "Specificity" is thus the primary quality measure for the supply firms such as Biotech.

Since the industry has historically focused on research, the primary market for these supply firms has been for research efforts. Since most research efforts require small amounts of antibody products, order quantities have been traditionally small, usually measured in milligrams. Therefore, the primary firms in the supply end of the industry are characteristically small, and they have focused much more on product quality than production quantity. Of these supply firms, only one can rival Biotech in terms of product quality.

However, as the primary focus of the industry transcends from research to commercialization, there is expected to be a major increase in "original equipment manufacturer" (OEM) relationships for suppliers. These OEM relationships will provide a tremendous increase in the number of bulk orders available to suppliers, and will likely necessitate an increased focus by suppliers on production quantity as order quantities go from milligrams to grams and even kilograms [3;8].

Several analysts foresee changes in production procedures as order quantities increase and scale up becomes necessary. More efficient isolation and purification procedures must be developed. The traditional animal-based methods become somewhat awkward as antibody production increases, leading several experts to believe that animal-free methods will replace animal-based antibody production technology [3].

SOCIOPOLITICAL ENVIRONMENT

As Edward Williams sipped on his coffee, he thought about the recent Department of Defense grant applied for by Biotech to develop a new antibody that would detect toxins in the environment. It is to be included in a diagnostic kit carried by soldiers to test the environment during warfare. Edward believed that biological warfare was one of the most complicated ethical issues the biomedical/genetics industry was facing. He also thought of other critical sociopolitical issues facing the industry. Animal rights groups focus a great deal of attention on biomedical research, and the myriad of federal agencies involved in regulating the industry is mind-boggling. The disposal of highly toxic substances such as radioisotopes and immunotoxins is also a crucial issue.

Probably the biggest environmental thorn in the side of the biomedical/genetics industry is Jeremy Rifkin. Rifkin, a well-known environmental activist and author of *Entropy* as well as other environmental books and articles, has filed several suits against the biotechnology industry. He recently won a suit against the Department of Defense which kept the army from building a high-containment biomedical testing laboratory in Utah to test biological and chemical defense items [7]. He has been successful so far in stopping experiments at the University of California involving the deliberate release of genetically modified organisms into the environment without first determining their effect [6]. Experts believe that deliberate release experiments may be the most controversial issue currently affecting the industry [13]. Rifkin has also filed suit against the USDA asking that super livestock research (research involving the use of growth hormone to increase the size and speed of farm animals) be stopped [10].

One of the most confusing sociopolitical issues of the industry is regulation. Discussing industry regulation is like eating a bowl of alphabet soup—FDA, EPA, DEA, OSHA, DOT, USDA, and DOD. The result is a chaotic patchwork of regulation which overregulates some areas and ignores others. Both EPA and USDA seem the most likely candidates to regulate the deliberate release of organisms into the environment [14], although the USDA is not yet prepared to carry out this responsibility according to the Government Accounting Office [9]. The FDA focuses its regulatory powers on the safety of biomedical/genetic products, but it ignores the processes involved in producing the products and disposing of the wastes. The Department of Defense regulates the export of certain biotechnology products and information to socialist countries [14]. The DEA is getting involved as diagnostic kits designed to test for abusive drugs are developed.

The issue of regulation is further complicated by the current anti-regulatory mood in government. The Reagan administration has stated that they do not want new laws passed tailored to the industry, claiming that current laws are sufficient; however, certain members of Congress disagree, saying that the issues of biotechnology are too unique for current laws [13]. The administration has formed the Cabinet Work Group on Biotechnology (CWB) for the purpose of sorting out current regulatory overlaps and omissions and weaving the different federal agencies together in the regulation of the biomedical/genetics industry. The CWB may be the first step in untangling the regulatory mess [14].

There is a great deal of motivation in the industry to develop effective regulatory procedures. It is clear that public fear of the industry is very high and occasionally irrational [14]. The public is concerned that the industry may threaten basic notions of morality, ethics, and environmental integrity. Also, as the industry transcends into more commercially viable ventures, regulatory agencies must begin to distinguish between the control of scientific experimentation and the control of industrial products and technology [12]. In short, the biomedical/genetics industry is new, it is growing, and it is perceived to be potentially hazardous in a variety of ways. All of these factors make the sociopolitical future of the industry quite uncertain.

CURRENT OPERATIONS OF BIOTECH, INC.

Structure

As he readies himself for the drive into the office, Edward Williams turns his attention to what is happening currently at Biotech. He now owns 26 percent of the firm and is its president and chief operating officer. He is primarily responsible for managing the daily technical operations of the firm. He also spends a significant amount of time promoting the product. Franklin Carroll, who also owns 26 percent, is currently the chief executive officer and chairman of the board. His primary responsibilities include finance, planning, and marketing. It is his job to develop investor and distributor relationships and to identify external opportunities. Leanne Jacobson is vice president for quality control. In this capacity she performs technical quality control procedures and provides technical assistance for customers. Dorothy Mays is vice president for production with primary responsibility for the day-to-day supervision of the production process. Leanne and Dorothy each own 11.5 percent of the firm. In addition to the four owners, the firm has hired John Tucker, Ph.D., to be its vice president for research and development. John has primary responsibility for the development of new products and new production techniques designed to improve the competitive position of the firm. In addition to these five officers, Biotech employs three laboratory technicians and a clerical worker who serves as secretary, receptionist, and bookkeeper.

As the firm has grown, the principals have found that they have had to focus their efforts more within their own areas of specialization and, as a result, have had less time to spend on overall operations. Because of this increased focus on specialization, the structure of the firm has informally evolved into two groups—business and scientific. Franklin is the primary principal in the business group, and Leanne, Dorothy, and John are the primary principals in the scientific group. Communication and trust often become problems between these two groups because of the diversity of the knowledge necessary to perform the functions. Edward Williams finds himself as a member of both the business group and the scientific group, leaving him with the often frustrating responsibility of bridging the communication and trust gaps between the two groups.

The firm is currently struggling with several structural options in an attempt to develop a more suitable system, but this has itself led to more conflict. Franklin Carroll feels that as the firm grows it needs a structure which has greater formal functional and procedural control. He would like to see more complete job descriptions and formalized production procedures. On the other hand, the scientific group is more interested in maintaining the less formal system currently in place.

Marketing

As mentioned above, Biotech is primarily a supply firm for the biomedical/genetics industry. Their basic marketing goal is to produce the highest quality antibody products in the industry, and they have been largely successful in achieving this goal. Twenty parent antibody products (classes of purified antibodies) are produced by coupling specific goat antibodies with specific antigens from four animals—mice, rats, humans, and rabbits. Each of these parent antibodies can in turn be treated and expanded into derivative products. Through the production and treatment of the 20 parent antibodies, Biotech can produce up to 364 different marketable antibody products. Of all the product lines, the ones that contribute most to sales are those parent antibodies and derivatives produced using mouse antigens (called goat antimouse antibodies).

Although Biotech markets these antibody products for both research and commercial purposes, the bulk of their sales are currently in the research segment of the industry. Most of their products go to university research laboratories and research institutes throughout the world. They also supply products to several of the commercial firms in the industry (including at least 15 of the large biomedical and pharmaceutical firms) for research and development purposes. However, as the relatively small research market becomes overshadowed by the much larger commercial market for diagnostic products, Edward Williams hopes that Biotech can expand into the commercial market by aggressively pursuing OEM relationships.

Biotech sells its products throughout the world. Besides the United States, they sell to firms and labs in Europe, Australia, India, Canada, Japan, Kenya, and the Middle East. All sales in countries outside the United States are handled directly by Biotech. Biotech originally gave exclusive U.S. distribution rights to the national scientific products distributor in return for a $100,000 purchase order. However, the distributor now allows Biotech to sell its products directly to customers in the United States as well as through the distributor. Since the primary focus of Biotech is on product quality, the firm believes that they also need a relationship with a scientific products distributor who has a reputation for carrying only high-quality product lines. Such a relationship is currently under consideration, and negotiations for expanding their relationship with their current distributor are also underway.

The products are promoted through the sales representatives of the national distributor and through the personal contacts and efforts of the principals—mainly Edward and Franklin. They expected the distributor to do all the selling when the exclusive relationship first began, but they soon found that they needed to personally sell the products because of the lack of technical knowledge and proper contacts by the distributor's sales force; hence, the modification of the original exclusive relationship with the distributor. Although one of Franklin's major functions is product promotion and sales, this is not true for Edward whose responsibilities are mostly internal.

The slick cover promotion brochure mentioned earlier is the primary advertising tool for the firm. It stresses the quality orientation of

---

EXHIBIT 1

BIOTECH, INC.
Consolidated Statement of Income

	1983	1984	1985	1986
Net sales	$26,157	$50,647	$192,829	$453,435
Cost of goods sold . . .	3,786	2,871	137,951	87,223
Gross profit.	22,371	47,776	54,878	366,212
Operating expenses. . .	7,991	30,417	79,705	349,389
Income before taxes. . .	14,380	17,359	(24,827)	16,823
Income taxes	2,400	2,000	(2,800)	4,000
Net income	$11,980	$15,359	$(22,027)	$ 12,823

---

the firm, and is itself a high-quality document. Further, it has a section on methodology which can be used as reference material by researchers. This encourages them to keep the brochure handy.

Finance

As mentioned above, the firm began in a small office/laboratory with $50,000 in seed capital. They then procured a $100,000, six-month purchase order from a large scientific product distributor. That purchase order, paid in advance, allowed them to move into new larger quarters for which they signed a three-year, $2,000 per month lease— a $72,000 obligation. Franklin Carroll said, "This was our first real gut check. You are betting the company on such a lease." They got another $100,000 purchase order from the distributor, although the distributor was having little luck selling the products. This second purchase order was given primarily because of "trust and friendship" according to Franklin Carroll.

Sales have climbed from slightly over $26,000 in 1983 to over $450,000 in 1986. Sales in 1987 are expected to reach from $1.25 million to $1.5 million. According to Franklin Carroll, the break-even sales point is approximately $700,000. The exhibits demonstrate the growth experienced by Biotech.

Production and Operations

As mentioned above, the 20 parent antibody products are produced by coupling specific goat antibodies with specific antigens from either mice, rats, humans, or rabbits. The firm owns a goat herd from which it procures its goat antibodies. The goats are not destroyed in this process, and they can be used to produce antibodies throughout their

---

EXHIBIT 2

BIOTECH, INC.
Consolidated Balance Sheets

	1983	1984	1985	1986
Current assets:				
Cash.	$ 2,113	$39,428	$ 8,836	$ 3,625
Accounts receivable	1,953	11,062	36,931	86,769
Inventories	9,327	15,743	73,284	118,773
Lab supplies	—	5,951	5,490	—
Prepaid expenses.	—	265	704	704
Refundable income taxes	—	—	3,800	687
Deferred interest	—	—	—	8,963
Total current assets.	13,393	72,449	129,045	219,521
Furniture and equipment	4,874	22,551	64,953	166,415
Less: Accumulated depreciation	547	1,812	8,170	12,130
	4,327	20,739	56,783	154,286
Other assets	287	306	150	150
Total assets	$18,007	$93,494	$185,978	$373,957
Current liabilities:				
Accounts payable.	$ 224	$ 9,930	$ 57,078	$123,332
Taxes payable	2,400	2,445	4,883	13,402
Notes payable	—	—	17,500	94,645
Current portion of long-term debt				
and capital lease obligation	—	480	2,362	—
Deposits on undelivered sales	—	—	45,201	45,855
Total current liabilities	2,624	12,855	127,024	277,234
Long-term debt and capital:				
Lease obligation	—	1,217	1,959	—
Deferred income taxes	—	400	—	—
Notes payable	—	—	—	22,904
Stockholders' equity:				
Common Stock, $1 par value,				
100,000 shares authorized, 800				
shares issued and outstanding . .	800	800	800	800
Paid-in capital	2,883	50,883	50,883	50,883
Retained earnings	11,700	27,339	5,312	22,136
	15,383	79,022	56,995	73,819
Total liabilities and capital.	$18,007	$93,494	$185,978	$373,957

---

lives. Rat, human, and rabbit antigens are purchased from other sources, but mouse antigens are produced in-house. The mice are destroyed in the antigen-harvesting process and thus can be used only once. Because each mouse costs up to $6, and because it takes significant time to tap the mice, the production of mouse antigens is expensive. The firm has recently begun to raise its own mice in order to cut this expense.

Production begins by immunizing a goat with a specific antigen. This causes the production of specific antibodies in the goat. Four to six weeks later, 250 milliliters of goat's blood (called serum) are collected. The antibodies from the goat serum are then grossly isolated in preparation for further isolation and purification into parent antibody products. This gross isolation process takes one day.

Next, these grossly isolated goat antibodies are filtered through columns (called affinity columns) which contain a gellike substance containing specific mouse, rat, human, or rabbit antigens. This process, known as affinity column passage, takes 7 to 14 days and results in the highly specific isolation of the parent antibodies. After isolation, the parent antibodies are then purified in a one-day process called affinity purification. The resulting affinity-purified antibodies are the nine parent antibody products offered for sale by Biotech. They can be grouped into four broad categories—goat antimouse, goat antihuman, goat antirat, and goat antirabbit. One milliliter of raw goat serum will yield from .5 to 2 milligrams of affinity-purified parent antibodies depending on the type being produced.

At this point, quality control of the parent antibody is performed. A small amount of the batch of affinity-purified parent antibodies is coupled with either fluorochromes or enzymes. The purpose of the coupling process, called conjugation, is to produce derivative products. If the conjugation is successful, then the batch of parent antibodies can either be sold or processed into derivatives. Also, the small amount of derivative products resulting from the conjugation process can be sold. If conjugation fails, the entire batch can be reprocessed through the affinity columns except for the small amount used in conjugation which must be scrapped. This quality control procedure takes two to three days.

Once the quality of the parent antibodies has been assured, these antibodies are either sold, kept in inventory for future sale, or processed into derivative products. This mutually exclusive option of either selling or processing the antibodies complicates inventory control. The parent antibodies will last from 6 to 12 months in inventory if refrigerated, and indefinitely if frozen.

The next step is to process those parent antibodies not sold or stored for future sale into derivative products. The same fluorochrome or enzyme conjugation procedures are used to process the entire batch that were used to test the quality earlier. The quality control procedure described above is then performed on the batch, and the resulting products—known as fluorochrome or enzyme-labeled derivatives—are then sold or stored in inventory. Each milligram of parent antibody yields an average of .8 milligrams of fluorochrome-labeled derivative and .9 milligrams of enzyme-labeled derivative. Fluorochrome-labeled derivatives can be stored six months if refrigerated and indefinitely if frozen. Enzyme-labeled derivatives can be stored indefinitely regardless of temperature.

When an order is received from a customer, it is entered into a computer to generate a packing list for shipping. If the product is in inventory, Edward Williams hand-packs it in styrofoam (using ice packs during warm weather), labels it, and ships it by parcel service to the customer. If the product is not in inventory, then Edward Williams informs production of what needs to be produced.

Each affinity column represents a production line. Currently, the number of lines is sufficient to produce enough antibodies to meet market demand. Each affinity column requires a capital investment of approximately $4,000, and equipment acquisition takes about four months.

FUTURE DIRECTIONS

As Edward Williams started his Volvo for the trip across the city to his office, he began to wonder where all of his hard work and risk taking would take him. He has goals—ambitious goals—for Biotech. His primary goal is to continue to produce and market affinity-purified antibodies of unparalleled quality. He also wants to aggressively pursue the bulk-order commercial market through OEM contracts. Further, he wants to continue research and development efforts in two areas: (1) developing antibodies for new areas of research, and (2) developing research and diagnostic test kits using existing product mixes. He sees Biotech serving a worldwide market made up of both research and commercial enterprises. He hopes that the next five years will see the firm continue to develop and produce the highest quality antibodies in the industry while at the same time landing several OEM contracts.

Although the other officers agree with Edward concerning the primary goal of Biotech (producing the highest quality antibodies), and although Franklin and Dorothy both want to continue to grow and expand into the diagnostic kit market, there has been little actual discussion among the officers about the future of the firm. Franklin believes that the company can eventually attract venture capital and grow to the point that it can go public, but none of the others seem to have the same ambitions. Leanne says she wants the firm to grow, but at the same time she says that Biotech has grown too fast. She says that Biotech should produce and market different variations of the current product line, believing that government regulation makes the diagnostic kit market too risky. John Tucker feels that his job is one of a scientist doing pure research. He does not believe that the future direction of the firm is any of his concern, although he did say that the firm's internal capabilities will restrict its ability to take advantage of its external opportunities.

Franklin Carroll and Edward Williams seem to be following a strategy that primarily involves building stronger relationships with distributors, pursuing OEM contracts, and seeking research grants. This strategy has evolved informally between them, and is not well articulated. As a result, it does not seem to have been communicated well to the others. None of the other officers seemed to have specific ideas for how Biotech might achieve its goals.

As Edward Williams enters the office, he is greeted by the good news that the firm has been awarded the Department of Defense grant. The paperwork for the grant is due in 30 days, but Edward doesn't have 30 days to complete it because he is leaving on a promotional trip to Europe in 18 days. But that's all right. One thing Edward Williams has never been afraid of is hard work.

REFERENCES

1. Bylinsky, Gene. "The High-Tech Race: Who's Ahead." *Fortune 114* (8) (October 13, 1986), pp. 26–37.

2. "Companies in a Leading Industry." *Investors Daily 3* (56) (June 26, 1986), p. 9.

3. Diamond, P. "Isolating and Purifying Mabs for Scale Up." *Genetic Engineering News 5* (4) (April 1985), p. 11.

4. Dougherty, P., B. McCormick, and R. Stanford. "Production Planning in a Biotechnology Firm: Framework for Analysis." *Proceedings of the Sixteenth Annual Meeting of the American Institute of Decision Sciences.* Toronto, Ontario, Canada, November 1984, pp. 516–518.

5. "Drugs: Above Average Growth Should Continue." *Standard and Poors Industry Surveys,* January 17, 1985, pp. H15–H22.

6. Elman, G. "NIH and Rifkin Claim Victory in Appeals Court Ruling on Environmental Releases." *Genetic Engineering News 5* (4) (April 1985), pp. 1, 15.

7. Elman, G. "Rifkin Wins Suit against Department of Defense; Construction of Biomedical Labs Banned." *Genetic Engineering News 5* (6) (June 1985), pp. 1, 15.

8. Gebhart, F. "Large-scale Monoclonal Antibody Processing: A Host of Choices." *Genetic Engineering News 5* (4) (April 1985), pp. 9, 30.

9. "Genetic Research Not Regulated: GAO." *Johnson City Press,* April 4, 1986, p. 18.

10. Graf, J. "Lawsuit Opposes Use of Genes in 'Super' Livestock; Charges Animal Cruelty." *Genetic Engineering News 4* (8) (November/December 1984), pp. 1, 5.

11. Holman, R. A., moderator. "Biotechnology: A TWST Roundtable Discussion." *Wall Street Transcripts,* March 17, 1986, pp. 81, 190–81, 229.

12. Jefferson, E. "The Biotechnology Industry Needs Regulations Tailored to Its Needs." *Genetic Engineering News* 5 (1) (January 1985), pp. 3, 43.

13. Johnson, R. "Biotech Regulations Debated by Committee." *Genetic Engineering News* 5 (1) (January 1985), pp. 1, 48.

14. Kenny, M. "Biotech Conference Targets Regulatory Questions." *Genetic Engineering News* 5 (6) (June 1985), pp. 3, 12.

15. Miller, L. I. "Biotechnology Mergers Signal Industry Consolidation." *Genetic Engineering News* 5 (2) (February 1985), p. 26.

16. Sterling, J. "Three Scientists Win Nobel Prize; Work on Immune System & Monoclonal Abs Lauded." *Genetic Engineering News* 5 (2) (November/December 1984), p. 26.

17. Stiff, D. "Biotechnology Becomes a Business in Transition." *The Wall Street Journal,* September 3, 1985, p. 6.

As Bill Axelrod looked at the results of the first half of the 1986 fiscal year, he could not help being satisfied with his efforts and yet he knew luck had been with Health & Beauty Products Company (H&B) also. Bill, the president, owned and operated the company along with John Schroeder, vice president of finance, and Tom Smith, vice president of sales. H&B is a small over-the-counter (OTC) pharmaceutical company which markets products in the diet-aid category. The numbers Bill enjoyed studying showed a net profit for the six months of $325,000 on net sales of $2,483,000, not bad considering net profit for the same period last year was $82,000.

Even more fantastic was the fact that the three owners had been able to pay off their large debt to the former parent company and buy out the fourth silent partner with $234,750 in cash which was accumulated from operations within a short span of three months in 1985. In spite of all of this good fortune and hard work, Bill confessed to being concerned about attaining the planned sales goal for fiscal year 1987 of $5,500,000 given the size of his company and the nature of the competition.

COMPANY HISTORY

In 1946 Richard Dumont founded Dumont Drug Specialties in Decatur, Illinois. Dumont, a returning veteran, decided to get into the marketing of OTC remedies to independent pharmacists. Among his products was an appetite suppressant with the chemical name of phenylpropanolamine hydrochloride (PPA). Dumont was moderately successful until the late 1950s when he stumbled upon the advertising concept, at the suggestion of one of his customers, that he provide her with money to run small classified ads in the local newspapers about his products. He tried her idea and that particular account grew rapidly so Dumont expanded the concept to other areas with the result that his business grew very fast. As his business grew, he began to use the telephone heavily in his marketing efforts and, in effect, was the forerunner of telemarketing. With all of his success he was unable to figure out how to get to the chain drugstores, who today control the business. His sales eventually reached $500,000 with substantial profits.

In late 1975 Dumont, who had become quite wealthy, decided to sell his company. Through a friend he became acquainted with an executive of a conglomerate who made him an offer for his company. He sold out and agreed to stay for a year until a new manager was located. After the sale the name of the company was changed to H&B in order to more descriptively reflect the nature of its products. In early 1976 Bill Axelrod, who had been working for a major regional drug wholesaler as vice president of sales, was hired to manage the company. When Bill started, the base of the business was small independent pharmacists. Bill's first moves were to expand the product line and repackage the products so that they could be favorably presented to drug wholesalers and chains. In effect, the company had been operating as a franchiser since one retailer in each town was picked to handle Dumont's products exclusively, ignoring the rest of the drugstores in the town. Having had extensive experience with a drug company that did franchise, Bill knew the risks of this strategy and wished to avoid them. The first two years under Bill's leadership were good, with sales reaching $1.5 million and profits before taxes of $260,000.

In 1978 because of the faddish nature of the business Bill decided to get into two weight-loss product lines: fiber concept and liquid protein. Both lines proved to be disastrous. The company, as did other companies in the business, took back all the liquid protein product when people died as a result of not eating regular meals, even though the labeling called out the need to do so. In the OTC drug business, companies not only stand behind their products but a sale to a drugstore is really not considered final by the drugstore until the product is sold to the ultimate consumer. Thus drug companies may have to take back products that do not sell well and certainly those that are risky as the liquid protein product proved to be. Within a matter of months sales and profits had plummeted and H&B was for sale by the conglomerate.

Bill had specified in his original employment agreement that he was to have the first opportunity to buy the company should it be placed on the market. In early 1979, Bill Axelrod and three others, John Schroeder who is now vice president of finance, Tom Smith who is now vice president of sales, and Don Black who was then a consultant to the company on product development, all remortgaged their houses, etc. in order to raise $120,000 for operating capital and proceeded to buy the company on a leveraged buyout basis. Bill owned 40 percent of the company, John and Tom owned 17½ percent each, and Don owned 25 percent. The buyout created a debt of $412,500 with monthly payments of $6,750 plus interest at 2 percent above the prime rate in Chicago. A sharing of the profits or a consulting fee if the company lost money was also required, which amounted to $1,500 minimum to $3,000 per month. These latter conditions subsequently were renegotiated to raise the profit sharing from 25 percent to 37.5 percent because the company was in arrears. As a further agreement among the four new owners, Don Black, who was to continue to act as a consultant, was to receive a "consulting fee" whether he consulted or not.

On March 1, 1979, the company was officially sold to the management. The conglomerate, as one of their last acts, terminated all of the employees so that the new management could hire back only those they wished to keep. Only about 20 previous employees were subsequently rehired.

In February 1982, the FDA Monograph Committee on weight control products sent its preliminary findings to the Food & Drug Administration (FDA) stating that PPA had been found to be a safe and effective appetite suppressant. Although a preliminary finding has no force of law, the industry typically reacts quickly to such recommendations, which happened in the case of PPA. Very quickly large companies such as Smith, Kline & French, American Home Products, and Lee Pharmaceuticals joined Thompson Medical, who had dominated the market, in the appetite suppressant business. Within two years all of the big companies dropped out because they were unable to make significant inroads on Thompson's market share. H&B suffered greatly from all of this competition and was near bankruptcy. In addition to the heavy competition, the company made some bad advertising decisions by trying to give the appearance of being a national company with national marketing clout without sufficient money to do the job. H&B was "grasping at straws to stay alive and grasped the wrong straw."

The strategy that brought the company out of this disastrous period was the 100 percent consumer rebate offer whereby the company offered to rebate the entire retail purchase price of the product. Although the company was terrified to make the offer, they found out what others had known for a long time—that people are procrastinators and few ever get around to sending in the rebate request. As a result the company became marginally profitable in 1984 and went on to profitable years in 1985 and the first half of fiscal 1986. Exhibit 3 shows the income statements for the fiscal years 1980 through 1985.

EXHIBIT 1 Total Drugstore Sales (in millions of dollars)

	1982	1983	1984
Prescription drugs	13,795.2	16,706.0	17,541.9
Over-the-counter drugs	3,270.9	4,250.9	4,510.0
Other merchandise	25,673.2	27,219.2	30,401.4
Total sales	42,739.3	48,176.1	52,453.3

SOURCE: *Drug Topics.*

Exhibit 4 shows the balance sheets for the same years. Exhibit 5 shows the income statements for the first half of fiscal 1985 and 1986.

The 100 percent rebate offer idea came from two sources, a manufacturer's representative from Chicago whom Bill Axelrod was working with, and a buyer from Revco, a large drug chain. The buyer, using another product's promotional material, showed Bill how it could be done for appetite suppressant products which had not been tried before. He told Bill that he was positive that the redemption rate would not exceed 15 percent of net sales. Bill tried the idea on Revco's 1,500 drugstores and it was a "blockbuster success." Although the redemption rate on the 100 percent rebate offer was about 10 percent which is high compared to coupon offers, the traffic and demand created in the stores was dramatic. Today Revco is H&B's biggest customer, accounting for over $800,000 worth of business.

THE INDUSTRY AND COMPETITION

The OTC drug market represented 8.6 percent of total drugstore sales in 1984 or $4.5 billion. Exhibits 1 and 2 show drugstore sales statistics for 1982 through 1984 by various categories. The diet-aid sales by drugstores in 1984 represented 38 percent of the total diet-aid sales of $711 million. Drugstores were a much less significant channel of distribution for diet aids which were popularly purchased from super-

EXHIBIT 2 Sales of Diet Aids (in millions of dollars)

	Drugstores			All Outlets		
	1982	1983	1984	1982	1983	1984
Diet aids						
Appetite suppressants	137.4	151.4	166.5	228.1	240.2	264.3
Metered calorie products	13.1	20.8	28.0	62.3	90.3	121.9
Synthetic sweeteners	24.7	39.0	58.5	130.7	195.0	292.5
Dietary supplements	13.0	13.7	15.1	28.8	29.7	32.1
Total diet-aids sales	188.2	224.9	268.1	449.9	555.2	710.8

SOURCE: *Drug Topics.*

EXHIBIT 3

HEALTH & BEAUTY PRODUCTS COMPANY
Income Statement
For Years Ending February 28
(in thousands of dollars)

	1980	1981	1982	1983	1984	1985
Sales	1,811.3	2,541.3	2,094.5	1,430.3	1,941.0	2,806.8
Less: Returns	138.2	124.4	219.4	146.3	169.3	145.5
Less: Discounts	60.0	58.1	37.1	35.0	41.6	64.5
Net sales	1,613.1	2,358.8	1,838.0	1,249.0	1,730.1	2,596.8
Cost of goods						
Material	489.8	675.9	583.3	523.4	701.0	1,038.3
Labor and overhead	156.7	226.2	187.7	47.1	37.2	63.9
Total	646.5	902.1	771.0	570.5	738.2	1,102.2
Gross profit	966.6	1,456.7	1,067.0	678.5	991.9	1,494.6
Less expenses						
Shipping	10.7	17.0	15.0	4.3	5.6	35.0
Marketing	459.4	1,150.4	779.5	351.6	518.0	717.8
General & administrative	374.6	409.2	371.4	285.6	358.4	461.3
Interest	64.7	84.0	113.3	73.3	78.3	63.3
Management fee	18.9	18.8	18.8	27.5	31.9	105.4
Total	928.3	1,679.4	1,298.0	742.3	992.2	1,382.8
Plus other income	2.2	2.0	3.6	2.9	2.0	−6.0
Net operating income	40.5	−220.7	−227.4	−60.9	1.7	105.8
Extraordinary items	16.1					
Federal income tax	−.8	−.8				
Forgiveness			127.3	7.3		50.0
Net income	55.8	−219.9	−100.1	−53.6	1.7	155.8

markets and discount stores than they were for other OTC items. Between 1983 and 1984, diet-aid sales in total increased by a large 28 percent. Most of the diet-aid sales increase came from outlets other than drugstores.

A significant industry development has been calcium supplements. Calcium supplements, continuing a trend begun in 1983, had an outstanding year due to the large advertising campaigns linking osteoporosis to a lack of calcium, particularly in the case of women. In 1985 researchers at the Oregon Health Sciences University at Portland, Oregon, announced preliminary findings that calcium lowered blood pressure. Private labeled calcium supplements sold the most of the combined units sold.

The diet-aid category was dominated by synthetic sweeteners in 1984 as shown in Exhibit 2. This segment in turn was dominated by G. D. Searle's NutraSweet. The next highest segment was appetite suppressants which was dominated by Thompson Medical Company who

EXHIBIT 4

HEALTH & BEAUTY PRODUCTS COMPANY
Balance Sheet
For Years Ending February 28
(in thousands of dollars)

	1980	1981	1982	1983	1984	1985
Current assets						
Cash	63.3	7.5	5.4	−10.9	21.4	78.2
Accounts receivable	264.5	393.1	265.1	112.7	200.7	460.9
Less: Allowances	−75.2	−99.1	−134.3	−143.8	−26.1	−43.3
Inventories						
Bulk drugs	107.6	175.7	137.6	153.4	130.8	76.4
Packaging supplies	97.9	111.2	116.3	113.6	113.8	95.6
Finished goods	95.8	75.0	30.1	35.6	73.7	113.0
Returned goods	12.9	12.8	12.6	12.6	19.4	20.8
Total	314.2	374.7	296.6	315.2	337.7	305.8
Prepaid expenses	45.2	79.7	8.0	13.0	4.8	8.3
Investments	.8	.8				
Total	612.8	756.7	440.8	286.2	538.5	809.9
Fixed assets						
Equipment	109.7	112.5	114.1	107.2	107.2	107.2
Furniture and fixtures	13.8	15.0	12.5	12.5	12.5	12.5
Office equipment	62.3	81.1	89.3	90.7	93.3	98.9
Leasehold improvement	13.7	20.2	20.9	20.9	20.9	20.9
Total	199.5	228.8	236.8	231.3	233.9	239.5
Less: Depreciation	43.1	73.7	103.4	132.1	164.0	192.2
Net fixed assets	156.4	155.1	133.4	99.2	69.9	47.3
Other assets	38.7	26.0	33.1	17.0	9.5	8.3
Total assets	807.9	937.8	607.3	402.4	617.9	865.5
Current liabilities						
Note—bank	6.8	150.0	112.5		25.2	
Accounts payable	109.7	397.5	240.0	200.6	165.6	247.1
Accruals	131.0	132.0	70.3	128.1	257.9	324.9
Current portion of long-term debt	75.2	82.2	32.6	87.7	221.0	228.8
Total	322.7	761.7	455.4	416.4	669.7	800.8
Long-term debt	368.2	279.0	354.9	242.3	202.8	163.6
Total liabilities	690.9	1,040.7	810.3	658.7	872.5	964.4
Equity						
Capital stock	37.5	37.5	37.5	37.5	37.5	37.5
Less: Treasury stock	2.3	2.3	2.3	2.1	2.1	2.1
	35.2	35.2	35.2	35.4	35.4	35.4
Retained earnings	81.8	−138.1	−238.2	−291.7	−290.0	−134.3
Total	117.0	−102.9	−203.0	−256.3	−254.6	−98.9
Total liabilities and equity	807.9	937.8	607.3	402.4	617.9	865.5

was thought to have about 80 percent of the market. Exhibit 6 shows the financial statements for Thompson from 1981 through 1984.

Thompson is a master marketer but contracts out all purchasing, manufacturing, testing, and warehousing of its products. In fact, the formulation of Thompson's products is contracted out as well. Thomp-

EXHIBIT 5

HEALTH & BEAUTY PRODUCTS COMPANY
Income Statement
For Six Months Ending August 31
(in dollars)

	1985	1986
Gross sales	1,521,948	2,820,350
Less: Deductions		
Freight	57,969	61,408
Returns and allowances	112,749	211,196
Discounts	30,335	64,829
Total	201,053	337,433
Net sales	1,320,895	2,482,917
Cost of goods sold		
Direct material	506,556	607,094
Disposed of goods	977	24,326
Direct labor	26,404	28,566
Temporary labor		30,757
Total	533,937	690,743
Manufacturing overhead		
Salary	17,540	21,671
Bonus	1,818	2,538
Maintenance	146	738
General plant expense	4,041	3,888
Quality control	437	1,350
Rent	1,433	1,770
Utilities	566	628
Depreciation	7,094	7,012
Payroll taxes	6,605	6,644
Group insurance	1,913	3,440
Auto expense	1,238	1,444
Total	42,831	51,123
Shipping department		
Labor	2,815	8,060
Supplies	3,192	3,599
Payroll taxes		513
Total	6,007	12,172
Sales department		
Inside sales salaries	6,889	3,930
Field sales salaries	18,653	21,371
Phone sales commission	2,890	2,318
Broker agencies commission	68,804	166,103
Bad debt expense	6,671	12,863
Telephone	10,309	7,557
Travel and lodging	7,941	8,001
Auto expense	1,852	379
Miscellaneous selling expense	4,718	3,437
Advertising bill backs	45,575	87,891
Sales promotion samples	3,507	3,975
Sales meetings	1,438	2,498
Payroll taxes	2,988	3,740
Group insurance	1,620	1,496
Coupon redemption	133	248
Total	183,988	325,807

EXHIBIT 5 *(concluded)*

	1985	1986
Marketing department		
Media expense	21,842	572,476
Classified	6,943	408
Production costs	21,801	13,034
Full manufacturing rebate	175,064	64,557
Total	225,650	650,475
General and administrative department		
Administrative salaries	17,156	24,671
Supervisory salaries	18,653	20,680
Office wages	28,424	28,232
Administrative bonus		74,175
Payroll taxes	7,768	8,969
Employee benefits	5,121	8,024
Group insurance	3,793	2,728
Medical reimbursements	1,751	2,953
Officers life insurance	2,349	9,803
Credit and collections	1,173	692
Employee IRA	4,593	5,063
Telephone	3,227	2,288
Travel and lodging	6,587	9,059
Dues and subscriptions	1,872	1,941
Building maintenance	2,518	3,674
Office maintenance	1,222	1,563
Equipment rent	614	633
Auto rent	3,602	3,056
Miscellaneous expense	518	465
Property taxes	4,858	4,884
State taxes	7,049	15,623
Office supplies	6,020	6,794
Postage	11,666	5,894
Insurance	11,745	29,374
Professional fees	49,730	45,000
Building rent	12,893	15,930
Utilities	5,098	5,651
Depreciation	6,674	7,063
Amortization	1,170	
Computer costs	6,375	8,195
Total	234,219	353,077
Other income and expense		
Interest income	−1,466	−8,052
Interest expense	32,508	5,437
Discount on purchases	−422	−6,341
Miscellaneous income	−720	−910
Miscellaneous expense	7,500	19
Outside consulting fees	15,936	
Forgiveness of debt	−40,994	−164,713
Total	12,342	−174,560
Net income before taxes	81,921	574,080
Income taxes		249,075
Net profit	81,921	325,005

EXHIBIT 6

THOMPSON MEDICAL COMPANY, INC.
For Years Ending November 30
(in thousands of dollars)

Income Statement

	1981	1982	1983	1984
Net sales	83,879	90,984	149,442	197,245
Less cost of sales	22,951	25,106	47,875	66,320
Gross profit.	60,928	65,878	101,567	130,925
Less: Selling and administrative				
expense.	41,021	45,963	71,925	91,097
Plus interest income.	1,208	2,508	2,592	2,642
Net operating income	21,115	22,423	32,234	42,470
Federal income tax	10,781	10,805	15,717	21,262
Net income	10,334	11,618	16,517	21,208

Balance Sheet

		1982	1983	1984
Assets				
Cash and investments		25,685	36,495	29,344
Accounts receivable		11,435	21,025	20,005
Inventories.		11,273	16,308	26,823
Due from officers			175	
Income tax refund receivable		474		
Prepaid expenses		601	698	1,165
Total current assets		49,468	74,701	77,337
Net property and equipment		803	1,282	1,769
Formulae and trademarks		3,241	2,745	2,183
Net cash value of insurance		761	798	846
Other assets.		2,074	2,455	3,153
Total assets		56,347	81,981	85,288
Liabilities				
Accounts payable		5,323	10,155	4,948
Income taxes		845	5,010	3,819
Accruals.		4,846	8,366	9,359
Total current liabilities		11,014	23,531	18,126
Equity				
Common Stock ($.10)		500	1,000	1,000
Paid-in capital		302	302	302
Retained earnings		44,531	57,148	75,496
Less: Treasury stock				−9,636
Total equity		45,333	58,450	67,162

SOURCE: *Moody's Industrial Manual.*

son's products include Dexatrim, an appetite suppressant, and Slim Fast, a meal-replacement product which was reformulated and reintroduced in late 1983 and accounts for about 90 percent of the meal-replacement subcategory. Thompson markets its products primarily through "appetite control centers" which are special display racks in drugstores, supermarket, and mass merchandise chains such as K mart, which is its biggest customer. Thompson puts approximately 30 percent of its annual revenues into advertising.

Acutrim, Ciba Geigy's appetite suppressant, has about a 10 percent market share, with the remaining 10 percent divided between Jeffery Martin's Aids, Allegheny's Permathene 12, Alva Amco's Thinz, O'Connor's Dex-A-Diet, and H&B's Dexathin.

According to Ted Gladson in the August 5, 1985, issue of *Drug Topics*, "Meal replacement sales almost doubled last year, coming close to $200 million." He believed moderate growth could be expected in 1985. Appetite suppressants had only a modest growth in 1984, although supermarkets had a 17 percent increase in unit sales. The typical space allocation to diet-aid products in a drugstore is four to eight running feet according to *Drug Topics*. Gladson projected total sales of diet products in 1985 to be $782 million, with drugstore sales of $375 million at a 35 percent to 40 percent gross margin.

In the August 19, 1985, issue of *Drug Topics* the role the pharmacist plays in recommending OTC products was discussed. As might be expected for products such as cold remedies, the recommendations follow a seasonal pattern, but in the case of nutritional supplements the recommendations are quite constant. In the case of calcium supplements 80 percent of pharmacists made recommendations for a total of 218,000 recommendations weekly. The median number of recommendations per week was three. In the case of weight-loss products, 74 percent of pharmacists made recommendations for a total of 147,000 recommendations weekly. The median number of recommendations per week was two and recommendations appeared to peak in the spring/summer periods. In April 1985, when recommending weight loss products, 38 percent of the pharmacists suggested some form of Dexatrim, 26 percent Acutrim, and 10 percent a store brand or generic. Acutrim appears to be gaining market share (from 16 percent) on Dexatrim, which dropped from 47 percent in October 1984, and store brands and generics may be gaining as well.

In the February 18, 1985, issue of *Drug Topics* the use and effect of cents-off coupons on drugstores was discussed. In 1983, according to data from Nielson, 143 billion coupons were distributed and the projection for 1989 is 350–400 billion will be distributed. The largest distributor, accounting for 49 percent, is the free-standing Sunday paper insert which has a redemption rate of 2.8 percent. A 1982 study by Arthur Anderson indicated that "92.5 percent of all coupons are redeemed in supermarkets, only 5 percent in drugstores." A nationwide 1983 study done by Point-of-Purchase Advertising Institute of 20,000 drugstore purchases showed that 4.8 percent of all purchases involved newspaper ads (either manufacturers' or retailers') while only .8 percent involved coupons from direct mailing, and .6 percent from magazines. Ad retailer coupons were used in 2.2 percent of the purchases. In another survey, double couponing was reported to be used by 15 percent of the druggists and 54 percent of the grocery

EXHIBIT 7 Nutritional Products Company Organization Chart

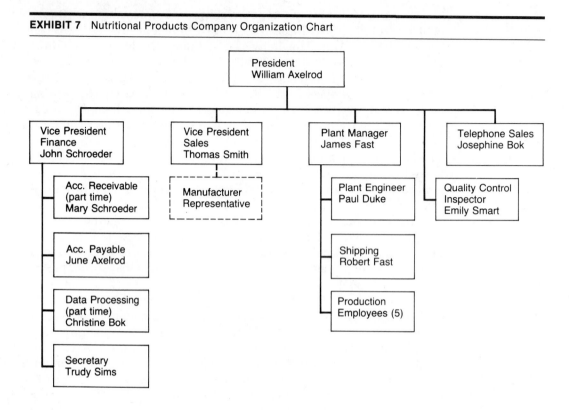

executives. Double couponing was thought to be profitable because, like any sale, it attracts customers who want to save money. In its present form coupons are somewhat of a nuisance because of handling and recording problems. However, new developments such as electronic coupons using banks as a clearing house or video couponing could ameliorate this nuisance problem.

MARKETING

Like most small companies in the diet-aid business, H&B is primarily a marketing organization. The responsibility for the marketing activities including sales is shared by Bill Axelrod, president, and Tom Smith, vice president of sales. The organization chart for the company is shown in Exhibit 7. Bill, who is 50 years old, is a graduate of the University of Illinois with a degree in commercial art. While attending school, he worked part time in a drugstore in Champaign where his father was the pharmacist. He received national recognition from a national wholesale drug firm from his door-to-door sales of vitamin products and subsequently went to work for them directly upon graduation. He worked in most of the marketing areas of the company and rose to the level of vice president before leaving to take over the management of H&B.

The company's products include the major category of diet aids which includes appetite suppressants containing PPA, appetite suppressants combined with vitamin C, a meal replacement powder, and the new fiber concept diet plan. The company markets its products through 18 manufacturer's representatives who in turn use about 50 salespeople to call on drugstores, drug chains, supermarket chains, and discount houses.

The manufacturer's reps are compensated by commissions which range from 5 percent to 10 percent averaging about 7½ percent based upon the product lines and their margin. The reps were selected based upon two characteristics, their entrée to good accounts and their follow-up. The company has about 10,000 accounts of which about 8,000 are small drugstores. The 25 large drug chains, 15 major discount chains such as K mart and the major supermarket chains make up 80 percent of the company's sales following Pareto's Law. Bill believes that manufacturer's reps are the only economical way to sell his products because a sales level of $200 million is needed to support an inside sales force. No in-house accounts are maintained.

In addition to his general management responsibilities, Bill spends about one day per week calling on top key accounts with manufacturer's reps. He also works on new product development with outside consultants and develops sales promotions and marketing sheets. The company uses a small Chicago advertising agency for whom H&B is the largest account. Package design under Bill's direction is done by a design firm in a Chicago suburb.

In 1985 the company spent about $196,000 on all forms of advertising. Although TV advertising is thought to be most effective, it is also the most expensive. Since the company has limited funds, it limits its TV advertising to spot markets selected by analyzing the various markets the company is engaged in. Radio advertising has not been found to be effective. The bulk of the company's advertising in the past has been devoted to cooperative advertising in omnibus newspaper ads, flyers, or coupon books. The company has used limited freestanding ads. As alluded to earlier, the company has used rebates extensively in its advertising. The company will reimburse retailers 100 percent of the actual advertising cost up to a maximum of 5 percent of the retailer's purchases. Various requirements are made for proof of expenditure, the use of the H&B brand names in the ad, and the type of media used.

The beginning of 1985 saw a shift in the advertising for the company. Because of the emphasis being put on the importance of fiber in the diet by physicians and the general public, the company resurrected an old product from 1978 that had "bombed" at that time. It uses the fiber concept for controlling weight; that is, the fiber swells in the stomach making the user feel full so less food is eaten. Fiber products typically do not contain an appetite suppressant. Sales sky-rocketed as a result of this product in the first six months of calendar 1985. The company spent about $450,000 on television advertising during the first six months of fiscal 1986 on this product.

Tom Smith, who is 42 years old, has been with Dumont and its successor, H&B, for his whole professional career since he completed two years of community college. He has handled all of the jobs within sales at one time or another. He visualizes the company as a promotional house which is similar or superior to a national brand house. In addition to the rebate strategy, he sees the company's strategy as offering a price to the retailer which is 25 percent below the leader in the product. The company projects a national brand quality image with a superior product packaged in a creative way. The company tries to tune into what the customer wants.

Tom notes that although the product leaders, such as Thompson in the case of appetite suppressants, will retaliate against H&B with rebates, the rebates are usually smaller but media expenditures are greater. The company has also used trial-size packages effectively since operations can package them efficiently with its packaging equipment. These trial-size packages of a three-day count are typically priced at 39 cents to 49 cents with a coupon worth 50 cents cash upon the purchase of a full-size package. Often the consumer will buy two samples for a six-day trial, so the price point is critical.

Sales for H&B are quite seasonal. Diet aids have a strong peak in the January through May period with a minor pickup again in the fall. This seasonal pattern makes it difficult to judge how well a new product is doing depending on what the season is.

Pricing followed the typical pattern outlined below.

- Retail price $4.29
- Warehouse price   2.29
- Distributor price   2.06
- Company price   .41

Tom sees the company's strengths to be its recently found financial strength, its building brand loyalty, the knowledge of its market niche, and good contacts that could be transferred to other drugstore items. In turn, he is concerned about the tough competition, the limited working capital to support advertising, and the inadequate activity of some of the company's reps. He describes Bill as "demanding but fun." Tom notes that the company is strongest in the Midwest and Southeast. The Southwest is reasonably strong and there are pockets of strength in the West. The Central section is relatively weak and the Northwest seems to be declining.

OPERATIONS

The operations department is managed by Jim Fast, plant manager. He is 35 years old and has been with the company since completing three years of college. In addition to managing the packaging operations, he is responsible for purchasing of all items needed for packaging including the bulk product. Bulk tablets and capsules account for about 65 percent to 70 percent of the cost of goods sold. They are purchased from six different formulators located in the Midwest and on the eastern coast. Quality for all of these suppliers is consistently good, so price and delivery is the determining factor on vendor selection. A perpetual inventory is maintained of the bulk stock which has a lead time of 10 to 12 weeks.

Other items purchased include printed folding boxes with a four- to six-week lead time which are supplied by two vendors as well as inserts, labels, bottles, caps, and clear wrapping film. There are about 120 inventory items in all, of which 50 to 75 are active and 30 are very active. A physical inventory is taken once a month. Jim knows the monthly usage of boxes from experience. He uses two times the lead time as a rule of thumb in establishing inventory levels on all items.

The building is leased with three years remaining on the lease and contains about 15,000 square feet and is 15 feet high. Office space takes up 2,800 square feet, excess storage space on a balcony over the office consumes 2,800 square feet, four production rooms utilize 1,800 square feet, and the balance of the building is used for storage of raw materials and finished goods. There is sufficient space for rent in the area should the company need to expand.

The plant operates on one shift and employs six women permanently for packing operations at $4.50 to $6.50 per hour plus fringe benefits which amount to about 30 percent of the labor costs. A maintenance man who has worked for the company for 10 years and is a backup for Jim Fast handles all maintenance and janitorial work as well as working part time in shipping and receiving helping the other full-time employee there. Other labor is hired on a temporary basis from Kelly at $5 per hour and no fringe benefits of course. Two temporary women are employed on the average except during the summer months. Up to 10 temporary women may be employed during the busy season from January through May. The company provides free cokes and coffee to all employees as well as a Christmas party and birthday parties. The company is not unionized.

The company has sufficient equipment for its needs. In fact, the machines run only half of the time as a general rule. There are two strip sealers for packaging 250,000 capsules or tablets per shift each, a bottle-filling line, a bagger, a cartoner which prints the lot number, and a shrink tunnel used primarily for bottles packed in trays. A new automatic blister-pack machine was considered for purchase recently which would cost $300,000 and had a three-year payback period based on utilizing 3 people in place of the 15 people now used to do the same job. The machine had a one-year lead time so it was not ordered because Bill and Jim were not that certain of the demand for its use, although it would improve the package by providing a higher quality, more attractive appearance.

The quality control function is run by Emily Smart who reports to Bill Axelrod in this capacity. She also does packing work in her free time. All incoming materials go immediately into a quarantine area until the certified assay is received from the manufacturer. The company does stability testing on all products using elevated temperatures for the two-year stability study. All products are shipped by lot number to facilitate recall should a problem be encountered. The FDA makes an annual inspection which has become routine because of the use of quality control manuals which were set up originally by Don Black.

Jim sees his ability to react quickly to packaging needs and to ship orders quickly as company strengths. He tries to ship orders the same day they are received. He believes the packaging needs to be improved, however, and would like to see the product line expanded.

FINANCE

John Schroeder, who is 40 years old, graduated from De Paul University with a degree in accounting. He worked for the drug division of a supermarket chain before joining H&B in 1978. John is responsible for all data processing, accounting, and personnel benefits for the company.

Data processing is done on an IBM System 36 computer with five terminals and two printers. In addition John has a standalone IBM PC which is tied into the System 36 for data accessibility. Software for the computer is provided by an outside firm. All accounting is done on the computer including billing, accounts receivable, inventory, payroll, accounts payable, general ledger, sales analysis, and sales performance. Auditing is done by a local outside CPA firm.

John believes the company has a strong receivables program. Terms are 2 percent/10, net 30. Statements are issued monthly and receivables are aged. Those past due over 60 days are called and then turned over to an outside agency if payment is not forthcoming. Most customers pay on receipt of their statement and 90 percent pay within the credit terms. There is an unwritten rule in the OTC business that returns will be taken back for full credit.

Recently an outside consulting firm was retained to completely review and reorganize the filing system which was accomplished with excellent results in eliminating costly duplication of records. John believes some work needs to be done to improve inventory control. The present system does not match the inventory to minimums or maximums. Finished goods inventory is tightly controlled by packaging to order, except for major products, with a one- to two-day turnaround.

John is involved in developing strategy and makes up the company's budget one year in advance based upon the forecasted volume of sales. Performance against budget is shown and variances calculated. During the first half of fiscal 1986 everyone was agreeably surprised by the fact that 50 percent of the volume was supplied by the recycled fiber diet product. John does formal cash planning using spreadsheet programs on his PC. Buying decisions are made at a monthly meeting, with the principle used being conservative but still able to supply products to customers as needed.

John sees the company's strengths as being Bill's and Tom's relationship with strong manufacturer's reps, strong telemarketing, and a strong lawyer for FDA work. As potential problems he sees competition, the FDA, the risk of the fiber product concept, the distribution chain is high, and the pipeline is changing. He sees supermarket and discount chains increasing in importance, which is not the company's strong marketing channel.

When thinking about goals for the company, he talks about growing at 25 percent to 50 percent per year while maintaining the present good profit margins. Diversification into health and beauty aids is mentioned by buying existing products which are being poorly marketed. Alternatively, he can see going public or even selling the company if the price were right. In any event, decisions are made by consensus and then everyone pulls together.

PRESIDENTIAL MUSINGS ABOUT THE LAST YEAR

As he thought about the last 12 months, Bill Axelrod continued to be amazed. The takeoff of the fiber product brought in an unexpectedly large amount of cash that allowed H&B's management to pay off its debt to the conglomerate of $178,500 and buy out Don Black for $56,250. The cash had accumulated after the year-end statements so that the conglomerate was unaware of it and was so pleased to escape from what it considered a risky situation that it forgave the rest of the fees and profit sharing that were still owing. Fortunately, Don Black did not probe either because of the risk he perceived.

But with those pleasant events behind, what about the future? Would the faddish fiber product prove to be enduring and profitable, particularly since others already were copying it? Diversifying seemed to make sense but good categories were hard to find and even harder to launch with big dollar expenditures required—more than the company had. He thought of buying some existing brand and even visited a broker in Chicago. Bill came away wondering if his situation was not good enough to sell instead of trying to buy. And yet the company could now break even at $1,500,000 in sales but it was vulnerable because of its size, product categories, and the strong competition. Finally, this was a family business. In fact, his daughter noted that it looked like nepotism was the policy. Bill's wife, John's wife, and Jim's brother, as well as two other employees who were related, all worked for the company.

Then there was the latest news about another product that could be solid or yet another fad. A small competitor had come out with a grapefruit appetite suppressant diet plan which was producing rapid sales. This competitor had piggybacked onto the interest created by a direct-response company's advertising in newspapers. And what about the interest in calcium supplements, a segment the company had not entered? At least there was never a dull moment or a time to relax.

The management of Western Breeders Limited was concerned about the future directions in which to take their organization. Based in Balzac, Alberta, a small farming community on the outskirts of Calgary, Western Breeders was established to distribute and supply semen for artificial insemination of dairy and beef cattle throughout western Canada. In the 15 years since their inception, they have expanded their semen sales to the United States, Latin America, Europe, and Eastern Block countries. They established a computer division, selling software and hardware to Alberta farmers, and became involved in the development of frozen embryo transplants. The task facing the management group in 1986 is that of determining which markets have the greatest potential for both long- and short-term growth, and then redefining their strategies to facilitate market penetration and expansion in those areas.

BACKGROUND—THE INDUSTRY

Technological advancements over the past several decades have provided opportunities for companies specializing in beef and dairy herd enhancement through genetic improvement techniques. Genetic improvement of any species is accomplished by selecting males and females with superior transmitting ability to be parents of succeeding generations.[1] Several measures of a bull's or a cow's traits are obtainable. These enable a breeder to select the cattle which will provide the greatest rate of genetic improvement to his herd. Although a single herd cannot excel in every trait, a farmer can choose which of the following traits he wishes to improve in his herd: milk production, fat percent, protein percent, bone structure, size, calving ease, and weight. The desirability of these traits will depend on whether the herd is dairy or beef. The goal of genetic improvement is to develop animals which will produce higher yields of milk or meat in shorter

---

This case was prepared by Michele Power and Karen Paul under the supervision of Dr. James B. Graham, associate professor, Faculty of Management, the University of Calgary, for the sole purpose of providing material for class discussion. Copyright © 1986, The University of Calgary.
[1] H. J. Bearden and J. Faquay, "Applied Animal Reproduction," Reston Publication Co., 1980.

EXHIBIT 1

A BUTLERVIEW MATTADOR

EXCELLENT
SUPERIOR TYPE

347993
70 HO 0188
Born: December 28, 1976
aAa: 213645
Milking Speed: Average
Calving Ease: Easy

A Northcroft Admiral Citation (Ex-Extra '75)
DSC'82·6082 Daus: M + 12 %F:.12
Type '82·6903 Daus: + 9

Butlerview Princess Matt (Ex-USA)
04-07 239 10347 468 4.5
3 Lacts.2 ×: 31884·1391-4.4

Rosafe Citation R (Ex Extra '64)
DSC'82 M + 4 %F-.09 Type'82 + 19
Northcroft Ann Admiral (Ex-USA 4E)
07-05 305 10650 351 3.3
No-Na-Me Fond Matt (Ex-USA GM)
DSC'84 M + 1 %F + 12 Type'84 + 11
Butlerview Keystone Princess (Ex-USA)
06-09 305 11794 379 3.2

DAUGHTERS

GERANN MATTADOR TREASURE (EX)
3Y 305 6890 253 3.7% (154-153)
Owner: Gerald & John Wynands, Cardinal, Ontario

OLD POPLAR MATTADOR HAZEL (EX)
4Y 305 7585 294 3.87% (153-159)
Owner: Butch Crack, Richmond, Quebec

Gail Snobilen

Sire Analyst's Comments

Mattador is now rated in the top 1% of the breed for type improvement at + 14. The Mattadors are large, dairy cattle walking uphill. He has the unique ability to sire dairyness with strength and capacity. His daughters show great angularity, being sharp over the shoulder and exhibiting an open, dairy rib. Note his high ratings in all the mammary system traits including median suspensory ligament. Although pins could be wider, rumps are otherwise quite desirable and loins strong. Mattador is destined to be a legend in his own time.

MILK	Avg Test				DIRECT SIRE COMPARISON				
	3.72	122 Daughters 88 Herds 87 % Rep		Milk +3	Fat +2	% Test Deviation -.05			
TYPE	117 daus.·63% GP+ (2EX 5VG 74GP 35G 1F)								
		FINAL +14	GEN APP +14	DAIRY CHAR +10	CAPACITY +10	RUMP +3	LEGS & FEET +11	% Test Deviation	
		Style +11	Loin +5	Dairyness +10	Chest +8 Muzzle —	Width −1 Pin Set OH	Bone Dual Set +6 Heel +5 Rear −3S		
	Rating: 108 daus./83 herds	81 Daughters 53 Herds 82 % Rep							
					MAMMARY +12	FORE (UDDER) +11	REAR +10	Protein +4	% Protein Deviation +.02
					Med Susp +13 Texture +8	Attchmt +10 Placemt +11	Attchmt +7 Placemt +11	SIZE +8	Stature +9

EASTERN

EXHIBIT 2

SDF HIGHLINER 1K

Reg. # MC 23836 **Tattoo:** SDF 1K **Semen Code:** 28CH0404
Birthdate: January 19, 1978
Owned by: Allan Sparrow, Box 256, Vanscoy, Sask. S0L 3J0
Mature Wt.: 2500 lbs.
Ht. at Hips: 61'' **Ht. at Shoulder:** 60''
Scrotal Circum.: 42 cm **Date:** August 29, 1984

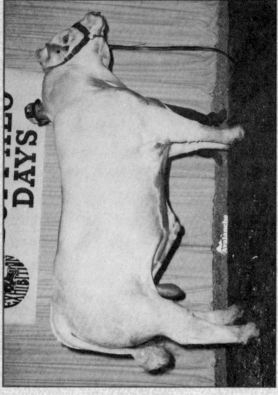

Hannibal FMC 1315
Sire: SDF Investigator 2H MC 19340
Sparlais A7 FC 3764

Sir Silver Dawn 18D FMC 1436
Dam: Miss SDF Silver Dawn 5F
Margaret Silver Dawn RFC 67248

SB Miss Highliner 21P

CHAROLAIS

HIGHLINER will put profit into your program. A son of Highliner topped the Sparrow Farms 1983 Bull Sale. He has the ability to turn pounds into profit. He is a fleshy, thick bull.

1983 CANADIAN BEEF SIRE MONITORING PROGRAMME				
Trait	* No. of Progeny	Predicted Difference	Repeatability	Rank
Calving Ease		− 2	47%	59/74
Weaning Weight	*42	**+30 lbs.	74%	4/154
Yearling Weight		**+67 lbs.	80%	1/128

* No. of Progeny provided for weaning weight only
** Canadian Growth Trait Leader

periods of time, thus decreasing feed requirements and improving the efficiency of the herd operation. Variation in the rate of herd improvement is dependent upon the degree to which certain traits are genetically inherited or are affected by such environmental influences as diet and disease. The length of the interval between generations and the intensity at which parents are selected or culled will also affect the rate of genetic improvement. Measurement of these factors can provide estimates of the rate of genetic progress per generation per year. Records are kept by individual farmers, breeding services, breed associations, and government agencies. From these records, bulls and cows are ranked against the average population. Exhibits 1 and 2 are examples of dairy and beef sires and their ratings, taken from Western Breeders Services' 1985 bull catalogs.

Genetic improvement in farm animals has been aided by more sophisticated methods of semen collection, storage, and artificial insemination procedures. More recently, applications of computerized record-keeping and modeling techniques have contributed to this process. The most exciting development is the commercialization of the embryo transfer procedure. Future opportunities include the use of genetic engineering techniques such as gene splicing and cloning.

Although genetic improvement has been used extensively in developed countries (Western), this has not been the case in Communist and Third World countries. Thus, an enormous potential export market exists because of Canada's superior genetics and stringent health standards.

BACKGROUND—THE COMPANY

Western Breeders Limited (WBL) was established in Balzac, Alberta, in 1968 to provide artificial insemination services to Western Canadian farmers. Initially, the company offered custom semen collection services for privately owned beef bulls. Western then began importing bulls and began marketing semen from their own and a number of leased bulls. Dairy semen was added about a year later when the Ontario Association of Animal Breeders (OAAB) joined Western Breeders Limited to create Western Breeders Services Ltd. as a marketing operation. During the years 1970 to 1974, beef semen sales grew rapidly because of the "exotic boom" created by the introduction of European breeds. Beef semen sales surpassed income from custom collection and dairy semen during this period, but by 1976, the boom in the exotics collapsed.

To replace lost beef semen sales, Western concentrated major efforts in expanding its dairy semen sales and diversifying its activities to encompass artificial insemination (AI) supplies and related products and services. Today, Western's services include the collec-

EXHIBIT 3

WESTERN BREEDERS LIMITED
Consolidated Balance Sheet
to September 30

	1984 $000s*	1983 $000s*
Assets		
Net working capital	$1,667	$1,194
Land, buildings, and equipment	1,043	1,079
Other long-term assets	495	160
	$3,205	$2,433
Liabilities		
Long-term debt	666	459
Due to affiliates	1,663	1,848
Other	145	220
	2,474	2,527
Retained earnings (deficit)	731	(94)
	$3,205	$2,433

* These figures have been disguised but reflect the company's actual standing.

tion, freezing, and evaluation of semen; AI training schools; development of breeding programs in dairy and beef cattle; marketing export programs for national and international clients; and most recently, the distribution of farm microcomputer systems and specialized farm management software. Gross sales volumes averaged $5 million over 1983 and 1984, establishing Western Breeders as the largest integrated AI unit in western Canada. Exhibits 3–5 provide financial information for 1983 and 1984.

Ownership of Western Breeders Ltd. is split between three men: Douglas Blair (president), Donald Stewart (vice president), and Donald Dufault (secretary-treasurer). Since its inception, the company has expanded and diversified, leading to the formation of several subsidiary companies. (See Exhibit 6 for an organizational chart and a description of the functions of the subsidiary companies.)

Western Breeders Services Ltd. is the major operating arm of WBL and employs about 50 people, including technical and professional specialists with expertise in herd management, genetic matching, semen collection, processing, distribution, and on-farm artificial insemination. These people are supported by a marketing, accounting, and administrative staff.

In 1976, the OAAB sold its interest in Western Breeders Services Ltd. to WBL and replaced it with an exclusive long-term distributorship agreement. Similar agreements have since been established with

EXHIBIT 4

WESTERN BREEDERS LIMITED
Consolidated Statement of Income and Retained
Earnings For the Years Ending September 30

	1984 $000s*	1983 $000s*
Income from operations**	$3,641	$2,592
Other income	380	270
	4,021	2,862
Expenses		
Administration	2,332	2,196
Barn	407	270
Laboratory	176	130
Computers	83	14
	2,998	2,610
Income before income taxes	1,023	252
Income taxes	198	9
Net income	$ 825	$ 243

**Income from Operations Source	Percent Contribution to Operating Income 1984	1983
Semen, certificates		
AI supplies and services	74.2%	101.1%
Computers	1.1	.2
Mating guide service	.3	.3
Embryo exports	.9	—
Other	23.5	(1.6)
Total	100.0%	100.0%

* These figures have been disguised but reflect the company's actual standings.

other AI units in Quebec, the Maritimes, and B.C., allowing for reciprocal exchange of genetics between all the major distributors of genetics in Canada. Today, most of the dairy semen sold in the prairie provinces is sold through WBS.

A company brochure provides a brief description of the facilities and services offered by Western Breeders at Balzac, Alberta.

Facilities at the Western Breeders head office include 125 open and closed bull pens, isolation barn, semen evaluation laboratory, packing and freezing room, distribution center, and accounting and management offices. Also, since 1981, Western Breeders has operated the only recognized animal quarantine center in North America used in the export of live cattle and frozen embryos to New Zealand and Australia.

EXHIBIT 5 Western Breeders Historical Sales Picture, 1969–1984

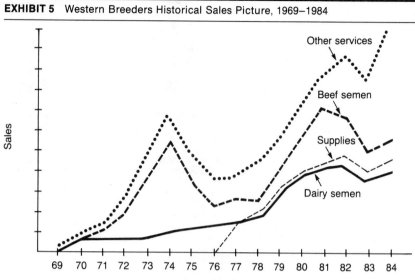

EXHIBIT 6 Western Breeders Group of Companies Organization Chart, 1984

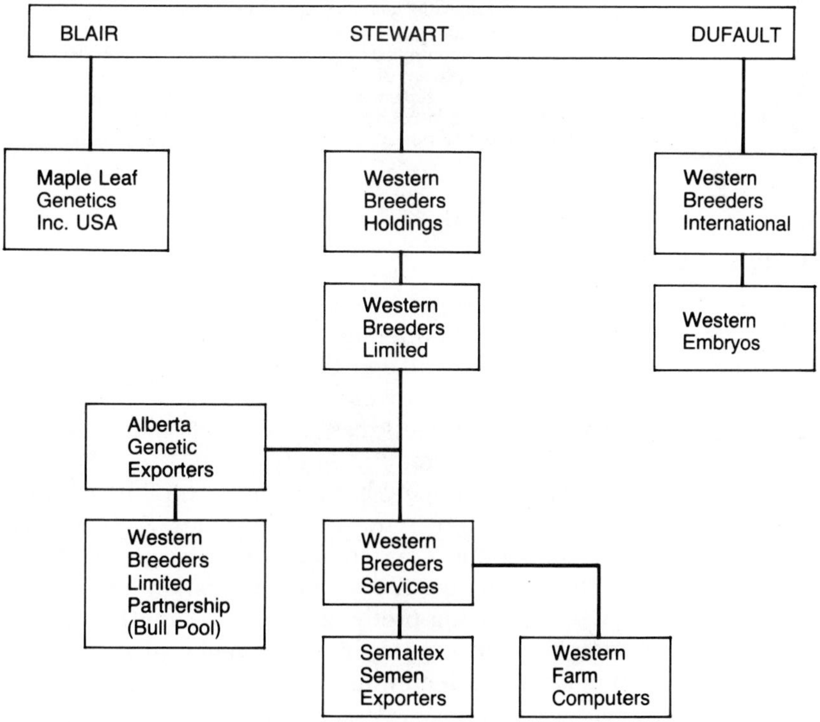

NOTES TO EXHIBIT 6 *(concluded)*

Maple Leaf Genetics Inc.
Incorporated in 1983, MGI is the American operating arm of WBL. Western has negotiated separate distribution agreements with each of the other AI units in Canada and represents these units through MGI in the U.S. market. MGI sells mostly Canadian dairy semen, but also supplies some beef semen.

Western Breeders Limited Partnership
A division of Alberta Genetic Exporters, WBLP was responsible for raising capital through the sale of shares in the Bull Pool.

Western Breeders Limited
WBL controls WBS and AGE. It has negotiated exclusive distributor agreements with the other major AI units in Canada regarding the reciprocal sale of semen from Western's unit-owned bulls to other provinces in Canada and, in turn, represents sires from these other units in the prairie provinces.

Western Breeders Services
WBS is concerned with the marketing of semen and related services to the prairie provinces and directly to Australia, New Zealand, and Cuba.

Semaltex Semen Exporters
Semaltex was set up in 1976 with Universal Semen Services Ltd. and BCAI to sell purebred breeding stock and beef semen to Central and South America and Mexico. Because of foreign exchange problems, expansion into these markets was limited. In 1981, WBS bought out USSL and BCAI's interest in exchange for a distribution agreement. Semaltex continues to maintain a strong distribution network and operates in Mexico, Argentina, Brazil, and Uruguay.

Western Farm Computers
WFC was formed in 1983 as a division of WBS to market microcomputer systems and software specifically geared to the agricultural market.

Western Embryos Ltd.
Western Embryos was set up in the winter of 1982–83 as an embryo production and quarantine facility to supply the emerging export market.

Semex Canada
Semex is not controlled by Western. Semex was formed in 1974 to promote the sale of frozen semen worldwide (except USA) on behalf of all Canadian AI units such as Western. This cooperative effort distributes semen to Europe, Africa, and Asia for Western. Semex also competes indirectly with Western in countries that WBL distributes directly, for example, Australia and New Zealand. Semex distributes mainly dairy semen to these countries.

Opportunities for Growth

The three owners of Western Breeders Ltd. were examining the avenues of growth open to their company in the next three to five years. They had established themselves in western Canada with AI sales and services but revenues from this area, particularly for dairy herds, had been relatively flat since 1980. One reason for this is that over time, through genetic improvements and better management, milk production per cow has increased, thereby decreasing the total dairy cow population required to produce a given quantity of milk. The demand for milk and milk products has reached maturity, contributing to the reduction in the potential market for dairy semen. On the positive side, rising production costs and milk quotas are pressuring the dairymen to improve the efficiency of their operations with better management techniques and improved genetics.

WBL felt their successes to date were due to the persistent efforts of the principals and the fact that they were leaders in many aspects of their industry. However, in light of rapid technological advancements in the industry and increasing competition, the management recognized that intensive efforts to produce superior breeding stock would be required to secure future growth through the supply of proven genetic material to local and international markets.

At the beginning of 1985, the three partners identified several potential areas of growth including further development of their AI services, embryo transfer programs, sales of arm computers and software, and expansion of their herd management consulting services. Each of these areas required further thought and investigation.

ARTIFICIAL INSEMINATION: BACKGROUND INFORMATION

History: Development and Use

The use of artificial insemination has for a long time been an acceptable and important means of expediting genetic improvements in a herd. The first attempt at AI in cattle was made in Russia about 1900. This followed experiments involving the artificial insemination of dogs and horses, dating back to 1300 with Arabian horse breeders.

In the late 1940s researchers and livestock managers recognized the potential gains that could be made through commercial breeding services. The importance of a high-ranking sire to improve certain traits in a herd created huge demands for high-ranking bulls to be used as studs. With artificial insemination, one bull can provide enough semen for as many as 200 to 300 progeny in each collection period. Also, the semen can be stored indefinitely, so supply is available at any time of the year, even after the bull's death.

Generally, commercial AI services collect semen from a young bull and store it for five years or until the bull is proven. If the bull has a high rating, determined by the genetic merit passed on to his sons and daughters, the breeding service can collect a high price for his semen. A dose of an unproven sire's semen may sell for $4 or $5 whereas an elite proven sire's semen may command $60 to $80 per dose.

Today AI is a multimillion dollar industry. The largest commercial operations, including exports, are located in North America. In 1982, about 60 percent of the U.S. dairy cow population was bred by AI.[2] Similar statistics apply to Canada. Less than 7 percent of beef

---

[2] J. K. Hillers, S. C. Thonney, and C. T. Gaskins, "Economic Comparison of Breeding Dairy Cows Artificially versus Naturally," Washington State University, 1982.

cows are bred by AI in North America, by comparison. World statistics show at least 150 million artificial breedings per year, half of which occur in countries with centrally planned economies excluding China for which no statistics are available. Often, the technology associated with improved genetics through AI is secondary—many countries continue to use local semen supplies instead of superior imports.[3] Exhibits 7–9 provide statistics for AI use in various countries, cattle population figures, and semen imports and exports per country.

The Artificial Insemination Procedure

Businesses selling AI services try to maximize the use of superior sires. This is accomplished by obtaining the maximum number of high-quality sperm from each collection. Care must be taken during each step of the AI process which is as follows:

1. Semen collection—accomplished by artificial vagina or electrojaculator methods, the latter of which can be used to collect semen from dairy bulls who have become crippled or have low sexual activity due to age. In beef, EJ is used to collect samples prior to the mating season and to check the quality of the bull's semen.
2. Laboratory analysis—to document volume, concentration, morphology, and sperm motility.
3. Dilution—with a buffer solution to prevent injury during freezing, to control bacterial contamination, and to maximize the number of doses from each collection.
4. Packing—in plastic straws and labeled with donor bull's full registration name, number, and company's name.
5. Storage—Straws are frozen in liquid nitrogen and can be stored indefinitely, enabling units to stockpile thousands of doses of a sire's semen, ensuring payback of the investment in the bull, even after he dies.
6. Insemination—Semen is carefully thawed and inserted in the cow's vagina. The cow must be in estrus (heat) at the time of insemination in order for conception to occur. Cows cycle every 21 days on average. AI results in a successful pregnancy about 60 percent of the time. In other words, an average of 1.6 inseminations per cow is required.

---

[3] "The Use of Artificial Insemination in Developing Countries," *Tenth International Congress on Animal Reproduction and Artificial Insemination*, June 10–14, 1984, Illinois.

EXHIBIT 7   World Farm Animal Statistics* by Selected Countries

Country	1,000 Head Cattle Total	1982 Statistics Dairy Cows	Sheep	FAO Estimates Pigs	Goats
World	1,257,489	217,471	1,145,547	767,849	474,640
Africa total	175,288	21,869	187,738	10,874	153,849
Canada	13,036	1,765	564	10,035	27
Cuba	6,200	750	365	2,000	101
Mexico	36,834	9,000	6,657	18,373	10,320
US	115,604	11,033	12,966	58,688	1,410
South America total	243,745	24,172	105,094	52,177	19,573
Argentina	52,717	3,050	30,401		
Brazil	123,488	14,500	18,000	33,500	
Columbia	24,495	2,600	2,749		
Uruguay	11,595	530	20,307		
China	55,328	730	109,466	298,528	78,441
India	181,540	25,600	41,700	8,600	77,500
Turkey	16,983	5,526	49,598	11	18,926
Europe total	133,281	49,963	142,287	177,057	12,347
Austria	2,530	973	194		
Belgium-Luxembourg	3,072	1,032	115		
Bulgaria	1,807	694	10,726		
Czechoslovakia	5,108	1,854	959		
Denmark	2,836	1,011	61		
Finland	N/A	683	104		
France	23,493	10,026	13,090		
Germany DR	5,745	2,118	2,169		
Germany FR	14,992	5,480	1,108		
Greece	N/A	340	8,316		
Hungary	1,945	666	3,137		
Ireland	6,688	1,458	3,476		
Italy	8,904	3,016	9,051		
Netherlands	5,241	2,430	776		
Poland	11,912	5,747	3,899		
Portugal	N/A	330	5,200		
Rumania	6,082	1,920	17,288		
Spain	5,074	2,031	17,133		
Sweden	1,938	666	430		
Switzerland	1,945	844	333		
UK	13,244	3,293	33,053		
Yugoslavia	5,464	2,730	7,398		
Australia	24,553	1,810	137,976	2,373	244
New Zealand	7,912	2,005	74,300	425	68
USSR	115,919	43,664	142,348	73,302	6,123

* *FAO Monthly Bulletin of Statistics*, Vol. 7, November 1984, Rome: Italy, Food and Agriculture Organization; United Nations.

USE OF AI IN OTHER FARM ANIMALS

Although AI has been used most extensively in dairy cattle, its use is becoming more widespread for genetic improvements in sheep, goats, swine, and poultry (see Exhibit 8). A new technique, whereby semen is deposited directly into the ewe's fallopian tube rather than in her

EXHIBIT 8   Artificial Insemination Statistics by Selected Countries (number of artificial breedings in recent years in thousands per year)

Country or region	Cattle	Sheep	Goats	Swine	Poultry*
Argentina	2,500	150			300
Brazil	2,000	525			1,200
Africa, (Botswana, Kenya, Egypt)	560				
Portugal, Spain	1,025				
Turkey, Greece	1,200	724	1.7	966	100
Eastern Europe	8,500	4,351	1.5	553.5	20
Scandinavia	3,200	2.7	1.4		
Austria, Belgium, France, UK, Denmark, France, UK, Ireland, Netherlands, Fed. Rep. of Germany, Switzerland	21,000	121.4	5.0	561.5	525
US, Canada	8,500			40	
USSR	30,000	50,000		2,400	10,000
China Statistics are not available, but AI is practised extensively on large dairy cattle farms.					

Trends in amount of AI with cattle in Europe 1949 - 1978

Number of inseminations in '000

22,000

15,000

7,500

0

1950   55   60   65   70   75   80

Frozen semen Solid CO2 refrigerant

Liquid nitrogen refrigerant

* Data are not complete for poultry, but it is a standard practice to use AI in large commercial breeding operations. The world total is approximately 150 million breedings per year.

EXHIBIT 9 Canadian Exports and Imports Semen (by selected country)

1983	Cattle	Swine
Canadian exports (doses) to:*		
Argentina	11,428	
Australia	75,600	3,285
Brazil	3,126	
Burma	21,560	
Columbia	11,612	
Czechoslovakia	2,520	
France	10,973	188
West Germany	108,181	
Great Britain	186,008	
Iran	63,894	
Italy	29,600	
Malaysia	10,400	120
Mexico	53,126	130
Netherlands	99,859	
New Zealand	23,476	
Philippines	18,000	
Switzerland	20,025	
USSR	96,526	
US	322,682	28
Venezuela	740	
Other	81,918	614
Total	1,251,354	4,365

Canadian exports ($)†		US exports‡	
Dairy semen	$10,621,000		
Other semen	1,715,000		
Total	$12,336,000	Total	$6,855,000

Canadian imports (doses) from:*	Cattle	Swine
Great Britain	640	
Australia	3,351	
Japan	25	
United States	228,439	60
Total	232,455	60
Canadian exports live cattle†	383,409 head;	$227,651,000

* Artificial Insemination in Canada: *Annual Report*, 1983 Agriculture Canada.
† Statistics Canada.
‡ United States Department of Agriculture.

vagina has improved the success of AI in sheep from 20 to 80 percent. A limited genetic base due to low numbers of domesticated sheep in North America has, however, limited the use of this procedure. Correspondingly, demand for AI services in sheep is relatively small in local markets.

AI is also limited in swine, because, as with the ewe, complicated reproductive systems create problems and render the procedure difficult. To complicate matters, boar semen can only be used in the fresh state.

Use of AI in breeding horses is limited because collection is extremely dangerous, the reproductive system is quite complicated, and registration of progeny resulting from AI is not allowed.

WESTERN BREEDERS SERVICES LTD.: AI ACTIVITIES AND OPPORTUNITIES

Western Breeders' traditional line of business, selling semen for AI and its related services to beef and cattle dairy owners accounted for approximately 75 percent of its revenues in 1984. It is from this product base that WBS has expanded and hopes to continue to grow.

THE MARKET

Western Canada

The absence of sales growth from beef and dairy semen over the past few years suggested to the directors of WBS that their existing market was saturated. Conversations with several Alberta farmers who use AI already use it on up to 100 percent of their lactating cows. This is particularly true of the elite breeders. On the other hand, among users of AI in beef operations, only about 15 percent of the lactating females would be serviced with AI. Logistics associated with breeding beef cattle prevent the owners from using AI on a larger scale. Increased revenues in this area, for any AI unit, depend upon their successful acquisition of a superior proven sire.

At WBS, they are hoping to increase semen sales by gaining new customers in their existing western Canadian markets. "We're in a mature industry," explained Don Dufault, "and our growth is going to be tied to population growth. There are three ways you can grow: with growth in the cattle population—which is tied to the Canadian population; by getting more people to use AI; or by taking business away from the competition."

Most dairy farmers use AI for their mature herd. They do not use AI in heifers (young cows bearing their first calf) because of management practices. AI requires more intensive management than does standard breeding. Western Breeders had nearly 80 percent of the AI market in their region. That is, they sold semen to 80 percent of the dairy farmers using AI in dairy herds. This accounted for about 60 percent of the cows kept on dairy farms.

Part of WBS' challenge is to convince beef breeders that AI is very necessary and worthwhile in the very competitive beef industry.

Beef AI

Stan Jones, a purebred Hereford breeder in Balzac, says he uses AI mostly to test new blood or to experiment on a high-ranking bull. Stan sites several problems or inconveniences associated with the use of AI on a beef herd. Firstly, it is too difficult and time consuming to check cows for estrus. For best results, cows should be inseminated within 12 hours of estrus. Thus, someone would have to check the cows at least twice a day. Unlike dairy cows which are, for the most part, kept inside barns and can easily be checked twice each day when they are milked, beef cattle roam the pastures and feed all day.

Stan had tried using some estrus-detecting aids, such as chin markers and paint balls, but this does not eliminate the task of checking the cows. He also tried to have his cows synchronized to come into estrus at the same time. However, the estrus-altering drugs affected his cows' cycles to such an extent that several of them were infertile for an entire season and just got fat in the pasture. He does not feel that enough is known about the drugs available, although the technology is advancing rapidly. The risks involved do not warrant the loss of a cow's productivity for a year.

The dryness of southern Alberta in the first half of the 1980s has provided another barrier to insemination for beef breeders. They have had to rotate the use of feed pastures to revitalize the soil. As a result, the herds have been kept further away from the farming operations wherever green pastureland is available.

AI is used most frequently for beef herd management by owners of smaller herds who utilize intensive management practices. These are most often the "elite" breeders whose goal is to achieve success in the show circuit. This does not necessarily mean that these breeders are after improved genetics. A filtering down process occurs through the other market segments—from the aspiring elite breeders who would like to be winners to the other purebred breeders and finally to the commercial operators. The difficulty is that a different set of criteria are used to evaluate the elite cattle which are used primarily for breeding stock as opposed to the commercial animals who must pass such traits as early calving, annual calving, calf size, etc. onto their daughters.

Dairy AI

Western Breeders has conducted research into the western Canada dairy semen market in an attempt to improve their position and realize growth. As with the beef market, dairy operators can be segmented into three distinct groups: the elite breeders, who make up 22 percent of the market; the mixed breeders with 41 percent; and commercial

EXHIBIT 10 Cattle Market Statistics, 1984

	Canada	Prairies	Alberta
Number of cattle	11,360,000	6,882,000	3,370,000
Dairy cows	1,731,000	411,000	157,000
Dairy heifers	665,100	125,000	45,000
Beef cows	3,236,100	2,660,000	1,290,000
Beef heifers	946,500	587,500	280,000

Number of Farms in Canada with Sales of
$2,500/year or more

	Canada	Prairies	Alberta
Dairy	41,905	7,514	2,743
Cattle	60,139	33,392	16,098
Livestock combined	9,054	5,727	2,515

SOURCE: Statistics Canada.

breeders with 37 percent. A survey conducted by WBS and directed toward these three segments indicated that most breeders are aware of WBS' products and services and hold the company in high regard. However, it also showed that dairymen are not particularly loyal to any one AI unit, preferring to use the company that can readily provide the desired product, at the desired time, for the lower price.[4] The elite breeders tend to be less price sensitive than the commercial breeders and are, correspondingly, more concerned about the quality of the product they are purchasing.

About 40 percent of the total dairy cow and heifer (first-service) population is bred by natural methods (the bull) rather than by AI. WBS currently estimates that it holds 80 percent of the AI market or 40 percent of the total potential market in the prairie provinces. The other 20 percent is supplied by competing AI units—the most predominant being the American Breeders Service (ABS) with about 10 to 15 percent of the market.

Each dairy herd is viewed as a potential customer. As noted previously, current users of AI use AI extensively on their herds. However, an opportunity does exist for WBS to sell present users better genetics at a higher price in order for dairymen to continue to improve their herds for the next generation. This, of course, is dependent upon WBL's ability to obtain superior proven sires. Exhibit 10 provides information on the Canadian beef and dairy semen market and Exhibit 11 presents WBS' semen sales.

As the Western Canadian Market will not be able to absorb all of the new sires WBL has in proving programs, new markets in Eastern Canada and export markets will have to be found over the next five

---

[4] "Marketing Plan, Western Breeders Services, Ltd., Prairie Provinces," D. Dufault, B. Kronemeyer, B. Moir, and W. Richardson, Winter 1986.

EXHIBIT 11 WBS Semen Sales (semen sold in the prairie provinces 1984)

	Dairy Semen	Beef Semen
Supplied by WBS' bulls	30,381 doses	23,000 doses
Sold by WBS for other suppliers	145,311	4,326
	175,692	27,326

Value of WBS' Semen Sales and Certificates by Territory
1984 in $000s

Domestic:			Export:		
	Alberta	$1,136		Semex & UK	$ 113
	Saskatchewan	477		USA	156
	Manitoba	423		Australia	36
	Total prairies	2,036		New Zealand	26
	B.C.	377		Semaltex	18
	Ontario	80		Total export	$ 316
	Quebec	14		Grand total	$2,849
	Maritimes	26			
	Total B.C. & East	497		Maple Leaf Genetics Inc.	
	Total Canada	$2,533		U.S. Dairy	$1,000

years. WBS plans to continue advertising and promoting their bulls through their association with other AI units in Canada and the Canadian export consortium, Semex. Semex represents WBL and the other Canadian AI units in such countries as Africa, China, Japan, the USSR, and the European Commonwealth. Semex distributes mainly dairy semen to these markets. Prior to the inception of Semex, WBS had made its own distribution arrangements in Australia, New Zealand, and through Semaltex, its own distribution entity, in South Central America and Mexico. Semaltex markets only beef semen for WBS. Sales of dairy semen to these countries are accomplished through Semex. Finally, WBL has established a subsidiary company to market dairy semen through the United States. This company represents semen from Western, as well as the other units in Canada with which it holds distribution agreements.

Sales through Semaltex have fallen off over recent years due to the serious foreign exchange problems experienced by the South American countries and Mexico. As Don says, "They can't afford to pay their bills." The majority of this market is made up of elite breeders who are interested in winning on the show circuit. Therefore, they are less price sensitive and want the best quality semen available.

Western has already been very successful in U.S. markets. Through their subsidiary company in Illinois, Maple Leaf Genetics Incorporated (MGI), they have sold over 70,000 units of dairy semen worth over $1 million during their first year of operation, 1984. They were able to achieve such success in their first year of business because they acquired a network of 150 dealers and distributors from an existing Minnesota firm, rather than starting from scratch. Western sells beef semen directly to the United States and sold $156,000 worth in 1984. They plan to use MGI's extensive distribution system to expand their U.S. beef semen sales.

The popularity of Canadian cattle in the United States, in particular dairy cattle, is due to Canada's advanced and well-balanced genetic improvement programs. Don Dufault explained the difference between Canadian and American genetics: "The United States's concentration over the last 10 to 15 years has been very highly centered toward milk production—without comparative improvement in physical characteristics of the animal—conformation, structure, strength, feet, and legs. So 15 years later you end up with a lot of cows that will produce a lot of milk, but won't last for more than two lactations because they're not strong enough to maintain that high volume of milk production. They've got narrow chests, they're shaped like pyramids and they've got poor feet. Our program is aimed at making more inroads into that particular weakness that American AI units have boxed themselves into."

Australia is another market that holds a great deal of promise for WBL. Canada's very high health standards have provided an international competitive advantage and have opened up opportunities for exporting genetics.

Exhibit 11 provides information on WBL's sales to eastern Canada and B.C. (through other AI units) and to their international markets.

PRICING

One of the major risks associated with the AI business centers is the pricing of semen. "If you price a bull too high, too fast," explained Don, "you'll kill his marketability. It's happened more than once where AI units get greedy. All of a sudden they see demand for a newly proven bull is fantastic and they'll price him about $10 higher than what they should. Everything stops. And then they don't know what to do anymore because they can't bring the price down. People are just not interested because it's very much ingrained in their minds that price is equal to quality."

Retail price is fixed for all semen sold by WBS that originates from bulls not owned by Western. These prices are negotiated between WBS and its suppliers so that virtually any Canadian buying a specific bull's semen from any AI unit will pay the same price. WBS has found that reductions in price may even lead to a decrease in demand because of the perceived price-quality relationship. Currently, WBS is selling its semen for an average blend price per unit of just under $10. Prices range from a low of $5 per unit to a high of $250. An additional amount of $25 to $150 is charged if a certificate is required for registration purposes.

In contrast to the pricing of semen, the pricing of services and secondary products is extremely competitive. For example, the WBS market report states that: "Our major competitor makes it a practice of undercutting WBS in the price it charges for services and secondary products. For example, the competition positions liquid nitrogen as a loss leader by pricing nitrogen at or below what we believe to be its cost. The competition also waits until WBS publishes its AI course schedule and then offers a similar course a week or two earlier at a slightly reduced price. This helps build rapport with dairymen and increases the perceived value of services."[5]

PRODUCT

WBS had an "inventory" of about 55 unproven Holstein sires in 1985. If several of these bulls are found to have highly marketable traits once they are proven, WBS could increase its beef or dairy AI market shares. The "inventory" of beef sires is 25–35, representing 10 or so different breeds.

WBS either leases or purchases their bulls, depending upon their market potential and/or what can be negotiated with the pure-bred breeder. As a general rule, Holstein bulls are purchased and beef bulls are leased, although Western does purchase beef bulls if they fall within purchasing guidelines.

Because the cost of maintaining and building up an inventory of sires is "horrendous"—it costs about $1,825/year to keep a bull—Western established a bull pool in 1983. The pool started with 25 of Western's Holstein bulls scheduled to get their proofs between 1984 and 1988. They sold 40 percent shares in the bulls for $8,000. With 110 limited partners participating, they raised $880,000. Canadian tax law provides incentives for individuals making such investments. For example, in a 50 percent tax bracket, an investor could write off $4,000 of the $8,000 investment at the time it is made. "The return is really long term," Don conceded, "but the banks are really not into this kind of lending. They just don't provide that service, and we needed to build up our capital base." The minimum cost to produce one proven bull is $50,000.[6]

Based on 25 bulls and a national average of 1 in 10 bulls being superior, projections given to investors were that at least 3 of the bulls

---

[5] Ibid.

[6] Charles Hickman, "Artificial Insemination in Livestock," *Ceres* 16, no. 5 (September–October 1983), FAO, Via delle Terme di Caracolla 00100, Rome, Italy.

would be superior. Don believes that "We can do better than that. It all boils down to the capability of people involved in trying to select out of the large North American population which sires are going to be superior. And we think we've got the best guy in Canada doing the selecting." Don figured that, at the optimistic end of the spectrum, "7 or 8 or even 10 will come out superior." In 1987 or 1988 Western plans to make a similar offering with 25 more bulls. Good results from the first pool would encourage further investment.

The importance of bringing up superior sires through their organization is reinforced by the fact that Western's top 20 sires represent about 80 percent of their business. Lack of growth in Canadian semen sales over the past few years has made the market very competitive and Don says, "If we had better bulls we might be able to make inroads in other parts of Canada and certainly in export markets."

Standard procedure at WBS is to collect 10,000 to 20,000 doses of semen from a young sire, and store those until the bull is proven four to six years later. For example, dairy sires are proven when their daughters reproduce and begin lactating, which is in the fifth year following breeding. About 6 to 12 months before a bull is officially proven, WBS would start building up the bull's semen bank, raising his inventory to 30,000 doses. If he obtained a good proof, collections of up to 4,000 doses per month would continue over the bull's remaining lifespan of four or five years. Exhibit 12 describes how beef bulls are ranked from their proofs and Exhibit 2 is an example of one of WBS' bulls out of their beef sire directory. Exhibit 13 gives the results of a comparative study of AI units entered into the Canadian Holstein Young Sire Proving Program. This exhibit shows that although WBL has entered relatively few sires, the genetics of these sires as measured by their pedigree indexes for fat, milk, and type are superior.

A related service WBS offers its customers is custom collection and private semen storage. WBS will also market semen through all its distribution channels for private individuals. This is a fairly popular customer service because it is used as an alternative to costly mortality insurance for private bull owners. If the bull dies, the owner can still market its genetics, which may in fact increase in value after the bull is dead. As demand for this type of service is expected to continue to grow in the years to come, and customer loyalty is strong, WBS hopes to increase its market share from its 1984 levels, estimated at 50 percent.

DISTRIBUTION

In terms of distribution systems, Don describes the AI units in Canada as a network of supermarkets. For example, if someone comes to WBS and asks for a bull owned by an AI unit in another province, Western

EXHIBIT 12 Canadian Beef Sire Monitoring Program

Trait	*Number of Progeny*	*Predicted Difference*	*Repeatability*	*Rank*
Refers to economic trait evaluation.	Reference included for weaning weight only.	The sire's performance proof appears under PD (Predicted Difference). Each proof estimates the genetic worth transmitted by a bull to its progeny for a given trait, in comparison to the average bull of the breed whose data is included in the summary.	The repeatability indicates how accurate the proof estimate is.	The rank for each bull is computed among all bulls listed by breed and by trait.

Trait	Number of Progeny	Predicted Difference	Repeatability	Rank
Calving ease	295	− 1	87%	313/514
Weaning weight		+26 lbs.	94	17/724
Yearling weight		+30 lbs.	94	32/646

a. Calving ease proofs are expressed as deviations from the breed average. Therefore a bull with a zero proof has an average genetic worth for calving ease in its breed. A producer using a bull with a plus proof for calving ease can expect a lower incidence of calving problems than he would from using an average bull of the same breed in his herd.

b. These proofs are expressed in pounds of gain from birth to weaning or birth to yearling. A producer using a bull with a +26 pounds in the PD column for weaning weight can expect the calves from this bull to gain 26 pounds or more on average than would the calves from an average bull of the same breed in his herd with a PD of 0 pounds. Yearling weight proofs can be interpreted similarly.

c. A proof is only an estimate of the genetic worth of a bull. The repeatability indicates how accurate this estimate is. The repeatability ranges from 0 to 100% and depends on the number of progeny per bull, their distribution across herds and the heritability of the trait. The higher the repeatability, the more accurate and stable the proof. A repeatability of 70% means that 70% of the variation in the true genetic worth of a bull is explained by its proof. If you decide to breed your whole herd to one proven bull, it is recommended that you choose one with both a high proof and a high repeatability.

d. Ranking is very important to consider when selecting a bull. The rank of each bull is computed among all bulls listed, separately for each breed and trait. You can use these rankings to select a bull that suits your goals. If you wish to improve calving ease in your herd, look at the rank for calving ease first. You can probably find a high-ranking bull for calving ease with an acceptable growth proof. If growth is what you are looking for, select a high-ranking bull for gain to weaning and gain to yearling, but stay away from very low ranking bulls for calving ease.

EXHIBIT 13 Canadian Holstein Young Sire Proving Program

	No. Sires Entered in		Pedigree Index		
Supplier	1983	1984	Milk	Fat	Type
BACI	21		3.95	5.43	4.48
		23	6.70	6.00	4.14
WBL	10		4.50	4.40	5.70
		14	6.00	7.28	5.92
NSAB	5		0.00	2.40	5.00
		8	4.38	4.88	6.25
EBI	33		5.03	5.36	5.33
		31	5.51	6.13	5.39
UBI	38		2.11	3.76	6.13
		49	3.25	3.86	6.02
WOBI	32		1.41	2.34	6.38
		37	1.65	3.62	7.08
CIAQ	105		4.67	4.22	3.67
		99	5.79	5.67	3.73
NBAB	8		1.25	0.25	5.50
		10	2.60	3.90	6.20
St. Jacobs	7		0.29	2.29	5.29
		5	0.20	2.00	8.75
Total	259	276			
Year proof expected	1986/87	1987/88			

This table is intended to show that on average young sires now on test are expected to be genetic improvers when returned to service since there is a high correlation between pedigree indexes and final proof.

SOURCE: A study of alternative genetic improvement programs for the Atlantic Provinces by Drs. E. B. Burnside, B. W. Kennedy, and Mr. H. M. Wilson, M.Sc., September 1985.

---

can get it for them. During the 1984 fiscal year, WBS sold 175,692 doses of dairy semen in western Canada, but only 17 percent of this came from WBS' own bulls. The remainder came from other Canadian AI units, with WBS taking an agreed-upon markup. WBS sold 27,326 doses of beef semen in western Canada, 85 percent of which came from their own bulls.

Several distributors operate in the prairie provinces through whom WBS distributes semen. WBS gives these distributors a 20 percent discount off retail prices which cuts into WBS' already slim margins. This group as a whole tends to be order takers and relies exclusively on WBS to create demand for the product through advertising and promotion. Many distributors also sell semen from the competition, and as a result, are not exclusively loyal to WBS.[7]

---

[7] "Marketing Plan, Western Breeders Services, Ltd., Praire Provinces," D. Dufault, B. Kronemeyer, B. Movi, W. Richardson, Winter 1986.

The transportation mode used to deliver semen depends on the distances involved. In western Canada, the semen can travel with regularly scheduled buses, or by diesel trucks on WBS' own bimonthly run through the prairies. For other points in Canada or the United States, most shipments travel by air, although bus delivery is used if the cost savings more than offset the added time of delivery. Export orders to overseas markets in Europe, South America, or the Pacific Rim are usually shipped by air. Adequate transportation insurance is carried on all shipments to cover losses resulting from breakage or loss of nitrogen due to accidents, loss of volume in the tank, and similar unforeseen events.

PROMOTION

WBS' prime method of promotion is via personal sales calls to various farms in the prairies by Western's own salespeople or by their distributors. Calls are made at eight-week intervals to these farms. During that time, perhaps one or two other competing AI unit representatives will call on these same farms. This is in contrast to the six or seven reps that may call on the average farm in the United States.

WBS relies on the other AI units in B.C., Ontario, Quebec, and the Maritimes to promote its semen; however, these units do rely on WBS' catalogs and product information to advertise their sires.

International marketing efforts also utilize WBS' catalogs and product information to promote their semen. In countries such as the United States, Australia, and New Zealand, WBS has appointed one or more local distributors to market semen on its behalf. Promotion is also accomplished by export organizations such as Semex.

Advertising includes direct ads placed in magazines and breeder journals, catalogs, and one-page flyers printed in-house or by using outside printers, radio spots, and other incidentals. Full-time marketing staff always attend major agricultural shows and fairs in western Canada where they display WBS products and services at a specially designed booth. Advertising expenditures amounted to over $183,000 in 1984.

THE COMPETITION

As a result of WBS having negotiated and obtained exclusive distribution rights throughout the prairie provinces from all the major suppliers in the other provinces, the competition within the target market has been restricted to American Breeders Services Ltd. (ABS) and a few small independent companies. Indirect competition does, however, exist among all AI units in the sense that each unit competes to produce the greatest number of sires with the best proofs in order to stimulate demand for their own unit sire's semen at the farm level.

EXHIBIT 14 Semex Canada Total Semen Sales, Fiscal Year 1983–84*

Unit	Number Doses	Amount
Cattle		
BCAI	63,587	$ 488,949
CIAQ	244,992	2,918,974
EBI	203,865	1,734,608
NBAB	18,563	105,833
NSAB	1,334	7,832
St. Jacobs	47,962	299,260
UBI	177,673	3,100,894
WBL	24,777	146,160
WOBI	135,779	1,190,400
Universal	110	2,965
Other & private	3,779	114,553
Total	922,421	$10,110,430

Note: Semex sells the greatest number of doses to the following countries: West Germany, United Kingdom, USSR, Netherlands, Switzerland, Mexico, Italy, Iran, and Australia.

* October 1, 1983, to September 30, 1984.

SOURCE: Semex *Annual Report*.

American Breeders Services Ltd. (ABS)

ABS is Western's major competitor with sales in the $2.0–$2.4 million range. It tends to carry higher priced semen with an average price per dose of $12. ABS is the largest AI unit in the United States and it "proves out as many bulls as all of Canada," says Dufault. "They're all over the United States and they've got a truck run (transporting semen) coming through Alberta. But ABS' program is different from the Canadian program and this (better genetics) is why we've been quite successful in the United States in competing against ABS and others."

Canadian competitors are mostly either government or cooperative member owned. In fact, WBL is the only privately owned unit among the group of majors with which it holds distribution agreements. The list that follows indicates who these other units are and where they operate. Again, refer to Exhibit 13 for comparisons on how these units rate in terms of sires entered into the Holstein Young Sire Proving Program and how their genetics compare. Exhibit 14 shows contributions to Semex's export sales by unit. This exhibit also illustrates that relatively low priced semen is marketed through Semex supplied from the substantial inventories of the various units.

Eastern Breeders Inc. (EBI). Located in Kemptville, Ontario, EBI operates under a provincial licensing agreement and supplies the northeast quadrant of the province.

United Breeders Inc. (UBI). Located in Guelph, Ontario, and services the south-central region of the province under license.

Western Ontario Breeders Inc. (WOBI). Operating out of Woodstock, WOBI services western Ontario, also under license.

Centre d'Insemination Artificielle du Quebec (CIAQ)

New Brunswick Central Artificial Breeding Cooperative (NBAB)

British Columbia Artificial Insemination Centre (BCAI)

Nova Scotia Animal Breeders Co-op Ltd. (NSAB)

Independent Units

A number of smaller units cover the remainder of the market and are in direct competition with WBL in the prairies.

Independent Breeders Services (IBS). Located in Airdrie, Alberta, five miles north of WBS, IBS competes with WBL mainly in the beef area. They do not own their own sires, but rather lease them and promote their semen. IBS is service oriented and specializes in custom collection.

Universal Semen Services Ltd. (UBS). Located in Cardston, Alberta, UBS has some of their own dairy sires. They also compete with WBL in custom beef-semen collection services.

Saskatchewan Artificial Breeders Cooperative Ltd. (SABC). Operating out of Yorkton, Saskatchewan, SABC is involved in the custom collection and sales of beef semen.

In addition to these units is a small independent organization operating in Ontario (St. Jacob's Artificial Breeding Cooperative) and three other units specializing in fresh swine semen collection and AI only; Centre d'Insemination Porcine du Quebec, Ontario Swine AI Association, and the Alberta Agriculture Swine AI Centre in Leduc.

EMBRYO TRANSFER: BACKGROUND INFORMATION

A major boon to the genetic improvement industry involving advanced breeding techniques is embryo transfer (ET). This technique is very useful for export purposes as the cost of transporting embryos is far below the cost of transporting live cattle and bypasses the costly quarantine period. There was virtually no commercial activity in this area before 1972. By 1979, the North American industry was generating revenues of $20 million a year from the 140-odd companies involved. The Science Council of Canada predicts that "by 1995 . . . genetic stock enhancements through embryo transplants will affect 30 percent of cattle."[8] According to the best predictions, the exportation of embryos—of goats, sheeps, swine, as well as cattle—is likely to grow to a billion dollar a year business (in North America) within the decade.[9] Several aspects of embryo transfer are in need of additional research, although the increased demand has accelerated the research process. For example, it is now possible using microsurgical methods to divide single cattle embryos into identical twins—a process called twinning.

Approximately 22,000 embryos were transferred in Canada in 1984, 7,000 of which were transferred in Alberta. Although this represents less than 1 percent of the total calves born in a given year, its popularity is increasing rapidly. The cost of an embryo transfer in 1981 came to about $2,500 per recipient. By 1985 that cost dropped to $800. As new technology leads to higher success rates and simplified procedures, embryo transfer will become less expensive and therefore more attractive to many breeders.

The Embryo Transfer Procedure

The commercial success of embryo transfer is dependent upon the successful combination of superovulation (stimulating the donor cow with drugs and hormones, resulting in the production of up to 12 ova on average instead of the usual 1) and artificial insemination. Several high-quality embryos can be retrieved from a donor cow after an AI service by a nonsurgical procedure called flushing. Fresh embryos can be stored for a few days, or frozen indefinitely in liquid nitrogen as is semen. About one third of the embryos, however, are damaged in the freezing and thawing process.[10] As many as 50 offspring from one cow are possible.

The purpose of embryo transfer is to increase the reproductive rates of valuable donor cows through less valuable recipient cows. However, the recipient cow must also possess certain desirable traits, such as ease of calving, adequate milk production, freedom from disease, and fertility. The largest cost of ET is in producing a suitable recipient and maintaining her in a nonpregnant state until an embryo is available for transfer. Because recipient cows are likely to develop infections, antibiotics are often used.

---

[8] David Helwig, "Selling Life," *Canadian Business Magazine,* vol. 59 (no. 11), November 1986.

[9] Harris Brotman, "Frozen Embryos Boost Beef, Milk," *New York Times,* April 17, 1983.

[10] George E. Seidel, Jr., *Science,* vol. 211 (no. 23), January 1981.

Commercial Applications of Embryo Transfer

The most important use of ET is to increase the number of progeny a valuable donor cow is capable of producing. By combining both the genetics of superior dams and sires, and duplicating these matches through ET, the rate of genetic improvement in a herd is accelerated. As George Seidel writes in his embryo transfer article, "Although artificial insemination usually is the method of choice for introducing new genetic material into indigenous cattle, it is slower than embryo transfer because three generations are required to produce an animal with seven eighths of the genetic makeup of the new breed. On the other hand, embryo transfer is considerably slower than importing breeding adults, if they survive."

Donor dams are usually chosen on the basis of anticipated commercial value of the calves rather than on the basis of direct genetic considerations. However, the rapid multiplication of scarce valuable cattle can oversaturate the market and decrease the profitability of the animal.

Another important use of ET is to obtain progeny from cows with certain types of infertility or injuries, namely valuable cows that can produce normal ova but cannot maintain a pregnancy.

In export markets, an added advantage to the low transportation costs is that the transferred embryos receive passive immunity to the specific country's bacteria through the first milk of the recipient cow. In this way, they are not as susceptible as exported cattle are to foreign diseases.

A secondary use of ET for commercial operations is testing bulls for undesirable traits. A cow with superior genes is superovulated and inseminated with the test bull's semen. The calves can be checked for many traits at 60 days of gestation. The recipient cows can be slaughtered at that time to speed up the test without harming the valuable donor. ET also allows for sex identification of the embryos when only six days old. Thus, if a breeder wanted to produce only superior females for his dairy herd, he could do so, without tying up his cows in the production of less desirable males.

ET has gained wider acceptance in beef than in dairy genetic improvement programs. Beef cows are easier to take out of production for embryo flushing, and there are far more beef cattle than dairy in production with a correspondingly broader selection of breeds. Beef breeders tend to be more speculative and entrepreneurial in their operations because the traits upon which beef cattle are judged tend to be more subjective, rather than the quantifiable milk production criteria dairy cows are judged by. Finally, a U.S. tax incentive program supported research into ET in beef. No such incentives were offered for dairy ET research because of the huge surplus of milk and milk products on the American market.

WESTERN BREEDERS SERVICES LTD.: ET ACTIVITIES AND OPPORTUNITIES

During late 1982, Western Breeders set up an embryo production and quarantine facility called Western Embryos. The first successful transfers of frozen embryos from this facility were completed in New Zealand in 1984 through a joint venture agreement with Masterbreeds, a company with offices in the United States, Australia, and New Zealand. Western is now negotiating embryo sales to such countries as China, the USSR, Hungary, and Czechoslovakia. An exceptional conception rate of 57 percent based on 63 pregnancies resulting from 111 frozen embryos exported was achieved by the end of 1984. Western's involvement in these exports contributed about $33,000 to their revenues in 1984.

Embryo transfer is a new product line which is a step away from the high-volume, low-ticket items that Western is accustomed to marketing. Costs to farmers of embryo transfers can range anywhere up to $3,500, depending on the program. The higher prices are due to the incorporation of superior genetics from both the male (based on his semen value) and the female. WBS has access to an extensive semen supply through their AI operations but must identify and lease superior females for the procedure.

Because of the high cost to farmers, the domestic market is very small, and Western does not deal in fresh embryo transfers locally. Domestic ET is generally left with the veterinarians or with Alberta Livestock Transplants Ltd. ALT operates on the forefront of embryo technology and supplies ET services to both the Canadian and U.S. markets, although they are expanding into foreign markets as well. Bovatech, another ET facility in Alberta, also possesses the required technical expertise. Both Bovatech and ALT have been involved in joint ventures with WBS and other facilities in the production of embryos to complete Canadian export contracts.

On world markets, Canadian embryos are gaining popularity. Exporting embryos is much less expensive than exporting live cattle, especially where air freight is involved. Trucking live cattle to the United States and through to Mexico, however, is still relatively cost effective. Western's 1985 business plan asserts that "Canada's genetics are in demand worldwide but the cost of shipping live cattle is often prohibitive. Frozen embryos can be obtained for a fraction of the cost and enormous potential exists in the field now that the technology of producing and freezing embryos is commercially viable." Selling to international markets does have its difficulties, however, especially if the country's agricultural practices are less sophisticated than ours, as is often the case. For ET to be widely accepted, the farmers must be educated on the benefits of ET as well as implantation procedures. ET is just one aspect of improved herd management through the introduction of superior genetics. Essential to the success of any improvement program is a complete and accurate record-keeping system to document gains and identify areas of weakness in the program.

Western's role in the New Zealand project was that of a middleman, to bring the buyer who was looking for superior genetics in touch with the seller. As Don describes, "Once the transaction was negotiated, they needed a place to quarantine the animals and somebody to manage the contract on their behalf. So we became the buyer's agent in Canada and our role was to make sure the cattle are maintained, quarantined, embryos collected, and for that we have our costs plus we get a management fee plus a percentage of the genetics." Western also used their expertise in freezing, storing, shipping, and insuring the embryos to facilitate the transaction.

The success of the New Zealand project was the direct result of extensive marketing efforts which secured the support of the Ninth World Hereford Conference. The conference, which was held in New Zealand, permitted the public auction of the embryos. The sale was well received because of the integrity of the breeding establishments involved. The results of the project were summarized in a management report: "The image portrayed in Australasia that Western Breeders is the firm to contact has already provided us with a number of inquiries for the forthcoming collection season." Exhibit 15 provides a cost breakdown for the New Zealand project as well as revenues for the first batch of exports.

Western Breeders has been particularly interested in securing a position in the Chinese market in 1985. Says Don Dufault, "China has an export market at the moment. It's one of those markets where there is so much potential that everyone is scrambling to get into it." Don traveled to China several times in 1984 in an effort to finalize an agreement with a potential Chinese partner. The joint venture would involve dairy and beef embryos as well as technology transfer.

CIDA (the Canadian International Development Agency) has been supportive of marketing efforts in China. By selling embryos and technology to the Chinese, a superior base of breeding stock can be established in one generation. These bulls and dams will be used to provide improved genetics to the various commercial herds. As the Chinese upgrade their herds, they will demand more superior genetics from Canada in the form of export semen and embryos. Many of the Chinese herdsmen are nomadic and their farming practices are vastly different than ours. Alberta Agriculture has been working on rangeland crop improvement programs in Alberta's sister province in north-

---

EXHIBIT 15 Embryo Transfer

Cost Estimate: Production of Frozen Embryos for Export from Canada to Australia and New Zealand

Assumptions:
1. New Zealand health protocol requires quarantine and testing 30 days prior to and 60 days after collection.
2. Each donor will produce an average of 10 embryos from 3 attempts at embryo collection.
3. Cost estimates based on 5 donors.
4. Variable costs of genetic material are not included.

Estimates: (per donor)		
1.	Housing and feeding under quarantine 210 days @ $10.00/day.	$2,100.00
2.	Health test.	400.00
3.	Embryo collection and freezing.	2,085.00
4.	Shipping 10 embryos @ $15.00.	150.00
5.	Insurance (assume embryo value of $5,000 each. If 5% premium, cost per embryo is $25).	250.00
	Total cost per donor (10 embryos)	$4,985.00 CON

Results of Initial Shipment of Embryos to New Zealand

Results based on: 60 embryos frozen
10 lost due to vials exploding in freezing
17 rejected upon post thaw examination
33 embryos transferred
9 pregnancies resulted

Total revenues	$750,000
Sales and promotion	25%
Genetics (dams or semen)	25%
Embryo production	50%

SOURCE: Masterbreeds Consultants, WBS, company memos.

ern China. The big problem in penetrating the Chinese market is in the lack of health protocol standards for imports. Therefore, extensive testing and quarantine of the dams is required. Canada is now negotiating what they hope will be a workable agreement with the Chinese. Competitors in the field of embryo sales to China include countries with advanced genetics, such as the United States, Great Britain, Holland, Belgium, and New Zealand. Don describes the process of marketing to countries with centrally planned economies as being long and trying, but one that can generate rewards in terms of large ongoing sales contracts once approved. For example, an agreement with Russia is now underway, following one and a half years of negotiation. Agriculture Canada and the Russian agriculture officials first met to discuss embryo technology. An exchange program was arranged whereby the Russians visited ET facilities and farms here, while the Canadians toured Russian operations. Eventually an agreement was struck and foreign exchange details were worked out between governments allowing for the commencement of Canadian shipments. Also in the Eastern Block, negotiations with Hungary and Czechoslovakia have included field trials of the ET procedure in Hungary. The Hungarians appear to possess the technological abilities to thaw and transplant the embryos shipped from Canada and are expected to provide this technology to the Czechoslovaks.

In countries which operate under the free-enterprise system, the marketing procedure is considerably different. Primary research in the target country is carried out by WBS staff. Breeding associations are contacted for their membership lists, government agricultural agencies are approached, trade journals are searched for advertisements and information about various breeders, and finally, select breeders are approached and negotiations initiated.

Sales of embryos to developing countries have not as yet been pursued. Semex markets semen to those countries and, consequently, WBS does not have any direct contacts on which to build. Many of the developing countries are so behind in the technology that it still takes major efforts by governments and industry to educate the farmers in the use of herd improvement techniques.

Western has utilized their semen distribution network and contacts in Australia and New Zealand to promote their embryos. Likewise, since Semaltex is still active in Latin America, WBS may choose to introduce embryos through that agency when the foreign exchange situation turns around.

Western expects embryo sales to increase by about a factor of five in 1985 and to average 25 percent growth in the following five or six years. To accommodate this forecast growth in their export trade, Western is investigating the possibility of building a dairy barn. "At the moment," Don Dufault explained, "most of the embryo work has been done with beef cattle because it is easier to take a beef cow out of production than a dairy cow. There are no embryo facilities available for dairy cattle where you can take a cow out of her herd of origin, put her into a quarantine facility, and milk her twice a day all the while that you are flushing her."

In order for a cow to get an official production record, she must be milked twice a day.

> A purebred breeder who has a superior cow is reluctant to put that cow out anywhere because he wants to maintain her production. He wants to make sure she has her record because that's the basis on which she is going to be able to show people that are interested in her calves that she is a superior animal. We have to be sensitive to that so when the cow comes to our place she is given classy treatment and treated just like she would be at home. But that's the major thrust I think we are going to move into in the next couple of years—to build a dairy barn—or rent one—

where we can bring in the high genetic cows in the province—what we call our home market, even B.C.—into this quarantine facility so we can collect those embryos for export markets.

It's a bit of a risky venture because you never know once you have collected an embryo and tested the cow and the sire for all the diseases whether that embryo will qualify for export markets in a year or three or four from now. So it's hard to bank embryos ahead of time because these regulations change. You play your game as you go along. You can put $150,000 into a new barn and produce all the cows you want, but if your product doesn't qualify under health regulations for export markets, you're out of luck. All you can do is sell them back to the domestic market.

FARM COMPUTERS: BACKGROUND INFORMATION

Alberta is one of two provinces in Canada that has a specialized farm computer department within its farm business management branch, the Department of Agriculture. The purpose of the department is to provide information and educational services to farmers in an effort to foster farm computer utilization through home study courses, publications, newsletters, and support of regional rural "computer fairs."

A 1983 survey indicated that approximately 5 percent of the 45,000 farms in Alberta having sales of $7,500 or more per annum owned personal computers and used them in their farm management programs. At the time of the survey, a further 20 percent of the farms said they expected to own a computer within three years. More conservative estimates suggest an actual ownership rate of between 12 and 15 percent by 1986.[11]

Microcomputers first became available in 1979 but it wasn't until 1983 to 1984 that sales began to take off. The reason for the delay was the large gap in knowledge between sellers and users and the lack of software on the market applicable to farm use.

The three most commonly used applications for farm computers in 1983 were firstly basic accounting functions, secondly for physical recordkeeping, and thirdly for word processing. With more specialized software packages coming on the market and prices dropping, applications for farm management are being purchased and utilized. These packages include such management functions as:

- Feed lot management for beef cattle.
- Crop production and marketing.
- Dairy herd management including production and breeding performance.
- Swine management programs.

---

[11] Bruce Waldi, Farm Business Management Branch, Alberta Agriculture, Olds, Alberta.

Another advantage of owning a farm computer is that a telephone linkup is possible with the Grassroots system. Grassroots is the Canadian agricultural videotex system offered by Infomart, a company owned by Southam and Torstar Corporation. Information is available through the system in several agricultural categories, such as weather, crop markets, livestock markets, farm management, special crops, chemicals, seed and feed, and the like. Unfortunately, much of the data is oriented to the Manitoba farmer as Grassroots is marketed through the Manitoba Telephone System. Another criticism is that many of the farm management programs that Grassroots offers are too simplistic and that independent specialized software packages are far superior.[12]

Until a few years ago, farmers were faced with the option of writing their own software for farm management applications or simply utilizing the basic business programs on the market. Several competing firms have recently entered the market with specialized farm management packages. Exhibit 16 is a condensed version of software offerings and prices.

WESTERN FARM COMPUTERS: ACTIVITIES AND OPPORTUNITIES

In April 1983, Western Breeders became the exclusive distributor for Homestead Farm Management Systems Limited in Alberta and B.C. Under WBL's western farm computers division, they sell IBM microcomputers and Homestead software directly to dairymen, ranchers, and grain operators throughout the two western provinces. WBL also gets royalties from Homestead every time a computer system is sold in Saskatchewan or Manitoba because their 20,000 catalogs which are distributed in western Canada contain Homestead advertising. Don Dufault described the computer as "a product that we've identified as being very easy to introduce. The customer base that we have in beef and dairy is the type of person that would buy a computer."

Nevertheless, this high-tech product line also represents a break from Western's traditional low-price, high-volume AI products, and initial response has been slow. Don Dufault explained: "This is a new kind of product that has a certain life cycle. We're in the innovative stage and our sales are not as high as they could be because we're still talking to people who don't know anything about computers. They know what they'd like to do. They're not sure that the computer will do it—they're looking around to see if anyone else in their area has one. So over the last three years we've been selling primarily to inno-

---

[12] "Compu Farm," Best of volumes 1–4, Agdex 818–23, Alberta Agriculture, Farm Business Management Branch, February 1985.

EXHIBIT 16 Farm Computer Software Comparisons

	Advanced Ag, Swine Brdg, Herd Mgt.	Agpro Dairy Herd Mgt.	Basic Business Systms, Crop, Land, Commodit.	Countryside Beef Cow/Calf Herd Mgt.	Countryside Hog Mgt.	Cutlass Herd Mgt. System	Dawson, Dau, Feedlot Mgt	Homestead Beef Herd Record Keeping	Homestead Dairy Herd Mgt. System	Homestead Crop Record Keeping	Homestead Feedlot Record Keeping	Marshall Dairy Mgt	Cattle Admin. Solutions
Dealer/manufacturer in Alta.	*					*	*	*	*	*	*	*	*
Training provided	*			*	*	*	*	*	*	*	*		*
Hardware: Apple II													
Commodore 64, 8000	*	*	*		*	*							*
IBM PC			*			*		*	*	*	*	*	*
other	*		*										*
Cost	$795	$1,200	$500	$550	$550	$1,495	$500	$1,000	$2,500	$1,000	$1,000	$1,150	$1,890
Cow/calf management programs													
Animal identification	*			*		*		*					
Breeding records	*			*		*							
Production records	*					*		*					
Reports	*			*		*		*					
Crop management programs			*							*			
Dairy management programs													
Animal identification									*			*	
Breeding records									*			*	
Production records									*			*	
Health records									*			*	
Reports									*			*	
Feedlot management programs		*					*				*		*
Swine management programs	*				*								

January 1985. Note: Tables are incomplete; software packages should be compared by feature for each function.

SOURCE: "Physical Record Keeping Software," Alberta Agriculture, AGDEX 818–26.

vative types." Sales in 1984 totaled $154,000—six times the 1983 sales.

Keith Jones graduated from the University of Alberta in 1982 with an agriculture degree. He is running a farm near Balzac with his mother and brother, as well as acting as a dealer for the Homestead computer package. He agrees that word of mouth is a very important selling tool for farm computers because "so much of farm business is built on reputation."

The directors at Western realized this and in 1985 were able to put testimonials about their computers in a company brochure. "With these testimonials," says Don Dufault, "we can maybe appeal to the early adoptors and laggars. But by then we'll have much more competition in the market. At the moment, we're fairly unique."

Keith Jones also discussed the difficulty most farmers have finding sufficient time to learn how to operate a computer. He suggested that when home computers first became popular in the early 1980s, a lot of farmers in western Canada bought them. They were never taught how to use them properly, however, and as a result, many computers are now sitting idle. He said those farmers who have the computers set up are pleased with the results; they feel computers are beneficial to their operations.

Most of Western's computer sales have been through direct retailing at their Balzac office. Sales are not accomplished through their semen distribution network. They do limited volumes through dealers because "they are not sufficiently motivated," says Don, citing that Keith Jones is an exception. Another dealer handles the Homestead line for WBL, but sells Sperry-Holland hardware (IBM compatible) because she is a New Holland farm machinery dealer and gets a better commission than what WBL can offer on IBM.

Dufault believes that having farmers selling to farmers gives them an edge over home computer retail outlets which cater to urban consumers. Western's salespeople are better able to relate to the farmers and their individual needs.

Stan Jones (Hereford breeder) confirmed Dufault's beliefs about why farm computer sales were starting out slowly. Stan feels computers can help a farming operation, that their widespread presence on farms is almost inevitable, and that he'll "probably own one someday."

Just how soon these early and late adopters choose to use computers to monitor their farm accounts and operations was a question foremost in the minds of the WBL directors. Approximately 50 customers had been sold systems or software by the end of 1984. As computers are now taught at the junior and senior high school levels, their presence on farms will probably become commonplace within 10 years. In the meantime, however, Western Breeders did not know how soon sales would take off and how much attention should be devoted to this high-tech farming field.

CONSULTING SERVICE

An area of Western Breeders that has been in existence for some time and that the directors would like to see expand in the last half of the 1980s is their consulting or mating guide service for AI users. The service has been confined to dairymen thus far. Resistance or lack of consumer interest in this program in the past probably stems from most farmers' desire for independence. Says Keith Jones, "It's just the nature of agriculture. Consulting is new and farmers aren't ready for it yet. They don't like being told how to manage their farms or cattle. It'll take a long time before farmers accept advice from professional consultants." Revenues in 1984 totaled about $10,000.

Don Dufault claims that none of the other local AI units are currently offering a consulting service. WBL has entered into joint venture agreements on a limited basis with various consulting engineering firms. One of WBL's prime functions in these ventures is to provide the genetic input (semen) for the genetic improvement program. Western employs three field representatives specially trained in dairy breeding programs. Don Dufault explains the consulting procedure: "We go into a herd, we analyze a herd on a per-cow basis, and we say 'now this cow—this is her major fault, what would you like to improve? You have a choice of one or two—you can't improve all her faults within the next generation—you've got to work toward an objective.' Then we select a bull or two or three that will have the highest probability of improving these faults in the next generation."

As Don explains, within any herd, you'll find a normal curve—some excellent individuals at the top, a broad range of average animals, and a few inferior animals at the bottom. The bottom end animals can be more productive if they are implanted with embryos from either the herd's top dams and sires or purchased embryos from a service if the farmer wants to introduce new genetics into his herd.

With the increasing complexity of the technology associated with herd improvement through genetic introduction, the popularity of the mating guide service is expected to improve. WBL is in an excellent position to advise the farmer how to balance optimal improvement with time and cost.

CONCLUSION

Western Breeders had their options set out for them. They wanted growth and their business plan for the remainder of the 1980s had to reflect this objective. The decision facing them was with what products and markets should they concentrate their efforts and funds.

45. Marion Laboratories

Michael E. Herman, senior vice president of finance for Marion Laboratories, had just received word that the board of directors was planning to meet in three days to review the company's portfolio of subsidiary investments. In particular, he and his senior financial analyst, Carl R. Mitchell, were to prepare an in-depth analysis of several of the subsidiaries for the board. The board would be considering these subsidiaries compatibility with Marion's overall long-range strategic objectives. The analysis was part of a continuing process of self-assessment to assure future growth for the company. At the upcoming meeting, the board was interested in a review of Kalo Laboratories, Inc., a subsidiary that manufactured specialty agricultural chemicals.[1]

Marion's future had been the subject of careful study following the first two years of earnings decline in the company's history. In fiscal 1975, net earnings for the company were 12 percent lower than in 1974. In fiscal 1976, Marion faced a more serious problem as earnings fell 30 percent below 1974 levels, while sales decreased 4 percent and cost of goods sold rose by 12 percent above 1974 levels.

Kalo was profitable and in sound financial shape for the fiscal year just ended. (See Exhibit 1.) But Kalo, their agricultural chemical subsidiary, was unique for Marion and Mr. Herman knew that Kalo's long-term status as a Marion subsidiary would depend on more than just profitability.

BACKGROUND

As a result of the interruption in the earnings' growth pattern, Marion sought to re-examine its corporate portfolio of investments. By fiscal year 1977, some results from the reappraisal were seen as earnings rose 28 percent from the previous year. Although sales continued to climb, earnings had not yet recovered to the 1974 level by the end of fiscal year 1978. Marion's long-range planning was an attempt to define what the company was to become in the next 10-year period. Current analysis of subsidiaries and investments were analyzed

---

This case was prepared by Kenneth Beck and Marilyn Taylor of the University of Kansas.

[1] Kalo Laboratories, Inc., was utilized as the case subject due to the nature of the information available in Marion Laboratories, Inc., SEC submissions.

EXHIBIT 1 Sales Profits and Identifiable Assets by Industry Segments ($000)

	Year Ended June 30				
	1978	*1977*	*1976*	*1975*	*1974*
Sales to unaffiliated customers:					
Pharmaceutical and hospital products	$ 84,223	$ 72,299	$59,236	$64,613	$54,165
Specialty agricultural chemical products	9,302	5,227	2,880	4,522	4,044
Other health-care segments	23,853	22,605	18,722	14,961	13,569
Consolidated net sales	$117,378	$100,131	$80,838	$84,096	$71,778
Operating profit:					
Pharmaceutical and hospital products	$ 27,900	$ 23,439	$18,941	$28,951	$25,089
Specialty agricultural chemical products	905	382	(328)	881	620
Other health-care segments	929	1,251	(593)	686	871
Operating profit	29,734	25,072	18,020	30,518	26,580
Interest expense	(1,546)	(1,542)	(898)	(97)	(83)
Corporate expenses	(5,670)	(4,474)	(3,106)	(2,795)	(2,475)
Earnings before income taxes	$ 22,518	$ 19,056	$14,016	$27,626	$24,022
Identifiable assets:					
Pharmaceutical and hospital products	$ 75,209	$ 69,546	$60,376	$43,658	$35,103
Specialty agricultural chemical products	3,923	3,805	1,801	1,942	1,790
Other health-care segments	14,635	14,875	13,902	14,229	12,217
Corporate	5,121	3,424	4,518	3,928	3,770
Discontinued operations	—	—	—	3,370	6,865
Consolidated assets	$ 98,888	$ 91,650	$80,597	$67,127	$59,745

SOURCE: 1978 *Annual Report.*

within this 10-year framework. As part of this long-range planning, Marion's Corporate Mission was defined as:

Statement of Corporate Mission

Statement of Corporate Mission

1. Achieve a position of market leadership through marketing and distribution of consumable and personal products of a perceived differentiation to selected segments of the health care and related fields.
2. Achieve long-term profitable growth through the management of high risk relative to the external environment.
3. Achieve a professional, performance-oriented working environment that stimulates integrity, entrepreneurial spirit, productivity, and social responsibility.

In addition to these more general goals, Marion also set a specific goal of $250 million. No time frame was established to achieve this goal, as the major emphasis was to be placed on the stability and quality of sales, but it was well understood that to meet stockholder expectations, the company must grow fairly rapidly. For example, on June 8, 1978, in a presentation before the Health Industry's Analyst Group, Fred Lyons, Marion's president and chief operating officer, emphasized Marion's commitment to growth. In his remarks he stated:

> We expect to grow over the next ten years at a rate greater than the pharmaceutical industry average and at a rate greater than at least twice that of the real gross national product. Our target range is at least 10–15 percent compounded growth—shooting for the higher side of that, of course. Obviously, we intend to have a great deal of new business and new products added to our current operations to reach and exceed the $250 million level.
>
> Our licensing activities and R&D expenditures will be intensified. . . . At the same time we'll undertake some selective in-house research business into Marion through the acquisition route. It is our intention to keep our balance sheet strong and maintain an "A" or better credit rating, to achieve a return on investment in the 12–15 percent range and to produce net after tax earnings compared to sales in the 8–12 percent range.

To finance this growth in sales Marion was faced with a constant need for funds. (See Exhibits 2 and 3.) Most of these funds in the past came from the company's operations. To finance a $25 million expansion in its pharmaceutical facilities, the company, in fiscal year 1976, found it necessary to borrow $15 million in the form of unsecured senior notes. The notes were to mature on October 1, 1980, 1981, and 1982, with $5 million due on each of those dates.

In regard to possible future financing, Mr. Herman made the following comments before the Health Industry's Analyst Group. "Most of you realize that industrial companies have a debt-to-equity ratio of 1 : 1 and, if we so desired to leverage ourselves to that level, we could borrow $66 million. However, we would keep as a guideline the factor of always maintaining our 'A' or better credit rating, so we would not leverage ourselves that far."

Although Marion was fairly light on debt, the potential for future borrowing was not unlimited. Besides maintaining an A credit rating, it was felt that a debt to equity ratio greater than .4 : 1 would be inconsistent with the pharmaceutical industry.

To analyze Kalo's future as well as the futures of the other non-pharmaceutical subsidiaries, Mr. Herman realized that he and his analysts would have to consider the impact of these financing constraints on Marion's future growth. With unlimited financing in the future he would have only had to make a "good" investment decision. However, to balance the goals of a strong balance sheet and a high growth rate, Mr. Herman was faced with making the optimal investment decision. It was with these constraints that Mr. Herman would eventually have to make his recommendation to the board of directors.

EXHIBIT 2 Ten Year Financial Summary (dollar amounts in thousands except per share data)

	Years Ended June 30									
	1978	1977	1976	1975	1974	1973	1972	1971	1970	1969
Sales										
Net sales	$117,378	$100,131	$80,838	$84,096	$71,778	$57,937	$49,066	$41,692	$35,322	$30,188
Cost of sales	43,177	37,330	29,315	26,078	21,715	18,171	14,932	12,262	10,622	8,985
Gross profit	74,201	62,801	51,523	58,018	50,063	39,766	34,134	29,430	24,700	21,203
Operating expenses	51,718	43,397	37,292	31,699	26,991	21,155	19,164	17,181	13,828	12,453
Operating income	22,483	19,404	14,231	26,319	23,072	18,611	14,970	12,249	10,872	8,750
Other income	1,581	1,194	683	1,404	1,033	722	709	599	630	328
Interest expense	1,546	1,542	898	97	83	109	116	88	198	260
Earnings										
Earnings from continuing operations before income taxes	22,518	19,056	14,016	27,626	24,022	19,224	15,563	12,760	11,304	8,818
Income taxes	10,804	8,404	5,628	13,295	11,791	9,297	7,730	6,364	5,899	4,493
Earnings from continuing operations	11,714	10,652	8,388	14,331	12,231	9,927	7,833	6,396	5,405	4,325
Earnings (loss) from discontinued operations	—	—	—	(3,617)	(120)	76	488	—	—	—
Net earnings	$ 11,714	$ 10,652	$ 8,388	$10,714	$12,111	$10,003	$ 8,321	$ 6,396*	$ 5,405	$ 4,325
Common share data										
Earnings (loss) per common and common equivalent share:										
Continuing operations	$ 1.38	$ 1.23	$ .96	$ 1.65	$ 1.40	$ 1.14	$ .90	$ .76	$ .65	$ .52
Discontinued operations	—	—	—	(.42)	(.01)	.01	.06	—	—	—
Net earnings	$ 1.38	$ 1.23	$ .96	$ 1.23	$ 1.39	$ 1.15	$ .96	$ .76*	$ .65	$ .52
Cash dividends per common share	.59	.53	.52	.48	.28	.21	.20	.16	.12	.12
Stockholders' equity per common and common equivalent share	$ 7.87	$ 7.09	$ 6.63	$ 6.29	$ 5.52	$ 4.16	$ 3.16	$ 2.52	$ 2.01	$ 1.47
Weighted average number of outstanding common and common share equivalents	8,475	8,640	8,707	8,708	8,689	8,715	8,651	8,396	8,377	8,354

* Before extraordinary charge of $916,000, equal to $.11 per common share resulting from the disposition of investment in affiliated companies.

SOURCE: 1978 *Annual Report.*

EXHIBIT 3

MARION LABORATORIES, INC.
Consolidated Balance Sheet, 1977 and 1978

	June 30	
Assets	*1978*	*1977*
Current assets:		
Cash	$ 381,116	$ 961,588
Short-term investments at cost which		
approximates market	2,561,660	10,028,297
Accounts and notes receivable, less allowances		
for returns and doubtful accounts of		
$1,845,466 and $2,305,793	28,196,199	20,576,412
Inventories	19,640,945	15,568,170
Prepaid expenses	2,305,403	1,461,367
Deferred income tax benefits.	757,585	895,110
Total current assets	53,842,908	49,490,944
Property, plant, and equipment, at cost:		
Land and land improvements.	2,832,588	2,935,671
Buildings	24,458,746	25,224,652
Machinery and equipment	19,671,607	18,110,907
Aircraft and related equipment	1,670,904	1,670,904
Construction in progress.	365,311	357,338
	48,999,156	48,299,472
Less accumulated depreciation.	10,725,533	8,585,190
Net property, plant, and equipment	38,273,623	39,714,282
Other assets:		
Intangible assets	4,774,055	2,042,762
Notes receivable (noncurrent)	890,692	11,589
Marketable equity securities, at market value	688,914	—
Deferred income tax benefits (noncurrent)	318,434	249,647
Miscellaneous.	99,597	141,232
Total other assets	6,771,692	2,445,230
Total assets	$98,888,223	$91,650,456

Liabilities and stockholders' equity

Current liabilities:		
Current maturities of long-term debt	$ 82,102	$ 95,004
Accounts payable, trade	3,979,341	4,224,105
Accrued profit sharing expense	1,752,515	243,096
Other accrued expenses	3,864,168	3,008,238
Dividends payable	1,260,612	1,198,938
Income taxes payable	4,391,252	5,030,219
Total current liabilities	15,329,990	13,799,600
Long-term debt, excluding current maturities	15,580,072	15,661,399
Deferred income taxes payable.	1,107,000	733,000
Deferred compensation	177,975	172,889
Stockholders' equity:		
Preferred stock of $1 par value per share		
Authorized 250,000 shares, none issued.	—	—
Common stock of $1 per value per share		
Authorized 20,000,000 shares; issued 8,703,346		
shares	8,703,346	8,703,346
Paid-in capital.	3,474,358	3,475,443
Retained earnings	58,358,925	51,604,550
	70,536,629	63,783,339

EXHIBIT 3 *(concluded)*

	June 30	
	1978	*1977*
Less:		
293,153 shares of common stock in treasury, at cost (189,500 shares in 1977)	3,819,243	2,499,771
Net unrealized loss on noncurrent marketable equity securities.	24,200	—
Total stockholders' equity	66,693,186	61,283,568
Commitments and contingent liabilities.		
Total liabilities and stockholders' equity	$98,888,223	$91,650,456

SOURCE: 1978 *Annual Report.*

COMPANY STRATEGY

In 1979, Marion Laboratories, Inc., of Kansas City, Missouri, was a leading producer of ethical (prescription) pharmaceuticals for the treatment of cardiovascular and cerebral disorders. (See Exhibit 4.) Marion also owned subsidiaries which manufactured hospital supplies, proprietary (nonprescription) drugs, eyeglasses, optical accessories, electrical home stairway elevators, and specialty agricultural chemicals.

Marion Laboratories was founded in 1950 by Ewing Marion Kauffman. Prior to establishing his own company, Kauffman held a job with a field sales force of a Kansas City pharmaceutical company. After four years on the job, Kauffman's sales were so successful that he was making more money in commissions than the company president's salary. When the company cut his commission and reduced his sales territory, Kauffman quit to establish his own firm.

In its initial year of operation, the new company had sales of $36,000 and a net profit of $1,000. Its sole product was a tablet called OS-VIM, formulated to combat chronic fatigue. The company's three employees, counting Kauffman, worked from a 13′ × 15′ storeroom that served as manufacturing plant, sales office, warehouse, and headquarters.

From the company's inception, the major emphasis for Marion was on sales and marketing. Kauffman was successful in developing an aggressive, highly motivated sales force. During the mid-1960s, the company's sales effort was concentrated on developing Pavabid, introduced in 1962, into the leading product in the cerebral and peripheral vasodilator market.

While other drug companies were spending large amounts on research and development, hoping to discover new drugs, Marion concentrated on the sales effort, spending very little on basic research.

EXHIBIT 4 Marion's Major Ethical Pharmaceutical Products

Product	Product Application	Estimated Market Size	Marion's Product	Share of Market
		($000,000)		
Cerebral and Peripheral Vasodilators	Vascular relaxant to relieve constriction of arteries	90–100	Pavabid®	22%
Coronary Vasodilators	Controlled release nitroglycerin for treatment of angina pectoris	90–100	Nitro-Bid®	12%
Ethical and OTC Plain antacids	Tablets for relief of heartburn	37	Gaviscon®	26%
Androgens-estrogens	Product for treatment of calcium deficiencies	12	Os-Cal®	46%
Topical burn Antimicrobials	Ointment for prevention of infection in third-degree burns	8	Silvadene®	57%
Urologic antispasmodics	Product for treatment of symptoms of neurogenic bladder	10	Ditropan®	10%

SOURCE: Smith, Barney, Harris, Upham and Co. Research Report (January 19, 1978).

Nearly all of its research expenditures were directed at improving its current products or further developing products licensed from other drug companies. This particular approach to product development was still being followed in 1979.

Beginning in the late 1960s, Marion decided to reduce its dependence on Pavabid which accounted for more than half of Marion's sales. In the pharmaceutical area, the company continued to minimize basic research and worked to develop new drug sources. Marion also began diversifying into the hospital and health products sector primarily by acquiring existing firms in those areas. (See Exhibit 5.) Taking advantage of the high market value of its common stock,[2] the company acquired several subsidiaries engaged in businesses other than pharmaceuticals.

ORGANIZATION

In 1979, Marion's operations were divided into two separate groups, the Pharmaceutical Group and the Health Products Group. (See Exhibit 6.) The Pharmaceutical Group's operations were a continuation of the original ethical drug line of the company. The Health Products Group was composed of subsidiaries purchased by Marion in hospital and health-related fields.

Fred W. Lyons, 41, was president, chief executive officer, and member of the board of directors. As president, Lyons was responsible for the total operation and performance of the corporation. This

---

[2] Price-earnings ratios for Marion in 1968 and 1969 were 46 and 52, respectively.

EXHIBIT 5 Summary of Subsidiary Acquisitions and Divestures

Name of Subsidiary	Type of Product(s)	Date Acquired	Date Divested
Marion Health & Safety	First aid and hospital products	1968	—
American Stair-Glide	Manufacturer of home stairway lifts and products to aid the handicapped	1968	—
Kalo Laboratories	Manufacturer of specialty agricultural chemicals	1968	Sold: 1978
Rose Manufacturing	Industrial fall protection devices	1969	Merged into MH&S: 1973
Mi-Con Laboratories	Manufacturers of opthalmic solutions	1969	Sold out: 1971
Pioneer Laboratories	Manufacturer of sterile dressings	50% in 1970	Discontinued operations, selling some assets: 1975
Signet Laboratories	Vitamin and food supplements	1971	
Optico Laboratories	Eyeglasses, hard contact lenses and related products	1973	Sold: 1978
Certified Laboratories	Manufacturer IPC products	1969	Merged into Pharmaceutical Division: 1979
IPC	Marketed IPC products	1969	—
Marion International	Distributor of pharmaceutical products	Incorporated 1971	Merged into MH&S: 1974
Inco	Industrial creams	1972	Discontinued operations: 1973
Occusafe	Consulting services; re: OSHA regulation & compliance	Incorporated 1972	
Nation Wide	Specialty AG-Chem products	1973	Merged into Kalo
Marion Scientific	Manufacturer and distributor of	Acquired by MH&S: 1973	—
Colloidal	Specialty agricultural products	1973	Merged into Kalo: 1974
WBC	Holding company for IPC	Incorporated 1976	Sold: 1978
SRC	Specialty AG-Chem products	1977	Merged into Kalo

EXHIBIT 6 Organization Chart

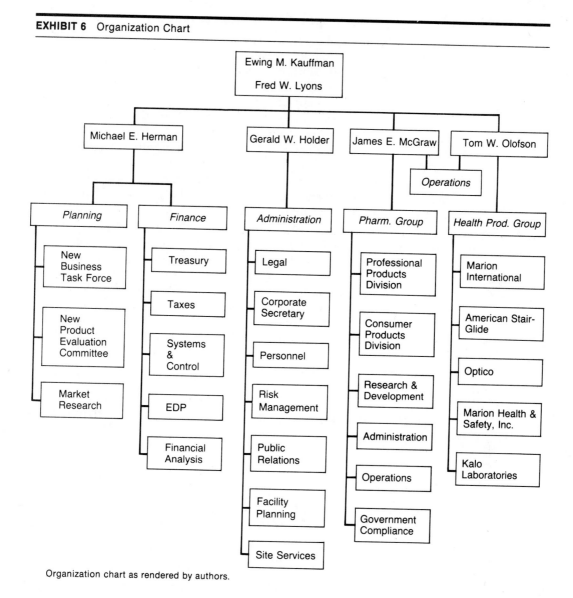

Organization chart as rendered by authors.

responsibility included the company's pharmaceutical operating group as well as all subsidiary operations, corporate planning functions, and corporate supportive activities.

Lyons joined Marion in 1970 as vice president and general manager, and director. He came to Marion from a similar position with Corral Pharmaceuticals, Inc., a subsidiary of Alcon Laboratories, Inc. Lyons was a registered pharmacist and received an MBA from Harvard University in 1959.

Also serving on the board of directors was senior vice president and chief financial officer, Michael E. Herman, 37, who joined Marion from an investment banking firm of which he was a founding partner. Herman started with Marion as vice president of finance in 1974, and in 1975 was named director of the company. His responsibilities were financial planning, financial control of operations, the management information systems, the treasury functions, product development, and strategic long-range planning. Mr. Herman was also chairman of the company's New Business Task Force Committee which was responsible for the financial review, planning, evaluation, and negotiation of acquisitions. Herman earned a bachelor of science degree in metallurgical engineering from Rensselaer Polytechnic Institute and an MBA from the University of Chicago.

Gerald W. Holder, 48, was the senior vice president in charge of administrative functions for Marion. Holder was responsible for all corporate administrative functions, including Marion's legal, personnel, facilities and engineering services, public relations, and risk management staffs. He joined the company in 1973, rising to the senior vice president level in March 1978.

James E. McGraw, 46, was senior vice president of Marion Laboratories, Inc. and president of the company's pharmaceutical group. He was responsible for the manufacturing, marketing, quality control, and accounting functions within the two operating units of the Pharmaceutical Group: the Professional Products Division and the Consumer Products Division. McGraw joined Marion in 1974 from a position as president of the General Diagnostics Division of Warner-Lambert Company.

Tom W. Olofson, 36, was a senior vice president and president of the Health Products Group. His responsibilities included financial and planning aspects for each of the subsidiaries in the group.

Within the described organization, Marion made some of its operating decisions in small group or task force settings that brought together corporate personnel from several different disciplines. The process of approving certain capital expenditures was an example of the review and analysis process.

Marion had a formal capital expenditure review program for expenditures on depreciable assets in excess of $10,000. At the option of the group president, the review program could also be applied on expenditures of less than $10,000 with the modification that in these cases only the group president was involved in the review process.

A form that forced the requesting individual to discount the cash flows of the project was required to be completed. If the net present value of cash flows was positive, the form was submitted to a corporate planning group. This group consisted of corporate accounting and facilities planning personnel who, since the company was operating with limited funds, decided which projects, based on financial and strategic considerations, should be forwarded to Lyons for final approval or rejection. This process occurred after the planning period and prior to the purchase of the asset. The capital expenditure review program was used for expenditures in both the Pharmaceutical Group and the Health Products Group.

PHARMACEUTICAL GROUP

Marion's ethical and over-the-counter drug operations were the major components of the Pharmaceutical Group. These operations were split into two divisions, the Professional Products Division and the Consumer Products Division. James E. McGraw headed the Pharmaceutical Group which also was made up of the functions of research and development, administration, operations, and government compliance. Although Marion had been exclusively an ethical drug maker prior to diversification efforts, the company had recently increased its operations in the proprietary drug area.

In 1978, Marion formed the Consumer Products Division from what had been International Pharmaceutical Corp. (IPC) to market its growing nonprescription product line. This market area, previously untapped for Marion, was expected to be a major ingredient for near-term growth. To aid in the marketing of its nonprescription line, Marion hired a full-scale consumer advertising agency for the first time in the company's history.

Sales for the Consumer Products Division were boosted when, in fiscal 1978, Marion purchased the product Throat-Discs from Warner-Lamberts' Parke-Davis Division. In addition, Marion also purchased two Parke-Davis ethical products, Ambenyl cold-cough products and a tablet for the treatment of thyroid disorders. Because of the timing of the acquisition, most of the sales and earnings were excluded from that year's earnings results. Sales for these three lines were expected to be nearly $8 million in 1979.

Marion's ethical pharmaceutical products were marketed by its Professional Products Division. The company sold its ethical product with a detail sales force of about 200 that called on physicians, pharmacists, and distributors within their assigned territories. The sales force was very productive by industry standards and was motivated by intensive training, supervision, and an incentive compensation system. There was very little direct selling to doctors and pharmacists, the main purpose of the salesman visits being promotion of Marion's products. In addition, Marion had an institutional sales force that sold directly to hospitals, institutions, and other large users.

In fiscal 1978, 80 percent of Marion's pharmaceutical products were distributed through 463 wholesalers. All orders for ethical drug products were filled from Kansas City, Missouri. Marion's pharmaceutical distribution system is diagrammed in Exhibit 7.

EXHIBIT 7

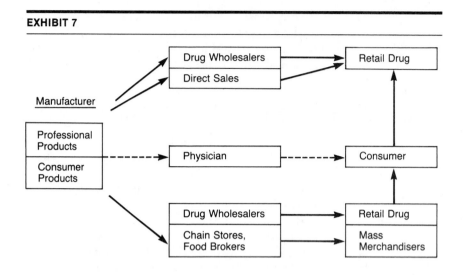

During 1978, the company decided to use its improved liquidity position to aid its wholesale drug distributors. Many wholesalers used outside financing to purchase their inventory and were unable to maintain profit margins when interest rates rose. By extending credit on key products, Marion helped its distributors maintain higher inventories and gave the company a selling edge over competitors.

One of Marion's major goals for each of its products was for the product to hold a market leadership position in the particular area in which it competed. This goal had been accomplished for most of the company's leading products. (See Exhibit 4.)

Capturing a large share of a market had worked particularly well for Marion's leading product, Pavabid, which in 1978 accounted for 18 percent of the entire company's sales. Marion was decreasing its reliance on Pavabid (see Exhibit 8) which, since its introduction in 1962, had been the company's most successful product. Through the 1960s, Pavabid had been responsible for almost all of Marion's growth. In recent years, as the product's market matured, sales growth had slowed, forcing the company to become less dependent on Pavabid. The decrease in sales of 3.9 percent in fiscal year 1976 was due primarily to previous overstocking of Pavabid and the subsequent inventory adjustments at the distributor level.

In April 1976, the Food and Drug Administration (FDA) had requested that makers of papaverine hydrochloride (sold by Marion as Pavabid) submit test data to support the safety and efficacy of the drug. Many small manufacturers were not able to submit the data and dropped out of the market. Marion complied with the request and had not yet been notified by the FDA of the outcome of the review by

EXHIBIT 8 Changing Product Mix

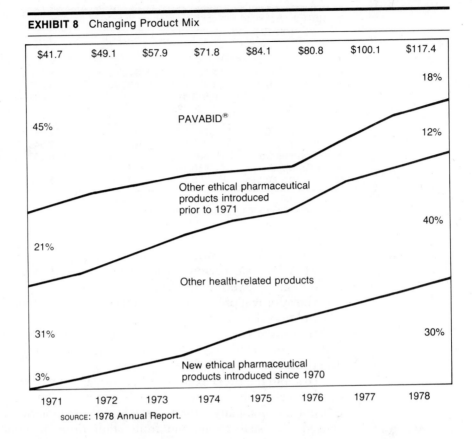

| $41.7 | $49.1 | $57.9 | $71.8 | $84.1 | $80.8 | $100.1 | $117.4 |

18%

PAVABID®

45%   12%

Other ethical pharmaceutical
products introduced
prior to 1971

                                                                        40%

21%

Other health-related products

31%   30%

New ethical pharmaceutical
3%   products introduced since 1970

1971   1972   1973   1974   1975   1976   1977   1978

SOURCE: 1978 Annual Report.

early 1979. A negative action by the FDA was not expected since it
had taken so long for a decision and papaverine had been used safely
for decades. However, if the FDA ruled that compounds such as Pavabid could not be marketed, either because they were not safe or were
not effective, Marion would lose its leading product.

In August 1977, the FDA requested that manufacturers of coro-
nary vasodilators, including nitroglycerin compounds like Marion's
Nitro-Bid, submit test data to prove product safety and efficacy. This
review was the same process that Pavabid was subject to and a negative ruling, although not expected, would adversely affect the company.

Proving its products to be safe and effective was only one area in
which the company dealt with the FDA. Before any ethical drug product could be marketed in the United States, Marion had to have the
approval of the FDA. Under the system effective at that time, the
company was required to conduct extensive animal tests, file an In-
vestigational New Drug Application, conduct three phases of clinical

EXHIBIT 9 Selected Ethical Drug Companies, 1977 (in thousands of dollars)

	Net Sales	Cost of Goods Sold	R&D Expenses	Net Income*
Pfizer, Inc.	$2,031,900	$978,057	$ 98,282	$174,410
Merck & Co.	1,724,410	662,703	144,898	290,750
Eli Lilly & Co.	1,518,012	571,737	124,608	218,684
Upjohn, Inc.	1,134,325	—	102,256	91,521
SmithKline Corp.	780,337	299,338	61,777	89,271
G. D. Searle & Co.	749,583	345,224	52,645	(28,390)
Syntex Corp.	313,604	132,710	27,648	37,643
A. H. Robbins Co.	306,713	122,374	16,107	26,801
Rorer Group, Inc.	186,020	59,606	5,174	18,143
Marion Laboratories	100,131	37,330	5,907	10,652

* After tax.
SOURCE: Drug and Cosmetic Industry, June 1978.

human tests, file a New Drug Application, and submit all of the data to the FDA for final review. With the FDA's approval, the drug firm could begin marketing the drug.

The approval process from lab discovery and patent application to FDA approval took from 7 to 10 years. Often a company had only seven or eight years of patent protection left to market its discovery and recover the average $50 million it had taken to fully develop the drug from the initial discovery stages.

To avoid the R&D expenses necessary to fully develop a new drug into a marketable product, Marion's source for new products was a process the company called "search and development." Marion licensed the basic compound from other drug manufacturers large enough to afford the basic research needed to discover new drugs. Generally, the licensors, most notably Servier of France and Chugai of Japan, were companies lacking the resources or expertise necessary to obtain FDA approval and marketing rights in the United States. Marion's R&D effort then concentrated on developing a product with an already identified pharmacological action into a drug marketable in the United States. By developing existing drug entities, Marion was able to shorten the development time required to bring a new drug to market at a lower cost than discovering its own drugs. This enabled Marion to compete in an industry dominated by companies many times its own size. (See Exhibits 9 and 10.)

In addition to the FDA, the federal government was also affecting the drug industry with its activities that promoted generic substitution. In early 1979, 40 states had generic substitution laws that allowed nonbranded drugs to be substituted for branded, and often more expensive, drugs. The U.S. Department of Health, Education and Welfare and the Federal Trade Commission had also recently proposed a model state substitution law and a listing of medically

EXHIBIT 10 Ethical Drug Industry Composite Statistics

	1978	1977	1976	1975
Sales ($ millions)	12,450	10,859	10,033	9,022
Operating margin (%)	22.5	22.2	21.9	22.1
Income tax rate (%)	36.5	36.4	36.2	36.7
Net profit margin (%)	11.8	11.7	11.7	11.6
Earned on net worth (%)	18.5	17.9	18.2	18.4

SOURCE: Value Line Investment Survey.

equivalent drugs. Under other federal programs, the maximum allowable cost (MAC) guidelines, reimbursement for medicaid and medicare prescriptions was made at the lowest price at which a generic version was available.

Generics accounted for 12 percent of new prescriptions being written and were likely to increase in relative importance. To combat the decreasing profit margins that were expected, the industry was looking to its ability to develop new drugs to offset the expected shortfall that was expected in the 1980s caused by a loss of patent protection on many important drug compounds.

The effect that generic substitution laws would have on Marion was unclear. The company had always concentrated on products with a unique pharmacological action rather than those that were commodity in nature. Generic substitution required an "equivalent" drug be substituted for the brand-name drug and there were uncertainties about how equivalency would be defined.

Marion's pharmaceutical operations had not produced a major new product for several years. Products that were in various stages of development were diltiazen hydrochloride, an anti-anginal agent; sucralfate, a nonsystemic (does not enter the bloodstream) drug for the treatment of ulcers; and benflourex, a product that reduced cholesterol levels in the blood.

HEALTH PRODUCTS GROUP

Subsidiaries selling a wide range of products used in health care and related fields made up Marion's Health Products Group. The company had bought and sold several subsidiaries since beginning to diversify in 1968 (Exhibit 5). By 1978, the group of subsidiaries was responsible for 39 percent of total company sales and 22 percent of earnings before taxes.

Several times after purchasing a company, Marion had decided to sell or discontinue operations of a subsidiary. The divestment decision in the past had been based on considerations such as a weak market position, low growth position, excessive product liability, or a poor "fit" with the rest of Marion.

In his presentation before the Health Industry's Analyst Group, Fred Lyons noted the importance of a subsidiary fitting in with the rest of Marion when explaining the company's decision to sell Rose Manufacturing. "You may have noticed that during this past year we determined through our strategic planning that Rose Manufacturing, in the full-protection area of industrial safety, did not fit either our marketing base or our technology base. Therefore, we made a decision to spin Rose off, and we successfully culminated its sale in November 1977, Rose, like Signet Laboratories three years ago, just did not fit."

In adjusting its corporate profile. Marion was always searching for companies that provided good investment potentials and were consistent with the company's goals. To provide a framework within which to evaluate potential acquisitions and to avoid some of the mistakes made in past purchases, Marion developed the following set of acquisition criteria to be applied to possible subsidiary investments:

Search Criteria for Acquisitions

Product area:	Health care
Market:	$100 million potential with 8% minimum growth rate
Net sales:	$3–30 million
Tangible net worth:	Not less than $1 million
Return on investment:	Not less than 20% pre-tax
Method of payment:	Cash or stock

The board of directors made the ultimate decision on the acquisitions and divestment of Marion's subsidiaries. At the corporate level, Mr. Herman was responsible for evaluating changes in the corporate portfolio and based on his analysis making recommendations to the board. Since Mr. Herman was also on the board of directors, his recommendations were heavily weighed in the board's final decision.

In early 1979, Marion had four subsidiaries in its Health Products Group: Marion Health and Safety, Inc., Optico Industries, American Stair Glide, and Kalo Laboratories. A brief description of each follows.

Marion Health and Safety, Inc. sold a broad line of hospital and industrial safety products through its Marion Scientific Corp. and Health and Safety Products Division. Recently introduced Marion Scientific products (a consumer-oriented insect bite treatment and a device for transporting anaerobic cultures) both showed good acceptance and growth in their respective markets. Distribution was generally through medical/surgical wholesalers and distributors who in turn resold to hospitals, medical laboratories, reference laboratories, etc. The Health and Safety Division manufactured and/or packaged primarily safety related products (hearing protection, eyewash, etc.) first-aid kits, such kit products as wraps, band-aids, and various OTC products. Sales of these products were made to safety equipment wholesalers/distributors who resold to hospitals, industry, institutions, etc. Sales of Marion Health and Safety, Inc. were estimated to have increased about 17 percent by outside analysts, to a level estimated at $19.0 million. Pre-tax margins were about 10 percent in this industry. Marion Health and Safety, Inc. was headquartered in Rockford, Illinois.

Optico Industries, Inc. participated in the wholesale and retail optical industry. Its main products were glass and plastic prescription eyeglass lenses and hard contact lenses. Outside analysts estimated this subsidiary recorded sales gains of about 26 percent for 1978 with sales estimated to be about $8 million. Optico had reduced profitability during 1978 due to expansion of its retail facilities. Pre-tax margins for 1978 were estimated at 6 percent, but this was expected to improve when the expansion program was completed. Optico's headquarters were located in Tempe, Arizona.

American Stair Glide Corp. manufactured and marketed home stairway and porch lifts and other products to aid physically handicapped individuals. These products were principally sold to medical/surgical supply dealers for resale or rental to the consumer. In some instances, distribution was through elevator companies. Sales were estimated at about $5 million annually by outside analysts. This subsidiary was expected to grow slowly and steadily and it had a very stable historical earnings pattern. The trend for greater access to buildings for the handicapped was expected to impact favorably on this Grandview, Missouri, based subsidiary.

Kalo Laboratories, Inc. operated in the specialty agricultural chemical market and provided products to meet specialized user needs. In the past, Kalo had been successful in marketing its line of specialty products. (See Exhibit 11.) In assessing Kalo's future, there were many risks to consider. These risks included competition from large chemical companies, governmental regulatory actions, and uncertain future product potentials.

KALO LABS

The United States' and Canadian agricultural chemical market was estimated to be $3.2 billion in 1978 and growing at more than 15 percent a year.[3] The industry was dominated by large chemical manufacturers, including Dow Chemical, DuPont, Stauffer Chemical, and Gulf Oil. The market was also shared by large ethical drug manufac-

---

[3] 1979 DuPont *Annual Report* and 1979 Upjohn *Annual Report*.

EXHIBIT 11 Kalo Laboratories: Sales, Investment, and Expense Information

	1978	1977	1976	1975	1974	1973
			Dollars in Millions			
Sales	$9.0 M	$5.0 M	$2.0 M	$4.0 M	$3.0 M	$2.0 M
Total assets	5.0 M	4.0 M	2.0 M	2.0 M	2.0 M	1.0 M
Total investment*	3.0 M	3.0 M	1.0 M	1.0 M	1.0 M	.5 M
			Expenses as Percent of Sales			
COGS	43%	54%	61%	53%	55%	48%
R&D expense	8	7	7	5	5	3
Marketing, selling and general administrative expenses	37	31	42	23	24	27

* Includes Marion's equity in Kalo and funds lent on a long-term basis.
Authors' estimates.

---

turers including Eli Lilly, Pfizer, and Upjohn. (See Exhibit 12.) Economies of scale allowed the larger companies to produce large amounts of what might be perceived as a commodity product (herbicides, insecticides, and fungicides) at a much lower cost per unit than the smaller companies. Diversification of and within agricultural product lines assured the larger manufacturers an even performance for their agricultural divisions as a whole.

Since smaller chemical companies like Kalo could not afford to produce large enough amounts of their products to match the efficiency and prices of the large companies, these firms concentrated on specialty markets with unique product needs. By identifying specialty chemical needs in the agricultural segment, Kalo was able to produce its products and develop markets that were very profitable, but weren't large enough to attract the bigger firms.

Products

Since the larger chemical companies dominated the large product segments, Kalo's products were designed to meet the specialized needs of its agricultural users. Kalo's product line was divided into four major classes—seed treatments, adjuvants, bactericides, and herbicides.

Seed treatments for soybeans accounted for the majority of Kalo's sales. One product in this area was Triple Noctin. Products in the seed treatment class were intended to act on soybean seeds to increase their viability once in the ground. Kalo manufactured seed treatments for soybeans only.

Adjuvants were chemicals that, when added to another agricultural product, increased the efficacy of the product or made it easier to

EXHIBIT 12 Total and Agriculture Related Sales, Selected Companies, 1979

	Total Sales (millions)	Agriculture Related	
		Sales (millions)	Earnings (before tax)
Eli Lilly	$2,520	$920*	28.6%
Pfizer	3,030	480*	9.8
Upjohn	1,755	280*	9.2
Marion (1978)	100	9	9.0

* Includes international sales.
SOURCE: Value Line Investment Survey.

use. For instance, Biofilmo prevented liquid fertilizer from foaming which made it easier to apply and Hydro-Wet enhanced the soils' receptiveness to certain chemicals, which reduced run-off into surrounding areas.

The newest product for Kalo was the adjuvant EXTEND, a chemical compound added to fertilizer that made it bind chemically with the soil or the plant. The binding process helped retain the fertilizer where it was applied making each application longer lasting and more effective. EXTEND was only recently introduced and its success was difficult to assess at such an early stage. Kalo's management was planning to build a family of products around EXTEND. Sales projections showed EXTEND contributing between 60–70 percent of Kalo's future growth through 1987.

Bactericides and herbicides were the final two product classes at Kalo. Bactericides were applied to the soil to either inhibit or encourage the growth of selected bacteria. One product, ISOBAC, was used to control boll rot in cotton. Herbicides, mainly for broadleaf plants, were used to control or kill unwanted weeds leaving the desirable crop unharmed.

In the past, Kalo had acquired several of its products by acquiring the company that manufactured the product. When it purchased a going-concern intact, Kalo was able to gain both manufacturing facilities and an existing distribution system. In the future, Kalo expected to diversify its product line in a similar fashion. To enlarge its existing product lines, Kalo was planning to use both internal and contract R&D. An example of enlarging the product family was the planned adaptation of its products to different numerous crop application.

Because Kalo did not have a well diversified product line, its operations were more cyclical than the overall agricultural sector. Two major factors beyond Kalo's control—the weather and spot prices for commodities—made its annual performance extremely unpredictable.

EXHIBIT 13 Kalo Laboratories: Forecasted Sales and Asset Turnover

	1979	1980	1981	1982	1983	1984	1985	1986	1987
Net sales $MM (current dollars)	12	16	20	25	30	35	40	45	50
Asset turnover	1.8x	1.8x	1.9x	1.9x	1.9x	1.9x	1.9x	1.9x	1.85x

Note: After-tax margin expected to increase to 7% by 1984.
Author's estimates.

Kalo's operating results were seasonal because its products were primarily intended to be applied in the spring months. It was not unusual for the subsidiary to show a net loss from operations for the nine months from July until March and show a large profit in the three months April, May, and June when the products were being purchased for immediate application. If the spring months were particularly rainy, Kalo's profitability was adversely affected. Heavy farm equipment could not operate on wet fields without getting stuck and application was impossible until the fields dried out. Once the fields were dry, Kalo's agricultural users often did not have time to apply the herbicides or other products even though it would have been economically advantageous to do so.

Competition and Industry

The other factor that affected the demand for Kalo's products was the spot pricing of commodities. The price of commodities relative to each other had a large effect on the total amount of each type of crop planted. Because the producer was free to switch crops yearly based on the spot prices, Kalo's demand for the upcoming planting season was uncertain and variable. Kalo was particularly vulnerable to swings in demand caused by the substitutability of crops since many of their products were applicable only to soybeans.

Distribution and Marketing

The end user of Kalo's products was usually the individual farmer. Kalo and the rest of the agricultural chemical industry had a distribution system like the one shown:

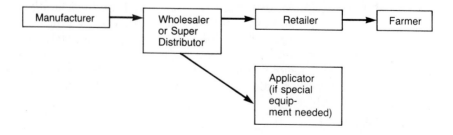

EXHIBIT 14 Kalo Laboratories: Balance Sheet, 6/30/78

Current assets	$2.5MM	Current liabilities	$1.4MM
PP&E (net)	1.9MM	Long-term debt	1.0MM
Other	.2MM	Capital	2.2MM
Total	$4.6MM	Total	$4.6MM

Author's estimates.

Kalo promoted its products with a sales force of about 30 salesmen. The main task of these salesmen was to call on and educate wholesalers/distributors on the advantages, unique qualities, and methods of selling Kalo's products. In addition, some end-user information was distributed to farmers, using "pull" advertising to create demand. A limited amount of promotion was done at agricultural shows and state fairs but because of the expense involved, this type of promotion was not used often.

Kalo's Future

Sales forecasts prepared by the staff analysts for Mr. Herman looked very promising as they predicted sales gains of from $4–6 million in each of the next nine years. (See Exhibit 14.) There were, however, some important assumptions on which the forecasts were based.

As mentioned earlier, 60–70 percent of the forecasted growth was to come from a product family based on the new product EXTEND. A great deal of uncertainty surrounded the product, however. Since it was new, the current success of EXTEND was difficult to measure particularly in determining how current sales translated into future performance. If the market evaluation for EXTEND and related products were correct, and if a family of products could be developed around EXTEND, then the sales potential for the proposed product family was very promising, provided Kalo was able to exploit the available sales opportunities.

Additional growth projected in the sales forecasts was to come from existing products and undefined future products that were to be developed or acquired. Approximately 20 percent of the growth was to come from the existing products in the next four to five years. Ten to 20 percent of the growth in the later years of the forecast was expected to come from currently unknown products.

For Kalo to realize the forecasted growth it was going to be necessary for Marion to provide financing. It was going to be impossible for Kalo to generate all the required funds internally. Kalo had been a net user of cash, provided by Marion, since 1976. (See Exhibit 11.) Marion's management did not consider the amount of cash provided through the first part of 1979 to be excessive so long as Kalo maintained adequate profitability and steady growth rates. In addition to the long-term funds provided by Marion, Kalo also required short-term financing of inventory during each year due to the seasonality of its sales.

Government Regulation

Another major uncertainty in Kalo's future was an unpredictable regulatory climate. Regulation of agricultural chemicals was under the jurisdiction of the Environmental Protection Agency (EPA). Compliance with the EPA was a similar process as with the FDA. The process of developing and introducing a new chemical product took from 8 to 10 years which included 2 to 5 years necessary to obtain EPA approval. The costs of developing and bringing a new product to market were generally from $5–10 million.

Once a product was on the market, the EPA had powers of recall similar to the FDA and could require the company to do additional research after the product was introduced. The prospect of having a product removed from the market was an added element of risk for Kalo if any of its products were affected. No problems were expected for Kalo although several of the subsidiary's products (particularly its herbicides and bactericides) had a relatively high potential for environmental problems, if applied incorrectly.

THE DECISION

Mr. Herman knew that in making his recommendation he would have to balance the immediate and long-term resource needs and the goals of Marion. Although Kalo looked promising from the forecasts, there were many uncertainties surrounding these subsidiaries' futures that had to be considered.

Since Marion had no new drug products ready to be introduced soon, the company would have to rely on other areas of the company to reach its growth goals. Kalo was growing, but it was also requiring a constant input of funds from its parent.

One possibility for growth was to purchase another drug manufacturer and add its products to Marion's, taking advantage of any distribution synergies that might exist. To make such a purchase, the company would need more resources. To sell a subsidiary could provide needed resources, but to do so quickly under less than optimum conditions would surely result in a significantly lower price than could be realized under normal conditions. The income and cash flow impact of this approach would be undesirable.

With the board meeting so soon, Mr. Herman was faced with analyzing the complex situation quickly. In three days he would have to make his recommendation to the board of directors.

The Corporate Environment

46. Lone Star Energy Division

INTRODUCTION

Ed Slovak had just graduated from State University with an MBA in management in June 1986. Since Ed's interests were in the personnel area, he had taken a position as personnel administrator at Lone Star Energy Division (LSED). He was excited by the challenge and diversity of his potential assignments in his new position. He wanted a job as a personnel generalist but wondered if his new position was "too general." As he sat at his new desk, he thought about the information he gathered during his employment interviews.

BACKGROUND OF LSED

LSED is an autonomous division of Lone Star Statewide Rural Electric Cooperative. The function of LSED is to furnish the parent organization with generating plants and transmission systems in order to service the requirements of 95,000 rural consumers in southern Texas. Presently, LSED acts in the role of a manufacturer and wholesaler of electrical energy to 17 local rural electrification membership cooperatives (REMC).

The headquarters of LSED is in Bryan, Texas, which is located approximately 100 miles from Houston. Together with its twin city, College Station, Bryan has a population of approximately 100,000. During the early 1980s the area has been heavily dependent upon the growth of a major university; there is increased industry locating in these communities, although the unemployment rate had been one of the lowest in the country. However, the collapsing oil economy had sent unemployment soaring.

The initial generating plant, Lone Star I, is located on the Brazos River near Navasota, Texas. With a population of 25,000, Navasota is located approximately 25 miles south of Bryan. In addition to the generating plant, there is being constructed approximately 1,400 miles of 60,000-volt transmission lines and 500 miles of 160,000-volt transmission lines throughout southern Texas. The estimated completion date for the plant and transmission lines is December 1988. When

---

This case was prepared by Dr. Tom Urban, ARCO.

in production, LSED's work force will increase from the present 35 to approximately 100 employees.

The purpose of LSED is to provide the member-users of the local REMC with an adequate amount of electric power at a lower cost than provided by commercial power sources. Since LSED is a division of Lone Star Statewide Rural Electric Cooperative, it is owned entirely by the recipients of its service—the rural residents of southern Texas. LSED is a nonprofit organization established to provide optimum electric service at the lowest possible cost to its consumer-owners. Thus, the establishment of LSED enables the cooperative members to integrate backward into the complete phases of electric service—generation, transmission, and distribution.

THE LONE STAR ENERGY-GENERATING PLANT

Lone Star I, the initial generating plant, will have a capacity of 300,000 kilowatts. Depending on the success of Lone Star I, it is planned to develop additional plants, Lone Star II and III, in order to meet increased energy demands of additional REMC.

In addition, LSED belongs to a power pool which can generate an additional 565,000 kilowatts. LSED is interconnected with rural electric generating plants in Louisiana and Oklahoma. Each of the plants will generate electricity for the pool, and the power requirements for each plant's member systems will be taken from the pool. Each plant can also generate additional energy which will be available as a pool reserve in order to provide maximum electricity for peak loads, emergency situations, and future growth.

The events leading to the construction of Lone Star I, the first consumer-owned generating and transmission plant in Texas, present an interesting episode in the political events of Texas. There has been constant litigation by the commercial power companies regarding the "public convenience and necessity" of the construction of a generating and transmission plant with the alleged "uneconomical and wasteful duplication of existing facilities." Prior to Lone Star I becoming operational, the local REMCs purchased electrical power from the commercial power companies at specified rates, specified sites, and specified load restrictions. The completion of Lone Star I ended these restrictions by providing full generation, transmission, and distribution facilities to the member REMCs.

ORGANIZATION OF LSED

The general manager is responsible to the operating committee of LSED. The operating committee consists of representatives from those member REMCs of Texas Statewide REC who receive or have contracted to purchase electrical energy from LSED. The operating committee is analogous to a board of directors in a profit oriented business except that the prime interest group represented on the committee has a consumer orientation.

This orientation is reinforced in the statement of the operating committee that the primary objective of LSED is:

> To promote and encourage the fullest possible use of electric energy in the state of Texas by making electric energy available to its members in the rural areas of the state at the lower cost consistent with sound economic and prudent management of the system.

The formal organization structure of LSED consists of the following departments:

1. Engineering Services
2. Power Production
3. Finance and Accounting

In addition to the managers of these three departments, the general manager and the assistant to the general manager compose the top management team of LSED. Organization charts depicting the present and planned formal organization are contained in the Appendixes 1A through 1D.

EMPLOYEE RELATIONS AT LSED

The effective utilization of the human resource is a high-priority objective at LSED. The operating committee has several subcommittees, one of which deals with employee relations. The responsibilities of this subcommittee include:

1. Review and revision of the administration of the LSED compensation program.
2. Review and revision of personnel policies
3. Review and revision of fringe benefit policies and programs.
4. Performance appraisal of management with recommendations for salary adjustments.
5. Review of attitude surveys, employee training and development programs, and management improvement programs.

This responsibility is reinforced in one of the objectives stated in the position description of the general manager, namely:

> To manage the human, financial, and physical resources of the division, guided by the policies of the operating committee, through operating objectives and policies which will achieve the purposes of the operating committee and fulfill the needs of employees for dignity and significance in their work.

The personnel function at LSED is primarily within the organizational role of the assistant to the general manager. This position is extremely broad with stated duties such as being administrative assistant to the general manager, coordination of purchasing activities, and special assignments.

However, the majority of the duties contained in the assistant's position description (Appendix 2) relate to the personnel function. These duties include:

1. Provision of central services in the recruitment and screening of applicants.
2. Development, implementation, and control of personnel policies and procedures.
3. Assistance and control in organizational planning, job descriptions, organization and policy manual development and maintenance, and implementation and control of the compensation and performance review plans.
4. Development, coordination, and implementation of training programs and accident prevention programs.

While LSED was in the construction phase, the majority of the time and effort of the assistant to the general manager has been directed toward special assignments. These duties have included lobbying, providing support material for litigation, and public relations work. In addition, the purchasing function has also occupied a significant portion of the time.

However, as the operational phase of LSED approaches, there is an increased necessity to devote effort to the personnel activity in order to meet the pressing problems of recruiting, employing, developing, utilizing, and maintaining an effective and efficient work force.

As previously stated, the operating committee policies had some general policies relevant to the personnel area. However, there is no written statement of personnel policies for LSED. No centralized source exists which would be of reference value to the employees as well as to management and supervisory personnel. The management services division of the National Rural Electric Cooperative Association will assist LSED in the compilation of job descriptions, position evaluations, and compensation plans. However, the management of LSED considers their other programs to be too mechanistic and restrictive in their scope. LSED is desirous of instituting personnel policies and procedures which would be more specifically tailored to the objectives and needs of LSED.

ASSIGNMENT AT LSED

Since the assistant to the general manager was unable to devote his efforts to the personnel area, he was authorized to hire a personnel administrator to assist in this area. The personnel administrator would have a generalist orientation with the initial assignment being the development of a personnel policy and procedures manual for LSED.

The assistant to the general manager told Ed that he didn't have to worry about job descriptions and evaluation or compensation. He gave Ed the outline contained in the Appendix 3 and asked Ed to see what he could do about developing these policies. The assistant was anxious to report to the operating committee on the development of the personnel policies.

APPENDIX 1 Organization Chart General Manager and Staff

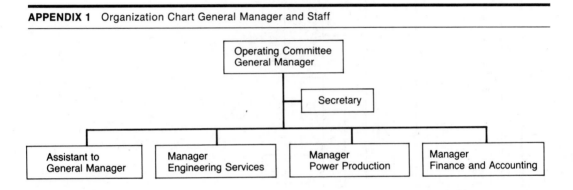

APPENDIX 1A Organization Chart Engineering Services Division

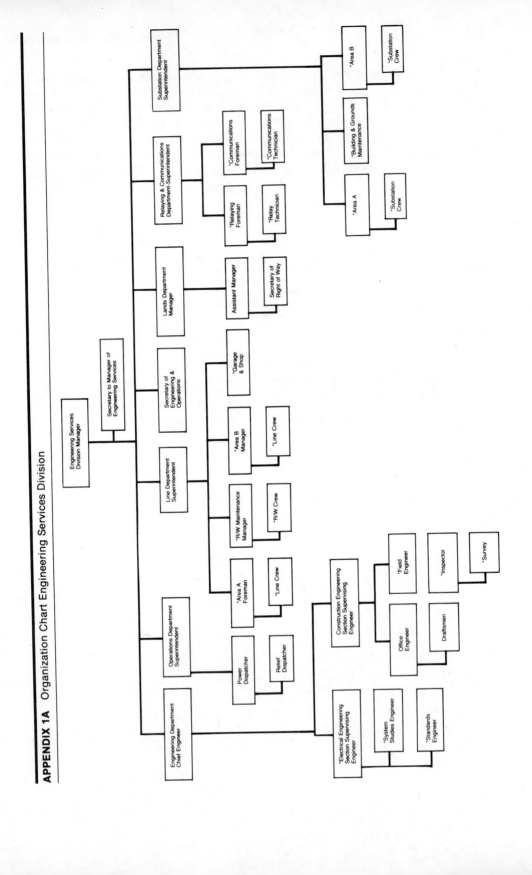

APPENDIX 1B Organization Chart Power Production

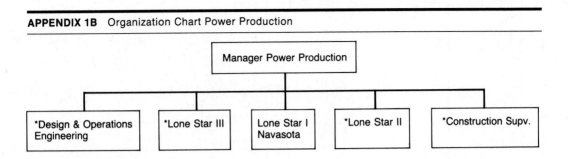

APPENDIX 1C Organization Chart Design & Operations Engineering

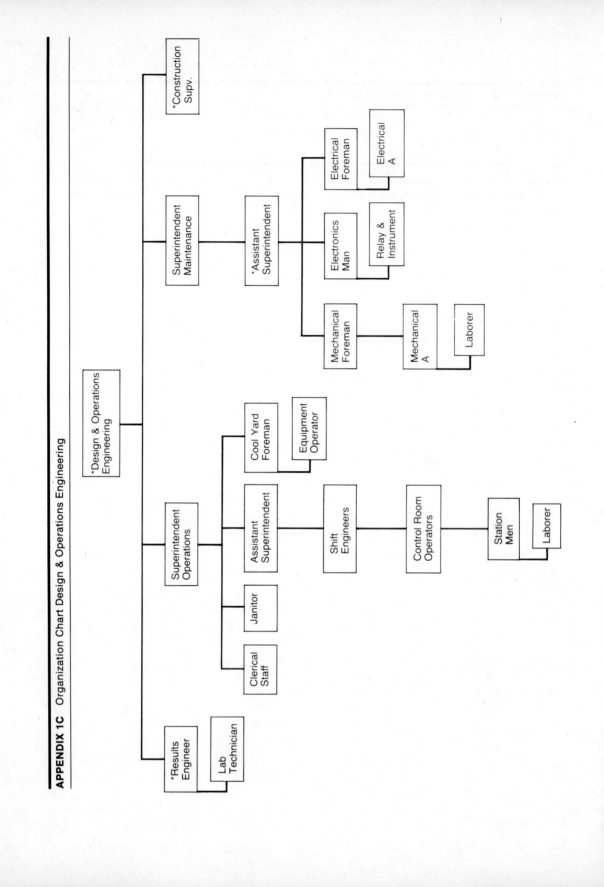

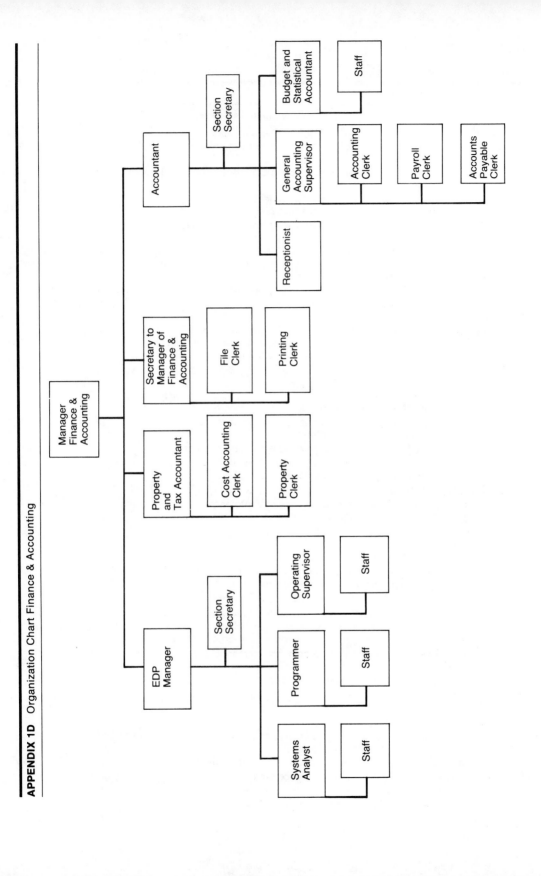

APPENDIX 2 Position Description

Assistant to General Manager

I. *Objectives*
   A. To act as administrative assistant to the general manager and carry out such responsibilities as assigned.
   B. To provide central personnel services to the Lone Star Energy Division in recruiting and screening applicants.
   C. To develop, implement, and control personnel policies and procedures to meet the needs for qualified, productive, and interested employees in all operations.
   D. To develop operating policies on purchasing and to coordinate purchasing activities which involve more than one department.
   E. To be a source of assistance and control in organization planning, job descriptions, organization, and policy manual development and maintenance, and the implementation and control of the compensation and performance review plans.
   F. To develop in coordination with division and department managers' training programs and accident prevention programs and to carry them out in cooperation with the managers.

II. *Responsibilities and authorities*
   Within the limits of operating committees policies, budgets, legal requirements, and operating policies, assumes responsibility and has commensurate authority, except as specified below, to achieve the objective stated below, including the following activities:
   A. *Planning*
      1. Develops and recommends programs, policies, and procedures on purchasing, employee recruitment and selection, employee relations and communications, training in operational skills and safety, compensation, and performance review.
      2. Develops plans and programs of coordination of management through assisting the general manager in planning staff conferences.
      3. Plans for change in organization structure in coordination with staff.
      4. Develops operational policies and procedures affecting more than one department or division and recommends to general manager.
   B. *Studying and Researching*
      1. Keeps up to date by study, research, and conferences on management and organization, purchasing, and personnel developments and improvements.
   C. *Organizing*
      1. Develops job descriptions and man specifications as required to meet the developing needs of the Lone Star Energy Division.
      2. Interviews, screens, and processes applications for all vacancies in the Bryan office and all supervisory positions in the field and refers qualified applicants to supervisors.
      3. Develops and trains field supervision in applying modern personnel techniques.
      4. Develops means of building employee understanding and morale.
      5. Provides control and coordination of organization and compensation charts and manuals, evaluation of positions through the job evaluation committee.
      6. Makes periodic wage, salary, benefit, and personnel practices surveys and recommends changes in compensation plan, benefits, and personnel practices for all groups of employees.
      7. Acts as secretary to the general manager in staff meetings; prepares agenda and keeps minutes.
   D. *Operating*
      1. *Performs Personally*
         a. Keeps up to date on general manager's activities so as to be able to carry on assigned duties to assist him.
         b. Recruits and interviews applicants for employment.
         c. Interviews salesmen in connection with purchase of interdepartmental supplies and equipment.
         d. Sets up and maintains employee records.

APPENDIX 2 *(continued)*

      e. Handles claims under insurance benefit plan.

      f. Attends meetings and conferences, makes presentations and addresses as required by general manager to represent him and relieve him of some of his duties.

      g. Investigates and reports to general manager on problems assigned.

      h. Performs other duties as required from time to time.

  E. *Controlling*

    1. Objective A

      Measured by appraisal by general manager of assistance rendered and success in carrying out assigned tasks.

    2. Objective B

      Measured by quality and quantity of personnel available when required by department and division managers.

    3. Objective C

      Measured by periodic review of each policy and program in application; by the availability of personnel for promotion, and by analysis of employee attitudes, complaints, etc.

    4. Objective D

      Measured by the effectiveness of purchasing policy and procedures in efficient and economic procurement.

    5. Objective E

      Measured by review of organization plan and manual, policy and compensation and performance review plan, in operation; by the understanding and support given by department and division managers in carrying out the intent of these programs and policies.

    6. Objective F

      Measured by the availability and use of training plans, accident prevention activities, as needed by management, and by the results of training and safety activities in providing competent and safety conscious employees to meet the needs of the organization.

III. *Relationships*

  A. *Internal*

    1. Line

      a. Reports to: General manager

      b. Directs: None

    2. Other

With Whom	For What Purpose	About What
a. Department and managers Division managers	To serve	Personnel and organization matters; purchasing
b. General manager's staff	To coordinate	Staff meeting Policy development
c. All employees	To advise	Personnel policies, benefits, training programs, safety activities

  B. *External*

With Whom	For What Purpose	About What
1. Officials of other utilities	Negotiate with, give and secure information	Agreements and contracts
2. REA officials and representatives	Cooperate with and secure advice	Loans and other matters
3. Operating committee and subcommittees	Represent the general manager	Policies, reports, and other matters
4. Management consultants	Secure help and assist	Management and organization, personnel, etc.

APPENDIX 2 *(concluded)*

5. Member cooperatives	To serve	Any matter as assigned by general manager
6. Public officials	To exchange information	Any matter as assigned by general manager
7. Sales representative	Exchange information, negotiate	Supplies, equipment and services
8. Texas statewide personnel	Exchange information	Any matters

Man Specifications

Position: Assistant to general manager

Scope: Assists general manager as his representative and by research and study as required. Coordinates organization, compensation, benefits, and performance review plans. Develops personnel and other policies. Recruits and interviews applications. Sets up training and safety programs.

Education: Graduation from a recognized college or university with a major in business or public administration, or industrial management of the equivalent is required. Completion of NRECA basic institutes plus workshops on job evaluation, staff assistant seminars I and II are desirable prior to accepting the position or soon thereafter.

Experience: Previous experience in the rural electrification program in positions such as manager, assistant to manager, or staff assistant is preferred. Experience in these positions with a generation and transmission organization is desirable.

Attitude: Must have an interest or develop an interest in the rural electric cooperative and public power program. Must be willing to coordinate and assist in the management program development at LSED with the understanding that he is staff and not line and results must be achieved by the persuasion of demonstrated competence.

Personal characteristics: Must be of highest personal integrity, in good health, and have a pleasant personality with good personal habits. Should create a favorable impression on people.

Knowledge:
The principals of management and organization
Teaching methods
Personnel administration
Accident prevention
Statistics
Report writing
Public speaking
Planning techniques

Salary grade: M–10

Benefits: Pension, insurance, medical, and hospital benefits in Texas statewide plans.

Location: Base headquarters in Bryan, Texas.

I. *Objective: Employment Function*

To assure that LSED generates, recruits, selects, and places the most qualified persons in available positions so that the interests and abilities of employees will be fully utilized in the achievement of LSED goals and individual satisfaction.

Policy Areas to Be Covered

1. Recruitment
    a. Internal
    b. External
2. Screening
3. Interviewing
4. Testing
5. Physical examination
6. References
7. Selection
8. Placement
9. Orientation
10. Personnel records
11. EEO

II. *Objective: Development Function*

LSED recognizes that its success is dependent upon the continuous development of the knowledge and skills of its members. It is our policy to assist qualified and motivated employees to engage in the requisite training and education for personal self-development and to enhance their positions and careers at LSED.

Policy Areas to Be Covered

1. Level
    a. Managerial
        (1) Executive development
        (2) Supervisory development
        (3) Professional development
    b. Operative
        (1) On-the-job training
        (2) Technical
        (3) Safety
    c. Clerical
        (1) On-the-job training
        (2) Special
2. Staff Assistance
    a. Preparation of
        (1) Training programs composition
        (2) Training and visual aids
        (3) Training manuals
        (4) Training standards
    b. Selection of
        (1) Training instructors
        (2) Training facilities
    c. Training Counseling and Guidance
        (1) Needs assessment
        (2) Program development
3. Sources
    a. Internal
        (1) On-the-job training—staff personnel
        (2) NRECA and statewide training programs
        (3) Library and reading racks
        (4) Communications, periodicals, newspapers, etc.
    b. External

III. *Objective: Utilization Function*

To pledge that LSED will respect the rights of employees so that fair and equitable treatment will be assured in order to promote every consideration in making employee utilization with LSED a rewarding and satisfying relationship.

APPENDIX 3 *(concluded)*

Policy Areas to Be Covered

1. Leadership
2. Employee motivation
3. Communication
4. Job satisfaction and productivity
5. Promotional opportunities

IV. *Objective: Compensation and Benefit Function*

To establish and maintain an equitable compensation program designed to maintain a balance in order to provide employee reward, incentive, and satisfaction and, at the same time, to contribute to LSED's financial stability.

Policy Areas to Be Covered

1. Wage and salary administration
2. Indirect pay practices
3. Employee benefits
4. Job evaluation
5. Merit rating

V. *Objective: Maintenance Function*

To maintain effective relations with LSED's employees by providing them with the conditions for the maintenance of physical, emotional, and corporate health and safety in order to ensure a high quality of work life.

Policy Areas to Be Covered

1. Health
2. Safety
3. Employee relations
   a. Absence
   b. Leave
   c. Discipline
   d. Termination
   e. Complaints, grievances, harassment, and discrimination
   f. Drugs and alcohol

VI. *Objective: Research Function*

To provide analytical data for managerial decision making regarding personnel matters in order to provide the optimal techniques and procedures for each function of LSED's employee relations policies.

Policy Areas to Be Covered

1. Surveys
   a. Opinion, attitude
   b. Audits
   c. Forecasts
   d. Wage surveys
   e. Exit interviews
   f. Special
2. Analysis
   a. Job classification
   b. Job evaluation
   c. Job specification
   d. Job descriptions
3. Publications
   a. Reports
   b. Manuals
   c. Forms
   d. Tests
   e. Budgets
4. Affirmative action plan

47. Telephones and Turbulence: Managing Information Systems in the Eighties

Maria Warren, information systems director at the Regional Telephone Corporation (RTC), glanced at her work schedule. A telephone call from the vice president of consumer marketing services had just jarred her into action. The vice president, her supervisor for the last six months, had described his meeting that morning with the president of RTC. During the meeting the president had reiterated his concern about the marketing strength of the corporation, especially in light of the company's reorganization as a marketing oriented organization.

Apparently the president had asked her new boss for an action plan which detailed steps toward making RTC into a competitive and successful telephone company. The vice president, in turn, had asked Warren to present her recommendations to him and to schedule an emergency meeting on Friday. She had three days to prepare for the meeting, a meeting for which she had hoped for a long time.

BACKGROUND

RTC provides telecommunications services to approximately 300,000 customers in the northeastern region of the United States. It also is involved in a joint venture with another company to provide cellular telephone service in five neighboring counties.

Since divestiture, RTC has attempted to enhance its marketing strategies. As Warren characterizes it, her company "has been awakened by competition." Buyers are now shopping for the best rates and services, and major competitors in the telecommunications arena are working hard to attract these buyers. Additionally, with RTC new to the cellular services and products market, 1986 is a challenging new world.

This case was prepared by Nannette S. Levinson, The American University, and Mignon Williams, Xerox Corporation.

ORGANIZATIONAL STRUCTURE

The information systems division has never had the status of a department at RTC. However, the director of this division has total responsibility for data processing and is, as Warren says, "the last word of authority for data processing at RTC." Prior to 1986, she reported to the vice president for operations. Now (as related earlier) she reports to the vice president of consumer marketing services, who, in turn, reports directly to the president.

As information systems director, Warren manages a staff of 100. She oversees computer services and applications development for revenue programs, customer information, toll and long distance services, and end-user application development. She is responsible for an information center and for setting standards for hardware and software.

Four people report directly to Warren: the manager of computer services and three managers for computer application development. Tim Cullihan, who manages computer services, has programmers, analysts, and two assistant managers on his staff. His unit is responsible for operating systems, data bases, and on-line and data communications. The other three managers are assigned specific areas of RTC's business, and each manager is similarly assisted by a group of analysts and programmers.

THE INFORMATION SYSTEMS DIVISION

Warren administers a budget of $8 million, or approximately 3 to 5 percent of RTC's total budget. Despite her control of the data processing budget and her total responsibility for data processing, she believes that her unit is "not serving the user community in the way that it should." She believes that users should be more accountable to the corporation and would like to implement a transfer pricing system. A feasible option would be a charge-back service, whereby users' departments would "pay" the information systems division for applications development work.

THE INFORMATION CENTER

A related concern is the information center. The center exists to promote end-user application and to generate systems-compatible solutions using microcomputers. In order to meet these objectives, center staff members work with users to determine the most appropriate microcomputer solution for a designated business application. The staff also supplies a list of preferred vendors, which is drawn up in conjunction with the purchasing department. The list is periodically reviewed by staff members of the information center and the purchasing department. Additionally, the information systems division supplies a list of standard hardware and software.

STANDARD HARDWARE AND SOFTWARE

Warren has designated five criteria for inclusion on the division's list of standard hardware and software: (1) current and envisioned needs of RTC users, (2) developments in microcomputer technology, (3) compatibility with the installed base of hardware and software, (4) RTC internal communications projects, and (5) RTC data processing objectives and project planning. The policy statement of the information systems division on microcomputers encourages users to utilize standard hardware and software.

"Selection from a list of RTC standard microcomputer hardware is strongly suggested," the statement reads. It continues, "Similarly, the information systems division strongly suggests selecting micro-based software from a list of RTC standard software," and adds, "every attempt should be made to utilize standard software."

COMPUTER LITERACY AND THE INFORMATION CENTER

Warren seeks to create a computer-literate employee population through the use of the information center. She wants to help RTC's employees to become comfortable with using microcomputers in their daily tasks. Accordingly, the center's staff, in coordination with the human resources division, provides training or recommends outside training in the use of standard hardware and software.

Herein is the point of divergence—even turbulence—at RTC. While Warren encourages employees to select and use standard hardware and software, her counterpart in the human resources division does not. Gale Vader, head of human resources, recommends solutions that are not compatible with existing hardware and argues for incremental information systems expenditures. Until recently she and her division, along with the other divisions at RTC, "viewed information technology as a necessary evil," in Warren's own words. Thus, an impasse exists between the human resources division, which represents the user perspective, and the information systems division, which seeks to manage information systems as a whole as it serves the user population.

INFORMATION SYSTEMS PLANNING

Currently there is no information systems planning at RTC. The only system in place, a project management system, follows the systems development life cycle, beginning with a project estimate. Warren's staff uses prototyping to shorten the development cycle. Also, users in systems development have no role in either short- or long-term planning. They are involved in a project only if the system costs more than $50,000 or takes more than six months to develop.

Warren finds little top-level support for or understanding of the potential of information technology at RTC. But now, with the paper she has been asked to write as a vehicle, she has the opportunity to impact organizational priorities and to create support for information technology at RTC. Her input, she hopes, can help to solve some of the corporation's information systems problems. Thinking about how to overcome the barriers to integrating successfully the information systems function with the mainstream of RTC, Warren drafts a background paper. This background paper will provide support for the oral presentation to the vice president and, ultimately, will be a part of a presentation to the president.

48. The Georgia Marble Company (A)

The Georgia Marble Company was established in 1884 to extract the marble from the Long Swamp Valley, near Tate, in north Georgia. Probably, outcroppings of this deposit had been first worked by the Indians. Recent excavations in the Etowah Mounds yielded figures made of marble which had similar characteristics.

The first known white artisan to extract and to fabricate material from this area had begun working it about 1835. The lack of adequate transportation facilities had retarded the industrial development, however, since the first customers had to be within a radius of ox cart delivery. In a deposit of dolomitic limestone in an adjacent area, a waterwheel had been set up as a source of power for use in the fabrication of stone. However, the work produced had been crude and, by the year 1884, this operation had terminated.

Upon this earlier background of the area, some additional events happened during the Civil War period which had a definite influence on the area and culminated in the establishment of The Georgia Marble Company. On a visit to the region as a member of "Morgan's Raiders," a Yankee military group in the Civil War, O.F. Bane observed the existence of a marble deposit. Another influential factor was the construction of the Marietta and North Georgia Railroad (later Louisville and Nashville Railroad) to Tate Station in the early 1880s. Then too there was a chance meeting on the train of Frank H. Siddall, a Philadelphia soap millionaire, and the brother-in-law of Oscar Bane, H. C. Clement, who was also a cousin of Percival Clement, active in Vermont marble. Quite by chance, the conversation drifted to the north Georgia marble quarries. A friend of Siddall, Mr. Dewar, had already made a trip to the area to survey the situation as to feasibility of investment. In this chance meeting and conversation, the inception of the firm had its roots.

Those present at the organization meeting were: Henry C. Clement, Frank H. Siddall, Charles Willoughby, Harry Dewar, and Oscar F. Bane. Mr. Siddall was elected temporary president and Mr. Bane, temporary secretary (see Exhibits 1 and 2).

This case was prepared by Curtis E. Tate, University of Georgia.

EXHIBIT 1 Initial Stock Subscription List*
May 1884

Subscriber	Number of Shares Held
Henry C. Clement	150
Oscar F. Bane	150
Charles L. Willoughby	50
David K. Hill	50
Levi B. Bane	50
Nathan L. Clement	50
Frank H. Siddall	250
C. M. Smith	83
Harry Dewar	162
J. A. Dewar	5

* Common stock with $100 par value; initial capitalization of $100,000.

EXHIBIT 2 Stockholders after Increase of Capitalization to $1 Million July 1884

Subscriber	Number of Shares Held*
Frank H. Siddall	2,500
Henry C. Clement	1,500
Harry Dewar	1,620
David K. Hill	500
Levi B. Bane	500
J. A. Dewar	50
C. M. Smith	830
Oscar F. Bane	1,500
Nathan L. Clement	500
Charles L. Willoughby	500

* Par value $100 per share.

H. C. Clement became the firm's first president. He was associated with the Banes in the wholesale clothing business in Chicago. With him to guide the new company were Frank H. Siddall, vice president, Levi Bane, secretary, and J. A. Dewar, general manager. O. F. Bane replaced Levi in 1885 as secretary.

The corporation, about 1884, arranged a mineral lease on a section of marble properties belonging to members of the Tate family, in whose possession this part of the property had been since 1835. The lease was on a royalty basis for 25 years with an option for renewal.

There was limited quarrying activity during the first year. Time was devoted, primarily, to the procurement of machinery, the removal of overburden, construction, setting in place of equipment, and additional capital procurement. Equipment and operational procedures were copied from the Vermont Marble operation, with some supervisory personnel imported from Vermont. During this period the board of directors met frequently, discussing and taking action on operations and problems of finance and activities. The corporate minutes indicate action and consideration by the entire group, with no one person playing a dominant role.

It was during the second year of operation that the decision was reached to procure the Kennesaw quarrying properties, and to establish a second operation there. In this decision it was understood that the Tate operation would continue to be the company's principal one.

During the years that followed, the company was moderately profitable to unprofitable, in terms of the accounting practice of the period.[1] Frequently disappointing results were encountered because of unanticipated difficulties in the quarrying operation. Poor quality sections of stone were found. It was not unusual for the company to be unable to supply all of the stone needed, either because of inadequate quantities produced or because of scarcity of grade. This was true, particularly, of the number 1 grade.

The primary objective of the company was to quarry, saw, and semifinish the marble. It soon became apparent that there was an opportunity for the establishment of independent finishing works. The Harrisons, McGraths, Keelers, Andersons, Sickelses, Bradys, Dewars, Norcrosses, and others, set up finishing plants in Marble Hill, Tate, Nelson, Ball Ground, Canton, and Marietta—all towns nearby.

The labor force of The Georgia Marble Company was paid off in scrip, by way of a side agreement between the company and the Tates who operated a store in Tate, Georgia. The scrip was redeemable in merchandise and cash at the store, the operation of which was bid on a five-year basis between the Tate brothers, William and Stephen C. The first reference to any of the Tate family as stockholders was shown at the stockholders' meeting of 1888, when Stephen C. Tate had 377 shares voted by proxy. In the meeting of the next year, Stephen voted by proxy 300 shares and William 100 shares by proxy. This stockholder relationship continued past the death of both of these men some years later. By 1900, two members of the family were serving on the board of directors.

Additional funds were provided along the way from the sale of bonds, preferred stock, and, on occasion, by notes given to some of the major shareholders. The bonds were 6 percent, but sold at 0.75+.

In an effort to obtain more profitable business during the 1890s, the company procured the necessary equipment and personnel to fin-

---

[1] No provision was made for depreciation. All items were carried on the books at cost.

ish and to set stone, both interior and exterior. Some Italian labor was imported to fill the labor requirements. After a contractual agreement was signed for the Montgomery Ward building in Chicago, the company was advised that it would not be permitted to use its nonunion craftsmen to set the stone. Following some negotiations, however, an accord was reached that permitted the use of the company's own labor, provided it paid the higher scale of the unionized stonesetters of Chicago. After this unfortunate experience, the company returned to the firm's original objective of quarrying, sawing, and semifinishing marble.

By 1887 stockholder distribution had increased. It continued to increase. But, in spite of its projected potential, the company had not had performance such as to attract capital with ease, in an adequate amount to satisfy the insatiable appetite of establishing a new extractive company working mineral deposits in a virgin territory. Records show that, for a period of some months, a Mr. Abbott held an option to purchase the company. It was never exercised.

A motion was tendered by Stephen C. Tate and accepted at the annual stockholders' meeting in May 1900 that the directors seek a buyer for the assets of the corporation, the reason being that there was needed a larger amount of capital to operate successfully in exploiting the deposits. The corporation had been under almost constant pressure since its establishment to raise additional funds. The need for employee housing, more equipment, better equipment, different equipment, the need to open new quarries, seems to have ever "dogged" the steps of the management (see Exhibit 3).

During the period from 1895 to 1905, Stephen C. Tate and his subsequent estate held the store operation contract. (This was the store where company payroll was redeemed.) It had been managed by his son Sam, a bachelor. "Col. Sam," as he was later known, had been thought of as something of a hell raiser in his younger years[2] but had settled down to Puritanical sobriety with considerable business acumen at the time he had taken over the store management.

In 1905, the William Tate estate won the store contract. A later associate of Col. Sam commented, "Col. Sam was quite concerned over what should be his future endeavor."

It was at this point he was approached by Henry C. Clement, president of The Georgia Marble Company, about his taking over the management of the company. To assume this position it was apparently necessary for Sam to acquire a sizable block of stock. During the period in which efforts were being made to work the financial details, Col. Sam gave some consideration to relying on family resources.

---

[2] William Tate, ed., *Documents and Memoirs, Genealogical Tables, The Tates of Pickens County* (Marietta, Ga.: Continental Book Company, 1953), p. 28.

EXHIBIT 3

THE GEORGIA MARBLE COMPANY (A)
Financial Statement of 1900
Balance Sheet

Assets

Real estate and leases	$1,576,289.80
Cash	7,953.80
Notes receivable.	21,324.61
Accounts receivable	40,712.22
Stocks and securities	57,500.00
Machinery and fixtures.	246,164.94
Railroads	78,132.75
Buildings	30,050.00
Marble (inventory)	116,391.07
Supplies	7,477.38
Total assets	$2,181,996.57

Liabilities

Capital stock	$1,500,000.00
Bonds.	500,000.00
Notes payable	13,950.00
Accounts payable	108,285.21
Profit and loss.	59,761.36
Total liabilities.	$2,181,996.57

Statement of Gains and Losses
(Income Statement)

Gains		
Sales	$132,260.05	
Less purchases. . .	11.10	$ 132,248.95
Rent		1,645.43
Railroad earnings		5,813.11
Increase in marble (inventory) . .		5,663.49
		$ 145,370.98
Losses		
Expense—maintenance		$ 14,477.71
Labor		47,180.94
Salaries		12,700.00
Freight		11,904.62
Royalty		7,591.58
Traveling		1,510.89
Insurance		694.89
Interest		34,442.88
Discount		622.63
		$ 131,126.14
Net gains		$ 14,244.84

Some discussions were conducted with the appropriate members, two of whom were cousins. Previously, he had given financial assistance to R. T. Jones of Canton Cotton Mills to help him achieve a personal project objective in establishing the cotton mills. In the final negotiations, it was this man who came in with the needed financial assistance to consummate the transaction. Col. Sam, at 45, became president and general manager of the company in 1905 with the acquisition of 6,791 shares of stock (see Exhibit 4).

The immediate consequence of the change in management was a drive for more production by adding equipment, changing procedures, clearing quarries, having the S. C. Tate estate construct additional tenant houses to make possible the procurement of additional labor. The results of the first year of the new management may be noted by examining the financial statement of 1906 (see Exhibit 5).

During the second year under Col. Sam's management, items of equipment and machinery which no longer had a useful life but whose value on the books was equal to the original cost were charged off. The Panic of 1907 brought a period of reduced sales for marble. As evidenced in the annual reports of the president-general manager given in 1908 and 1909, all employees were continued on the payroll and customer accounts were carried. In the face of adversity the company continued to pay its short- and long-term obligations. It was evidence of a "gilt-edged" company in Col. Sam's opinion. Taking care of employees and customer needs in a period of such adversity brought much personal pride and satisfaction to him. Dean William Tate tells us in his memoirs:

> No man has more respect and reverence for women or more love for children; yet he has never married. It was a delicate subject, but I went straight at the heart of the big, serious man in an unguarded moment and he made a confession.
> "I have thought about marriage," he said, "but with it always comes the thought of the children here in these hills, hundreds of them, who need me; I have thought that perhaps if I had children of my own I might neglect this greater number of other children."[3]

Justification for continued utilization of the total work force was the need to retain the men in order that future business commitments might be met most advantageously.

The year of 1909 saw the expiration of the initial 25-year lease of marble properties from the S. C. Tate and William Tate estates. Some of the executors of the William Tate estate saw an opportunity to dispose of their property by way of sale. After a period of impasse in negotiations (the initial lease contained an option of renewal clause)

---

[3] William Tate, ed., *The Tates of Pickens County*, p. 21.

EXHIBIT 4

THE GEORGIA MARBLE COMPANY (A)
Financial Statement of 1905
(Balance Sheet)

Assets

Real estate and leases	$1,748,639.80	
Cash	18,790.09	
Notes receivable.	19,673.14	
Accounts receivable	49,026.83	
Stocks and securities	1,500.00	
Machinery and fixtures.	265,487.50	
Railroads	89,739.85	
Buildings	31,066.00	
Marble (inventory)	108,099.76	
Supplies	7,512.68	
		$2,339,535.65

Liabilities

Capital stock	$1,500,000.00	
Bonds.	500,000.00	
Improvement notes	130,000.00	
Notes payable	1,785.39	
Accounts payable	65,590.08	
Profit and loss.	142,160.18	
		$2,339,535.65

Statement of Gains and Losses
(Income Statement)

Gains		
Marble, as per inventory	$ 108,099.76	
Sales	206,066.34	$ 314,166.10
Inventory, April 30, 1904 . .	91,326.54	
Purchases.	258.25	91,584.79
Gains on marble and sales . . .		222,581.31
Rents		1,675.55
Railroad earnings		9,600.02
Gross profits		$ 233,856.88
Losses		
Expenses—maintenance	$ 32,712.50	
Labor	56,490.13	
Salaries	8,700.00	
Freight	16,339.70	
Royalty	14,712.12	
Traveling	981.34	
Insurance	1,408.33	
Interest	39,518.97	
Discount	3,985.89	$ 174,848.98
Net profit		$ 59,007.90

EXHIBIT 5

THE GEORGIA MARBLE COMPANY (A)
Financial Statement of 1906
(Balance Sheet)

Assets

Real estate and leases	$1,747,989.80	
Cash	44,210.43	
Notes receivable	46,725.77	
Accounts receivable	39,251.22	
Machinery and fixtures	272,860.50	
Railroads	91,966.90	
Buildings	31,566.00	
Marble (inventory)	115,679.05	
Supplies	9,832.68	$2,400,082.35

Liabilities

Capital stock	$1,500,000.00	
Bonds	500,000.00	
Improvement notes	130,000.00	
Accounts payable	8,246.49	
Profit and loss	261,835.86	$2,400,082.35

Statement of Gains and Losses
(Income Statement)

Gains		
Marble as per inventory	$ 115,679.05	
Sales	283,830.28	$ 399,509.33
Inventory, April 30, 1905	108,099.76	
Purchases	228.42	108,328.18
		291,181.15
Rents		1,826.25
Railroad earnings		11,588.39
Gross profits		304,595.79

Losses		
Expenses—maintenance	$ 29,034.32	
Labor	68,719.69	
Salaries	5,700.00	
Freight	18,702.90	
Royalty	17,735.66	
Traveling	1,088.18	
Insurance	1,298.26	
Interest	34,975.96	
Discount	7,019.85	$ 184,274.82
Net profits		$ 120,320.97

the terms of sale were agreed upon: $324,000 to be paid: $60,000 cash at once (1909), $20,000 per year 1910 through 1921, final payment of $24,000 to be made in 1922. The deed was to be held in escrow until the final payment was made. This transaction made The Georgia Marble Company joint owners with the Stephen C. Tate estate of certain marble properties.

At this point, the company was, to a great extent, dependent for sales volume on the local finishing plants. On occasion, joint contracts were undertaken, but, primarily, the activities of the finishers determined the sales of The Georgia Marble Company.

The Georgia Marble Company (B)

The marketing activities of The Georgia Marble Company were confined primarily to the sale of cubic stock. Advertising promotion carried on by the company was directed toward this objective. Demand for the company's number 1 cubic stock was strong: "We have demand for every No. 1 block we can produce. . . ." There was a problem in marketing the number 2 and number 3 grade blocks, however. At this point the company was not carrying on any finishing activities. This, in effect, made its activities dependent on the whims of the finishing trade.

In a discussion of the utilization of funds procured from $1,500,000 in bonds issued in 1911, Col. Sam expressed the feelings he had had for some time.

> I have had it in mind for quite a while that the wisest and most profitable thing to be done for those interested in The Georgia Marble Company is that the company control the manufacture of their product and I have therefore made provision in the new issue of bonds for $500,000 of same to remain in the treasury to acquire additional property and I would recommend that if deals can be made whereby The Georgia Marble Co. can exchange these bonds at such price as necessary to acquire The Blue Ridge Marble Company, The Geo. B. Sickels Marble Co., The Kennesaw Marble Co. and The Georgia Marble Finishing Works plants, when it can be done. As it now stands, we are entirely dependent upon these finishers to market our product, and we find they often push the sales of such materials as they can find a ready sale for without any efforts to dispose of any surplus we may have and oftentimes they demoralize the business, to some extent, by making unnecessarily low prices in order to get business. I believe the profits of The Georgia Marble Company, as well as all the finishers, could be increased not less than 25 percent by the consummation of a trade of this kind.[1]

None of the above mentioned organizations owned or operated any quarries. They purchased their marble stock from The Georgia Marble Company. The company was showing a continued interest in keeping its assets directed toward the extraction and fabrication of stone.

---

[1] President's Report, 1911 (The Georgia Marble Company: Official Record, No. 2, pp. 15–17).

EXHIBIT 1

THE GEORGIA MARBLE COMPANY (B)
Financial Statement of 1912
(Balance Sheet)

Assets

Real estate and leases	$2,247,400.00	
Cash	31,464.67	
Notes receivable	1,681.53	
Accounts receivable	95,385.52	
Stocks and securities	49,000.00	
Machinery and fixtures	271,899.27	
Railroads	128,027.85	
Buildings	69,054.40	
Marble (inventory)	197,599.17	
Supplies	13,333.06	$3,104,845.47

Liabilities

Capital stock	$1,500,000.00	
Surplus	500,000.00	
Guarantee fund	50,000.00	
Profit and loss	347,693.28	
Real estate purchase notes	231,500.00	
Bonds	400,000.00	
Notes payable	51,200.00	
Accounts payable	23,091.19	
Dividend account	1,361.00	$3,104,845.47

Statement of Gains and Losses
(Income Statement)

Gains		
Marble as per inventory, April 30, 1912	$ 197,599.17	
Sales	337,921.32	$ 535,520.49
Marble as per inventory, April 30, 1911	167,863.79	
Purchases	198.48	168,062.27
Gains on marble		$ 367,458.22
Rents		4,106.58
Gross profits		$ 371,564.80
Losses		
Expense, maintenance	$ 48,265.83	
Labor	95,319.59	
Salaries	17,200.08	
Freight	17,135.67	
Royalty	18,606.40	
Traveling	1,204.48	
Insurance	1,909.35	
Interest	35,232.93	
Discount	1,725.78	
Wm. Tate—Real estate purchase	3,395.47	$ 239,995.58
Less for depreciation		23,557.02
Net profit		$ 108,012.20

EXHIBIT 2 Schedule of Acquisition of Finishing
Operations

The Southern Marble Company	May 1916
Amicalola Marble Company	October 1916
The Kennesaw Marble Company	February 1917
The Blue Ridge Marble Company	February 1917
The George B. Sickels Marble Company	February 1917

From the beginning of the new management under Col. Sam in 1905, The Georgia Marble Company responded to the individual drive and personality of its president-general manager with improved profits and greater growth (see Exhibit 1). An age at which he desired retirement was soon reached by Mr. George B. Sickels. The stock of his company was acquired by Col. Sam Tate, Mr. H. L. Litchfield, corporate secretary, Walter Tate, vice president and brother of Col. Sam, all of the company, and J. M. Eaton, a Marble Hill merchant.

The Blue Ridge Marble Company was purchased from the Harry Dewar estate and two or three minor stockholders after an unsuccessful attempt by the widow and son to continue the operation of the firm. Most of the stock of this firm was purchased by Col. Sam and his brother-in-law Alex Anderson. It continued as an independent operation under the direction of Anderson.

A gentlemen's agreement determining pricing policy made more pleasant the company dealings with The Kennesaw Company, principally owned by a Mr. Newell of Boston. It continued to operate independently.

Another operation, the Southern Marble Company, continued along independent lines with both quarrying and finishing facilities. Mr. O. W. Norcross, a contractor of Worcester, Massachusetts, owned this company.

Hampered somewhat by the general economic conditions, and later by World War I, The Georgia Marble Company continued to hold its own and made some advance. The years of 1916 and 1917 were important years in the history of the company. It was during this period that it acquired all of the adjacent independent finishing companies with the exception of The Georgia Marble Finishing Works of Canton, Georgia (see Exhibit 2). These acquisitions enabled the company to assume a more positive and directed course in achieving greater sales results (see Exhibits 3 and 4). Still another significant factor, when the dust had cleared, was that Col. Sam was then voting 13,112 shares of the 20,000 shares of outstanding stock.

The termination of the war came and the following key personalities were in officer positions, places that they were to fill, in most cases, for the next decade and a half or longer:

EXHIBIT 3

THE GEORGIA MARBLE COMPANY (B)
Statement of Gains and Losses for Year Ending
April 30, 1916

Marble as per inventory April 30, 1916	$239,206.57	
Sales for year	246,017.64	$485,224.21
Marble as per inventory April 30, 1915	$244,372.64	
Purchases of marble for year	218.06	$244,590.69
Gains on marble		$240,633.52
Rents		3,649.28
		$244,282.80

Losses

Expenses	$31,774.28	
Labor	76,165.39	
Salary	17,400.00	
Freight	13,662.48	
Royalty	14,941.07	
Traveling	1,046.30	
Insurance	2,912.05	
Interest	25,080.84	
Discount	5,751.31	
Wm. Tate purchase E. & E.	46.82	188,781.34
Net profit		$ 55,501.46

Col. Sam Tate, president

Alex Anderson, vice president, manager of the Nelson Plant (Blue Ridge Marble Company plant)

A. V. Cortelyou, vice president, manager of the Kennesaw Plant

Harry Miles, vice president, manager, New York sales office

Walter Tate, vice president

H. L. Litchfield, vice president

A. B. Bayless, general manager (The first time since Col. Sam became president that a separate general manager had existed.)

G. M. Atherton, secretary and treasurer, manager of Monumental Operations at Tate, Georgia

While conditions of the company somewhat followed the pattern of the business cycle, it prospered in the 1920s. After Col. Sam's arrival in New York City in 1924 on a trip around the world, the board of directors voted that the company pay his expenses as a token of appreciation for his services and to give him opportunity for a much-needed rest to regain his health.[2] In an interview for a story in a

---

[2] In 1927, the board again voted a trip to renew his health, this time a cruise in the Mediterranean.

EXHIBIT 4

THE GEORGIA MARBLE COMPANY (B)
Summary of Income and Profit and Loss, 1919

Sales		
Rough blocks	$ 118,520.96	
Monumental	1,107,095.57	
Interior.	211,180.18	
Exterior	132,454.37	
Scrap and sundries.	22,676.42	
	$1,591,927.50	
Less returns and allowances	41,567.37	
Net sales.		$1,550,360.13
Cost of goods sold	$1,414,749.71	
Less inventory of marble		
Materials, supplies, and so on, December 31, 1919	330,551.29	
Net cost of goods sold		$1,084,198.42
Gross profit from sales		$ 466,161.71
Selling expenses		40,157.63
Net profit on sales		$ 426,004.08
General expenses		77,329.70
Net profit on operations.		$ 348,674.38
Other income		28,846.38
Gross income		377,520.76
Income charges		
Interest on bonds.	$ 62,000.00	
Amortization of discount and expense on bonds	11,025.12	
Interest on notes payable	18,835.37	
Cash discounts on sales	24,435.51	
Interest on notes receivable discounted	254.03	$ 116,550.03
Net income.		$ 260,970.73

---

national magazine of that year, Col. Sam was estimated to be worth 165 million dollars.[3] The marble deposits were estimated at that time to be "a solid mass, from five to seven miles long, one-half mile wide, and in some places estimated by geologists to be 2,000 feet deep."[4]

Certain policies followed during this period were to have a profound effect in the future on the company's operations. While the president was known to be very autocratic in his rule, a considerable amount of decentralization did exist. Vice presidents in charge of individual operations were expected to follow the wishes of Col. Sam. While there was not as much "looking over the shoulder" as might have been expected, he, who had given up his quart a day and his pipe and cigar, was strongly opposed to the consumption of alcoholic bev-

---

[3] W. O. Saunders, "He's King of Hearts in Georgia," *Collier's* 74 (December 6, 1924), pp. 12–13.

[4] William Tate, *The Tates of Pickens County*, p. 4.

erages or tobacco. An officer now in the company jovially recalls that he was made to understand there would be no advance in grade or pay if Col. Sam ever caught one smoking. The result was a swallowing of cigarettes on six or seven occasions. From the point of view of some onlookers, it seemed that politics existed too in the upper echelons of the company, where favoritism might have been shown in the parceling out of orders.

There were other factors pertinent to the future course of history of the company. Some mausoleum work was done for which securities were taken instead of money. Certain officers of Georgia Marble, and others, made purchases without payment, either directly charging to the company or at one of the two company stores. Members of the Tate family, with others, became involved in the development of "Tate Mountain Estates," a mountain resort hotel and golf course, constructed in an inaccessible mountain area. And, Mr. Willie Anderson, brother of Alex, both of whom were formerly with Blue Ridge, became involved in the Tennessee Pink Marble Company, heading this operation.

Some 6,000 acres of land was purchased with the objective of developing a water power plant to supply the company's power needs. Two or more engineering surveys were conducted. A new steam power plant was constructed. But, at this point, a contract was made with the Georgia Power Company to supply power needs. The power plant was used very little and the land for the water power plant was later to be of value for its stand of timber. The farm depression adversely affected the sale of monuments in the rural South. And the increasing use of no-monument cemeteries in the North and Northeast began to be felt in the company.

But the late 1920s and early 1930s had their good days too. Among them were contracts for the New York Stock Exchange building and a large number of new post offices and other public buildings. Dividends were paid through 1931.

During the year 1933 the company lost $225,000 on its operation, according to the report of the audit. While, in the early years of the depression, the company had successfully countered the trend, early in 1934 orders fell away. The Kennesaw plant was closed early in 1934 and continued so except for one brief period. A member of the administrative group at Kennesaw at that time says, "I sat for six weeks with nothing to do." Seeing nothing in view, he quit to find other employment, and, when he tendered his resignation, was thanked by the manager for saving himself the pain of the termination.

Many projects were undertaken during the depression years to provide employment for the work force. Some were carried on at cost, or less: the road to the Tate Mountain Estates, the marble residence of Col. Sam and his unmarried sister, the $75,000 to $100,000 of marble given for use in the buildings at Wesleyan College in Macon, Georgia. And there were other such projects.

By September 1934, in order to continue operations, even on a curtailed basis, Col. Sam had pledged 10,000 shares of his stock for loan from a group of Atlanta banks. Interests of the banks had to be represented and protected by the establishment of a position of executive vice president. This officer was to be responsible for the business, operation, and sales of the corporation. Mr. E. W. Gottenstrater was elected as executive vice president. Officers at this time were:

Col. Sam Tate, president
E. W. Gottenstrater, executive vice president
Alex Anderson, vice president
A. V. Cortelyou, vice president
Harry H. Miles, vice president in charge of New York sales office
Herbert L. Miles, vice president in charge of Atlanta office
H. L. Litchfield, vice president
Walter E. Tate, vice president and general manager

Gottenstrater's tenure of office lasted from September 26 to November 14 at which time he resigned. The banks (voting trustees) decided to permit Col. Sam to return to active management of the company.

During early 1935 a decision was reached to apply for a loan from Reconstruction Finance Corporation of $709,000. When RFC proposed a loan of only $500,000, the terms were unacceptable to Col. Sam and the application was withdrawn.

An effort was made to sell the company through the Robert R. Otis Company at a price of $3,000,000. Nothing came of this.

Again in 1936, the bank group asked that the office of executive vice president be filled with a person of their choice, W. C. Cram. The comment made by an observer affiliated with the company was, "It took Col. Sam about a month to eat those fellows up. He began working on them as soon as they arrived and, by the end of the month, he had them eating out of his hand. He was just that kind of man—a strong, personable individual."

When illness struck Col. Sam in 1936, Mr. Cram continued to serve (though some questioned his effectiveness). In 1937, the corporate articles were amended and Col. Sam was elevated to chairman of the board. His brother-in-law, I. P. Morton, became president. In October 1938, the curtain of an era closed as Col. Sam died.

Now the courts had their role to play, along with the heirs, the creditors, and the corporation. The organization continued to function, but was hampered by the haze of uncertainty and lack of strong leadership. The management, under court order to elect no directors until Col. Sam's estate was settled, left existing practices generally unmolested. One attempt was made to sell the stock held by the receivers at public cry, but the bid was inadequate in the eyes of the court. During a second public auction in April 1941, the stock was purchased by a syndicate of individuals who joined together to form the Georgia Marble Holding Company. Immediate needs were a stockholders' meeting, election of directors, and taking steps to reorganize the corporate charter in keeping with the more recent revision of Georgia corporation laws.

The first stockholders' meeting found the Georgia Marble Holding Company in possession of 13,121¹⁄₁₂ shares of the 20,000 shares outstanding. The board of directors elected follow:

Alex Anderson	Granger Hansell[5]
C. H. Candler, Jr.[5]	H. L. Litchfield
J. R. Cowan	I. P. Morton
Clement A. Evans[5]	James D. Robinson, Jr.[5]
Wilbur Glenn[5]	L. E. Tate

Mr. Cowan was brought in by the new controlling group to be executive vice president until he could be moved into the president's position.[6]

Here was an organization in which the operating procedures, the physical facilities, the personnel policies, the assets, had been permitted to deteriorate steadily since 1929. A portion of assets had been used for the personal benefit of some officers and employees, a part of which was covered by personal notes.

The value and continued utility of some assets carried on the balance sheet were questionable. The Marietta (Kennesaw) plant had been idle since 1934, with the exception of six months in operation in 1936. Taxes, insurance, building maintenance, watchman wages, salaries for the plant manager and his assistant, continued to run costs up. There was the power plant with its idle boiler and turbine. Parcels of real estate that were no longer useful were scattered here and there. Tenant houses for employees were in need of paint, repairs, and some lacked electric lighting. What should be done about the company's first mortgage 6 percent sinking fund gold bonds, amounting to $407,000 as of December 31, 1940?

There was the question of what should be done about the school facilities for the children of the area. It had long been the custom of

---

[5] Member of Georgia Marble Holding Company.

[6] An engineer by profession, he had served as coordinator on the building of the Mellon National Gallery of Art, Washington, D.C., followed by a period as president of the Ross-Republic Marble Company, Knoxville, Tennessee. At this time Ross-Republic was bankrupt, but its failure could not be attributed to Mr. Cowan's action as president. A controller with the company since 1927 makes this appraisal of Cowan: "An engineer first, a real good businessman, handy with a slide rule in analyzing statistical information."

the company to provide the physical facilities and the funds for faculty salaries. The Nelson store was having a monthly loss of $400. Also, there was a question of what to do about the Godfrey plant, its real property and improvements in Atlanta, the mausoleum accounts, Grand Rapids, Michigan, Oak Ridge Abbey Mausoleum, Chicago, and one in Enid, Oklahoma. These facilities had been constructed in the 1920s and the company, in lieu of cash payment, had accepted claims against the respective assets.

What should be the status of property jointly owned by The Georgia Marble Company and the S. C. Tate estate?

In dealing with the issues at hand, there were to be considered the economic consequences upon the community which would result from a drive on improved efficiency. While stringent action might, in theory, improve earnings, how would the company fare if these policies should cause a mass exodus of the workers and their families? The demands of the national defense effort were also taking ever-increasing gulps of manpower.

In the face of these conditions, what should be the policy of the company relating to sales, to personnel, to the community, toward operations, and toward its methods?

The Georgia Marble Company (C)

Under the control of the new ownership, an executive committee was established in The Georgia Marble Company to act for the board of directors between meetings of that body.[1] The board formulated the policy which the company should follow and a letter was issued by the president, Mr. Morton, interpreting the policy to the officers and employees.[2]

April 23, 1941

To Officers and Employees of The Georgia Marble Company:

I am very happy to announce to you that the period of uncertainty which has beset this company has at long last definitely ended. Colonel Tate's controlling interest in the company has passed into strong hands and the prospects are most promising.

A new board of directors was selected by the stockholders on April 14. This board has met and I have been reelected president. Mr. J. R. Cowan, now of Knoxville, Tennessee, was chosen first vice president and general manager. Mr. Litchfield was made secretary. Other officers have been reelected.

I want to quote from the minutes of the board of directors showing their proceedings as follows:

A discussion of the future policy of the company then took place, after which it was moved, seconded and unanimously

Resolved:

1. That the directors earnestly desire a continuance of the cordial relations that have always existed between the officers, stockholders, and employees.

2. That the directors pledge themselves to use their best efforts to reestablish this company in the commanding position it is accustomed to occupy in the business and financial field, and request the officers and employees to cooperate to this end.

3. That the management aim at increasing the demand for and sales of marble as a means of taking up the slack in employment and absorbing

---

[1] Membership of this executive committee consisted of:

I. P. Morton	James D. Robinson, Jr.
J. R. Cowan	Wilbur Glenn
Clement A. Evans	

[2] Minutes, directors' meeting, April 14, 1941; The Georgia Marble Company (official record), April 14, 1941, to May 29, 1946, p. 22.

the full time and talents of all officers and employees; to the end that loyal and efficient persons may be assured of steady work.

4. That all officers and employees are invited to make constructive suggestions as to new uses of marble, improvements in the method of quarrying or finishing, and ways in which the community life may be made more pleasant and the general welfare improved.

I believe that these resolutions are self-explanatory. I feel sure that they express the genuine sentiments of the board and the management.

Cordially,

President

Company affairs demanded the attention of the executive committee rather frequently during the remaining months of 1941. Decisions had to be reached concerning certain problematical situations, concerning the disposition of certain assets. It was truly a year of action in the company.

- a. An office was established in Atlanta along with continued maintenance of the office in Tate, Georgia.
- b. Several parcels of real property were sold (in some instances mineral rights were reserved; they were not held back in other cases).
- c. Consideration was given by the executive committee to the application of new sales techniques to procure more business and to the loss of sales brought on by "no-monument cemeteries."
- d. The need to establish an independent pricing policy as well as a satisfactory pricing structure was recognized and action taken.
- e. Continuation of the company's employee group life insurance program was authorized, but it excluded people who no longer had active company status unless they paid the entire premium cost.
- f. Compulsory retirement at 65 was established for officers and employees. All beyond this age at the time had December 31, 1941, set as a retirement date for them.[3]

---

[3] The board of directors, upholding action of the executive committee, provided for the retirement of Mr. Alex Anderson among this group, with the title of senior consultant. Stipulations for his stay in Florida for three months in the interest of his health carried a continuation of his salary of $500 per month through that period with an extra bonus upon his return: cancellation of a $1,700 note which the company held against him. But the board also felt it desirable to stipulate that if Anderson failed to go to Florida, his salary would be cut to $225 per month on the retirement date. Or, if he cut his stay short of three months, the salary cut was to be effective upon his return.

g. A satisfactory agreement with the bondholders was evolved.

h. For a saving of $1,000 a year, the listing of the company bonds on the Baltimore Securities Exchange was withdrawn. It was informally understood that an Atlanta securities organization would make a market for these bonds.

i. The board authorized the sale of all miscellaneous securities owned by the company.

j. A $46,000 claim against the Acacia Mausoleum in Chicago was sold for $12,000. The statute of limitations prevented any other action.

k. Claims against the Light Pink Marble Company were settled with an agreement for payment of $5,000 cash and the shipment of 20 carloads of light pink marble.

l. A settlement was reached with certain of the Tate estate beneficiaries for a $45,000 note.

m. The power plant was disposed of for $26,000.

n. Lands jointly owned by the S. C. Tate estate and the company were divided and appropriate deeds were drawn.

o. A more accurate accounting system was ordered for the Nelson plant, one that would truly reflect the profit and loss relationship.

p. Consideration was given to the opportunities for improving profits through utilization of waste stone. Decisions relating to the Serpentine properties at Holly Springs had to be given. Production of medicinal calcium from sawing and rubbing bed waste was considered.

q. In the management structure, weaknesses were pinpointed: certain employees were relieved of their responsibilities or retired and new personnel was procured.[4]

r. Building improvements were made at the Tate plant, with a concrete floor added; some production bottlenecks were eliminated through layout changes.

s. A number of employee houses were provided with electric service.

---

[4] Among new personnel brought into the company at this time was Mr. William Vance. A loan officer with The Trust Company of Georgia, he had been brought into the company as monumental sales manager. This was not his first association with the company. An engineer by profession, he had, during the 1920s, worked in the Florida boom. Then, he began a seven-year period of employment with the company in the Marietta plant. During this period he was involved in many different kinds of activities, from which he probably got "marble dust in his veins." But he joined GMAC where he says "I received my degree in business administration." After another short spell with the Marietta plant of the company, and an interval in the banking business, he indicates he welcomed the opportunity of reassociation with The Georgia Marble Company under the new management.

    t. For handling marble in the yards, tractors were substituted for mule power with a cut of 50 percent in manpower requirements in this area.

    u. Various alternatives were considered relating to the status of the Nelson and Marietta plants.

    v. War defense enforcement of material allocation made necessary the seeking of defense work in order to procure an adequate supply of saw blades. It had to be recognized, however, that there was a serious shortage in procurement of this type of business.

The opportunity came, in early December 1941, for acquisition of the business, assets, and personnel of The Georgia Marble Finishing Works at Canton, Georgia. It had always had operations related to those of The Georgia Marble Company, and it has been reported that each company attempted to exploit its position in dealing with the other. The Finishing Works was dependent on Georgia Marble as its source of stone. And, likewise, the company had, under Col. Sam's management, depended on banking associations of some officers of the Finishing Works.

Now, the efficiency of the production at the Canton plant was never under criticism, either in years of high-volume sales ($600,000) or, even in the latter years of low-volume sales ($200,000), when the Finishing Works was caught in the yoke of a price squeeze on its cubic stock and when management's vocal anti-Roosevelt attitude resulted in the calling of all salesmen in off the road. During its period of operation, 1904–41, the Finishing Works had sales of $20 million, with a net profit of $4 million. What reasons could be given for the acquisition of a company which seemed destined to close its operation and to liquidate its assets?

Fifty-one percent of the stock of the Finishing Works was tied up in the R. T. Jones estate, which was understood to be confronted with the need to raise cash for tax purposes. The first plus factor for acquisition was that the Finishing Works had, among some of its key management personnel, people with desirable management proficiency, particularly in the area of production.[5] The Finishing Works also had an inventory of 40,000 cubic feet of silver gray marble; this was a second feature making this company desirable for acquisition. At this time The Georgia Marble Company quarries were not producing any silver gray, a type of marble which was in considerable demand.

The best terms seemed to be: a cash payment of $25,000 and an issue of $62,500—5 percent preferred stock of The Georgia Marble

---

[5] Two of these were S. E. Hyatt, their plant manager, and George Doss, who was production manager of The Georgia Marble Finishing Works.

Company;[6] a one-year lease on the plant facility at Canton with the option of cancelation after this time upon a 60-day notice. A stated conservative value of the equipment and machinery of the Finishing Works was estimated at $30,000. The transaction was consummated, effective December 31, 1941.

The advent of war with its continued pressure on the civilian sector of the economy had its impact on The Georgia Marble Company. The demand for monumental products continued strong, but the cutback in civilian construction, with little demand for marble to be used in defense construction, necessitated certain changes in production and administration of the company. The field sales force was cut back; the Atlanta office was maintained with a minimum force to handle those few situations that did arise in the structural field. Production was chiefly in monumental products.

Mr. Cowan, now president, continued the task of rebuilding the company.[7] A bonus arrangement, dependent on company profits, was worked out with him. Since the freight cost of shipping marble blocks from the quarries to the Marietta plant added 50 percent to production costs, it was decided that the liquidation of the Marietta plant was an economic necessity. Also, the local electric distribution system serving Tate, Marble Hill, and Nelson, Georgia, communities, which had been owned by the company, was sold to the local Rural Electrification Administration. Other liquidations were carried out as well.

Because of the policy of management in the liquidation of all assets not useful in goal achievement, there was criticism that efforts were being made to strip the company of all salable assets to recover costs of investment incurred by the Georgia Marble Holding Company. The stockholders were given a six-months' report in 1943 as an answer to this criticism (see Exhibit 1). In addition, the board of directors passed a resolution which provided that no director should purchase company assets unless these had been first offered to the public on a bid basis.

Efforts to set up a school district at Tate, Georgia, and to float a $50,000 bond issue to enable the company to sell the school building were unsuccessful. Finally, the building was turned over to the school district for a $1,000 promissory note.

In January 1943, the board of directors authorized an advertising budget of 2 percent of anticipated sales (see Exhibit 2). Also, upon recommendation of the auditing firm, $930,000 was written off from the surplus account to more nearly represent actual conditions. This had accumulated during early years of operation through discounts on

---

[6] The cash payment of $25,000 was to be obtained from the bond trustee who had received the $26,000 proceeds from the sale of the power plant.

[7] Mr. Morton had been elevated to chairman of the board of directors.

EXHIBIT 1

To the Stockholders of The Georgia Marble Company:

Six months of 1942 having past, your management believes that an interim report would be both appreciated by you and would help you to understand what has been accomplished in this time.

These six months have each shown a net operating profit. It is impossible to make any dependable forecast of what will be the result of the next six months. Conditions brought about by the war make it absolutely impossible to forecast and extremely difficult to establish any plans. We can say that we are being as conservative as possible and are making our plans to meet any conditions that may arise, as far as possible. Total business in these six months is considerably greater than last year, due in a large measure to the acquisition of the Georgia Marble Finishing Works.

Under the authority of the board of directors our electric distribution system, furnishing electricity to the tenant houses of the towns of Tate, Nelson, and Marble Hill, was sold and the money received from this was applied toward reducing our first mortgage bonds.

Your management, with the approval and under the direction of the board of directors, has been liquidating certain plant items which have not been absolutely essential to the operations of the company. Two large compressors from Tate and a crane and runway from Marble Hill, along with some other items, have been sold at very good prices. Some of these items had not been used for many years and no use could be seen for them for some years to come; other items would not be used for the duration of the war and after the war is over can probably be replaced to better advantage at lower prices.

Your board of directors decided that it was inadvisable to continue maintaining the Marietta plant any longer and it was decided to liquidate it. This has, in a large measure, been accomplished and fair prices received for most of the machinery. The market for critical machinery items made it possible to secure the best prices. As a large part of this had been depreciated, a net profit from the sale of these capital assets has been made. The proceeds from these sales were applied toward reducing the outstanding 6 percent first mortgage bonds. This resulted in reducing the number of outstanding bonds to a point where it was deemed best to refinance. The directors authorized this to be done and your management has succeeded in placing bank loans at more favorable rates of interest, the proceeds of which have partly been used to retire the balance of these first mortgage bonds. This operation will be completed by August 1, 1942, and the mortgage on the properties is now being released.

Monthly payments toward retiring the 5 percent preferred stock issued at the end of last year to finance the purchase of the Georgia Marble Finishing Works resulted in over half of the amount owing on this preferred stock being retired by June 1. It was therefore decided to retire the balance of this stock, which has been done as of July 1, so that after that date none will be outstanding.

We have also paid in full the deficiency in the income and excess profits tax for the year 1936 and the interest accumulated on this since that time. This tax

---

EXHIBIT 1 *(concluded)*

---

case was contested and finally decided in March of this year, which resulted in establishing a certain saving to us in the amount claimed by the government.

Very truly yours,
The Georgia Marble Company

James R. Cowan,
President.

Directors' Meeting, July 16, 1942. (The) Georgia Marble Company. (Official Record.) April 14, 1941 to May 29, 1946, p. 130–131.

sale of company bonds, sales of stock, and writing up of railroad asset value.

By late 1943, Mr. Cowan estimated that proceeds from the liquidation of the Marietta plant were in the neighborhood of $150,000. At this time the value of the timber on the Amicalola Dam site property was $100,000, with an estimated 12 million feet of timber suitable for cutting. The board concurred with Mr. Cowan in making the stock currently held in the company treasury available to executive employees on an at-cost basis.

The sale of burial vaults had reached such proportions by early 1944 that the establishment of a position of vault sales manager was considered. Then, it was decided to move to a vice presidency certain officers with considerable areas of responsibility. This was not a new policy, since Alex Anderson, manager of the Nelson plant, had been vice president also. And Mr. Litchfield, whose place in the organization was really that of corporate secretary, was at this time vice president. Upon the recommendation of Mr. Cowan, president, Mr. William Vance became vice president in general charge of sales and Mr. S. E. Hyatt, vice president in general charge of production. Throughout the period the market demand was primarily for monumental stone, with the market for building and construction marble negligible.

But war conditions were changing and seemed to indicate a conclusion. In anticipation of this, the officers could see the revival of a market for structural stone. There seemed to be a need for launching a plant and equipment modernization program that would also encompass production for this area. In preparation for such a program, T. J.

EXHIBIT 2

THE GEORGIA MARBLE COMPANY (C)
Consolidated Income Statement, 1941, 1942

	1941	1942
Gross sales		
Monumental sales	$ 693,710.82	$ 989,815.91
Interior and exterior sales	294,530.93	235,263.95
Rough blocks, scrap, and sundry sales . .	134,042.71	85,671.56
Total sales.	$1,122,284.46	$1,310,751.42
Less freight, discounts, returns, and		
allowances	67,305.51	80,392.22
Net sales	$1,054,978.95	$1,230,359.20
Cost of sales.	851,402.93	974,944.81
Gross profit on sales	$ 203,576.02	$ 255,414.39
Deduct		
Selling expenses.	$ 81,127.66	$ 91,159.63
General and administrative expenses . . .	116,856.41	110,648.58
School and dwelling maintenance.	55,715.46	54,694.68
Dwelling rentals	41,192.87 (L)	36,732.18 (L)
	$ 212,506.66	$ 219,770.71
Net profit or loss (L) from operations . .	$ 8,930.64 (L)	$ 35,643.68
Other income	$ 11,230.52	$ 12,717.47
Less miscellaneous income deductions . .	$ 17,403.11	$ 9,604.49
Other income (net)	$ 6,172.59 (L)	$ 3,112.98
Net profit or loss (L) before other		
deductions	$ 15,103.23 (L)	$ 38,756.66
Other deductions		
Interest on bonds	$ 23,278.24	$ 11,616.17
Interest on notes payable, and so on . . .	5,198.20	6,262.31
Amortization of debt discount and		
expense	1,649.44	668.49
	$ 30,125.88	$ 18,546.97
Less net profit from disposition of capital		
assets		
Net profit from disposition of buildings		
and equipment.	$ 37,966.52	$ 73,295.08
Net loss on disposition of investments. . .	—	62,679.59
	$ 37,966.52	$ 10,615.49
Other deductions (net)	$ 7,840.64 (L)	$ 7,931.48
Net profit or loss (L)	$ 7,262.59 (L)	$ 30,825.18

Durrett, Jr., was employed as a consulting engineer to work out the details.

Also, there seemed to be a need to reestablish a sales organization to cover the structural stone market. Previously, it had been company policy to maintain sales offices in the major population areas of the

North and Northeast. Now, the company, after some extensive investigation, entered into a sales contract with Huntley-Kretzmer, a sales engineering firm. The organization represented the Alberene Stone Corporation of Virginia. There was a bilateral benefit from this arrangement. It gave an engineering sales agency a group of complementary products, while it provided The Georgia Marble Company with an established sales organization in the heavily populated areas of the North and Northeast.

After 40 years of service with the company, Mr. H. L. Litchfield retired on July 31, 1944. Shortly afterward, two others, the treasurer and the manager of the Nelson plant, were elevated to the vice presidency. Among other important considerations during 1944 was the need to negotiate a new lease with the S. C. Tate estate. (The existing lease was due for expiration in 1959, but no satisfactory planning and execution of capital expenditures could be achieved until the status of a new lease was established.) The executive committee allocated $200,000 for new machinery, repairs, and equipment in that year; a derrick was purchased for the quarries. The CIO was recognized as the bargaining agent for the workers and a contract was signed. Final disposition was made of the mausoleum assets which had been carried over from the 1920s. Option was taken on some Elberton granite properties.

More efforts were directed toward preparation for meeting the market demands that would come with conversion after the war. The year 1945 brought ordering of new equipment, authorization of more capital expenditures, financial arrangements for the modernization program. Durrett's performance was quite satisfactory; and, as chief engineer, he was made a vice president early in the year. Consideration was given to the opening of the company's granite quarry property at Elberton. Sanitation facilities were authorized to be provided at the Tate plant and at the Tate high school. Absence of satisfactory medical services at Tate pointed out the need for the establishment of a clinic there to attract adequate and competent medical personnel. As an incentive to this project, up to $10,000 was to be contributed by the company.

The manpower situation improved and, by the latter part of 1945, orders were being received for building and structural marble. Among these orders was an $85,000 order for blocks to be used in the St. Patrick's Cathedral in New York City. And President Cowan was authorized to investigate the possibility of acquiring a lease on the travertine deposits in Randolph County, Georgia. But, lease negotiations with the S. C. Tate estate collapsed without further explanation from the Tate estate. The next year the board of directors accepted Mr. Cowan's proposal to establish a Delaware corporation to operate the company-owned timber lands.

The program of renovation was moving ahead under the thoughtful deliberation of officers to place The Georgia Marble Company as an organization of which Georgians and the South could be proud. Directors and management of the company perceived such a position as one objective. However, there was yet another end in view. The potential of the company being what it was, it could well serve as a nucleus about which to add other related activities.

Because of postwar shortages, it was necessary to look for many items of equipment by way of government surplus property sales.[1] It was not possible to move directly from coal-fired to diesel-powered locomotives and railroad cranes. Because of deferred delivery, it was expedient to make the transition by way of oil-fired steam units, equipment which was subsequently replaced by diesel-powered units. As rapidly as the "old-fashioned" equipment had replacements, it was sold.

During this period, thought was given to what might be done with scrap and waste marble. The company's contract with Thompson-Weinman Company, signed in 1937 for a period of 10 years, was only about 18 months from its terminal point. The Georgia Marble Company had the option of renewing the agreement which made provision that Georgia Marble should not grind finer than a "200 mesh-screen," while Thompson-Weinman should not grind stone coarser than this size. Because of the company's inability to supply Thompson-Weinman's demands during the war period, the latter company had gone to Alabama to acquire some marble properties there.

Renewal of the Thompson-Weinman contract was a controversial point. Construction of a plant to convert the waste to lime was being considered. Likewise, officials were thinking of the expediency of establishing grinding facilities and exploring the chemicals market for powdered and marble granules.

---

[1] Mr. William B. Tate, Jr., was a part of the modernization program in scouting out these items. He joined the company after having completed his military service with the navy. A graduate engineer, a son of a cousin of Col. Sam, his employment had actually preceded his military service by about 10 days. His first assignment was that of assistant to Mr. Durrett, the chief engineer. In this position he aided in the renovation projects for the railroad, water supply, quarry pumping, and other general engineering work.

The Dorr Company was employed to make a research study surrounding the establishment of a lime plant. About the middle of 1947 this study was completed.[1] Using it as a basis, company officials decided not to renew the lease with Thompson-Weinman but immediately to start construction of facilities to produce up to "347" powdered screened marble. The large calcite deposits under company control seemed to dictate this as the best course.

It became the responsibility of Mr. John W. Dent, soon after his alignment with the company, to implement the decision, as he headed the newly begotten calcium products division. Conditions seemed to dictate first construction of a dry mill plant. The stringency of equipment and construction materials procurement made this a difficult undertaking. Because of postwar shortages, structural beams had to be of wood instead of steel; electric motors, frequently being of obsolete types, were picked up as one of a kind here and there. Pilot runs of this first dry-ground plant began in February 1948, and the plant went into full production the next month. Already, plans were being carried out for the construction of a wet-ground plant.

It was William B. Tate, Jr., who served as the sales force of the calcium products division, later becoming its sales manager. His confidence in the future of chemical applications of marble had dated back to the time of Col. Sam. Bill had told him that this was the area where a bright future lay for the company. But to Col. Sam this had been only a sound of a young engineering graduate who needed a practical viewpoint. Bill sold to the cast stone dealers, to the chicken feed manufac-
...ers, and to other similar consumers of crushed marble.

When the wet-ground plant began to feed the production stream, the division flexed its muscles and grew with amazing rapidity. The addition of other production facilities became necessary. Soon the division's products were going into items other than brick, chicken feed, cast stone, terrazzo, and so on. Rubber goods, chewing gum, paints, and numerous other items were becoming a part of the growing spectrum of its uses.

During the period when the calcium products division was being

---

[1] In April 1947, Mr. John W. Dent resigned from the production-managership of Thompson-Weinman, a position he had held for six years. He became affiliated with The Georgia Marble Company in June 1947.

established, the structural and building stone operation was moving ahead. The monumental province continued to hold its own in dollar sales, but, as was to be expected, it became a less important phase of the company's total operation.[2] The lease on the plant building of The Georgia Marble Finishing Works in Canton, Georgia, was terminated in 1949, with its equipment being transferred to the structural division at Nelson.

Officials of the company, in early 1951, became aware of the possibility that they could acquire the physical properties of the Rockwood, Alabama Limestone Company. Possessing limestone deposits, this company was producing stone for exterior building work and for agricultural limestone. While the sales force of The Georgia Marble Company was adequate to absorb these additional products, at the same time it gave an opportunity to meet the price demand for exterior stone at about half of the price of marble.

A wholly owned subsidiary corporation, The Alabama Limestone Company, was formed in November 1951, to take over the limestone operation. James R. Cowan was elected chairman of the board, S. E. Hyatt was made president, William L. Vance, Jr., vice president in charge of residential sales, and G. W. Putney, vice president and general manager. Shortly after the coalition, it became necessary to shift from surface to underground quarrying operation because the surface stone deposit was almost depleted. This change in method of quarrying was an innovation in the limestone industry.

By way of merger, The Georgia Marble Company acquired the Tennessee Marble Company of Knoxville, Tennessee, in midyear 1953.[3] This organization had owned finishing plant facilities which fabricated highly decorative interior marbles from its quarries at St. Genevieve, Missouri. Also acquired in this merger were the plant and quarries of the Green Mountain Marble Company of West Rutland, Vermont. This latter operation gave to The Georgia Marble Company additional quantities of white marble and other color types that it did not previously have. The proximity of this facility to the northeastern markets gave an added transportation advantage.[4]

---

[2] Sales were made in both rough block and finished form. Monumental sales in 1950 accounted for 51 percent of gross dollar sales, building marbles 23 percent, and sundry 4 percent. In 1950 calcium products sales comprised 22 percent of total sales.

[3] This was accomplished through exchange of stock and a lease interest in one of the less valuable granite quarries in Elberton, Georgia. The company continued to own very valuable granite properties in the Elberton area. The Tennessee Marble Company had been owned by the Coggins group who were primarily interested in granite operations.

[4] At the time the Green Mountain operation was taken over, its quarry activities were being carried on underground. The average time taken to move stone to the surface after its extraction was eight hours. Under the new ownership, a tramway was installed and the time of removal was reduced to 10 minutes.

James R. Cowan, at 63, was approaching the age of retirement. It was time to give consideration to the selection of a successor. The person selected would be made an executive vice president for a year, at the end of which time he would assume the presidency with Mr. Cowan being elevated to chairman of the board.

To find a new president, some eligible person could be brought in from outside the company, as had been done with Col. Sam and when Mr. Cowan became president. However, four top contenders in the company seemed young and vigorous enough to give the company a dynamic leadership.

John W. Dent had a varied background, some years in a college agricultural training program, a commercial school course in bookkeeping and shorthand, a correspondence course in cost accounting. He had also been a hotel clerk, a bookkeeper in a textile mill, city clerk, city manager, production manager of a crushed marble operation, and, most recently, head of the calcium products division of the company since 1947. His obvious competence in originating this new division had won for him the admiration of co-workers, subordinates, and superiors.

S. E. Hyatt had spent a year in railroading, after which he moved into the Georgia Marble Finishing Works at Canton. Here he had moved up the ladder to become plant manager. When this organization was consolidated with The Georgia Marble Company in 1941, he had gone ahead in production management, proving his competence with a broadened scope of responsibility until he had become responsible for the company's entire production operations.

William L. Vance, Jr., was in charge of sales for the company. An engineer, he had worked at this profession in Florida during the boom of the 1920s. He had spent seven years in the Marietta plant of The Georgia Marble Company in sundry roles as clerk, estimator, and so on. After a satisfactory period with GMAC and affiliation with the Trust Company of Georgia as loan officer, he rejoined the company in 1941 and had been responsible for rebuilding its sales organization into the creditable place it now held.

Thomas J. Durrett, Jr., an engineer by profession, had been a state engineer under the Works Progress Administration. It had been his responsibility to design and to implement the company modernization program in the postwar period. These activities brought his recognition within the company and he was placed in charge of the Tennessee operation when the Tennessee Marble Company was acquired in 1953.

These four men were vice presidents. They had been placed in a position of equal status in 1952 in salary as well as in a small profit-sharing plan. The ages of these men covered a range of only about three years. Each of the four candidates was given an opportunity to discuss with Mr. Cowan the possibility and the desirability of his own election to the presidency. The directors, who were not officers in the company, then were given a voice.

The Georgia Marble Company (F)

In early 1954, Mr. John W. Dent was made executive vice president, it being understood that the following year he would assume the presidency. T. J. Durrett was shifted to head the calcium products division, filling the vacancy created by the elevation of Mr. Dent.

Willingham-Little Stone Company, an organization concerned with high-volume production of white fine-grain dolomitic limestone (actually recrystallized marble), was acquired in September 1954. The quarries and plant of this company were located 15 miles to the north of the Tate operations. The purchase seemed desirable for a number of reasons. Its proximity made possible executive supervision with limited amount of travel. Acquiring this company would enable The Georgia Marble Company to serve a broader market by sale of a material that was the accepted standard for chips used in white terrazzo. The physical characteristics of the items produced by the calcium products division made them undesirable for this purpose. The nearness to the Florida construction market would make this material a welcome addition. The "fines," a byproduct, were unsurpassed in quality for use as agricultural limestone. There was an available market for this also.

From December 1941 to 1955, J. R. Cowan had had a long laborious task but his fellows concluded that, in many respects, he had done it well. He had taken a sick company and moved it on the way toward becoming the giant of its industry. He had to do many things which, it is reported, were to him unpleasant, but, in the interest of all, he did what to him seemed best. Statements about him indicate that he was a driver for efficiency and a good judge of men. He apparently acted also on the premise that a man had to be past his 40th birthday to achieve his best potential. A month after becoming chairman of the board, Mr. Cowan died. Mr. John W. Dent became president.

The board of directors, at their August meeting in 1955, authorized the establishment of a stock option plan for Mr. Dent, 4,000 shares, for Mr. Hyatt, Mr. Vance, and Mr. Durrett, 2,000 shares each. The market at this time was $30 per share and under Internal Revenue regulations, the price was $25.50 per share. These men were given five years to exercise their options.

Two significant personnel changes occurred in 1955. Bill Tate, who had resigned in 1953 to become sales manager for Thompson-Weinman, was brought back to the calcium products division as sales manager. Soon after, he was made a vice president of the company. By this time, the growth and future of the company seemed to dictate the procurement of a financial officer who was a recognized authority on income tax. Arthur Andersen, who had been serving as auditor for the company for a number of years was requested to make some recommendations, as was the accounting firm of Ernest and Ernest. Each recommended two or three potential candidates. As Harry Mathewson of the latter firm brought in one of their recommended candidates for interview, he himself was spotted as the man for whom the company had been searching. Subsequently he became financial officer of the company.

It had been the general policy through the years, as new acquisitions were made, to continue operation of each newly acquired organization as a division. In fact, to a considerable extent, these companies were carried on as separate entities. No consideration had been given to establishment of a uniform policy of depreciation, of centralized control over accounting, credit, purchasing, capital expenditures, cash, labor relations, and so on. It seemed that this general policy needed to be reexamined in the light of certain conditions that had been noted. Several weeks were required for auditing the records of each division, a fact which added to the cost of this auditing operation. Also, individual customers, dealing with more than one division, were occasionally paid up on a current basis with one division while very delinquent with another division of the company.

Facing officials of the company was the question of centralization versus decentralization. There was a need to centralize operations without impairment of the effectiveness of the various divisions, or, alternately, a need to correct inefficiencies in the various operations, leaving them as they existed at the time.

The Georgia Marble Company (G)

The company elected to centralize. The effectiveness of centralization, in terms of savings through reduction of personnel, seems to have been obscured by the continued growth of the firm. But it has been concluded by management officials that the very real problem of obtaining and developing personnel to assume the increased responsibility which has accompanied the growth experienced in the various divisions has been lightened considerably by the centralizing processes.

There had been a change in the ownership of Huntley-Kretzmer, which was now Albermar Agency. Some of the top people of that firm had been brought into the company as new partners. The Albermar Agency was becoming concerned about the effect of present trends at Alberene Stone Corporation of Virginia on its own operation. The corporation was eight months in arrears in delivery; it seemed to be in need of an improved management.

Here for The Georgia Marble Company was a further opportunity to diversify its activities in the stone field. Eighty percent of the Alberene production went into chemical laboratory installations; the remaining 20 percent was serpentine, going into structural work. This serpentine would complement other sales of the company in the structural field. Another apparent advantage would be control over all products included in Albermar sales. Controlling interest in the Alberene Stone Corporation of Virginia was obtained by The Georgia Marble Company.

Not long after, rumors began to circulate that the stone deposits owned by Alberene were nearing depletion. This brought a hurried huddle at The Georgia Marble Company. An extensive core-boring survey of the Alberene properties was conducted. This was something that the company had never attempted to carry out on its own properties. The results of the survey refuted the rumor and proved quite disturbing to the previous owners of Alberene Stone. It made possible more positive planning and action in the operations. Subsequently, delivery time was reduced from eight to two months. This experience made the company aware of benefits to be gained from carrying such an exploratory survey on in its other properties.

The services of a professional geologist were procured later for a core boring survey for Georgia Marble properties. Some officials see, in retrospect, this program as a not too effective operation because of

EXHIBIT 1 Organizational Chart, 1960

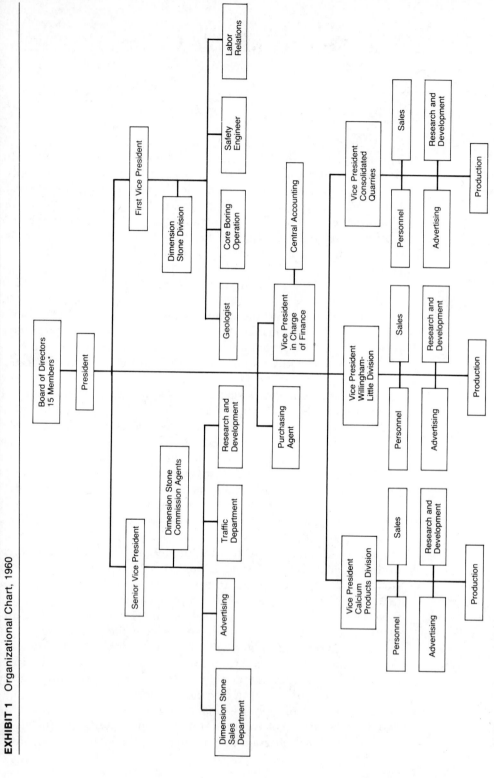

* Five are officers of the company.

the lack of competent drilling crews and equipment, though these deficiencies were finally corrected.

In 1957 the board of directors authorized the creation of a major medical insurance program for all executives and salaried employees, the company paying the cost for the individual employee, the employee, the cost for each dependent. The insurance company was to pay 80 percent of the cost of medical bills up to $10,000; the employee, 20 percent. A life insurance program for the executives and salaried employees equal to 1½ times the employee's annual salary had already been provided.

The board of directors approved the establishment of a profit-sharing program for salaried employees in 1958. To be eligible for participation the employee must have been in the company for a period of three years. The basis of computation is 15 percent of the employee's annual salary, excluding any bonus. In addition, an employee may contribute up to 7 percent of his salary from his own funds, if he so elects. Upon termination of service prior to retirement, the employee, after a period of five years, may draw out 10 percent per year, and increasing increments of 10 percent per year, until all benefits have been withdrawn.

At the same time that the profit sharing was established, provision was made for the compulsory retirement of salaried employees at 65, for members of the board of directors at 70. Permission was granted to those who had not at this point accumulated funds in the profit-sharing program to continue their employment. There were about seven people affected; they were retired early in 1960.[1]

The greatest emphasis in the postwar period had been placed on the Nelson plant and on the calcium products division.[2] Modern methods and equipment had not been as extensively utilized in the monumental division at Tate. Some changes here were undertaken in 1957. Additional equipment and production lines were set up. However, no changes were made in the marketing concept: dependence on the large dealer as a primary source of sales for this division.

Another change in the company policy during this period was the launching of a program to employ a number of young engineers. Contrary to his predecessor's belief, Mr. Dent did not adhere to the fact that a man had to be in middle age before he could achieve his opti-

---

[1] Each received 20 percent of his annual salary for those years not covered by profit sharing. This, with social security benefits and income from investments, was a substantial accrued earning.

[2] After considerable wooing by a former college classmate, Tom Durrett resigned from the company to become involved in a different industry. He was replaced as division manager of the calcium products division by William B. Tate, Jr. Bill, already a vice president, was soon appointed to the board of directors.

Durrett had exercised only 1,000 of his 2,000 shares of stock option given him in 1955.

mum productivity. But the modernization program and the employment of young engineers met resistance at the Tate plant. It seems that a higher proportion of older workers had accrued to this plant than at the other operations. A common attitude was, "If it was good enough for Col. Sam, it's still good enough for me." Many of the workers did not see any reason for change. Their basic distrust of "outsiders" did not simplify the task of the engineers. Such conditions have retarded progress in the monumental division more than in other areas. It was never the intent of the company to eliminate jobs but, through improved operations, to create more jobs. The rank and file seem to lack an appreciation for the economic results of Col. Sam's policies.

For a period of time the calcium products division had depended on the laboratory control program established by Dr. Milton Gallagher of the industrial chemistry department in the University of Chattanooga. Dr. Gallagher had acted on a consulting basis until 1957, when he became a full-time employee of the company. At the same time, Bob Hall, a paint chemist was also brought to the company. It was intended that these two would carry on a research program. However, the technical service demands made on them left little time for the achievement of basic research in production and product improvement, in the research laboratory that had been equipped for this purpose. Though research project objectives were established, nothing was reported back.

In midautumn 1959, the board of directors approved the capital expenditure for the construction of a research laboratory facility, to be located separate and apart from any of the company's operational activity. Past experience had proved that close proximity to operations might be advantageous for operations but not conducive to basic research, of which the company had immediate need. To give the research center project a fitting send-off, 24 of the company's top officers were assembled into a brainstorming session. The objective of this conference was to gain support of all officers in this endeavor, and to map out a *collective* program of research for the company.

The Mineral Bluff operation to the north of Tate was acquired in 1958. In January 1960, in an exchange of stock, the company acquired the outstanding stock of a joint venture operation, Consolidated Quarries. It was a 1,700 acre granite deposit near Atlanta with little or no overburden. The object of this acquisition was the continuation of diversification in the stone industry. Located near a thriving market for concrete aggregate for ready-mix concrete, road aggregate for the road-building boom ahead, chicken grit, and so on, this operation was capable of producing 600 tons of crushed stone per hour. One 35,000 pound charge of dynamite provided a three-months' supply of stone for the crusher.

EXHIBIT 2

THE GEORGIA MARBLE COMPANY (G)
Balance Sheet
December 31, 1959

Assets

Current assets
Cash	$ 1,476,153
Receivables, less reserves of $166,716 in 1959	2,338,680

Inventories, at average cost, not in excess of market
Stone and stone products	1,758,039
Materials and supplies	444,251
Total current assets	$ 6,017,123

Investments, and so on
Investments and miscellaneous receivables	$ 496,127
Prepaid expenses, and so on	125,094
	$ 621,221

Property, plant and equipment
Quarry lands, owned and leased, at cost.	$ 2,176,179	
Less: Reserve for depletion.	1,333,247	$ 842,932
Land, buildings, and equipment, at cost.	$11,094,803	
Less: Reserve for depreciation	5,613,080	5,481,723
Total assets		$ 6,324,655
		$12,962,999

Liabilities

Current liabilities
Accounts payable	$ 290,849
Accrued wages and other expenses.	657,103
Accrued federal and state income taxes	534,442
Installment on mortgage notes payable within one year.	25,000
Total current liabilities	$ 1,507,394

Mortgage notes on $1,065,000 of Vermont properties, 6 percent, payable $25,000 annually and $16,319 in 1969 (noncallable)	$ 216,319
Deferred income taxes for accelerated depreciation . .	$ 118,000
Minority interests in a subsidiary company.	—

Stockholders' equity
Preferred stock, 5 percent cumulative, $10 par value, authorized and outstanding, 94,901 shares (convertible, under certain conditions, into 5 percent subordinated notes)	$ 949,010

Common stock, $10 par value
Authorized, 1,000,000 shares
Issued and outstanding, 748,175 shares on December 31, 1959.	$ 7,481,750
Paid-in surplus.	574,016
Earned surplus.	2,116,510
	$11,121,286
Total liabilities	$12,962,999

EXHIBIT 3

THE GEORGIA MARBLE COMPANY (G)
Income Statement for the Year Ended
December 31, 1959

Income
Net sales	$17,560,265
Other income, net	50,377
	$17,610,642

Costs and expenses
Wages, salaries, and other compensation	$ 7,157,186
Materials, supplies, power, repairs, insurance, and other services and costs	6,824,108
Social security and general taxes	400,583
Depreciation, depletion, and royalties	720,105
Provision for income taxes	520,000
	$15,621,982
Net income	$ 1,988,660

A project being done for the nation's Capitol building in Washington had overloaded the structural facilities at Nelson so that the excess need for production was spilled over into the monumental division. This necessitated curtailed sales activity in this area. Many new sizable contracts were made in 1960. Among these was a joint venture to supply marble for the House of Representatives office building in Washington. The Capitol job, in 1960, moved toward completion, and the company made ready to chew into the "House office building job," the largest stone contract made in American history.

But there remain problems:

1. How to lighten the work load of the men in the top echelon.
2. How to fill the gap in the organization of "number 2 men" without dampening the enthusiasm of "number 3 men."
3. Though the research center is in operation, how to destroy the research and development lag.
4. What to do about transportation costs and improved markets.
5. How to make the calcium products division less susceptible to the swings in the construction industry's cyclical pattern.
6. How to reduce quarrying cost.

In the thoughts and discussions of the board of directors and of the officers of the company are methods of exploiting to best advantage all of the resources at the disposal of the company. Finding new ideas and promoting self-improvement are two major needs of the company.

49. Conoco

It was the Fourth of July weekend in 1981 and time for the tennis championships at Wimbledon, but for a handful of corporate executives from Conoco, Inc., and their aides and advisers, the fireworks outside were nothing compared to what was going on inside their headquarters at an industrial park in Stamford, Connecticut. According to reporters from *The Wall Street Journal*, work sessions that weekend usually started about 8 A.M. and ran past midnight. As many as 15 people were on hand, including Conoco chairman Ralph Bailey and three or four other top Conoco executives, and Morgan Stanley's managing director Robert Greenhill, his assistants, and attorneys from three law firms. Most of the time, they were dressed casually and ate sandwiches, soft drinks, and coffee. By the end of the July 4th weekend, they had put together the terms of a $6.9 billion purchase of Conoco by the Du Pont Company.

According to a Conoco director, the weekend pace was strenuous. For a while, top Conoco people, Morgan Stanley people, and lawyers would all assemble in the same conference room. At other times, they worked in smaller groups, taking occasional breaks for sandwiches, coffee, and phone calls to partners and aides. All but a couple of Conoco directors were on hand each time the board convened; the others participated by means of a speaker-phone system.

On Sunday, July 5, the Conoco board met to vote on the proposed merger. By now everybody was wearing suits. The meeting did not end until late evening. After the board approved the deal, Conoco's Bailey telephoned Du Pont Chairman Edward Jefferson in Wilmington, Delaware, to tell him the news. Jefferson offered to fly up to Stamford to sign the agreement. Bailey accepted. So the Du Pont chairman and a few of his aides flew up in the company turboprop, arriving about midnight. The papers were signed at 1 A.M. Monday, July 6.

Of course the Du Pont-Conoco merger agreement was subject to the approval of the stockholders of both giant corporations. However, the agreement reached between the boards and top management of Du Pont and Conoco was part of an almost bizarre series of efforts by several large companies to acquire Conoco. The offers by Dome, Sea-

---

This case was prepared by Timothy M. Singleton and Robert McGlashan, both of the University of Houston at Clear Lake City.

grams, Mobil, Cities Services, and Du Pont to acquire Conoco captured the business headlines as these suitors bid and rebid for Conoco in what might be described as a "time-telescoped auction."

THE DU PONT–CONOCO PREMERGER STANCE

Du Pont and Conoco had a friendly working relationship since 1978 when they formed a natural-gas exploration partnership in Texas. In 1980, the two companies embarked on a second gas exploration venture in nine southern and southwestern states, which involved a joint expenditure of $300 million over five years. "That's how the two companies got to know and like each other," Irving Shapiro, retired Du Pont chairman, is quoted as saying. "We developed high regard for Ralph Bailey and his people." Mr. Shapiro said he and Bailey had been friends as members of the Business Roundtable and in business dealings. Mr. Shapiro, who continued as a director of Du Pont and as chairman of its finance committee, said he was involved in "shaping" Du Pont's proposal but was not in the actual negotiations with Conoco.

It was a phone call on June 24, 1981, this time from Edward Jefferson of Du Pont to Ralph Bailey, that started the Du Pont-Conoco merger talks. The details came from documents filed with the Security and Exchange Commission and sources available to *The Wall Street Journal* reporters. Jefferson had called Bailey to ask if Du Pont could play any "constructive role . . . in the light of the public reports of merger discussions by Conoco." Bailey replied that if merger negotiations failed with a smaller company, he would get in touch.

The next day, June 25, Jefferson and Bailey were talking business. Seagram Company had announced its $2.55 billion bid for 41 percent of Conoco's common stock, and merger talks between Conoco and Cities Service Co. (the smaller company) had ended, reportedly due to Seagram's announcement. Bailey then asked, "Might Du Pont be interested in merging?"

On June 26, Mr. Jefferson answered yes. Du Pont would study the possibility over the weekend of June 27 and 28. From the 28th through the 31st, representatives of both companies, and their investment bankers, had meetings and telephone conversations about possible terms.

Du Pont's directors met on July 1. After this meeting, Jefferson telephoned Bailey to report that the directors had approved the merger on essentially the terms later announced on Monday, July 6. The weekend of July 2 through 5 was spent in negotiating final terms by executives of the companies and their legal and financial advisers. During the weekend negotiations, Jefferson told Bailey he would recommend that Bailey and three other members of the Conoco board of directors join the Du Pont board after the merger. On Sunday, July 5, the Conoco board approved the merger, and on Monday the formal agreement was signed.

CONOCO BACKGROUND

Conoco was a broadly based energy company. Petroleum operations included exploration for and production of crude oil and natural gas, transportation and refining of crude oil, and marketing of refined products. Through Consolidation Coal Company, a wholly owned subsidiary, Conoco held a major position in the U.S. coal industry. Conoco Chemicals Company was engaged in the processing and marketing of chemicals and plastics. The company was also engaged in mineral exploration, principally uranium. Conoco employed over 41,000 people in over 20 countries. In addition to being the ninth largest oil company, it was the second largest coal concern in the United States. In 1980, the company had net income of $963 million from revenues of $18.3 billion.

CONOCO'S OPERATIONS

What made Conoco so attractive that it sparked the biggest bidding war in Wall Street history? Why were several companies considering a multibillion dollar takeover of the nation's ninth largest oil company? These are some of the reasons:

1. Conoco had about 398 million barrels of untapped oil in seven western states. Its U.S. natural gas supplies amounted to about 2.681 trillion cubic feet, or the energy equivalent of about 477 million barrels of oil.

2. Conoco had huge unrecovered coal reserves currently amounting to 14.3 billion tons. The value of the reserves was conservatively estimated at between $2.3 and $3 billion.

3. Conoco's chemical division, which had 1980 reserves of about $850 million, amounted to about 5.5 percent of Conoco's $18.3 billion in sales and 4.3 percent of 1980's $1 billion earnings. Chemical plants and equipment were valued at $705 million.

4. Conoco's domestic holdings in uranium and copper were estimated at $30 million. The company planned to begin production in 1982 to extract 1,350 tons of uranium ore per day, or about 900,000 pounds per year, in a joint venture with Wyoming Mineral Corporation.

5. Conoco was managed by professional managers who owned less than 1 percent of their respective company's stock.

6. Conoco's stock sold at high discounts to net asset value. Conoco's asset value ranged from $120 to $150 per share, but the

stock was trading on the New York Stock Exchange at around $49 in early May 1981 (before the price began climbing in response to the flurry of merger interest).

COMMON ATTRACTIONS FOR ALL BIDDERS

good for Buyer

The acquisition of Conoco had many attractive features for all its bidders. The corporation had huge reserves of coal, oil, and natural gas. In view of current market prices, Conoco's reserves would cost less for an acquirer than the cost of exploration for new energy reserves.

Conoco's coal assets were valued at $2–$3 billion and measured at 14.3 billion tons. This amount of coal reserves was equivalent to twice the entire U.S. petroleum reserve base. Earnings from the coal assets were $105.2 million in 1980, which was 11 percent of Conoco's total earnings. Even if an acquirer of Conoco were unable to utilize the coal operations, the resale of them with retention of the coal reserves was still a valuable asset.

Conoco's petroleum reserves provided another valuable asset in the corporation's sale. At that time, Conoco's petroleum reserves were considered low priced—as current bids placed their crude reserves at $5 to $8 a barrel. One attractive feature to all bidders was Conoco's ability to produce enough crude oil (458 million barrels) to cover its refining capacity.

By most standards of major oil companies, Conoco was considered mediocre; however, one more attractive feature to bidders was its $1 billion in cash assets.

CONOCO'S SUITORS

Dome Petroleum, Ltd.

sold off Hudson Bay division

In early May 1981, Dome Petroleum Limited of Canada was pressing its move to acquire a big part of Conoco, Inc. common stock. Dome's subsidiary, Dome Energy, Ltd., intended to purchase 22 million Conoco shares in a transaction worth $1.43 million. The purchase would give Dome a little more than 20 percent of Conoco's 108 million outstanding shares. The acquisition, however, faced legal and political opposition in the United States. Conoco did not plan to appeal a denial of its request for a stay of an order issued May 26, 1981, in a federal court in Oklahoma City that could have paved the way for Dome to acquire the Conoco common stock. United States District Judge Lee West ruled that Conoco failed to meet its burden of proof that Dome's tender offer would inflict irreparable harm and failed to prove allegations that Dome's statement contained omissions and misrepresentations. Conoco had alleged that a loan agreement between

Dome and four Canadian banks would violate Federal Reserve Bank regulations in the United States. Conoco further charged that Dome did not truthfully represent its financial condition. Because Dome planned to take control of Hudson's Bay, a Conoco subsidiary based in Canada, a compromise was later negotiated in the legal skirmish surrounding Dome Petroleum Ltd.'s takeover.

In its deal with Dome, Conoco transferred its controlling 52.9 percent interest in Hudson's Bay to Dome for 22 million shares of Conoco common stock valued at $1.43 billion which would be retired. Dome made a cash payment to Conoco of $245 million for Conoco's 40 million Hudson's Bay shares. The deal made Dome Petroleum one of the largest oil companies in Canada. At the time Dome bought 20 percent of Conoco, more stock was offered to Dome than it needed, signifying that Conoco stockholders were willing to sell.

Seagram

Seagram's move toward acquisition of Conoco was not singularly motivated. In mid-1981, Seagram (a Canadian firm), was in a cash-heavy position, with nearly $3 billion gained by the sale of its Texas oil and gas properties. Bidding for Conoco was a result of the hunt for new acquisitions with its liquid assets. Seagram was thought to be in search of a long-term investment with which it could wait for a good return. Conoco seemed to fit this strategy. Buying Conoco would be an acquisition of some magnitude for Seagram since it was one seventh Conoco's size. Seagram was additionally attracted by Conoco's past earnings capacity of approximately $1 billion/year. Seagram's bid for Conoco, however, was out of line with Canada's new nationalistic energy policy. The policy was designed to give Canada some domination in the oil industry since the major U.S. oil subsidiaries dominated Canadian turf. The Canadian government wanted its private firms to buy oil properties in Canada; however, Seagram viewed Conoco as a better investment.

Mobil

The acquisition of Conoco met many current and future goals for Mobil. Mobil, unable to produce enough crude for its refineries, had been buying large amounts of crude on the open market. Since Mobil was "crude poor," the purchase of Conoco would boost its supplies. The merger of Conoco and Mobil was also felt to provide mutual comfort for both corporations. Typical of many oil companies in 1981, Mobil had the overflowing profits with which to buy and Conoco had the valuable deposits in the ground. A merger between Conoco and Mobil would create a substantial market share in gasoline retailing.

good move for mobil

The Mobil/Conoco merger would make the combined corporation almost as large as the industry leader—Exxon. The wide range of energy reserves in Conoco would result in a fully integrated energy company for Mobil. This integration met a long-term strategy held by Mobil. Buying Conoco would be an acquisition that Mobil could not feasibly build by themselves for decades.

Du Pont

similar size.
Heavy debt
for Dupont
Prior business.

Du Pont planned to obtain Conoco as a wholly owned subsidiary even though Conoco was somewhat larger than Du Pont. Conoco's 1980 revenues were $18.3 billion with earnings of $963 million (not including Hudson's Bay Oil and Gas Company which was sold earlier in the year). In comparison, Du Pont's revenues were $13.7 billion with earnings of $695 million.

Conoco and Du Pont already had a friendly working relationship as a result of the natural gas exploration partnership. Du Pont's chairman Edward G. Jefferson felt the merger would reduce Du Pont's problems with fluctuations in the price of energy and hydrocarbons. Du Pont's earnings in 1980 plunged 24 percent as a result of rising petroleum costs. Petroleum made up 80 percent of the raw materials in Du Pont's products. While the merger would create a heavy debt for Du Pont, it was felt by analysts that there would be no dilution of earnings.

SUMMARY

golden Para chute
for Conoco's top exec.

Even though the Du Pont bid did not provide the largest immediate return to Conoco shareholders, it was considered by management to be in their best interest. No matter which company was successful in acquiring the Conoco assets, the final outcome would have an impact on both the Conoco management and shareholders.

It seemed that the Conoco management had a lot at stake in the event of a merger. The board of directors of Conoco in mid-1981 announced that Conoco's top executives would receive their annual salaries until 1984, and sizable stock options in the eventuality they were fired or resigned after a merger had been completed. Generally, it was felt that if Seagram took over Conoco, the top executives at Conoco would lose their jobs.

There were several possible reasons that Seagram would fire the Conoco management. Seagram had vigorously opposed the employment contracts which were issued to Conoco management. A less obvious reason for removing the Conoco management might be because of the difference in strategies that exists between the two companies. Seagram was a highly diversified company that used a leveraged position to make acquisitions. If Seagram succeeded in acquiring Conoco, it could sell a sizable portion of its coal assets in order to pay for the takeover. This plan would be diametrically opposed to the Conoco management strategy. The conservative strategy of Conoco management was to develop their company into a fully integrated energy company. It was felt that as their oil stocks become depleted, they could be substituted with their sizable coal reserves.

Surprisingly, the Mobil takeover bid for Conoco was challenged by Conoco management—they attacked the bid on antitrust grounds. Conoco stated a Mobil merger violated the Clayton Antitrust Act, which prevents unlawful mergers. Even though a Mobil takeover provided the most return to the Conoco shareholders, the Conoco directors claimed that it was not in the best interest of the shareholders. There was another less obvious reason for Conoco management's not sanctioning the Mobil merger; Mobil had given Conoco management no assurance that they would be replaced following a merger. A merger between Mobil and Conoco had some synergistic advantages. Mobil was considered to have a shortage of crude, while Conoco was considered to be crude rich. If the companies were merged, they would form the second largest oil company, placing it behind only Exxon in total revenues.

Conoco management saw Du Pont as a "white knight," and had recommended that a Conoco-Du Pont merger would be in the best interest of the shareholders. Obviously, a merger with Du Pont would be highly advantageous to Conoco's top management. In fact, the Conoco management had been assured that they would keep their jobs after the merger had been completed. Since the Du Pont merger was backward integration and Du Pont was primarily interested in Conoco's feedstocks, the Conoco management would be more likely to have a great deal of autonomy.

The combining of Conoco and Du Pont would have a synergistic effect and the maximum future earning potential would be expected from a merger. Du Pont had a need for Conoco's hydrocarbon reserves since 80 percent of their products are petrochemical based. In addition, Du Pont (with its existing technology) could assist Conoco in the development of coal gasification and oil recovery. Also, Du Pont could use Conoco's coal reserves as a secondary source of raw materials once the coal gasification process was perfected.

APPENDIX

Legal Environment for Mergers in 1981

The early Reagan administration appeared to be sympathetic to the growing sentiment in Congress to broaden antitrust immunity for exporters and to reduce certain antitrust penalties. William E. Baxter, Reagan's chief of the antitrust division of the Department of Justice, spoke against the guidelines issued in 1968 that spelled out when the Department of Justice will or will not be likely to challenge a corporate combine. Between March and July 1981, Baxter's trustbusters had filed only four new suits, compared with the 25 started during the same period in the Carter administration. Baxter, in late June 1981, dropped two of the antitrust cases inherited from Carter, one against Mack Trucks and the other involving two firms in the brick-selling business. The antitrust division appeared likely to take a narrower approach than the Justice Department to any investigation. It would probably stress conflicts involving "horizontal" competition (where companies involved in a merger directly compete with one another). Baxter was seen to believe that vertical mergers—where, for example, a producing concern acquired a supplying concern—could stimulate competition. A former deputy assistant attorney general in the antitrust division said he did not think Baxter would look favorably on a motion to stop the Conoco-Du Pont merger simply because it has some vertical effects.

Even during the last year of the Carter administration, the government brought fewer than 3 percent of the 1,496 civil antitrust cases filed in the federal courts. Baxter, a former legal consultant and professor of law at Stanford University Law School, had indicated his plan to enter these suits that pit one company against another. He felt a bad precedent had been set; he had seen too many companies walk away from proposed deals that would have added vigor to competition because top brass were frightened of antitrust challenges. He believed a wide pattern of business activity got directed into less efficient modes because current antitrust laws cast doubts on their legality.

Merger Consultants

Many companies trying to engage in merger activities use the services of one of Wall Street's investment bankers. These services do not come cheap. In the Du Pont purchase of Conoco for $7+ billion in cash and stock, its investment banker First Boston Corporation would pocket $15 million. Even if Du Pont did not succeed in buying Conoco, the investment banker would still get $750,000 for a few weeks' work.

First Boston's chairman answered the question, does a bigger merger mean more work for investment bankers by saying, "You bet your neck it does—you have to have crews of people—lawyers, accountants, bankers—and they work around the clock. There have to be people who make out the strategies, people who massage the figures and do the layouts. Everybody from the chairman to the associates gets involved." In a major takeover, the single largest professional fee is usually the investment banker's fee. If a transaction involves several hundred million dollars, the banker advising the buyer could receive a fee of $1.5 million to $3 million. The banker advising the seller usually gets a good deal more. Each deal is different. Morgan Stanley's agreement with Conoco used a sliding scale in which the fee percentage decreased as the value of the transaction increased. But even with this sliding scale, a bigger deal meant a bigger fee for Morgan Stanley. Sometimes merger specialists save their clients millions of dollars in the course of a takeover fight. One of the investment bankers cited instances where his client, the acquiring company, was willing to pay millions of dollars more than the price the investment banker was able to negotiate. In many cases, such savings more than outweigh the fees.

Mergers—Social Benefits

Some economists fear, however, that what is good for the Wall Street merger makers is bad for the economy. Says Walter Adams, professor of economics at Michigan State University, "Merger managers are playing short-term games that will not create a single new job, build a single new factory, or add anything to U.S. technology. The economy is likely to be hurt by merger activity that is senseless and, in fact, creates corporate monsters with no need to compete or push hard." A *Wall Street Journal* analyst stated that there is no such thing as a deal in which you pay dearly but suffer no added expense. Those who pay the premiums draw them from their companies' stockholders' equity. The shares of the bidders in a takeover contest often fall, while the shares of the company being sought often rise, spectacularly.

Merger Shareholders—Winners or Losers?

Corporate Data Exchange, New York, a research concern, in 1981 published a stock-ownership directory listing the largest holders of stocks in 456 of the Fortune list of the 500 largest industrial companies. The interesting point of this was that many of the biggest shareholders of Conoco were also among the biggest shareholders of Du Pont, and many of these also were among the biggest shareholders of Mobil. Data from Computer Directions Advisors, Silver Springs, Maryland, showed a number of institutional owners of Conoco, Mobil, and Du Pont also had holdings in Seagram as of March 31, 1981. The effect of all of this, according to Michael Locker, president of Corporate Data Exchange is, ". . . the same shareholders will be deciding the fate of this merger on both sides of the transaction." All of this raises questions about the concentration of stock ownership in relatively few hands (see Exhibit 1).

EXHIBIT 1 Interested Parties

	Stock Ownership (Shares)		
	Du Pont	*Conoco*	*Mobil*
Prudential Insurance	2,144,900	762,800	2,060,000
Manufacturers Hanover	2,005,478	1,512,616	1,389,397
J. P. Morgan & Company	1,765,000	424,000	4,864,000
Teachers Insuracy Annuity—College Equities Retirement Fund	1,454,087	1,187,700	1,450,000
Citicorp	1,341,253	2,390,000	1,393,014
N.Y. State Teachers Retirement Fund	1,163,000	871,000	522,200
California Public Employees & Teachers Retirement System	992,700	1,051,300	430,000
Girard Trust	847,264	377,320	728,379
Wells Fargo	762,500	636,385	1,267,296
Provident National	741,585	473,038	616,162
Chase Manhattan Bank	627,508	501,859	2,450,438
U.S. Steel Pension Trust	624,906	917,760	544,410
First Union Bancorp	578,748	398,289	638,711
Bankers Trust*	510,314	5,629,206	13,337,329
Fidelcor	504,456	283,601	739,083
Walter E. Heller International	496,449	414,707	741,770
Batterymarch Financial	427,500	225,100	536,368
U.S. Trust Company	422,701	616,204	785,589
Texas Teachers Retirement System	385,200	233,700	556,884
Metropolitan Life	347,775	229,250	432,500
Ameritrust	338,082	394,822	862,525
First Pennsylvania	324,613	227,841	797,981
Bank of New York	318,541	729,291	816,563
N.Y. City Teachers Retirement System	256,200	222,800	466,632

* Mostly employee plan holdings.
SOURCE *The Wall Street Journal,* July 28, 1981.

In Washington, Representative Berkley Bedell, an Iowa Democrat and chairman of the House Small Business Subcommittee on Energy, said the Conoco bidding "illustrates how incestuous the relationships have become" among big companies. "Thirty-six of the top 65 holders of Conoco stock also are listed among the biggest investors in Mobil and Du Pont," he said. "The problem is a situation where shareholders are able to sit on both sides to vote on purchases at higher than market prices to benefit themselves."

Representative Bedell has asked the Federal Trade Commission to investigate the role of institutional investors in the current wave of mergers among major corporations. He was concerned that in the case of some of the largest banks, the question was compounded by the fact that some of the same institutions were deeply involved in the financial arrangements attendant to pending mergers.

Besides these negative comments about mergers, Federal Reserve Board Chairman Paul Volker criticized major banks for contributing to the "contagious mania" of takeover bids by providing corporations with some $25 billion in credit lines. Some of the credit extensions should not have been made—in his opinion. On the other side of the coin, however, were comments by Yale law professor Robert Bork: "When I see business managers deciding to merge, and I can see that it doesn't eliminate competition, then the only thing it does do is increase business efficiency. Anything that increases business efficiency helps—at home and in foreign markets."

The Reagan administration agreed with Bork. In fact, Bork's writings were required readings for incoming Justice Department antitrust attorneys. This was, of course, in agreement with William E. Baxter's views. He was a disciple of the conservative "Chicago school" of economics which long contended that antitrust laws overprotect inefficient small businesses and bar business growth and business arrangements that increase efficiency—all to the detriment of the consumer.

Are mergers good for the economy? John Cunniff wrote in the *Houston Post* on July 19, 1981: "To say they are is as empty of real content as the claim that big is bad merely because it is big. The issue obviously needs more discussion, and it probably will get it."

50. First National City Bank: Operating Group

John Reed paced along the vast glass walls of his midtown Manhattan office, hardly noticing the panorama of rooftops spread out below his feet, baking in the September sun. One of 41 senior vice presidents of the First National City Bank, Reed, at 31, was the youngest man in the bank's history to reach this management level. Reed headed the bank's operating group (OPG)—the back office, which performed the physical work of processing Citibank's business transactions and designing its computer systems, as well as managing the bank's real estate and internal building services. Today, musing to himself about the forthcoming 1971 operating year and his plans for the next five years, John Reed was both concerned and angry.

He was concerned that his recent reorganization of the operating group, though widely recognized as a success, was not sufficient. His area still followed the traditional working procedures of the banking business, and OPG continued to be seen by the rest of the bank as a "necessary evil" which, given enough tolerance by its more intelligent brethren, should "muddle along" the way it always had. After a year and a half with the group and five months as its head, he still had few concrete measures of its performance. But most of all, John Reed was concerned that his initial concept of what the group needed— massive new computerized systems for coping with a growing mountain of paper-based transactions—might be both impractical and irrelevant. Reed's new staff assistant Bob White had been pushing hard for a change in management approach, to emphasize budgets, costs, and production efficiency instead of system development.

And, uncharacteristically, John Reed was angry. He looked again at the management report he had received the day before. Here it was, September of 1970, and he was only now learning that his manpower had grown by 400 people in July and August. Maybe Bob White really had something in his stress on control and management.

9-474-165 First National City Bank: Operating Group (A) Copyright © 1974 by the President and Fellows of Harvard College. This case was prepared by John A. Seeger under the direction of Jay W. Lorsch as a basis for class discussion rather than to illustrate either effective or ineffective handling of an administrative situation. Reprinted by permission of the Harvard Business School.

FIRST NATIONAL CITY BANK

The operating group was one of the major divisions established in a reorganization of Citibank at the end of 1968. The five market oriented divisions, shown in the organization chart in Exhibit 1, generated varying demands for OPG services; all of them were looking forward to continued growth in 1971, and all were pressing for improved performance by the Operating Group.

Citibank's personal banking group, (PBG) with 181 branches and 6,000 employees, provided a full range of services to consumers and small businesses in the metropolitan New York area. As the area's leading retail bank, PBG projected a 3 percent annual growth in checking account balances, and a 2 percent annual growth in savings accounts over the next several years; in addition to an increase in number of accounts, PBG anticipated continuation of the recent trend toward more activity *per* account.

The investment management group, with 1,700 employees, managed assets for personal and institutional investors, and provided full-banking services to wealthy individuals. In this latter category, the group currently carried some 7,000 accounts, and hoped to increase its customers by 25 percent in the next four years.

The corporate banking group, itself subdivided into six industry-specialist divisions, served big business (generally, companies with more than $20 million in annual sales), financial institutions, and government accounts within the United States. CBG aimed at an annual growth rate over 5 percent, but qualified its ambitions: In order to gain market share in the increasingly competitive world of the major corporations, the bank would have to improve both its pricing structures and the quality of its services. Operating group errors, CBG said, had irritated many major accounts, and their reputation for slow inaccurate service made expansion of market share very difficult.

The commercial banking group operated 16 regional centers in the New York area to serve medium-sized companies, most of whom did not employ their own professional finance executives and thus relied upon the bank for money advice as well as banking services. The fastest growing group of the bank, commercial banking projected an annual growth rate of about 10 percent.

The international banking group operated some 300 overseas branches in addition to managing several First National City Corporation subsidiary units concerned with foreign investments, services, and leasing. Although IBG conducted its own transaction processing at its overseas centers, still its rapid growth would present new demands on the operating group in Manhattan. All business originating in New York was handled by John Reed's people, and the IBG complement of 160 New York-based staff officers was expected to double in five years.

EXHIBIT 1 First National City Bank: Institutional Organization, 1970

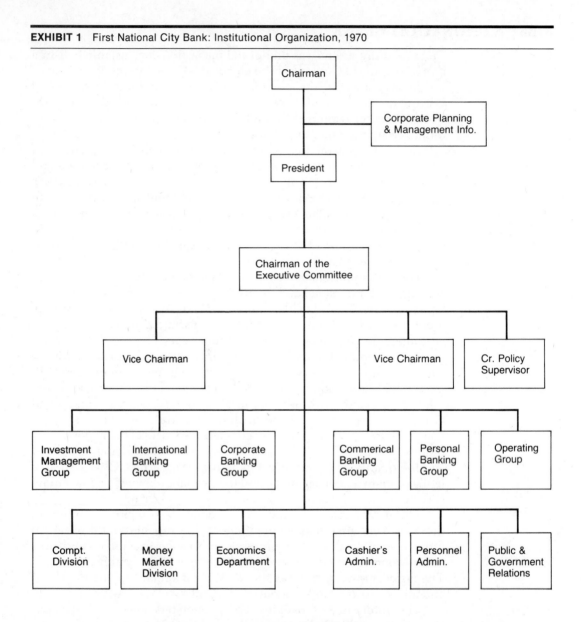

Worldwide, First National City Corporation had shown assets of $23 billion in its financial statement of December 31, 1969. Earnings had been $131 million, after taxes (but before losses on securities traded). The corporation employed 34,000 people, having doubled its staff in the previous 10 years, while tripling its assets. Citibank's published goals for financial performance presented another source of pressure for improvement in the operating group: Board Chairman

Walter B. Wriston had recently committed the bank to an annual growth rate of 15 percent in earnings per share of common stock. President William Spencer had made it clear to John Reed that OPG was expected to contribute to this gain in earnings.

THE OPERATING GROUP'S FUNCTIONS

As the bank had grown, so had its back office. Increases in services offered, in customers, in volume per customer, and in staff all meant added transactions to be processed by the operating group. As the volume of paper flowing through the bank increased, so did the staff and budget of the back office. In 1970, John Reed had some 8,000 people on his group payroll, and would spend $105 million on the direct production of the bank's paperwork. For several years, transaction volume had increased at an annual rate of 5 percent; the operating group's total expenditures had grown faster, at an average of 17.9 percent per year since 1962.

Operating group's headquarters was a 25-story building at 111 Wall Street, several miles south of the bank's head offices at 399 Park Avenue. The volume and variety of work flowing through this building was impressive; in a typical day, OPG would

- Transfer $5 billion between domestic and foreign customers and banks.
- Process $2 billion worth of checks—between 1.5 and 2 million individual items. (A stack of 1.5 million checks would stand as tall as a 66-story building.)
- Start and complete 900 jobs in the data processing center, printing five million lines of statements, checks, and other reports.
- Process $100 million worth of bill and tax payments for major corporations and government agencies. (And during the 16 weeks between February 1 and May 30, the group also processed 50,000 income tax returns per day for the city of New York.)
- Handle 102,000 incoming and outgoing telephone calls and 7,000 telegrams and cables.
- Mail out 30,000 checking account statements and 25,000 other items, accounting for $10,000 a day for postage.

OPERATING GROUP ORGANIZATION

In 1968, John Reed had transferred into OPG from the international banking group to become a vice president of the bank and to set up a task force pointed toward reorganization of the group. He had assembled a team of young, technically oriented managers (most of them relatively new to OPG) to analyze and rearrange the basic functions of the group. Systematically, this task force had examined the structure and function of each OPG subdepartment, working with the line managers to question where the subgroups fit in the organization; to whom their managers reported and why; what processes and technologies they shared with other groups; and how the physical output of each group affected the operation of the next sequential processing step. The result of this study was a complete realignment of reporting responsibilities, pulling together all those groups doing similar work, and placing them under unified management.

A leading member of OPG's "systems management" team during this reorganization effort was Larry Small, who had followed John Reed from the planning staff at the IBG in 1969. Small, a 1964 graduate of Brown University (with a degree in Spanish literature), set the keynote for the task force approach with his concept of basic management principles. Small elaborated:

> Managing simply means understanding, in detail—in *meticulous* detail—where you are now, where you have to go, and how you will get there. To know where they are now, managers must measure the important features of their systems. To know where they are going, managers must agree on their objectives, and on the specific desired values of all those measured factors. And, to know how to get there, managers must understand the processes which produce their results. Significant change demands the participation of the people involved, in order to gain the widespread understanding required for success. Management is essentially binary; all change efforts will be seen as either successes or failures. Success follows from understanding.

Few major changes in equipment or physical space were required by the new organization, and the approach characterized by Larry Small's statement made the transition an easy one. By late 1969, the operating group was running smoothly under a four-area structure as shown in Exhibit 2.

Area I was the "operating" part of operating group; these were the people who processed the transactions which constituted the bank's business. Area I operated the computer systems, processed checks for collection from other banks, posted the accounts for Citibank's customers, transferred funds from one customer to another, and prepared customers' bank statements.

Area II encompassed system design and software for computer operations. It was the "intellectual" side of operating group, developing new computer systems for the use of Area I. The subgroups in charge of operations analysis, management information systems, and data control also belonged to Area II, as did the programming group in charge of ALTAPS, a new automated loan and time payment-processing system.

EXHIBIT 2 First National City Bank: Basic Organization

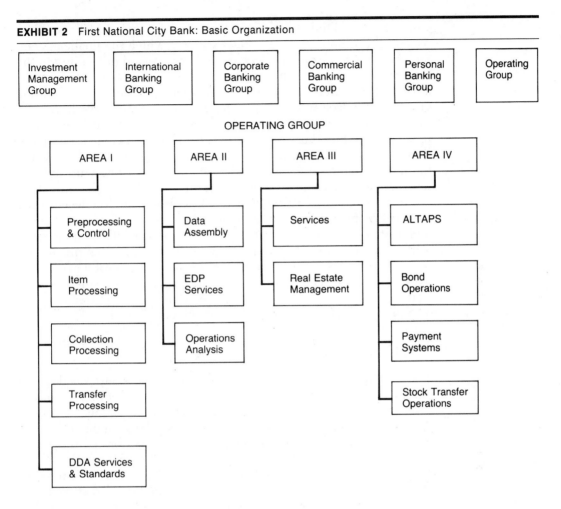

Area III, quite removed from the paper oriented processing groups in the operating group, was a free-standing organization in charge of Citibank's real estate, physical facilities, and building services. (When he was not concerned about processing transactions in the back office, John Reed could worry about the quality of cafeteria food, and the cleanliness of the bathrooms.)

Area IV was composed of the relatively low-volume, high-value, transaction-processing departments—stock transfer, corporate bonds, corporate cash management, mutual funds, and government services.

In addition to the routine of day-to-day operations, Reed was responsible for the long-range development of both hardware and software systems. For several years, a subsidiary of the bank, with operations in Cambridge, Massachusetts, and in California, had been working on the kind of on-line systems and terminals which would be required to support the "checkless society" which the financial community expected would replace paper-based record processing in the long-range future. Reed had decided to maintain the separation of this advanced research and development activity from the operating group. "Let's face it," he said, "the computer systems we have now will never evolve into the systems needed for point-of-sale transaction processing. When those new systems come, they'll come as a revolution—a total replacement of existing technology. We should develop the new systems, sure. But we shouldn't let them screw up the systems we need today and tomorrow in the meantime."

In September of 1970, John Reed, feeling comfortable with the overall structure of OPG but impatient with its lack of measured progress, had assigned Larry Small to head Area IV. Small's demonstrated skills in management of change held out the promise that this highly sensitive area, where any errors could cause major problems for the bank's most important customers, would soon be under more effective control. Now Reed was considering the future course of Area I, where even more people and dollars were involved.

AREA I: THE DEMAND DEPOSIT ACCOUNTING SYSTEM

The largest single job performed by the operating group was demand deposit accounting (DDA), the complex process of handling the physical flow of paper and communications, posting transactions, distributing processed items, and producing the bank's daily statement of condition. Some 2,000 employees of OPG's Area I performed this work. The process was composed of three parts: The "front end," which received, encoded, and read transactions onto magnetic computer tapes; the data center, which sorted the data and printed statements; and the "back end," which microfilmed and filed the checks of Citibank's own customers, prepared and mailed their statements, and handled accounting exceptions.

Around the clock, mail sacks containing checks, deposit slips, travelers' checks, transfer vouchers, credit memos, and other paper transaction records arrived in the eighth floor receiving room at 111 Wall Street to enter the "front end" of the demand deposit accounting system. The first step of that process was to weigh the bags, in order to gauge the volume of work coming in: one pound of mail equaled about 300 items to be processed.

Each incoming mailbag contained a control sheet, listing the various bundles of checks in that shipment and the aggregate totals of the bundles. As each sack was opened, its contents were checked against its control sheet to ensure that all the bundles listed were actually received. This marked the first step in Citibank's system for proving the books; from this point onward in the DDA system, each batch of material was signed for whenever it moved from one area of responsibility to another. The records of these transfers, together with any changes in batch totals as discrepancies were discovered or generated, were accumulated by a "proof clerk" on each operating shift. The following morning, these proof worksheets were consolidated into the bank's daily report of its operating condition, as required by the Federal Reserve system.

Materials arriving from other banks and check-clearing houses were already partly processed, but items from domestic Citibank branches, the head office, mail deposits and lockboxes had to be encoded with machine-readable information. These papers were distributed to one of the 150 magnetic ink encoding machines, where operators would key the dollar amounts into a keyboard. The machines would print these amounts on the checks, accumulating batch totals for each 300 checks processed. Some machines had several pockets, and sorted the work into different pockets for different kinds of media, adding up separate control totals for each pocket. As the pockets filled up, the paper was unloaded into conveyor trays, to be transported to the next operation, where the checks were read by machines and sorted by their destination, while the information from them was recorded on computer tape.

Encoder operators were generally women, who worked on an incentive pay arrangement and processed 800 to 1,100 items per hour. No direct record of keypunching accuracy was kept, and operators were not penalized for errors.

At the read/sort machines, on the floor above, the paper media were sorted into two major classifications. On-us checks—those written against the accounts of Citibank's own customers—were directed to the back end of the DDA system; transit checks, written on other banks, were directed to the various check-clearing houses and exchanges. Firm deadlines held for these exchanges. For example, the major Manhattan banks met at 10 each morning to trade checks with each other, and to settle the differences between the checks paid and collected for other banks. This meeting had been a New York tradition for well over a hundred years; banks were not late for the exchange.

About 600,000 checks each day entered the back end of Citibank's process, where they were microfilmed, screened for exceptions, and filed by customer for rendition and mailing of statements.

Overdrafts, stop payment orders, and no-post items were listed by the computer and referred to exception clerks, who searched through the incoming paper for the offending items, in order to route them to the proper offices for special handling. No-posts were especially troublesome; about 1,300 items per day, with an average value of $1,000 each, would flow into the back end, destined for accounts which had been closed, or were burdened by attachments, or had invalid numbers, or belonged to recently deceased owners, or were suspected of fraudulent activity. On a typical day, the exception clerks would fail to find between 50 and 100 of these checks, and the cases would be referred to the investigations unit.

In the filing and signature-checking section, women worked at 158 large filing machines, where each operator was responsible for 5,000 to 7,500 accounts. In addition to simply filing the day's flow of checks, each operator handled telephoned check-cashing authorizations; reconciled full sheets (the first pages of multipage monthly statements); compiled the daily activity of medium-volume accounts (between 25 and 125 items per day) into SMUT listings[1]; and ruled off the accounts scheduled for next-day statement rendition.

Nine clerks in the breakdown section received the checks for tomorrow's statements from the filing clerks, collated them with the statements arriving from the computer printer, and prepared the work for the rendition group the next day. The 60 women in rendition confirmed the count of checks to go with each statement, observed special mailing instructions, and sorted the outgoing mail into heavy, medium, and lightweight classifications.

Throughout the DDA process, errors could be generated in a variety of ways. Any of the machines could eat a check if the machine were out of adjustment. Multipocket encoders could add a check into the total for one pocket, but sort the paper into a different pocket, creating a shortage in one batch of material and a corresponding overage in another. Conveyor trays could be spilled, and loose paper could be stored in desk drawers, or shoved under furniture, or swept out in the trash. The bank's proofing system recorded variances in all the processing steps, and accumulated the errors in the difference and fine account—commonly called the D&F.[1]

THE OPERATING GROUP STAFF

By tradition, the operating group was a service function to the customer-contact divisions of the bank. Citibank's top management attention was directed outward—toward the market. Operations was expected to respond to change as generated and interpreted by the customer-contact offices. As a consequence, tradition held that the career path to the top in banking led through line assignments in the

---

[1] The Citibank executives interviewed for this background material were generally young men who had served with OPG for only two or three years. They did not know the antecedents of the acronym SMUT-list. Similarly, the source of the name D&F for the variance account was obscure—although one manager thought there might once have been a monetary fine levied against the bank which failed to balance its accounts perfectly.

market oriented divisions. "The phrase 'back office' is commonly assumed to mean backwater," said John Reed. "Operations is a secure haven for the people who have grown up in it; it's a place of exile for people in the other divisions."

In 1970, most of the operating group's management was made up of "career men" who had spent 15 to 25 years with OPG, often beginning their service with several years of clerical-level work before advancing to supervisory jobs. Through years of contact with "their" outside divisions of the bank, managers had built up rich personal acquaintanceships with the people they served. Frequent telephone contacts reinforced these relationships. Dick Freund, OPG's vice president for administration and a veteran of 42 years' service with the group, commented on the close interaction between OPG people and the customer-contact offices:

> Problem solving here is typically done on a person-to-person basis. For example, an account officer in International Banking, faced with tracing some amendment to a letter of credit, would know that Jerry Cole, an assistant vice president on the 22 floor, could find the answer. He'd call Jerry, and yes, Jerry would get him an answer. Whatever else Jerry was doing in the letter of credit department could wait; when a customer needs an answer, our men jump. They're proud of the service they can give.

Recruits for the managerial ranks of the bank typically came directly from the college campus. Dick Freund described the process:

> We hire people straight out of college—most of them without business experience—and shuttle them around in a series of low-level jobs while they learn the bank. The Yale and Princeton and Harvard types eventually settle in the customer-contact offices; the Fordham and St. John's and NYU types come to operating group. We don't have the glamorous jobs that IBG and corporate can offer, but even so there's a lot of prestige to working for First National City, and the security we offer means a lot to some of these people. I know one officer who bases his whole employment interview on security. "You come to work for us," he says, "and put in a good day's work, and you'll never have to worry about your job. Never."

While management ranks remained stable, the characteristics of the clerical staff had changed dramatically over the previous decade. Through the 1950s OPG relied on the local parochial high schools as a source of well-trained clerical applicants. Those women would typically work for one to five years before leaving to raise a family; some stayed on to form the experienced core of the staff. By 1970, however, applicants for work in lower Manhattan were predominantly black and Puerto Rican graduates of New York's troubled school system. The middle-class population had migrated from lower Manhattan by 1970, and its schools had followed it.

MANAGEMENT SUCCESSION AND THE CHANGING ROLE OF OPERATING GROUP

Dick Freund traced the recent succession of top managers at the operating group.

> From 1964 to 1968, when he retired, we had a top man who convinced the policy committee that our operating capabilities were becoming more and more important—that we simply couldn't afford to take them for granted. There was a tidal wave of paperwork coming—the same wave that swamped so many brokerage houses in '68—and we had to pay attention. Until 1968, nobody cared much.
>
> The first clear signals that management attitudes toward the operating group were changing came in 1968, when Bill Spencer was appointed executive vice president in charge of operations. Mr. Spencer was generally regarded as a prime candidate for the bank's presidency. It was plain that his appointment wasn't some form of punishment. He had to be here for a reason, and the reason had to be that operations was, after all, an important part of the corporation.

It was Mr. Spencer who recruited John Reed to move from the international banking group to operations, and who promoted Reed to senior vice president later in 1969.

"And that was another sign that things were changing," Reed said. "For one thing, nobody my age had ever made SVP before. But more important, I wasn't a banker in the traditional sense. Most of operations management had been in the group for 15 to 30 years; I'd only been with Citibank for five, and none of that was with OPG."

John Reed's undergraduate training had been in American literature and physical metallurgy. After a brief job with Goodyear Tire and Rubber, and a tour in the United States Army, he had taken a master's degree in management at MIT, and then joined the IBG planning staff, where he applied systems concepts to the international banking field with impressive results. That his rise in the organization was atypical was illustrated by the following comments from other bank officers:

"I've spent all my life in the bank," said a gray-haired senior vice president from the corporate banking group. "I was trained by assignment to different departments every two years; then, when I went into a line position, I had enough experience to correct something by doing it myself. At the very worst, I always knew people in the other departments who could straighten out any problem."

"I started with Citibank as a night clerk in personal banking," said a PBG vice president. "It was 10 years before I reached supervisory ranks, and by then I'd had a lot of experience in credit and in operations as well."

"I joined the bank as a naive liberal arts graduate, and spent three years in clerical work before making first-line supervision," said a newly appointed assistant vice president in the operating group. "After eight years as a supervisor, you get a pretty good feeling for what's happening around you."

In May of 1970, to the surprise of no one, William Spencer was named president of First National City Corporation. John S. Reed—youth, nonbanking background, and all—was selected to head the operating group.

OPERATING GROUP COSTS

By tradition, the method of meeting increased workloads in banking was to increase staff. If an operation could be done at the rate of 800 transactions per day, and the load increased by 800 pieces per day, then the manager in charge of that operation would hire another person. It was taken for granted. Financial reports would follow, showing in the next month-end statement that expenses had risen, and explaining the rise through the increased volume of work processed.

But in the late 1960s the workload began to rise faster than the hiring rate could keep up, and in addition there was a decrease in productivity per operator. Backlogs of work to be done would pile up in one OPG department or another, and would require overtime work in order to catch up. Even with extensive reassignment of people and with major overtime efforts, some department would periodically fall behind by two or even three weeks, generating substantial numbers of complaints from customers. Three or four times a year, special task forces would be recruited from other branches of the bank to break the bottlenecks of these problem departments. Trainees, secretaries, junior officers, and clerks would be drafted for evening and weekend work, at overtime pay rates. "The task force approach is inefficient, annoying, and expensive, but it gets us out of the hole," said Dick Freund. "A lot of these people don't *want* to work these hours, but it has to be done." In 1970, OPG spent $1,983,000 on overtime pay.

There were other sources of expense in the operating group, which did not show up on financial reports. John Reed described a major area of hidden costs.

If we have cashed a $1,000 check drawn on the Bank of America in California, we are going to be out $1,000 until we send them the check. If we miss sending the check out today, it will wait until tomorrow's dispatches to the West Coast, and we'll wait a day longer for that $1,000. There are rigid deadlines for each of the clearinghouses; even a relatively small number of checks missing these deadlines can cost us a great deal of money. If each day only 3 percent of the $2 billion we handle is held over, then we will lose the interest on $60 million for one day. That turns out to be something like $3 million a year in lost earnings. We call it "lost availability."

That's a big number. Yet, until a few months ago we were making no effort to reduce it, or even to measure it. No one had thought of it as a cost. Check processing has always been treated as a straight-line operation, with bags of checks going through the line as they were received. Whatever wasn't processed at the end of the day was held over, and cleaned up the following day. It was just another clerical operation.

In 1970, lost availability amounted not to 3 percent of the value of checks processed, but to four.

OPERATING GROUP QUALITY

"Quality is something we really can't measure," said Dick Freund. "But we can get perceptions that the level of service we're providing isn't acceptable. For all our outlay of expenses, it seems we are not improving, or even maintaining our performance."

Indications of poor service came to the operating group in the form of customer complaints, usually voiced through account officers from the market-contact divisions of the bank. Failures could take many forms, including loss of checks after they had been posted, late mailing of statements, miscoding of checks, payment of checks over stop orders, misposting of transfers, and, on occasion, loss of whole statements. Since any kind of error could cause inconvenience to the customer, the people in direct touch with the market were highly sensitive to quality. These account officers frequently assumed the role of problem solvers on the customer's behalf, traveling to the 111 Wall Street office to work directly with operating group staff to remedy specific errors affecting their accounts. A separate section had been set up to analyze and correct errors in customer accounts; its backlog of unsolved inquiries was a major indicator to management of OPG's quality level. In the fall of 1970, this investigations department faced a backlog of 36,000 unsolved cases.

The importance of error-free operation to the customer-contact officers was pointed out by several officers from outside the operating group.

"Sure, I know the volume of paper has gone up," said a vice president from corporate banking group. "I know we have 750,000 accounts, and most of them are handled for years without a mistake. But operations has to perform at 100 percent, not at 99 percent. Errors can be terribly embarrassing to the customer; repeated errors can lose customers for us. I have 600 checks missing from last month's statement for a major government account . . . and there were 400 missing from the previous month's statement. Now, how can I sell additional services to that account, when we can't even produce a correct monthly statement for him?"

"We tell the customer that his canceled check is his legal receipt," said an assistant vice president from personal banking, "and then we lose the check. What am I supposed to tell the man then? I can get him a microfilmed copy of the check, but that's not very useful as a legal document, is it?"

"Just getting a simple transfer through the books can generate a whole family of problems," said an account officer in International Banking Group. "Here's a typical case. A translator at 111 Wall Street miscodes the original transaction (it was written in Portuguese), and the transfer goes to the wrong account. When that customer inquires, we trace the error and reverse it. But before the correction goes through, a follow-up request comes in from Brazil; it's a duplicate of the first request, and our people don't catch the fact it's a follow-up, so they put through another transfer. Now the same item has gone through twice. Where does it all end? My customer is tired of writing letters about it."

"If our operations were perfect," sighed a CBG vice president, "we'd have a tremendous tool to go out and sell against the competition."

THE "TECHNOLOGICAL FIX"

"The customer-contact side of the bank," said John Reed, "and to some extent the top-management group, shows a natural tendency to press in the direction of great, massive, new, total computer systems— bringing the ultimate promise of technology into instant availability. It has been natural for all of us to blame mistakes and daily operating problems on inadequate systems; after all, if the systems were perfect, those mistakes would be impossible. But maybe we've all been brainwashed. Maybe we expect too much."

Fifteen years before, Citibank had acquired its first computer—a desk-sized Burroughs machine used to calculate interest on installment loans. For the four years following, the operating group had cooperated in an extensive research program on automated check processing, based on equipment developed by International Telephone and Telegraph to encode and sort mail in European post offices. This experimental system had progressed to the point of pilot use on the accounts of First National City's own employees when, in 1959, the American Banking Association adopted magnetic ink character recognition (MICR) as an industrywide standard approach to check processing. Citibank immediately dropped the ITT system, and installed MICR equipment.

Although the computer facilities had grown immensely in the ensuing decade, the basic process performed by the operating group remained the same. "For example," said Reed, "people used to verify names and addresses against account numbers by looking them up in paper records. Now they sit at cathode-ray tubes instead, but they're still doing the same operation."

Reed's computer people had reported to him that Citibank's use of machines was already highly efficient. Operating group was—and had been for several years—at the state-of-the-art level of computer usage. A new survey by the American Bankers Association seemed to verify this conclusion: where the average large bank spent over 30 percent of its back-office budget on machine capacity, OPG spent less than 20 percent.

Reed paused beside his corner window. "Think about this for a minute," he said. "We've been running this operation as if it were a computer center. We've been hoping for some Great Mother of a software system to come along and pull the family together. Well, she's slow. None of us children has heard one word from her. Maybe she's not coming.

"What if it's *not* a computer center we have here? What other point of view could we take, that would result in running the operating group differently? Better?"

Reed turned. "What if it's a *factory* we've got here?"

THE FACTORY CONCEPT

Through much of August 1970, John Reed had worked with Larry Small and Bob White to develop the implications of viewing the operating group as a high-speed, continuous-process production operation. White, working without an official title, had just joined Reed's staff after six years' experience with Ford Motor Co., most recently as manager of engineering financial analysis for Ford's product development group. At the age of 35, with an Ohio State Bachelor of Science degree and an MBA from the University of Florida behind him, Bob White brought to the operating group a firm conviction that the McNamara philosophy of budgets, measurements, and controls was the only way to run a production operation.

Now, in early September, Reed was trying some of these ideas on Dick Freund to get a sense of their impact on the traditional banker. Freund, with more than four decades in the organization, was serving as a sounding board; Reed had almost decided to carry a new program to the policy committee of the bank, and wanted to anticipate their reactions.

> We know where we want operating group to be in five years' time. For 1971 and 1972 we want to hold expenses flat; in spite of the rising transaction volumes we'll keep the same $105 million expense level as this year,

and after that we'll let costs rise by no more than six percent a year. By 1975, that will mean a $70 million annual saving compared to uncontrolled growth at 15 percent. At the same time, we want to improve service, and eliminate our bottlenecks and backlogs, like the jam-up in investigations.

To accomplish those goals, though, we will have to put over a fundamental change in outlook. We must recognize the operating group for what it is—a factory—and we must continually apply the principles of production management to make that factory operate more efficiently.

It is not important for the people in the factory to understand banking. We'll take the institutional objectives and restate them in terms of management plans and tasks that are quite independent of banking. The plain fact is that the language and values we need for success are not derived from banking, and we couldn't achieve what we want in terms of systems development and operations if they were.

To control costs, we must think in terms of costs. That means bringing in management people trained in production management—tough-minded, experienced people who know what it is to manage by the numbers and to measure performance against a meaningful budget. We have to infuse our management with a new kind of production oriented philosophy, and the process has to start with new outside points of view. Good production people in here can provide a seed crystal and the present management staff can grow around the seed. Some of them will make it; others won't. Our headhunters can find the top factory management people to start the reaction. From there on, it's up to us.

Our costs are out of control because we don't know what they are, let alone what they should be. Our quality is criticized when we don't have any idea what quality really is, or how to measure what we're already doing. Our processes run out of control and build up backlogs because our efforts are aimed at coping with transactions instead of understanding what made them pile up in the first place.

I'm not talking about turning the operating group *into* a factory. I'm talking about recognizing that it *is* a factory, and always has been. The function isn't going to change, but the way we look at it and manage it must.

Reed turned to Dick Freund, who has been listening intently. "What will they say to that, Dick?"

Freund smiled, and his eyes sparkled. "They'll go for the stable budget idea, and in spite of skepticism they will hope you can do it. They'll love the idea of improved service, but they'll know you can't pull that one off if you're holding costs down. And the factory management idea?

"There's one other bit of history you should know, John. The first engineer we ever hired came to work here in 1957, the year after we bought our first little computer. He was an eager guy, really impressed by the challenge of managing back office operations. He poked around for a few days, and then came back to the head office to declare that this wasn't a bank at all. It was a factory, he said. Nothing but a goddam paperwork factory.

"That was after just two weeks on the job.

"It was his last day on the job, too."

Reed grinned broadly, and turned to face Bob White. "Are you ready to move out of the office, Bob? This concept is going to fly, and we're going to need someone down at Wall Street who can make it happen. Why don't you get yourself ready to take over Area I?"

Index